MONEY-DRIVEN
MEDICINE

ALSO BY MAGGIE MAHAR

Bull! A History of the Boom and Bust,
1982–2004

MONEY-

THE REAL REASON

DRIVEN

HEALTH CARE COSTS SO MUCH

MEDICINE

MAGGIE MAHAR

HarperCollins books may be purchased for educational,
business, or sales promotional use. For information, please write:
Special Markets Department, HarperCollins Publishers,
10 East 53rd Street, New York, NY 10022.

FIRST EDITION

Designed by Kathryn Parise

Library of Congress Cataloging-in-Publication has been applied for.

ISBN-13: 978-0-06-076533-0
ISBN-10: 0-06-076533-X

06 07 08 09 10 DIX/RRD 10 9 8 7 6 5 4 3 2 1

To Michael and Emily

CONTENTS

ACKNOWLEDGMENTS

When I began writing *Money-Driven Medicine,* my goal was to tell the story of health care in America through the eyes of the doctors, patients, hospital administrators, health care executives, economists, and Wall Street analysts who understand firsthand the messy realities of a marketplace where money drives medicine.

This meant relying on the generosity of countless strangers—very busy strangers—who, over the past two-and-a-half years, have agreed to share their time, their stories, and their insights.

In particular, I want to thank Liz Dreesen, Bruce Vladeck, Lynn Schnurnberger, Lazar Greenfield, Ed Dench, Charles Rosen, Gerard Anderson, Lawrence Casalino, John Wennberg, Elliott Fisher, Thomas Riles, Robert Rosen, Donald Lefkowits, Diane Meier, George Lundberg, Kenneth Kizer, Mark McDougle, George Halvorson, Robert Califf, James Robinson, Thomas Rice, Andrew Weisenthal, Jay Crosson, Kim Adcock, Jack Mahoney, David Polly, Jonathan Skinner, Lisa Schwartz, Steve Woloshin, Bill Weeks, Sheryl Skolnick, Richard Evans, Neil Calman, Steffie Woolhandler, Jim Moriarty, Steven Hunt, Tony Ginocchio, Bob Wooten, John Cherf, George Cipolletti, Peter Gross, Bradford Gray, Patrick Malone, Arthur Kellerman, Genie Kleinerman, Katherine Baicker, Amitabh Chandra, Kenneth Thorpe, Jeff Villwock, Scott Wallace, Barry Hieb, J. B. Silvers, Joan Richardson, John Stobo, Karen Sexon, Ben Brouhard, Vindell Washington, John Harold, Sid Abrams, Joanne Andiorio, Clifford Hewitt, Evan Melhado,

James Orlikoff, Roger Hughes, Kenneth Cohen, Kenneth Wing, Deborah Weymouth, and Dugan Barr. Without them, this book would not exist.

In addition, I owe thanks to the journalists who graciously shared their sources and their knowledge, including Susan Dentzer, Tom Linden, Melissa Davis, Steve Twedt, and Joanne Kaufman. These are only a few of the outstanding writers and reporters who have contributed their ideas and stories to this book; I have tried to acknowledge their help throughout, both in the footnotes and in the text.

Special thanks go to those who have offered comments on all or part of the manuscript. In particular, I want to single out Larry Martz, a superb editor who can remove two words from a sentence and make it instantly better, and Michael Klotz, who read the entire manuscript twice, questioning contradictions, flagging infelicitous phrases, all the time refusing to be rushed. ("No, wait—there's a better way to put this.") The fact that he is my son makes his patience all the more extraordinary. As I raced toward a final deadline, Elizabeth Woodman and Maureen Quilligan also offered much-needed encouragement and counsel.

Anne Greenberg, who copyedited the manuscript, did a meticulous job, not only copyediting but fact-checking hundreds of names and details. Any errors that remain are mine and mine alone. Meanwhile, Alex Scordelis, the editorial assistant who worked on the project, smoothed the path to production without letting me feel the bumps along the way.

Finally, I want to thank my editor, Marion Maneker, who believed in this book from the very beginning. His unflagging enthusiasm and confidence made the hard work of writing much, much easier.

Who Is Paying?

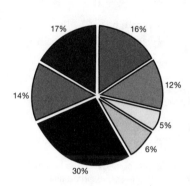

■ TAXPAYERS Medicare 17%

■ TAXPAYERS Medicaid & SCHIP 16%

□ TAXPAYERS Other public spending (including veterans' programs, public hospitals, school programs) 12%

□ TAXPAYERS buying private insurance for government employees 6%

■ PRIVATE INSURANCE 30% (paid primarily by private sector employers and employees, as well as the self-employed buying their own insurance)

■ PATIENTS out-of-pocket spending 14%

□ CHARITY and philanthropy (includes private money for construction) 5%

"Other public spending" includes programs such as workers' compensation, public health activity, Department of Defense, Department of Veterans Affairs, Indian Health Services, state and local hospital subsidies, and school health. "Out-of-pocket spending" includes direct consumer spending for all health care goods and services such as co-payments, deductibles, and any other amounts not covered by insurance. Premiums are included under "Private Insurance." This chart does not include revenues that the government loses while subsidizing employer-based insurance. (See "Where We Are Now," p. 325.)

Source: Centers for Medicare and Medicaid Services, *2005 Report on National Health Expenditures,* reflecting $1.7 trillion total health care spending in 2003.

What Are We Paying For?

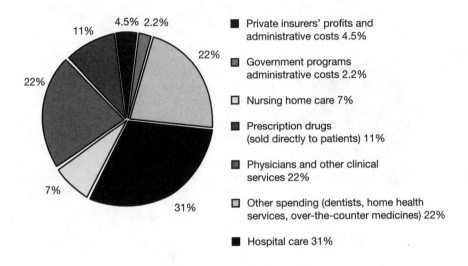

Due to rounding, numbers will not add up to 100%.

"Prescription Drugs" includes only drugs that patients buy "retail" at a pharmacy or other outlet; it does not include the cost of drugs that they receive in a hospital or a doctor's office. "Other Spending" includes dentist services, other professional services, home health care, durable medical products, over-the-counter medicines and sundries, public health, research, and construction.

Source: Centers for Medicare and Medicaid Services, *2005 Report on National Health Expenditures*, reflecting $1.7 trillion total health care spending in 2003.

roughly $1,400 for each vehicle that it manufactured. This is a major reason why GM's profit per vehicle made in North America came to just $178. And when compared to its domestic rivals, GM was doing well: Chrysler and Ford both lost money on every vehicle that they turned out that year.

By contrast, Japanese auto maker Nissan showed a profit of $2,402 per vehicle, while Toyota tacked $1,742 onto the bottom line each time it rolled out a new car. "For all the time Washington has spent discussing how U.S. companies are losing ground to counterparts in places like China, little attention has been given to how skyrocketing health-care costs are putting U.S. companies at a disadvantage to competitors in developed countries," Wall Street's paper of record observed.

By the end of 2005 Toyota was on track to set a record net profit for the fourth year in a row. Meanwhile, GM lost more than $3 billion in the first nine months of the year.[13] In June, when GM chairman and chief executive officer Rick Wagoner announced that the company planned to eliminate some 25,000 U.S. jobs by 2008, he cited the high cost of health care benefits.[14] GM just couldn't afford to keep its employees. And it is not only large, unionized manufacturers like GM that are running into trouble. In 2004 small businesses reported that health costs had become their No. 1 problem according to the National Federation of Independent Business (NFIB).[15]

"Japan, like most industrialized nations, has national health insurance," The Wall Street Journal observed back in 2004. And while providing coverage for all of its citizens, the paper noted, Japan "spends about half as much on health care as a percentage of GDP, yet has a higher life expectancy at birth and a lower infant mortality rate. Somehow one doesn't want to chalk it all up to the benefits of drinking green tea."[16]

Why does the United States spend twice as much as Japan? Few would argue that our health care system is *twice* as good.[17] And why is it that no matter how much we spend, it never seems to be enough to provide consistent, high-quality care for all Americans?

The conventional wisdom has it that health care costs so much in the United States because, in contrast to most other countries, we don't ration care. In other developed nations, governments limit the supply of health care resources by capping total spending, controlling the spread of medical technology, limiting the number of hospital beds that can be built, and restricting the number of physicians who can enter certain specialties. As a result, would-be patients in Canada, Europe, Australia, and New Zealand can wait months for elective surgery. In our more generous system, Americans have better access to timely care, and so, quite naturally, we spend 53 percent more than Switzerland—the next-highest-spending country in the Organisation for Economic Co-operation and Development (OECD)—and 140 percent more than the average OECD member.[18]

Or so the theory goes.

But when researchers at the Bloomberg School of Public Health at The Johns Hopkins University put this hypothesis to the test by looking at the 15 procedures that account for most of the waiting lists in Australia, Canada, and the United Kingdom, it turned out that those 15 procedures represent just 3 percent of health care spending in the U.S.—not nearly enough to explain the enormous difference in spending levels.[19]

Looking at the question from another angle, researchers compared the supply of hospital beds, doctors, and CT scanners in the United States to the supply in other countries. Again, a surprise: while some U.S. markets boast an embarrassment of specialists and hospitals, overall the number of hospital beds per capita in the United States ranks in the bottom quartile of OECD countries, while the number of physicians per capita and the number of CT scanners also falls below the OECD average. Though, the researchers noted, U.S. health care providers tend to favor more intense care: the United States has fewer hospital beds, and hospital stays are shorter, but patients undergo more treatments and procedures.

A second, popular explanation for our sky-high health care bills is that the threat of malpractice litigation forces American doctors to practice defensive medicine. But here again, the numbers muddy the story. While Americans file 50 percent more malpractice claims than patients in the United Kingdom and Australia, and 350 percent more than in Canada, malpractice payments—including both awards and settlements—are significantly lower, on average, in the United States than in either Canada or the United Kingdom.[20]

Moreover, while the size of malpractice payments has been growing at a stiff pace in the United States—rising by an average annual rate of 5 percent over inflation from 1996 to 2001—over the same span, malpractice awards in Australia, Canada, and the United Kingdom were outstripping inflation by an eye-popping 10 to 28 percent.

What is most striking is that in all four countries—including the United States—*malpractice payments represent less than 0.5 percent of health spending.*[21]

Admittedly, these figures do not capture how much physicians spend ordering tests and procedures that are not absolutely necessary in order to protect against the danger of finding themselves in court. The cost of defensive medicine is all but impossible to pin down. Inevitably, physicians have many motives—both conscious and unconscious—when deciding to order that extra test. Genuine concern for the patient and a desire to leave no stone unturned can blend, confusedly, with fear of malpractice. Not surprisingly, government estimates of the cost of defensive medicine are all over the ballpark.[22]

None of this is meant to minimize the financial burden that malpractice insurance premiums places on individual physicians in the most vulnerable specialties. Excellent doctors have been driven out of the profession. But given the size of malpractice awards in other countries, added to the fact that payments in Australia, Canada, and the United Kingdom are growing faster than in the United States, it seems likely that physicians in those countries also might be inclined to order the extra test.[23] Thus, fear of litigation does not begin to solve the question at hand: why is health care becoming unaffordable for so many Americans?

Not long ago, Karen Davis, president of The Commonwealth Fund, a nonprofit research organization that focuses on medical care, put the answer in nutshell: "Health care spending in the U.S. is higher because:

- we pay higher prices for the same services,
- have higher administrative costs,
- and perform more complex, specialized procedures.

Sick adults in the U.S. report higher rates of medical errors," Davis added, "are more likely to go for duplicate tests, and are less likely to have their medical records available when they go for care compared with similar adults in other major English-speaking countries."[24]

Davis's answer, while both factually accurate and impressive for its lack of rhetoric, still begs the larger question: why is medical care in the United States so extravagantly inefficient—and why is it that even while prices are rising, quality seems to be sliding?

Some blame consumers for wanting too much health care (particularly when they are spending other people's money). Others denounce drugmakers, insurers, doctors, and hospitals for charging too much; government for interfering too much; and trial lawyers for stirring the pot. In recent years each group has taken a turn as the villain in the play. But the truth has less to do with the individual actors, and more to do with the larger economic forces that determine the rules of the game.

Put simply, over the past 25 years, power in our health care system has shifted from the physician to the corporation. A professional, the physician pledged to put his patients' interests ahead of his own financial interests. The corporation, by contrast, is legally bound to put its shareholders' interests first. Thus, many decisions about how to allocate health care dollars have become marketing decisions. Drugmakers, device makers, and insurers decide which products to develop based not on what patients need, but on what their marketers tell them will sell—and produce the highest profit. "There is a saying in the drug industry," one Wall Street analyst notes. "A pill you take once is good; a pill you take every day is better."

Even not-for-profit hospitals are expected to keep an eye on the bottom line when deciding whether to invest health care dollars in a new heart pavilion, valet parking, or palliative care for the dying. "Is there a business case for palliative care?" hospital administrators ask.

Ideally, market forces would be making our health care system more efficient. We should be getting a bigger health care benefit for each dollar that we spend. But this is not the case. Instead, the best available evidence suggests that *up to one out of every three health care dollars is squandered on unnecessary tests, unproven procedures, and overpriced drugs and devices that too often are no better than the less expensive products that they have replaced.*

Why is money-driven medicine so wasteful? Because rather than collaborating, health care providers compete. Rather than sharing knowledge, drugmakers and device makers divide value. Rather than thinking about long-term collective goals, corporations respond to the imperatives of an impatient marketplace and focus on meeting Wall Street's short-term expectations. And so investments in bleeding-edge medical technologies have crowded out investment in information technology that might, over the long run, not only reduce errors but contain costs.

Many point to medical technology as the prime mover behind health care inflation. As Davis observes, U.S. hospitals and doctors are inclined to perform "more complex, specialized procedures" than health care providers in other countries. We may have fewer hospital beds, and hospitals stays may be shorter, but more happens to you while you are there.

This is in part because we adopt the newest medical technologies sooner than other countries, in part because American patients believe that the latest, most sophisticated medical care is always best, and in part because the pressures of a competitive fee-for-service market encourage aggressive care: when in doubt, don't wait, medicate. Operate. Investigate.

That said, only a Luddite would fail to appreciate the wonders of 21st-century medical technology. Thanks to extraordinary advances in medical science, we can hope, not just to live longer but, more importantly, to live better. Clearly, the more aggressive, intensive, and expensive care that U.S. doctors and hospitals offer is often the most effective care.

But not always. This is what is less obvious. It would seem that by spending so much more, we would be buying the best care on earth. But the evidence shows that, often, we are not. And therein lies the conflict at the heart of our money-driven health care system: while more health care equals more profits, it does not necessarily lead to better health.

Knowing that there is waste in the system is one thing; finding it is another. In the pages that follow, I look at the hospitals, doctors, drugmakers, device makers, and insurers who together make up what we somewhat euphemistically call our health care "system." In each case, I ask the same questions: where are our health care dollars going? How are they allocated—and does that allocation make sense? In other words, is more health care spending improving our health?

For insight, I have turned to physicians, patients, hospital administrators, policy makers, researchers, corporate executives, and other insiders who are in a position to see on a daily basis how both health care and business decisions are made. They, better than anyone, can describe the fierce struggle for market share that has come to define American medicine—and explain why instead of lowering costs, competition seems only to be making health care more expensive.

In the course of these interviews, I was surprised by just how many physicians returned my calls. The great majority did not know me; I expected responses from perhaps 20 percent. Instead four out of five called back. Most talked for 30 minutes—or longer. To a man and to a woman, they were most passionate about what many saw as the declining quality of health care. With few exceptions, I was struck by their genuine concern, not only for themselves, but for the plight of their patients, the state of their profession, and their own inability to cope with the problems.

"We want someone to know what is going on," explained one prominent Manhattan physician as he described how much care had deteriorated at many of New York City's major hospitals. "But please don't use my name," he added. "You have to promise me that. In this business, the politics are so rough—it would be the end of my career."[25]

Health care economists also contributed their wisdom to this story. To test some of their theories, I widened my net to consult those who understand financial follies best: the Wall Street observers who follow health care as a business and can offer field reports based on close observation of how these businesses actually work in the not-always-efficient, not-always-honest marketplace.

Ultimately, the questions that this book tackles are not simply financial puzzles, but political and ethical conundrums. Economists may sometimes pretend that theirs is an objective, value-free science. But as most would acknowledge if pressed hard enough, economic decisions about health care cannot be separated from the political priorities and moral judgments that drive them. In the end, we have to face some tough questions:

Is health care a right or a personal responsibility? If it is a responsibility, does that mean that control over health care spending should be turned over to individual consumers? What if consumers don't spend their family's health care dollars wisely—is this society's concern?

On the other hand, if health care is a right, does that mean that it is society's responsibility to guarantee that every citizen has the same level of care? How do we ensure quality? Should we pay certain hospitals and doctors more for better care? Would pay for performance lead to a two-tier system? And if so, what would count as "good enough" at the lower tier?

In the end, given finite resources, must we ration health care, and if so, on what basis: ability to pay? Age? The likely odds of treatment achieving a cure? Or instead of rationing services, should we try to bring down health care prices?

In the summer of 2004, the National Coalition on Health Care, an alliance of almost 100 of the nation's largest businesses, unions, provider groups, insurers, pension funds, and consumer and religious organizations shocked many in the health care industry by calling for price controls.[26] At the top of the list was a proposal that has long been taboo in the United States: national health insurance. To make it affordable, the report recommended an independent board, overseen by Congress, that would set limits for reimbursement rates paid to physicians and hospitals for a set package of core medical benefits, and restrict increases in insurance premiums.[27]

The proposed reforms went far beyond anything Congress was prepared to do.[28] And if it had come from any other organization, it would have been dismissed as a hopelessly out-of-touch liberal solution.

But the coalition enjoys unusual credibility. A rigorously bipartisan alliance of for-profit and not-for-profit organizations, it claims former presidents Gerald Ford, Jimmy Carter, and George H. W. Bush as its honorary chairmen. That such a group would suggest such extreme measures underlines the size of the health care crisis. "We don't see anything in the national debate now that's big enough or ambitious enough to address the problem," said coalition president Dr. Henry Simmons, a top health official in both the Nixon and Ford administrations.[29]

Although *Money-Driven Medicine* does not offer final solutions to what is shaping up as the nation's most pressing and most personal financial crisis, it does try to spell out the assumptions implicit in our current system—and the questions that we need to make explicit before attempting anything like reform.

If we are not willing to let government regulate prices, if we are not ready to ration care, and if we don't want to take the risk that we (or our children and grandchildren) might wind up on the second tier of a two-tier system— what are we willing to give up in other areas in order to fund open-ended health care spending?

Before facing the challenges of making such choices, it is worth considering how we got where we are today. Only then can one fully appreciate the contradictions built into our current health care system. With that end in mind, chapter 1, "The Road to Corporate Medicine," offers a brief history of how, over the course of the 20th century, what was once a profession evolved into a $2 trillion industry, while chapter 2, "Market-Driven Medicine: The Cost of Competition," explores what happened when the managed competition of the 1990s was replaced by the unmanaged competition of the 21st century.

MONEY-DRIVEN
MEDICINE

1

The Road to
Corporate Medicine

The story of health care in America is, first and last, a story about power. This, Paul Starr made clear in 1982 when he published his landmark study of U.S. health care, *The Social Transformation of American Medicine.*

Starr's history opens with a single, stark statement: "The dream of reason did not take power into account."[1] Medicine, perhaps more than any other science, epitomizes the "dream of reason"—the Enlightenment hope that, in the end, the human mind can tame nature and find order in chaos—or, in the case of medicine, make sense of flesh. But that pure, scientific endeavor does not unfold in a vacuum. It takes place in society, in a world of men. Inevitably, those men will jockey for position.

Throughout most of the 20th century, the nation's physicians won the battle to control American medicine. For decades, they held virtually unchallenged economic, moral, and political sway over what we now call the "health care industry." Doctors were able to gain dominion, in part because their patients wanted them to rule the nation's health care system, and in part because the market's normal laws of supply and demand do not apply to medicine.

In most industries, supply responds to demand. When it comes to deciding what to produce—and in what quantity—the supplier follows the customer's lead. Or as UCLA economist Thomas Rice puts it in *The Economics of
Health Reconsidered,* "In the traditional economic model, demand is key; supply is essentially along for the ride."[2] But in the case of health care, the supplier (traditionally, the doctor) plays a much more active role in determining
what consumers believe they want—or need. Indeed, health care providers
enjoy nearly unparalleled influence over demand for the very services that
they sell.

This is completely understandable. Health care is different from other
"purchases" in large part because the customer faces so much ambiguity. Dr.
Atul Gawande, a surgeon at Boston's Brigham and Women's Hospital puts it
best in *Complications: A Surgeon's Notes on An Imperfect Science:* "Medicine is an
enterprise of constantly changing knowledge, uncertain information, falli-
ble individuals. . . . the core predicament of medicine, its uncertainty, [is] the
thing that makes being a patient so wrenching, being a doctor so difficult,
and being part of a society that pays the bills so vexing."[3]

While *Consumer Reports* can rate midpriced refrigerators briskly and
clearly, in a way that makes comparisons easy, it is all but impossible, even for
a physician, to be positive of the relative benefits of a great many medical
procedures.

"Uncertainty as to the quality of the product is perhaps more intense
here than in any other [market]," Kenneth Arrow, the Nobel laureate economist who launched the study of health care economics, observed in 1963.
"Recovery from disease is as unpredictable as its incidence . . . and further
there is a special quality to the uncertainty: it is very different on the two
sides of the transaction. The information possessed by the physician as to
the consequences and possibilities of treatment is necessarily very much
greater than that of the patient, or at least so it is believed by both parties."[4]

This is what makes the purchase of health care so different from any
other purchase: it is a transaction based on trust.

Granted, today both physicians and patients enjoy access to far more information than ever before, and "with all that we know nowadays about people and diseases and how to diagnose and treat them, it can be hard to . . .
grasp how deeply the uncertainty runs," Gawande writes. Yet as anyone who
has ever been seriously ill knows all too well, the more one learns about a dis-

ease and the odds of success with possible treatments, the more ambiguous the situation can become.[5]

A Transaction Based on Trust

It is not just the complexity of the human body, but the uniqueness of each body that makes it so difficult to predict health care outcomes. Put simply, health care is not a commodity. While two consumers may derive pretty much the same value from the same midpriced refrigerator, a particular course of treatment can have a drastically different effect on two different bodies. This makes it difficult for heath care "shoppers" to rely on their friends' experiences the way they might when choosing, say, a computer or a car.

Nor can the consumer rely on his own past experience. Three out of four health care dollars are spent on products and services that the patient has rarely, if ever, purchased before—and probably hopes never to purchase again.[6] To make the consumer's dilemma even more wickedly difficult, when purchasing health care, he knows that there are no warrants and no guarantees. The patient cannot return an unsuccessful operation. And if he winds up unhappy with the outcome, he may find himself stuck with something far worse than a bad haircut.

The patient wants to believe—needs to believe—not only that his doctor possesses superior information, but that his doctor is committed to putting the patient's interests ahead of his own. As a customer, he is in a uniquely vulnerable position: he cannot sample the product beforehand; there is real possibility that the product will do him more harm than good; and yet, even if it proves useless, he is expected to pay for it. How could he go forward with the purchase if he did not trust the seller?

As Arrow emphasizes, whether the buyer's belief in the supplier's superior knowledge and complete professionalism is wholly justified is not the question.[7] It is simply that without it, the health care market could not function. This is one marketplace where "caveat emptor" cannot apply.

This is not to say that the 21st-century health care consumer places blind faith in his physician. Today brave-hearted patients research their own conditions, and armed with computer printouts, many participate in each treatment decision. But the truth is, however one strains against surrender, even the 21st-century patient has no choice but to place considerable faith in his doctor.[8]

The Physician's Autonomy:
The AMA Takes On Capitalism

Still, the physician's dominion was not easily won. Over the course of the 20th century, as American physicians struggled to maintain their position, they had to fend off both government and corporate intervention.

Almost everyone knows that the American Medical Association spearheaded the battle against government intrusion, or what it called "socialized medicine." Following World War II, most Western nations granted governments a major role in organizing their health care systems. In the United States, by contrast, the population's distrust of big government combined with the AMA's fierce insistence on autonomy effectively quashed any talk of a national health care system.[9]

But not everyone realizes that the medical profession also fought tooth and nail to resist the forces of capitalism—what the AMA termed "corporate medicine." The doctors' guild made its opposition to the basic tenets of capitalism startlingly clear in 1934 when it adopted a code of ethics that declared it "unprofessional" for a physician to permit a "direct profit" to be made from his labor. This is not to say that the AMA believed it wrong for doctors themselves to profit from their work. What the AMA objected to, was "for anyone else, such as an investor, to make a return from physicians' labor."[10]

Here, the AMA struck at the very heart of a capitalist system. Under capitalism, the entrepreneur who owns the means of production (the real estate, the equipment, the raw materials needed to make the product) profits from the labor of the individual worker. The worker is guaranteed a wage, while the capitalist, who takes a larger risk by paying for the costs of production, reaps whatever return is left after those costs have been met.

The AMA, in its wisdom, erased the capitalist from the picture. In the association's view, "the full return on physicians' labor had to go to physicians, and consequently, by implication, if medicine required any capital that doctors themselves could not provide, it would have to be contributed gratis by the community, instead of by investors looking for a profit," Starr explains.

"In other words, physicians must be allowed to earn whatever income the capital contributed by the community might yield to them." [11]

And so the community provided doctors with the real estate and equipment that they needed—i.e., the community hospital—free of charge. In retrospect, the arrangement may seem inevitable, but in fact, things could easily have worked out differently. Hospitals might have charged physicians fees to use their equipment, or they could simply have hired doctors as salaried employees. Insurance companies also might have hired physicians, paying them to provide services to their beneficiaries. But for most of the 20th century, the AMA won its battles, and the solo practitioner avoided being swallowed by the hospital, the insurer, or any other institution that might want to absorb him into its hierarchy.

Of course doctors are not unique; other highly skilled workers might well have wanted to avoid becoming cogs in a larger corporate machine. Why did doctors succeed? The answer, some would suggest, lies with the advance of science and technology, which lent the medical profession ever-greater authority. Yet the march of progress could just as easily have had the opposite effect. Rather than strengthening the physician's position, it might have reduced professional autonomy by making doctors dependent upon organizations that could provide the capital that they needed. After all, few scientists remained independent; most became salaried employees of universities or industries that could provide them with labs and equipment. And as technology advanced, modern medical practice would require huge capital investments. [12]

What insured the physician's autonomy was not technology, but rather his intimate relationship with his patient—even when medical care took place in the hospital. Hospitals, after all, do not "have patients." Doctors "have patients"—whom they may or may not refer to a particular hospital. Thus, hospitals depend on doctors to fill their beds. Even today, the average doctor sends 90 percent of his patients to a single hospital. [13]

As for the commercial insurers, here the AMA protected the doctors' sovereignty by insisting that, rather than paying doctors directly, insurers would reimburse the patient for his medical expenses on "fee-for-service" basis. In this way, physicians maintained their direct relationship with the patient—and avoided any system of payment that would force them to negotiate with a single organized payer. [14]

The doctors' lobby also objected violently to the idea of prepaid medical clinics—even when they were run by doctors. During the thirties and forties a number of such "medical cooperatives" sprang up across the country. Typically, they were structured as group practices, and rather than charging fees for individual services, they accepted a lump sum prepayment of, say, 85 cents per patient per month. But the AMA rejected any model other than fee-for-service, insisting that physicians should be free to set prices for each procedure, thus leaving total health care costs open-ended.

As usual, the doctors' guild prevailed, and by 1950 most states had passed laws that barred the co-ops. Prepaid plans like Kaiser Permanente and Group Health Cooperative of Puget Sound would survive only on the West Coast where doctors controlled prepaid plans and built their own clinics and hospitals.[15]

When it came to the pharmaceutical companies, the doctors once again used their cultural authority and strategic position to become gatekeepers. They and they alone decided when medicine should be prescribed, and in what dose. Understanding the importance of their power, physicians blocked efforts by drug manufacturers to market their products directly to the public, arguing that such advertising would threaten public safety and interfere with the doctors' control over their patients' health. Some would argue that the AMA was trying to withhold information from consumers while ensuring that all drug purchases were channeled through doctors. But, to be fair, physicians were not simply guarding their own position; they were also watching over their patients. Many of the drugs that the manufacturers of the day wanted to peddle to the public were, at best, worthless, and at worst, dangerous.

Ultimately, pharmaceutical companies, hospitals, and insurers came to accept the power that flowed from the physician's intimate relationship with his patient: he, after all, directed the flow of health care dollars. Rather than trying to capture and control the physician, they learned instead to court his goodwill—which meant letting him be his own boss.

Make no mistake, from the patient's point of view, there was much to be said for guarding the direct relationship between doctor and patient, without allowing a third party to intrude. While many of the AMA's most self-serving pronouncements displayed a surprisingly frank combination of cupidity and self-righteousness, physicians were driven, by and large, by something more than pure self-interest. Most saw themselves as members of a healing profession. And as professionals, the majority lived up to the expectation that they would put their patients first—even when they knew those patients would not be able to pay the bills. "When I was a child, we lived next door to a doctor, and I can remember seeing him coming home from visiting patients, carrying pans of baklava," recalls a medical reporter who grew up in the fifties.[16]

As for patients, they wanted their physicians to be all-powerful. Then, as now, trust was essential not only for the transaction to take place, but to medicine's healing power. Without it, a querulous, uncertain patient would be far less likely to respond to even the most skilled laying on of hands.[17]

Insurers Open the Door to Health Care Inflation

That said, allowing physicians so much autonomy all but guaranteed that the cost of health care would soar. Because the doctor was a free agent, he was responsible only to himself and to his patient. The patient wanted as much care as possible; the physician had been trained to provide the best care possible. The price was not his concern. To the contrary, from a purely economic point of view, it was in his interest to see health care spending climb.

Moreover, from a totally disinterested point of view, most physicians would say that when more of a society's resources are devoted to medical care, everyone benefits. After all, what could be more important than health care? Today medical expenses soak up roughly 16 percent of the gross domestic product. Even so, in the eyes of some doctors, the competing claims of housing, food, clothing, education, and national defense pale by comparison: "If someday health care accounts for 25 percent of GDP, so be it," declared one Manhattan physician in 2005.[18]

The only plausible check on rising health care costs was the patient's ability to pay. Up until the 1930s, most patients paid for almost all health care services out of their own pockets—which meant that many medical bills went unpaid. But even this restraint was overcome when employers stepped into the breach, offering health care insurance.

In the aftermath of the Crash of '29, it became clear that the nation's hospitals were in trouble: by 1930 receipts per patient had fallen from $236.12 to $59.26.[19] As the Great Depression deepened, fewer and fewer patients could afford care. One hospital executive recalled how hard it was just trying to stay open: "People brought chickens in and meat to pay their bills. They would paint or do work around the hospital of some kind . . . Nurses would come in and beg us to give them a job without pay, for room and board, because they were starving."[20]

By 1932 the American Hospital Association warned that the U.S. hospital system was on the verge of a breakdown. That year the AHA approved prepaid hospital insurance as the only practical solution to the crisis. Thus, from the bowels of the Great Depression, Blue Cross, a not-for-profit insurer that offered hospital coverage, was born.

Historians usually point to a health care plan set up by Baylor University Hospital in Dallas as the prototype for what would later become Blue Cross. In 1929 a group of Dallas schoolteachers approached the hospital with the idea of establishing a "sick benefit fund" that would provide 21 days of hospitalization in a semiprivate room for an annual premium of $6. Before long, Baylor offered the same arrangement to other groups, and the plan grew to cover several thousand people. Other hospitals followed suit, with some variations on the original model. In Dallas, for example, Methodist Hospital hired a private firm to solicit business. The company, which called itself the National Hospitalization System, charged $9 a year for insurance, keeping $3 to cover its own expenses and profits, while turning over just $6 to the hospital—thus providing one of the earliest examples of how much insurance company middlemen could add to the cost of care.[21]

In 1937 the first meeting of Blue Plan executives from around the country was held in Chicago and Blue Cross was officially born. From the beginning, the American Hospital Association laid down some ground rules for the new hospital insurance plans: they must be nonprofit, they must emphasize the public welfare, and they must cover only hospital charges. They were not to invade the AMA's territory. Blue Shield, a plan that offered insurance to cover doctors' bills, would not be founded until 1939.

Professionals in the for-profit insurance industry were shocked to see Blue Cross succeed. Up until this point, commercial insurers had avoided offering health insurance, believing that because the risks of poor health are so hard to measure, it would be all but impossible to price the product. Moreover, they feared that hospital insurance would attract subscribers who needed it—i.e., individuals who were likely to become ill. (This is a worry that would continue to haunt the industry.) But once Blue Cross blazed the trail, private insurance companies followed, "half dragged, half lured" into the field.[22]

The AMA kept a wary eye on the burgeoning industry. On the one hand, if insurance covered hospital bills, patients were more likely to have the money to pay their physicians. On the other hand, many feared that voluntary insurance plans might lead to compulsory insurance—with the government setting limits on what health care providers could charge.

In fact, by the end of the decade, the governor of California was proposing compulsory health insurance for all workers earning less than $3,000 a year—or roughly 90 percent of the state's population. In response, the California Medical Association decided to sponsor its own voluntary insurance plan to cover doctors' services. Before long, physicians in other states were forming similar plans, and in 1939 the AMA reluctantly approved the idea, laying down guidelines for what would ultimately become Blue Shield.

The AMA gave Blue Shield its blessing in large part because Blue Shield agreed to pay any qualified provider that the patient chose. In other words, the insurer made no attempt to use its purchasing power to extract discounts by setting up a closed network of doctors. Nor would doctors be required to charge all patients the same fee. At the time, many physicians were accustomed to using a sliding scale, charging well-heeled customers significantly higher prices. Under Blue Shield, they could continue that practice, billing patients for the difference between what they chose to charge and the amount reimbursed by the insurer.[23]

Meanwhile, Blue Cross helped pave the way for health care inflation by reimbursing hospitals on the basis of their costs—an early example of the perverse incentives that would fuel health care spending for the rest of the century. Any hospital that tried to be more efficient and managed to reduce the cost of doing business would find its income reduced by an equal amount "possibly for years to come," Paul Starr explains, "since the record of past costs affects future reimbursement levels . . . Thus hospitals were encouraged to solve financing problems, not by minimizing costs but by maximizing reimbursements."[24]

At the outset, employers were well pleased with the system. "Employers often found that an extra dollar devoted to insurance benefits earned a greater return in attracting, retaining and motivating conscientious employees than an additional dollar devoted to cash wages," notes James C. Robinson, a health care economist and author of *The Corporate Practice of Medicine.*[25]

By and large, workers thought of "fringe benefits" as extra compensation—icing on the cake, so to speak. They did not consciously realize that they were receiving a $1 worth of benefits instead of an extra dollar of pay.

Union leaders, of course, were aware of the trade-off, but if their members preferred $1 worth of extra benefits, they were happy to oblige. No doubt many believed that, over the long term, having medical insurance was, in fact, more valuable than this year's raise.

The IRS also blessed the system, subsidizing that extra dollar by letting employers deduct the cost of benefits from their corporate income tax— just as they deducted the cost of wages. The difference was that while employees paid income taxes on the wages, they did not have to declare the value of those benefits. In other words, no one ever paid a tax on the revenue that a company used to fund employees' health care.

In the 1940s an accident of history gave employer-based health insurance yet another boost. During World War II the government imposed wage and price controls in order to contain inflation, making it difficult for employers to attract workers in a tight labor market. But the War Labor Board recognized the problem, and so in 1942 it decreed that fringe benefits up to 5 percent of wages would not be considered inflationary. As a result, total enrollment in group hospital plans spiraled from less than 7 million to about 26 million subscribers—one-fifth of the population.[26] This set the precedent, and when the war ended, unions would fight to widen coverage. By the end of 1954, over 60 percent of the population had some type of hospital insurance; 50 percent were covered by surgical insurance; and 25 percent by medical insurance—though often it paid doctors' bills only for in-hospital services.[27]

At first the Blues dominated the market, but after World War II commercial insurance companies began to take an increasingly active interest in the business. For private insurers, employer-based insurance proved a boon, in part because it cherry-picked a pool of relatively healthy subscribers: those too old or too sick to work were automatically excluded. As an added bonus, employer-based insurance saved the insurance companies the administrative costs of collecting premiums: the money was deducted from employees' paychecks before they ever received them.

Medicare, Medicaid, and Madison Square Garden

In the early 1960s the percentage of Americans covered by some form of insurance continued to grow. By 1965 more than 70 percent of the population had hospital insurance. Still, those most likely to need care were excluded: the poor and the elderly. More than half of the nation's senior citizens had no coverage whatsoever.[28] Even retirees who could afford the premiums often found it impossible to purchase insurance—carriers frequently refused to cover individuals with a history of illness.[29]

In 1961 a newly elected President John F. Kennedy set out to remedy the situation, sending a letter to Senator Pat McNamara, chairman of the Special Committee on Aging, promising to give health insurance for the elderly the "highest priority" in the next session of Congress. A few weeks later, Abraham Ribicoff, the secretary of health, education, and welfare, publicly pledged "a great fight across the land" for a program that would become known as Medicare.[30] By the time the second session of the 88th Congress convened in January of 1962, the administration's push for Medicare had picked up speed. Politically, the issue looked like a winner: Gallup polls showed public support running as high as 69 percent.

Predictably, the AMA howled, calling the government-sponsored insurance program "the most deadly challenge ever faced by the medical profession."[31] To the guild, Medicare sounded like the first step on the slippery slope to socialized medicine.

To be fair, the AMA objected in part because it realized that Washington was greatly underestimating the cost of the new program. "AMA lobbyists warned that the entitlement program would lead to out-of-control spending and would change the way medicine would be practiced," recalls Dr. George Lundberg, a pathologist who would go on to become a controversial editor of *The Journal of the American Medical Association*. "And, frankly, the AMA was right on that point," Lundberg admits. "But," he added, "the fact that this was valid as a prediction does not mean that it was valid as an objection." Speaking in 2004, Lundberg still saw Medicare as "one of the great achievements" of the U.S. health care system.[32]

Meanwhile, public debate intensified, coming to a climax on Sunday, May 20, 1962, when President Kennedy addressed a crowd of nearly 20,000 in New York's Madison Square Garden. The president's speech was broadcast live and free over three television networks and reached an estimated home audience of 20 million. The AMA asked the networks for equal free time but was turned down. Nevertheless, the association did manage to buy time on one network for the following evening and arranged to rent the Garden for its rebuttal.

Balloons, banners, and debris left over from the president's speech lay strewn over the chairs and aisles. Against that background, the AMA's Dr. Edward Annis made an impassioned speech to empty seats, hoping to dramatize the association's supposed "underdog" status.[33] In fact, estimates suggested that some 30 million people watched the speech; 42,000 sent letters to the AMA.

Two months later the full Senate voted on the bill, and Medicare was defeated, 52–48. Once again the AMA had steamrolled the opposition.[34]

Still, the bill was not dead, only dormant. After Kennedy's assassination in November of 1963, President Lyndon B. Johnson resurrected it. Johnson knew he had a chance: the martyred president's tragic death had led to a groundswell of grassroots support for his legislative initiatives. A year later, when Johnson went back to the White House with the largest plurality in U.S. history, he was certain: Medicare's time had come.

But Johnson also recognized that the opposition would be fierce. In an effort to bring both doctors and hospitals on board, administration officials followed the precedent set by the Blues. They caved.

Like Blue Cross, the government agreed to pay hospitals not what a service might be worth, but whatever it cost them to provide the service— which meant that the least efficient hospitals would be paid the most. Any hospital that managed to cut the cost of providing a service would trim its own income as well; those that reported the highest costs would receive the highest reimbursements.

As for doctors, they would be paid fee-for-service, just as they were by most private-sector insurers. Those fees would be based on what they had charged in the past. The only ceiling: what was "usual and customary" in their community. "This left doctors free to create the baseline for higher fees. And they did this by hiking their fees," point out Howard Wolinsky and Tom Brune in their history of the AMA. "As a result of the higher fees and the increased number of patients, the average physician's earnings rose to its highest level ever—$32,170."[35]

The Johnson administration's domestic policy advisor, Joseph Califano, later recalled the moment of capitulation:

"The key meeting I remember vividly. I mean, we sat in President Johnson's little green office and he said, 'We've got to get this bill out of the House Ways and Means Committee. What will it take?'

"And Larry O'Brien [then the administration's congressional liaison] said,

'We have to give the doctors what they want and the hospitals what they want.' Johnson said, 'What will that cost?' O'Brien said, 'Half a billion dollars a year.'

"Johnson said, 'Only $500 million a year? Give it to them. Let's get the bill.' "[36]

At one point in the debate, Republicans argued strongly that the whole program should be means-tested so that middle- and upper-income individuals would not qualify. This version of the bill failed in the Ways and Means Committee by just one vote. The Democrats would continue to fight income limits because they feared that a program targeting only poor retirees would lose general public support and wind up underfunded, becoming a "poor program for the poor."[37]

As the measure wended its way through Congress, more and more legislators left their thumbprints on it, and in the end, the almost-finished product included not only all citizens over the age of 65, but at least some of the nation's poorest families. Under a three-tiered proposal that combined Democratic and Republican initiatives, the plan included compulsory hospital insurance for the elderly (which would become known as Medicare Part A) and government-subsidized voluntary insurance to cover doctors' bills (Medicare Part B), while also expanding assistance to the states with the aim of helping them provide care for impoverished families with children (later known as Medicaid.)

It had taken thousands of hours of negotiating and bullying, wheedling and compromising—but finally, in March of 1965, the legislation passed the House by a resounding majority: 313–115. It then went to the Senate, where the Senate Finance Committee tacked on 75 amendments of its own before submitting the bill for a vote by the full Senate early in July. Again, it passed by a comfortable margin: 68–21. The final compromise was approved by both houses later that month.

When word of the new law reached the AMA, some physicians swore that they would boycott the programs, and in October of 1965 the AMA held an emergency meeting. "Its members were hostile to Medicare and cool to their own leaders," Wolinsky and Brune report. But by the end of the two-day meeting, the AMA membership decided to go along with the new program. Once it went into effect, the profession would discover that while Medicare might be "government run, bureaucratic, and even a tad socialistic," it would present an unparalleled opportunity. In 1966—the first year of Medicare—the average physician's earnings rose 11 percent.[38]

The story was different with Medicaid, however. While Medicare allowed physicians to charge more than the program would pay, Medicaid did not, and many physicians refused to participate.[39]

The Rise of the Specialist

At about the same time, medical school enrollments doubled, thanks to a generously funded federal program. The Johnson administration hoped that as the supply of physicians rose, more would be forced to practice in underserved inner cities and rural areas—and that as supply met demand, doctors' fees would fall. Of course, this would never happen. As usual, health care ignored the laws of supply and demand.

"What no one seemed to notice was the trend in medicine toward specialization," recalls Dr. George Lundberg, who graduated from the Medical College of Alabama in 1957. "By the time I was an academic physician in the late sixties and seventies—first at the University of Southern California and then at the University of California—a large percentage of [medical] students knew well before matriculation exactly what they wanted," Lundberg adds.

What they wanted, he says, was simply "money," and that was pouring disproportionately into the specialties—"especially surgery, anesthesiology, pathology, radiology, and the new and expanding discipline of oncology.

"This is not to say that money wasn't a motivator before Medicare," Lundberg acknowledges, with the candor that sometimes raised hackles when he served as editor of *The Journal of the American Medical Association*. "In the fifties a lot of people applied to medical school in part because they thought they could make a good living. But it is fair to say that by the seventies money was a greater motivator because, after Medicare, there was more money in the system."[40]

So instead of producing more general practitioners, the new federal dollars dramatically increased the number of specialists—and as their numbers increased, so did their fees. For as time went by, the definition of "usual and customary" compensation inevitably rose, especially among surgeons.

Lundberg remembers how it happened: "While surgeons were barred by law from fixing fees, they knew what the going rate was [in their region]. When new surgeons entered the community, they learned what prevailing fees were for given procedures, and then they set their fees at a higher level.

"Adam Smith might have predicted that a newcomer to a community would set lower fees in order to attract patients," Lundberg continues, "but medicine was beyond supply-and-demand market rules. When new surgeons set higher fees, they not only got away with it, but also drove up the prevailing fees for all surgeons." [41]

Before long, the economic advantages of the new government programs became clear even to those health care providers who had been most horrified by the idea of government involvement. Billions of tax dollars now poured into the system. At the same time, federal subsidies of hospitals and medical research fueled an explosion, both in the growth of medical technology and in the use of hospital services.

Enter the Entrepreneur

By the late 1960s, the funds available for health care in America seemed limitless. The financial arrangements among insurers, employers, the government, and taxpayers created the illusion that no one was paying for the cost of medical care. Insurers handed rising costs off to employers in the form of higher premiums. Employers deducted those costs from their taxes, thus passing a good chunk of the cost on to the government. (The more the employer spent on medical benefits the bigger the tax break.) Government, in turn, would hand the cost on to the taxpayer, who remained largely unaware that he was now subsidizing not only Medicare and Medicaid but employer-based health care—whether or not he received benefits at his own job.

With both government and private insurers greasing the wheels of commerce, medicine was quickly turning into a high-growth business. That meant there was money to be made, and inevitably, in the 1960s the for-profit hospital was born. One of the most successful would be Humana, formed by two young lawyers who began their foray into the healing arts by investing in nursing homes. Humana went public in the go-go market of the late 1960s. Within a year the stock sailed from $8 to $84.

At this point, it appeared that anyone who could afford the initial capital investment was all but certain to make money by investing in medicine. In most industries, as supply grows and more competitors enter the fray, prices fall. But when it comes to health care, greater supply (in the form of new technologies, new treatments, and new specialists) only excites greater demand. This, in turn, encourages suppliers to provide more: more hospitals, more drugs, more services.

"Research done during this era shows several reasons why competition in the hospital industry was quite different from what neoclassical economic theory would predict," explain the authors of a study published in *Health Services Research* in 2003. "Physicians were a primary purchaser of hospital services on behalf of patients, but they were 'imperfect agents' because they might benefit financially or non-financially (in terms of patient satisfaction and loyalty) from ordering more, relatively expensive hospital care. . . . Second, private purchasers of hospital services were not organized, so even if they were more concerned about cost they had little leverage with which to negotiate. . . . Finally, employers and patients had little or no information about clinical quality, limiting their ability to search for value and make cost-quality tradeoffs." And because the majority of patients' bills would be paid by insurers, most didn't even ask in advance what their hospital care would cost.

Hospitals competed, "not on price, but by building a reputation for having the latest technology and 'hotel-like' amenities such as private rooms, better food and shorter waiting times. At this point, hospitals also began advertising to build brand name image and loyalty among physicians as well as consumers."

Ultimately, the market dynamic led to a "medical arms race," which swiftly became a game of duplication and one-upmanship as hospitals in the same city added technology and services that their competitors either already provided or were expected to offer in the near future.

"This resulted in service duplication and excess hospital capacity, particularly in markets with many competitors," the study's authors note. "The game of one-upmanship helps explain why, contrary to conventional economic theory, *the most competitive markets showed higher costs per case per day* than in communities with fewer hospitals." (emphasis mine)[42]

Throughout this period, the nation's appetite for health care could not be sated. And no wonder. Thanks to advances in research and technology, the quality of modern medicine was improving by leaps and bounds. No matter how many new products came to market, demand would always meet or beat supply—insuring ever-higher prices. No one tried to impose a budget on the health care system. No one sat down to say, "Given finite resources, how shall we allocate health care dollars?"

On the surface, the system worked swimmingly—at least until the late sixties. Indeed many physicians would look back on the sixties and early seventies as the "golden age" of medicine, an era when television programs from *Dr. Kildare* to *Marcus Welby, M.D.* seemed to reflect widespread contentment with the nation's health care system, at least among those families lucky enough to have full insurance coverage.

But away from the cameras, costs mounted. From 1960 to 1970 the nation's health care bill rose from $27 billion to $73 billion.[43] Along the way, the government's share soared; in 1965 taxpayers shelled out $10.8 billion for health care; five years later they paid $27.8 billion.[44]

1970: A System in Crisis

By 1970 it was becoming clear that no matter how much Americans spent on health care, it never seemed to be enough. Although Medicare was less than five years old, Congress already had been forced to hike Medicare taxes by 25 percent. A report by the Senate Finance Committee blasted the way the government set physicians' reasonable charges. The law said Medicare should not pay any more than local insurance companies. But according to the report's survey of eight common procedures performed in 1968, the government sometimes paid far more. In Illinois, for example, the most Blue Shield would pay for cataract surgery was $165; Medicare paid an average of $444. In Florida, Blue Shield paid at most $117 for a hernia operation; Medicare forked over $255.[45] This, of course, does not necessarily mean that Medicare was overpaying; Blue Shield might well have been underpaying.

But it did seem that some health care providers were gouging the system. The report described "gang-visiting" of patients in hospitals and nursing homes: "A physician may see as many as 30, 40 and 50 patients a day in the same facility—regardless of whether the visit is medically necessary or whether any service is furnished. The physician in many cases charges his full fee for each patient, billing Medicare for as much as $300 or $400 for one sweep through a nursing home."[46] Again, it is not certain that physicians were taking advantage of the system. A charge of $400 to visit 40 patients means that the doctor was billing only $10 per patient. From a distance, it is impossible to determine whether such visits were "medically necessary." Nevertheless, politicians assumed the worst.

What is certain is that, despite enormous government outlays, many Americans still lacked access to medical care, particularly in rural counties and urban ghettos. Even middle-class families found that the family doctor who made house calls and accepted a pan of baklava for payment had all but disappeared. He had been replaced by high-priced specialists that only the wealthy and very well-insured could afford. While nearly 80 percent of Americans now had insurance to cover hospital bills and surgery, only slightly more than half were covered for even part of doctors' bills for office visits.[47]

Even worse, skeptics now questioned the quality of U.S. health care. Research suggested that, at one level of society, some Americans were getting too much health care in the form of unnecessary surgeries and hospital stays. Doctors had a financial incentive to treat their patients in hospitals where, studies showed, they earned 50 to 60 percent more per hour than if they performed identical services in their offices. For their part, patients had an incentive to prefer treatment in the hospital, where their hospital insurance would cover doctors' bills.[48] In 1970 a *Fortune* magazine editorial declared: "The time has come for radical change. . . . The management of medical care has become too important to leave to doctors, who are, after all, not managers to begin with."[49]

At the other end of the equation, some Americans seemed to be getting too little care: even if one excluded underserved minority populations, research revealed higher infant mortality rates among white Americans than among most Europeans.[50]

Meanwhile, specialists' fees continued to levitate, despite the fact that, in some cases, their services, measured in hours of labor, had narrowed. In *The New England Journal of Medicine,* a cardiac surgeon estimated that in 1980 members of his specialty were earning an average of $350,000 a year on cardiac bypass operations alone. Add in the other operations that they performed, Dr. Benson Roe wrote, and "it is conservative to estimate that their average gross income exceeds $500,000"—a handy sum in 1980. At the same time, the surgeon's work had become increasingly specialized. In the past, he had been expected to take care of the patient from diagnosis through postoperative care. Now technicians and other assistants took over most of those services—and of course, billed separately. "Under these circumstances," Dr. Roe noted, "one might expect the surgeon's fee to have dropped considerably, but it has not. On the contrary, fees for cardiac surgery have escalated at a rate that far exceeds the inflation factor." [51]

In January of 1970, a *Fortune* magazine cover story summed up the growing suspicion that the nation's health care dollars were being squandered. "Much of U.S. medical care, particularly the everyday business of preventing and treating routine illnesses, is inferior in quality, wastefully dispensed, and inequitably financed," *Fortune* charged. "Medical manpower and facilities are so mal-distributed that large segments of the population, especially the rural poor and those in rural areas, get virtually no care at all—even though their illnesses are most numerous and, in a medical sense, often easy to cure.

"Whether poor or not, most Americans are badly served by the obsolete, overstrained medical system that has grown up around them helter-skelter," the magazine concluded. "The time has come for radical change." [52]

Fortune was not alone. That same month *Business Week* ran a cover story that compared medical care in the United States unfavorably to national health care systems in Western Europe. As for the general public, a 1970 survey found that three-quarters of those polled agreed with the statement "There is a crisis in health care in the United States." [53]

The alarm already had sounded in the White House. "We face a massive crisis in this area," President Richard Nixon declared in 1969, "and unless action is taken, both administrative and legislative, to meet that crisis within the next two to three years, we will have a breakdown in our medical care system, which could have consequences affecting millions of people throughout this country." [54]

The next year Nixon announced a "new national health strategy" that put health maintenance organizations (HMOs) at the center of reform. The key to the administration's plan: HMOs would provide health care for a fixed fee, avoiding the perverse incentives of fee-for-service medicine. In the past, liberals had championed prepaid medical co-ops where doctors, who worked on salary, provided comprehensive care for a lump sum. Now Republicans embraced the notion as a prudent market solution to out-of-control spending, and in 1973 Congress passed the HMO Act, legislation that entitled nonprofit HMOs to receive financial assistance from the federal government in the form of grants, loans, and loan guarantees.

Nixon's Health Plan

Never a predictable president, Nixon then took a leap to the left. In 1974 he stunned his cabinet by coming out foursquare in favor of a sweeping plan for national health insurance developed by his new secretary of Health, Education, and Welfare, Caspar Weinberger. Under this proposal, employers would be required to provide private insurance for their employees, with employer and employee sharing the cost of the premiums. A separate government system would provide exactly the same benefits for the rest of the population.

Thirty years later a Democrat who dared suggest such a plan would have been labeled a Canadian. Under Nixon's Comprehensive Health Insurance Plan (CHIP) co-payments would be pegged to income: families earning over $7,500 a year would pay 25 percent of medical bills—up to a maximum of $1,500 per family a year. There would be only one tier of health care for all, covering hospital and doctor bills, lab tests, ambulance services, catastrophic illness, and mental illness. In the last category, a generous President Nixon included alcoholism and drug abuse.

"I believe that comprehensive health insurance is an idea whose time has come," Nixon told the nation in February of '74. "I believe that some kind of program will be enacted [this year]. There's long been a need to assure that no American is denied high-quality health care because he can't afford it. As prices go up, that need becomes more pressing."[55]

Up until this point, Senator Edward Kennedy had spearheaded the liberal push for health care reform. Now he gave Nixon's plan a respectful nod, calling it "a serious and carefully worded proposal."[56]

At the time, Senator Kennedy and Representative Wilbur Mills, the powerful chairman of the House Ways and Means Committee, supported a plan that was enough like the president's to make compromise possible. The president's proposal gave private insurance companies a much larger role; nevertheless the Kennedy and Weinberger staffs seemed to be closing in on a deal.

One major obstacle remained: labor unions insisted that health care should be free—without any cost-sharing by the patient. They also wanted fee-for-service medicine to be replaced, across the board, with HMOs. Finally, they were adamant that private insurance companies should have no role in the new national health insurance system. And they rejected any compromise. Livid at Kennedy's move toward the center, unions labeled him a "sellout" and announced they would oppose anything but his original single-payer bill.[57]

At the other extreme, the AMA struggled to preserve fee-for-service payment, pushing for "Medicredit"—a plan that would have the federal government provide tax incentives to help individuals buy private indemnity insurance. Under this scheme, there would be no cost controls whatsoever. But the AMA no longer represented the profession. The guild's prestige had fallen when it lost the Medicare battle with Washington in the midsixties, and membership dropped. It didn't help that the AMA had opposed a bill that ultimately raised doctors' incomes. Meanwhile, by the late sixties, some liberal young doctors were refusing to join a guild that they saw as reactionary. By 1971 only about one-half of all U.S. physicians belonged to the AMA.[58]

Behind the scenes, Congress and the White House were making headway. In the spring of 1974, Nixon's plan won an unofficial show of hands at a Ways and Means Committee meeting. In June, Kennedy announced, "A new spirit of compromise is in the air." [59]

It was not to be. For June of 1974 was, of course, the beginning of Watergate summer, a time when Congress was aboil over Nixon's impeachment. "If the name on the administration's plan had not been Nixon and if the time had not been the year of Watergate, the United States might have had national health insurance in 1974," Starr observed. "This was the last moment in the 1970s when any such program had a serious chance of adoption." [60]

Meanwhile, labor unions continued to resist compromise, and some liberal Democrats argued that if they just waited another year, they would have a chance at passing a plan that the unions could accept.

They were wrong. In the year that followed, a severe economic recession would dispel any thought of the government financing major health care reform. Nevertheless, in his first message to Congress in August of 1974, President Gerald Ford followed Nixon's lead, asking for passage of national health insurance. Then, two months later, came the final blow: on a late October night police discovered Ways and Means Committee chairman Wilbur Mills with a red-haired stripper named Fanne Foxe, who proceeded to leap from his car and throw herself into the Tidal Basin on the National Mall. When Mills resigned as chairman of the Ways and Means Committee, national health insurance lost its strongest champion in the House. In his 1976

State of the Union address, Ford withdrew the administration's plan, saying it only would make inflation worse.

The political moment had passed. In 1978 some 26 million Americans remained uninsured. Many more had only limited coverage. Then, as now, they would discover just how inadequate it was only when they fell seriously ill.

The 1980s: A Market Solution

The fact that some Americans were shut out of the system did not mean that medical spending was slowing. By 1980—the year that Ronald Reagan was elected president—the nation's health care bill had more than tripled in just ten years, climbing to $257 billion, up from $73 billion in 1970.[61]

As for the taxpayer's share of the tab, over the course of the 1970s, Medicare and Medicaid spending had snowballed, growing by nearly 600 percent. "For too long, the federal government has had a blank-check mentality," Reagan declared in 1981. "The hospitals simply filled in the amount they wanted, and then Uncle Sam—or to be more precise, the hard-pressed American taxpayer—paid the bill."[62]

In 1983 Reagan strategists took matters into their own hands. Medicare, they declared, would no longer pay fee-for-service. Instead, they divided hospital treatments into broad categories and set a fixed price for each. From then on, Medicare would pay only so much for each "diagnostic related group" (DRG).

Ten years earlier, national health care reform had catapulted to the top of the national agenda. Now the idea of a national health care system had vanished into the thin air of shifting public opinion. (This is a pattern that had been—and would continue to be—repeated throughout much of the 20th century as public enthusiasm for national health insurance waxed and waned.)

In Washington, the political winds had shifted. "Basically, the federal government backed away from its responsibility as government," Dr. Stuart Altman, deputy assistant secretary of Health, Education, and Welfare from 1971 to 1976, later charged. "It said, 'Health care is . . . the market's responsibility. It's the community's responsibility. It's the state's responsibility. It's not the federal government's responsibility.' "[63]

Others would argue that rather than ducking its duty, Washington had made a bold decision to place its faith in free market competition. With Reaganomics came a fervent belief in market forces as the solution to many, if not all, economic problems. Deregulation was the order of the day. The belief that the private sector does best without any government intervention was entrenched and would carry through to the end of the century.

That ideology dovetailed with the material reality of the eighties. Thanks to a constant flow of government and private insurance dollars, combined with the rising cost of health care, there was now enough money on the table to make medicine truly interesting as a business proposition. Quick to recognize the opportunities, entrepreneurs began building and acquiring for-profit hospitals, nursing homes, ambulatory surgical centers, renal dialysis centers, diagnostic laboratories, home care services, and—most important to the future of health care—for-profit health maintenance organizations (HMOs).

When Congress passed the original HMO Act in 1973, it did not bar investor-owned HMOs—but neither did it encourage them. The law made federal grants and loans available only to nonprofit operations. Not suprisingly, in 1981, 88 percent of all HMOS were nonprofits. But in the early eighties, Washington cut off the stream of federal financing. Searching for an alternative source of capital, many nonprofit HMOs turned to the markets and converted themselves into profit-making enterprises. By 1986 the share of nonprofits had fallen to just 41 percent.[64]

Drug companies also benefited from the laissez-faire spirit of the times. Beginning in 1980, Congress enacted a series of laws that helped them gain exclusive rights to new products. One of the most important, the Bayh-Dole Act, was designed to speed the translation of research into marketable products. Under the new law, universities and small businesses doing research sponsored by the National Institutes of Health could patent their discoveries and then grant licenses to large drug companies eager to piggyback on their findings.

Previously, research sponsored by taxpayer dollars had remained in the public domain, available to any company that wanted to use it. Now the pharmaceutical giants could claim exclusive rights to the fruit of publicly funded research. New legislation also let the NIH enter into deals with drug companies that would directly transfer NIH discoveries to industry.

The legislation turned into a windfall for Big Pharma: "These laws meant that drug companies would no longer have to rely on their own research for new drugs, and few of the large ones do," observes Dr. Marcia Angell, a former editor of *The New England Journal of Medicine,* and author of *The Truth About the Drug Companies.* "Increasingly, they rely on academia, small biotech startup companies, and the NIH for that. At least a third of drugs marketed by the major drug companies are now licensed from universities or small biotech companies, and these tend to be the most innovative ones."

Bayh-Dole was not Washington's only gift to the pharmaceutical industry: in 1984 Congress passed the Hatch-Waxman Act, extending monopoly rights for brand-name drugs. "The law was meant mainly to stimulate the floundering generic industry by short-circuiting some of the FDA requirements for bringing generic drugs to market. But Hatch-Waxman also lengthened the patent life for brand-name drugs," Angell explains. "Since then, industry lawyers have manipulated some of its provisions to extend patents far longer than the lawmakers intended."

With Washington's wind at its back, Big Pharma cruised. Over the course of the eighties, drugs stocks soared, along with profit margins. By the end of the decade, the top 10 drug companies boasted profits equal to nearly 25 percent of sales.[65]

The Coming of the Corporation: 1982

In 1982 pharmaceutical companies constituted just one corner of a burgeoning health care empire. Health care spending now accounted for more than 10 percent of GDP—up from 7.1 percent a decade earlier. (It is perhaps no accident that *St. Elsewhere,* a prime-time television program that married medical drama to black humor, premiered that year. *Marcus Welby* had been relegated to late-night reruns, replaced by an edgy, often gritty look at an inner-city hospital that reflected growing skepticism about the nation's health care system.[66])

By now employers, insurers, and taxpayers were alarmed. All agreed that health care costs could no longer grow "helter-skelter." Some 10 years earlier, *Fortune* had set the tone when it declared that "the management of medical care was too important to be left to the doctors." Now it seemed certain: medicine must be subjected to the discipline of the marketplace.

The irony, of course, is that the very entrepreneurs who promised to rein in health care costs were in fact attracted by the sea of green—the seemingly unlimited flow of health care dollars. This might have served as a warning, but it did not.

Nineteen eighty-two also turned out to be the year that Paul Starr published his watershed study, *The Social Transformation of American Medicine*. Starr ended his book with a warning: "Those who talked about 'health care planning' in the 1970s now talk about 'health care marketing.' . . . The 'health center' of one era is the 'profit center' of the next . . ." In a final chapter titled "The Coming of the Corporation," Starr expressed his concerns that while physicians had won their battle against government intervention, they may have succeeded all too well. While prevailing in the war against socialized medicine, they had lost their battle with capitalism, or what the AMA called "corporate medicine." By so jealously guarding their autonomy, health care providers had set the stage for untrammeled spending—and now power was shifting from the physician to the private sector where for-profit HMOs were gaining power. Nearly everyone agreed: the physician and his profession must now bow to the rigors of free market competition.

To Starr, "the coming of the corporation" seemed all but inevitable: "The failure to rationalize medical services under public control meant that, sooner or later they would be rationalized by private control. Instead of public regulation, there will be private regulation, and instead of public planning, there will be corporate planning." The goal driving that planning, Starr suggested, would no longer be better health, but rather "the rate of return on investments."

In 1982 Starr hoped that his sketch of the future would turn out to be a "caricature."[67] In fact, Starr's vision proved prescient: over the next 20 years, doctors, hospitals, and patients would find themselves, along with the rest of the nation, swept up in a celebration of the corporation that would put it at the very center of the culture. There, corporate executives would become both the wealthiest and the most powerful actors on the new cultural stage. In health care, as in other industries, CEOs, not physicians, would make the decisions—except in those somewhat confusing cases where the physician was also a CEO, watching over his patients' interests while simultaneously keeping an eye on the store.[68]

The Charm of a Bull Market

As the 20th century drew to a close, "managed competition" became the mantra of modern medicine: HMOs, we were told, would compete, both on quality and on price, to provide optimal care.

Not everyone wanted to give the market exclusive control. In the early nineties, some of Washington's politicians once again flirted with the idea of letting public policy makers play a greater role in setting the rules of the game. Under President Bill Clinton's Health Security Plan, managed care would have to meet a certain standard. Moreover, the government envisioned creating large regional purchasing alliances that would enroll public and private employees, the self-employed, the unemployed, and Medicare and Medicaid patients. Because of their size, these alliances would have the clout to negotiate with managed care plans, demanding quality care at an affordable price.

No surprise, the insurance industry was appalled at the very idea of regulated competition. And since the Clinton plan was conceived behind closed doors, the public never had a chance to weigh in. All that most people knew was that the 1,364-page bill sounded complicated—very complicated. "The whole thing blew up at the grassroots level. There was so very little information out there that the insurance industry was able to fill in that vacuum with fear," recalls Richard Evans, a health care analyst at Sanford C. Bernstein & Company who served as an executive at Roche Pharmaceuticals throughout much of the nineties.[69]

The secrecy that shrouded the Clinton health care plan doomed it to oblivion, but even if the process had been public, the timing was less than propitious. The health care system that would evolve in the nineties was founded, in large part, on the bull market's faith in corporate America. In 1993—the year that the administration proposed its plan—the Dow rose by 13.7 percent. In its own way, health care fell under the bull's charm. The conventional wisdom of the time held that markets are rational. No wonder so many believed that as American medicine became more corporate, market forces would work their magic, creating a health care system that offered the highest quality at the lowest possible cost.

This has not happened. Market forces may work well to do many things, but creating a sustainable, affordable health care system does not appear to

be one of them. It is not just that by the end of the 1990s both doctors and patients questioned the quality of managed care. Free market competition had not even succeeded in doing what it is supposed to do best: manage costs.

Granted, in the mid-1990s, health care inflation plateaued—briefly. But by the end of the decade, health care costs were once again rising far faster than inflation.[70] Meanwhile, the baby boomers were aging. Early in the 21st century, it became apparent that we had reached a turning point: In 1960 the nation spent $27 billion on health care—roughly 5.1 percent of gross national product. By 2005 the tab approached $2 trillion, or 16 percent of GDP.

"Managed competition" had seemed such a clean, clear idea, and on paper, it was. Looking back on the nineties, Dr. Lawrence Casalino, a physician who had practiced family medicine for 20 years before becoming an assistant professor of health studies at the University of Chicago, could not help but remember a question that a reporter once asked Mohandas Gandhi:

"What do you think of Western civilization?"

"I think it would be a very good idea," Gandhi replied.

"The same," Casalino observed, "could be said of managed care."[71]

This, of course, is no reason to give up on the idea of Western civilization. Nor is it a reason to give up on the hope that, under different circumstances, free market competition could help to create a rational health care system.

The "Business" of Selling Dreams

Still, the question remains: why does the price of health care continue to spiral? Some blame galloping technology. In many other industries technology saves money; in the world of health care, increasingly sophisticated technology usually leads to ever more expensive treatments. Often these treatments save lives; in many other cases, benefits are uncertain. Or as one young doctor puts it: "There are so many things we can do—and so we do them." Again, when it comes to health care, supply leads demand around by the nose.[72]

But technology remains only a partial answer. Beneath the explosion in medical technology lies a deeper truth: what is good for business is more business.

As medicine becomes more corporate, it is, quite naturally, driven by the quest for profits. A corporation's first responsibility is to its shareholders. And corporate planners know that, with some luck, more sales will lead to higher earnings. (Or at least that is the conventional wisdom, especially during a boom.) But more health care—more devices, more drugs, more procedures—does not necessarily lead to greater health. Quite the opposite, as some of the latest research confirms.

Comparing Medicare patients in regions of the country where Medicare spending is highest to patients in areas where spending is lower, a study published in *Annals of Internal Medicine* in 2003 found that more visits to the doctor, more tests, more attention from specialists, and more hospitalization did not result in lower mortality rates or improved health. In fact, in some cases, more care seemed to produce higher death rates. "Our finding suggests that up to about a third of medical care is devoted to services that do not provide any detectable benefit," Dr. Elliott S. Fisher, the Dartmouth Medical School researcher who led the study, concluded.[73]

This, then, is the contradiction that lies at the very heart of the idea of "corporate medicine." Insofar as health care has become a growth industry, "the pressure is to increase total health-care expenditures, not to reduce them," observes former *NEJM* editor Marcia Angell. But here corporate goals conflict with society's need to make health care affordable. "Presumably, as a nation we want to constrain the growth of health costs," Angell adds. "But that's simply not what health-care businesses do. Like all businesses, they want more, not fewer, customers—but only if they can pay."[74]

In the final decades of the 20th century, this drive for profits, coupled with the advance of modern technology, fed that century's boundless appetite for unlimited growth, unlimited progress, and unlimited resources. "The medical marketplace is in the business of selling dreams," Daniel Callahan, cofounder of The Hastings Center, an independent research institute that focuses on bioethics, observed in 1998. "The union of technological medicine and the market has intensified the belief that . . . when all seems lost, medicine can rescue us."[75]

But by now it is apparent that the millennial vision of transcendent, unlimited growth was part of the myth of the nineties—part of the delusion that allowed us to believe that corporate profits could rise, year after year, by 15 or 20 percent, that the U.S. trade deficit could grow to the heavens without harming anyone, and that the stock market could forever postpone its

rendezvous with fair value. The reality is that in the material world, there are limits. In the physical world, nature eventually catches up with us. And in the world of money, just as in nature, resources are always finite.

This is something those who truly understand markets recognize. And this is why some of the most experienced market-watchers on Wall Street believe that the U.S. health care system is heading for a cliff. "The genie's out of the bottle," says one money manager. "The system's running out of money."[76] Sanford Bernstein's Richard Evans agrees: "There is no rational scenario where the status quo can continue. It can't happen economically or politically. Something has to give."[77]

2

The Cost of Competition: An Overview

In all parts of the healthcare system, the providers of care see themselves as competing businesses struggling to survive in a hostile economic climate, and they act accordingly. The predictable result is a fragmented, inefficient, and expensive system.

—Arnold S. Relman, MD[1]

Over the past 25 years, market forces have splintered the U.S. health care system, converting what was, at its best, a network of collaborative relationships among patients, doctors, and hospitals into a vast and competitive marketplace.[2] In theory, free market competition should reduce the cost of a product. But economics is as much a belief system as it is a science, and economists' theories do not always pan out in the material world.[3] In practice, the scramble for health care dollars has proved extraordinarily expensive—both in terms of the quality of care and in terms of its cost.

The result is a Hobbesian marketplace where a war of "all against all" pits the health care industry's players against one another: hospital vs. hospital, doctor vs. hospital, doctor vs. doctor, hospital vs. insurer, insurer vs. hospi-

tal, insurer vs. insurer, insurer vs. drugmaker, drugmaker vs. drugmaker. In this adversarial environment, "competitors do not create value, they divide it. And sometimes, they destroy it," says Michael Porter, a Harvard Business School professor well-known for his writings on market competition. "Health care plans, hospitals, doctors and payers . . . all are trying to assemble bargaining power so that they can strike a better deal for themselves while shifting cost." But passing costs like a hot potato, from one player to another, creates no net value. Instead, gains for one participant come at the expense of others'—and frequently with added administrative costs.[4]

Managed Competition

Of course many would argue that, in the health care industry, market forces have never really been given a chance to work their magic. As the 20th century drew to a close, managed competition was supposed to provide a laissez-faire solution, but by the end of the decade most agreed that the experiment had failed. Under managed care, the market's invisible hand was manacled to an insurance company's all-too-visible bureaucracy. Rather than allowing doctors and patients to choose the best course of treatment, insurance companies tried to dictate the care a patient would receive.

This was not what was supposed to happen. Managed care's architects had envisioned a health care system that could contain costs while simultaneously lifting the quality of care. Traditional fee-for-service medicine leads to health care inflation, its critics argue, because it encourages caregivers to maximize the number of procedures they perform, while scanting or ignoring preventive care. Doctors and hospitals are not paid to keep patients well; they are paid to treat them when they are sick—the more treatments the better. Meanwhile, caregivers who try to improve medical outcomes watch their income drop. For example, when Duke University Hospital created an integrated program to treat congestive heart failure, its patients were healthier, but because there were fewer complications, there were fewer admissions— and the hospital lost money.[5]

Managed competition set out to erase the perverse incentives of fee-for-service medicine. Rather than paying for each treatment, HMOs would pay caregivers a fixed amount to treat a patient over the course of a year. This, in turn, would encourage doctors and hospitals to find the most cost-effective

way to care for each patient—emphasizing low-tech and preventive measures, while limiting unnecessary surgery and visits to specialists. The result seemed all but inevitable: better care at a lower cost.

Dr. Lawrence Casalino (the physician who compares managed care to Western civilization—a "good idea" but difficult to implement), explains why, over the course of the nineties, managed care failed on both counts: "Early on, I think managed care did provide savings, but these were the easy pickings—keeping patients out of hospitals who really didn't need to be there, or not hospitalizing patients with low-back pain for traction, for example, as we used to do when I was first in practice. I mean, at the time that was just routine. 'Oh, your back hurts, we'll put you in the hospital for traction.'

"So eliminating these kinds of practices did generate one-time savings," Casalino continues. "But over the long run, managing care is a matter of creating *processes* that can really improve the care of patients with congestive heart failure or diabetes or asthma or other chronic diseases. That's hard, and that's just barely begun to be done."[6]

Even the prepaid HMOs of the nineties did not reward the kind of continuous, preventive care needed to manage chronic diseases. As Joanne Andiorio, the former president and CEO of Pittsburgh's Mercy Health System, points out: "The HMO paid the doctor the same fixed amount to care for a patient, whether the patient went to the doctor or not. As a result, most doctors continued to practice episodic medicine—seeing a diabetic, for example, only when he became ill. True 'managed care' would encourage continuous visits that allowed the doctor to monitor the patient's ongoing condition."[7]

But developing the systems needed to provide ongoing high-quality preventive care requires time, money—and a long-term perspective, says Casalino, who practiced family medicine for two decades in Half Moon Bay, California, before joining the faculty at the University of Chicago. "For instance, if a group practice of physicians invests a lot of money in lowering patients' cholesterol or in getting screening exams for diabetics for retinopathy, that costs the group money this year," Casalino observes, "but it isn't going to save any money this year. It's going to save money years down the line."[8]

Hospitals also focus on the short term, says Andiorio, a former nun who served as president and CEO of Mercy for most of the nineties. "Today's

hospital CEOs are bottom-line oriented. Increasingly, they're MBAs," she adds. "Their forte is not process or the kind of long-term outcome evaluation that is most needed to control quality."[9]

Nor did the for-profit HMOs of the nineties reward caregivers for saving money "down the line."[10] After all, in what has become a spot market for employment, a patient might well change jobs and switch health care plans in two or three years. Why, then, would an insurer want to invest in screening a diabetic for retinopathy when, in all likelihood, another company would reap the benefits? Even if, by chance, the patient stuck with the original plan, a for-profit insurer's first obligation is to its investors, and Wall Street demands earnings growth *now*—not in two or three years.[11]

It should come as no surprise then, that rather than taking the high road and competing on quality, most managed care plans began to compete solely on price. And in order to offer employers the lowest possible price, they skimped on what many patients and doctors argued was necessary care. Primary physicians who were assigned the role of gatekeeper refused referrals to costly specialists; if a patient did manage to scale the gate, the HMO might well deny payment for the surgery that the specialist recommended.

The media reveled in the resulting headlines about care denied and lives ruined. No doubt some of the stories were exaggerated, but many were true. Both patients and doctors revolted against managed care, and the intensity of the backlash made one thing clear: *Insurance companies possess neither the expertise nor the standing to set the nation's health care priorities.*

By the end of the nineties, insurers had no choice but to begin loosening restrictions. Originally, managed care's advocates had envisioned HMOs with distinct networks of doctors and hospitals vying for customers. But employers soon discovered that employees wanted access to all of a community's important hospitals, not to mention a long list of doctors. In response, HMOs broadened their networks to a point where employees were left with a "choice" between two or three plans offering access to virtually the same hospitals and doctors—undermining the very idea of discrete groups of caregivers going head-to-head on quality and price. In the process, as managed care plans gave up the power to exclude doctors and hospitals, they surrendered the clout needed to negotiate discounts. There was, however, one important advantage to more inclusive networks: patients enjoyed greater continuity of care. By 2000, if an employee changed

health care plans, there was only a 50-50 chance that he would have to switch doctors.[12]

Responding to a combination of lawsuits and bad press, the most popular managed care plans also became more liberal about approving sophisticated procedures. Ultimately, many plans began to rubber-stamp virtually every treatment that patients requested: "The social compact was that managed care would make careful decisions about costs; instead, they became a cost-through vehicle," says one Wall Street observer.[13] In some cases, this meant paying for questionable surgeries like bone marrow transplants for breast cancer patients—risky, costly procedures that could turn out to be of little or no benefit.[14]

Inevitably, as insurers eased restrictions, costs levitated, along with premiums. From 2000 to 2005 the cost of family coverage jumped 73 percent. Over the same span, wages rose by 15 percent.[15] But despite soaring premiums, most patients and doctors were more than happy to see the HMOs retreat.

"Unmanaged Competition"

As the new millennium began, tightly managed competition gave way to what health care economist James C. Robinson calls "unmanaged competition." As Robinson describes it, unmanaged competition begins to sound more like truly untrammeled, free market capitalism, creating a marketplace "notable not only for its turbulence, but also for its creativity, as freewheeling competition fosters innovation" while "medical groups, hospital systems and health care plans, come together, dissolve and re-group."

Robinson acknowledges that in a market roiled by "turbulent cycles of expansion and contraction, diversification and refocusing, merger and divestitures," the melee can turn rough. After all, he points out, "health plans are not selfless sponsors [operating] for the social good. They wrestle with purchasers for higher revenues, with providers for lower costs, and with each other for brand name recognition, market dominance and profit leadership."[16]

Nevertheless, Robinson applauds the virtues of a vibrant marketplace, which promises consumers "a complete menu of choices, a chaos of oppor-

tunities, a cacophony of sales pitches." Through it all, Robinson suggests, "the American consumer reigns sovereign."[17]

At the same time, his alliterative language betrays his reservations about a form of unmanaged competition that shifts more and more responsibility to the consumer. A "cacophony of sales pitches" sounds very much like the cascade of unfiltered investment information that was supposed to help the individual investors of the nineties sort through their choices. As it turned out, some of that information was true, some of it was false, and much of it was slanted to show only a slice of reality.

"This is a double-edged sword," Robinson acknowledged in a 2005 interview. "Some consumers are not in a position to make wise choices. I don't know how many—say 10 percent. But these will be the poorest and the sickest—the cancer patient who is in a coma. . . . I worry about them, because their need for health care is greatest."[18]

Moreover, even if the consumer is able to sort through the laissez-faire chaos of conflicting and sometimes misleading sales pitches, the number of customers who can afford the full menu—or even part of the menu—is shrinking. As employers shift the cost of health insurance to employees, a growing number will find premium hikes too steep for their budgets: from 2000 to 2005, the average worker's share of premiums for family coverage climbed by $1,091.[19]

Granted, not everyone believes that middle-class Americans are being priced out of the health care market. "If people can take their children to Disney World, why can't they afford health care? What's more important?" one doctor grumbles. But when the cost of health care is set against the average family's income, it becomes clear why so many fear that they won't be able to afford insurance next year.[20] Faced with monthly premiums that approach the mortgage payment on a small house, more and more households are likely to fall back on "pared-down" plans that leave them seriously underinsured. In 2003, Texas, for example, became one of eight states that allow insurers to offer no-frills plans that exclude certain benefits. Among the "frills" eliminated: coverage for complications during pregnancy; treatment for HIV and AIDS; contraceptives; treatment for serious mental illness, diabetes, speech and hearing impairment; and home health care.

"Patients might walk around with a card showing that they're insured. But how much coverage do they really have? That's the frightening part," says Patricia Kolodzey, the Texas Hospital Association's director of insurance and managed care. "The big concern is the lack of a clear definition on what kind of basic health care should be covered," adds Dr. Lewis Foxhall, a physician at the M. D. Anderson Cancer Center in Houston. He argues that when plans limit treatment of AIDS or chronic diseases like diabetes, "patients just wind up getting sicker and end up costing the system [i.e., the taxpayer] more in the end."[21]

A Hostile Economic Climate

The consumer's dilemma only heightens the economic pressure on health care providers. With 15 percent of the population uninsured and countless others underinsured, competition for patients who *can* pay their bills is not merely robust—it is fierce. And this is precisely what worries Dr. Arnold S. Relman, a former editor of *The New England Journal of Medicine*. Rather than collaborating, "hospitals and physicians see themselves as competing businesses struggling to survive in a hostile economic climate," Relman warns. "And they act accordingly."

While Robinson applauds the vibrancy of the marketplace, Relman fears that free market competition has turned into a free-for-all, with providers wrestling for scarce health care dollars while hundreds of private insurers "constantly seek to reduce both their payments to providers and their financial obligations to sick patients. The predictable result," Relman concludes, "is a fragmented, inefficient, and expensive system."[22]

Ultimately, so much competition isn't even good for the investors who sink their savings into health care stocks. A 2003 report by the Institute for Health and Socioeconomic Policy, an independent watchdog association, calls "the internal profit war within the health care industry" both "self-destructive" and "the real genesis of the current crisis in escalating health care spending."

At the same time, public support for corporate health care is eroding. IHSP stresses the importance of public perception: "The industry's survival as an industry is linked to its ability to be widely seen as legitimate, fair and trustworthy by both the general public and the nation's caregivers." But in 2003, the report warned, consumers see health care companies as "guilty of opportunistic price-gouging," and this perception fosters "a growing sense among workers, retirees and the general population that the health care industry simply is not fair." [23]

A 2004 Harris poll asking how well 15 industries serve consumers confirms widespread distrust of corporate health care. At the very bottom of the scorecard, managed care companies tied with tobacco companies (with only 30 percent of those surveyed saying that either does a good job). Insurers and drugmakers placed just a notch above oil companies (with just 36 percent of respondents giving the nod to insurers and 44 percent to drugmakers). Of all the sectors in the health care industry, only hospitals ranked in the middle of the list, with 70 percent of those surveyed saying they did a good job—and even so, hospitals had slipped in the polls, down from a 77 percent approval rating in 1997. Banks, computer companies, and airlines all scored higher. [24]

Hospital vs. Hospital

Not only are hospitals sinking in the polls, many are swimming in red ink. As the number of Americans without full coverage grows, unpaid bills mount: by 2003 a PricewaterhouseCoopers survey of hospitals showed that bad debt had climbed to nearly 10 percent of revenues—up from 7.9 percent in 1999. [25] That same year another survey revealed that nearly one-quarter of all large hospitals reported that they had either "run a deficit or been unable to stay in budget" during the past year, while 30 percent said that their current financial condition was "insufficient to maintain current levels of service." [26]

Backs to the wall, 21st-century hospitals have revived the "medical arms race" of earlier decades. In the 1970s and early 1980s, hospitals tried to dazzle both doctors and patients by spending lavishly on the latest technology, even if that meant duplicating the equipment that the hospital down the street already had. [27] In the nineties, the arms race slowed as HMOs put their stamp on a new, more frugal marketplace. Hospitals hoping to win business from managed care plans had to compete primarily on price—which meant they resisted the lure of superfluous or redundant technology. But by the end of the decade, HMO enrollments were heading south, and in 2001 researchers found that U.S. hospitals were once again pouring millions into the newest in high-tech inpatient and outpatient services—even though "many admitted [these services] duplicated existing services in their communities." [28]

"Hospitals are adding a service because a competitor already offers it or is expected to do so in the near future," explains Kelly Devers, a health researcher for the Center for Studying Health System Change who helped oversee the survey. "As the battle for doctors and patients becomes more intense, the mimicking and one-upmanship of the eighties is returning."[29]

Inevitably, duplication fuels health care inflation. When a half dozen hospitals in a single city invest in the same multimillion-dollar equipment, some of it will be underused—or, even worse, overused. One way or another, in order to cover the purchase, each hospital must pass the cost on to its patients—and to the taxpayers and employers who pay for their care.

As they struggle to offset mounting debt, rival hospitals fight for market share in the most profitable high-tech lines of businesses. In particular, they aim to capture customers in the most lucrative niches: cardiology, orthopedics, and oncology. As a result, three or four hospitals within a single city can easily wind up investing in dueling cardiology centers. Meanwhile, a cadre of local cardiologists may decide to set up their own freestanding surgical center—specializing in the very same procedures.

Specialty Hospital vs. Community Hospital

In cities across the nation, physician-owned specialty hospitals have been popping up like Starbucks. The theory behind these so-called focused factories is a good one: research shows that when surgical teams repeat the same procedure thousands of times, outcomes improve.[30] Surgeons agree. "Physicians believe [excellence depends on] practice, not talent," writes Dr. Atul Gawande, a surgeon at Boston's Brigham and Women's Hospital. "People often assume that you have to have great hands to become a surgeon, but it's not true. When I interviewed to get into surgery programs, no one made me sew or take a dexterity test or checked if my hands were steady. . . . Attending physicians say that what is most important to them is finding people who are conscientious, industrious and boneheaded enough to stick at practicing this one difficult thing day and night for years on end."[31]

Yet while focused factories offer the promise of "Practice makes perfect," there is a downside to freestanding centers. Critics accuse for-profit physician-owned surgical centers of threatening the financial stability of nearby general care hospitals by skimming the most lucrative business while leaving the community hospitals to provide much-needed but unprofitable services such as trauma centers and burn units. "We're being plundered by our orthopods. They joined a surgery center started by a plastic surgeon and took 3,000 surgeries out of the hospital," says one CEO.[32]

The surgeons who own the centers enjoy an unfair advantage, community hospitals say, because they can cherry-pick patients, based on ability to pay, "steering" the easiest, best-insured cases to their facilities. "I sit on the board of a surgical center where the physicians regularly talk about sending some patients to the [community] hospital, and other better-paying patients to our surgery center," one doctor confides.[33]

In retaliation, hospitals like Mount Carmel Health System in Columbus, Ohio, have threatened to revoke admitting privileges for doctor-investors who divert profitable patients to their new $30 million for-profit orthopedic clinic. "You cannot stand by and watch people rip whatever profitable veins there are in the institution away from you," declared Michael Curtin, Mount Carmel's board chairman.[34]

Curtin has a point. The effect on a general acute-care hospital can be devastating. Traditionally, cardiac services have accounted for 25 to 40 percent of a hospital's net revenues, while orthopedic services have been the most important source of revenue for hospitals that do not have cardiac services.[35] Meanwhile, the new competition is serious and growing fast. Nationwide, the General Accounting Office reckons that between 1990 and 2003 the number of inpatient surgical centers tripled, to more than 90—with 20 more under development. Over the same span, the number of physician-owned ambulatory surgical centers providing outpatient care doubled to 3,371, closing in on the 3,859 outpatient surgery departments owned by larger hospitals.[36] In November of 2003, Congress stepped into the fray with an amendment to Medicare legislation, ordering an 18-month moratorium on new physician-owned specialty hospitals. In June of 2005, the moratorium expired, but the Centers for Medicare and Medicaid said that it would need the rest of the year to review procedures for enrolling specialty hospitals.[37]

At its best, the competition has inspired some general care hospitals to develop new products and services within their own walls. In one case, a hospital responded to its obstetricians' plans to open a women's specialty hospital by finding out what the doctors wanted (more beds, more operating rooms, and improved services for patients) and then initiating a major capital expansion to provide these upgrades.[38] Instead of competing, they collaborated.

But a competitive threat works to improve care only if the added capacity is needed. Facilities that siphon dollars from general care hospitals by replicating existing services while offering only minor improvements in the quality of care (more convenient parking, for example, or larger rooms for patients) serve only to weaken a community's total health care system.[39]

The real problem, argues Michael Connelly, president and CEO of Catholic Healthcare Partners, is not the competition but the fact that "flawed reimbursement systems" make some lines of business so much more profitable than others: "It doesn't make sense to have a system that creates huge margins in open-heart surgeries and other complex surgical procedures," says Connelly, "but little or no margin for the treatment of pneumonia and other medical conditions."[40]

Connelly's point is indisputable, and in June of 2005 the Centers for Medicare and Medicaid said it would review reimbursements to specialty hospitals. But even if the way private insurers and government reimburse hospitals were fixed, critics argue that redundant facilities can lead to overtreatment. "The physician-owned hospitals tend to fill their beds, even [in a city where] you have excess capacity," adds Bob Taylor, a principal and senior health care analyst at Banc of America Securities. Physicians tend to find the illnesses they are looking for, and so "if you lock up the top orthopedic group in town, your facility is going to be full, because the physicians are going to drive the demand and steer the patients into it," Taylor explains.[41]

One might expect that the duplication of services would set off price wars. But again, the health care industry differs from most others. Because suppliers drive demand, excess supply rarely drives prices lower. Instead, more hospitals beds create demand for more surgeries, more tests, and more procedures, ramping up the cost of care. "Build the beds and they will come. Look at radiology costs," says Kelly Devers. "We're seeing MRIs and CTs proliferating, and when we look at utilization, it's skyrocketing."[42]

Certainly, heart surgery did not become appreciably cheaper in Indianapolis when The Heart Center of Indiana threw open the doors to a new facility in 2002. The for-profit center, which is jointly owned by a group of physicians and St. Vincent Health, added 60 new heart-care beds to the area—and the competition was not far behind. Over the next two years, In-

dianapolis's four primary hospital systems spent $220 million building, reno-
vating, expanding, and in the end, adding roughly 15 to 20 percent new capacity to the city's heart services.[43] Five adult open-heart surgery programs
now serve a population of just 1.6 million potential patients.

Available evidence suggests that the population had little immediate need
for more heart surgery programs. Open-heart surgery volumes in the area
have been on a downward slide for at least four years. In 2000, before the
two specialty hospitals existed, the area's four open-heart programs performed 4,377 procedures. Today many patients are opting for less invasive
procedures: by 2002 the number of open-heart surgeries had dropped to
3,310, a 24 percent decline.[44]

Yet Indianapolis's hospitals felt compelled to expand their heart-surgery
programs, the Center for Studying Health System Change reports, because
area cardiologists had threatened to partner up with MedCath, a national
for-profit cardiovascular service company, to build a cardiology center of
their own. "Only if demand increases will new specialty hospitals and general hospitals both have enough volume to provide high-quality, low-cost
services," warns the center, a nonprofit Washington think tank.[45]

Nevertheless, in 2004 Tom Malasto, executive director of the Cardiac
and Vascular Care Center at St. Francis Hospital, was not worried about
overcapacity, pointing out that lifestyle factors in central Indiana indicated
that demand for cardiology services will continue to grow. "The most recent
CDC stats place Indiana as one of the top five states for obesity and prevalence of smoking," he observed.[46]

No one was talking about what would happen if some of the millions
poured into new cardiac centers over the past few years had been funneled
into preventive care that might reduce obesity and smoking rates. This is understandable: traditionally, open-heart surgery promises high profit margins.
Preventive medicine does not. And so it's little wonder that doctors in Indianapolis were more interested in investing in cardiac centers than in smoking
clinics. It's hard to imagine a better illustration of the medical industry
watching health deteriorate and, instead of stepping in to prevent it, making
plans to cash in on the decline.

Or as medical ethicist Daniel Callahan points out, *"The market is far better at
meeting immediate short-term private interests than long-term collective needs."* (emphasis mine)[47]

Indianapolis does not stand alone as the Midwest's mecca for heart surgery. Milwaukee boasts no fewer than 13 adult cardiology centers. Leo Brideau, president and CEO of Columbia St. Mary's health system, is candid: "These for-profit centers don't propose to serve inner-city regions. They want the high-profit, easier-to-take-care-of patients." But in February of 2004, Brideau told *HealthLeaders* magazine that he wasn't yet worried about the competition. "There is still enough [profit] margin in cardiovascular services" to offset any underutilization of facilities, the magazine explained.[48] For-profit margins on cardiovascular surgery are rich: nationwide, insurers were paying hospitals an average of $29,300 for a coronary bypass in 2002 according to John Birkmeyer, an associate professor of surgery at Dartmouth Medical School, and out of that, the institutions netted an average of $6,800 in profit.[49]

Meanwhile, fat margins mean that more health care dollars are spent on advertising. Incredibly, Milwaukee-area hospitals outstripped both fast-food restaurants and banks in ad spending in 2003, laying out $7.4 million. "The cardiac advertising is so intense. In our competitive market, people are confused about who is who," admits Ann Saqr, Covenant Healthcare System's vice president of marketing and advertising.

"But don't look for hospitals to advertise based on the price of health care services," notes the *Milwaukee Journal Sentinel.* "Milwaukee's highly competitive market doesn't mean patients can shop for low prices. On the contrary, hospitals typically don't compete on price but on amenities: marble lobbies, paintings, tapestries and even fireplaces and indoor waterfalls, things that make health care even more expensive" in a town where "health costs are among the highest in the country."[50]

Finally, there is the very real danger that, rather than sharpening the quality of care, too much competition can lead to unneeded surgeries. A wave of studies done from 1998 through 2001 show Americans undergoing four times as many bypass operations and five times as many angioplasties as the citizens of other developed nations. What sets the United States apart is the number of surgeries performed on patients over the age of 80. Because so many factors affect a patient's health—especially in the case of older patients—it is extraordinarily difficult to compare outcomes. But researchers have found little evidence that elderly patients in the United States fared better than those who had less surgery. Indeed, one comparative study published in *The New England Journal of Medicine* found that one year after the U.S.

patients received surgery, mortality rates in that group were nearly identical to mortality rates among a group of Canadian patients who did not go under the knife.[51]

This is not to suggest that bypass surgery is inappropriate for all patients over 80. But octogenarians tend to suffer from more than one ailment simultaneously, and these complications, combined with the risk of surgery, make some health care providers question whether it is wise—or even kind—to put certain elderly patients through the ordeal.

"Do we do more procedures than are necessary? Absolutely," says Dr. Thomas Riles, a cardiovascular surgeon and chief of surgery at New York University Medical Center. "Recently, I lectured in Korea and Japan," Riles confides, "and over there, they do a fraction of the surgeries we do—perhaps 10 percent. I would say they do too few, but we're at the other end of the spectrum. We do too many."[52]

But the threat is not just that a medical arms race can lead to unnecessary surgeries and wasteful spending. Too much competition can dilute the quality of care. If too many facilities in a single city are trying to specialize in heart surgery, the surgical teams at these hospitals do fewer procedures. They may draw enough business to turn a nice profit—but not enough to remain at the top of their game.

Cincinnati, Ohio, for example, weighed in with eight open-heart surgery programs in 2002—so many that only two of the eight programs performed more than 400 coronary artery bypass grafts that year. Such low numbers undermine the very notion of a "focused factory." The Leapfrog Group, an alliance of employers that monitors patient safety, contends that hospitals performing fewer than 450 coronary artery bypass grafts experience higher surgical mortality rates. Six of Cincinnati's programs did not make the cutoff.

"There was a time when we made a valiant attempt to limit coronary bypass care to certain facilities, or 'centers of excellence,' " recalls Dr. Jack Mahoney, a corporate medical director who oversees health care strategy at Pitney Bowes. "But then the lobbyists from the AMA and the AHA came in, saying that the way to improve health care was to stimulate competition. The U.S. is one of the only countries I know that has made health care a purely entrepreneurial activity," adds Mahoney, who served as White House physician during President Gerald Ford's administration.[53]

Doctor vs. Hospital

In what Dr. Arnold Relman rightly describes as an increasingly hostile economic climate, it should come as no surprise that the social contract between doctor and hospital also is fraying—and this too carries a price. Not only are entrepreneurial physicians battling hospitals for patients, some are refusing to fulfill traditional hospital duties without compensation. The chief operating officer of a rural community hospital recalls a conversation with a young doctor who walked into his office and informed him that he would no longer be willing to be on call for the hospital's ER.[54]

When the doctor had signed on with the hospital, he, like all of the other physicians, had agreed to be available to treat ER patients one week a month. Typically, this meant coming into the hospital three or four times during that week. But now, he explained, he wanted to spend more time at home with his children. He was not willing to continue answering the calls unless the hospital would pay him $80,000 a year for the service.

The COO was nonplussed. He did not ask how the doctor had calculated that quality time with his children was worth $80,000. "But we have a contract," he protested.

The young doctor nodded. "Times change," he said easily.

The COO knew that, legally, the hospital had a responsibility to have specialists on call to cover emergencies. He also knew that if he paid one doctor, he would have to pay all of them—adding millions in additional expenses to a budget that was already under water.

Yet it is not surprising that the doctor wanted to be paid, says James Orlikoff, a health care consultant who has been advising hospitals and insurers for more than 20 years. "In the past, a physician with privileges at a hospital enjoyed substantial economic benefits from that relationship, and so he was willing to fulfill certain obligations to the hospital without compensation," he explains. "But today privileges don't carry the same benefits."[55] A hospital administrator in Arizona agrees: "There was a time when a doctor might well pick up new patients by treating people in the ER. But these days patients are likely to belong to a managed care plan, and they'll go to a doctor in their plan for follow-up treatment."[56] Or worse, the patient will turn out be uninsured, making him a less than ideal "new patient."

Still, in this case, the doctor was demanding a very high price for his services. Based on past experience, the COO knew that, in all likelihood, the young doctor would be needed only two or three times a week during the 12 weeks of the year that he was on call. An additional $80,000 would work out to payment of roughly $2,200 to $3,300 each time that he came in. Nevertheless, the COO did not even try to negotiate. He knew that if he refused to pay the amount asked, he risked alienating not only this physician, but all of the others who practiced at the hospital. In response, they might well begin referring some of their most profitable business to a hospital in a city just an hour and a half away. He had no choice but to agree.

This is not an uncommon situation; covering ERs has become a problem nationwide. "Emergency room patients often must wait hours—or sometimes days—for treatment from specialists, largely because many doctors resist coming in unless they are assured adequate payment," according to a 2003 report by the California Senate Office of Research. Fewer doctors are willing to work for the rates offered by Medi-Cal and other health plans, the report explained. "In some cases, patients are shuffled from hospital to hospital until an appropriate specialist is found."

As an example, the study cited the case of a man suffering from internal bleeding who came into the emergency room of an unidentified California hospital. Over the next three hours, six gastrointestinal specialists refused to come to the hospital to treat the patient. Finally, the director of the emergency room lured a specialist to the hospital with a promise of $500 cash. The specialist then performed the needed procedure, and the bleeding was stemmed.[57]

"Across the country, doctors are blackmailing hospitals," says Orlikoff, the national advisor on governance and leadership to the American Hospital Association and Health Forum. "The hospitals just don't want it to get out. It underlines how precarious the entire U.S. hospital system is."[58]

Doctor vs. Doctor

"When we were in training, they warned us that things were changing," recalls Dr. Robert Rosen, who graduated from medical school in 1976. "But there's been much more change in the past five years than in the previous 25."[59]

"Today everyone is very open about treating medicine as a business,"

Rosen, the director of interventional radiology and endovascular surgery at New York University Medical Center, explains. "The business model has trumped all of what we used to consider the normal perspectives on how we do things." When he became a physician, he recalls, "You would be embarrassed to mention money. It just didn't come up in polite medical conversation about how to treat a patient. But in the eighties and nineties, the whole country shifted gears and the corporate paradigm took over. Unfortunately, that has affected medicine along with everything else."

What Rosen describes is more than a cultural shift: in recent years, the economic realities of U.S. health care have begun to close in on the profession. In 1990 the nation spent $700 billion on health care. By 2006 the tab had tripled. And as medical spending spiraled, employers, state governments, insurers, and taxpayers began to rebel. "There is just an awareness of the cost of things that wasn't around 10 years ago," says Rosen.

"There used to be more than enough work for everyone," he adds. "Physicians in different specialties weren't vying for patients—so turf issues weren't so important. Usually, there was agreement among doctors about what procedure was best for the patient." Today, however, some physicians are less willing to collaborate.

A sign of the changing times: in 2004 Rosen found himself in the middle of a turf war that pitted doctor against doctor at NYU Medical Center. "People I've known for 25 years aren't talking to me," he said, sounding both discouraged and resigned to a situation that he did not expect would change.[60]

The trouble began, says Rosen, when minimally invasive techniques became a popular alternative to standard open surgery, and the hospital's "interventional cardiologists" and "interventional radiologists" began to compete with cardiovascular surgeons. Rather than cutting the body open, "the interventionalists use devices like catheters and stents [tiny metal scaffolds that prop arteries open] to treat cardio and vascular disease," Rosen explains.

Thanks in large part to these devices, by 2003 the number of bypass surgeries performed in the United States had plunged by 20 percent in just nine years. Meanwhile, *The Wall Street Journal* reported, Medicare had slashed its reimbursements. In 2002 a surgeon earned $1,850 for a bypass, down from $4,000 in 1987.[61] Private insurers also cut fees. Bypass had been a big business—a very big business. Tempers began to flare, and the battle for patients escalated. "Many physicians—especially the middle-aged guys who entered the profession when reimbursements were highest—began trying to make it up on volume," one young surgeon in Chicago explains.[62]

At NYU, Rosen says, "We set up the cardiovascular center in 2001 so that surgeons and other cardio and vascular specialists could work together to decide which procedure was most appropriate for an individual patient." In some cases, surgery would be needed; in other cases, the less invasive procedure would make more sense. "Then we planned to assign the procedures to doctors based on who was best qualified and pool the fees."

Sharing the fees was the key to making the economics of the collaboration work, Rosen claims: "It wouldn't matter how many procedures any individual doctor did—at the end of the year, we would all share in the profits. But now the surgeons are backing out. They say that they have learned to perform the new procedure using stents and catheters themselves, and that they can do it just as well as the interventionalists who specialize in using these devices—even though they don't have the experience. The surgeons are learning on the job."

The dispute isn't solely about money, he explains: "There are egos involved. Doctors want to feel that they're in control, that there's nothing that someone else can do that they can't do. But they also want the business. And they don't want to share fees. They want to be paid per procedure. So they're fighting us for patients."

Dr. Thomas Riles, NYU's chief of surgery, offers the surgeons' side of the argument. "The financial arrangements were always up in the air," says Riles. "There were at least eight different proposals. For a period of time—maybe a year—there was an idea that surgeons would have access to interventional facilities, and in return we would share income with them. But things never did quite work out. We were never given access to the interventional space—I'm not quite sure why," says Riles, acknowledging that somewhere along the way, discussions broke down.[63]

While Rosen argues that minimally invasive procedures require "a totally different skill set," Riles maintains that "surgeons aren't practicing on their patients. Learning how to do all of these procedures is now part of a surgical resident's training—they know how to do them when they come out. And some of the older surgeons have gone back for training."

A surgeon who has learned how to perform the new procedures is understandably reluctant to refer patients to someone else, Riles argues, especially when he or she has an ongoing relationship with the patient. "If you're a surgeon who can do the stent," he asks, "at what point do you say, 'I'm going to send the patient to someone else, someone who hasn't been following this patient for six months'? It was easier when surgeons weren't trained to do this." He adds, "The lines for referral were clearer."

Riles believes that there is an advantage for patients when surgeons follow the case from beginning to end. "Interventional radiologists are trained to do procedures, but they are not trained to manage a chronic disease over a period of time," he says. "And one of my concerns is that people trained to do procedures may have a tendency to do too many of them. They aren't trained to do the clinical work of admitting a patient and following up afterward—they don't see the whole spectrum of the illness. By contrast, if I do a procedure and it doesn't turn out well, I have to live with that for the next 20 years. This person continues to be my patient." That said, Riles believes that in the United States cardiovascular surgeons also perform far too many operations.[64]

When medical care is in flux—as it always is—the questions at the center of a controversy like this one are not easily resolved. "As technology evolves, the only way to determine the best treatment for a particular group of patients is through randomized studies—studies in which a control group of patients does not get the new procedure," says Riles. "This, of course, is difficult. You can imagine—if you were the one asked to have your course of treatment determined by pulling a card out of a box. But it's the only way to develop the information needed for evidence-based medicine."

A 2003 story in *New York* magazine leaves no doubt that the contest for patients has turned rancorous. A cardiac surgeon who requested anonymity described the condition of a 51-year-old diabetic who had been seeing an interventionist. "He'd had way too many stenting procedures," the surgeon confided. "I just performed a triple bypass on him, and his arteries were scarred and blocked. I'm concerned about his long-term prospects because [they] were so badly damaged."

"For every one of those patients, I could cite you 10 who've been messed up through bypass surgery," countered Jeffrey Moses, chief of interventional cardiology at Lenox Hill Hospital. "I could give surgeons tit for tat," Moses told *New York,* and went on to charge that certain medical centers around the city push surgeries "because the economics are more favorable and they want to get their numbers up. I'd like to put up a sign in Times

Square: IF YOU'VE BEEN RECOMMENDED FOR BYPASS SURGERY, LET US LOOK AT YOUR FILMS."[65]

Such disputes over patients are not limited to Manhattan, nor are they confined to cardiovascular surgery. Nationwide, "as technology favors one subspecialty over another, you get very, very large turf battles" over who treats patients, says Kevin Schulman, professor of medicine and business at Duke. "We're going to see more of these battles where you can literally put some doctors out of business, and very quickly."[66]

Rosen agrees. "Several years ago, there were lots of seminars about getting cardiology and vascular together. Every time you turned around, you got a brochure about another meeting. It was like the Middle East when people were talking. There are now, at best, a handful of these collaborative centers around the country, because conflicts broke out everywhere."[67] In the end, he concludes, "The whole idea of a center where specialists work together has fallen apart." All of this, he adds, "is an unfortunate result of the state of American medicine. Everyone has been so much under the gun that there's a ruthless, no-holds-barred approach."

When elephants fight, says a Swahili proverb, the grass suffers. Similarly, in a war among doctors, patients are the most likely losers.

"Two years ago," says Robert Rosen, "if a patient came in with cramping in the leg for lack of blood flow, the vascular surgeon would call me or an interventional radiologist in to consult—to decide which procedure was most appropriate. Today he probably wouldn't even mention to the patient that such a thing as interventional radiology exists."

What does all of this have to do with providing the best care for the patient? "Nothing," Rosen says flatly.

It is not only doctors, he adds, but hospitals that have been affected by the war for profits: "At hospital meetings, instead of talking about patient care, everyone talks about how we can increase our market share. *But the odd thing is, the more we use the business model, the less successful we seem to be as a business. Health care is going broke.*"

Drugmaker vs. Drugmaker

The pharmaceutical industry has always been ambitious. But the race to medicate America picked up speed in the second half of the nineties when

HMOs set out to contain costs by restricting the use of expensive prescription drugs that, in many cases, were no more effective than less costly rivals. At that point, drugmakers decided that the best way to peddle their product would be by advertising directly to the consumer, bypassing both doctors and the HMOs. And in 1997 the FDA gave the industry its blessing, removing most prohibitions on such advertising. Over the next four years spending on ads aimed at the patient would triple.[68]

By 2005 the industry's budget for direct-to-consumer ads had ballooned to $4.1 billion—from $2.5 billion in 2001.[69] "Drug companies are spending far too much on sales and advertising—and they know it," said Richard Evans, a global pharmaceutical analyst at Wall Street's Sanford Bernstein. Evans, who served as an executive at Roche, the Swiss pharmaceutical giant, before joining Sanford Bernstein in 1999, speaks as an industry insider when he says, "If given the chance, virtually any CEO in the industry would slash his sales force by a third. But no one wants to be the first to do it. If you step out in front and cut promotion, you lose market share."[70]

So in 2003 market giant Pfizer poured $2.84 billion into promoting its products, making the pharmaceutical giant the fourth largest advertiser in the United States—right behind General Motors, Procter & Gamble, and Time Warner Inc. Pfizer was not the industry's only prodigal advertiser: Bristol-Myers Squibb, the biggest U.S. producer of AIDS drugs, laid out $778 million for ads, "a bit less than candy maker Mars Inc.," *Bloomberg News* reported, "but $2 million more than brewer Anheuser-Busch Cos."[71]

This is not to say that drugmakers gave up on doctors. In 2001 the industry acknowledged that it spent $5.5 billion to send some 88,000 sales representatives to doctors' offices, bearing trinkets, food, and "educational" materials detailing the advantages of their companies' drugs.[72] In 2005 Pfizer alone employed some 38,000 sales reps—an advance guard roughly the size of three army divisions.[73]

But while pulling out all the stops, the pharmaceutical industry had reached a point of diminishing returns. "Up until 1998—and for many companies through 2000—you were being paid to hire that next sales rep; you were being paid to do that next consumer ad," says Evans. "You were generating return for your shareholders by doing that." After 2000, however, even industry insiders privately admitted that billions were being wasted. In 2002 pharmaceutical companies laid out some $30 billion for promotion—or roughly one of every seven dollars that they took in.[74] By the beginning of

2005, drugmakers were beginning to mutter about cutting back on their television advertising.[75] Yet no company wanted to risk market share by being the first to rein in its marketing budget.

In other words, drugmakers had painted themselves into a corner. And now "they can't exactly get together in a room and agree that on October 1, they'll all slash marketing by 30 percent," Evans observes. "That would be illegal." Usually, in a situation like this, the company that would be hurt least steps out and makes the first deep cuts. In this case, the market leader is Pfizer. But, Evans adds, "Pfizer would be the last to do it."[76]

In the end, the bill for these ads is being paid by the public, observes Dr. Jerry Avorn, chief of the Division of Pharmacoepidemiology and Pharmacoeconomics at Brigham and Women's Hospital in Boston, and author of *Powerful Medicines: The Benefits, Risks, and Costs of Prescription Drugs.* "It is not just the cost of all that airtime, the magazine pages and the advertising firms," Avorn points out. "It is also the cost of using a more expensive patented product when nearly identical generics are available, and the cost of wasted physician time spent convincing a patient that her heartburn will respond as well to a generic drugs as it would to the latest 'purple pill.' And it is the emotional cost to the cancer patient who learns that his fatigue and weakness are due to the malignancy itself, and will not disappear with a $1,500 dose of Procrit as the television commercials imply."[77]

At Pitney Bowes, Dr. Jack Mahoney, the director of the company's health insurance program, saw just how powerful the blare of advertising can be in 2003, following a $233 million advertising blitz by AstraZeneca Pharmaceuticals promoting Nexium, its popular heartburn pill. In the fall of that year Procter & Gamble had begun marketing Prilosec, a less expensive over-the-counter medication originally developed by AstraZeneca that Mahoney knew was a perfectly good alternative to Nexium. The former White House physician tried to encourage Pitney Bowes's employees to choose Prilosec by setting the co-pay for a month's supply at just $25 or less. Nexium would cost employees $50. Nevertheless, Nexium remained so popular that by the end of the year it ranked as the company's third-highest drug expenditure, right after antidepressants and Lipitor, Pfizer's blockbuster anticholesterol drug.[78]

From 1993 to 2003, prescription drug prices rose by an average of 7.4 percent a year—more than twice as fast as inflation.[79] But when questioned about price hikes, Big Pharma is reluctant to say exactly how much it spends on marketing, preferring to talk about research and development. The consumer who pays $80 for 10 pills funds lifesaving research, the industry's backers explain, pointing out that 99 products out of 100 never make it out of the laboratory, and the price of successful medicines must include the cost of those that fail.

The truth is this: in today's pharmaceutical industry, marketing trumps research. By some estimates, drug companies spend more than twice as much on ads, marketing, and administration as they do in labs. In 2002, when Families USA, a nonprofit health care consumer advocacy group, reviewed the financial reports submitted to the SEC by nine of the largest U.S.-based pharmaceutical companies, the group's analysis showed drugmakers investing only $19 billion in R & D, while shelling out some $45 billion for marketing, advertising, and administration. Meanwhile, the industry pocketed $31 billion in profits.[80]

In recent years the gap between investment in research and outlays for marketing has been widening. In 2003 promotional spending jumped by nearly 20 percent, according to *Bloomberg News,* while funding for R & D rose by just 7.1 percent. Over the preceding five years, drugmakers boosted promotional spending by 103 percent while R & D climbed by only about 58 percent.[81] And those numbers probably don't tell the whole story. Drugmakers guard details of their R & D expenses, and most observers think the R & D numbers include at least some costs that most companies would count as marketing.[82]

That the pharmaceutical industry finds itself laying out more for marketing than even it thinks reasonable says something about the cost of competition. But sky-high advertising bills turns out to be only one reason why the nation's tab for prescription drugs tripled from 1990 to 2001.[83] Wooing politicians is another top priority, and here, Big Pharma is more than generous.

In 2002 drugmakers laid out over $91 million to support a legion of lobbyists—more than one for every congressperson.[84] The next year lawmakers passed Medicare legislation pledging that the government would never attempt to negotiate lower drug prices. (This was truly a landmark government purchasing agreement. Even the Defense Department makes at least a pretense of haggling with military contractors.) By 2005, the industry had spent $800 million on lobbying in just seven years.[85]

But the problem is not just that a money-driven health care system forces drugmakers to waste too many dollars on promotion and politicians. The larger cost of the "drug wars" is this: in a dog-eat-dog market, rivals do not share research. As a result, they inevitably duplicate one another's efforts, wasting both millions of dollars and millions of scientist hours.

Even the war on cancer is marked by "isolated problem-solving" instead of "cooperation," *Fortune* reported in 2004, as "hundreds of cancer drugs are thrust into the pipeline . . . even though their proven 'activity' has little to do with curing cancer." The magazine quotes Andy Grove, the chairman of Intel and a prostate-cancer survivor who serves as a member of several cancer advisory groups: "It's like a Greek tragedy. Everybody plays his individual part to perfection, everybody does what's right by his own life, and the total just doesn't work." [86]

To make matters worse, as each company races to fill its own pipeline, a fragmented industry spawns more possible cures than oncologists can keep track of. In 2004 the Pharmaceutical Research and Manufacturers of America reported that over the previous couple of years some 395 cancer drugs had entered clinical trials. "Oncologists say it is becoming difficult to run all the clinical trials needed to test [these drugs] and to determine the best sequences and combinations in which to use them," *The New York Times* reported. One sign of physicians' frustration: in June of 2004 a session of the American Society of Clinical Oncology's conference was titled "Therapy for Metastatic Colorectal Cancer: What Do We Do with So Many Options?" [87]

Too much competition and too little collaboration makes it difficult for oncologists to sort out which drugs are most effective alone, which should be used together—and in what sequence. Genie Kleinerman, chief of pediatrics at Houston's M. D. Anderson Cancer Center, recalls a time when she was doing work on two drugs made by different companies: "Together, they seemed to do a better job of targeting malignant cells of osteosarcoma, a bone cancer that occurs in children. In the lab, we had shown that you could combine the two agents. Scientifically, it was fine, but now we needed the companies to do clinical trials. My lab work was being provided free, but in order to get approval from the FDA, they needed to invest in trials and collect the data.

"But we just couldn't get them to do it," she recalls, reliving the frustration. "The lawyers for the two companies couldn't come up with an agreement on who would own the rights to the combination and who would pay for what." That was a number of years ago, says Kleinerman. "Today it would be the same situation—or probably worse. The pharmaceutical industry has become so protective of who owns the intellectual property. You probably couldn't even get them to sit down at the same table."[88]

Instead, companies pursuing parallel research squander millions producing me-too tumor-shrinking drugs that "don't perform much better than existing treatments," oncologists report—though they always cost more.[89] Part of the problem is that Big Pharma's pipeline is drying up: "We have a shortage of good ideas that are likely to work," acknowledges Bruce Johnson, a Dana-Farber Cancer Institute oncologist who runs lung cancer research for institutions affiliated with the Harvard Medical School.

But even if the pharmaceutical industry boasted a pipeline chock full of revolutionary ideas, clinical trials that aim at real breakthroughs would take far longer than the time needed to try out a me-too drug—and Wall Street frowns on leisurely trials. Drugmakers are, after all, "public companies . . . with shareholders demanding a return on investment," *Fortune* points out. Their aim is to produce drugs that are likely to win quick FDA approval. So the companies focus not on breakthrough treatments, but on incremental improvements to existing classes of drugs. The process does not encourage risk taking or entrepreneurial approaches to drug discovery. It does not encourage brave new thinking.

Once again, the market tends to be much more efficient at serving short-term private interests than at addressing the long-term public interest. "It's really, really hard to set up competition in a way that is socially beneficial," acknowledges Larry Casalino, the physician who quotes Gandhi. "But that doesn't mean that it's impossible."[90]

Meanwhile, as redundant new drugs crowd the marketplace, these new nostrums gobble up needed health care dollars. Paying for them is straining the system, health care providers warn, especially since some of the newest cost tens of thousands of dollars for a course of treatment. In 2004 Bain & Company, a management consulting firm, estimated that paying for all the cancer drugs in development would require $60 billion a year—up from $10 billion at the time. "Who's going to pay for that? It's just going to become unaffordable," says Elgar Peerschke, head of the North American health care practice at Bain.[91]

Genie Kleinerman believes that if government gave drugmakers incentives to pool their research, they might be able to produce fewer, far more effective, and affordable remedies at a lower cost.[92] But that is not how free market competition normally works—at least not according to the conventional wisdom of the late 20th century.

In an era hooked on growth, the corporate strategists of the nineties saw head-to-head competition as the best catalyst for innovation. Even within a single institution, they argued, divisions and departments should be kept distinct so that they could compete. Rivalries would stir up creative juices. The idea that innovators should talk to one another, share their views, and debate ideas was out of vogue.

General Instrument's onetime CEO, U.S. Secretary of Defense Donald Rumsfeld, summed up this point of view on *The NewsHour with Jim Lehrer* in 2004. Cautioning against the hazards of centralizing national security, Rumsfeld pointed to corporate R & D as his model: "I was in industry, and I was involved in research and development. And anyone in that field knows that *what you don't want is all of your R & D people in the same place, going to lunch together* . . . That is not the way to get innovation or creativity or differing views." (emphasis mine)

Lehrer's expression didn't change, but he did sound nonplussed: "Why not?" he asked. "Why not?"

"It just doesn't work," Rumsfeld replied, making it clear that that the topic brooked no discussion.[93]

Insurer vs. Insurer

In 2003 President George W. Bush asked Congress to strengthen the role that private insurance companies play in the Medicare system. Under the Medicare Prescription Drug, Improvement, and Modernization Act, the president proposed funneling some $460 billion of federal money into managed care plans over 10 years, a cash infusion that would help insurers cut premiums and hike benefits as they tried to attract more seniors into their managed care plans. When the bill passed, the president predicted that within four years, some 35 million of the nation's 40 million Medicare beneficiaries would switch from traditional Medicare to private insurance plans. On Wall Street, investors bet that the new legislation would lift the industry's after-tax profits by 2–5 percent.[94]

At the time, most taxpayers naturally assumed that the decision to send more Medicare business to commercial insurers was based on evidence that the private sector can deliver more cost-effective health care than Washington's swollen bureaucracy. In truth, experience shows just the opposite: insurance companies that already offered Medicare were spending 2½ times more on administrative overhead than the traditional Medicare program run by the federal government.[95]

How could this be?

Former *NEJM* editor Dr. Marcia Angell describes what happens to the health care dollar as it wends its way through the insurance industry: "Private insurers regularly skim off the top 10 percent to 25 percent of premiums for administrative costs, marketing and profits. The remainder is passed along a gauntlet of satellite businesses—insurance brokers, disease-management and utilization-review companies, lawyers, consultants, billing agencies, information management firms and so on. Their function is often to limit services in one way or another. They, too, take a cut, including enough for their own administrative costs, marketing and profits." In the end, Angell reports, "as much as half of the health-care dollar never reaches doctors and hospitals."[96]

An insurance company's administrative expenses begin with enrollment. "Under private insurance the enrollment and disenrollment process is very complicated," says Bruce Vladeck, the man who ran Medicare while serving as administrator of the Health Care Financing Administration from 1993 to 1997. "The average employer insurance contract has an annual turnover of 20 to 25 percent, and as people change jobs, they change plans. By contrast, Medicare's enrollment costs are zip. The Social Security Administration does it. But even if you allocate what Social Security spends on Medicare enrollment, it's very, very low. And it's a one-time operation. Once you're in Medicare, you're in. People don't switch in and out." But they will move in and out of managed care plans offering Medicare.

"For private insurers, this front-end stuff is very expensive," Vladeck adds. "Even very efficient insurers spend 5 percent of their premiums just to do it right, though in a sense, it's a pure waste."[97] "Pure waste" because the cost of moving patients in and out of plans usually does little to improve their health—though it does boost the amount that society as a whole pays for health care.

"Then there is the cost of processing claims," Vladeck continues. "Medicare enjoys enormous economies of scale: once you have the software written and the people trained, you're set." Add on the dollars that private insurers spend on advertising and lobbying, and it becomes clear why the industry's overhead is steep.

But a private insurer cannot worry about the cost of competing with its rivals: legally, its first allegiance must be to its investors.[98] And if the company hopes to hit a home run with investors, it must meet Wall Street's short-term expectations. As every insurer knows, Wall Street rewards those with the lowest "medical loss ratio"—the industry's somewhat chilly term of art for how much the company "loses" when it pays out promised medical benefits.

In 2003 Forbes.com columnist Robert Maltbie illustrated how investors value insurance company stocks by recommending Oxford Health Plans, in part because the company's "medical loss ratio, a key measure of HMO profitability tracking, [had] improved in the first quarter [falling] to 78.9% from 79.9% a year ago."[99] In other words, Oxford was now spending only 78.9 percent of every premium dollar on medical benefits, while keeping 21.1 percent to cover administrative costs and profits. From Wall Street's point of view, the low ratio stood as proof of Oxford's efficiency, solvency, and creditworthiness. Needless to say, some subscribers took a different view of Oxford's parsimony.

A managed care plan can keep its medical loss ratio low in two ways: by raising premiums or by keeping a tight rein on benefits. Most try to do both, and in 2003 the HMO industry as a whole succeeded, reporting total earnings of $5.5 billion, up 83 percent from $3 billion in 2002, according to Weiss Ratings, a firm that assesses the strength of financial institutions, including banks and insurance companies. "Profitability continues to improve as insurers raise premiums and restructure policies to reduce costs," observed Weiss vice president Melissa Gannon—though she was candid about the larger cost to society: "While this bodes well for the industry's overall health, rising premiums have forced many consumers to select more restrictive health plans or opt not to purchase insurance entirely."[100]

In 2004 the industry's earnings jumped another 10.7 percent to $11.4 billion, and in the summer of 2005 industry leader WellPoint told investors that it expected its profits to continue to levitate by 15 percent a year, on average, for at least the next five years.[101] That same week WellPoint announced its plan to boost average premiums by 16.7 percent in 2006.[102]

Premiums have spiraled in recent years, in part because investors expect soaring profits, and in part because the industry spends so much on administration. Totting up all the extra costs that private insurers must cover, Vladeck sympathizes with the challenge managed care plans face: "In order to provide precisely the same services that Medicare offers at the same costs, private plans have to either be at least 15 to 20 percent more efficient in their use of services, or else extract prices from providers lower than those Medicare pays . . . something that is no longer possible in most communities. While private managed care plans are often more economical in their use of services than the traditional [indemnity] insurance, documented evidence of a 15 to 20 percent differential is extremely hard to come by."[103]

"This is why, when I was in Washington, some of us talked about giving people age 55 to 65 the opportunity to voluntarily enroll in Medicare—letting them pay premiums to the government in exchange for the full Medicare coverage," Vladeck recalls. "Donna Shalala, who was Secretary of Health and Human Services at the time, said to me, 'You really want to compete with the insurance companies don't you?' And I said, 'You bet.' Simply because our costs were so much lower, I knew I could beat them."[104]

On top of high overhead, private insurers must lay out princely sums to lure the best executives to their corridors—or so they claim. In 2005 modernhealthcare.com, a leading trade website, dropped a small bomb when it announced that the previous year, CEOs at the nation's 10 largest insurers had strolled home with salary and bonus packages that averaged $3 million. "Critics of some insurance executives . . . say their pay packages are too lavish at a time when Congress is considering legislation to restructure Medicare by moving more beneficiaries into private managed-care plans," the website noted. It quoted Ron Pollack, executive director of Families USA, who pointed out that in 2002 Tom Scully, the Centers for Medicare and Medicaid Services top administrator, was paid just $130,000. That was 456 times less than the highest-paid health insurance company executive, Oxford's Norman Payson.[105]

Scully was not the only government health official earning far less than his corporate counterparts. Former Medicare director Bruce Vladeck confides that one reason he left Washington in 1997 was that his second child was entering college. "Combined tuition, room, and board for the two of them equaled 60 percent of my gross salary," he recalls.[106]

Caught in the Crossfire: Patients and Whistle-Blowers

At the extreme of the Hobbesian struggle of all against all, some health care providers view even the patient as fair prey.

In 2001 Dr. Chae Hyun Moon, the cardiology director at Redding Medical Center in Redding, California, was so eager for business that he persuaded 52-year-old Sandy Holtz to undergo heart surgery—surgery that she didn't want and didn't need. "He said you got two choices: You can have it done and live or you can go home and die," Holtz recalls. "That's what he told me."

"Chest cut open, pried apart, heart's operated on—darnedest thing I've ever seen," says her lawyer, Dugan Barr.[107] But Dr. Moon did not stop there. After Holtz had her bypass operation, he persuaded her 71-year-old mother, Pearl Stewart, to have one too.

Unfortunately, Moon was not a lone rogue practitioner. Dr. Fidel Realyvasquez Jr., chair of Redding's cardiology department, also was charged with performing countless unnecessary surgeries. In an FBI affidavit, at least three other physicians testified they had warned hospital administrators that "too many heart procedures" were being done. But both doctors were rainmakers who brought in millions of dollars of business. Moon had so many patients lined up that he would rush through delicate heart procedures, one nurse recalls: "We used to call them fire drills because he was always in a hurry."[108]

By 2004 Holtz and her mother were just two of more than 500 patients suing both the doctors and Tenet Healthcare, Redding's corporate parent.

Much more remains to be told about both Redding and Tenet.[109] But first, one should note that while Redding stands out as an extreme example of criminally reckless care, it is not as uncommon an example as one might hope. At too many institutions, physicians report, hospitals and even other doctors turn a blind eye when "high-volume" physicians put financial interests ahead of patients' interests. The root of the problem, they say, is that the peer review process designed to monitor the quality of care has broken down.

The tradition of physicians policing themselves goes back to 1918, when the American College of Surgeons decided that something had to be done about the quality of hospital care. At that point the surgeons were not quite ready to declare that they themselves might need oversight, but over time the Hospital Accreditation Program evolved into the Joint Commission on Accreditation of Healthcare Organizations, and the JCAHO directed hospitals to set up peer review programs that would let physicians monitor their colleagues.

But today, as medicine becomes more corporate and competitive pressures mount, economic relationships can create conflicts of interest that turn peer review inside out. "The assumption that peer review is always only about quality and not about economic or intra-professional political struggles is less and less realistic as the economics of the health care industry become more competitive," Sallyanne Payton, a University of Michigan health law professor, observes.[110]

If a physician makes a sizable economic contribution to a hospital, for example, he can become a major power among staff physicians: some of his colleague may depend upon the "heavy-hitter admitter" for referrals. As a result, "these doctors are frequently reluctant to take action," even when the star shows signs of sloppiness, says longtime hospital consultant James Orlikoff.[111]

Meanwhile, hospital administrators may be even slower to rein in a rainmaker, fearing that discipline might drive him away or backfire by damaging the hospital's reputation. "In some cases, a hospital peer review takes a stand against one of its their own and revokes a physician's hospital privileges, only to be circumvented . . . by publicity-shy hospital executives," says Bill Monnig, a suburban Cincinnati urologist who has served as chair of the AMA's Organized Medical Staff Section, the group that serves as a liaison between the AMA and the medical staffs of hospitals nationwide.

"Is there a risk that doctors will support big producers and rainmakers?" Monnig continues. "Yes. But I think there's an even greater risk of a hospital CEO or board basing their decisions on economic factors, and overruling the [peer review committee's] opinion. The physicians on staff may want to hold the institution responsible for providing good quality care, but if the hospital wants to maintain its standing in the community, it won't necessarily want those kinds of complaints to surface. Before the current economic climate muddied the waters," Monnig adds, "the relationship between medical staff and hospital administrators was a good and mutually beneficial one clearly defined by the hospital board and medical staff bylaws."[112]

That relationship has broken down. Indeed, these days, a physician who expresses qualms about the quality of a colleague's care may find himself the target of a hospital investigation. Sometimes, doctors who try to stand up for patient safety are labeled "disruptive" and "uncollegial." Ultimately, the patients' advocate may wind up unemployed.

That is exactly what happened to Ed Dench when he began questioning standards of care in the anesthesiology department at Centre Community Hospital in State College, Pennsylvania, the primary hospital not only for the 38,000 permanent residents of State College, but also for Penn State's 40,000 students.[113] Dench, who graduated from the University of Pennsylvania's medical school in 1971, was an experienced physician when he came to the hospital in 1985. "I recognized right away that some things in the anesthesiology department were not being done by the book," he recalls. In particular, Dench was troubled when he realized that a senior colleague was in the habit of working three and four surgeries simultaneously, leaving nurse anesthetists in charge as the phantom practitioner glided from one operating room to another.

"The difference between having a nurse anesthetist in the room instead of an anesthesiologist may be only 1 in 100," Dench acknowledges. "In most cases, the nurse can handle any problems that arise. But if you happen to be that one . . . and it isn't always the sickest patients. It can be a very healthy person who dies. On the other hand, if you view medicine as a business, and don't care about the individual life . . ." In that case, Dench suggests, "1 in 100" might seem a tolerable degree of error, and any subsequent lawsuits part of "the cost of doing business."

When Dench first came to Centre Community Hospital in 1985, he refused to participate in the game of musical operating rooms. "I told the hospital's chief administrator that I couldn't supervise anesthesiology for surgery on the third and fourth floors simultaneously." He explains his reasoning: "It's unethical; the patient isn't getting what he's paying for; and if you're billing Medicare for a procedure and you're not there, it's probably illegal. The administrator looked me in the eye," Dench remembers, "and said, 'I understand. I realize that. But don't worry, you won't get caught.'

"That's how some administrators think," Dench adds. "As long as they don't get caught, it's fine to violate what they see as just 'rules and regulations.' Medical ethics don't matter," he adds, touching on the tension between medicine—a profession traditionally based on trust—and commerce, where "caveat emptor" always applies.[114]

Some would say that the "physician-businessman" is an oxymoron. Others argue that it is a redundancy: of course doctors are businessmen, they say. Doctors perform a valuable service and in return expect to be paid. Dench steers a middle course: "Doctors aren't monks. Like everyone else, they like to make money. Even 100 years ago, the country doctor had the nicest carriage, the nicest house in town. But most doctors go into medicine to help patients. Businessmen don't respect the same professional rules—rules that say the patient's interest always has to come ahead of financial interests. At best they have business ethics—which," he says cheerfully, "is all about winning."

In 1991 Dench decided to write a letter to the hospital's chief administrator. "I was president of the Pennsylvania Anesthesiology Society at the time, and we were told that Medicare was cracking down on fraud. So I suggested that the hospital should be concerned about a physician billing Medicare for supervising surgeries on two different floors at the same time." And, Dench recalls, "that's when things turned bad for me."

The administration did not appreciate the warning. The anesthesiologist who ran the department was, after all, a good friend of the hospital's CEO. Dench, who tells his story without bitterness, knew this: "Like most sociopaths, he was a good socializer," he recalls. "He was a great partygoer, he ran fund-raisers for the hospital, he played golf and tennis . . . though some surgeons would complain that if he was on the golf course, they'd call him to come in for an emergency, and he'd say, 'I'm not coming.' You could tell he was a sociopath because he felt no compassion, no remorse. He did only what was good for him.

"Meanwhile, things got tough for me," Dench continues. "I was told that I was 'uncooperative,' and instead of investigating this other fellow, they began investigating me. They told the nurses to document anything I did wrong. For example, one time, when I had been up for 36 hours straight, I advised a patient either to postpone her surgery or to use another anesthesiologist. Fifty percent of my cases came by request—the patient asked for me," Dench explains. "But in this case I told her I hadn't had any sleep, and I was concerned about her safety."

Dench knew that when sleep-deprived doctors practice medicine, risks multiply geometrically. "When I was a resident, if someone came in who needed a cardiac catheterization, and there had been some narrowing of the artery, the hospital would schedule them immediately. At 2 a.m. we'd be doing open-heart surgery! Now, it's true that 2 percent of the patients might die if you waited. But they finally did a study which showed that the death rate was 5 percent when you operate in the middle of the night—as opposed to the 2 percent mortality rate you'd have if you waited until morning."

On one occasion when Dench himself was the patient, he waited for a fresh crew. "I diagnosed myself with appendicitis and showed up at the ER at 4 a.m.," he recalls. "But I told them, 'I don't want you to call anyone in to operate. I want you to confirm the diagnosis—but it's not going to rupture instantaneously. I *don't* want to be operated on until the regular schedule starts.' I knew there was a difference in care."

To Dench's dismay, his patient insisted that she didn't want anyone else to supervise the anesthesiology, and she didn't want to postpone the procedure. She had already hired a babysitter, she explained. "I thought she was wrong," says Dench. "But I did it." The operation went smoothly. Nevertheless, an incident report was filed about Dench's attempt to dissuade the patient. He was, after all, turning away business. Moreover, he was acknowledging that a hospital focusing on volume might allow physicians to do just one more operation—even if they were not at their best.

Robert Martin, the hospital's legal counsel for 35 years, disputes that the hospital objected to Dench's candor: "An incident report is filed whenever *anything* unusual happens," he stresses. "No corrective action was taken."

A year after Dench blew the whistle on the senior anesthesiologist in his department, 33-year-old Dr. Danae Powers came to Centre Community Hospital. She, too, was an anesthesiologist, and she remembers being warned about Dench: "They told me he was a troublemaker."[115]

"I was happy to see her join the department," Dench recalls. "She came from Emory, and generally, academic hospitals are much better about peer reviewing quality of care. Residents at a good teaching hospital are constantly evaluated. But I didn't talk to her after she came to the hospital—I thought I had no business prejudicing her. It wasn't until the end of the year that she came to me and said, 'What's going on here?' "

Powers would later tell *The Pittsburgh Post-Gazette*'s Steve Twedt that she noticed patients being wheeled into surgery without standard preoperative workups that might alert the surgical staff to problems. Some arrived in surgery with inaccurate information about their condition. Nurses also told her that some anesthesiologists would go to lunch in the middle of a surgery, leaving responsibility for monitoring the patient to a nurse anesthetist.

Powers spoke to her department chair. He told her not to worry about it. But Powers continued to be disturbed, and in March of 1994, she wrote a memo to the hospital board and chief of staff, detailing the problems and dangers of what she considered sloppy medicine. After that, she recalls, "My life became miserable at the hospital. The scheduling became absolutely unbearable. They started trying to slander me . . . I got written up for the first time since I had been there."

Later that year Powers was deeply troubled by the death of a patient following elective knee surgery. To avoid unnecessary bleeding during the operation, a tourniquet had been applied above his knee. But once the operation was done, doctors could not restore blood flow to his leg. Powers had not been present during the original operation, but she was called to help with emergency surgery on the 69-year-old patient's deteriorating leg. When she checked his chart, she saw that he had a history of systemic atherosclerosis—hardening and blocking of his arteries. That, she believed, should have precluded use of a tourniquet, and probably the surgery. Later that weekend his heart stopped and he died.

Upset, Powers went to her department chief and other administrators. Again, she was told not to worry. And in May of 1995 she received a letter from the hospital president, rebuking her for "derogatory, if not slanderous, remarks relative to other physicians." The next month, she received a critical evaluation, saying she did not always adhere to medical staff bylaws, rules, and regulations. "By then the anesthesiology department had divided into warring camps," says Martin, the hospital's lawyer. "The doctors were bickering over schedules and refusing to cover for each other." He describes Powers and Dench as "uncooperative." [116]

Thirteen months later, on June 24, 1996, 73-year-old William Curley, the retired director of Penn State's food service and father of Penn State athletic director Tim Curley, entered Centre Community for a routine hip replacement.

A day later he was dead.

Curley's widow, Florence, sued. Ultimately, the suit revealed that a nurse anesthetist had suggested the surgery be postponed while Curley, a diabetic with heart disease, high blood pressure, and unstable angina, was evaluated. But the anesthesiologist refused to delay the operation, and it appeared that he did not do a pre-op workup. In depositions for the civil suit, two colleagues said the doctor "had admitted to them that he did not perform preoperative evaluations because he was not paid for them." Despite his condition, Curley received "the same dosage of anesthesia as would have been provided to a healthy, young male," precipitating his death, according to court documents. The jury awarded Florence Curley $750,000. An appeals court upheld the judgment.

After the Curleys learned about Powers's earlier complaints, they also sued the hospital board. This second suit was settled for an undisclosed sum. This, the hospital's attorney emphasizes, did not constitute an admission of guilt. "We settle a lot of cases," Martin explains.[117]

Perhaps because of the Curley family's prominence on the Penn State campus, the case caught the attention of state officials. In July of 1997, the hospital was cited by the Pennsylvania Department of Health. State inspectors found that patients were not evaluated before or after surgeries. Moreover, they reported a "lack of established criteria for safe administration of anesthesia." Four months later state inspectors again chastised the hospital "for not actively pursuing" quality improvement in the surgical and obstetrics departments. For a second time, they found that there was no record of pre-anesthesia evaluation. This time the patients in question were expectant mothers.

That summer hospital president Lance Rose notified Powers and Dench that the hospital was reorganizing its anesthesiology department, and "all current anesthesia privileges granted to members of the Anesthesia Department will terminate on Jan. 1, 1998." Rose explained that the hospital planned to contract out exclusive anesthesia service to a selected group of physicians. Dench and Powers would not be included in the group.

At about the same time, roughly 150 members of Centre Community's medical staff elected Powers chief of staff. Despite her run-ins with the hospital administration, it was clear that she had strong support among many other doctors. "Everybody was hoping Danae could do something" to raise quality, plastic surgeon Dr. John Newkirk told Twedt.[118] But six months later Dench and Powers were no longer practicing at the hospital. Both sued—and both eventually settled for the usual undisclosed sum. "I had to settle," says Dench. "The hospital knew they could outspend me. I spent $400,000 in legal fees—they spent a million. Of course, they were spending the patients' money."[119]

The publicity dampened local enthusiasm for Centre Community Hospital, and some patients canceled elective surgeries. Rallying around the institution, 98 members of the medical staff—including some who had recently voted to elect Powers chief of staff—signed their names to a full-page ad supporting the hospital's quality reviews.

Dench is philosophical: "This is their livelihood. In a large city, doctors can move to a different hospital. Here it's a total monopoly." Dench says that he does not expect most doctors to be whistle-blowers. "People criticize doctors for not talking—what world are they living in?" he asks. "There are only so many heroes in the world. In any environment, maybe 10 percent of the people are honest, 10 percent are crooked, and 80 percent do whatever they have to do to survive. The 80 percent will follow the people who are winning. The public needs the good doctors to be winning."

In theory, peer review should discourage doctors who cut corners. But the problem is that when doctors who work together in a given hospital are asked to pass judgment on their colleagues, professional relationships come into play. While some doctors depend on one another for referrals, others are fierce rivals. "Today we're all either competing with each other for patients—or else we're business partners," Dench observes. "Either way, local peer review within a hospital doesn't work."[120]

This is why Dench advocates statewide peer review, done by doctors from other hospitals who have never met one another but practice in the same specialty. "You need some distance," he says. "Local peer review has become nothing more than a popularity contest. If you're friends with the administration and you make a mistake, it's no problem. If you're not popular, and you slip up, you'll be crucified. I worked there for 15 years, terrified of making a mistake.

"Doctors often make mistakes," Dench acknowledges. "And if no one dies, the doctor often doesn't tell anyone. It's okay to report on machinery making a mistake—that's machinery, not a doctor's judgment. But the truth is that we're all going to make a lot of mistakes. We need a way of collating those errors and publishing them so that we can learn from each other. But hospitals are not interested in trying to get to the heart of a problem and correcting it. Their interest is in covering it up, or in scapegoating someone and getting rid of that person."

Dench, who has been a pilot all of his life, contrasts peer review in a hospital to the way pilots share information about errors. "I took my first solo flight when I was 16," he says, "and from the time I began flying, I learned from other pilots' mistakes. I once found myself going across an active runway," he recalls. "I was staring at an airplane coming right at me. Nothing happened, but I filed a report. So they would know. Sometime later, another plane did the same thing—a lot of people were killed. By putting the two incidents together, they could see that there was a problem there.

"But once you become a doctor, the system discourages learning from other doctors' mistakes. Because of the economic pressure on hospitals, they have convinced physicians that it's better to keep it quiet. They can't afford for the public to be afraid of their hospital. But of course that means that errors are perpetuated."

In 2004 Centre Community Hospital changed its name to Mount Nittany Medical Center. In April of that year an AMA newsletter featured Powers and Dench speaking out about how hospitals retaliate when physicians raise concerns about care. Mount Nittany officials protested, calling the article, "a grievous misrepresentation."[121] Martin, the hospital's counsel, argues that in 2004, the two doctors had no way to know what was happening at their former hospital: "Neither Dr. Dench nor Dr. Powers has practiced at the hospital for the last six years."

But at hospitals across the nation, questions about peer review and medical errors continue to fester. After Steve Twedt wrote a story about what had happened at Centre Community Hospital in the *Pittsburgh Post-Gazette*, he heard from hundreds of physicians, telling stories of how they, too, were intimidated when they tried to warn of unsafe conditions or a colleague's poor work. "Instead of receiving praise or even support for trying to improve care," says Twedt, "they're disciplined or dismissed for being 'disruptive' or for violating patient confidentiality.

"I don't think this happens at most—or even very many hospitals," Twedt adds. "But if word gets around that it happened at another hospital in town, it can have a chilling effect.[122]

A five-country survey of hospital executives published in the medical journal *Health Affairs* in the summer of 2004, confirms that when mistakes are made, hospitals tend to draw up the bridge. "The most important barrier to disclosure and discovery of [medical errors] in hospitals is the endemic culture of secrecy and protectionism in health care facilities in every country," the report declares. "There is a pervasive 'club culture' in which at least some doctors and other health care professionals prioritize their own self-interest above the interests of patients," while some hospital executives "act defensively to protect the institution rather than its patients."[123]

Why are flight crews quicker to share information about mistakes and near-misses? "Fear of punishment serves as a disincentive to reporting in both contexts, but flight crews have one strong incentive for reporting that health care professionals lack," suggests Mary Anderlik, now an assistant professor of medicine with the Center for Medical Ethics and Health Policy at Baylor College of Medicine, "—namely the knowledge that *their* lives are on the line." (emphasis hers)[124]

The *Health Affairs* study elaborates on why safety seems to be taken so much more seriously in other industries: "First, a major service failure in an industrial plant, airline or oil exploration company may close down production . . . and entail huge commercial costs to the organization and its staff . . . As a result, these organizations have developed cultures that are [keenly aware of] the probability of failures and have embedded systems for constant diligence and awareness. In contrast, health care organizations usually carry on with their work even after the most serious failures, and the staff are rarely harmed or even much affected. Patients bear nearly the entire cost."[125]

Second, "the health care industry is unique in that many of its customers are already or will be harmed by the disease that brings them to the hospital. No other industry deals with morbidity and mortality as a routine part of the production process. This presents a unique challenge in distinguishing between [harm caused by the disease and harm caused by medical errors]." Moreover, health care workers become *"inured to such harm. It is normal for patients to die and for treatments to fail, and so we become accustomed to such events. When things go wrong it is then more difficult to step outside the normalizing mind-set and see the problems for what they really are: evidence of major health care failures."* (emphasis mine)

Finally, the study observes, "health care organizations . . . are controlled by powerful, producer-led interests. The dominant position of health care corporations and professionals gives them the political and economic clout to block changes" that would reduce their power and make them more accountable "even in the face of pressure from government, patients and the media."

A second study published in the same issue of *Health Affairs* suggests that in intensely competitive markets, executives may be all the more reluctant to disclose errors. When hospital administrators in Australia, Canada New Zealand, the United Kingdom, and the United States were asked whether hospitals should be required to make information about medical errors, infection rates, and mortality rates available to the public, the share of respondents who opposed the idea was highest in Australia and the United States—the two countries where hospital executives expressed the greatest fears about losing patients to their competition.

Concern about the rising cost of malpractice insurance also rated higher in the United States and Australia than in the other countries, and the study's authors suggest that this influenced attitudes about disclosure. Yet malpractice ranked much lower on the hospitals' lists of worries, with only 11 percent of U.S. hospital administrations and 6 percent of their Australian counterparts naming it as "one of the two top problems faced by your hospital." By contrast, nearly two-thirds of U.S. hospital executives and over 40 percent of those in Australia revealed that they were "very concerned" or "somewhat concerned" about losing patients to other hospitals.[126]

As for Dench, looking back he says, "I wish I hadn't felt that I needed to speak out. But I did."

Since leaving the hospital, Dench has watched his income slide. "I clearly understood that it would be hard to get a job at another hospital. I didn't try. I just knew it," he says matter-of-factly. As of the summer of 2004, Dench was freelancing as an anesthesiologist, providing services to doctors in their offices.

"Something like this destroys marriages," he adds. "You're feeling stress, and your spouse is going to feel it too. My wife said, 'You used to be fun.'" Dench laughs. "Well, I used to make money, too."[127]

The Cost of Consolidation

Turf wars between specialties . . . An arms race among hospitals . . . Billions spent on pharmaceutical ads . . . These are a few examples of how too much competition has created a fractured health care system, riddled with redundancies, weighed down by high administrative costs, and shrouded in confusion.

At the same time, in a Darwinian struggle for survival, too much competition can easily turn into too little competition, as the strongest players consolidate, "bulking up" to gain the clout needed to command the highest possible price. This already has happened in many parts of the country, as both hospitals and insurers concentrate their power. In some regions, insurers dictate the terms of engagement. In others, hospital chains gain near monopoly power. "Antitrust policy can prevent outright price fixing, but hospitals with market power have no need to break the law to set high prices. A quiet monopoly is perfectly legal," write the authors of a study of health care systems published in *Health Affairs* in 2004.[128]

"They'd never let Microsoft have that kind of power, but they think it's okay in medicine," observes Dr. Ed Dench.[129]

In theory, consolidation should reduce the cost of doing business. At this point, it should come as no surprise: it doesn't work that way in the health care industry.

The 700 hospital mergers consummated between 1996 and 2000 were supposed to give large chains an opportunity to capitalize on economies of scale, while minimizing the need to duplicate services. "If there were fewer hospital competitors, hospitals would not have to invest as heavily in similar services and advertising . . . there would be fewer Joneses to keep up with," explains Kelly Devers, a researcher at the Center for Studying Health System Change.[130]

In practice, however, field surveys demonstrate that economies of scale are achieved only when two hospitals fold into one—and one of them closes its doors. Mergers that stitch institutions together to form a hospital chain show no significant savings after the first year of operation.[131]

Such mergers often lead to duplication. Physicians do not like to relinquish fiefdoms, and so when two hospitals marry, two departments in the same specialty frequently remain open, "even when the facilities are close to one another," points out Harvard's Michael Porter. He sees hospital consolidation as yet another example of how rivals in the health care system divide value rather than creating it.

For when hospitals merge, their true goal is not to reduce costs, Porter argues. Instead, "hospital groups aim only to boost their bargaining power vis-à-vis health plans and other system participants."[132] Once again, they are simply shifting costs within the system. A 2004 study of Southwest and Midwest hospitals that merged between 1998 and 2000 seems to confirm Porter's thesis. Comparing hospital fees one year before the merger to prices hospitals charged one year after the deal was completed, researchers found no savings. Instead, "most consolidating hospitals [surveyed in the study] raised prices by more than median price increases in their area."[133]

Why? "Because they can," says Sid Abrams, chairman of the health benefits committee of CalPERS, the giant California Public Employees' Retirement System.[134]

In the spring of 2004, CalPERS took a stand against hospitals that overcharge, announcing that it was dropping 38 hospitals from a network used by more than a third of its 1.2 million beneficiaries. The decision meant that if state employees wanted to retain coverage at those institutions, they would have to switch from CalPERS's HMO to its PPO (preferred provider organization)—a plan with higher deductibles and out-of-pocket expenses.

Of the 38 hospitals that CalPERS said it would drop, 13 were operated by Sutter Health, a nonprofit network of doctors and hospitals that has become a giant force in California's health care system. CalPERS charged Sutter with gouging, citing "an analysis of claims data that showed the Sutter hospitals charged 80 percent more than the average hospital in Blue Shield's California network, and 60% more than other hospitals in Northern California."[135]

Sutter did not take the news graciously. "They placed full-page ads in newspapers, gave their doctors a script to read to their patients, and sent a mailing to everyone in the system saying that this is nothing less than the end of the world," Abrams complained a few months later. "To my mind, they were taken by surprise."

CalPERS's move only underlines a swelling nationwide rebellion against skyrocketing hospital charges. All told, hospitals accounted for 53 percent of the growth in overall health care costs in 2003.[136] Abrams expresses hope that other larger purchasers will be inspired to join CalPERS in excluding hospitals that they believe are overcharging. "That's what has scared Sutter," he says. "They're worried that other purchasers might follow our lead. The pressure from their doctors would be enormous."

Pitney Bowes might seem a likely candidate to join in the revolt. In recent years the mailing-equipment and services company has been doing its best to moderate the cost of coverage for its employees, and in 2003 Jack Mahoney, the firm's corporate medical director, was pleased to see that average hospital stays remained level at 3.7 days. Nevertheless, the average cost of each hospital visit jumped 9 percent to $10,500. How could this be?

With a little research, Mahoney identified the major source of the hikes:

ever-more powerful large hospital groups in California, whose price increases pushed the company's average cost of a hospital admission in that
state to $20,500, twice what it paid elsewhere.[137] Sutter, it turns out, is one of
the largest hospital operators in northern California, where most of Pitney
Bowes's 2,000 employees in the state live and work.

At the time, Bill Gleeson, a Sutter spokesman, argued that the hospitals'
charges must climb just to keep pace with the rising cost of serving the uninsured, meeting regulations regarding staffing levels, and conforming to
state-mandated requirements to make buildings earthquake resistant.[138]

Critics charge that Sutter is poor-mouthing: The nonprofit hospital
group posted a net operating income of $265 million in 2002, followed by
net income of $389 million in 2003, bringing Sutter's profit margin for that
year to 7 percent.[139] Gleeson retorts that these fat years followed 10 years of
famine: from 1992 to 2001, Sutter operated with a margin of just 2.4 percent. Still, even during that lean decade, the hospital chain was operating in
the black.[140]

Moreover, in 2003, when the California Nurses Association commissioned a study of the 100 most expensive hospitals in the United States, it
discovered that high profits are linked not to quality or high efficiency, but to
high markups. Among the hospitals mentioned, Sutter Health's Memorial
Hospital in Modesto, California, marked up what it charged for hospital services by an average of 525 percent over what it cost the hospital to provide
those services—more than double the average hospital markup of 206
percent. The report documented a direct correlation between fat markups,
handsome profits and consolidation, and what it called the "growing corpo-
ratization" of the health care industry. Ninety-five of the 100 most expensive hospitals belonged to chains. By contrast, 69 of the nation's 100 least
expensive institutions were independent.[141]

Pitney Bowes's Mahoney expresses his own skepticism about Sutter's
soaring prices. On a trip to California, he made the rounds and heard each
hospital in turn complain that it was bearing the brunt of serving the poor
and uninsured. "By the third visit, I was thinking, 'Now, wait a minute, you
can't all be that same hospital,' " Mahoney recalls.[142]

Yet Pitney Bowes is not prepared to join CalPERS in excluding some of
Sutter's priciest hospitals from its network. "The company just isn't powerful enough to move hospital prices," says Mahoney. "We can isolate certain
phenomena and try to act on some and advocate policy for others," he adds.

"But when you come right down to it, even the biggest company out there will tell you they don't have much influence on the market."

Large employers would have more clout at the bargaining table if they joined together to negotiate directly with health care providers. But as health care economist James Robinson points out, large firms with a young, healthy workforce usually prefer to bargain alone, hoping for sizable discounts on their premiums. "It's an every-man-for-himself mentality," says Mahoney. "We were willing to partner with other employers, but every company has its own priorities."[143]

Inevitably, Robinson argues, there will always be "self-interested individuals" who resist any attempt to form alliances. These include "the middle managers who run the benefit programs and corporate consulting firms that put corporations together with insurers." Such individuals "could lose their jobs, status and consulting fees if large firms were to pool premium contributions and delegate decision making to an alliance."[144]

If employers are going it alone, insurers are not. Like the hospitals, health care plans are consolidating: between 1995 and 2002 some 384 managed care plans merged or were acquired.[145]

"Ten years ago in the midnineties, we had 900 healthcare plans—we actually had a price war in health insurance," recalls Norm Fidel, senior vice president of Alliance Capital Management, a large mutual fund company. "At the time, literally hundreds of plans were created by health care providers, mainly hospitals, as well as physician groups, which had little underwriting capability"—in other words, they were not well-versed in avoiding the ill. "Virtually all of those provider-based health plans have been washed out. Today the number of health plans is less than half what it was eight years ago."

In 2005 the 10 largest insurers controlled 48 percent of the insured population, up from 27 percent in 1995.[146] In the market, might makes right: from 1998 to 2002 health insurance premiums rose 42 percent, more than double the overall rise in medical inflation (17 percent) and triple the increase in overall inflation (10 percent).[147] Meanwhile, the number of not-for-profit plans shrank: "For-profits now represent about 45 percent of all the health plan members today—versus only about 25 percent in the late '90s," Fidel noted in 2004. "So there is more concentration in fewer hands, and those fewer hands are more focused on the bottom line."[148]

Not all of the health insurance industry's Goliaths are Wall Street darlings. Some nonprofit Blues also began to concentrate their power: "The Blue Cross Blue Shield plan in my area has 85 percent of market share; it's a huge gorilla with complete control over what product I can bring to the market," complains Deborah Weymouth, COO of Thompson Health System, a community hospital in Canandaigua, New York. "We're a small rural hospital, and I take it as my mission to be able to provide mammograms, to work with schoolchildren with asthma . . . I need to have free cash flow to do so many programs," she adds.

But her cash flow depends on how well the Rochester-based Excellus Blue Cross Blue Shield is willing to reimburse her hospital for its services. "I have to go to Blue Cross and beg them for money to go out and teach children with asthma how to use their inhalers," says Weymouth.[149]

Meanwhile, critics like CalPERS's Sid Abrams argue that as hospital chains and insurance companies bulk up, they have begun to play ball with each other. Rather than representing the interests of employers and subscribers when negotiating with health care providers, large insurers pass on whatever rate increases the hospitals demand. "We've morphed into a situation where the insurance middlemen like Blue Cross are more interested in preserving their own business than in helping the clients save money," says Abrams, a pension consultant for more than 30 years.

Taking the path of least resistance, insurers now often agree to include all large hospitals in their network. "They quickly realized that, instead of negotiating with individual hospitals, it would be cheaper for them to set up one broad network," he explains.

"Today we've created a situation where a hospital proposes a ridiculous rate, and then we have to hire a middleman—Blue Cross, or some other insurer—just to get us back to retail. The insurance company will brag, 'You're paying only 45 percent of the proposed charges,' but of course, it's nonsense—because there is no limit on the proposed charge."[150]

Creative Destruction

As health care economist James Robinson describes it, mergers in the hospital and insurance industries are merely moments in the systole and diastole of unmanaged competition: "The most visible feature of the corporate system of health care is ceaseless acquisition and divestiture, integration and outsourcing, combination and recombination."[151] Indeed, the history of corporate America shows that cycles of consolidation are usually followed by periods of deconstruction.

Such cycles are part of the process of "creative destruction" that economist Joseph Schumpeter famously described as "the essential fact about capitalism."[152]

Unfortunately, in the nineties, Schumpeter's phrase became a buzzword for the "New Economy." And the more people repeated it, the less they thought about it. Most had never read Schumpeter, yet, as *Wired* magazine reported, the bumper sticker was bandied about until it became "all the rage" in Washington, where Schumpeter's ideas were cited by everyone from Federal Reserve chief Alan Greenspan to House majority leader Dick Armey.[153]

Yet the very fact that a glib notion of creative destruction helped inflate the bubble economy of the late 20th century might give one pause when thinking about applying the phrase to U.S. health care in the 21st century.

If the nation's aim is to build a sustainable health care system that emphasizes fewer errors, greater access, and the continuous, preventive care needed to manage chronic diseases, it is not clear that what Schumpeter rightly calls "the pervasive gale" of creative destruction is either desirable or affordable.[154]

In Silicon Valley, where new technologies are built on the rubble of the companies that preceded them, fierce and even ruinous rivalries may well be essential for innovation. And without question, in the decades ahead, small biotech firms will lead the way on the frontiers of medical research. The survivors will become the Microsofts of the 21st century, and they will have the deep pockets to develop new technology. Initially, many will be funded by forward-looking venture capitalists able and willing to speculate on the cutting edge of medical science. Most of these companies will disappear into the gyre of creative destruction. A few will survive and make invaluable contributions to the future of medical care.

But while venture capital plays angel to the future, the bulk of the nation's health care dollars will be needed to heal the larger health care system. For over the long run, when it comes the raising the overall quality of care, reducing errors, and widening access to treatment, what Robinson describes as the dance of "medical groups, hospital systems and health plans" forever "coming together and coming apart" is simply not conducive to producing a coherent system of care.[155]

Changing times demand new strategies. In the final decades of the 20th century, corporate medicine put its emphasis on innovation as drugmakers, device makers, and health care providers strove for the next new medical breakthrough. The linear dream of open-ended and unlimited technological progress dominated as researchers poured billions into end-of-life treatments. Some of those treatments would prove miraculous. But others only encouraged the "therapeutic relentlessness," of postmodern medicine, spawning what the renowned physician and writer Lewis Thomas once described as "half-way technologies [that] save our lives but do not make us well." [156]

In the 21st century, innovation must make room for consolidation. Much needs to be done to build on the advances of the last 100 years. Rather than engaging in an endless search for the next new drug, the next new device, the next new high-tech procedure, we need to invest in learning how to use the information that we already have to provide safer, more effective care.

Today "mistakes in the use of medical technologies account for an estimated 400,000 deaths each year," according to the bipartisan National Coalition on Health Care. "Two-thirds [of these deaths] can be attributed to preventable 'health care accidents.' *These numbers do not include the impact of failing to treat what we know how to treat,"* the coalition observes in its 2004 report. *"Nor do they include the impact of overzealous use of the care. Were fatalities from these additional sources added to those from accidents, the number of deaths would climb significantly."* (emphasis theirs) [157]

To reduce errors, the coalition proposes gathering together existing knowledge about the impact of new technologies and procedures, and creating a central database, which in turn could be used to shape national guidelines for the best practice of medicine.

By the same token, information on the comparative risks and benefits of various drugs needs to be drawn together into a single electronic database, says Dr. Jerry Avorn, speaking from his experience as an internist, a geriatrician, and a drug researcher. Lacking such a central database, Avorn confesses, "physicians are left to try to piece together an enormous patchwork of disparate findings as best they can . . . Studying drugs is what I do for a living, and I still have trouble finding a reliable way to compare a given medicine with its alternative in terms of effectiveness, safety and price . . . The most damning evidence of this problem is the fact that the most commonly used source of prescription drug information in the country is still the *Physi-*

cians' Desk Reference, the dense, 3,500-page tome that's simply a compilation of indigestible, industry-produced package inserts."

True, tech-savvy doctors can refer to the information stored on their Palm Pilots, but, Avorn observes, while "these databases offer useful listings of a drug's doses, indications and side effects, they are not as helpful in proving the higher-level information needed to choose *which* drug to prescribe." (emphasis his) For in the United States at present, no one is responsible for pulling together and synthesizing the kind of comparative information physicians and patients need.[158] Instead, prescribing decisions are left to what Avorn terms "the general disarray in the marketplace of ideas and products that marks American medicine as a whole."[159]

The story of Vioxx, the popular arthritis drug withdrawn from the market in 2004, illustrates the physicians' dilemma. That summer Merck & Co., the maker of the $2.5 billion drug used by some 20 million Americans, acknowledged that when taken for more than 18 months, Vioxx might double the risk of heart attack or stroke.

The news should not have come as a complete surprise to the company. Over the preceding four years, warnings about Vioxx had been published in three separate articles in three different medical journals.[160] In all likelihood, had the known information about the drug been pulled together in one place, some physicians would have stopped prescribing it long before 2004—preventing some of the estimated 30,000 to 100,000 heart attacks and strokes allegedly caused by the drug.

But as Avorn points out, "important news of the risks or benefits of [any drug] might appear in any one of dozens of journals," embedded in "arid reports . . . visually just a little more appealing than a phone book." Keeping up with all of this literature "is an arduous task that few of us have the time or the stamina to perform comprehensively,"[161] Avorn admits—which means that in all likelihood, only a handful of practicing physicians actually read, weighed, and synthesized the information in all three key articles about Vioxx.

Meanwhile, for patients, any rumor of risk was drowned out by a $195 million ad campaign featuring testimonials from former skater Dorothy Hamill and music by the Rascals, all aimed at aging baby-boomer patients. Given what the company knew, " 'Why didn't they [at least] stop the direct-to-consumer marketing?' " Cleveland cardiologist Eric Topol, a longtime critic of the drug, asked in 2004. 'That's the tragedy here.' "[162]

What Avorn describes as the "laissez-faire chaos of the marketplace" is not likely to create the electronic touchstone doctors need. For one, drug-makers tend to avoid head-to-head clinical trials, preferring to test their newest nostrums against placebos rather than comparing them to existing, often less expensive treatments.[163]

As a sometimes bewildering array of drugs and devices pour into the marketplace, there is only one way to synthesize the information regarding their long-term risks and benefits into a coherent whole: someone must con-solidate the evidence gathered in thousands of randomized, long-term clin-ical trials. And these ongoing trials need to outlast the vicissitudes of a marketplace where mergers and acquisitions can interrupt long-term re-search. Moreover, such trials need to be organized and overseen not by a corporation's marketing arm, but by physicians who have absolutely no fi-nancial interest in the outcome.[164]

For in the end, the aim of a health care system is not to create entrepre-neurial opportunities for doctors, profits for investors, or full employment for investment bankers who oversee a seemingly endless stream of mergers, acquisitions, and spin-offs. Profits and jobs are desirable by-products in any industry, but the raison d'être of a health care system is singular: to enhance the quality of our collective lives by making us healthier.

Or, as medical economist Rashi Fein once observed, "We live in a society, not just in an economy."[165] Corporations, on the other hand, live only in the economy. And properly so: this is their mandate.

If anyone thinks otherwise, consider a 2004 headline on the Dow Jones Newswires: "Health Care Seen as Growth Area for Buyout Firms." The story explains that "bad health is good news for U.S. buyout firms" and goes on to quote industry players who point to "wealthier patients" as "a good cash-generative source for private equity operators of high-margin ser-vices," particularly "surgical, heart and women's procedures."

Best of all, the story continues, "the sheer breadth of sub-sectors within the health care industry means that at any given time there will be . . . sectors presenting good buying opportunities and others where it's a good time to sell."[166] In other words, a fragmented health care system spawns layers of businesses, some on their way up, some on their way down, all providing endless opportunities for hot money.

But is churning the health care industry really likely to lead to better health?[167]

As the history of the eighties and nineties attests, what deal makers sometimes bill as "creative destruction" does not always add value. At times, a chain letter of financial transactions can destroy far more wealth than it creates—both for an economy and for a society. In the chapter that follows, the history of for-profit hospitals offers a stunning case in point.

3

For-Profit Hospitals: A Flaw in the Business Model?

I n 2005 health care spending in the United States topped $2 trillion. To fully appreciate the magnitude of that sum, put it in an international context: the United States spends over 50 percent more per person than Switzerland, 85 percent more than Germany and Canada, roughly twice as much as countries like Australia and the Netherlands, and nearly two and a half times as much as the United Kingdom.[1] At well over $6,000 per person, "we spend more on health care than the Chinese spend on everything," observes health care economist David Cutler—"including all the tea in China."[2]

Begin with the largest piece of the pie. As the chart on p. xii demonstrates ("What Are We Paying For?"), more than 30 percent of all health care dollars flow to the hub of the health care system: the hospital. Over the past 15 years, hospital stays have become shorter, and far fewer patients stay the night; nevertheless, inpatient and outpatient services together still absorb nearly one-third of the nation's health care budget, thanks in part to the spiraling cost of the drugs and devices that hospitals buy. And the hospital system's slice of the pie is expanding. In 2004 hospitals accounted for one-third of the total rise in health care spending.[3]

If the quality of care were rising, many Americans might be willing to accept higher prices—even while knowing that spending more of the nation's resources on hospitals leaves less for everything else. But whether you rely on statistics or doctors' anecdotes, all available evidence points in the opposite direction. While hospital bills climb, the quality of care remains—at best—the same.[4]

Nursing shortages, tight-fisted HMOs, unpredictable politicians, uninsured patients, alienated doctors, and antiquated systems—all are blamed for putting 21st century hospitals under enormous pressure. Despite breathtaking advances in medical technology over the past quarter century, patients are becoming more and more aware of the hazards of a hospital stay.

Not only are patients alarmed, some doctors are bitter. "There isn't a hospital in New York City where I would want to operate on any of my patients—it doesn't matter who you are or how much money you have," says a Park Avenue ophthalmologist, his voice cracking with anger. He now performs surgeries in a specialty surgical center and blames managed care for hospital understaffing: "When you don't have enough people, and you ask them to do more than is humanly possible—eventually, they stop caring."[5]

At the same time, hospital bills head for the heavens. In 2003 hospital spending climbed by 7.5 percent; in 2004 outlays for inpatient and outpatient services jumped by another 8.6 percent.[6] The popular wisdom has it that hospital spending is levitating because the Pepsi generation is graying. But surprisingly, the aging population accounts for "only about 10% of the recent growth in real hospital spending," says Princeton health care economist Uwe Reinhardt.[7] "The bulk of the rapid annual growth in national spending is driven by factors that increase per capita spending for *all* age groups," Reinhardt explains. Here he lists the spiraling cost of new technologies (including those halfway technologies that do not cure us, but keep us alive); a shortage of hospital workers, which leads to higher wages (boosting payrolls by 6 percent in 2004); and finally, the fact that in the health care industry, suppliers have such enormous sway over demand for the services that they sell.[8] In other words, if you happen to reside in a city well-endowed with hospitals, you are likely find yourself spending time in one of them.[9]

A Tough Business

Yet even as hospital revenues mount, most institutions barely manage to break even. In 2004 roughly one-third of the nation's 5,700 hospitals were operating in the red. The average hospital reported an operating margin of just over 4 percent. Add in profits from investments, and the industry averaged a little over 5 percent. Meanwhile, it was getting harder to eke out the 4–6 percent that a hospital needed to be considered financially healthy: in just three years, the average hospital's operating costs had climbed by 14 percent.[10]

That the hospital business is a tough business should come as no surprise. Consider, for a moment, how difficult it is to run a restaurant or a hotel. Now imagine that all of your guests are sick, most are more than a little grumpy, and some are threatening to sue. Many cannot pay their bills. Meanwhile, you are expected to make huge capital investments in equipment that threatens early obsolescence. Finally, the success of the whole operation depends on your ability to attract, and keep, highly skilled unionized workers—nurses and technicians who happen to be in very short supply. Labor accounts for up to 60 percent of your expenses, and while many industries have been able to cut costs and increase productivity by downsizing, hospitals have learned that if they try to trim nursing staff, patients die.[11]

Indeed, as NYU economist William Baumol pointed out more than 40 years ago, in certain labor-intensive industries like hospitals and schools, the *quality* of work is closely tied to the *quantity* of the workers, a phenomenon economists now refer to as "Baumol's cost disease." In these industries, it is difficult to raise productivity by downsizing. Despite advances in technology, it is no easier for a teacher to teach 25 students—or for a nurse to tend to 25 patients—than it was 25 years ago. In a classroom with a high student-teacher ratio, just as in a hospital with a high patient-nurse ratio, students and patients suffer.[12] In the future, as hospitals make greater use of information technology, nurses may spend less time chasing lost paperwork. But as medical technology becomes more sophisticated, a nurse's job becomes more complicated: in high-tech 21st-century hospitals, the need for hands-on caregivers is rising.

Of course, there was a time when no one expected a hospital to turn a profit. Originally, the hospital served as a place for the poor to die. In the late

19th century, "patients with adequate means were treated in the physician's office or, most often, in their home," explains Kenneth Wing, co-author of *The Law and American Health Care.* "Abysmal hygienic conditions, over-crowded wards, and the primitive state of medical knowledge made the hospital the choice of only the most desperate."[13]

As medical science grew, conditions improved. In 1890, for example, William Halsted at Johns Hopkins became the first physician to wear rubber gloves during surgery; until then, doctors had delved into the body bare-handed.[14] Meanwhile, the hospital evolved from a warehouse for the poor to a place where the middle class might seek relief from pain and suffering. By the 1920s approximately one-half of a hospital's patients were paying fees for services. Nevertheless, hospitals still could not begin to support themselves on patient revenues.[15]

It was not until the 1960s that hospitals found a reliable pool of paying customers. Many commentators assume that Medicare provided the funding that turned health care into a potentially lucrative business. But as discussed in chapter 1, it was the spread of employer-based health insurance that set the stage. By 1958 two-thirds of the U.S. population was covered by some form of hospital insurance.[16] Eight years later, with the passage of Medicare, senior citizens joined the ranks of the insured. And following the precedent set by Blue Cross, Washington, too, promised to pay hospitals on an open-ended fee-for-service basis.[17] At last, the industry could count on a seemingly endless stream of revenues from the deepest of pockets. Now laser-eyed entrepreneurs saw an opportunity to turn the hospital business into a moneymaking proposition.

The Rise of the For-Profit Hospital

In 1968 a father-and-son team of surgeons, Dr. Thomas Frist Sr. and Dr. Thomas Frist Jr., joined forces with Jack Massey, the promoter who turned Harland Sanders's recipe for Kentucky fried chicken into a fast-food emporium, and formed Hospital Corporation of America. The next year, they sold shares to the public. Later known as HCA, the company would become the nation's first investor-owned hospital chain.[18]

Success seemed within reach. The idea of a for-profit hospital was no longer an oxymoron. The industry's founders began with a nearly doctrinal conviction that their investors would reap a profit. In a competitive market, they reasoned, innovative businessmen would make the hard-headed decisions needed to streamline a notoriously wasteful industry. And as health care costs climbed, nearly everyone agreed that what hospitals needed was a good dose of market discipline. Sure enough, in the 1970s, Paul Starr points out, the hospital business "grew faster than computers" making the for-profit hospital "the first beachhead" in the march toward corporate health care.[19]

In palmier days, hospitals had been run, de facto, by doctors. But investor ownership "introduced managerial capitalism into American medicine," Starr explains. "Strong central management was the key to the model." At not-for-profits, the hospital board might hold sway. But at investor-owned hospitals, just as at most large corporations, boards made up of outside directors held limited power. Inside the company, corporate executives were calling the shots.[20] Welcome to an era where hospital CEOs would rack up salaries that made neurosurgeons look like pikers.

During this period, savvy executives introduced some much-needed practical reforms. From the beginning, they realized that there was money to be saved by buying in volume, and as they assembled their chains, they began snapping up everything from wheelchairs to laundry services in bulk. Over time, not-for-profits followed their example. The Mayo Clinic, for instance, consolidated its purchases by asking its orthopedic surgeons to agree on a single company as their source for artificial hips. The result: Mayo took the average cost per hip down from around $2,200 to roughly $1,000.[21]

It was not always easy to persuade doctors to comply. "Every surgeon had his preferred surgical glove, and in the past he could usually find someone in the hospital to order it for him," says Sheryl Skolnick, a stock analyst at Fulcrum Global Partners, a New York–based independent research firm.[22] But as the for-profit model took hold, hospital executives learned to herd cats.

Publicly traded hospital chains also enjoyed access to the capital needed to upgrade aging facilities and equipment—a particular boon in the South, where most communities lacked the capital base needed to build state-of-the-art hospitals. "In those states, even religious organizations didn't have the money that they had in the Northeast," explains Jeff Villwock, who follows health care at Caymus Partners, an investment-banking firm in Atlanta.[23] Meanwhile, Starr observes, deep pockets gave investor-owned hospitals an edge when it came to coping with an alarming pile of regulatory paperwork. As Washington tried (vainly) to contain health care spending, the complexity of the regulatory environment grew, and large organizations were better able to adapt to new regulations.

And beyond being able to handle the changing rules, the chains were in a better position to *shape* the new regulations. "This is the problem of political feedback," Starr observes. "Once powerful organizations become established, they find the political means to sustain themselves." Ultimately, political decisions would be driven by lobbyists, not health care professionals, and these decisions would set the nation's health care priorities.[24]

But even the best lobbyists cannot ensure profits, and before long the entrepreneurs who had set out with such confidence were finding out that it was not so easy to turn hospital care into a moneymaking endeavor. While a not-for-profit needs only to remain solvent while caring for its patients, a publicly traded hospital also has a legal responsibility to make money for its shareholders. And as the industry took off, those shareholders expected what Wall Street had promised—that those returns would not be meager. After all, the hospital industry was a growth industry, just like computers. Moreover, although not-for-profits were exempt from both property and corporate income taxes, investor-owned hospitals were expected to ante up, just like any other for-profit corporation.

But for-profits did enjoy one signal advantage over their not-for-profit rivals: they could pick and choose where to build or buy, avoiding the inner cities and poverty-stricken rural areas where so many not-for-profits struggled to stay afloat.

In the early years, the industry flourished: by 1986 for-profits had captured 14 percent of the nation's acute-care hospital market. But then the sector began to plateau. Whatever efficiencies a new breed of hospital operators may have introduced, hospital care remained a labor-intensive business that demands enormous capital investments. By 2004 the industry's market share remained under 16 percent—up less than 2 percent in nearly two decades.[25]

Despite initial success, for-profit hospitals seemed unable to break out of a self-destructive boom-and-bust cycle. Time and again, a promising company would gather strength and begin to flourish, acquiring one hospital after another until its empire stretched coast-to-coast—and then implode. Success was followed by forced sell-offs. Scandal stalked the sector.

Indeed, in recent years, the nation's leading hospital companies have joined the likes of Enron and WorldCom in the lists of corporate crime. *Time and again, it seems that the most successful investor-owned hospitals have been able to make their numbers only by making them up.* Some bilked taxpayers; others bribed doctors, still others gulled investors. In the most harrowing cases, health care providers resorted to kidnapping patients.

To be sure, not all publicly traded hospitals have stooped to turn a profit. Many have remained clean. Nevertheless, the industry's checkered history sums up the contradictions at the very heart of corporate medicine. A close look at the history of three of the largest investor-owned chains—National Medical Enterprises, Tenet, and HealthSouth—suggests that there may be a fatal, and perhaps fundamental, flaw in the business model.

National Medical Enterprises: Shanghaiing Patients

In 1992 National Medical Enterprises' CEO and cofounder Richard K. Eamer took home more than $17 million—a sum that made him the best-paid executive in California.[26] A lawyer and CPA, Eamer had founded NME in 1969 with two other attorneys, Leonard Cohen and John Bedrosian. The trio started out with just six hospitals and some $25 million raised by selling stock to the public. Within six years the company owned, operated, and managed 23 hospitals.

From the beginning, it was Eamer's insatiable ambition that drove the enterprise. A maverick, Eamer had dropped out of school at 14, worked as a truck driver, stevedore, and wrangler, and then returned to school at 22. Nine years later he completed his law degree.

Although none of the three had any direct experience in the health care industry, Eamer declared his independence from the conventional wisdom about health care delivery, telling the *Los Angeles Times,* "We don't care what the pack does."[27] John Bedrosian threw down the gauntlet for corporate medicine in a public debate with *New England Journal of Medicine* editor Arnold Relman—the physician who worried that in an increasingly hostile and competitive environment, health care was becoming a war of all against all. Bedrosian shrugged off Relman's concerns, arguing that medical services can be traded in the marketplace, just like any other commodity. Existing medical paradigms, he declared, were obsolete.

Ultimately, Eamer would build NME into a $4 billion empire boasting 143 hospitals on four continents. But along the way, he hit a snag: one of the deepest pockets feeding the for-profit boom was becoming less bountiful. Nineteen eighty-one was the year President Reagan declared that Medicare had been issuing "blank checks" for too long, letting hospitals "fill in the amount they wanted."[28]

Congress agreed, and Washington set out to rein in health care spending, decreeing that, from that point forward, the government would no longer pay hospitals whatever they chose to charge on a open-ended fee-for-service basis. Instead, Medicare set "per-case" rates, defined by the patient's diagnosis, plus any other factors that might affect cost—such as the patient's age or complications from other diseases.[29]

Nationwide, hospitals felt the squeeze. But Richard Eamer was not about to be stymied. Looking around, he realized that while payers were clamping down on payments to general care hospitals, cost controls were virtually nonexistent at psychiatric and substance-abuse facilities. In these areas of health care professionals often did not agree on the usefulness of various therapies, making it difficult for payers to lay down clear-cut rules for admission and treatment. At the same time, more and more states were requiring employers to include treatment for mental illness and substance abuse in their health care packages—which meant that demand for these services was climbing.

Eamer knew a lucrative niche when he saw one. Without hesitation, he began culling general hospitals from his portfolio, replacing them with more profitable and less regulated specialty hospitals. By 1991 NME owned 86 psychiatric and substance-abuse facilities. And NME was not the only for-profit chain to trade in its general hospitals for psychiatric and substance abuse facilities. From 1984 to 1989 the share of investor-owned hospitals that were specialty hospitals doubled from roughly one-quarter to over 50 percent.[30]

Inevitably, success led to excess, and by the late eighties, billing fraud at the nation's psychiatric hospitals had become too flagrant even for head-in-the-sand insurers to ignore. In the past, insurers often had looked the other way when health care providers put a thumb on the scale—the extra charge could always be passed along in the form of higher premiums. But now employers were beginning to rebel, and managed care companies were competing on price. Both private insurers and Medicare began tightening rules for admission and reimbursement, and with the easy money drying up, occupancy rates at most psychiatric hospitals plunged.

But not at NME. At Eamer's hospitals, 84 percent of the beds were full in 1989—up from 75 percent in 1987. "We all thought it was the quality of care that was keeping the beds filled," said John Hindelong, then a health care analyst for Donaldson Lufkin & Jenrette. "It looked on paper like such an attractive story," he added wistfully.[31]

In fact, Eamer kept his beds full by setting financial targets for his hospital executives. Their jobs would hang on meeting these targets.

On the surface, NME's CEO seemed a rather blasé manager. Sporting a ponytail, the 60-something executive drove flashy cars, raised thoroughbred horses, and cruised the halls of NME's executive offices on a scooter. At senior-level meetings, *The Wall Street Journal* reported, the aging playboy sometimes could be seen clipping his fingernails or playing with his black retriever.

When it came to profits, on the other hand, Eamer was far from nonchalant. Hospital executives who met their profit targets could count on bonuses that would double their salaries. Those who failed could expect a verbal beating. "Dick gives you all the room you want—but he will castrate you if you make any errors," said John Bowen, who served as a National Medical executive and consultant for 18 years. Another executive added: "I can count on one hand the times I have been intimidated in my life. Several digits go to Dick Eamer. There were times he reduced me to emotional rubble."

NME gave its managers plenty of help in meeting their quotas. According to numerous ex-employees, the company paid "bounty fees" of as much as $2,000 to school counselors, probation officers, and clergymen who referred young patients to its psychiatric hospitals. Sometimes the company sent its own "counselors" into schools to "recruit" patients. NME even turned doctors into recruiters. In Tennessee, physicians who moved their clinics onto NME land were given 50-year leases for just $1 a year. "It's an unwritten agreement for patient referrals," one surgeon explained.[32]

Company guidelines also spelled out how long to keep the patients, according to William McCabe, a psychologist and former executive director of a NME chemical-dependency facility in Lakewood, Colorado. In 1990, McCabe reported, a senior vice president of NME handed him a new "continued stay" admissions policy: from that point forward, a patient's stay would be determined not by his medical needs but by how much insurance he had available. Patients whose insurance paid less than 30 percent of billings were to be bounced within 10 days, while those with at least 60 percent coverage were to be confined for a minimum of 28 days. McCabe refused to implement the policies, was fired, and sued for wrongful termination.[33]

The Patients

NME's legal troubles began in 1991 when families of some young patients in Texas claimed that private security guards had taken children to National Medical Enterprises' psychiatric facilities against their will. Once the hospitals had the patients under lock and key, investigators alleged, they began overbilling both insurers and the federal government, charging exorbitant prices for medications and treatments that were never provided. Or, worse yet, provided but never needed.

Investigators would later charge that some patients were held until their insurance ran out. One such victim, John David Deaton, later testified at a congressional hearing that after his girlfriend jilted him, a physician had persuaded the depressed 17-year-old to go to a psychiatric hospital in Dallas. The teenager did not know that the physician was on the hospital's payroll and that his income depended on how well he succeeded in filling its beds. According to Deaton, once he was hospitalized, the doctors transferred him to the hospital's long-term care unit. There, he got into an altercation with a nurse and soon found himself restrained to his bed—confined in a mesh body net that stretched from his neck to his ankles.

For most of the next 11 months, he remained pinioned to his hospital bed. "Each of my limbs was secured to one corner of my bed. I was completely covered by the netting," Deaton recalled in testimony before the House Subcommittee on Crime and Criminal Justice. "I was never allowed more than one limb free to take my meals. I was not allowed outside for a breath of fresh air for nearly a year. I got no exercise."

When it came time for group therapy, Deaton was wheeled into the room where the group met—still tethered to his bed. "I never could understand why, if I was so out of control that I had to be tied to my bed for my own protection, I was still able to go to group therapy five days a week, and benefit from it enough that my insurance company could be asked to pay for it," he recalled. In the end, Deaton testified, the treatment cost his insurance company $250,000. He was released only when his insurance was finally canceled. At that point he was transferred to a state institution where doctors determined that the teenager was not in need of hospitalization.

By then his leg muscles had atrophied to the point that he could no longer stand up.[34]

Jim Moriarty, a Houston attorney who represented 625 former NME patients, recalls another victim, a high school senior who found herself locked into one of NME's psychiatric facilities just weeks before she was scheduled to graduate as the valedictorian of her senior class. A Texan who doesn't mince words, Moriarty is quick to acknowledge that it isn't always easy to verify claims of abuse: "Ninety out of 100 of these psychiatric patients would drive you crazy. But in 10 cases out of 100, you could see exactly what was going on. In this case, a 17-year-old girl had been sexually abused by her father for years. Finally, a friend comes to stay overnight, and the next day, the friend's mother calls the girl's mother, and says, 'If he's hitting on my 17-year-old, he's probably hitting on your 17-year-old.' The mother confronts the girl; she admits what is going on and is sent to counseling.

"The mother assumes that psychiatrists are caring, compassionate people. But her daughter goes to a crooked doctor who tells her, 'We really need to get you hospitalized.' The girl then spends the next 60 days as an involuntary patient in the hospital—this, during the time when she should have been going to her senior prom, graduating, making the valedictory speech. She's the completely innocent victim of outrageous family abuse, but the father goes free and the daughter is incarcerated. Meanwhile, the hospital staff immediately recognizes that she is very capable, so during the time she's there, they put her in charge of the program for the little kids who also are involuntarily held."[35]

But it was Christy Scheck's case that ultimately forced NME to admit responsibility for mistreating a patient. Testifying before the House committee, Scheck's parents described how they had followed the advice of a psychiatrist when they entrusted their 13-year-old daughter to San Diego's Southwood Psychiatric Center in November of 1991. At the time, the

Schecks did not know that Southwood was part of a chain of 76 hospitals owned by NME. Nor did they did know that in January of 1991, Southwood's corporate parent had embarked on a vast cost-reduction program. As a memo sent out to the hospitals' regional administrators explained: "No area of expenditure is sacrosanct."

Before long, licensed personnel were replaced by paraprofessionals—including unpaid interns who were working to earn units toward a degree. At Southwood, management cut corners by hiring "at the bottom of the pay scale in the professional health community," says Alan Sidell, who headed up a marketing team for child and adolescent services at the facility. Southwood mental health counselors were paid between $7 and $9 an hour while unit clerks received an hourly wage of $5 or $6. None of the mental health counselors in the early-adolescent program where Christy was housed were certified mental-health professionals. Too late, Bob Scheck realized that the people watching over his daughter were "22-year-old college grads, or student interns attempting to get their degrees. Inexperienced girls."

Certainly the attendants did not pay enough attention to Christy on the evening of March 6, 1992, four months into her stay, when she gave one of her caretakers a note saying: "I am feeling very unsafe. I don't want to run. I want to hurt myself." Despite the warning, the staff left the 13-year-old alone that evening—just long enough to end her life. They found her hanging from her bathroom door, the sash of her terry-cloth bathrobe around her neck, the Tootsie Pop that she had been sucking on when she hung herself still stuck in her throat.[36]

Christy had attempted suicide before. Why then, was she left alone? The hospital stonewalled Christy's parents. "We knew that something was very wrong because we were only able to contact the hospital through letters after Christy's death," Bob Scheck recalled. No one would answer their phone calls. "We weren't even able to pick up her things from her room. We felt so strongly that this should *never* happen to any other parent, and we knew the only way we could bring it to the attention of other parents was by a lawsuit."[37] Bob and Merry Scheck charged both Southwood and its parent company, NME, with negligence, medical malpractice, and wrongful death. Less than a week before the case was scheduled to go to trial, NME settled—and stunned observers by publicly accepting corporate responsibility for the girl's death.

"Hire Sleazeballs . . ."

This was NME's first specific mea culpa, the first admission of responsibility in any of the nearly 150 lawsuits alleging physical mistreatment and abuse that NME had faced since the late 1980s.[38]

By the fall of 1991 the scandal had spread, and investigators in New Jersey and Florida were looking into charges that hospitals owned by NME were kidnapping patients, committing them to mental institutions, and then milking their insurance companies.

Did NME's top management know just how aggressive the company's "recruitment" had become? At trial, Jim Moriarty and other attorneys produced damning internal memos including one from an executive medical director at a California hospital warning Eamer that the attitude at the company's psychiatric hospitals was to "put heads on beds at any cost." In a separate deposition, a senior vice president reported that he had been told by the head of the psychiatric chain to "fill the beds at any cost. Hire sleazeballs . . . anything it takes."[39]

By 1993 NME was sinking fast in mud of its own making. As the investigation heated up, Eamer remained unapologetic, appearing at one media interview wearing a sweatshirt that proclaimed his message to the world: "I'm not arrogant, I'm just always right."[40] But he would not be able to bluff his way out of the scandal. Federal investigators uncovered evidence revealing that NME had engaged in virtually every form of health care fraud imaginable, from fleecing insurers to paying kickbacks to doctors willing and ready to commit adolescent patients to the company's psychiatric hospitals.

Ultimately, a dozen of the nation's largest insurers would sue NME, claiming that the company had defrauded them of some $750 million. Meanwhile, more than 130 patients brought their own suits against the hospital chain, accusing it of fraud, physical mistreatment, and false imprisonment.[41] By 1993 NME faced a slew of civil lawsuits—plus 14 separate federal and state investigations. Rumor had it that criminal indictments were on their way. NME's shares had fallen from a high of $25 to $6 and change. Richard K. Eamer was losing his grip on his empire. Enter Jeffrey C. Barbakow.

Jeffrey Barbakow: "Composure Under Fire"

On a Friday night in April of 1993, Richard Eamer phoned Jeffrey Barbakow, a longtime friend and NME board member, and asked for a meeting the next day. Barbakow knew the company well—so well that critics would later charge that he must have had an inkling of just how NME made its money. After all, while working as an investment banker at Merrill Lynch Capital Management in the seventies and eighties, Barbakow had helped finance NME's growth. "This was my favorite company when I was with Merrill," he later recalled. "It was a star on Wall Street."[42]

When Eamer sat down with Barbakow in his den on Saturday afternoon, Barbakow assumed that his friend wanted financial advice. But Eamer surprised him. He wanted more, much more: he asked Barbakow to take over as NME's CEO. The request came as a shock. Less than two years earlier, Eamer had declared that he had no intention of retiring. Even when it was time for him to go, NME's flamboyant CEO boasted, no single individual could replace him. He resisted talking about a succession plan. But now the 65-year-old CEO had no choice.[43]

Barbakow must have been flattered. During the years that he worked at Merrill Lynch, the young banker had described himself as "in awe" of Eamer's entrepreneurial zeal, and even after Barbakow left Merrill in 1988 to become chairman and chief executive of MGM/United Artists Communications, the two men remained in touch.[44] While at MGM, Barbakow's job was to engineer the sale of the ailing studio, and in 1990, he did just that, pocketing $20 million in the process. That same year Barbakow joined NME's board of directors. And now many assumed that Eamer was asking him to do what he had done for MGM: dress the company for sale.

After all, as the *Los Angeles Times* pointed out, Eamer's hand-picked successor "knew next to nothing about hospitals." Best known as a Wall Street deal maker, Barbakow had made his reputation crafting eighties-style leveraged buyouts. Nevertheless, he embraced the challenge and vowed to salvage the hospital chain—in part, some observers speculated, out of loyalty to his mentor. At Eamer's retirement dinner, Barbakow described his predecessor as a "hero." When he picked up the reins of the struggling company, he again proclaimed his allegiance, saying, "I think the world of him."[45]

Despite Barbakow's lack of hands-on health care experience, many on Wall Street saw the 49-year-old as an ideal candidate for the formidable task ahead. At Merrill Lynch, *The New York Times* observed in a warmly written profile, colleagues admired Barbakow for his "cool composure under fire."

By 1994 the celebrity CEO profile had become a popular and well-honed form, and this one was a classic. The *Times* story was headlined, "The Job, Thankless; the Challenge, Huge. Let's Go," and it painted Barbakow as a tireless Wall Street warrior: "His face gaunt from 20 years of running 25 miles a week, Mr. Barbakow is tall and spare. As if to keep from telegraphing his message, he remains still when speaking and his voice has a gravelly edge. A spider-web of lines spreads across his cheekbones when he smiles."

A self-made man, Barbakow had grown up in South Central Los Angeles, where his father owned a struggling truck-parts shop. "Mr. Barbakow . . . credits his father with instilling in him a strong moral compass and work ethic," the paper noted. From there, Barbakow made his way through college, earned a masters degree in business from the University of Southern California, and was on the verge of earning a PhD from the Wharton School at the University of Pennsylvania, when his wife, Margo ("a vivacious, dark-haired former advertising account manager from California") accidentally threw out the research for his dissertation on computer-aided portfolio management. Nevertheless, when he returned to Los Angeles in 1972, Barbakow quickly made his way to the top, becoming the rainmaker for Merrill Lynch's West Coast investment banking arm.[46] Now, he would have the opportunity to show his mettle at NME.

And he would need all of the composure that he could muster. Just two months into the job, at 7:30 a.m. on the morning of August 26, 1993, NME's new CEO received a phone call informing him that the FBI was raiding his company. Some 600 agents had descended on the company's Santa Monica headquarters and nine of its hospitals, searching for evidence of billing fraud and malpractice. Once inside, investigators scooped up truckloads of documents. In Louisville, Colorado, the *Rocky Mountain News* reported, agents were still loading boxes of records into white vans at 7:30 p.m. when cocaine addicts began filing into Centennial Peaks Hospital for their weekly Cocaine Anonymous meeting.[47]

When investors heard that a horde of FBI agents had swept NME's facilities, they did not hesitate: in one day NME's shares plunged by 30 percent. Wall Street put the stock on a "death watch." Springing into action, Barbakow spent the days that followed on the phone—not with the hospitals' directors but with Wall Street bankers and analysts, assuring them that the company could be salvaged. Barbakow was not a health care specialist; he was a financial specialist. From his perspective NME was not a chain of hospitals, it was a stock.[48]

As he struggled to reassure investors, Barbakow focused on selling off assets and negotiating settlements with insurers as quickly as possible. His knack for wrapping up agreements soon earned him a nickname among NME employees, who called him "Monty Hall" (after the host of the hit television show *Let's Make A Deal*). Certainly, Barbakow had an incentive to work quickly: the bulk of his compensation was tied to the price of the stock. And he succeeded: within a year, NME's share price had bounced back from $7.75 to over $17—putting Barbakow on track to take home $5.7 million in 1994.[49]

In July of 1994, Barbakow sealed a settlement with state and federal agencies. NME pleaded guilty to eight criminal counts and paid fines totaling $379 million—a record in the annals of health care fraud—closing the books on a long list of charges that included kickbacks, bribes, unnecessary medical treatments, and false billings at psychiatric hospitals in some 30 states. As part of the deal, the company agreed to either shutter or sell off more than 70 psychiatric hospitals.

Did Insurers Look the Other Way?

In the medical marketplace—as in virtually any marketplace—corruption in one sector almost inevitably infects another. In this case, insurers who saw no evil created the climate for pervasive fraud. In 1993, when 10 large insurance companies sued NME, alleging that a "substantial portion" of the $1 billion they paid out in psychiatric claims over a period of years was for services that were neither needed nor provided, *The Wall Street Journal* asked the logical question: Why didn't the insurers act sooner?

"It appears that health insurance companies, with some exceptions, are content to pass the cost associated with fraud along to their customers in the form of higher premiums," Louis Parisi, director of the New Jersey insurance department fraud division, replied in testimony before a congressional subcommittee. Workers who process claims often get paid by volume. This gives them an incentive to let questions slide; some even take to "plugging in things that make the claims fly," Parisi added.

Robert F. Stuckey, the former medical director of the alcoholism unit at an NME hospital in Summit, New Jersey, backed Parisi's story, telling government investigators that when he informed The Prudential Insurance Company of possible insurance fraud, company executives merely laughed, saying that for them large bills meant large premiums and big bonuses. A Prudential spokesman denied that story, maintaining virtuously, "When fraud is alleged, we actively investigate it." Yet according to Russell Durrett, former controller of NME's Twin Lakes Hospital in Denton, Texas, "We would crank out bills of between $18,000 and $75,000 and we would never see an insurance auditor.[50]

Eamer Walks . . . Rebuilding the Empire

In the end, no one went to jail. Even when Pete Alexis, a regional officer who oversaw NME's psychiatric hospitals in Texas, admitted that he had conspired to pay $20 million to $40 million in bribes to psychiatrists, psychologists, and others in exchange for patient referrals, he was sentenced to only five years' probation and 200 hours of community service. (As part of a civil settlement, Alexis also agreed to give up $220,000 in assets that included his collection of Cartier jewelry, furs, antiques, and art.)

Alexis had cooperated with the FBI and prosecutors, testifying that top NME officials shared information about soliciting and paying for referrals. Yet none of these officials would serve time either. "For a deal that started at the highest levels of the company, to get a few middlemen is ridiculous," observed Jim Moriarty, the Houston attorney who represented more than 600 former NME patients.[51]

As for Richard Eamer, he walked away from NME with a severance package that included a lump sum of $2.66 million, $250,000 a year for five years in consulting fees, stock options valued at $790,500, and the promise of retirement payments of $527,600 per year.[52]

Meanwhile, Eamer's successor, Jeffrey Barbakow, had embarked on a multibillion-dollar shopping spree. In 1994 he laid out $3.3 billion to purchase American Medical Holdings, a chain known for running a clean operation. Two years later Barbakow engineered the acquisition of OrNda HealthCorp for $3.1 billion, adding another 50 hospitals to what was already the nation's second-largest hospital chain. Unfortunately, OrNda did not possess such a sterling reputation: in 1998 it would agree to pay more than $12.6 million to settle allegations of kickbacks and Medicare fraud.

Nevertheless, with 126 hospitals in 22 states, Barbakow's new empire had become a force to be reckoned with in much of the South. His strategy was to buy hospitals only in markets where the company could be one of the largest players. Size gave the hospital chain the muscle Barbakow wanted: when it came time to negotiate fees, insurers and employers had no choice but to accept his terms.

At the time, Barbakow was not the nation's only deal-happy hospital executive. Throughout the industry, CEOs had learned that the easiest way to boost cash flow was through mergers and acquisitions: "Growth. There's nothing investor-owned hospital chains are quite as obsessed with," *Modern Healthcare* reported in 1996.[53] And the deal making continued: "From 1996 to 2002, the hospital industry saw 1,076 mergers, acquisitions and other types of marriages."

Not everyone was equally enthusiastic about the hospital industry's M & A binge. Often, making a deal is far easier than making a deal work. Some of the acquisitions were well planned, others were haphazard. "OrNda is a house of cards. [They are] buying properties that are a piece of crap, that are going to take a lot of skill to be able to operate effectively, if they can be operated well at all," said Todd Richter, senior vice president of Dean Witter Reynolds.[54]

Barbakow had fallen into the nineties trap of seeking growth for growth's sake. The new hospitals would inflate cash flow, but would they be profitable? Critics also argued that incessant deal-making was undermining the hospital industry. *New England Journal of Medicine* editor Dr. Arnold Relman pointed to the OrNda acquisition as an example of the inherent "instability and unpredictability" of the investor-owned hospital industry. "A community that believes it is selling its hospital to one particular set of owners and managers may wake up one morning to find it is dealing with another set of managers, and one never knows whether there's a commitment to the community in the long run."[55]

Undaunted by his detractors, Barbakow forged ahead. Along the way, he changed NME's name to Tenet—a label meant to convey the company's new commitment to high principle. "It's very warm," said Barbakow. "It'll grow on you more and more." [56]

Some observers were not soothed. Constance Clarke, a former Wall Street analyst who had followed the scandal closely, wrote a letter to *The New York Times* protesting what she saw as its overly kind profile of the company's new leader: "Mr. Barbakow was a long-time friend of NME's founder, was involved in health care financing, and had been on the board of NME since 1990," Clarke pointed out. "If he was not aware of what was taking place, he was a fool; if he was, he was a villain. It may be telling that after Mr. Barbakow took the helm at NME, 13 insurers suing the company accused it of witness tampering. . . ." [57]

But all such warnings were brushed aside—and like many of his colleagues in the for-profit medical line, Jeffrey Barbakow used Tenet's seeming success to justify an increasingly regal standard of compensation for himself. In theory, financial incentives motivate managers at for-profit hospitals to work harder than their peers at not-for-profit institutions. This is hard to prove. In fact, some evidence suggests that, throughout corporate America, executives who receive the fattest perks turn in the worst performance— perhaps because their attention is so focused on their compensation. [58]

What is indisputable is that CEOs of for-profit hospitals are better paid. In 2001 Barbakow raked in $4.5 million in salary and bonuses, plus perks that included personal use of a Tenet corporate jet (valued at $66,962) and $34,090 for a company car. Granted, in recent years, CEO salaries at some not-for-profit hospitals also have begun to raise eyebrows: in 2003, for example, Douglas French, the CEO of Ascension Health, the nation's largest not-for-profit chain, collected $1.6 million in salary and benefits. At the very top of the heap, Memorial Sloan-Kettering's Harold Varmus, winner of a Nobel Prize in medicine, earned $2.3 million. A handsome sum, to be sure, but still only about half of Barbakow's 2001 take-home. And Barbakow was not ever a contender for a Nobel. [59]

All told, over the course of his tenure at Tenet, Jeffrey Barbakow would pull down roughly $400 million in salary, bonuses, and options—an amount, the California Nurses Association noted, that would cover 320,000 uninsured Californians for a year. [60] Even on Wall Street, some criticized Barbakow's compensation, saying that such lavish pay became a statement of the company's values. "When you pay the CEO so much money, you're saying, 'That's the game. Make as much money as you can,' " says Clifford Hewitt, who was a health care analyst at Legg Mason at the time. "At some point there's a spillover effect. We can't calculate it, but this kind of excess . . . gets reflected somewhere in the behavior of the organization." In any industry, Hewitt argues, egregious executive pay indicates that the CEO sees the corporation as "[his] own private piggy bank." And, he says, such compensation is especially inappropriate in hospital companies, since "These are low-margin businesses. If you want to make $110 million, maybe you go into high-tech—you don't go into the hospital business."[61]

In the end, who footed the bill for Barbakow's $4.5 million paychecks, his corporate jet, and his company car? The taxpayers, employers, and patients who paid Tenet's inflated bills. A 2002 survey of the nation's 100 most expensive hospitals would show that Tenet owned the top 14 slots, and 64 of the top 100.

Captain Kirk's Career Peaks

Yet if Barbakow was overpaid, his reputation only grew with his salary. This is true of most CEOs: it is not that we pay them so much because they are so much smarter than everyone else. Rather, we assume that they must be very, very clever because we pay them so much. And, of course, in one way, they are.

So in January of 2002, just seven years after Jeffrey Barbakow stepped up to become Tenet's CEO, *BusinessWeek* crowned him one of the nation's 25 top managers. As a tribute to his success, Tenet's Hollywood Medical Center saluted the CEO with a touched-up photo of the *Star Trek* crew, featuring Barbakow as Captain Kirk, a gift the magazine described as "one of his prized possessions."

"While the gift was given in good fun," *BusinessWeek* continued, "the image of the 57-year-old as a valiant captain isn't that far off. Since Barbakow took the helm in 1993, Tenet has blossomed from a struggling chain of 35 hospitals into a goliath with 116 hospitals in 17 states, revenues of 12 billion . . . and profits of $643 million, up 113% in just two years."[62] Over the next nine months, Tenet continued to dazzle, and on October 3 the company's shares hit an all-time high of $52.50. Unfortunately, that splendid moment would prove the apogee of Barbakow's career.

Just a day earlier, UBS/Warburg analyst Ken Weakley had called Tenet with a few questions regarding payments that the hospital chain had been receiving from Medicare. In particular, Weakley was interested in a steep rise in "outlier" payments. These were supplemental reimbursements that Medicare paid to hospitals that appeared to be taking particularly difficult cases—patients who were sicker than average or suffering from several illnesses simultaneously.

Thanks to dramatic growth in these outlier payments, Tenet had been posting stellar profits. But, Weakley wondered, was the trend sustainable? Why were Tenet's outlier payments so rich?

It would turn out that Tenet's outlier payments were growing, not because the hospital was treating more difficult cases, but because the company was gaming Medicare's reimbursement formula. Beginning in 2000, Tenet had set out on an aggressive campaign to hike its sticker prices—the rack prices that hospital charge before discounts. Few patients actually pay these retail prices; the vast majority receive a group discount. Nevertheless, Medicare used the undiscounted prices in complex formulas that determined how much it would pay in supplemental fees for outliers.

Tenet's scheme succeeded: its outlier payments more than doubled in just two years, climbing from $351 million in 2000 to $763 million in 2002.[63] The effect on the company's bottom line was impressive: according to Tenet's shareholder committee, outlier payments made up at least 25 percent of Tenet's total earnings in 2001 and 2002.[64]

Some would argue that Tenet got into trouble because Medicare's rules are so Byzantine. Caymus Partners' Jeff Villwock disagrees: "It's true that the rules of Medicare are very complicated, and whether you're a for-profit or a nonprofit it's easy to step over the line," says Villwock.[65] "But what Tenet did was deliberate. They raised their sticker prices or 'gross charges'— the prices that no one ever pays except the uninsured.[66]

"Someone at Tenet figured it out," Villwock continues. "If you raised these nominal prices rapidly enough, that would automatically trigger huge outlier payments." And Tenet's sticker prices were eye-popping. Doctors Medical Center, a Tenet hospital in Modesto, California, placed first in the 2002 survey of hospital prices, setting sticker prices some 1,092 percent over what it cost the hospital to provide services. In other words, if the hospital spent $1,000 on a patient's care, it would charge fees totaling more than

$11,000. Nearby, Tenet's Doctors Hospital of Manteca placed second, with average markups of 920 percent.[67]

The campaign to jack up Tenet's prices had been overseen by two of Barbakow's most trusted lieutenants: chief operating officer Thomas Mackey, a holdover from NME who had joined the company during Eamer's reign in 1985, and David Dennis, an investment banking sidekick who had worked at Merrill Lynch. When Dennis became Tenet's chief financial officer in February of 2000, he stepped up the pressure. And at that point the two men began to compete, setting ever higher performance targets for hospital executives. Managers who succeeded could expect a hefty bonus: in 2001 the average chief executive of a Tenet hospital doubled his $200,000 salary.

"We make cash flow an important part of our incentive compensation system," said Dennis—apparently unaware that this was precisely how NME had motivated its executives to "put heads on beds."[68] At Tenet, just as at NME, an executive's bonuses was directly linked to his hospital's financial performance. Neither quality of care nor patient satisfaction figured into the calculation.

Wall Street applauded Tenet's aggressive strategy—at least until late October when Ken Weakley, the UBS/Warburg analyst who had called at the beginning of the month with a few questions about Tenet's Medicare reimbursements, published his report. Weakley's analysis sent shock waves down Wall Street. First, he downgraded Tenet's shares from "hold" to "reduce." Then he explained why: the special outlier payments now accounted for nearly 25 percent of the reimbursements Tenet received from Medicare—up from 7.7 percent just three years earlier. Over the same period, the average for all urban hospitals had held steady at 5.6 percent to 5.7 percent. Something was clearly wrong.[69]

Wall Street did not welcome the insight. "When you say anything bad about a company, you upset two constituencies—the company's management and the institutional investors who own the shares," observes Caymus Partners' Jeff Villwock. Yet everyone knew that Weakley was a straight shooter. "I knew he was right," Villwock adds. "I had been wondering how it was that Tenet's average payment per patient per day kept on rising. Then I read Ken's report, and I thought, *That's* how they've been doing it."[70]

Ken Weakley put his report out on the Street on Monday, October 28, the beginning of what would turn out to be a truly terrible week for Jeffrey Barbakow. On Tuesday Tenet's shares shed 14 percent of their value. On Wednesday the second shoe dropped when 40 FBI agents raided a Tenet hospital in Redding, California.

Barbakow had been through this before. But when FBI agents had swooped down on NME's offices and hospitals nine years earlier, they were looking for evidence of overbilling and incarcerating patients until their insurance ran out. This time, the accusations were even more chilling. The investigators who descended on the Redding Medical Center were pursuing charges that Dr. Chae Hyun Moon, Redding's director of cardiology, and Dr. Fidel Realyvasquez Jr., chief of cardiac surgery, had been performing unnecessary operations on hundreds of unsuspecting patients.

Over the course of a year, the 238-bed hospital was doing about 1,000 cardiac procedures, including angioplasties, heart catheterizations, and open-heart surgeries. According to an FBI affidavit, competing cardiologists charged that as many as half of the heart surgeries and tests performed by the pair were "unnecessary by commonly held medical standards." In an estimated one-quarter of the cases, they claimed that Redding's rainmakers were operating on patients who had no serious heart problems whatsoever.

Some of those patients did not survive. Others were crippled. All suffered some form of psychological trauma.

Redding's Victims

Tony Ginocchio, a 57-year-old Wal-Mart truck driver describes the aftermath of his triple bypass: "I still have pain in my chest . . . especially when I cough or sneeze. I've been told it's probably a wire poking me. When they put your rib cage back together, they use wire, and they think it broke," he explained early in 2005. "I'm scheduled for another operation next week, to see if they can fix it."

As for posttrauma stress, "How can you go through a triple bypass and not have some sort of mental suffering, especially when you find out you didn't even need it?" he asks.

"I have a lot of fear about going to doctors," Ginocchio adds, "fear that they are going to do to me what Dr. Moon and Dr. Realyvasquez did to me. Just for money. Or to up the stock of the hospital they work at. It's hard to trust after someone who has taken an oath to care for people chooses to fatten their pocketbook on someone else's life and suffering.

"Also, I have a lot of fear of actually having a heart attack now. I worry a lot about the possibility of losing my job and not being able to get medical insurance due to what is now a preexisting condition. . . . On the road I worry if I don't have my nitro pills with me. I worry that there may be some undetectable damage to my heart and arteries from the actual surgery. I worry about my family if something happens to me. I hardly ever worried about anything before. I worry about everything now." [71]

Like NME, Redding virtually dragged patients in off the street. Seventy-nine-year-old Shirley Wooten's story began with an ordinary doctor's appointment, recalls her husband, Bob: "On the first Wednesday of February of 2002 she went to our family doctor with a slight pain in her left shoulder. That doctor referred her to Dr. Moon for a checkup. Moon gave her some tests and told her she had a plaque build-up and if it got stopped up she would die.

"The next day she had a two-way bypass," her husband continues. "She was in the hospital four or five days and seemed to be doing pretty good." But within a few days, he recalls, the pain in her chest suddenly got much worse. When her husband took her to the hospital, he was told that she needed a second operation.

"The main artery from the heart had torn loose and she was bleeding to death inside," he explains. "She was in the operating room all that night and at 5 a.m. the doctors told me she wasn't going to survive.

"Well, she did," Wooten says, with some pride. But his wife spent a month in intensive care—"she couldn't talk. She had a tracheal tube in her neck."

When Shirley Wooten finally came home, she had lost her sense of balance, and after four or five days, she fell and broke her hip. "They had to put in four pins," says Bob. "Had her home another four or five days and she fell again, and they had to put 27 stitches in her head." Ultimately, Bob quit his job to stay home and take care of his wife.

In 2005 he reported that Shirley was still using a walker. "Her sense of balance is coming back, but it's very slow," he explained. "And she never needed the operation in the first place—that's the bitter part." [72]

Why didn't Redding's patients get a second opinion? In retrospect, no doubt most wish that they had. But a patient who suddenly finds himself in the throes of a medical crisis may not feel in a position to second-guess his doctor—especially if he is told that delay could be fatal.

Thirty-eight-year-old Steven Hunt recalls going to the Redding hospital for help two days before Christmas of 2001. "I had high blood pressure, and my left eye was blurry—so I knew something was wrong. And the doctor said that, just by chance, they had an opening to do a bypass Christmas Eve morning.

"If I waited, the doctor told me, I could have a heart attack just walking across the hospital parking lot. And, because of where the problem was in my heart, I could die. They gave me no choice but to do the operation. Do it or die. What do you do when a doctor tells you something like that?"[73]

Today many would argue that a patient who does not question his doctor abdicates personal responsibility for his own health. But the brutal reality of a medical emergency is this: a patient faced with his own mortality has had the ground cut out from under him. Shocked, in pain, and facing enormous uncertainty, he may well want to put his life in the hands of an experienced, knowledgeable professional.

Moreover, Redding Medical Center had a sterling reputation: in 2002 its cardiac treatment center received a five-star rating from HealthGrades, the Colorado-based health care information company, for the fifth year running. According to HealthGrades, Redding's California Heart Institute had the best cardiac surgery record in the state.[74] A conscientious consumer who did his or her homework would have had every reason to believe that Drs. Moon and Realyvasquez were among the best in their field.[75]

Trust

Everything comes back to the fact that patients need to trust their doctors. Recent research suggests that in a medical crisis "elevated levels of trust are desirable for therapeutic reasons," says Mark Hall, a professor of law and public health who specializes in patient-physician relationships. Hall points out that a growing interest in the relationship between the mind and the body has led some scientists to suspect that, in a medical crisis, high levels of trust "may be a necessary defense mechanism"—a response that enables patients to "cope with the psychological distress of illness" while simultaneously "activating internal healing mechanisms."[76]

In other words, when experiencing a heart attack, trust may be a more adaptive response than suspicion. To be sure, not everyone agrees—and the vexed and vexing question of patient autonomy will receive more attention later in this book.[77] For the moment, suffice it to say that Hall is probably correct when he says that while trusting the physician may or may not be "desirable for therapeutic reasons," in a crisis it is probably "inevitable for psychological reasons."

Jim Moriarty, the attorney who represented Steven Hunt in his suit against Redding agrees:

"If you talk to these patients, you have to realize how unbelievably diabolical it is for Tenet's attorneys to suggest that people have free will in a situation like this," says Moriarty, who speaks from personal experience. "I remember what happened when my own brother-in-law had a heart attack, two or three years ago. There I am, down at the hospital at two o'clock in the morning, and these two doctors come out and say 'We've gone in and done a cath, and we've decided he needs heart surgery.'

"I see his wife turn ashen white—she has to make a life-and-death decision. And I realize that she is no more able to make that decision than the man in the moon.

"This heart surgery is elective," adds Moriarty; "in many cases, most of the issues that could be resolved by open-heart surgery can also be resolved by drug therapy—but they don't bother to tell you it's really a lifestyle choice. They don't make any money by telling you that."[78]

Lawyers and doctors don't always see eye to eye on best medical practice, but many cardiologists agree with Moriarty, complaining about what they call a "fireman's mentality" among some of their brethren. "We are very aggressive when we think a patient needs angioplasty or bypass surgery," says Dr. Thomas Graboys, president of the Lown Cardiovascular Center in Brookline, Massachusetts. "But the vast majority of folks undergoing interventional procedures in the United States don't really need them."[79]

Yet while Moriarty might have been skeptical about his brother-in-law's need for surgery, he couldn't be certain: "There is just no way that you can know—ultimately, the decision has to be based on trusting your doctor. With what I now know about open-heart surgery, making a decision under those circumstances seems crazy," he adds, "but we weren't given any options."

How can a patient know when he should wait for a second opinion, and when he should listen to the doctor who tells him that he must be hospitalized immediately?

It is all but impossible for a layman to know. Immediate action may have been necessary, says Dr. Tom Riles, head of surgery at NYU Medical Center. This is the same Tom Riles who, in chapter 2, declared that he, too, believes that far too many heart procedures are done in the United States. "But I can think of scenarios where I'd be worried about the artery clotting 100 percent—and, absolutely, I'd want to get the patient into the OR as quickly as possible.

"At some point, you have to—and one hopes that you can—trust in the total professionalism of your physician," Riles says.[80] Once again, in the most important moments, everything comes down to that compact between doctor and patient which makes the purchase of health care different from any other commercial transaction.

That night Moriarty's sister gave her permission. She could not be certain whether or not she was right. No more could Steven Hunt—back in 2001 at the Redding hospital—which is why it is so understandable that he put himself in his doctor's hands.

The tragedy is that Steven Hunt's surgeon violated his trust. Hunt's high blood pressure and blurred vision did not justify a bypass operation. Four years later, in January of 2005, he was still suffering from high blood pressure, but he had found that it could, indeed, be controlled by medication. And his other symptoms had disappeared.

Yet, as a result of the surgery, he could no longer work. He was just 42. "I was a rancher," he explains, "and I developed a hernia on the incision where they cut open my chest. After the operation, I couldn't do the physical work needed to survive—buck hay, fencing work. . . . All [of my] upper body strength was gone. I lost the ranch—everything."[81]

According to the FBI's affidavit, local cardiologists had tried to raise a red flag at Redding. One said that he warned Steve Schmidt, who was chief executive of the hospital at the time, of a "serious problem" with unnecessary heart procedures as far back as 1998. Another physician alerted his successor, Hal Chilton, during the summer of 2001. He quoted Chilton's response: "We have heard that, but we're not sure how to handle it."[82]

A Year Before the FBI Raid

Looking back, health care analyst Sheryl Skolnick realizes that Tenet's COO had been fudging Tenet's numbers at least a year before the Redding scandal broke. "I remember a meeting in L.A. late in October of 2001," says Skolnick. "Tenet was hosting an 'investor day,' and we sat there listening to the company pat itself on the back. Cash flow had turned around. Margins were up. It was the first investor day they had had in a long time.[83]

"And then, in one of the sessions, Mackey puts a slide up on the screen. I've forgotten exactly what was wrong with the numbers, but at the time I knew it didn't make sense. Something was missing.

"I asked him a question about the detail underlying the slide," Skolnick recalls. "And he stonewalled me, saying, 'That's not relevant.' So I asked the question again."

A petite mother of one in her early 40s with a brown belt in karate, Skolnick likes to get her facts straight. "At the time, I had a 'buy' recommendation on the stock," she recalls, "and I just wanted to know what was going on. So I kept asking: 'How do we know that these earnings are going to be sustainable?' To me, the question seemed obvious.

"But Mackey was getting really angry; his face was turning red. I asked the question five different ways—until it became apparent that either he was going to kill me or explode. Finally, I said 'Maybe someone on your staff could look into this and get back to me.'

"Later on, after the presentation was over, I went out to have a cigarette and ran into Paul Russell, Tenet's head of investor relations," Skolnick remembers. "And when he saw me, he just started to laugh.

" 'I told Mackey he wouldn't get away with that slide,' Russell said.

"You told him some pushy analyst from New York would call him on it?

" 'I bet him that it would be you.' "

In other words, Russell had bet Mackey that Skolnick would spot the discrepancy. This suggests that Mackey knew that he was lying—and so did Tenet's head of investor relations. And they expected that the analysts at the meeting would let them lie—either out of ignorance or out of an instilled sense of tact. (Offend a company, and it won't return your calls.) Unless Skolnick, or someone like her, stood up.

Blacklisted on Wall Street

It had taken Sheryl Skolnick a while to find her calling in life. After earning a PhD in economics from Washington University in St. Louis in 1985, she worked first in the antitrust division of the Justice Department, then for the Labor Department, in the Bureau of Labor Statistics. "That was a complete and total waste of time," she says with crisp disgust. "I was bored out of my mind. They didn't have anything for me to do. They had one project—I finished it in 35 days. So they told me to do it again. Basically, they just needed a female PhD economist to sit in a seat."

Following her foray into public service, Skolnick tried financial services, joining a small brokerage in 1988. A year later she was working for a larger regional brokerage and had begun covering health care stocks. By 1993 she had snagged a job at Robertson Stephens, a San Francisco–based investment banking firm.

There, she became known as the analyst who asked the tough questions. "While I was at Robertson Stephens, HMA [Health Management Associates] wanted me to put a 'buy' rating on their stock, and I refused," Skolnick remembers. "After that, they wouldn't return my calls." By then Skolnick had won the *The Wall Street Journal*'s "Best on the Street" award twice. Nevertheless, HMA (a for-profit chain based in Naples, Florida) shunned her. Skolnick was left off the list of analysts covering the company on the HMA website. Over a period of three years, she did not receive a single invitation to the company's investor meetings. At least, not until CNBC featured Skolnick in a story about how some corporations retaliate when analysts issue "sell" ratings. "After that," Skolnick recalls, "HMA's CEO called me."[84]

In the meantime, she was becoming disillusioned with Robertson Stephens. "In the late nineties, the firm jumped on the technology bandwagon, just before the sector tanked," she recalls. "At the same time, they dropped their health care coverage—just before the industry began a two-year bull run." Skolnick also was becoming uncomfortable with the implicit conflict between the firm's desire to build its investment banking business— which meant cozying up to companies that might bring it banking deals— and its responsibility to offer investors the best possible advice.

"I turned down some investment banking deals—which meant my revenues weren't up to snuff," Skolnick recalls. "At about the same time, it was becoming clear that the firm was no longer going to stand behind its longtime philosophy—that analysts have the right to say no." (In 2003 Robertson Stephens would pay $33 million in fines to settle allegations that it had charged inflated commissions and issued biased research.)[85]

In January of 2001, Robertson Stephens decided that it no longer wanted to cover health care services. "They wrote me a very nice check, and I began to look for another job. At that point, I didn't have to work—but I sure wanted to," she remembers. This is when Skolnick discovered that she had been blacklisted on Wall Street. Recruiters who dropped her name at the big brokerages were told: "We understand from our clients that she is not a team player."

Six months later, in June of 2001, Skolnick finally landed at Fulcrum Global Partners, an independent research boutique based in New York. There, she found her niche. Fulcrum does no investment banking business. "It is pure at Fulcrum, and there is only one client—the shareholder," says Skolnick. A nurse's daughter, she likes to see a bed made with hospital corners—especially if she is going to climb into it. "It is an opportunity to get paid for doing the work and sharing your opinion," Skolnick adds. "It is simple and straightforward."

With Fulcrum behind her, Skolnick felt free to take on Mackey in the fall of 2001. "It was the fact that he couldn't be questioned—that was what made me nervous—very nervous," she recalls.

How Much Did Barbakow Know?

That fall Skolnick heard a ticking bomb, and a year later, in October of 2002, it exploded. First, Weakley issued his damning report; two days later the FBI paid a call on Redding. By the end of the week, Tenet's investors had lost a stunning $6 billion. But as is often the case when a corporation implodes, key insiders managed to duck.

Tenet's chief operating officer, Thomas Mackey, for example, sold 277,500 of his Tenet shares—all but 15,000 of the shares that he owned—on October 4, 2002, just two days after Ken Weakley made his first call questioning the outlier payments. Unloading his stock at $51.50, Mackey, who had been a holdover from NME, turned a neat profit of just under $10 million. Roughly a month later (when the stock had been sliced nearly in half by investigations and downgrades), the 54-year-old executive abruptly retired from his $3-million-a-year job.[86]

Mackey was not the only insider who began jettisoning Tenet shares in 2002. In January, Jeffrey Barbakow had made some of Tenet's investors uneasy by selling shares worth $111 million. Just two weeks earlier, he had been touting Tenet's shares on CNBC: "We're in a sensational period right now in terms of our operations," he told the network's viewers. "Everything is going really well for us. And it's a really exciting, fun time."[87]

Two weeks later Barbakow bailed out of the fun, selling two million of his own Tenet shares. And then ten months later, in the fall of 2002, the company blew up. Granted, executives who receive generous stock option packages often trim their holdings in order to diversify their portfolios. But in 2002 Tenet insiders headed en masse for the exits.[88] Perhaps the top brass sensed that they were running out of road. Looking back, one Tenet executive marveled at the simplicity of management's strategy to goose its revenues—and the futility. "This would have bounced back eventually," he said, referring to the inflated outlier payments. "It was not sustainable and we would have had to give the money back."[89]

Meanwhile, Jeffrey Barbakow insisted that he had been unaware of the impact of the outlier payments on his company's bottom line. The Tenet Shareholder Committee headed by Dr. M. Lee Pearce, a Florida physician who began challenging Barbakow's management of the company in 2002, found this claim incredible. In a 2003 report, the committee marveled at Barbakow's supposed ignorance. If Tenet's CEO had been a physician, someone might believe that he just didn't have a head for numbers. But Barbakow was an investment banker, surrounded by his hand-picked team of lieutenants, including Mackey and chief financial officer Dennis, another Merrill Lynch veteran. And yet he claimed to be unaware that 45 percent of Tenet's total earnings in the 2001 fiscal year and 41 percent in 2002 were attributable to outlier reimbursements. "Didn't he ask his team to explain exactly how Tenet produced such extraordinary free cash flow, and nine consecutive quarters of 20%, or higher, earnings growth from operations as of February 28, 2002?" the committee asked.[90]

Nevertheless, Skolnick believes it is possible that Barbakow was not aware of the details of the outlier payments. "He was a very ambassadorial kind of manager," she explains. "That's how he saw himself—almost as if he were a university president, the organization's head cheerleader and fundraiser. I can see him not peeking under the covers."

Skolnick remembers how, two days after Weakley dropped his bombshell, Barbakow still appeared clueless. It was a Wednesday, October 30, 2002, and Tenet was hosting a lunch for analysts at the St. Regis Hotel in New York to try to undo the damage. "We're sitting there while they're laying out all of the information about the outlier payments. But in fact, they're just dancing around the issue."

Finally, Skolnick lost patience. "At this kind of function, I often try not to ask questions," she says. "After all, I'm surrounded by my competitors. It's not my job to share my ideas. But sometimes my right arm can't help itself. It shot up.

" 'What we really want to know is: did you or did you not commit Medicare fraud?' " Skolnick asked. Then she explained what was bothering her: " 'Here you are, patting yourselves on the back because your outlier payments have been so high—but Medicare created outlier payments to keep hospitals from going *bankrupt* when they treat too many very sick patients.' " (In other words, a high volume of outlier payments suggests a money-losing mix of patients.) Then she asked Barbakow the $64,000 question: " 'So the question is, are you making money on your outlier payments?' "

As she waited for a response, the scene turned into a cartoon. "You almost saw a lightbulb go off over Jeff's head," Skolnick remembers. "Suddenly, he realized, 'Oh my God—we shouldn't have been making money on outliers. . . . And if we did, something was very wrong.' " Indeed it was. In truth, Tenet's hospitals had not been treating an unusually large number of very sick, money-losing patients. But the company had been raising its sticker prices high enough and fast enough to fool the complicated formula that Medicare used to estimate how much it owed hospitals for outliers.

In 2005 Skolnick still wasn't certain whether Barbakow was dissembling or whether he really didn't understand the outlier payment scheme until that very moment: "Either he was very foolish—or he is a fabulous actor." But she agrees with his critics: if Tenet's CEO didn't "peek under the covers," it was because he did not want to know.

The Tenet Shareholder Committee would never accept the notion that Barbakow knew nothing about Redding. It stretched credulity, the committee said, to believe that he never had questioned "the inherent implausability that $94 million could be legally earned [in just one year] at a rural hospital located in Redding, California."[91]

"Some outsiders, without Barbakow's unlimited access to company records, figured out plenty about Tenet's [Redding Medical Center] on their own," observed TheStreet.com's Melissa Davis. "Researchers at Dartmouth Medical School said they flagged the high surgery rate at Tenet's Redding

Medical Center years ago. An ongoing study, conducted by Dartmouth's Center for the Evaluative Clinical Sciences, showed that Redding had the highest rate of heart bypass surgeries among Medicare beneficiaries in the 1990s." [92]

Settlement or Cover-up?

In October of 2002, Tenet promised full disclosure. A few days after the FBI raid, the company announced that it was "hiring the Mercer Consulting Group, a respected, independent medical utilization expert to assist in reviewing treatments performed by the two doctors at Redding." The company assured investors that Mercer "would, in turn, hire independent, expert cardiologists to review patient records and internal documents regarding the cases."

The report never saw the light of day.[93] Rather than disclosing precisely what had gone wrong at Redding, Tenet's management moved as quickly as possible to put the story to rest. Less than 10 months after the FBI raid, Tenet struck a deal with the government, agreeing to pay $54 million to settle charges that needless cardiac procedures performed at the Redding hospital between January 1, 1997 and December 31, 2002 were billed fraudulently to Medicare, Medicaid, and other government programs.

The agreement was careful to stipulate that Tenet was paying the $54 million "without admitting any wrongdoing"—leaving it unclear how so many healthy patients wound up on Redding's operating tables. As one Tenet watcher observed: "Settlements, by their nature, cover what actually happened."[94]

But the Redding case was not over. In the fall of 2004, the company still faced civil lawsuits by hundreds of former patients. Jim Moriarty, who had represented many of the patients who sued NME, now was the attorney for many of Redding's victims. And he did not see how Tenet's management would be able to hide the truth: "We have medical records," he said. "We have case after case after case validated by independent cardiologists showing that the operations were unnecessary," Moriarty declared in the fall of 2004. The facts are so clear, Moriarty said, that in trying to hide them, Tenet's managers look "like a cat trying to bury a turd on concrete."[95]

Yet Tenet would manage to silence the headlines without letting all of the grisly details become public. In December of 2004, the company announced that it was paying 750 Redding patients $395 million. The victims' attorneys had won a substantial sum for their clients, yet Moriarty could not help but wish that the case had gone to trial. Once again, a settlement buried the facts.

Redding's doctors also escaped criminal prosecution. In November of 2005, federal officials conceded that they could not gather enough evidence to warrant criminal charges. Instead, they announced that they had agreed on a series of multimillion-dollar civil penalties against four doctors accused of performing unnecessary heart procedures and surgeries at the hospital. "Oh, I'll be damned," said 78-year-old Shirley June Connelly, who sued after a 2002 surgery she now believes was unnecessary. "That's a shock." According to U.S. attorney McGregor Scott, penalties and settlements were expected to exceed $506 million. In addition, heart surgeon Fidel Realyvasquez Jr. and cardiologist Chae Hyun Moon agreed never again to perform procedures or surgeries on patients covered by Medicare, Medi-Cal, or TRICARE military insurance.[96]

What had happened to the peer-review process that is supposed to prevent a hospital's physicians from running amok? Who was protecting Redding's rainmakers? Had the order come down from Tenet's headquarters? "No one will ever know," says Moriarty, his voice filled with the frustration of someone who has been fighting the same battle for many years. Yet he does not sound resigned.

Tenet was predictably pleased with the outcome. "By settling all the cases at once," Trevor Fetter, Tenet's new CEO announced, "we put this matter behind both the plaintiffs and us and bring closure to this unfortunate event."[97]

Perhaps Fetter could put the matter behind him. Many of the injured patients could not.

Another Protégé

When Jeffrey Barbakow finally resigned his post as captain of a sinking ship, Trevor Fetter took the helm at Tenet. In choosing Barbakow's successor, Tenet fell back on tradition. Just as NME had picked Richard Eamer's protégé, Jeffrey Barbakow, to replace him, Tenet tapped one of Barbakow's favorite pupils, Trevor Fetter.[98]

Barbakow and Fetter first met in 1986 when they worked together at Merrill Lynch's Los Angeles office. When Barbakow left to become chairman of MGM, Fetter followed and served as his senior vice president. When Barbakow took over NME in 1993, Fetter initially remained at MGM. But two years later Barbakow persuaded his friend to join him, making Fetter the hospital chain's chief financial officer, a position that he would hold until 2000. That year, Fetter left corporate headquarters to run Broadlane, a cost management services firm spun off from Tenet, and David Dennis, another friend from Merrill, became Tenet's CFO.

Fetter later recalled that in 1995, when he first came to Tenet, he "knew nothing about health care." But this shortcoming had never fazed anyone at either NME or Tenet. And after holing up in a hotel room with health care consultants from McKinsey & Company for an entire day, Fetter declared himself "absolutely fascinated with [the hospital industry] from an intellectual point of view." [99] By "intellectual," presumably he meant financial. For like Barbakow, Fetter was a lifelong dealmaker. You could tell by the deal he cut for himself as Tenet's new CEO: a starting salary of $6 million.[100]

As for Barbakow, he left the hospital chain with his pockets full. On top of the $111 million that he had collected when he cashed in his stock options a year earlier, Barbakow took home $1.3 million in severance, another $585,000 in prorated salary for 2003, and $60,000 "for the use of an automobile."

Perhaps not content with his final payday, a year later Barbakow set out to score once more, this time filing a lawsuit against another sullied corporation: WorldCom. It seems that Barbakow had owned some 1.5 million shares of WorldCom's stock, and when the stock tanked he sought unspecified damages to help cover "tens of millions of dollars' worth" of losses that he had suffered. A Wall Street pro, Barbakow nonetheless cast himself as an innocent, claiming that he would have sold his WorldCom stock if he hadn't been tricked into believing that the company was "vibrant" and "financially secure" through "a series of representations spanning several years."

The Tenet Shareholder Committee gagged on the ironies: "Barbakow's gall is breathtaking," the committee observed, noting that even as Tenet was heading for disaster, Barbakow himself was cheerfully touting the stock on CNBC every bit as enthusiastically as WorldCom had huckstered itself.[101]

The Charges Mount

Despite Fetter's optimism that Tenet had put "unfortunate" events behind it, other Tenet hospitals would continue to make headlines:

The Kickback Game

In June of 2003 a federal grand jury indicted Barry Weinbaum, the CEO of Tenet's Alvarado Hospital Medical Center, in San Diego. According to the U.S. attorney in San Diego, Weinbaum had paid some $10 million in kickbacks to physicians who referred patients to Alvarado.

The indictment charged that during his 13 years at the hospital, Weinbaum had recruited more than 100 doctors to the area served by the hospital by paying them "relocation bonuses." Many were specialists in high-margin businesses such as obesity, orthopedics, and cardiology. Under some circumstances, such bonuses are legal—if, for example, the physicians are paid to move to an underserved rural area. But the Alvarado center was located in a middle-class San Diego neighborhood. And while hospitals are allowed to sign personal-services contracts with physicians, under the antikickback statute governing federal health care programs, they are not allowed to directly pay doctors in exchange for sending patients their way.

Many would argue that the line between a gift and a bribe remains murky. If money changes hands, is this a kickback, or must there be an explicit agreement about referrals? The indictment argued that Weinbaum had clearly crossed the line. In one case, for example, he agreed to pay "Dr. B.G." $70,000 to improve her office space and buy equipment, $180,000 for office expenses, and $132,000 for a one-year "collections guarantee." [102]

At the end of a four-month trial that began late in 2004, a federal jury deadlocked, and the judge had to declare a mistrial. The government reopened the Alvarado case for retrial in May of 2005. Eight months later, the second trial still had not ended. Meanwhile, authorities investigated relationships between physicians and other Tenet hospitals in Louisiana, Tennessee, and Texas.[103]

Germs on the Wing

In 2004 Tenet's Palm Beach Gardens Medical Center came under the microscope when more than 100 patients and survivors sued, alleging that the hospital performed open-heart surgeries in such unsanitary conditions that patients wound up with serious infections. Reportedly, dust and dirt covered some surgical equipment. Trash cans and soiled linens were stored in hallways. IV pumps were spattered with dried blood. One patient's wife said she saw a medical assistant tear surgical tape with his teeth.[104]

Then there were the bugs. When TheStreet.com's Melissa Davis dug into the story, she obtained documents which revealed that over a period of years the hospital had struggled with but failed to contain an insect problem in its operating rooms: "Correspondence between multiple exterminators and the hospital repeatedly mention, in some fashion, a 'flying insect issue in the O.R.,' " Davis reported. "The exterminators identify specific insects—crazy ants, fruit flies, fungus beetles, gnats—and offer remedies to the problem. Their comments appear to grow more urgent as time goes on."[105]

The gruesome infections contracted in the operating room led to open, draining chest wounds. In some cases, the only remedy was "radical reconstructive surgery—including the complete or partial removal of the patient's sternum and advancement of muscle flaps to fill the large hole left in the patient's chest," according to one complaint.

In a four-year period, 106 heart patients at Palm Beach Gardens developed infections after surgery, according to lawsuits and government records. More than two dozen were readmitted with fevers, pneumonia, and serious blood infections. The lawsuits included 16 patients who died.

Yet the hospital continued to do a brisk business. "Statistical records show that the hospital's mortality rate for open-heart surgeries exceeds both local and national averages," Davis observed, even though at one point "the federal Centers for Medicare and Medicaid Services (CMS) actually threatened to shut the hospital down if it didn't clean up its act."[106]

State regulators fined Palm Beach Gardens $323,800 in March of 2003—but then quickly reduced the penalty to $95,000. As usual, Tenet agreed to the fine without acknowledging any wrongdoing. "It would be inaccurate to conclude that all of the patients who were readmitted came back because of infections acquired during surgery," the company declared. Hospital officials claimed their infection rate was about equal to the national average and that some results of the inspections were misleading. "There is no aggregate clinical evidence to show that these infections occurred as a result of care provided at the facility," Tenet said in its statement.

Nevertheless, in 2004 Tenet forked over $31 million to settle more than 100 civil lawsuits—again without admitting wrongdoing.[107] The company posted a loss for the year. Meanwhile, Trevor Fetter took home $4.8 million in total compensation.[108]

The Pattern Repeats

Kickbacks to doctors, patient abuse, Medicare fraud . . . It all sounded so familiar. Supposedly, when Barbakow rescued NME in 1993, he cleaned house. In fact, he just painted the front door and gave the company a new name, but left the business plan in place. NME's corporate culture never really changed. Even the cast remained the same. As late as May of 2003, "eight out of twelve senior management positions at Tenet were held by holdovers from NME," observed Senate Finance Committee Chairman Charles Grassley.[109] And of course when it came time to replace Barbakow, Tenet didn't reach outside the company for a leader. Instead, it picked Fetter, Tenet's former CFO.

Over the course of two lawsuits, attorney Jim Moriarty came to know the players who created the NME/Tenet culture all too well. "These are some of the most intelligent people I've ever met in my life," Moriarty confided in 2004. "They're tremendously capable. They have insight, vision, and they're smart, smart, smart. But they have the moral and ethical sense of sea slugs. Zero compassion. To them, patients are billing opportunities."[110]

If Tenet and NME were the only investor-owned hospitals smudged by scandal, one might blame the entire episode on the NME culture—or a few rogue CEOs. But corporate fraud is not about personalities. As the late nineties revealed, it is systemic.[111] And in the hospital sector it has become epidemic: in recent years three of the nation's largest have confessed to a depressingly familiar string of federal charges—Tenet; HCA, the nation's largest; and HealthSouth, the largest owner of rehab hospitals and outpatient surgical centers.[112] Together they own more than half of the nation's for-profit hospitals.

This is not to suggest that all investor-owned hospitals operate outside of the law. Even within a chain, standards can vary widely at different hospitals. And some chains have avoided scandal altogether. Universal Health Services, for example, has managed to keep its skirts clean while slowly acquiring 100 facilities in 21 states—though like many for-profits, it has struggled to find a sustainable business model.[113]

Nor do publicly traded hospitals enjoy a monopoly on fraud. Not-for-profits have been charged with avaricious behavior that ranges from gouging the uninsured to gaming Medicare—leading some observers to suggest that, in today's hostile economic climate, the only difference between a for-profit and a not-for-profit is that the latter is not required to pay taxes. The CEO of one California not-for-profit acknowledges that there is some truth to the charge: "These days, we do act more like for-profit hospitals. But," she adds, "they *really* act like for-profits."[114]

That said, both the scale and the consistency of the for-profits' offenses stand out as nothing short of remarkable—especially since it is not the industry's laggards but its front-runners that time and again have succumbed to fraud.

Columbia/HCA: Fast-Food Health Care

When Rick Scott teamed up with Fort Worth financier Richard Rainwater to form Columbia Healthcare Corporation in 1987, his medical experience was limited to helping health care companies buy and sell each other. A mergers-and-acquisitions lawyer from Dallas, Scott had cut his teeth on deals involving radio stations, fast-food businesses, and oil and gas companies before focusing in on the money to be made by acquiring hospitals. Initially, he made a run at Health Corporation of America; in '87 he and two partners put together $5 billion and made an unsolicited offer to take over the chain founded in 1968 by Dr. Thomas Frist Sr., Dr. Thomas Frist Jr. and Jack Massey. HCA brushed them off.

But then along came Rainwater, asking Scott to join him in launching a hospital empire that would try to "do for hospitals . . . what McDonald's has done in the food business" and "what Wal-Mart has done in the retailing business."[115] Rainwater's goal was to combine volume with low cost. By 1991 Columbia Healthcare had 11 hospitals and $500 million in revenues. Flash forward three years, and Columbia was in a position to gobble up

Scott's original target: Hospital Corporation of America (HCA). Following the merger, Scott became CEO of the newly christened Columbia/HCA Healthcare Corp. while HCA's Thomas Frist Jr. stayed on as chairman.

Only three years into the marriage, disaster struck in the form of an FBI raid. In July of 1997, federal agents swarmed Columbia/HCA hospitals and offices in five states. Within weeks, three executives were indicted on charges of Medicare fraud, and the board had ousted Scott, naming HCA cofounder Dr. Tommy Frist both chairman and CEO.

What had gone wrong? Scott was obsessed not just with winning, but with money. A lean man with a receding hairline and a hungry look, he had grown up in Kansas City, Missouri, where his mother helped support five children by selling encyclopedias door-to-door, doing other people's laundry, cleaning telephone booths, and clerking at J. C. Penney.[116] Little wonder that when he became a hospital executive, his goal was to lay claim to 25 percent of the nation's hospitals.[117] Like Eamer, he bullied his subordinates. "My father owned and operated a millinery factory in the garment district, and [even in that tough garmento environment] I never witnessed such an extent of demeaning, debasing, and devaluing behavior as I personally experienced at Columbia," Mark E. Singer, administrative director for medicine at Michael Reese Hospital and Medical Center in Chicago told *The New York Times*.[118]

Personal testimony by disillusioned employees was not the only evidence of the company's priorities. Internal records showed that at Columbia/HCA, just as at many other for-profits, executive salaries hinged not on such criteria as reducing infections or lowering death rates, but on meeting financial targets like "growth in admissions and surgery cases." In 1995 one-fourth of Columbia's administrators won bonuses equaling 80 percent of their salaries—or more.[119] When bonuses become that large, some critics charge, they no longer function simply as incentives. They invite fraud.

To be fair, a business is supposed to set goals, and shareholders rightly expect those targets to focus on market share, revenues, and earnings. Many praised Scott's focus on the bottom line, and not a few hospitals—not-for-profit as well as for-profit—emulated his model.

But Scott's detractors claimed that his cost cutting threatened patient care and safety: "Gloves come in only one size, and rip easily," complained hospital workers in Florida. In California, nurses protested "filthy conditions," and being "stretched to the limit" as the company slashed the ratio of nurses to patients.[120] Since labor costs were the company's largest expense, Columbia/HCA took pride in "right-sizing," trimming staff to a point that "I sometimes had to watch 72 heart patient monitors at a time," recalled Columbia technician Susan Marks. "I was told you either do it or there's the door."[121] In Indianapolis, nurses complained to state authorities, babies in the neonatal unit were left unattended for as long as three hours. In one case, the only nurse caring for seven infants was so busy that she failed to hear an alarm when a baby stopped breathing. According to a state report, a parent rushed in and saved the infant. The hospital was fined $25,000.[122]

Rebutting its critics, Columbia/HCA stressed that health care is a commodity, like any other. "This industry's not any different than an airline industry or a ball bearing industry," said David T. Vandewater, Columbia's chief operating officer. "You run at 40 percent of capacity or at 60 percent of capacity, you're not getting the maximum value out of your assets."

Scott himself declared that the United States had too many hospital beds, and that he looked forward to a time when a shakeout would cut the number in half, leaving Columbia with a large slice of what was left. To be sure, excess capacity was a problem in some areas, and for-profits have taken the lead in closing failing institutions while some money-losing not-for-profit community hospitals remain open for purely political reasons. But Scott's solution was chillingly Darwinian. In his vision of the future, the hospitals most likely to succumb to competition would be "teaching hospitals and children's hospitals"—institutions where operating costs are highest.[123] His business plan left no room for unprofitable hospitals that nonetheless serve vital needs.[124]

Scott also questioned whether hospitals should throw their doors open to one and all: "Do we have an obligation to provide health care for everybody? Where do we draw the line? Is any fast-food restaurant obligated to feed everyone who shows up?" he asked.[125] "To Scott, patients were customers— period. He had a 'take no prisoners' attitude," recalls Clifford Hewitt, a health care analyst at Legg Mason at the time. "There was no nuance."[126]

Rarely troubled by a lack of nuance, Wall Street scrambled to finance the company's growth. "The market was very good to Columbia/HCA," says Gerard Anderson, director of the Center for Hospital Finance and Management at Johns Hopkins University. "Throughout most of these years Wall Street gave the company a price-earnings multiple of 18—which meant that if the hospital earns $10 million, the stock market values it at $180 million, or 18 times earnings."

This, in turn, meant that "Columbia/HCA could multiply a hospital's value simply by acquiring it. If the target hospital was valued at six times earnings, it would be worth three times as much when it became part of the Columbia/HCA family—and then the company could use the paper gains to buy more hospitals," Anderson explains. "So it keeps on buying hospitals. And as long as its price-earnings multiple is at 18, and it can buy hospitals at six, it can continue to acquire more hospitals and not do anything more efficient—not do anything different—it just keeps on buying." [127]

Growth for the sake of growth—this was the mantra of the 1990s. Though the music stopped for Columbia/HCA in 1997 when federal investigators exposed the fact that Columbia/HCA, like NME/Tenet, had been bilking Medicare while simultaneously handing over kickbacks and perks to physicians who steered their patients to its hospitals.[128]

The company did not fight the charges. In 2000 HCA (which, no surprise, had by now expunged "Columbia" from its name) pleaded guilty to no fewer than 14 felonies. Over the next two years, it would pay a total of $1.7 billion in criminal and civil fines.

The Frist Family Empire—How Much Did Dr. Frist Know?

When the FBI raided Columbia/HCA in 1997, Rick Scott took most of the heat. He was never charged, but the board was quick to banish the aggressive deal maker, replacing him with HCA cofounder Dr. Tommy Frist Jr., a country-gentleman surgeon who was seen as above suspicion.[129]

Frist's critics demurred, arguing that he was, in fact, the ultimate insider. Not only had he run HCA, he stayed on after its merger with Columbia in 1994, serving first as chairman and later as vice-chairman, while earning a total of $800,000 in the 1995 and 1996. It was only in 1997—a few months before the first FBI raid—that Frist began to disassociate himself from the company. That year he stopped attending management meetings and took a pay cut to $50,000.

Frist denied knowledge of any wrongdoing, and when he took Scott's place, he pledged to sever financial ties between hospitals and physicians.

Nevertheless, *The Wall Street Journal* pointed out, "As a senior corporate officer, board member and owner along with immediate family members of about 25 million Columbia shares, it is awkward for him to argue that he didn't know what was going on at the company, or was largely powerless to curb any excesses."[130]

Key shareholders doubted Frist's claim that he was out of the loop while Scott was CEO: "The real question is why should we feel confident that Dr. Frist will put the proper [reform] measures in place now, when he was on the board the whole time these abuses were taking place?" asked New York State Comptroller H. Carl McCall who filed a shareholders' suit on behalf of the state's $90 billion public-employee pension fund.[131] McCall also pointed out that the federal probe went back to the years preceding the merger, noting that "some of the hospitals that are under investigation were HCA's."[132]

Indeed, HCA's books were smudged. Some of the abuses were small but flagrant. In 1991, for example, the company had charged Medicare for such items as $18,000 worth of liquor, $15,000 worth of Tiffany pitchers for HCA executives, and $28,000 for a humanitarian award given to two HCA staffers.[133] On Wall Street, HCA's defenders tried to argue that the hospital was simply "tripped up" by Medicare's arcane accounting rules—an argument that would be rendered absurd by the discovery that HCA kept two sets of books.

In 1993, the year before HCA merged with Columbia, James Alderson, an accountant who served as chief financial officer of a small HCA hospital in Whitefish, Montana, blew the whistle on the accounting scheme. Alderson would testify that his bosses at the rural hospital had asked him to keep two sets of ledgers: one set showing the expenses the hospital claimed when billing Medicare, the second containing more accurate information regarding reimbursement claims. When Alderson refused the bookkeeping assignment, he was fired. Out of work and short on money, Alderson's family was forced to sell their home. Their children's college fund evaporated, and Alderson would find himself locked in a battle with his former employer that lasted for years. "I never had any doubt that I was right, and I think that is what kept me going," he said later. In the end, Alderson helped the government recapture $1.7 billion, and under the whistle-blower law, he won an $8 million reward.[134]

On Wall Street, Sheryl Skolnick agrees that HCA had set the pace for accounting practices long before Rick Scott met Frist: "It was the HCA accounting bible that had them keeping two sets of books. Did Scott ever go in and clean up the accounting? Absolutely not. Did he create it? Absolutely not."

When the scandal broke, "Frist sure moved fast to get Scott out of there," Skolnick adds. "Scott talked about fighting the government. Frist did not want that. He did not want anyone to go to jail." [135]

Another Wall Street observer agrees: "Unlike, say, Martha Stewart, Frist understood that when federal prosecutors have you in their sights, you don't fight them. The best thing you can do is kneel down and kiss the ring—especially if you're guilty." Accordingly, Frist urged employees to cooperate with investigators, vowing that he wanted to "work with the government. . . . The government did us a favor," he added. "It heightened other people's awareness that it was time to change management." [136]

In December of 2002, HCA finally settled its case with the government—shortly before attorneys were scheduled to depose Dr. Frist. Some questioned the timing of the settlement. As it happened, at that moment Dr. Frist's brother, Senator William Frist, had just emerged as the administration's candidate to replace Trent Lott as Senate majority leader. [137]

Skeptics suggested that the White House urged investigators to wrap up the settlement before the senator's brother was deposed. Others argued that it was HCA that was eager to close the deal, and that the company threw in the towel to avoid the spectacle of Dr. Frist being questioned about the family business. "[Tommy] Frist didn't want to be put under oath to explain what they knew about the worms under the rocks that were being uncovered," speculated Stephen Meagher, a San Francisco attorney who represented two HCA whistle-blowers. Company spokesman Jeff Prescott denied charges that politics determined the timing, saying that the company agreed to settle because it was "comfortable" with the amount it would have to pay: "It was about the numbers," he declared. [138]

Whatever else, the company's denouement produced a definite sense of déjà vu. Following industry tradition, Columbia/HCA changed its name (back to HCA), no one went to jail, and Rick Scott waltzed away with $10 million in severance pay plus $324 million in company stock. [139]

As for the Frist family, as of 2004 Thomas F. Frist Jr. held over 5.5 million shares of HCA stock, worth approximately $240 million, while Senator Bill Frist, his wife, and children reportedly owned shares worth up to $30 million.

How Much Did Senator Frist Know?

Those shares would come back to plague Senator Frist. Although the price of HCA shares plummeted during the federal fraud investigation in 1999 to under $20, the stock started to recover in 2000 and then began a steep climb at the end of 2004. By January of 2005, shares were changing hands at roughly $40. Six months later HCA hit $58 and change.

Top HCA executives cashed in on the run-up, exercising options and selling shares worth some $165 million during the first six months of 2005. In June Senator Frist joined them, instructing the managers of his blind trust to sell all of his HCA shares. And by July 8, Senator Frist's shares had been liquidated, along with shares owned by his wife and children.

Five days later—on July 13—HCA announced that its second-quarter earnings would fall below Wall Street projections because of lower than expected hospital admissions, combined with rising numbers of uninsured patients. That day the stock fell 9 percent, to $50.05 a share. In the months that followed, HCA continued to trade below $50.

Senator Frist had asked the managers of his trust to begin unloading his shares just nine days before the stock peaked at $58. "Good fortune, isn't it?" remarked John C. Coffee, a professor of securities law at Columbia Law School. Of course, Senator Frist had every right to sell his shares—unless he had received inside information from his brother or other HCA executives that earnings were going to disappoint. "There is no prohibition against a family member's dumping his stock in a company, unless it can be shown that the family member was tipped as to material nonpublic information," Coffee observed. "That seems to be the missing link." [140]

Meanwhile, the Tennessee Republican—who many believed was weighing whether to run for the presidency in 2008—said he sold off his stock simply to dispel any appearance of conflict of interest. But Democrats on the other side of health care issues had been crying "conflict of interest" for years. The fortuitous timing of the sale piqued widespread interest, and in the fall of 2005 both the SEC and the U.S. Attorney's office in New York were investigating Frist's sales. [141]

HealthSouth Follows the Leaders

Less than two years after Columbia/HCA confessed to 14 felonies, investigators descended on the Birmingham, Alabama, headquarters of Health-South, the nation's largest chain of rehabilitation hospitals and outpatient surgical centers. They found what they were looking for: six months later HealthSouth founder Richard M. Scrushy faced a 58-count indictment alleging that he was the mastermind behind a $2.7 billion accounting imbroglio.

While poring over HealthSouth's books, investigators also noted evidence of Medicare fraud. According to the Justice Department, the billing irregularities included items like the "lavish entertainment and travel costs" incurred while sending hospital administrators to a meeting held at Disney World. To settle the Medicare case, HealthSouth paid the government $325 million in December of 2002.[142]

But fleecing taxpayers would turn out to be the least of HealthSouth's sins. Allegedly, the company's specialty was duping shareholders. When Scrushy's case came to trial in January of 2005, prosecutors would claim that from 1997 through the middle of 2002, HealthSouth's CEO had schemed to inflate his company's earnings by a mind-bending $2.7 billion. The government argued that Scrushy had good reason to try to kite HealthSouth's stock: his own compensation was tied to the company's share price. For example, in 1995, when HealthSouth's shares rose by 60 percent, Scrushy raked in $7.5 million, more than twice his 1994 pay.[143]

Just as at NME and Columbia/HCA, management at HealthSouth set sky-high profit goals and pressured executives to meet them, without regard to the methods used. NME called its system "meeting plan." Columbia/HCA used scorecards. At HealthSouth, the prosecutors alleged, Scrushy set targets to exceed analysts' goals and insisted that accountants work backward to meet the numbers.

A larger-than-life CEO known for a swashbuckling lifestyle that included seven corporate jets, four mansions, a 92-foot yacht, and nearly three dozen cars (including a bulletproof BMW), Scrushy made a juicy target. By the time he went to trial, 15 former HealthSouth employees—including no fewer than five former chief financial officers—already had confessed to fraud. The fact that in the months before the scandal broke, HealthSouth's CEO slashed his stake in the company by one-third only added to suspicions. The sales began in May of 2002 when Scrushy cashed in $74 million of Health-South stock at $14 a share. In July he dumped another $2.5 million worth of shares at $10.

Less than a month later, the company roiled Wall Street by announcing that its earnings would be $175 million short of what analysts had predicted. In two days the stock plunged to $5, and HealthSouth was delisted from the New York Stock Exchange. Shareholders were blindsided. Roughly two weeks before selling off the first chunk of his holdings, Scrushy had told analysts that he was "very comfortable" with their estimates that HealthSouth's profits would grow by 39 percent that year.[144]

When the 52-year-old faced a jury in January of 2005, Scrushy denied any knowledge of flimflam accounting. Scrushy's defense attorneys argued that the executives who had pleaded guilty carried out the accounting scheme without Scrushy's knowledge, and now were trying to pin the scheme on their boss in order to win lighter punishment for their own crimes.

Over the course of the trial, HealthSouth's original CFO, Aaron Beam, claimed that in a conversation about the fraud, Mr. Scrushy once told him: "If we are ever caught, I'm going to deny everything, and you guys are on your own." Former CFO Michael Martin testified that once, after he described a new technique in the accounting to Mr. Scrushy, the CEO replied: "Damn, you guys are good."[145]

But the fact that Scrushy's accusers received featherweight sentences in exchange for testifying undermined their credibility. Of the 10 HealthSouth former executives sentenced before the CEO's trial, only one received even a brief jail term. Most were given home detention or probation. During cross-examinations of the former CFOs, Scrushy's attorneys emphasized the light sentences and stressed that no e-mails, memorandums, or other physical evidence clearly linked him to the fraud.

After 21 days of deliberation, a Birmingham, Alabama, jury cleared Scrushy of all 36 criminal charges, including conspiracy, securities fraud, mail fraud, and a single charge under the Sarbanes-Oxley Act, the statute that mandates penalties for CEOs and finance chiefs who sign false financial filings. Scrushy, who spent $25 million on his defense, walked out of court with most of his $300 million fortune intact.

Meanwhile, HealthSouth's shareholders continued to pay. A few weeks earlier HealthSouth had agreed to hand over $100 million to settle a civil complaint filed in 2003 by the Securities and Exchange Commission.

"Sometimes, I feel like a complete failure—because these bastards keep getting away with it," said Jim Moriarty, the Houston attorney who settled suits against both NME and Tenet. "They're all the same people, operating under the same business plan. The companies pay the fines and deduct them from their taxes—which they can. To them, it's all part of the cost of doing business. And they're not going to change. Not until the government says, 'We'll put you in jail if you do this.' "

For-Profits Lead Hospital Prices Higher

Some 40 years after their debut, for-profit hospitals still struggle to fulfill the promises of corporate medicine—that bright hope once expressed by hospital pioneer Richard Rainwater that someday for-profit hospital chains would do for health care "what Wal-Mart had done for retailing and McDonald's has done for food," by offering customers a reliable product at an affordable price.

Study after study shows that for-profit hospitals have succeeded only in leading hospital prices higher.[146] According to a 2003 survey, the majority of the nation's most expensive hospitals are concentrated in just three states—California, Florida, and Pennsylvania, all dominated by corporate hospital chains. A canvass of charges at these market leaders showed that in 2002 they were marking up their sticker prices by an average of 525 percent. In other words, the hospitals were charging 525 percent more than it cost them to provide the services. Granted, all hospitals charge a substantial premium over their costs in order to cover the bills that are never paid. But nationwide, the average hospital markup in 2002 was only 206 percent. And in New York State—where for-profit have been barred from the market as a matter of state law and public policy—the average hospital charged just 181 percent more than it spent.[147]

But what about economies of scale? Health planners had hoped that by consolidating, investor-owned chains would streamline operations in ways that would help stem runaway hospital spending. Instead, research suggests that when hospitals bulk up, they use their size to muscle larger rate increases from insurers. "The balance of power has indeed shifted toward hospitals," *Health Affairs* reported in 2005. "In some cases, hospitals [have] walked away from negotiations." And for-profits were not the only hospitals using size to push prices higher. By 2005 nearly half of all not-for-profit hospitals had followed the for-profits' example by forming hospital systems, and they, too, charged more than their stand-alone rivals.[148]

If the for-profit model did not lead to lower prices, did it create a better product? Measuring the quality of medical care remains a very rough science—the ambiguity of data on medical outcomes makes comparisons treacherous. That said, the 2005 *Health Affairs* report, like virtually every other study that has preceded it, suggests that "higher prices . . . do not translate into either higher quality of inpatient care or greater efficiency of care delivery."[149]

The Stocks That "Some People Love to Hate"

But if publicly traded companies have failed to lift the overall quality of care at their hospitals, they did provide the capital needed to modernize hospitals in many areas. And along the way, the industry's supporters point out, they have managed to generate profits for investors.

On this score, however, the industry's success is debatable. In too many cases, it seems that investor-owned hospitals have returned a profit not by improving operations but simply by ratcheting up their prices—a short-term solution that may actually impede long-term profitability. In its heyday, Columbia/HCA, for instance, charged the average patient 8 percent more than the industry norm, even after factoring in discounts to insurers, differences in regional wages, and the mix of cases.[150]

For shareholders, this is discouraging news. Inflated prices can keep a stock aloft for only so long—until reality (or an FBI raid) pricks the balloon. This helps to explain why, over the years, the history of so many hospital stocks has followed the plot of a Russian novel: Great Joy followed by Great Sorrow.

Indeed, companies like Tenet, HCA, and HealthSouth have taken investors on a hair-raising ride. In the fall of 2005 Tenet, for example, had plunged from a 2002 high of over $50, coming to rest where it had traded a decade earlier—at $10. HealthSouth changed hands for a little over $4, down 75 percent from its high four years earlier. Meanwhile, in 10 very volatile years, HCA has gained "only about 60 percent," Skolnick observed in October of 2005. Over the same period, the S&P 500 has more than doubled.

Granted, some hospital companies had better luck: from 1995 through the end of 2005, Universal Health Services gained roughly 500 percent—but almost all of that progress was made in 2000, when the stock took off. Over the five years ending in December of 2005, UHS returned less than 10 percent. Even Community Health Systems—which had performed very well in 2005—was up only about 30 percent over five years, and it, too, turned out to be a roller-coaster stock: an investor who had the misfortune to sink $10,000 into the company at its high in 2001 would find that two years later his nest egg had been cut roughly in half.

In other words, everything depended on when you got in and when you got out. For a speculator with the nerves of Richard Rainwater and a talent for bottom-fishing, there was good money to be made in hospital stocks over the course of the decade. But for the long-term investor, there were far safer ways to double a nest egg in 10 years: "This," Skolnick acknowledges, "is why some people love to hate hospital stocks."[151]

For society as a whole, the implications are even more troubling. The industry's harrowing boom-and-bust cycle has led to a recurring pattern of aggressive shopping sprees followed by wholesale sell-offs. For example, when Dr. Tommy Frist Jr. took over Columbia/HCA from serial acquirer Rick Scott, he liquidated its home health care business and unloaded 100 of its hospitals. Such cycles of expansion and contraction sound very much like the "unmanaged competition" that health economist James Robinson described in chapter 2: a laissez-faire chaos "notable not only for its turbulence but its creativity . . . as medical groups, hospital systems and health care plans come together, dissolve and re-group."

But the "comings and goings" of hospitals have brought turbulence without many creative benefits, Robinson acknowledged in 2005. "Their track record has been terrible. The mergers and divestitures have been disruptive—and costly."[152] When hospitals change hands, CEOs collect bonuses, and investment bankers scoop up fat fees—costs that, one way or another, are passed on to the taxpayers, patients, and employers who foot the bill for medical care.

Meanwhile, a local hospital is put on the block and a community is left in limbo, with effects "ranging from rumor and speculation to actual changes in management, data systems, budget procedures and policies," observes Bradford Gray in *The Profit Motive and Patient Care*. Describing two hospitals that changed hands six times in a dozen years, he remarks, "One can only

speculate on the consequences of a hospital being under six different owners in twelve years."

Yet the free movement of capital lies at the heart of free markets. Indeed,
beginning in the 1980s, the U.S. corporation came to be seen as a "salable
bundle of liquid assets rather than a producer of goods and services,"
says Gray, quoting sociologist Paul Hirsch. With that model in mind, "executives' incentives [were] channeled to accord top priority to . . . shareholder
value and price goals over and above a commitment to the firm's product or
products."

But "when the product is health care," Gray notes with remarkable understatement, "this dynamic raises some special concerns."[153]

A Brief (and Misleading) Golden Age

Looking back on the disappointing history of the for-profit industry, Sheryl
Skolnick declares that both investors and managers have consistently
made the same error: *"They mistook the hospital business for a high-profit, growth
business."*[154]

The mistake was understandable. When for-profit hospitals came on the
scene in the late sixties, third-party payers were chucking tens of millions
into the system. Thanks to Medicare, Medicaid, and the rise of employer-
based insurance plans like Blue Cross, 80 to 90 percent of the U.S. population suddenly had hospital coverage. This was the good news.

The downside was this: the system invited extravagance. Both private insurers and the government reimbursed fee-for-service for virtually every pil-
low, pill, and procedure that a hospital provided. As discussed in chapter 1,
the more services a hospital lavished on a patient, the more it would be paid.
There was no incentive to economize.

Hospitals were reimbursed, not just for the services they provided but
for a share of the capital they invested in new equipment. "Medicare compensated a hospital for costs, which included capital costs, while Blue Cross
paid a hospital based on what it charged—and hospitals would build those
capital costs into their charges," explains Bradford Gray.[155] The open-
handed system encouraged lavish investments in new technology, even if a
hospital was merely duplicating equipment already available at another facility in town.

The payment system also encouraged churning: each time a hospital changed hands, Medicare reimbursed for interest and depreciation—based on the purchase price that time around. This meant that "the flow of dollars to an institution generally increased whenever it was acquired by a new owner," Gray points out. In other words, a hospital automatically became more valuable to its new owners than it had been to its sellers—which, quite naturally, stimulated turnover at ever-rising prices.[156]

All in all, a business that had begun as a charity had turned into an irresistible investment opportunity. Think of it: the more hospitals a company bought, the more money it made. The more services it provided, the more money it made. The more equipment it purchased, the more money it made. And there was little risk: the reimbursements were guaranteed, and the pockets they came from seemed inexhaustible. "From the late 1960s until the early 1980s it was difficult *not* to make money operating hospitals," Gray observes, "so long as they were located away from concentrations of low-income populations and in states that did not regulate hospital income." This meant that for-profits spread "mainly in the South and the West."[157]

During this halcyon period, investor-owned chains married and multiplied. By 1983 publicly traded hospital companies owned more than 13 percent of the general hospitals in the United States and managed another 6 percent.[158] On Wall Street, profits turned heads. During the 1970s and the early 1980s, a dollar invested in an investor-owned hospital returned nearly 40 percent more in earnings than the average for all other industries.[159]

This is when cowboys like Richard Scrushy discovered the health care business. "His big break came in 1979, when he was hired by a Houston-based company called Lifemark," *Fortune* would later report. At the time, "there were tremendous opportunities for a certain kind of entrepreneur. 'These people were mercenaries,' says one person who knows both the industry and Scrushy. 'He fit right in, and he had to have been saying to himself, "Holy cow, I can do this!" ' "[160]

Of course, most hospital CEOs were not con men, but many were deluded into overestimating both their own abilities and the willingness of payers to continue fattening their margins. At this early point in the industry's history, "executives from the investor-owned companies spoke with considerable certainty about two matters," Gray recalls. "One was that their steady increases in earnings and corporate growth were due to their [own] managerial ability, and the financial incentives built into the organizations. The other was that the bulk of their payments came from sources that were solid and predictable."

So hospital companies continued to acquire faltering hospitals and build new ones, "even when the need for beds was marginal," says Gray, "which helps to explain why their occupancy rates were persistently 10 to 15 percent lower than those in nonprofit hospitals."[161]

What nearly everyone had forgotten, Gray adds, is that *historically, hospitals have been unprofitable institutions*: "In 1963 the average hospital was losing $6 for every $100 of patient care revenue that it took in." Even after Medicare and Medicaid were passed, hospitals continued to lose money. It was not until the 1980s that the American Hospital Association reported that the average hospital was in the black.[162]

The industry's golden age would be short-lived. As hospitals began to make more money, legislators took notice and "inevitably," Gray notes dryly, Congress "found things on which it would rather spend tax revenues than on paying hospitals amounts that exceeded their costs by 15 to 20 percent."[163] This was when Congress decided that rather than reimbursing for each service a hospital provided, Medicare would pay a set amount per patient, based on the patient's diagnosis. The legislation, which passed in 1983, allowed hospitals to keep any difference between their costs and the government's established price, thus creating an incentive to find more efficient ways to treat patients. The next year, legislators quite sensibly decided that from that point forward, taxpayers would pay only once for the depreciation of a hospital, no matter how many times it changed hands.

At first, Medicare reimbursements were set at a rate that let the average hospital reduce expenses and continue to grow its profit margins—largely by sending patients home sooner. But with time and mounting budget pressure, Medicare reimbursements slid.[164]

As the government withdrew its largesse, hospital stocks lost their sizzle. By 1985 investor-owned hospitals began announcing that earnings would not meet expectations. And "by mid-1986," Gray reports, "the clear consensus among observers was that the era of high profitability in the business of running general hospitals had passed." As the decade drew to a close, commercial insurers also began tightening the purse strings. Meanwhile, hospital chains began to shrink; by 1987 HCA, AMI, and Humana—the largest chains of the time—all were unloading properties.

The seventies and early eighties had marked a period of brief and un-precedented prosperity for hospitals, an era that overlapped neatly with the growth of investor-owned hospitals. The serendipity created the impression that for-profit hospitals were doing something innovative—that they had found a winning formula. But in retrospect it would become apparent that they had grown, "not because of managerial magic but as a result of the skilled use of the incentives [to overtreat] that had been built into [pay-for-service] payment systems," Gray explains. "As those incentives were changed in the early nineties, it became clear that the companies' growth strategies were now obsolete." [165]

The Flaw in the Business Model

By the fall of 2005, few investors saw hospitals as a sure bet. Many blamed the industry's woes on the uninsured, or what *Medical Economics,* a journal aimed at physicians, referred to as "dead-beat patients" in a helpful 2003 article titled "How to 'Fire' a Patient: When You Dismiss a Patient, Choose Your Words Carefully. Here's What to Say." [166]

To be sure, patients who cannot pay their bills have left hospitals saddled with a heap of unpaid debt. Each year, the number of uninsured and under-insured middle-class Americans grows. In 2004 HCA was forced to set aside $688 million—or 11.9 percent of its revenues—to cover uncollectible bills. Nationwide, hospitals reported providing $25 billion of free care in 2003—roughly twice as much as in 1990.[167] But this is far from the whole story. Even if the ranks of the uninsured suddenly shrank (a remote possibility), the sorry history of the hospital industry's best and brightest suggests a deeper, structural flaw in its business model.

The problem, Sheryl Skolnick suggests, is inherent in the way for-profit hospitals are financed: "Hospitals simply can't generate the year-after-year earnings growth that Wall Street wants. Wall Street rewards 15 to 20 percent growth, and you just can't get that from a labor-intensive, real-estate-based business.

"Hospitals are essentially real estate plays," she continues. "They're boxes, and within those boxes, you provide certain services. But once you've added all the services you can add, and have attracted all the physicians you can use, you can't grow much more than the population grows—maybe 2 percent."

At best, Skolnick calculates, "unless they're adding capacity, hospitals cannot expect much more than 6 to 7 percent top-line growth [of revenues]—maybe 10 percent bottom-line growth [of profits]—through leverage, strict cost controls, and retirement of debt. And then you're doing *very* well." Meanwhile, real estate requires maintenance: "You need constant, strong cash flow just to keep the buildings from falling down." In 2004, for example, Tenet announced that it was jettisoning a block of its California properties, in part so that it wouldn't have to spend the $1.6 billion needed to retrofit them to meet the state's updated earthquake standards.

Smaller chains have fared better, particularly in rural areas where labor costs are lower and competition virtually nonexistent. But what happens down the road? History shows that as investor-owned hospitals mature, profits hit a ceiling. "The only way for the company to continue to grow is to buy another hospital, fix it, grow it—and do it again," says Skolnick.

In other words, to survive, a hospital company must follow Rick Scott's model and become a serial acquirer. The catch is that as for-profit hospitals consolidate, the quality of hospitals up for sale is likely to decline. "The nonprofit hospitals most likely to offer themselves for sale are in need of major investments of capital and managerial attention" says James C. Robinson, a professor of health economics at the University of California, Berkeley.[168] And as the supply of viable hospitals dwindles, bidding wars can drive up prices.

Skolnick blames corporate management for hyping hospital stocks. "What investors did not understand—and the company executives pushing stock did not explain—is that what appeared to be phenomenal growth was based more on mergers and acquisitions than on the day-to-day profitability of health care firms," says Skolnick.

"I have no problem with hospitals being for-profit," she adds. "But I have lots of problems with CEOs who try to force their companies into the high-growth mold. Running a hospital may not be as exciting as running a high-margin business, but when CEOs try to turn a hospital into something it isn't, they're going to suffer the consequences. By putting that strain on the organization, they create fraud, alienate doctors, and fail patients."

"Stock Market Exuberance"

Yet, James Robinson observes, hospital management is only responding to Wall Street's need for growth—a seemingly unquenchable thirst that puts publicly traded hospital companies under relentless pressure "to increase revenues and earnings at a rate that can drive firms to repeat past cycles of overexpansion, financial shortfall, and stock-price collapse."

On this score, Robinson contrasts for-profit hospitals with not-for-profits. Unable to tap the stock market for financing, not-for-profits traditionally have relied on the tax-exempt bond market where a far more conservative pool of investors look only for steady returns. Bond market investors are "far more concerned with stability," than growth, Robinson explains. Their main concern is that hospitals avoid excess and maintain a stable credit rating. Thus, he suggests, "bond-market skepticism may save not-for-profits from themselves." [169]

By contrast, Robinson says, "stock market exuberance" drives for-profit hospitals to overreach. If a hospital chain is successful, this only seems to whet investors' appetite for ever-higher returns. To satisfy those spiraling expectations a company must continue to expand, and since hospital companies often use their own stock to make acquisitions, this doubles the pressure to keep share prices high—at any cost.

As a result, for-profits are more likely to take excessive risks and pile up debt. "Risk-taking" is "embedded in a managerial culture" where a hospital administrator's salary can double if he pushes his numbers, Robinson observes, "but it also derives from equity investors' expectations for continual growth."

None of this is inevitable. Wall Street can accommodate slow-growth industries, Robinson emphasizes—as long as growth is steady, risks are minimal, and price-to-earnings ratios remain low. But, he explains, the hospital industry is "a roller-coaster industry, driven by Washington's political funding cycles overlaid on Wall Street cycles." And in that context, a few years of 15 percent growth when Washington is generous with Medicare reimbursements can too easily spur unreasonable expectations, leading investors to mistake a "modest-growth industry" for a go-go industry. [170]

There Should Be a Way to Cut Costs, but . . .

Under this kind of pressure from investors, it's little wonder that when for-profit hospital chains bulk up, they use their leverage to charge insurers more, says Johns Hopkins's Gerard Anderson. "But to be fair," he adds, "hospitals have continued to raise their prices, not simply because they have the clout, but because they just haven't been able to find a better, more economical way of providing bedside care."

Logically, both Skolnick and Anderson are quick to acknowledge, hospital care *could* be made less expensive: "There's a lot of money in hospitals—and there's a lot of inefficiency in hospitals," says Anderson. "So in theory you should be able to pull a lot of money out and still maintain quality. But no one has been able to figure out how to do it."

Early in the history of the for-profit industry, for-profit chains were able to contain costs by consolidating purchases. But now that not-for-profits have followed their lead, forming their own purchasing alliances, "for-profits no longer enjoy a distinct advantage," says Anderson. "And they don't seem to have any other innovative solutions." He returns to the hard fact that labor accounts for as much as 60 percent of the average hospital's expenses, "with nursing a major part of that. And so the question becomes, can they find a way to use fewer nurses and still provide the same quality of care? The data says no."[171]

Skolnick agrees: "To try to cut costs on the backs of the nurses is clearly not feasible—and probably just isn't prudent. Some states are already looking at mandatory staffing levels." But she thinks costs could be cut without reducing bedside care. "You're going to have to look at administration, and the processes that lead up to the bedside. One wonders whether more efficient use of information technology, inventory management and controls, and automated delivery of medications could drive efficiency."

In the long run, it seems certain that information technology could reduce hospital errors—and over time, contain health care spending. But the start-up costs are daunting, and in a fragmented market where every player is jockeying for position, relatively few hospitals have been willing or able to make the long-term investments that would best serve the big-picture needs of both hospitals and patients.[172] "A lot of things have been tried," Skolnick notes, "but nothing has succeeded in a sustainable way."[173]

A Supply-Side Problem?

Some would say that patients themselves are responsible for much of the waste in hospital spending. Received wisdom has it that the hospital industry is inefficient because when someone else is paying the bills, patients demand too many services: using the ER when they're not seriously ill, asking for CAT scans that they don't really need, malingering in a hospital bed when they're well enough to go home. This is why so many policy makers recommend raising deductibles and co-payments—so that patients will have some skin in the game.

But rather than blaming consumers for demanding too much, UCLA economist Thomas Rice looks at the other side of the equation: *"Most of the waste,"* Rice argues, *"can be found in the many services that a hospital provides which do little or no good in improving a patient's health."* (emphasis mine) In other words, Rice suggests, in a corporate culture hooked on growth, waste may be a supply-side problem.[174]

After all, most hospital patients do not demand the open-heart surgeries, hysterectomies, angioplasties, and biopsies that in too many cases prove unnecessary at best and, at worst, harmful. Few insist on a third round of chemotherapy, a daylong gauntlet of tests, or yet another surgery. Fewer still call out for feeding tubes, ventilators, or the opportunity to spend the final week of life in an ICU.

This is not to suggest that demand plays no role in driving unnecessary hospital spending. In truth, supply and demand are caught in a widening gyre, with rising demand leading to greater supply—which in turn stimulates greater demand. But as Rice points out, in the health care industry, more than in any other, supply takes the lead, with the supplier playing a far more active role in determining what consumers believe they want—or need.[175]

Finally, it would be a mistake to assume that wasteful spending is the special province of for-profit hospitals. As the chapter that follows will illustrate, today *all* hospitals operate in a Darwinian arena where revenues depend upon volume and size equals power.

As a society, we might want to put a brake on runaway medical spending, but as health care comes to be seen as a business like any other, even the most prestigious not-for-profits are encouraged to follow the corporate mantra: What is good for business is more business. The market does not reward a hospital for doing less, only for doing more.

And if that lingering late-20th-century devotion to growth for its own sake leads to a medical arms race that produces too many ICU beds, too many specialty surgical centers, and an embarrassment of redundant (and sometimes unproven) technology, no matter. In a culture where patients have been sold on the idea that more health care equals better care, "the market," we are told, will absorb the excess.

4

Not-for-Profit Hospitals: "No Margin, No Mission"?

In the 1980s, when Nashville's Baptist Hospital trawled for maternity patients by promising prospective parents steak and champagne, it raised some eyebrows.[1] But by the spring of 2004, when Miami's Mercy Hospital ran a 30-second spot during the Oscars broadcast, no one blinked.

"It's part of our long-term branding campaign aimed at the baby boomers," Orlando Alvarez, Mercy's chief marketing officer told *The Miami Herald*. "We really want to put us on the map as a player." With that goal in mind, Mercy "is not waiting passively for patients to walk in," the newspaper observed approvingly. Instead, it "hammers its theme home with live web casts of surgery, full-page newspaper ads and health fairs . . . because . . . as a stand-alone hospital, it is battling in a world where all the advantages appear to go to the large chains [like] HCA and Tenet."[2]

In the crucible of a fiercely competitive market, the differences between for-profit and not-for-profit hospitals have all but melted away. For both, survival depends on revenues and "the right patient mix"—a polite way of saying that if a hospital hopes to remain solvent, it must reach out for well-heeled customers. Mark McDougle, chief operating officer of Brooklyn's Maimonides Medical Center, is blunt: "For hospitals, competition means trying to take affluent, well-insured patients—and the doctors who treat those patients—away from other hospitals. It is not a good thing."[3]

Ideally, says McDougle, hospitals would work together, dividing the pie, with each doing what it does best. But ruinous competition may be the order of the day in an era of corporate medicine "driven by the premise that all participants are supposed to work the system for their own benefit—and, if necessary, at the expense of the other participants," observes Dr. Jerry Avorn, a Harvard medical school professor and author of *Powerful Medicines: The Benefits, Risks, and Costs of Prescription Drugs.*[4]

We Do Botox!

Given the pressure, it is little wonder that so many hospitals have begun to emulate drugmakers, pitching their products directly to the consumer, as they trumpet the benefits of everything from Botox to bariatric surgery (aka stomach stapling). A 2005 study published in *Archives of Internal Medicine,* offers a sampling of some of the more entertaining, sometimes brazen, headlines:

- "25% of all adults are habitual snorers. Fortunately, we have a solution."
- "FDA Approves Deep Brain Stimulation Therapy for Parkinson's Disease."
- "How a revolutionary heart procedure helped Carol take on the Rockies."
- "The more you know about uterine fibroids, the better you'll feel."

Who were the hospitals hawking their wares? Here comes the surprise: the study was describing the marketing strategies employed by the 17 academic medical centers that made *U.S. News & World Report*'s 2002 honor roll of "America's Best Hospitals." Of the 17, only the Mayo Clinic told researchers that it relied on "word of mouth" to bring business through the door. The other 16 took promotion seriously, running some 122 newspaper ads in 2002 alone.[5]

The study's authors—all doctors at the Veterans Affairs Medical Center in White River Junction, Vermont—are not saying that hospitals shouldn't let the public know what services they offer. But they do question the methods many institutions use when they try to drum up new business. According to the report, 60 percent of the ads surveyed played on a potential customer's emotions, appealing to his fears, hopes, and anxieties. Less than 1 percent mentioned cost. Less than 2 percent mentioned safety. Most tellingly, less than 5 percent used statistics like "one in four," "two out of three," or "80 percent." Instead, the ads seemed to imply that virtually everyone might benefit from whatever treatment the hospital was touting.

Chastising the marketers for headlines that might well raise "false hopes and unrealistic expectations," the researchers point out that of the 21 ads promoting a single service, most were thumping the tub for unproven (38 percent) or cosmetic (28 percent) procedures. And while more than three-quarters of these ads highlighted potential medical benefits, even for cosmetic surgery (e.g., "improving not just the appearance of your nose, but the function"), only one mentioned or even implied potential risks.[6]

By packaging specific services like MRIs as "product lines," and aiming their headlines at healthy patients, the ads "create a need in medical consumers' minds where one might not have existed," says Dr. Robin Larson, the study's lead author. "These messages increase the likelihood that services will be used inappropriately."

When pharmaceutical companies use similar techniques, they are sternly criticized for creating demand while failing to present balanced information on the benefits and risks of their products. But academic medical centers have, until recently, gotten a free pass. It's one thing to beat up on Pfizer, another to suggest that The Cleveland Clinic might be putting its own interests ahead of its patients'.

Yet medical center ads can be far more insidious than a pitch for Viagra, the study points out, because the consumer is likely to take a drugmaker's ad with a grain of salt. The financial interests of pharmaceutical companies are apparent to everyone, "and may invoke a healthy degree of skepticism among viewers." Academic medical centers, by contrast, are supposed to be driven not by the quest for profits but by their "mission" to improve the health of their communities.

But "realistically," the study concedes, "academic medical centers do have another mission—to succeed financially." Ask the CEO of virtually any not-for-profit hospital and he will tell you: "No margin, no mission." Today every self-respecting institution is expected to show a profit margin—though not-for-profits call it a "surplus." Without that margin, there is a real danger that the hospital won't be able to treat anyone.

S&P Doesn't Give Points for Charity Care

This was not always the case. In the first half of the 20th century, hospitals were not expected to be self-supporting. As discussed in chapter 3, it was assumed that philanthropy and government would provide whatever additional capital hospitals needed—which they did. In 1900 most hospitals boasted only a small number of paying patients. Even in the 1920s, only about one-half of hospital patients were paying fees for their services.[7]

It was not until World War II, as more and more employers began to offer health insurance, that a hospital could expect to survive on the sale of its services. Even so, as recently as the late 1960s, government grants provided more than half of the capital hospitals needed to construct new facilities.

But as health care became increasingly sophisticated, neither government nor philanthropy could keep up with the levitating costs of a high-tech industry. Meanwhile, in the early 1970s Washington began to question what many saw as runaway hospital spending. Luckily, at about this time, the bond market decided that it would be more than happy to provide the capital that not-for-profits needed—for much the same reason that the stock market was eager to finance the first for-profit hospitals. With revenues pouring in from both Medicare and the private-sector employers who financed commercial health insurance, hospitals seemed a sure thing.

In 1968, Standard & Poor's rated its first health care bond. By the late 1970s nearly 50 percent of hospital financing was done through tax-exempt bonds. Ten years later, 80 percent of construction funds for not-for-profit hospitals would come from borrowing—up from 40 percent 20 years earlier.[8] By 1981 philanthropy and government grants funded less than 8 percent of hospital construction.[9]

The change meant that not-for-profit hospitals have had to redefine their mission. The expectations and demands of a bond investor who entrusts his savings to a hospital are, after all, quite different from the hopes and goals of a philanthropist who bids only for immortality: the bond investor expects a return on his money.

As Bradford Gray notes in *The Profit Motive and Patient Care,* the hospital industry's traditional sources of funding "had at least some concern for the institution's charitable activities and community service." By contrast, a bondholder's "primary concerns are [quite understandably] risk and expected return."[10]

This changes a hospital's priorities. In the past, when a hospital board decided how to allocate its resources, board members saw themselves as running a social service. When they looked in the mirror, they didn't see a crew of savvy entrepreneurs; they saw pillars of the community. Their goal, they believed, was to meet local health care needs. Of course, as Gray acknowledges, "obvious discrepancies have long existed between reality and the highest ideal of non-profit organizations and medical professionals."[11] Sometimes the community's medical needs blended into other community imperatives: the need for jobs, for example, or prestige or political power.

Still, the economic reality is this: 45 years ago, the market did not set a hospital's priorities because hospitals did not rely on the market in order to survive. Today not-for-profits rely on borrowed money for more than half of their capital.[12] And the cost of much of that money pivots on how well rating agencies such as Standard & Poor's view a hospital's balance sheet. An institution that looks shaky will have to pay dearly—if it can raise money at all.

At the same time, not-for-profit hospitals still are expected to operate as charitable institutions. This is why, unlike for-profit hospitals, they are exempt from both property and corporate income taxes. And in fact, not-for-profits do provide more charity care than investor-owned hospitals, not because for-profits turn patients away (they, too, must stabilize any patient who walks into their emergency rooms), but because for-profit corporations rarely build or buy hospitals in neighborhoods where they expect the majority of their patients to be uninsured.[13] Traditionally, not-for-profits have served these communities, with government-owned public hospitals and teaching hospitals located in low-income urban centers shouldering most of the burden.

Not-for-profits also are more likely to offer the unprofitable yet essential services that *everyone* uses, such as trauma centers, burn units, and emergency psychiatric services.[14] For teaching hospitals, the "mission" includes educating the next generation of physicians—which means investing in the next generation of technology while simultaneously engaging in cutting-edge biomedical research.

Yet, as Gray notes, bond rating agencies cannot be expected to give extra points to hospitals that provide large amounts of community service or free care to indigent patients. To the contrary, he observes, when an analyst evaluates a hospital's creditworthiness, it must actually "penalize" a hospital that "provides too many unprofitable services" to insured patients or cares for too many uninsured patients, "creating a double bind for institutions that try to adhere to the charitable aspects of the traditional mission of hospitals."[15]

"Not the Game that Hospital Executives Are In"

This is why today, when a not-for-profit sets out to invest in new plant and equipment, decisions are likely to be market driven, but not necessarily mission driven. Ideally, hospitals would add beds and build new units based on the local population's medical needs. In practice, candid hospital administrators concede, that's not exactly what happens. When deciding where to invest they must first ask themselves: "What's profitable and what isn't?"

For instance, even though nearly everyone agrees that end-of-life hospital care is, in the words of a 2004 study published in *The Journal of the American Medical Association,* "woefully inadequate"—with one in four patients receiving too little pain medication, and one in two receiving too little emotional support—just 20 percent of community hospitals invest in "palliative care" programs staffed by doctors and nurses who specialize in easing the pain and terror of dying.[16] Only recently have physicians like Dr. Thomas J. Smith, an oncologist at Virginia Commonwealth University Medical Center, been able to make "the business case" for this more humane alternative, persuading hospital administrators that although it is labor-intensive, palliative care may in the end cost the hospital less than standard treatments.

"It is as important to get to 'the money men' and explain the cost benefits as it is to persuade doctors about the treatment's approach," Smith, who founded a palliative care wing at VCU, told *The Wall Street Journal.* "Money talks," Smith added. "Unless you can make [a palliative care unit] break even, it won't fly in today's health system."[17]

At some hospitals, the quest for revenues dominates every discussion. Roger Hughes, executive director of St. Luke's Health Initiatives, a Phoenix-based health care foundation, describes how resources are allocated in his hometown as local hospitals chase affluent newcomers moving into the city's "Valley of the Sun": "Today hospitals plan the way that Wal-Mart plans—they use the same metrics and the same principles," Hughes explains. "Here, hospitals are following the rooftops," into an area that has been described as "a retailer's dream."[18]

In 2005 four brand-new hospitals were going up in the Valley, three of them crowding into an 11-mile stretch of the southeast Valley, a fast-growing region where a young, well-educated workforce boasted the highest median income in Arizona. Not to be left behind, existing hospitals had embarked on major construction projects. All told, hospitals new and old were adding 1,180 beds to the local inventory as they responded not to current needs, but "to the demand that they anticipate will materialize as the local population grows," Hughes observes.

He describes visiting a new hospital that has been open for just six months: "It's like a luxury hotel, and it's all electronic—you can reconfigure rooms on a dime. When you look out the windows, on three sides you see farm fields—on the fourth, a huge housing development." Yet, despite the new housing, Hughes reports, "the hospital hasn't yet realized the inpatient volume it expected." Nevertheless, he says, "If they can continue to float the bonds and get the funding, hospitals in this area will continue to build, based on projections of expected use over the next three to five years." In other words, the bond market will decide how many beds they add.

Are they overbuilding? No one knows.

Before the new hospitals began breaking ground, Hughes explains, Phoenix was already a "cutthroat" market that had seen a surge in physician-owned hospitals and specialty surgical centers that can take lucrative business from larger acute-care hospitals. "By expanding and modernizing, acute care hospitals are looking to compete with those facilities. It's going to be kind of messy over the next 10 to 15 years as they figure out how to do that,"

Hughes acknowledges. But hospitals feel that they must stake their claim: "They're rushing to get into areas where the population is beginning to expand, thinking, 'If we don't get in there, the other guys will beat us.'

"The land-rush mentality doesn't always take into account planning for the community's needs," Hughes adds. "When it comes to breaking down the health needs of the population by age and chronic diseases in order to try to decide what mix of ambulatory, inpatient, and home health care will be required. . . . This," he observes, "is not the game that hospital executives are in."

Instead, hospitals focus on attracting "the right patient mix" which, Hughes explains, makes "complementary alternative medicine" (such as massage and acupuncture) popular among hospital planners. "These are low-margin services," he says, "but they serve as 'loss leaders' to draw young well-insured patients who have the resources to select from a boutique of offerings."

If local hospitals invest in loss leaders, will they have enough cash left over to cover the soaring costs of staff and vital services? Although Arizona hospitals have boosted nurses' salaries, 15 percent of registered-nurse positions in metro Phoenix remained unfilled in 2005. By 2007 an additional 500 extra nurses will be needed just to cover new hospitals in the East Valley.[19] To fill those posts, hospitals will, no doubt, have to sweeten salaries.

Adding to the financial pressure, Phoenix hospitals, like many hospitals nationwide, have found that they must offer orthopedists handsome bonuses if they want them to be on call for their ERs, and even then, "If you're in an accident and suffer a hand injury, getting a hand surgeon is next to impossible," says Hughes. "Things won't change until some powerful congressman gets into a car accident, winds up in an ER at 3 a.m., and can't get treated."

Building to Survive

In 2005 Phoenix represented just one battlefield in a nationwide building boom. A year earlier a *Modern Healthcare* survey showed that in that year alone, acute care hospitals had completed $13 billion worth of construction, "with projects worth billions more in the pipeline." And the industry was still in the first quarter of an 8-to-10-year rebuilding cycle, according to Robert Levine, health care construction for vice president of Turner Construction Company, one of the country's largest construction firms: "It's occurring all over the country. There are no soft spots."[20]

Hospitals are expanding even while much of the industry struggles to break even. As noted in chapter 3, nationwide, reimbursements are sliding while the number of uninsured climbs—along with unpaid bills. Nevertheless, the race is on to lure well-insured patients with new pavilions, valet parking, and private rooms. Some observers suggest that it is precisely because of the financial pressure that even hard-pressed institutions feel that they have no choice but to follow the mandate of the late-20th-century corporation: grow or die. "If you're a hospital, you're really in a funny place," says Rick Wade, vice president of the American Hospital Association. "Everybody that pays you tries to give you less, but all your patients expect more."[21]

In many regions, suburban hospitals are reaching for big-city business. "What we have to do to maintain our position in the market is to keep adding services," explains Westchester Medical Center CEO Ed Stolzenberg. "That's the whole reason we went into liver transplants."[22]

Did the residents of Westchester need a local hospital doing liver transplants? Just how many liver transplants will a Westchester hospital do? Would such patients be better off at a high-volume medical center in Manhattan, where "practice makes perfect"? These questions don't seem to come up. Transplants will raise the hospital's image. Yet, even if suburban hospitals buy the newest equipment, they may not have the best surgical teams. "High-volume places tend to be better, in part, because they attract surgeons who love what they do. They just want to do a lot of them, all of the time," Maimonides' Mark McDougle explains.[23]

Other hospitals are scrambling to stay in the game by offering high-margin services to cardiac patients, even though they don't have a cardiac surgeon on site. A 2004 study that appeared in *The Journal of the American Medical Association* looked at 600,000 Medicare patients who underwent a nonsurgical cardiac procedure designed to unblock coronary arteries by using a balloon to open the constricted artery and a wire stent to keep the artery clear. The procedure, which is called percutaneous coronary intervention (PCI), has become popular at hospitals that have catheterization laboratories—but don't have surgical back-up.

"The problem is, if the artery collapses, the ambulance may not make it to a hospital that can do a bypass in time," says a New Jersey hospital executive. "Yet they're doing the procedure all over the state." [24] He is right to be concerned. According to the *JAMA* study, patients in the 178 hospitals surveyed that performed PCIs without onsite cardiac surgery stood a 29 percent higher risk of dying. [25]

Waterfalls and Chutney as Come-Ons for Neonatal ICUs

Another way to woo well-insured patients is to invest in luxury maternity suites. In Gastonia, North Carolina, for instance, Gaston Memorial Hospital recently opened a 120,000-square-foot maternity ward which features a two-story glass atrium with a 60-foot waterfall; a children's library where siblings can play; and 52 private rooms with Internet access, whirlpool baths, and sofa beds for expectant dads. [26]

Although the profit margin on maternity services is depressingly slim, hospitals bent on luring "more discriminating customers" see deluxe maternity suites as yet another loss leader, *The Rocky Mountain News* explained. The paper describes how Denver-area hospitals were sprucing up their maternity suites: installing Jacuzzis, offering moms free massages, and serving dinners that include entrees like roasted sea bass with citrus chutney. "A hospital that doesn't offer luxury perks risks attracting only patients who can't pay their bills," the paper explained. [27]

Meanwhile, low-margin maternity suites attract patients who will use the hospital's lucrative neonatal intensive care services. Neonatal ICUs filled with well-insured babies can achieve decent margins, *The Rocky Mountain News* reported, which may explain why "at least seven metro-area hospitals offer Level III neonatal intensive care, the highest and most intense designation." [28]

Denver is not an outlier. Nationwide, the proliferation of neonatal ICUs commands attention as a startling demonstration of how marketing strategies—rather than the population's *medical* needs—can dictate a 21st-century hospital's investment decisions. Although ICUs for newborn patients are extremely expensive to set up and maintain, they serve as profit centers and have become de rigueur at hospitals that hope to attract upscale, suburban customers who prefer to give birth in a relatively small, well-carpeted hospital near home—but want the assurance of knowing that it has an intensive care unit.

The result, according to a 2002 study published in *The New England Journal of Medicine,* is that hospitals bent on "establishing prestigious birthing services" have established "more neonatal intensive care resources than are needed in many regions."[29] And this, *NEJM* reported, is not only pricey but potentially dangerous for the babies.

The researchers found little or no health benefit in communities that boast an embarrassment of infant ICUs: after adjusting for other demographic factors, infant mortality rates were no lower. Meanwhile, researchers point to the danger that the existence of the pricey facilities will mean that "infants with less serious illness might be more likely to be admitted to the ICU." Thus excess supply could lead to overtreatment, exposing somewhat vulnerable newborns to the hazards of being "subjected to more intensive diagnostic and therapeutic measures, with the attendant risks of errors and iatrogenic complications [complications cause by medical care] as well as impaired family-infant bonding."

In an editorial that accompanies the study, Dr. Kevin Grumbach of the University of California at San Francisco comments: "The saga of neonatology is emblematic of how a market-driven health care system with inadequate public planning produces too much of a good thing."[30]

Approaching a Perfect Storm?

In the end, who will pay for the waterfalls, the free massages, the private rooms, and the extra ICUs? The answer, of course, is "everyone." As hospitals pour hundreds of millions into new construction, insurance premiums, deductibles, and co-payments soar.

Rising hospital prices help fuel those increases. In 2003 hospitals charged 8 percent more for inpatient and outpatient services than they had a year earlier; in 2004 prices jumped another 7 percent. Meanwhile, a combination of increased use and higher charges has meant that total spending on outpatient services has risen by at least 8 percent each and every year from

1999 through 2004.[31] Given the plans on the drawing board, plus the rising cost of medical technology, there is every reason to believe that hospital prices will continue to climb faster than either wages or GDP. Which makes one wonder: where will we find the money to bankroll a ballooning hospital system?

"Good question," says Roger Hughes as he watches Phoenix hospitals break ground for new facilities within a stone's throw of each other. "They figure they'll just go head to head," he adds. "But if you just rely on relentless growth—simply believing the money's going to be there—you're probably in for a rude surprise."[32]

On Wall Street, health care industry analyst Sheryl Skolnick agrees: "When cost is not zero, demand is not infinite," she declares.

In theory, an aging population guarantees that demand for hospital services will soar. But "you can't just look at the demographics in a vacuum and say more people equals more health care," says Skolnick, who doesn't see where either the government or the boomers themselves will find the funds needed to keep pace with rising costs. "I certainly don't know who is going to pay for all of the health care I'm going to need over the next 40 years," she adds. And Skolnick is not just talking about boutique offerings: if health care inflation continues at the current rate, it is not at all clear how taxpayers, employers, or the average patient will fund necessary care.[33]

Skolnick suggests that inflation will slow, perforce, as payers cut back. "There is a real possibility that the impact of the baby boom on the hospital industry is more likely to be negative than positive," says Skolnick. "We see a margin squeeze just at the time when hospitals should be enjoying unprecedented volume growth. There will be so many more people to be paid for by Medicare and private insurance that the unit reimbursements may be lower. The profitability of a baby-boomer patient is going to contract."[34]

Plainly, employers like General Motors can no longer be expected to foot the bill for unfettered spending. In the first quarter of 2004, GM spent more on health care than it spent on steel. "We need to reflect on what that means," says Jerry Mathis, an employee-benefits consultant in San Antonio, Texas. "If steel is what drove the automobile industry and the automobile industry is what drove America, and now steel is a secondary to the cost of health care for General Motors retirees and employees, you realize that you have reached a watershed."[35]

Some employers are getting out of the benefits business altogether. In 2005 just 60 percent of all firms offered health insurance to their employees—down from 69 percent in 2000.[36] At one time, even early retirees could count on employer-sponsored health insurance: as recently as 1997, 40 percent of 55–65-year-old retirees had employer-sponsored insurance; by 2002 that number had dropped to 28 percent. That's another 10 million Americans who have to find their own insurance plan.[37]

And today those plans not only cost more, they cover less. "We're moving toward high-deductible, lower-paying insurance plans," says Sheryl Skolnick, and this, she believes, will cap demand. Patients who face 20–40 percent co-payments are less likely to sign up for an optional CT scan—or schedule elective surgery.

Whether the consumer will have the clairvoyance to skip the test or treatment that really isn't needed is a question to be explored later—optimists hope that the Internet will lead him to the right decision. What is certain is that even when the need for a hospital's services is clear, many patients will find that some of the new "affordable" plans contain holes that spring open, like trapdoors, when they become sick. Some policies don't cover physical therapy. Others offer only a limited benefit for "skilled nursing." (A patient is likely to find out exactly what "limited" means only after he is in a hospital.) Still others have no annual limit on how much a patient might be required to shell out in co-pays and deductibles.[38]

For hospitals, this means more unpaid bills. The reality is that most American families cannot afford the $5,100 deductible approved by Congress in 2003, plus a 20 percent co-payment on a cancer drug that costs $12,000 a month—or the $14,000 in out-of-pocket expenses that David Koch faced in 2004 while his 18-year-old son recovered from surgery for a brain tumor. When someone explained the intricacies of his health insurance policy, it turned out that only $700 of the $14,700 in out-of-pocket expenses could be applied to the policy's $1,500 per person, $5,000 per family deductible.[39]

The average American's nest egg just isn't big enough to cover five-figure hospital bills. A 2005 survey by the Employee Benefit Research Institute (EBRI) finds that more than half of all working Americans report total savings and investments—including 401(k)s and other retirement accounts that they can tap only by paying stiff penalties—of less than $25,000. Nearly two-thirds said that they had less than $50,000 squirreled away.[40] Meanwhile, the average American in his 40s or 50s is carrying roughly $20,000 in debt—not including a home mortgage.[41]

Could Americans save more? Some could. But with median household income hovering around $44,000 in 2005, many could not. A worker grossing, say, $22,000, has little in the way of extra cash to sock away for medical emergencies.[42]

According to EBRI, only about 1 in 10 workers—and less than one-fifth of all retirees—are sitting on nest eggs worth $250,000 or more.[43] These are the patients who, in most cases, will have the wherewithal to cover rising out-of-pocket expenses—plus the extras, like private rooms or acupuncture, that their insurance doesn't cover. But it is not at all clear that 10 percent to 20 percent of the population will be able to keep the hospitals of the future in the black.

Nor is it likely that the government will pick up the tab for the waterfalls. In the face of an ongoing Medicare/Medicaid crisis, both Washington and state governments will no doubt continue to pare reimbursements whenever hospitals begin to lift their heads above water. Even Robert Levine, who is in the business of building hospitals, is concerned: "I believe the pressure's going to be put on hospitals when they can least afford it," he says. "Something's going to have to give and it's going to be construction. It's not a perfect storm, but I see some head winds."[44]

For the time being, however, the ads are working. Hospital spending climbs, and most not-for-profits, like their for-profit peers, stay busy—doing their best to generate demand for everything from full body scans to C-sections. Still, observers like Dr. Donald Berwick, cofounder of the Institute for Healthcare Improvement, can't help but worry that as not-for-profit hospitals focus on their "margin," they're losing sight of their "mission." Berwick recalls phoning a hospital in Houston to learn about its reportedly successful innovations in pneumonia care, and being told that "the gains were enormous but that the methods could not be reported to the public—excellent pneumonia care offered the hospital local competitive advantage."

He was stunned. "The enemy is disease," he told his audience of physicians and health care executives at IHI's sixth annual National Forum on Quality Improvement in Health Care. "The competition that matters is against disease, not one another. The purpose is healing." Yet, "in the storm of the health care crisis," Berwick acknowledged, "it is so easy to forget why we trouble ourselves in the first place. It is so easy—frighteningly easy—to become trapped in the sterile thesis . . . *that our true, deep purpose is to gain and preserve market share in a vacant terrain of others whose purpose is precisely the same."* (emphasis mine) [45]

In other words, it is all too easy to forget the patient.

A Map of Medicare Spending

During the Final Six Months of Life, Medicare Patients in High-Spending
Regions Receive 60% More Care.[1]

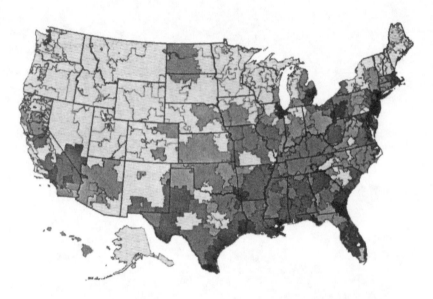

End-of-Life Spending, Lowest to Highest

	1 (Lowest)	2	3	4	5 (Highest)
End-of-Life Spending in Dollars*	9,074	10,636	11,559	12,598	14,644
Per capita Medicare spending in dollars†	3,922	4,439	4,940	5,444	6,304
Medicare enrollees in HMOs, %	12.1	6.8	7.3	7.7	15.3
Residents in metropolitan areas, %	77.5	81.9	82.3	79.2	97.4

* Average age-sex-race–adjusted per capita fee-for-service spending on hospital and physician services in the hospital referral regions within each quintile for Medicare enrollees age 65–99 years who were in their last 6 months of life.

† Average age-sex-race–adjusted 1996 annual per capita fee-for-service spending in the hospital referral regions within each quintile on all Medicare services among enrollees age 65–99 years.

Source: www.dartmouthatlas.org.

5

When More Care
Is Not Better Care

As she sat in the back of the ambulance, holding her father's hand and listening to the siren clear their path, Maureen Silverman knew that she had made a terrible mistake. She never should have called EMS.

The EMS worker was trying to reassure her: "We think your father has had a stroke," he said, "but don't worry, the hospital we're taking you to has the best stroke unit in New York City. There is nothing that they can't do."[2]

Nothing that they can't do. What did that mean? Her father already had been through so much—too much. What would they do? What would he want?

Of one thing Maureen was certain: he would not want to wake and find himself in an ambulance. Over the past five years, Lew Silverman had been in and out of hospitals. Three years earlier he had spent two grueling months in the very hospital where they were now heading.

But what else could she have done? When her mother called at 7 a.m. to say that she couldn't wake him, Maureen had rushed to their apartment. Her mother was right: he wasn't dead, but he wasn't moving. Maureen pinched his arm: no response. Then she phoned for the ambulance. Just before it arrived, her father regained consciousness long enough for her to tell him what was happening. He couldn't speak, but his eyes were pleading: "Why are you doing this to me?"

When the EMS workers arrived, Maureen answered their questions. In one month Lew Silverman would be 76. He was a type 1 diabetic. He was legally blind. Three years ago he had gone through a series of amputations. A year after that, he suffered a heart attack. He was in a lot of pain, both from his kidneys and his legs. He was depressed, but, no, he was not the least bit forgetful. Put simply, he was a 75-year-old diabetic with a sound mind padlocked in a dying body. And the mind wanted out.

As the ambulance rolled up to the hospital, Maureen knew what would happen next. They would wheel her father away, and he would be swallowed up by "the system," just as surely as if he had entered a prison.

To be fair, Maureen Silverman realized that the EMS worker was right: Mount Haven was an excellent hospital—one of New York's best.[3] Three years ago the surgeons there had managed to save her father's legs. Because diabetes damages blood vessels and nerves, diabetics like Lew Silverman often have problems with their feet. They are not always able to sense an injury to the foot, which means that what begins as a minor scrape can go unnoticed until the foot is badly infected. Compounding the problem, diabetes alters the immune system, making it more likely that a small infection will spread rapidly, leading to the death of skin and other tissue—and ultimately to the amputation of all or part of a limb.

But thanks to an experimental treatment, Lew Silverman was able to keep his legs—though just barely. Weekly, the surgeons sliced away portions of his feet, until in the end he was left with two toeless stumps. Using a walker he could just about wobble across a room. Often he fell. When that happened, he could not get up.

As the disease took hold of his body, Lew Silverman had coped. When he went blind, he began listening to books on tape. When he could no longer go out alone, his daughter took him to the bank, and he flirted with the teller, complimenting her on how pretty she looked. The teller knew he couldn't see her, but even so, she was pleased.

But now the pain was constant and debilitating. He couldn't even listen to his audio books. The pain was too distracting; he couldn't concentrate. Every day—every hour of every day—became a struggle, not to live but simply to exist. Depression settled over him like a shroud.

A few hours after they arrived at the hospital, Lew Silverman was finally settled in his room. There Maureen found him, his body riddled with tubes. A particularly nasty-looking line ran from his stomach up through his throat, pumping bile out of his nose. Dr. Hadley, the private-practice internist who had treated him for years, prescribed a morphine patch.

But before long it became clear that Lew was getting too much morphine. The next day it was hard to know how much he understood. Eventually, the dose was adjusted. A third day passed, a fourth, and a fifth. Then another crisis. When Maureen arrived at the hospital in the morning, they told her, "Your father has gone into renal failure."

"Without dialysis, he will die," the doctors said. In addition, they told Maureen, there was some sort of bowel obstruction. They wanted to do emergency exploratory surgery and then put him on dialysis.

But by now Lew Silverman's morphine dose had been reduced. He was lucid, and he was adamant: he would have none of it. "How much time would the dialysis buy?" he asked. "And for what? I don't want more surgeries," he added. "And I don't want to be hooked up to machines."

It fell to Maureen to fight Dr. Johnson, the renal specialist. "We can save your father's life," he declared. "You have to let us do the bowel surgery and then put him on dialysis. Otherwise, he's going to die in three days, maybe four."

"But dialysis is not what he wants," Maureen protested.

"This is the treatment," the doctor replied. "This is the procedure."

The message was clear: this is what we do. He was not interested in talking about what Lew Silverman wanted, his quality of life, or what stage of life he had reached. When Maureen Silverman refused to give in, Dr. Johnson turned on his heel and left the room.

Meanwhile, the hospital's medical ethics committee had decided that Maureen could become her father's health care agent. (Overwhelmed, her mother did not want the responsibility.) This gave Maureen the power to serve as his advocate and exercise his right to refuse surgery and dialysis. Nevertheless, she could not help but feel the glare of institutional disapproval boring down on her.

The next day an intern stopped her in the hallway: "I wouldn't let *my* father die," she said. Shaking, Maureen retreated to her father's room. There, Dr. Johnson once again cornered her: "I can save your father's life," he all but hissed.

Maureen paged her father's internist. It was her day off, but Dr. Hadley responded. She had heard from Dr. Johnson: although earlier he had insisted that dialysis was the only solution, now he wanted to try an alternative. There was a drug that he could put into her father's IV; meanwhile they would continue to provide nourishment through a feeding tube. "Let them do it," Dr. Hadley advised. "Though, frankly, if he lives another 24 hours, it will truly be a miracle."

The next day Lew Silverman fell victim to a miracle. In the morning he appeared to be going downhill. The kidney failure combined with his meds had made him delusional. He saw cars on the ceiling. He cried out—they were crashing into him. But by the afternoon he was calmer. He looked better. Once again he was lucid.

"How long is this going to take?" he asked. "I thought I was supposed to die. What the hell is going on here?"

As it turned out, the drug had worked. His kidneys had recovered. And what the doctors thought was a bowel obstruction had cleared up on its own. Dr. Johnson, the renal specialist, sailed into the room. "I told you we could save your father," he crowed, smiling smugly. For a moment fury rendered Maureen speechless—then she found words:

"No, you told me that he needed surgery and dialysis, and that without both, he would die. Why didn't you suggest the IV drug first? Dialysis is expensive and painful. My father is tired—very, very tired."

By now Lew Silverman was also very angry. So angry, his daughter could not comfort him. "I shouldn't have let the doctors give him the new drug," she told a friend. "And I should have had the courage to refuse the feeding tube."

Stung by guilt, she turned to her father for reassurance: "Daddy, did I do the right thing?" Lew Silverman growled—a long, drawn-out guttural sound—and slowly dragged a finger across his throat.

That night at 3 a.m., the phone rang. "Your father passed away several minutes ago," said the voice on the other end of the line. "He died in his sleep of a heart attack."

"They say that news in the middle of the night is never good," Maureen later told a friend. "But in this case, they were wrong."

* * * * * * * * * * * * * * *

Location, Location, Location

While millions of uninsured and underinsured Americans receive too little medical care, others, like Lew Silverman, stand a fair chance of receiving too much care in the form of unnecessary tests, questionable procedures, and end-of-life treatments that bring neither comfort nor cure.

Up to one-third of our health care dollars are squandered on ineffective, sometimes unwanted, and often unproven procedures, says Dr. Jack Wennberg, director of the Center for the Evaluative Clinical Sciences at Dartmouth Medical School.[4] That's right—more than $65 billion lost to overtreatment. And much of that waste can be traced to a hospital culture where technology and training support a reimbursement system that favors intervention over what some call "thinking medicine"—i.e., talking to and listening to the patient.

A controversial and courageous figure, Wennberg has spent the last 30 years investigating how medical practice varies in different parts of the country. And what he has discovered, to the chagrin of many in his profession, is that in some parts of the country, patients receive far more aggressive care than their counterparts in other states—and yet, in the end, those who enjoy the most intensive care fare no better than those who receive less lavish care.

Like UCLA economist Thomas Rice, Wennberg believes that waste is, to a large degree, a supply-side problem. It is not a matter of consumers in certain regions demanding more care, but of hospitals and specialists in some areas recommending more care. In other words "standard practice" is far from standard nationwide. How much care two equally sick patients receive when being treated for the very same disease seems to depend, to an astounding and irrational degree, on where they happen to live.

To test this theory, Wennberg and his colleagues at Dartmouth have spent thousands of hours over the last dozen years comparing the care that similar patients receive in 306 hospital markets nationwide. What they have found is that for reasons that have little to do with the dictates of medical science, the severity of a patient's illnesses, or his or her preferences, patients in places like Manhattan and Miami receive far more aggressive care than their counterparts in Minneapolis or Missoula, Montana.

Medicare records lay bare the differences. In Ogden, Utah, for instance, billings show Medicare patients spending an average of just 4.6 days in the hospital during the final six months of life, while seniors in Newark, New Jersey, rack up an average of 21.4 hospital days over the same period. In Miami and Manhattan, 30 percent of patients see 10 or more specialists in the six months before they die—compared to just 7 percent of Medicare beneficiaries residing in Iowa City, Missoula, or Portland, Oregon. The pattern holds true when it comes to winding up in an ICU: one study shows that terminally ill patients in Miami are three times as likely to find themselves in an intensive care unit as patients in Sun City, Arizona.[5]

More aggressive care is, of course, more expensive care: "Over the course of a beneficiary's life, Medicare spends more than twice as much per patient in 'high-treatment regions,' " reports Dr. Elliott Fisher, a professor of medicine at Dartmouth who served as lead author on a watershed 2003 study of regional variations in health care that appeared in *Annals of Internal Medicine*.[6] And it is not just Medicare spending that seems tied to geography; research reveals similar spending patterns for BlueCross BlueShield.[7] When patients receive more care, hospital spending soars—whether those bills are paid by taxpayers or by private insurers.

When one looks at the map of Medicare spending at the beginning of this chapter, a larger pattern emerges: during the last six months of life, hospitals in parts of the Northeast and Southeast seem to pull out all the stops. Patients in the Northwest, by contrast, receive far less expensive care—even after adjusting for demographic differences such as age, sex, and race, as well as local prices. And, the Dartmouth researchers point out, what happens during the final six months of life serves as "an excellent marker" for how much Medicare lays out in a given region throughout the average patient's life.[8]

On the face of it, the concentration of spending in the East might not seem too surprising. After all, as practically anyone in Nebraska could tell you, consumers on the East Coast are spendthrifts. But as Wennberg observes, it is not only in the Northeast that hospitals lavish more care on their patients. Medicare records show that "spending in some rural regions in the South is as high or even higher."

"And the dollar transfers involved are enormous," the Dartmouth team reported in a 2002 study. "The difference in lifetime Medicare spending between a typical sixty-five-year-old in Miami and one in Minneapolis [is] more than $50,000, equivalent to a new Lexus GS 400 with all the trimmings."[9]

Demographics? Fear of Malpractice?

It may seem logical that seniors who reside in Ogden, Utah, are less likely to spend their final days in a hospital than their counterparts in Newark, New Jersey.[10] Surely, higher levels of poverty, violence, and air pollution in Newark account for the difference. As for the different spending levels in Miami and Minneapolis, perhaps seniors who choose to live out their twilight years enduring Minnesota's cold winters are simply a hardier lot than those who retire to Florida's beaches.

Not surprisingly, researchers have considered these variables. When comparing the intensity of care in different parts of the country, they bend over backward to adjust for differences in race, age, and overall health of the population. They acknowledge, for example, that salubrious conditions in Grand Junction, Colorado, one of the healthiest regions in the United States, imply that per capita Medicare outlays there should be about 20 percent below the national average. By contrast, the comparatively poor health of Medicare beneficiaries in Birmingham, Alabama, one of the least healthy communities, suggests that spending in that city should be nearly 25 percent above the national average. Nevertheless, even after factoring in these differences, researchers find that the underlying health of the populations accounts for only about one-quarter of the enormous disparities in Medicare spending.[11]

Fear of malpractice suits in particularly litigious states also springs to mind as a reason why hospitals in some regions would be more zealous than others. Yet, even proponents of tort reform claim that statewide caps on malpractice awards reduce hospital spending by only 5–9 percent—not enough to explain twofold differences in the cost of care.[12] Moreover, when researchers drill down and look at individual hospitals within a high-treatment state, they find significant differences in how aggressively some academic medical centers manage dying patients—even within the same city.[13] If fear of the local plaintiff's bar drove end-of-life care, this would not be the case.

"Stubborn, Embarrassing" Inconsistencies

It is not only spending on end-of-life treatment that varies dramatically across regions. When it comes to a wide range of procedures, it appears that geography is destiny. "Wennberg's work has shown, for example, that the likelihood of a doctor sending you for a gallbladder-removal operation varies 270 percent, depending on what city you live in, for a hip replacement 450 percent . . ." observes Dr. Atul Gawande, author of *Complications: A Surgeon's Notes on an Imperfect Science*. "What he has found," Gawande adds, "is a stubborn, overwhelming and embarrassing degree of inconsistency in what we do."

"Embarrassing," because outcomes are just as good for those who receive more conservative care. A study of nearly 1 million patients published in *Annals of Internal Medicine* in 2003 sums up the findings: "higher spending did not result in higher quality care, lower mortality, better function outcomes, or greater patient satisfaction." [14]

In fact, "more care may even lead to worse outcomes," says Dr. Elliott Fisher, the lead author of the study. When he and his colleagues tracked mortality rates for Medicare patients who had fractured a hip, suffered a heart attack, or been hospitalized with colorectal cancer, they discovered that "among older patients who were treated for a heart attack or colorectal cancer, there actually was a small but statistically significant increase in the risk of death as intensity [of care] increased." [15] In other words, more care is not simply wasteful; it could be hazardous to your health.

Dr. Donald Berwick, cofounder of the Institute for Healthcare Improvement, summed up Fisher's findings at the 15th annual National Forum on Quality Improvement in Health Care in December of 2003: "If you divide American hospital markets according to the intensity of their services, and then study the quality of care in each area several different ways . . . here's what you find: More intensity doesn't get you any more quality of care," and "at the top level, outcomes are worse. This is a frightening finding," Berwick added, "with imponderably large implications for American health care. In fact, nobody powerful in American health care seems to want to touch this one with a ten-foot pole." [16]

Granted, a correlation between more intense care and higher mortality rates does not establish a causal connection: there is no proof that more patients died *because* they received more aggressive treatment. Yet, as Fisher points out, the sheer "number of physicians involved in a given patient's care, the number of minor tests performed, and the amount of time that patients spend in the hospital and intensive care unit" all expose the patient to a greater risk of complications or medical errors. It is not only that frail elderly patients stand a greater chance of contracting infections if they spend more days in an ICU. There is also the danger that when a dozen or more specialists "consult" over the patient, they may not consult with one another.

Along the way, the more specialists a patient sees, the more likely he is to be subjected to a battery of tests, with "more frequent testing leading to more diagnoses," says Fisher. "And physicians rarely stop with a diagnosis."

The problem today, he goes on to explain, is that advanced diagnostic testing has become so refined that it can pick up what scientists call "pseudodisease," disease that would never become apparent to patients during their lifetime without the diagnostic test. For example, microscopic examination of specimens from women in their 40s reveals that as many as 40 percent of them may have ductal carcinoma in situ of the breast [a preinvasive form of breast cancer]. Similarly sophisticated testing shows that half of men in their 50s have adenocarcinoma of the prostate [prostate cancer]. In such cases, Fisher reports, physicians often differ on what should be done, with pseudodisease leading "not only to physician disagreement and unnecessary patient worry and disability, but also to unnecessary treatment."[17]

All in all, says Fisher, "Hospitals are dangerous places—especially if you do not need to be there."[18]

Mount Sinai vs. the Mayo Clinic

That said, Wennberg and colleagues are quick to acknowledge that some of the differences in the ways hospitals in different regions treat patients arise because of completely legitimate disagreements on "best practice." In some cases, clinical evidence proving which treatment is better is missing, and until randomized clinical trials fill in the blank spaces (a never-ending task), physicians will continue, quite rightly, to disagree.[19] But in other cases, Wennberg observes, different practice styles "appear unrelated to scientific controversy. Physicians in some hospital markets practice medicine in ways that we know are more costly, without any clear benefit. Whatever the reason, it is certainly not because of adherence to medical standards based on clinical outcomes."[20]

Even at the nation's finest academic medical centers, Medicare records illuminate unsettling disparities in how patients are treated—with no discernible difference in how well patients fare. Since these teaching hospitals are seen as setting the standard for best practice nationwide, one might well assume that treatment would not vary too much from one part of the country to another. One would be wrong.

A recent study comparing how patients were treated six months after fracturing a hip revealed, for example, that patients at teaching hospitals in high-spending regions enjoyed 82 percent more physician visits, 26 percent more imaging exams, 90 percent more diagnostic tests, and 46 percent more minor surgery than their counterparts at equally prestigious academic medical centers in low-spending regions.[21] A separate four-year project took a look at the seven medical centers rated best for geriatric care by *U.S. News & World Report* only to discover wide variations in how aggressively hospitals like Johns Hopkins, Duke University Medical Center, Mount Sinai, and the Mayo Clinic treated terminally ill patients.[22] Patients at Manhattan's Mount Sinai, for instance, spent almost twice as many days in the hospital as similar patients at the Mayo Clinic in Rochester, Minnesota. And during that time, Mount Sinai's patients were twice as likely to see 10 or more specialists. Yet, by all accounts, the Mayo Clinic's customers were no less satisfied with their care.

Admittedly, questions about patient satisfaction lead to murky answers since the patient cannot know with any certainty how happy he would be if he had not had the treatment (after all, a great many ailments, like Lew Silverman's bowel obstruction, clear up by themselves) or if he had had a different treatment (for example, the drug that Silverman ultimately received instead of dialysis). Thus, it is difficult, even for the patient himself, to measure whether his health care dollars were well spent.

Complicating matters further, patients who receive the most aggressive care may be inclined to exaggerate their satisfaction: "Patients who have experienced a great deal of trauma and cost often are reluctant to acknowledge to themselves or to researchers that it was all in vain," observes health care economist Victor Fuchs."[23] No doubt he is right—human beings will go to great lengths to avoid regret.

At the same time, the uncertainties of medical science make it impossible to say that longer stays at hospitals like Mount Sinai had no appreciable benefit for any individual patient. But stepping back and looking at the evidence in the aggregate, it seems clear that, on average, high-treatment regions have reached—and moved past—a point of diminishing returns.[24] "The bottom line is that a considerable amount of the care delivered in the United States is 'flat-of-the-curve' medicine," explains Fuchs. In some areas, we've reached "a level of intensity of care that provides no incremental health benefit."

Forgetting the Little Things

To make matters worse, high-tech care that brings little benefit may distract health care workers from doing the quotidian things that we *know* work—like giving aspirin to heart attack victims. In a stunner of a study published in *Health Affairs* in 2004, two Dartmouth economists uncovered what appears to be an inverse relationship between expensive care and low-tech effective care.

The chart on p. 166 illustrates their findings. Here, "quality of care" (the vertical axis) is measured using 24 yardsticks of effective care developed by the Medicare Quality Improvement Organization. The list focuses on treatments for which there is strong scientific evidence and professional consensus: for instance, everyone agrees on the importance of giving antibiotics to a patient suffering from bacterial pneumonia within eight hours of admission, and giving beta-blockers to heart attack victims within 24 hours. Meanwhile, the horizontal axis shows how much Medicare lays out per beneficiary in each state.[25] States that spend more appear on the far right of the chart. States that provide the highest quality care are clustered at the top.

Compare spending to quality, and the results are astounding. Someone who has suffered a heart attack seems to stand a better chance of receiving an aspirin in states like New Hampshire, Vermont, Maine, North Dakota, Utah, Iowa, Hawaii, Wisconsin, Minnesota, Oregon, and Montana (where Medicare spends less than $5,500 per person), than in Louisiana, Texas, California, Florida, New Jersey, and Oklahoma (where Medicare lays out $7,000 to over $8,000 per enrollee).

One caveat is appropriate: these 24 yardsticks cannot hope to capture overall quality of care. They serve merely as markers for specific procedures. Nevertheless, they do say something about an institution's attention to vital

The Relationship Between Quality and Medicare Spending, 2000–2001

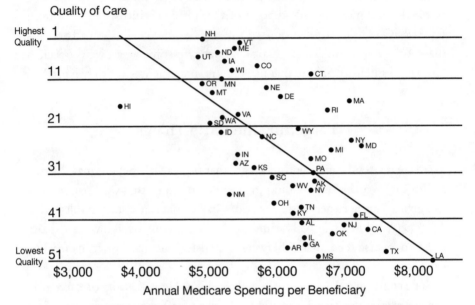

Sources: Medicare claims data; S. F. Jencks et al., "Change in the Quality of Care Delivered to Medicare Beneficiaries, 1998–1999 to 2000–2001" *Journal of the American Medical Association* 289, no. 3 (2003): 305–312, Baicker and Chandra, "Medicare Spending," *Health Affairs,* 7 April 2004.

details—details that can be forgotten even at the most sophisticated hospitals. A study at Duke University Medical Center, for example, revealed that when patients arrived at the hospital short of breath, feverish, and suffering from bacterial pneumonia, fewer than half received antibiotics in a timely fashion. And while current best practice dictates that pneumonia patients who are elderly or suffering from a chronic illness like emphysema should receive a vaccine to protect against another bout of the disease, none of Duke's at-risk patients got the shot.

Most physicians were unaware of the holes in their routine. If asked, they would have said, "Of course, we always give the vaccine." When they saw their record, they were flabbergasted. "It's like the Elisabeth Kübler-Ross stages of grief," says Dr. Robert Califf, a professor of medicine at Duke. "First you're in shock, then denial, and then you gradually come to terms with what needs to be done."[26]

No one is certain why more expensive care seems to go hand in hand with these lapses in basic care. But Elliott Fisher points to one clue: in high-spending regions there tend to be more specialists and fewer general practitioners. "And if there are five specialists treating you," Fisher speculates, "each one is going to be slightly less likely to take overall responsibility for your care, and more likely to think that another doctor has prescribed the aspirin."[27]

Greedy Geezers?

Still, the question hangs: why do patients in some parts of the country see more specialists?

If demographic differences don't justify regional variations in care, one might suspect that what Dartmouth's researchers have uncovered is, at bottom, a cultural difference. Perhaps the worried wealthy in places like Miami and Manhattan simply demand more care than stoic Minnesotans. Indeed, some patients proudly describe themselves as avaricious consumers: "We're New Yorkers—we want the best," one Manhattanite declares.[28] And why not? Especially when Medicare picks up the tab.

It becomes tempting to blame greedy geezers for wasting resources, especially after reading newspaper stories that describe retirees in places like South Florida lining up for all that Medicare can provide. A colorful and well-documented piece in *The New York Times* tells how, in the gated communities near Boca Raton, "doctor visits have become a social activity. Many patients have 8, 10 or 12 specialists and visit one or more of them most days of the week. They bring their spouses and plan their days around their appointments, going out to eat or shopping while they are in the area. . . . They know what they want; they choose specialists for every body part. And every visit, every procedure is covered by Medicare . . .

" 'It is easy to find all these specialists,' one retiree confides. 'You get recommendations at the clubhouse, at the swimming pool. You go to a restaurant here and 9 times out of 10, before the meal is over, you hear people talking about a doctor or a medicine or a surgery.' "

And of course, "there are the other patients in all those waiting rooms," the *Times* noted, eager, no doubt, to share their dance cards. "Boca Raton," the article concluded, "is a case study of what happens when people are given free rein to have all the medical care they could imagine."[29]

In a nutshell, the story illustrates what insurance companies fear most: "moral hazard" (a term originally coined by the fire insurance industry to describe the risk of losing money due to the poor moral character of the insured—i.e., the danger that he might turn out to be an arsonist). These days, health care economists have stretched the phrase: "moral hazard" now refers to the risk that when insured patients are spending someone else's money, they will cheerfully sign up for $1,000 worth of services—even though, if they were reaching into their own pockets, they might assess those same services as worth only $500, and reduce their use accordingly. (Whether using the health insurance that you have paid for really ranks as a "moral failing" will be discussed later.)

What is certain is that when Medicare spends more in some regions, retirees in other regions receive less.[30] And this breeds resentment, not only among Medicare beneficiaries but among taxpayers. "On equity grounds, we have problems with the idea of single working mothers in Nebraska (often themselves lacking health insurance) footing the bill for gold-plated health care provided to high-income Medicare enrollees in Miami," says Jonathan Skinner, a Dartmouth economist who works with Jack Wennberg, "Leaving equity aside, on efficiency grounds, why should Medicare continue to pay billions of dollars every year on health care that does nothing for longevity, nothing for patient satisfaction and nothing for better access to care?"[31]

But Medicare beneficiaries in Minnesota enjoy the same level of moral hazard as retirees sunning themselves in Miami: they, too, can order anything that they want from the Medicare menu. Yet somehow—they don't. Is it simply because Minnesotans are more frugal, less self-indulgent, or less sociable than seniors in Manhattan or Miami?

It is hard to imagine that a twofold difference in lifetime spending can be explained by widespread regional character flaws, especially when many of health care's high rollers live in Louisiana or Texas—cultural milieus that bear little resemblance to either Miami or Manhattan.[32]

Nevertheless, the majority of health care economists continue to focus on the demand side of the equation when analyzing the excess in health care spending: we spend so much on health care because well-insured Americans simply use too much care—this is the reigning ideology.

Not everyone agrees. Former Medicare administrator Bruce Vladeck rejects what he sees as a worn formulation. Vladeck attributes our tendency to "blame the consumer" first to "our Puritan ethos," which "rebels at the thought of all of those overinsured consumers frivolously using up all of that valuable health care—and if the consumers are using health care because they're sick, then that's probably their own fault, too."

But that is only one reason why economists finger the consumer, says Vladeck. The other, he suggests, is political: "If we focus on [how much care consumers use] we don't talk about prices—or incomes—and thus don't directly threaten the existing structures of power and prestige within the health care system or the political system." In other words, we don't ruffle the feathers of those on the receiving end of a $2 trillion industry— the drugmakers, device makers, hospital CEOs, and entrepreneurial health care providers who see themselves as businessmen first and professionals second.

By blaming the consumer, we also avoid flustering the many politicians who receive handsome contributions from a grateful health care lobby. As Vladeck puts it, "focusing on utilization permits both health care providers and payers to change the subject away from the more embarrassing discussion of who's getting paid, by whom, and how much."[33]

Build the Beds and Someone Will Fill Them

This is what makes UCLA economist Thomas Rice's work so refreshing. Rather than tiptoeing around those imposing structures of power and prestige in the middle of the room, Rice turns the spotlight on the supply side of the equation. Indeed, as noted in chapter 3, Rice goes so far as to attribute "most of the waste in health care spending" to "the many services that a hospital provides which do little or no good in improving a patient's health."

And he is not at all convinced that what he calls "patients' druthers" explains the waste. Instead, Rice points to excess capacity as one of the major factors driving the misuse and overuse of health care resources.[34]

The Dartmouth research puts flesh on the theory that supply creates demand by providing empirical evidence that patients receive more intensive care in regions flush with hospital beds, surgeons, and subspecialists. Using data from the watershed study of nearly 1 million patients published in *Annals of Internal Medicine* in 2003, researchers divided the nation's hospital markets into five quintiles, ranging from those where Medicare spent least during the final six months of life to those where it spent most, and then compared resources in those regions. As the table below shows, high-spending regions boasted 32 percent more hospital beds per capita, over 60 percent more subspecialists, roughly 25 percent more surgeons, and nearly 20 percent fewer family practitioner/general practitioners.[35]

The numbers only confirm what the Dartmouth team already knew: "The supply of resources governs how frequently they are used," says Jack Wennberg. Over the years, the Dartmouth project has consistently shown a positive association between the supply of staffed beds per 1,000 residents and hospitalization rates, with "supply-sensitive" care accounting for at least 50 percent of Medicare spending.[36] So in towns like Lubbock, Texas, or Hattiesburg, Mississippi—where there are twice as many hospital beds per 1,000 residents as in the average low-spending region—patients are far more likely

	LOW-SPENDING REGIONS	HIGH-SPENDING REGIONS
*Spending per person**	*$3,922 per person*	*$6,304 per person*
Hospital Beds per 1,000	2.4	3.2
Physicians per 100,000		
Medical subspecialists	27	44
General internists	21	37
Family practioners/GPs	36	27
Surgeons	44	56
All other specialists	57	78

* Average per capita spending on Medicare enrollees during their last six months of life adjusted for age, sex, and race.

to land in an ICU, seeing 10 or more specialists during the final six months of life.[37]

But not all medical decisions are driven by supply, says Wennberg. When it comes to elective surgeries, such as knee and hip implants, there is another figure in the carpet. While the number of specialists available can be a factor, it is doctors' preferences for certain surgeries over others—rather than the number of beds available—that holds sway.[38]

"Supply is most likely to drive decisions when physicians are treating chronic illnesses like congestive heart failure, chronic lung disease, and cancer," Wennberg points out. In these cases, "differences in the frequency of hospitalizations, physicians visits, stays in intensive care units, referrals to specialists, and the use of imaging and other diagnostic tests" add up— which explains how Medicare manages to spend twice as much in markets where there are plenty of beds, and plenty of specialists.

Subliminal Decision Making

Does this mean that specialists book patients into hospitals the way airlines fill empty seats?

Just as it is tempting to blame "greedy geezers" for spiraling Medicare costs, it would be easy to take the numbers above as evidence that money-hungry physicians in gold coast towns like Manhattan and Miami simply count the beds in their communities and then grimly set out to fill them.

But the Dartmouth team rejects the easy explanation. Wennberg simply doesn't believe that the average specialist in a high-treatment area "looks for and recommends more procedures—even if the physician knows that these procedures are not particularly beneficial—making trade-offs between quality of care and take-home income." Nevertheless, he insists, "we believe that physicians, along with willing hospitals, are at the root of over treatment" in high-spending regions.[39]

As Wennberg sees it, the number of hospital beds in a community plays an unconscious role in a physician's decision making. While "physicians don't really know how many hospital beds are available," supply has "a subliminal influence on utilization," says Wennberg. "If there's a bed available, naturally you'll use it."

He points out that this is in part because when deciding whether or not to hospitalize a chronically ill patient, "physicians are not applying a well-established remedy to a well-understood problem, such as doing an appendectomy on a patient with appendicitis."[40] When it comes to treating some of the most serious chronic diseases, there is no rule book. When should a 65-year-old cancer patient who also suffers from congestive heart failure be admitted to the hospital? When is she better off at home? There are no cut and dried answers.

Convenience also influences the decision, says Fisher. From the physician's point of view, it is often easier to manage care in an inpatient setting. Once the patient is admitted, his doctor no longer has to worry about answering late-night calls or arranging for visiting nurses and follow-up office visits. Meanwhile, hospitalization lowers the threshold for further intervention: it is now simpler to obtain tests, perform minor discretionary surgeries, or consult with other specialists.[41] So, one thing leads to another.

In other cases, hospitalization can serve as "the path of least resistance" for a physician treating a terminally ill patient: "It is often easier for a busy doctor to hospitalize a patient or institute treatment than to have an always difficult and poignant discussion acknowledging the possibility that the patient is dying, and discussing alternatives such as home care and hospice," notes a recent study on end-of-life care.[42]

When it comes to how frequently a patient sees a specialist, the uncertainties of medical science once again come into play. How often should a patient suffering from congestive heart failure be examined by her physician: every two months? Every four months?

"The doctor will sort it out based on how sick an individual patient is and how many openings he has in his schedule," Wennberg explains. "Specialists tend to fill their appointment books to capacity," and so it is easy to see how a doubling of the supply of cardiologists would mean that patients would see their physicians twice as often. "From a systems perspective the phenomenon makes sense," Wennberg observes. Though because most specialists keep their calendars full, "they are not able to see emergency patients, and wind up sending them to an ER—the worst place for these sickest patients to be treated."[43]

Uncertainty, convenience, the automatic tendency to use whatever resources are available—whether time, beds, or technology—all help explain how supply drives a doctor's decision making. The process proceeds quite naturally. Yet none of the factors shaping these decisions seem to have much to do with either medical science or the needs of the patient. Each step of the way, an individual doctor may or may not be overtreating a particular patient. But once again, an aerial view of aggregate outcomes suggests that, on average, those who receive more supply-driven care are no better off than similar patients who enjoy a certain degree of benign neglect.[44]

Supply and Demand: The Chicken and the Egg

Admittedly, untangling supply and demand remains a tricky business. If supply influences a physician's decisions, so do a patient's expectations. "Patients in Miami come to expect full-bore health care as the norm, and they worry when they cannot see multiple specialists or if they are not provided with an array of diagnostic tests," says Dartmouth economist Jonathan Skinner. "They wonder, what's wrong? Doesn't he care? Doesn't he like me?"

"Our most recent studies suggest that in areas where supply is high, consumers do demand more care, because that is what they're used to," he confides. "When you think about it, it's obvious—people like what they're getting. So if you ask someone in Miami, 'Do you feel more comfortable with a specialist than with a primary care physician,' they reply, 'Why, of course.' In Minnesota, where there are far fewer specialists, patients are more likely to say that they feel most comfortable with the primary care physician who they see most often."[45]

Which comes first, supply or demand? The Dartmouth team remains convinced that supply leads the dance, in part because they have studied what happens when Medicare beneficiaries move from one region to another. "People are always shuffling around," says Skinner, "which creates a natural experiment. And what we've found is that, even if people leave an area, the beds stay—and somehow they get filled, despite the fact that there are now more beds per person." It is hard to imagine that the remaining residents suddenly develop what economists call a "taste" for more time in a hospital bed.

Too Many Oars in the Water

Although Wennberg began his work on geographic variations in treatment some 30 years ago, the whole issue of how much care is the right amount of care is "only beginning to emerge as a topic for medical discourse at medical rounds and in scientific journals and textbooks," he observes. "With the exception of a few studies of chronic disease management, patient-level studies that might shed light on the question simply haven't been done."[46]

Dr. Diane Meier, director of the Center to Advance Palliative Care at Manhattan's Mount Sinai School of Medicine, agrees: "Evidence-based standards of practice that could guide physicians' treatment choices for many of the complex and chronic medical problems that Medicare patients face do not exist. In the absence of such data, doctors continue to do what they were taught during their training and what the culture of clinical practice in their region expects."[47]

Why has it taken so long for the health care system to begin to follow up on the questions that the Dartmouth research raises?

When Wennberg first attempted to publish his findings on geographic variation, in the early seventies, the medical community was less than enthusiastic. Not only was he suggesting that hospitals might be wasting health care dollars, he was reminding everyone that medicine is a highly inexact science. "Most people view the medical care they receive as a necessity provided by doctors who adhere to scientific norms based on previously tested and proven treatments," Wennberg points out. But his work suggests that many medical decisions are driven by something other than science. The "conventional medical journals sent me form-letter rejections," Wennberg recalls. "*Science* was the journal of last resort, but we were delighted to get the paper accepted there.

"The paper was very important for me," he continues, "because it described a set of problems that have occupied me every since: what are the causes of unwarranted variations in care [variations that seem to have little or no connection to either medical science or the patient's needs or preferences]? What are the consequences? When is more better? When is there too much care and the likelihood of iatrogenic illness [illness inadvertently caused by what a physician say or does, or by a medical treatment]?"[48]

Thirty years later, these questions remain unanswered. And Wennberg understands why. "The system is stubborn," he acknowledges, "because it is, after all, more than 15 percent of the economy. There are a lot of oars in the water, and information per se is not going to change the fundamental economic incentives."[49]

In other words, there is no "business case" for learning how to do less.[50] Or, as Dr. Robert Califf, professor of medicine at Duke University, puts it, "There's a lot of money being made on things that don't work well." Sorting out what works and what doesn't is extremely difficult, Califf explains, in part because "most of what we do has a modest effect. In rare cases, a new technology will have a major curative effect," he adds, but "for the most part new therapies add incrementally, if at all, to clinical outcomes."

In the world of medicine, "technology" refers not just to devices and equipment, but to high-powered drugs and sophisticated surgical techniques.[51] And Califf's point is that as these new technologies become more refined, their effects are subtler. Measuring the benefit of a given drug or procedure is further complicated because today there are likely to be multiple therapies available for a given chronic disease, and as Califf observes, any one of them is likely to make only a "small, marginal difference." As a result, he says, "the only way to get a reliable answer about the benefits of a treatment is by enrolling a large number of patients in randomized controlled trials."

But such clinical trials are costly and not always practical. Moreover, "if you are making a ton of money being reimbursed by Medicare," says Califf, "the last thing you want to do is put your treatment to a test."[52]

"Awash in Novelty"

Nevertheless, Jack Wennberg argues, the cost of large randomized clinical trials should be weighed against the hundreds of millions wasted on unproven procedures: "Clinical medicine is awash in novelty, but without the capacity to distinguish what truly works. . . . The employer community, the tax-paying community and the Centers for Medicare and Medicaid Services need to understand that their cost problems [can be traced] to a large extent, to unevaluated technologies. They need to give political support to a major upgrade for funding the Agency for Healthcare Research and Quality

[AHRQ]," he adds, referring to the federal agency originally charged with spearheading clinical research.[53]

Unfortunately, Wennberg realizes that this is not likely. The AHRQ committed political suicide in 1995 when it made the mistake of releasing a set of policy guidelines that discouraged surgery in the management of lower back pain. "A number of politically active surgeons took offense," recalls Dr. George Lundberg, who was then editor of *The Journal of the American Medical Association,* "and aggressively lobbied members of Congress, demanding the agency back off. . . . At the time, there was talk of eliminating AHRQ entirely but Congress finally settled the matter by slashing its budget."[54]

As a result, today AHRQ is "irrelevant to the problems that I was interested in having it address," says Wennberg. "It's a tragedy—the whole program got knocked out. Congress gives them $300 million—that's a laugh. They're out of the business of determining the scientific basis of clinical practice."[55]

Indeed, as Fisher points out, the lion's share of both private and public sector medical research continues to concentrate on developing new technologies and treatments while "relatively little effort is devoted to evaluating current clinical practices, identifying their limitations, and advising clinicians about what *not* to do."[56]

Meanwhile, overinvestment and malinvestment in cutting-edge technologies serves as a catalyst for overtreatment. "Lurking behind variations in patterns of care are often huge hospital investments in expensive technologies," says Wennberg. "Many have not passed the muster of a clinical trial," and "even those that have [are used] in many unevaluated ways. What is done with a new technology once it's in the market depends on the inventiveness of physicians, and they're terribly inventive."[57]

Lundberg, editor of *The Journal of the American Medical Association* from 1982 to 1999, agrees: "Too many medical technologies are based on uncertain science. All too often," he adds, "good clinical trials are not conducted before a new technique is almost universally used."

To illustrate the problem, Lundberg, who is now editor-in-chief of the online medical journal *Medscape,* points to bone marrow transplant technology, which was used in conjunction with high-dose chemotherapy for stage 4 breast cancer while it still was an experimental procedure. It became standard treatment more than a decade before studies showed that it was no more helpful than regular chemotherapy. In fact, Lundberg points out, "the procedure was dangerous, debilitating and expensive. Between 15 and 20 percent of the patients died from the drugs used . . . Many others had permanent injuries including heart damage and hearing loss." [58]

Despite the lack of medical evidence that the treatment worked, pressure from patients, state legislatures, and courts forced many insurers to begin providing coverage for the procedure, and this only compounded the problem. Because insurers would pay for the treatment, few patients were willing to enroll in randomized clinical trials, fearing that they would be assigned to the conventional therapy group rather than the experimental transplant group. As a result, the clinical trials were delayed for five years. Ultimately, the nation squandered roughly $3 billion while an estimated 4,000 to 9,000 women died, not from their cancer but from the therapy.

"Nobody got cured," says attorney Alice Philipson, referring to the five women whom she represented in suits against their HMOs. "I put them through litigation when they were dying. Then if I won, they got to have a bone marrow transplant. You can't raise your head, you are so sick, and it's so horrible and so hard, and you don't have time to say good-bye to the people you love. I had to decide for myself whether I was going to take these cases anymore, and I decided not to. It was a cure that didn't work." [59]

In the end, the National Breast Cancer Coalition, the largest advocacy group for breast cancer patients, felt forced to issue a position paper warning that hospitals, oncologists, and certain corporations had a financial interest in promoting this unproven treatment: "Unfortunately, based on early and limited studies, many oncologists have strongly recommended the treatment to patients with metastatic breast cancer outside of clinical trials," the coalition cautioned. "Eventually, women with non-metastatic, but very high-risk early breast cancer were encouraged to get the treatment as well. At $80,000 to $200,000 per treatment, hospitals, oncologists, and even private corporations brought in huge revenues. . . . For years, many women were told that it was their only hope for survival, although no one really knew if the treatment worked.

"Hospitals and the oncology community should recognize that they have a financial stake in [this procedure]," the coalition added, "and may not be in a position to make unbiased assessments of the research and of the future use of this treatment." [60]

A Solution to the Medicare Crisis? But No Quick Fix

If you believe the Dartmouth research which says that one in three health care dollars is wasted, the conclusion is inescapable: the real reason Medicare appears to be headed for bankruptcy is not because the nation is graying, nor even simply because the cost of new technology is skyrocketing. *The problem lies not in the cost of progress, but in the way we are using—and overusing—that technology* in a money-driven system where device makers, drugmakers, some hospitals, and even some doctors all seem to be selling something—and selling hard.

Over the long run, aging boomers will hike Medicare spending, but they don't have to break the bank. As noted earlier, the aging of a generation born over nearly two decades (1946–1964) is, by definition, a slow process. Health care costs are ballooning far faster than the boomers are shriveling: the aging of the population is not the prime force propelling health care inflation.

In fact, the boomers are just beginning to push sixty. We have time to save Medicare, says Princeton economist Uwe Reinhardt, and the Darmouth research could provide the key: "If the gradual aging of the U.S. population over the next three decades could be accompanied by a gradual switch in medical practice styles from those now preferred in the high-cost regions to the more conservative practice styles preferred in the lower-cost regions (such as Wisconsin, Minnesota, and Oregon)," then, Reinhardt suggests, "the United States might be able to manage the impact of its retiring baby-boom generation."[61]

That said, learning how to practice medicine the way they do in Minnesota is a little harder than learning how to make bagels the way they do in Manhattan. As Jack Wennberg observed in an address to The New York Academy of Medicine in January of 2005, the Dartmouth research provides only a "provisional answer to the question of when and where more care is or isn't better care. . . .

"In most parts of the country, we probably have an excess capacity of both physicians and hospital beds, in terms of what is most beneficial for the population, but we don't know what the supply of specialists, particularly surgeons, *should* be. We know what the supply is now, and we know that it's fully utilized, everywhere, no matter how much there is."[62]

In the end, the only way to weed out the excess is by taking a long, hard look at scientific evidence of what works and what doesn't. This will require researchers willing to accept the fact that not a few oxen will be gored in the process. And it will take time. Thoughtful investigators recognize the danger that outcomes research, which compares how patients fare under different regimens, could turn into an entrepreneurial industry that produces Instamatic report cards:

Snapshots of medical data can lead to suboptimal policy decisions, warns Mark Fendrick, a professor of internal medicine at the University of Michigan. He paraphrases sports announcer Vin Scully: "The data's utility resembles the benefit a drunk derives from a lamppost in the dark, 'support, not illumination.' "[63]

In-depth analysis of medical outcomes requires long-term risk-adjusted clinical trials. Even then, medicine will always be plagued by uncertainty. "Much of medical practice remains in gray areas without unambiguous scientific evidence and is likely to remain so for quite some time, warn researchers from the Center for Studying Health System Change, a Washington-based research group that has been tracking U.S. health care markets for a decade. Hard choices about competing social resource uses and social values in the face of irreducible uncertainty lie ahead. Better data on quality and effectiveness would improve the knowledge base underlying these choices, but the choices will be hard in any case."[64]

In other words, not only is this a long-term project, it will take leadership. "Academic medical centers should make this a top priority." says Jack Wennberg, "but there is no money and no prestige in evaluating how science plays out in everyday practice."[65] Nevertheless, at 71, Wennberg remains passionately, doggedly determined to get to the bottom of variations in care. And if he has not found final answers, the Dartmouth project has at last succeeded in focusing attention on the need to distinguish between "more care" and "more effective care." Today, Jack Wennberg no longer seems a voice in the wilderness.

"For too long, we have substituted volume for a measure of quality," says Dr. Ralph Horwitz, dean of Cleveland's Case Western Reserve University School of Medicine.[66] Karen Davis, president of The Commonwealth Fund, an independent foundation that supports health research, agrees: "In the past the idea that high quality means high costs [has been] a matter of faith in the United States. Indeed, our health care system is perceived to be the best in the world in part because we spend more than any other country.

Yet startling new evidence suggests the absence of a systematic relationship between cost and quality." [67]

Making It Happen—"The Will to Excellence"

Dr. Donald Berwick, cofounder of the Institute for Healthcare Improvement, goes a step further, calling the Dartmouth research "the most important work that's been done in this area. . . . There's a big agenda here," he declares. "To help create a public awareness that 'more is not necessarily better.' Frequently it's worse. I have said it before and I'll stand behind it," he proclaimed in January of 2005: "The waste level in American medicine approaches 50%." [68]

Make no mistake: Berwick is outbidding the Dartmouth suggestion that one in three health care dollars is wasted. He is saying that fully half of the over $2 trillion that we spend on health care does nothing to relieve pain. To the contrary, says Berwick: "Much of it adds to suffering." [69]

Berwick's opinion matters. In 2005 *Modern Healthcare,* a leading industry publication, named him the third most powerful person in American health care. A clinical professor of pediatrics and health care policy at the Harvard School of Public Health, Berwick runs the Institute for Healthcare Improvement (IHI), a nonprofit organization that spearheads pilot projects aimed at providing more effective care. In contrast to the others on *Modern Healthcare*'s list, Berwick "is not powerful because of the position he holds," notes Boston surgeon Atul Gawande. (Former secretary of Health and Human Services Tommy Thompson ranked no. 1, while Thomas Scully, the head of Medicare and Medicaid Services, captured the second slot.) "Berwick is powerful," Gawande explains, "because of how he thinks." [70]

At 57, Berwick is a soft-spoken, spellbinding orator. Over the past 13 years, his keynote addresses at IHI's annual National Forum on Quality Improvement first became legend, and later, a book *(Escape Fire: Designs for the Future of Health Care).* His style is colloquial, intimate, and absolutely riveting—probably because his thinking is as passionate as it is original.

Since 1995 IHI's Breakthrough series has targeted problems like asthma care or safety in coronary surgery, and then invited teams of medical workers from hundreds of hospitals to collaborate in "results-oriented, clock-ticking projects," which may last six months or a year. Berwick describes the process: "A hundred teams working to improve cardiac surgery outcomes, 70 teams working to reduce Emergency Room waits, 160 teams working on better pharmacy use—guided by teams of faculty from around the country or around the world, meeting regularly in learning sessions that are diagrammed here [at IHI] and going home, sharing what they're learning, combing back together here, sharing again."

About half of the organizations that participate achieve true breakthroughs. He gives a few examples: "York Hospital in York, Pennsylvania, reduced the inappropriate use of ICU bed days by 90 percent, from 35 percent to fewer then 3 percent, in one year. A team at Lawrence General Hospital in Lawrence, Massachusetts, reduced cesarean section rates by more than 30 percent in one year, without compromising maternal and infant outcomes . . . Nash Health Care Systems in Rocky Mount, North Carolina, nearly abolished ventilator-associated pneumonia."[71]

Berwick's vision is generous: progress comes through collaboration, not competition. And he absolutely believes that a sufficient number of doctors, nurses, technicians, and health care executives possess the will and imagination to transform our health care system through "continuous quality improvement."

"It will not happen because someone buys right, or pays right, or judges right," Berwick told his audience at the Forum on Quality Improvement in 1993. "It will happen if and only if we, the people in this room, decide to make it happen." Five years later he could cite dozens of cases where IHI's Breakthrough program had made a difference: "The local gains are big: a clinic reduces its waiting times by 80 percent; a hospital reduces its unnecessary use of albumen by 95 percent; a nursing unit cuts medication errors in half. This is good stuff. But," Berwick admitted, "it is not enough. Not nearly enough. The system as a whole remains stuck."

Since then IHI's initiatives continue to save lives, yet progress remains episodic, confined to pockets of the system. Nevertheless, nine years later, when Berwick once again addressed the National Forum on Quality Improvement in Health Care, it was clear that his passion had not been broken. He continues to believe that within the health care professions, there are enough like-minded people to create a revolution: "The will to excellence is present everywhere in health care," Berwick declared. "The will to do well— the quest for pride, the joy of achievement, the warmth of serving—these are natural capital, human traits. Not of all human nature, not all of the time, but enough, plenty enough. We can waste them and we can deplete them . . . But the will to have pride in work is not scarce; it is everywhere abundant."[72]

Some would say that Berwick has lost touch with the times. In the waning decades of the 20th century, the notion that pride in a job well done drives excellence was dismissed by a new wave of economists as simply sentimental. People are motivated, we were told, by financial incentives. If we want a CEO to perform, a seven-figure salary is not enough; we must give him a bonus. In this context, Berwick may well sound naive. Yet it is difficult to find anyone in the health care industry who wants to call him that. The sheer authenticity of his presence commands tremendous respect.

Hazardous Waste

When Berwick talks about "the phenomenal waste" in our health care system, his expertise extends well beyond his credentials as a doctor and scientist. In 1999 painful first-hand experience confirmed what Don Berwick had known until then only in theory.

It happened suddenly. In early March, Berwick recalls, his wife, Ann, an environmental lawyer, "competed in a 28 kilometer cross-country ski race in Alaska. Two months later she couldn't walk across our bedroom." She had been struck down by a rare and serious autoimmune spinal cord problem. From April to September she would be hospitalized six times. Over the course of the summer, the pain grew, she lost her ability to walk, and ultimately, became a prisoner of her own bed. Worst of all, "for most of that time," says Berwick, "nobody could tell us exactly what was happening or what her prognosis was."[73]

Ann was treated in what Berwick describes as "three of the finest hospitals in our nation," and he stresses that throughout their ordeal, he was impressed by the "goodwill, kindness, generosity and commitment of the many nurses, doctors, technicians, housekeepers, dieticians, volunteers and aides of all sorts" who cared for his wife. Nevertheless, he says, the system failed them. "Put very, very simply, the people work well, by and large, but the system often does not. Above all," he says, "we needed safety—yet Ann was unsafe. The errors were not rare; they were the norm."

Don Berwick began his career in medical quality control in the eighties when the Harvard Community Health Plan made him vice president of quality improvement measures. By the mideighties he was so frustrated that he almost quit his job. In 1991 he cofounded IHI. So by the time his wife became ill in 1999, he knew the system's shortcomings all too well. As a result, what he witnessed while sitting at her bedside day after day for two months "did not actually surprise me," Berwick acknowledges. "But it did shock me." To read about medical errors is one thing; to experience them triggers a more visceral response.

He offers a few mind-bending examples. When Ann was admitted to one hospital, the neurologist told them: "By no means should you be getting anticholinergic agents [drugs that block or oppose the action of acetylcholine, a substance that is involved in the transmission of nerve impulses in the body]." A medication with profound anticholinergic side effects was given that afternoon.

At another hospital, "the attending neurologist told us by phone that a critical and potentially toxic drug should be started immediately," Berwick recalls. "He said, 'Time is of the essence.' That was on Thursday morning at 10 a.m. The first dose was given sixty hours later—on Saturday night at 10 p.m. Nothing I could do, nothing I did, nothing I could think of made any difference. It nearly drove me mad."

A physician himself, Berwick still could not make the system work, even for his own wife. And he realized that if he pushed too hard, there could be repercussions. "Time and again, Ann and I were migrating to the edge of the label 'difficult patient.' " If that label stuck, Berwick knew, the system might well take it out on Ann.

The list of errors mounts: When Ann was admitted to one hospital, the doctor ordered that she should no longer receive Colace [a laxative]. Nevertheless, the nurse brought Colace every single evening for the 14 days that Ann spent at that institution.

In another case, Ann was supposed to receive five intravenous doses of a very toxic chemotherapy, but dose three was labeled dose two. For half a day, no record could be found that dose two had been given, "even though," Berwick recalls, "I had watched it drip in myself. I told the nurse. She just assumed I was wrong. If I had been 10 years old, she would have been patting me on the head, saying, 'I know, I know, don't worry, honey.' I almost wanted to grab her by the lapels and say, 'Listen! I know something!' " (The nurse eventually checked the record, and discovered that he was right.)[74]

In all, during the 60 days that Ann spent in three hospitals, "no day passed—not one—without a medication error," says Berwick. "Most weren't serious. But they scared us."

Talking to the roughly 50 physicians involved in Ann's case proved equally disconcerting. From the outset it was clear that the doctors did not talk to one another—or read one another's records. "Drugs tried and proven futile in one admission would be recommended in the next as if they were fresh ideas," says Berwick. "Complex, serial information on blood counts, temperature, functional status and weight"—the very information that was being used to make risky and expensive decisions—"was collected in disorganized, narrative formats, embedded in nursing notes and daily forms.

"As far as I know, the only person who ever drew a graph of Ann's fevers or blood cell counts was me," Berwick reports. "As a result, physicians often reached erroneous conclusions, such as assuming that Ann had improved after a specific treatment, when in fact she had improved before it, or not at all.

"We needed continuity," he continues. "Ann's story was extremely complex and evolved over many weeks." Yet each hospital where Ann was treated seemed, to Berwick, a "Tower of Babel," with each doctor speaking his own language and relying on his own judgment.

Berwick values the individual physician's autonomy—but only up to a point. "A system fundamentally committed to autonomy places the individual doctor's mind between the patient and the best knowledge anywhere," he observes. "I would place a commitment to excellence—standardization to the best-known method—above clinician autonomy as a rule for care."

But in our medical culture, too many physicians see themselves as Lone Rangers. "The problem goes back to the way we train doctors," says an executive at one of New York City's most respected hospitals. "We teach them to be solo operators. If you're a resident and you're not sure what to do, you don't call the senior attending physician. That would suggest incompetence."[75]

Because they did not collaborate, most of Ann's physicians approached her as if they were the first to see her. "We often felt that the only real memories in the system were ours," Berwick recalls. "Times of transition were especially trying. On one first of the month the new attending physician walked into Ann's room, introduced himself, and asked cheerfully, "So how long have you had MS?"

Ann did not have MS, nor had anyone ever suggested that she did.

Unfortunately, Berwick knows that his experience was not unique. He recalls a senior health care executive recounting his own ordeal when his wife's mother spent 60 days as an inpatient, and a physician new to the case began suggesting treatment options. One by one "we rejected them," the executive recalled, "because every one had been tried previously with no positive results and often adverse consequences." Finally, the physician, still jovial, made a suggestion: "Maybe I should read the chart!"[76]

What Must the Average Hospital Be Like?

At the end of Ann's hospital odyssey, Berwick recalls, "We received the bills. They were covered by our insurance, for which we are immensely grateful." But still, Berwick understood that at the end of the day, we all pay everyone else's hospital bills—through taxes or higher insurance premiums—and so he was interested in the details.

"Remember the Colace that was discontinued but brought anyway?" he asks. "There it is pill by pill, charges for all the days on which the nurse opened the unneeded packet and threw it in the garbage . . . Radiology charges of $155 per film for second readings of fourteen films transferred from one hospital to another."

Why couldn't the hospitals share their readings? Because in a market-driven system, hospitals are not collaborators, they are competitors, and every hospital needs every reimbursement that it can get. But it is not even that most would object to sharing the information; it is just that the system is not set up that way. Hospital records do not talk to each other.

Then there were the tests: "MRI scans over and over again for $1,700, $2,000, $2,200 per procedure. Ann's case has been billed at perhaps $150,000, so far, at a minimum," Berwick reported a few months after she had been released from the last hospital at the end of 1999. "And the bare fact is that of all that enormous investment, a remarkably small percentage—half at best, probably much less—stood any chance at all of helping her. The rest has been pure waste. Even while simpler needs—for a questioned answered, information explained, a word of encouragement, or just good and nourishing food—have gone unmet.

"Not all of these flaws in care were equally present in all of the hospitals," says Berwick. "But some of these defects existed everywhere, and this was in some of the best hospitals in America. . . . We are causing harm and we need to stop it.

"The people [in the hospital] know this," he adds. "Not just the people in the beds, but the people doing the work too. The doctors and nurses and technicians and managers and pharmacists and all the rest know—they must know—the truth. They see it every day, and even if their defensive routines no longer permit them to say what they see, they do see it: errors, delays, and nonsensical variation, lack of communication, misinformation."

Ann Berwick was to be one of the lucky ones. Slowly, she recovered. Two years after she left the hospital she was once again able to walk, though she was still in pain. The cause of her illness remained a mystery. Had the hospital care helped her? No one knew.

"If I had stayed in a lovely hotel and been waited on hand and foot for three months, maybe I would have gotten better faster," Ann confides. "It would have been more pleasant, much cheaper, and more fun. I had two really major medical interventions. They may have saved my life or maybe were just terribly invasive and didn't do anything."[77] Perhaps her body had healed itself. What is important is that her story has a miraculous ending: by 2005 her illness had virtually disappeared.

Don Berwick does not blame the hospitals that treated his wife for failing to diagnose a confounding disease. Modern science has not (and almost certainly never will) crack the code of all illnesses. His complaint is not that the system did too little but that it did too much, putting his wife through the serial ordeal of painful, ineffective, and redundant treatments that, in his view, stood "no chance at all" of helping her. But it is not just that these hospitals couldn't cure her. They didn't care for her:

"On at least three occasions Ann waited alone for over an hour, cold and frightened on a gurney in the waiting area outside an MRI unit in a subbasement in the middle of the night," Berwick recalls. Another time, "an emergency room visit for a diagnostic spinal tap that should have taken two hours evolved in an eleven-hour ordeal of constant delay." On yet another occasion, "my wife had a surgical procedure and awoke in the recovery room, asking for me. I was not permitted to join her for almost ninety minutes, even though she repeatedly asked that I be allowed to comfort her.

"If what happened to Ann could happen in our best institutions," Berwick adds, "I wonder more than ever before what the average must be like."

"For a Few Procedures, We Are the Best on Earth"

Berwick's testimony is striking because he is known for his optimism. As Dr. Frank Davidoff, IHI's executive editor, points out, Berwick has turned quality improvement in medicine on its ear by avoiding "the blame game," and shifting the focus "to a process of continuously learning from errors ('every defect is a treasure')."[78] But when the conversation turns to waste, Berwick pulls no punches:

"Let's start with the basics," he told his audience at the 14th annual National Forum on Quality Improvement in Health Care in December of 2002. "America spends 40 percent more dollars per capita on its health care than the next most expensive nation, and twice as much as most. For this glut of funding, it gets nowhere near the top health status in the world—we are maybe tenth, or twentieth, depending on how you count it."

It is not just that uninsured and underinsured Americans lack access to care. When it comes to treating specific conditions, he explains, other countries often do a better job: "For a few procedures, we are the best on Earth, but not for most. At a lower cost—far lower cost—many other nations and health care systems get better end-of-life care, better mental health care, better infant mortality rates, better asthma control, better physical rehabilitation, better primary prevention, and much more comprehensive primary care than we do. In cystic fibrosis outcomes we are not the best in the world. We are number two. Denmark is number one."[79] "When compared to the U.K., Australia, New Zealand, and Canada," he adds, "we are worst among these five countries in kidney transplant survival; we are second worst in colon cancer survival."[80]

And when it comes to controlling pain, we lag countries that invest far more in palliative care.[81] A 1999 IHI study measured how long terminally ill patients had to wait after being admitted to a hospital before receiving their first dose of pain medication. The wait averaged 110 minutes. "The number haunts me," Berwick says. "Have you ever been in severe pain? Pain that you feared would not go away? Can you imagine lying on a gurney in an emergency room in pain, as an 'expected admission' [someone who the hospital knew was coming], there for relief of your pain, and having 110 minutes tick by before your first dose? Sometimes, instead of a speech, I think I will just tell that story, and then sit quietly with my audience for 110 minutes, waiting."[82]

Berwick knows that this is hard to hear. For decades we have been told that we have the best health care system in the world. It is not just that we take pride in that reputation; it makes us feel safe. But as a doctor, Berwick recognizes that the dangers his wife and other patients face are real, and that the system cannot be mended unless we face up to the harsh fact that "today in the United States of America, even those with insurance cannot count on receiving high-quality care. Most, if they are sick enough for long enough, will experience and suffer from poor quality—not just errors, but poor quality."[83]

Privately, many physicians in the field agree. "The public doesn't care because most people are not sick," says an oncologist who practices at one of the best hospitals in southern California. "And so they don't realize what is happening to people who are sick—what they're going through. It is only when they, or a loved one, becomes seriously ill that they begin to realize." And then it is too late. Meanwhile, the system rigidly resists change and unleashes the fury of its immune system on any internal critics. "If you use my name," the oncologist adds, "this will end my career."[84]

Yet Berwick remains unabashedly, quixotically hopeful. In truth, his hope is pragmatic. He believes that we have no choice: this is a problem that must be solved. Berwick can sustain that hope because he knows, as he told his audience in 2002, we are working not "from scarcity" but "from plenty."

Both in terms of financial capital and in terms of human capital, the United States is lucky. We have more than enough. "To say that we spend 15 percent of our gross domestic product on health care and that that is not enough—that that is scarcity—is ridiculous," says Berwick. "It is dishonest. We have enough. We have plenty. What we lack is not social resources; it is honesty."[85]

"A Vast Cultural Delusion"

When it comes to taking an honest look at the hazardous waste in our health care industry, nearly everyone agrees that a good place to begin is with the medical arms race described in chapter 2. Today dueling institutions spend millions on the latest diagnostic tools—even while admitting that they are merely duplicating services that other hospitals in their community already offer.

Lucas County, Ohio, for example, boasts more than 250 magnetic resonance imaging (MRI) units. "We always joke that it's surprising your car doesn't start veering if you're driving on Monroe or Secor, there are so many magnets out there," Dr. Peter Royen, a radiologist and medical director of Regency Imaging Center in Toledo, says, chuckling. Dr. Kenneth Bertka, a Toledo family physician and past president of the Ohio Academy of Family Physicians is decidedly less enthusiastic: "We don't need this many MRI scanners in Toledo; there's no question about that." [86]

Meanwhile, nationwide, supply seems to stimulate demand: in 2005 spending on imaging services and new machines added an estimated $100 billion to our national health care bill—up from $80 billion in 2003. [87]

Both patients and physicians find it hard to resist the lure of tomorrow's technology. We are drawn to the newest inventions because we believe, almost as an article of faith, that more advanced technology equals greater certainty. After all, high-tech diagnostic technologies offer up hard-and-fast data, fostering the illusion that the physician has vanquished medicine's ambiguity.

But in truth, advanced diagnostic tools, like earlier tools, can miss critical information. The problem is not the technology, but how we interpret the data. The more refined the technology, the more likely it is to produce false positives (suggesting that the patient is sick when he isn't). Some observers even suggest that the newest and most sophisticated tools are more likely to produce false negatives (wrongly concluding that no disease is present), simply because doctors accept the results so readily. [88]

Misplaced confidence in tests may help to explain why, when patients die in the hospital, autopsies reveal major misdiagnosis about 40 percent of the time, according to three studies done in 1998 and 1999. "For example, the attending physician may have been treating a person for heart disease when the real problem was cancer, or vice-versa," former *JAMA* editor George Lundberg explains. And in about one-third of those cases the patient would have been expected to live if proper treatment had been administered. [89]

Calling our blind faith in bleeding-edge technology a "vast cultural delusion," Lundberg, who trained as a pathologist, buttresses his argument with a stunning fact: despite extensive use of modern diagnostic imaging techniques, autopsy studies reveal that misdiagnosis of terminally ill patients has not improved since at least 1938. [90]

A physician's first impulse is to say that this can't be right. There must be some mistake. "With all the recent advances in imaging and diagnostics, it's hard to accept that we not only get the diagnosis wrong in two out of five of our patients who die, but that we have also failed to improve over time," confesses Boston surgeon Atul Gawande. He describes how a group of doctors at Harvard decided to do a study to see if this really could be true:

"They went back into their hospital records to see how often autopsies picked up missed diagnoses in 1969 and 1970, before the advent of CT ultrasound nuclear scanning and other technologies, and then in 1980, after those technologies became widely used," Gawande reports. And to their dismay, "the researchers found no improvement. Regardless of the decade, physicians missed a quarter of fatal infections, a third of heart attacks and almost two-thirds of pulmonary emboli in their patients who died.

"In most cases," he adds, "it wasn't technology that failed. Rather the physician did not consider the correct diagnosis in the first place. The perfect test or scan may have been available, but the physician never ordered it.[91] Instead, he ordered another test—and believed it.

"We get this all the time," says Bill Pellan of Florida's Pinellas-Pasco County Medical Examiner's Office. "The doctor will get our report and call and say: 'But there can't be a lacerated aorta. We did a whole set of scans.'

"We have to remind him we held the heart in our hands."[92]

End-of-Life Care: Doctors Are Not Trained to Listen

All too often, hospitals employ some of their most sophisticated tools crudely, even callously, in futile end-of-life care. While roughly 80 percent of all Americans hope to die at home, 75 percent end their lives in hospitals or nursing homes. Of those, a third die after 10 days in an ICU.[93] This helps explain why roughly one-quarter of all Medicare dollars are spent during the final year of a patient's life, thanks in part to the cost of drugs and devices that prolong not just life but pain and suffering.

End-of-life treatment can be relentless, says Dr. Ellen Fox, director of the National Center for Ethics in Health Care at the Veterans Health Administration, because doctors are trained "to assume that diseases demand treatment, an assumption that applies even to treatments that are unlikely to work, as in the case with experimental chemotherapy and cardiopulmonary resuscitation. As long as any possibility of recovery remains on the horizon, no matter how remote, it is assumed that continued treatment is the right path to follow. And once the wheels of 'Doctor Think' are in motion, it acquires a momentum that is difficult to restrain." [94]

"The problem, of course, is that we don't know who is in their last year," says Mount Sinai's Dr. Diane Meier, a palliative care specialist who has devoted her career to treating the terminally ill. "The fact that we spend so much on these patients in what often turns out to be the final months of their life is not necessarily a bad thing," she adds. "These are the sickest people, who need the most sophisticated care. *We shouldn't say, 'We're wasting money on the dying.' But,*" she adds *"we should be asking: 'Is this the best care? Is it appropriate care?' "* (emphasis mine) [95]

For many, palliative care offers a middle road between pulling out all the stops and giving up hope. Like hospice care, palliative care focuses on comfort rather than cure, emphasizing pain management and easing the emotional trauma of facing death, both for the patient and for his family. But there are important differences: in contrast to traditional hospice care, palliative care includes procedures aimed at treating the symptoms of the disease. In the past, says Meier, physicians have seen caring for a terminally ill patient as an either/or situation: "Either we are doing everything possible to try to prolong your life—or when there is 'nothing more that we can do,' only then do we make the switch to providing comfort measures. This dichotomous notion—that you can do one thing alone and then the other thing alone later—has nothing to do with the reality of what patients and their families go through."

For example, a palliative care team "would offer dialysis to a patient like Lew Silverman, in order to hear what he wants," says Meier. "But if the patient didn't want it, we wouldn't do it. And we would help the daughter negotiate with the hospital system as the patient's advocate. Palliative care is about making patient and family aware of their options—and the limits to their options—sitting down and talking to them, while listening to their hopes and fears."

Why do doctors continue to intervene, even when a patient like Lew Silverman makes it clear that he no longer wants to be poked and prodded?

Doctors are taught to view death as the ultimate enemy: "Defeating death at any cost—that is the priority. It comes ahead of reducing suffering, or considering the quality of the patient's life," says Meier. "If you look at NIH funding," she points out, "you see that is where the money goes—to cure cancer, to prevent all heart disease and stroke."[96]

"This is why it has been so much easier to find money to search for a cure for cancer than to find money for better palliative and home care for those suffering with terminal cancer," adds medical ethicist Daniel Callahan. "In the face of budgetary pressures, the care of the chronically ill of all ages—those who are proof against the miracles of medicine—have trouble gaining adequate support. . . . The caring function of medicine, once its center, has been displaced to the sidelines," he observes. "It is not a major source of money, prestige or research awards."[97]

Meanwhile, physicians have been trained to *do* whatever can be done, says the VA's Dr. Ellen Fox: "Doctors like to fix whatever is fixable, and as a result, many patients die in intensive care units with their blood chemistries in perfect order. Insofar as doctors view patients as puzzles to be solved, they can be remarkably vested in finding information for its own sake, regardless of whether new information will alter a particular patient's circumstances. . . .

"I recall a patient with widely disseminated lung cancer and confirmed metastases to the brain who was admitted to the hospital when he could no longer care for himself at home due to progressive confusion," she continues. "A brain scan was performed revealing a new and unexplained lesion near the nasal septum. An ear, nose and throat specialist was immediately consulted, and he recommended a biopsy be performed to explain the new radiological finding. The various doctors involved in the case seemed to share an overwhelming desire to find out the nature of the unexplained lesion, even though doing so would be of no benefit to the patient."[98]

Sometimes, too, physicians focus on what they *can* do—order another test, another round of chemo, recommend another surgery—as a way of circumventing the impossibly sad conversation about what they can't do.

"It's hard for a doctor to say, 'I'm sorry I don't know of any treatment that will help you'," explains Harvard's Dr. Jerry Avorn, who trained as a geriatrician. "After all, most of us went into medicine because of our desire to help people who are suffering, and our eagerness to use science to do so. Admitting that we aren't aware of anything useful for a given problem means we fail on both counts."

As a geriatrician, Avorn recognizes that in some cases, what a patient like Lew Silverman needs most of all is simply a physician willing to listen. "During my training in primary care," Avorn remembers, "a wise clinician once said, 'One of the best and hardest things to put into practice . . . is the precept "Don't just do something—sit there!" ' " [99]

But doctors are not trained to listen. Their impulse, by instinct and education, is to intervene. And hospitals are organized around that assumption.

Nor Are They Paid to Listen

In truth, it is not only that physicians are not trained to listen; they are not paid to have long conversations. "Unfortunately, American medicine has come to rely much more on diagnostic testing than on knowledge and cognitive thinking," Dr. Bob LeBow, the former head of three community health centers in Idaho, wrote in 2002. "And this makes economic sense," he added, "since reimbursements for diagnostic tests are much better than for cognitive efforts . . . 'Thinking clinicians' might get reimbursed $35 for talking to a patient for half an hour about multiple medical problems, but pass a tube to somebody's stomach (it can be done in ten minutes) and the payment can be $900. Illogical, but that's our system." [100]

Perhaps it should come as no surprise that the current payment system was devised by a practitioner of the dismal science—William Hsiao, an economist from Harvard. To be fair, when Hsiao was commissioned in 1985 to measure the amount of work involved in the thousands of treatments that doctors provide, he faced a Herculean (not to mention thankless) task. In an effort to rationalize the process, Hsiao decided that work should be measured not just in terms of the time it took to perform the procedure, but by the mental effort and judgment involved, the technical skill and physical effort required, and the stress entailed.

Usefulness was not on his list. But he did factor in overhead and the cost of training to learn how to perform the task at hand.

After interviewing thousands of doctors, Hsiao's team determined that cataract surgery involves slightly less work than performing a hysterectomy on a woman with cervical cancer, but nearly five times as much work as offering 45 minutes of psychotherapy to a patient suffering from a panic attack. The hysterectomy takes only about twice as much time as the session of pychotherapy, yet Hsiao's team reckoned that the surgery demands four times as much mental effort, is nearly five times as risky (a measure of stress), and requires five times as much technique and physical effort. (Though one might speculate that listening to anguished patients suffering from panic attacks, severe depression, and obsessive-compulsive disorders, day in day out, week after week, could take a comparable toll on a doctor's mind, body, and soul.)

In 1992 Medicare adopted Hsiao's fee schedule, and before long, private insurers followed suit.[101] That schedule is not carved in stone: a subsequent commission has fine-tuned the amount of work involved in more than 6,000 services, and the master schedule will no doubt always remain a work in progress, rather like a cathedral that outlives its original architects. But Hsiao laid out the basic parameters for measuring the value of a physician's services.

Ironically, Hsiao himself had intended to try to redistribute some of the wealth from surgeons to GPs. When he finished his work, he predicted that family doctors would get a 60 percent raise from Medicare, while heart surgeons would see their income cut in half. But once his formulas were applied, it didn't work out that way: an analysis by the federal Physician Payment Review Commission found that in the first six months of the new program, average Medicare fees paid to family physicians rose just 10 percent while surgeons' fees fell 8 percent.[102]

"The problem with the system is that it is still so weighted toward doing procedures—and it's so easy to make out like a bandit—that almost inevitably, we do too many procedures," says Dr. Elliott Fisher. "I think we need to get to a reimbursement system that rewards doctors for overall health outcomes, rather than paying them for piecework. Ideally, doctors would be on salary, plus a bonus for better outcomes. That way," he explains, "cardiologists would be rewarded for getting involved in efforts to persuade their patients to stop smoking."[103]

But today counseling patients is a low-margin activity. For instance, "when a palliative care team spends 90 minutes in a meeting with a family, Medicare would probably pay $130 to $140—for all three people," says Mount Sinai's Meier. "And Medicare is one of the better payers." This explains why Meier earns $100 for every several thousand dollars that her husband, an invasive cardiologist, takes home. "Though," Meier says mildly, "it would be hard to say that one of us is practicing more sophisticated medicine."[104] Both are operating on the frontiers of medical science. Perhaps the biggest difference is this: her patients are dying, his are anesthetized.

The ICU

Talking to the families of the dying is a major part of Meier's job, and one that some physicians avoid at all costs—especially in the intensive care unit, says Dr. Liz Dreesen, a surgeon who spent the late nineties doing double duty as medical director of the ICU at a hospital in Lincolnton, North Carolina, a small mill town near Charlotte. "A lot of doctors schedule their ICU rounds at 6 a.m. or midnight, when the families aren't there," Dreesen confides, "so that they don't have to talk to them about the big issues—the decisions that are hardest for the family of a terminally ill patient." [105]

Unless a doctor is trained in palliative care, he may not be comfortable with those end-of-life discussions, says Dreesen. "If he does run into the family, the easiest thing to say is, 'Do you want us to do everything possible for grandma?' That's much easier than saying: 'There are various places where we can draw the line . . . ' It takes a lot of time to explain those lines. But you're not going to be paid to have those conversations; you'll probably make more just billing every day for a critical care visit."

Often the situation is complicated by disagreements within the family. "Middle-aged children may be especially reluctant to let elderly parents slip away," says Kenneth Boyd, a medical ethicist from the University of Edinburgh in Scotland. He points to a study published in the *Journal of the American Geriatrics Society,* which showed that most offspring "believed that medications, food and fluids should be continued," and a quarter "wanted to initiate resuscitation, mechanical respiration and dialysis" for their terminally ill parents—*even when it was not what the parents had wished, nor what the offspring would wish for themselves.*" (emphasis mine) [106]

The death of a parent can be most difficult for a middle-aged child to accept, Boyd suggests, because "it is in middle age, when awareness of one's mortality surfaces, that the fear of death is strongest." In the years that follow, most adults make their peace with their own mortality. As a result, he points out, "The elderly are no more afraid of death than people in other age groups." But in middle age, letting go of the dying parent means looking over the edge of the cliff, "losing the ambiguous parental buffer which lies (sometimes literally) between death and themselves." [107]

Following the family's request, Dreesen often found herself putting feeding tubes into demented, unconscious patients who would never leave the hospital. "In many cases, I felt it was the wrong thing to do," she confesses. "Sometimes it was hard because the patients were so contracted and curled up in a fetal position—it was hard to get them to lie flat enough to do it . . ." Nevertheless, she did it because "this was what the family wanted," sometimes out of a moral conviction that life should be preserved at all cost—a conviction that Dreesen would not question. But in other cases, the family requested extraordinary lifesaving measures because no one had laid out the alternatives or discussed the pros and cons of each option.

"The idea of grandma starving to death sounds terrible," Dreesen acknowledges. "The family would rather say that she died from an infection. But there is more and more evidence in the hospice literature that you can do things to make a patient who isn't taking food or water comfortable. You keep their lips moist with Vaseline; you give them something moist to suck on. From what we can tell, they are not that uncomfortable."

By contrast, the patient who survives on the feeding tube may suffer for weeks. "The relatives agree to things without knowing what goes on in an ICU," says Dreesen. "They visit twice a day—as often as they can—before and after work. But if they spent one full day in the ICU and saw how many times patients get stuck for blood . . . How often they moan when you roll them over . . ."[108]

In the face of such suffering, there are no easy answers. But most observers would agree with palliative care specialist Diane Meier that "the choice belongs to the patient, not to the system."[109]

When the Technology Defines the Patient

In the end, perhaps the greatest hazard of the medical arms race is not the waste of health care dollars, but the danger that the heavy armament of high technology will obscure the physician's view of the patient. Frequently, the specialist is trained to see not the whole human being but the part that he can cure, through the prism of a diagnostic imaging machine, a new form of chemo, or an innovative surgical procedure.

In these cases, "diseases are defined in terms of the technologies we have to treat them," says Mark Hanson, a medical ethicist at The Hastings Center in Garrison, New York. He quotes Dr. Eric Cassell's seminal essay on medical technology, "The Sorcerer's Broom":

"Technologies came into being to serve the purposes of their users, but ultimately, the users redefine their goals in terms of the technology. . . . A saying that makes the point has become popular among physicians, 'To the man with a hammer, everything is a nail.' Doctors who have mastered a technology tend to use it as often as possible," he adds, "not necessarily for reasons of profit, but because they love their skills and technologies.

"This is not an antitechnology essay," Cassell stresses. "In medicine, one can no more be antitechnology than antiscience. There is no going back to a prescientific or nontechnological medicine—who would want to? The issue is how to solve the difficulty epitomized by Emerson's observation, 'Things are in the saddle and ride mankind.' Technology is not the problem; it is the relationship to it of those who employ it that is problematic." [110]

When the supply of tools at hand inspires medical decisions, the patient is redefined not in terms of what he needs, but in terms of what is technologically possible.

So Lew Silverman, a blind diabetic who could no longer walk with any confidence, was redefined as a kidney patient. Physicians had done all that they could to treat Lew Silverman's diabetes; they had run out of experimental treatments. Nor could they cure his despair. But they could treat his kidneys with dialysis. So someone called in a renal specialist, who, quite naturally, was eager to use the technology that he felt certain would work. Of course dialysis would do nothing to cure Silverman's larger medical problems.

The story illustrates what Dartmouth's Elliott Fisher describes as the one of the "unintended consequences" of having 10 or more specialists hovering over a single patient: "Because there are more diagnoses to treat and more treatments to provide, physicians may be more likely to be distracted from the issues of greatest concern to their patients." [111] In such cases, it's all too easy for the patient to get lost in the crowd.

6

"Too Little, Too Late": The Cost of Rationing Care

While well-insured Americans face the hazards of overdiagnosis and overtreatment, millions of uninsured patients routinely receive care that the Institute of Medicine describes as "too little, too late."[1] And in the long run, "too little, too late" proves expensive, not just for the patient—who may pay with his life—but for everyone in the health care system.

Who are the uninsured?

Recent surveys show that one in eight children has no insurance.[2] The majority live in low-income working households with barely enough money to meet the rent and pay for groceries.[3] In theory, the State Children's Health Insurance Program (SCHIP), passed by Congress in 1997, covers the thousands of children who fall through the holes of a catch-as-catch-can safety net. But "SCHIP entitles participating states, rather than children, to receive federal contributions for children's health assistance," leaving states "with broad discretion to define assistance in terms they deem most appropriate," notes *Health Affairs* editor John Iglehart.[4]

In other words, states can decide how much of the money to spend, depending on how much they are willing to match—and cash-strapped states have not always been generous. Many have made it difficult for eligible children and families to secure coverage by freezing SCHIP enrollments, raising premiums, and/or requiring parents to renew their application for SCHIP every six months.[5]

Florida, for example, froze SCHIP enrollment in July of 2003. By year-end, the waiting list of children who were deemed eligible but denied benefits had grown to 90,000. Some were seriously ill. When the media tumbled to the story, an embarrassed state legislature scrambled to approve a measure covering the 90,000 already on the list. At the same time, legislative leaders changed the rules of the game in a way that would sharply limit future enrollments. From that point forward, there would be only two 30-day windows each year during which parents could try to enroll their children in SCHIP. Moreover, the law stipulated, the state could, at any time, cancel even those enrollment periods "for budgetary reasons."

As for the tell-tale waiting list, legislative leaders solved that problem quite neatly: they did away with the list. "Politically, what that means is that nobody—not us, not you, not anyone—would be able at any point to say that 30,000 or 50,000 or 80,000 or 100,000 kids are on the waiting list because there would no longer be any record," observes Robert Greenstein, director of the Center on Budget and Policy Priorities.[6]

Uninsured vets are easier to count. In 2003, nearly 1.7 million U.S. veterans had no health insurance. Many had seen combat in Vietnam, the Gulf War, Afghanistan, or Iraq. Most were employed, but in many cases, either their employer didn't offer insurance or they couldn't afford it.[7]

Too young for Medicare, they were not eligible for Medicaid—either because they earned too much or because they didn't happen to have children. Under federal law, states are not required to offer Medicaid to childless adults under 65 unless they are pregnant, blind, or disabled. Some states do extend Medicare to these adults, but even in relatively open-handed states like New York, a childless adult who earned more than $9,570 in 2005 (the poverty threshold at the time) was considered "too rich" to qualify.

A few years earlier, these 1.7 million uninsured vets could have turned to a VA hospital or clinic for care, thanks to a bill signed by President Clinton in 1996, just three weeks before the presidential election, pledging to "furnish comprehensive medical services to all veterans."[8] But the bill did not require Congress to *fund* care for all veterans, and in January of 2003 Washington announced that it was no longer enrolling veterans in the system if their medical condition was not connected to their service, and/or they earned more than $25,000 a year.[9]

In the summer of 2005, as vets trickled home from Iraq, the number of uninsured U.S. veterans was moving closer to 2 million. For them "less care" would mean fewer opportunities. "The armed services are aggressive in encouraging people to join the military to serve their country and to 'be all you can be,' " says Dr. Sidney Wolfe, director of Public Citizen's Health Research Group. "But after leaving the service, veterans do not have the right to health care; in a way [they're] being discarded by the government after serving their country. Without access to health care, no one can be all that they can be."[10]

At Risk: 47 Million Plus

Those uninsured veterans represent just a fraction of the more than 47 million Americans who lacked coverage in 2005—and their ranks are swelling. From 1995 to 2003, the number of uninsured grew by 7 million—to 17.7 percent of the population under the age of 65. Economists project that by 2013 another 11 million Americans will be "going naked," bringing the total to 58 million, *or more than one-fifth of Americans under 65*. And these projections are based on the relatively optimistic assumption that in the years ahead, health care inflation will slow, while personal incomes rise twice as fast as in recent years, making insurance more affordable.[11]

Make no mistake, the uninsured are at risk. A 2003 study published in *Health Affairs* paints a stark portrait of a two-tier system. When care is measured in dollars, uninsured cancer patients under the age of 65 receive half as much care as those who have insurance. When researchers looked past the dollar value of the care to the services received, the results confirmed what spending patterns suggested: the uninsured are admitted to the hospital less often, see fewer physicians in their offices, and even log fewer emergency room visits.

At the same time, the uninsured pay more than twice as much out-of-pocket for their care. "They're paying more of their own money for the limited services that they do get," says Kenneth Thorpe, chairman of the health policy department at Emory University and the lead author on the cancer study, even though "the uninsured usually are treated at public hospitals and don't have access to some of the cancer specialists that are typically available to insured patients."[12]

And it's not just cancer patients. When it comes to a wide range of procedures, "we know that the uninsured receive about 60 percent as much care as the insured," says Thorpe. "In this study we focused on cancer because we wanted to see how much less care they receive even when they are very sick and their needs are very clear."[13]

But wait—if Dartmouth's Jack Wennberg is right, and up to one-third of health care dollars are squandered on ineffective or unproven treatments, is it really clear that those who receive less care are deprived of essential care?

Some economists point to the waste in the system to argue that "health care is an ordinary and not always very useful commodity," paving the way for the argument that health care is neither a right nor a necessity, but a discretionary item "of uncertain value," observes Evan M. Melhado, a professor at the University of Illinois College of Medicine. In that way, "they strip health care of the special character that, in the past, invested it with the importance typically accorded food, clothing and shelter," he says, and instead lump medical care together with luxury items like a brand-new SUV or a $40 steak.[14] Some people can afford them, some can't. Is a two-tier system really so bad?

Yes—if on the bottom tier patients receive less care than they need to survive. The "more care is not necessarily better care" argument applies only when a group of patients hits a very high plateau on the health care curve. On the way up to that point of diminishing returns, health care is as necessary as food, water, or shelter.

A 2003 study comparing mortality rates among insured and uninsured cancer patients makes the point painfully clear: uninsured cancer patients are 1.2 to 2.1 times more likely to die, depending on the type of cancer.[15] And this is just one of dozens of studies published in medical journals in recent years that demonstrate that the uninsured receive less preventive care, are diagnosed at more advanced stages of the disease, and once diagnosed, tend to receive less therapeutic care. In its 2002 report *Care Without Coverage* the Institute of Medicine observes that even "uninsured car crash victims receive less care in the hospital and have a 37 percent higher mortality rate than insured patients."

Overall, the institute notes, uninsured adults face a "25% greater risk of dying." That translates into 18,000 extra deaths among Americans under the age of 65 each year—about the same number as die of diabetes or stroke.[16]

Show Me the Money

Most Americans assume that hospital emergency rooms serve as the ultimate safety net for the uninsured, guaranteeing that when someone *really* needs care, he will get it. Unfortunately, that belief is grounded in faith, not fact. While federal law requires hospitals to "screen" and "stabilize" patients, it does not oblige the ER to treat them—as Michael Martinez discovered when he staggered into Denver Health medical center, one of Denver's two public hospitals, in April of 2003.

Martinez had been badly beaten. The doctor who saw him confirmed that he had three broken ribs and a fractured jaw. But the same doctor refused to give Martinez so much as a painkiller because the 38-year-old didn't have insurance, didn't have cash, and couldn't produce proof that he was a resident of Denver County. The fact that Martinez was a U.S. citizen did not give him a right to health care in Denver.[17]

Martinez's next stop was University of Colorado Hospital, the city's only other full-service public hospital. There, the nurse proved equally implacable: he'd have to pay up front before a doctor could fix his jaw.

By the time he arrived at the third hospital, Martinez was slurring his words through the clenched teeth that still clung to his shattered jaw. He was drooling because each swallow meant excruciating pain. His face muscles twitched.

"This time, they'll help me," he told himself as he walked toward the ER reception desk at the Rose Medical Center.

He got lucky. Dr. Donald Lefkowits recognized an emergency when he saw one. "This guy had been through the wringer," he recalls. "He was in obvious pain, and his pain was getting worse. He couldn't eat or drink because he couldn't open his mouth, so he was getting dehydrated. And he was starting to run a fever." The fever worried Lefkowits because he knew that given the injuries to his mouth and jaw, Martinez ran a real risk of infection—perhaps even in his jawbone, which could prove fatal.

"Was he going to die that night? Probably not," says Lefkowits. "But unless someone tended to his jaw, it was going to heal in a way that wouldn't allow him to eat properly unless he had it reset"—which would mean breaking the jaw again, then setting it.

Lefkowits got Martinez hooked up to an IV, gave him painkillers and paged the on-call oral surgeon. "I kept thinking to myself, 'There was this thing they called the Hippocratic oath. . . . ' "[18]

Isn't There a Law?

How could Denver's two public hospitals turn away a patient like Michael Martinez? What about the law that obliges *all* ERs—public or private, for-profit or not-for-profit—to at least stabilize the patient?

University Hospital and Denver Health were adhering to the letter if not the spirit of the federal Emergency Medical Treatment and Active Labor Act. Commonly called the antidumping law, EMTALA was created in 1986 to prevent hospitals from rejecting, transferring, or refusing to treat patients either because they are unable to pay or because they are covered under low-paying government programs such as Medicaid (the government program for the poor) or Medicare (which, depending on the procedure and the region, may also pay significantly less than a commercial insurer).

But while the law says that emergency rooms must screen everyone who walks through the door and "stabilize" those who need "emergency" care, the language of the act, like most legal language, is just precise enough to leave plenty of room for interpretation. According to EMTALA, an emergency is "a medical condition manifesting itself by acute symptoms of sufficient severity (including severe pain) such that the absence of immediate medical attention could reasonably be expected to result in—

i) placing the health of the individual (or with respect to a pregnant woman, the health of the woman or her unborn child) in serious jeopardy, or

ii) serious impairment to bodily functions, or

iii) serious dysfunction of any bodily organ or part."

As for a doctor's duty to stabilize a patient, according to EMTALA, a patient is stable if "no material deterioration of the condition is likely, within reasonable medical probability."

In the past, most hospitals translated EMTALA to mean that anyone who was injured or in severe pain must be treated, regardless of his ability to pay. "That was fine 19 years ago when hospitals had higher profit margins and most people were insured, but that's not the case today," observes Peter Young, a health care strategist in Fort Myers, Florida. "Times are changing."[19]

Screening the Sick

Denver Health and University Hospital began screening ER patients based on their ability to pay in 2002. Denver Health drew the line at nonresidents—unless the case is considered life-threatening, its ER won't treat an uninsured patient from outside Denver County. As for University Hospital, it decided to ask for partial payment up front before treating patients, like Martinez, who are deemed "nonurgent." For someone with good insurance, that might mean a small co-payment. But for someone who is uninsured or underinsured, the charge can run to a few hundred dollars. If the patient can't make the payment, he's given a list of low-cost clinics and shown the door.

"When they hand them this list of clinics they know very well there's little chance that they'll be welcome—the clinics also ask for a down payment," says Lefkowits. "I don't know how they live with themselves," he adds, referring to doctors at University Hospital. "Denver Health at least tries to make referrals; University just sends them out on the street with the yellow pages. That's not what ERs are about. If someone walks through your door and needs help, you help. I don't stop and think, 'What's their insurance?' "[20]

"I've talked to the docs at University about this," Lefkowits confides, "and they say, 'This is what the administration wants us to do.'

"I say, 'You're the doc—you're the one who has to look the patient in the eye and say: "I know what's wrong with you. I know what you need. But unless you give me cash, I'm not going to tell you." ' Sure, the system is broken, but you don't try to fix it on the backs of the most vulnerable patients."[21]

Local physicians say that Martinez is not the only serious case that University Hospital has bounced back on the street. Dennis Beck, copresident of CarePoint, the physician group that staffs Rose Medical and six other freestanding emergency rooms in the Denver area, recalls a patient who fell down a flight of stairs and wound up with neck pain and tingling in one arm.[22]

Dr. David Glaser, head of Exempla St. Joseph Hospital's ER, remembers a young woman complaining of nausea, vomiting, diarrhea, and cramping. Although she was pregnant, the University Hospital nurse who screened her deemed her "nonurgent," declaring that the patient suffered from "irritated intestines." When she got to St. Joseph's, doctors there determined that she was suffering from gastroenteritis, an inflammation of the digestive tract that can cause severe cramping and dehydration.

And, Glaser points out, it could have been much worse: "There are snakes in the grass hiding behind every minor complaint . . . To me, it's a scary prospect that they have nurses weeding out the sick from the non-sick. At some point, they're going to miss and miss big."[23]

Denver is not the only city where ERs have begun to parse EMTALA.[24] In Florida, where ERs are rethinking their open-door policy, Tampa health care consultant Peter Young points to overcrowding as the rationale for screening walk-ins. Otherwise, he argues, ERs will be swamped with patients suffering from relatively minor complaints. "Hospitals are in the business of taking care of people with life-threatening situations," says Young, "not in the walk-in clinic business, not in the 'I think I have an ear infection business.'"[25]

He has a point. Certainly, it makes sense for ERs to refer nonurgent cases to a primary care clinic. At some hospitals, patients in need of immediate attention find themselves waiting four or six hours while nurses and doctors tend to headaches and hypochondriacs.

At the same time, it's worth noting that contrary to urban myth, it is not the uninsured who are crowding emergency rooms. "Our findings indicate that emergency departments serve as a safety net, not just for the poor and uninsured, but for mainstream Americans, and in particular those with serious and chronic illnesses," says Dr. Ellen Weber, a professor of emergency medicine at the University of California at San Francisco and the lead author of a 2004 study of ER use published in *Annals of Emergency Medicine.*"[26]

Other recent studies reveal that more than 80 percent of patients seen in emergency rooms are covered by insurance, with insured patients driving the recent surge in ER visits.[27] Many say that they couldn't get an appointment with a specialist. As Jack Wennberg points out, specialists tend to keep their calendars full, and patients who don't have regularly scheduled visits often have to wait weeks for an appointment.[28]

"If we tell those chronically ill patients, 'Don't come to the emergency department unless you're dying'—that's exactly what they'll do," adds Dr. Arthur Kellermann, chairman of the emergency department at Grady Memorial Hospital in Atlanta. "If no one else is willing to take care of a diabetic patient, then we are very unwise to turn that person away. The likelihood that he will get care elsewhere in 24 to 36 hours is slim to none."[29]

Nevertheless, Dr. Norman Paradis, head of University of Colorado Hospital's emergency room in 2003, acknowledged that his ER was routinely telling patients suffering from complaints ranging from "broken bones and Hodgkin's disease" to "cancerous lumps and detached retinas" to seek care elsewhere on the grounds that they "need more than emergency care."[30]

No doubt these patients would be better off having their complaint diagnosed in a specialist's office. Yet plainly, they require medical attention—which raises a question: are ERs sending patients away because they're too crowded or because the patients can't pay?

A Tale of Two Patients

In 2004 *The Washington Post* described a typical Monday morning at University Hospital's ER, where Molly Turner, 27 and uninsured, and "Debbie," 45 and insured, waited to see a doctor. "Debbie asked that her name not be published because her insurer might object to her ER visit," the paper explained.

But whether or not her insurer would approve, Debbie received treatment for what turned out to be hives. Although Dr. Paradis, who saw both patients, ruled her case "not an emergency," Debbie was told that she could stay because the health insurance provided through her husband's employer carried neither a deductible nor up-front charges. (And presumably if the hospital entered the right code when submitting its claim, the insurer would pay, even though Debbie was a little hazy on whether her policy covered "nonurgent" ER visits.)

Turner, a mother of three who sells sod at a farm, did not receive quite as warm a welcome when she explained that she had dropped her health insurance after the premium jumped to $390 a month. Like Debbie, she had had a tough weekend, coughing and wheezing while battling a sore throat.

Like Debbie, Molly Turner was not in critical condition. But while Debbie was invited to stay, the financial desk informed Molly that if she wanted treatment she would have to produce $250. Turner chose to go home and tough out what Dr. Paradis diagnosed as "seasonal allergies." Down the road, the hospital would mail Turner a bill for $50 to cover the cost of "screening her out." (To be fair, for her $50 Turner also went home with a list of low-cost clinics, plus Paradis's opinion that she was suffering from un-specified allergies.)

Molly Turner was philosophical: "You get what you pay for," she said. "If I wanted to pay $250 I'd have had a full-blown work-up. But he's telling me it's not necessary, so I'm comfortable with that."

Meanwhile, Debbie stayed and professed herself well pleased with her treatment. "I've been to emergency rooms where there are crying babies and the whole drama," she said. "I'm amazed how quiet it is." No babies. No drama. No Michael Martinez.

"Because of her insurance, our institution will make money on her visit," explained Paradis, also well pleased.

"In a perversion of the system," *The Washington Post* observed, "insured patients such as Debbie are welcome to stay, no matter how trivial the prob-lem."[31] Of course, an ER is an expensive place to treat hives. But Debbie's insurer would no doubt do its best to find a way to pass the cost on to an-other payer.

An Unfunded Mandate

Admittedly, many hospitals already offer more free care than they can af-ford. In 2004, U.S. hospitals provided some $25 billion in uncompensated care.[32] While government provides some assistance, a recent study suggests public programs cover only about one-third of the total cost of the uncom-pensated care that hospitals and doctors supply—leaving health care providers with billions in unpaid bills.[33]

"The problem is that this is an unfunded mandate," observes Loren Johnson, a California doctor with the American College of Emergency Physicians. "The government says anyone who goes to the ER must be ac-cepted for treatment. That's fine. But who's going to pay for that? The

American public has been given this free ticket, and everybody is having trouble financing it. Good will and medical ethics is about all that's holding the system together, and that's not going to last."[34]

Major teaching hospitals and public hospitals like Denver Health and University Hospital provide the bulk of uncompensated care, and they're cracking under the strain. Nationwide, "there is no single or stable source of financial support for public hospitals' service to their communities," observes a 2005 study of Medicaid and the uninsured by The Henry J. Kaiser Family Foundation.[35]

Denver Health is typical: in the first five months of 2005 it lost $6.4 million; by midyear, it was forced to trim its budget by $15 million, laying off workers, closing clinics, and putting restrictions on what drugs it could offer to patients. "More and more people who never thought they'd be without health insurance are finding themselves on our doorstep," says Dr. Patricia Gabow, Denver Health's chief executive.[36] At University Hospital, spending on uninsured patients skyrocketed, climbing 35 percent in the twelve months ending June of 2005 to a staggering $68.2 million.

"We can't do everything for everyone," said Dr. Norman Paradis, head of University's emergency department at the time. "Other hospitals, clinics and private physicians find ways to limit care covertly," Paradis added. "We are overt. It's rational rationing."[37]

Shunning and Dunning the Poor

Whether or not rationing at University Hospital is rational, Paradis is right: it shocks us because it is so overt. Other hospitals find subtler—if no less effective—ways of discouraging unwanted traffic.

Rather than rejecting uninsured patients outright, some hospitals simply demand top dollar, knowing full well that needy patients will be scared away. Indeed, in recent years hospitals have come under fire for gouging uninsured patients by charging those who can least afford it sticker prices that are two or three times higher than the discounted rates private insurers and government agencies negotiate for insured patients.[38]

Another way to deter uninsured customers is to threaten those who can't pay with debtor's prison. In 2003 The Wall Street Journal published a series of stories outlining the Dickensian tactics that some hospitals have adopted as they try to collect unpaid debts: garnishing wages, freezing the bank accounts of minimum-wage workers, and even arranging to have debtors arrested who failed to appear at a court hearing—a practice known in some parts of the country as "body attachment."

In one case, the *Journal* reported, Carle Foundation Hospital, a not-for-profit that serves as the primary teaching hospital of the University of Illinois, had a diabetic truck driver arrested in the middle of the night—handcuffed while his wife and son stood by—over a $579 bill. In another case, the hospital obtained an arrest warrant for an uninsured single mother, who missed two court hearings on a $1,678 debt she incurred for a miscarriage. In a third case, Carle went after an uninsured part-time musician whom it had treated for a gunshot wound in a suicide attempt. When the man missed a hearing on his $7,718 hospital bill, Carle asked the court for a warrant.[39]

Why would hospitals make such aggressive efforts to collect relatively small amounts from patients who quite clearly do not have the funds to pay their bills? Richard Scruggs, the lead attorney on a series of class-action suits charging not-for-profits with abusive billing practices, explains that a number of hospital financial officers told him that they used the tactic to discourage indigent patients from returning to their hospital.[40] In other words, dunning becomes a form of shunning.

"Even hospitals whose [stated] mission includes treating indigent patients are reluctant to make the process too easy or too public for fear of becoming magnets for the uninsured," *The New England Journal of Medicine* observed in March of 2005. In New York City, for instance, few hospitals post any information about charity care, discounts for indigent patients, or patient payment plans. After all, who wants to be known as the softest touch in town?

When New York's Legal Aid Society surveyed 22 New York City hospitals regarding discounts for the uninsured and underinsured in the summer of 2003, it discovered that the majority would not even give Legal Aid copies of their sliding fee policies. "This is a hospital. We can't give out that information," one institution explained. And although 17 of the 22 hospitals acknowledged that they had sliding fee scale programs, it turned out that only three actually applied them to inpatient bills—where discounts are most needed. The others offered a sliding scale only to outpatients.[41]

Moreover, at eight of the hospitals, Legal Aid's surveyors learned that

uninsured patients were regularly asked to pay 100 percent of their antici-
pated bill prior to admission. "Such 100% up-front deposit requirements result in the outright denial of medically necessary care to the uninsured and
underinsured," the report noted. Meanwhile, New York State had allocated
over $300 million in Bad Debt and Charity Care (BDCC) funds for New
York City hospitals to help cover the cost of caring for the poor. Yet, the report revealed, "none of the 22 hospitals had a process for uninsured and underinsured patients to apply for and access BDCC funds."

"New York City is a self-touted 'Medical Mecca,' " the report concluded.
"But for the uninsured and the underinsured, securing access to affordable
care is not only a confusing, frustrating and uncertain process, but an exercise in futility . . . Unlike consumers who are shopping for cars, uninsured
and underinsured health consumers have few consumer protections when
they confront a medical crisis."

Indeed, when a surveyor inquired about BDCC funds at NYU Medical
Center, an institution that had received $4 million from the state, a financial
representative at the hospital told him that NYU is "a private hospital" that
normally refers uninsured patients to Bellevue Hospital, a government-
owned public hospital a stone's throw from NYU.

In fact, while NYU Medical Center is not owned by the government, it is
a not-for-profit, exempt from both property and corporate income taxes—
just like Bellevue. Nevertheless, NYU's financial rep told the surveyor:
"NYU Hospital is a *corporation,* people have to *pay* for the services they receive here . . . if they can't pay, they have to just get the hell out!" (emphasis
mine)

However unwittingly, NYU's financial representative may have put his
finger on the crux of the problem. As noted in chapter 4, the analysts at S&P
who rate hospital bonds can't give points for charitable care. And today, investors expect all hospitals, including not-for-profits, to strive for corporate
efficiency—which means maximizing revenues and minimizing losses. A
well-managed hospital is expected to remain solvent, which is to say that it
must learn to avoid customers who can't pay their bills.

The inevitable tension between a not-for-profit's sense of mission and
the requirements of the market sums up the contradiction at the very heart
of "corporate medicine." Do we expect a hospital to operate like a business,
or do we see it as a community service, charged with fulfilling a social mission? Increasingly, it seems, we expect both.

If a not-for-profit operates at a loss, year after year, we accuse it of poor management. If it remains solvent by shunning the poor, we sue it for failing to live up to its responsibility as a charity.

By 2004 some 370 hospitals had become the targets of class action lawsuits charging them with failing to provide enough charity care, thus violating the provisions of their not-for-profit status. Why should they be exempt from property and corporate income taxes, plaintiffs' attorneys ask, if they are not caring for the poor?

Not an unreasonable question. But lawsuits won't solve the problem, declares John Kitzhaber, a former emergency room doctor who in the 1990s became a two-term governor of Oregon. The suits stand as "a classic example of treating symptoms rather than causes," says Kitzhaber, who now serves as president of the Estes Park Institute, a nonprofit organization that conducts education conferences for health care leaders. "Clearly the mission statements of these hospitals speak to treating the poor. . . . But the reality of the matter is that a hospital cannot absorb an unlimited burden of uncompensated care and remain economically viable. Although the tipping point is different for each institution, there is a tipping point."[42]

"My point is that instead of arguing about the amount of charity care provided by a hospital . . . instead of battling it out in court, we should be focusing on the real problem—the policies which result in so many uninsured and underinsured Americans," Kitzhaber added at an Estes Park conference in 2004. "Lawsuits do not create resolution—they create winners and losers—and they do not reduce the number of people who cannot afford to pay for their care."

Everyone is trying to shift the cost of caring for the uninsured onto someone else, Kitzhaber adds. Hospitals try to pass the costs onto private insurers; insurers, in turn, shift costs to employers by lifting their premiums, while employers pass on the hikes to employees by boosting their share of that premium. "These actions are apparently based on the assumption that if we simply stop paying for people's health care needs, they will somehow go away and as a society we can avoid the cost," says Kitzhaber. "But this only works if you are also willing to repeal EMTALA [the law which requires emergency departments to stabilize patients] and let people die on the ambulance ramp for lack of insurance coverage. But we don't do that. Congress will not advocate for that; nor will state legislators or the business community. They simply shift the *responsibility* for dealing with the problem to hospitals and then sue them when they are unable to fulfill that responsibility."

No Cash, No Cure

The barriers that the uninsured and marginally insured face only begin with the ER. Even if a patient manages to jump that hurdle and get the urgent care that he needs, that doesn't mean that he will have access to the follow-up treatment that the physician in the ER recommends, says Dr. Liz Dreesen, recalling her experience as a surgeon and intensive care specialist in Lincolnton, North Carolina.

After graduating from Harvard Medical School in 1987, Dreesen finished a trauma fellowship at Johns Hopkins in Baltimore. There, she met her husband, also a surgeon. "We didn't really like academia, so after I completed the fellowship, we decided to 'light out for the territories,'" says Dreesen. They landed in Lincolnton, a mill town near Charlotte, where they practiced for nine years.

"One of the most poignant cases that I remember involved a good-looking, vigorous 60-year-old patient named Buddy Rich," Dreesen confides. "He came to the ER one day because he felt terrible—his red blood count showed that he was profoundly anemic. This means either your bone marrow isn't making blood, or you're losing blood, gradually.[43]

"First we find out that his bone marrow is working—so now we assume that he's bleeding. But when this happens, all you know is that it is somewhere between the mouth and the anus. It could be anywhere in between. And there are many feet of small intestine that we can't scope. Generally, this is not much of a problem," she adds. "Very few people are bleeding from their small intestine. Usually it's the stomach or the colon.

"The next day, we admitted him and gave him a blood transfusion," Dreesen recalls. "The day after that, we scoped him. But we couldn't find the source of the bleeding. Because he had the transfusion, he was over the immediate problem," she explains. "But still he needed some sort of study to find out what was going on. When we discharged him, we told him that he needed to come back to the hospital's outpatient clinic for testing. But he never came back."

Why? "Because he had no insurance, and he didn't have the money to pay out of pocket," says Dreesen. When Rich went to the hospital's outpatient clinic to be tested, he was told that before he could be treated, he would need to make a cash down payment. "I don't know whether they told Buddy he needed $1,000 or $500," says Dreesen. "It doesn't matter—these are people getting their single-wides [trailers] repo'd. They don't have $1,000 *or* $500 cash.

"I would have continued to treat him for free, but it's difficult if a person needs outpatient testing," she explains. "If I refer him to the hospital as an outpatient instead of as an inpatient that automatically means it's not an emergency. And so the hospital doesn't have to provide care.

"If I had known what would happen I would have admitted him as an inpatient to have those studies done," she confesses. "But it's not a very cost-effective way to do tests. It's much less expensive for the hospital to do the studies at an outpatient clinic. It was obvious that he needed them—somewhere, he was bleeding internally. If we had done them, we might have caught the cancer . . ."

A year later, Buddy Rich returned to the hospital with an intestinal blockage. "That's when we found out that he had a small bowel cancer," Dreesen recalls. "By the time we operated on him, it had metastasized. It wasn't clear how long he might live. We knew that ultimately he would die of it, but patients can survive for years."

A few months later, Rich went to his oncologist—the abdominal pain was getting worse—much worse. The oncologist sent him to the outpatient clinic for a CAT scan. "The oncologist could have admitted him as an inpatient, but he was trying to be responsible," Dreesen explains. "He didn't want to put him in the hospital when he didn't need to be there. But of course when Buddy appeared at our outpatient clinic, he was told, 'It's not an emergency—you need to come up with $1,000 before we can do a CAT scan.'

"So Buddy went home to tough it out," says Dreesen. "Most of these very poor people don't make waves," she adds.

"Whenever I saw him, he was never angry," she recalls. "He was just really, really sad. He couldn't believe that it was all happening; he had always been so healthy. He worked outdoors—doing landscaping, I think. He didn't drink or do drugs. He was, as we say in medicine, 'a citizen.' "

Over time, Buddy's pain became unbearable. "At this point, he'd been turned away from our hospital's outpatient clinic twice, and so he went to a hospital in Charlotte, 40 miles away," Dreesen continues. "There, he was operated on by people who knew nothing about him or his medical history. He probably just showed up in the middle of the night."

There was little that the doctors in Charlotte could do. "His intestine was totally blocked," Dreesen explains, "and so he couldn't stop throwing up. Anything he tried to eat just came back up. Sometimes you can bypass the blockage, but he had too much cancer for that. All they could do was put a tube into his stomach, so that he could drink—for comfort—and not be dried out. But whatever he drank came out the tube into a bag, or onto the floor. . . .

"The only reason I found out what had happened to him is that after the operation, the doctors in Charlotte said, 'We realize it's difficult for you to get here for your follow-up care; you can follow up with your regular surgeon close to home.'

"So he came back to see us," says Dreesen, who was in practice with her husband. "I was out of town that day, but my husband knew him, and they talked.

"Later, my husband wrote a poem about it. In the poem, he describes how Buddy's stomach contents came through the yellow tube and onto my husband's shoe—both of them looking at each other, knowing that this was the last time that they were going to see each other. . . . The poem begins: 'The dead gather around my bed at night.' "

Access to Specialists

Asking for payment before performing a procedure is becoming common-place at outpatient clinics nationwide. In 2004 Atlanta's Grady Health System, Georgia's largest public hospital, put a new billing system in place: patients scheduled for procedures are called in advance and informed of their co-pay, among other charges. "If patients can't afford to pay up front, their procedures are postponed until they can," says Teresa Finch, Grady Memorial Hospital's chief financial officer.[44] University Community Health Inc., a network of four Tampa Bay–area hospitals, gives employees scripts to help them diplomatically ask for money when people are admitted. If patients balk, hospital employees try to be polite but assertive, says Arnez Wotring, who oversees hospital admissions.[45]

But it is not just hospital outpatient clinics that avoid the needy. A growing number of physicians refuse to see both the uninsured and Medicaid patients. From 1997 to 2001, the proportion of doctors offering charity care fell a full five percentage points—from 76.3 to 71.5 percent, according to the Center for Studying Health System Change. Over the same span, the share willing to treat Medicaid patients declined from 87.1 percent to 85.4 percent.

A study published in *The Journal of the American Medical Association* in 2005 illustrates just how difficult it is for uninsured and Medicaid patients to find someone willing to provide follow-up care—even if they are seriously ill. Researchers at the University of Chicago hired graduate students to call 430 physicians' offices, community clinics, and hospital clinics in nine cities, posing as patients in need of an appointment. They were instructed to say that they had been seen at an ER and had been told that they needed urgent follow-up care for one of the three following conditions: pneumonia, hypertension with blood pressure greater than 110, or possible ectopic pregnancy (low abdominal pain, vaginal bleeding, and an indeterminate ultrasound).[46]

Callers emphasized the need for an urgent appointment (e.g., "I went to the ER last night for a cough and they told me I had pneumonia. I'm a diabetic and I've had some kidney problems, so the ER doctor wanted me to follow up . . .") and asked for an appointment sometime in the next week. Of callers who said that they were covered by Medicaid only about one-third were able to get an appointment within the next seven days; by contrast, two-thirds of those who claimed that that they had private insurance were booked. If patients admitted that they were uninsured but offered to bring $20 at the time of the visit and arrange to pay the balance later, three-quarters were still turned away. If, on the other hand, they said they were uninsured but could pay cash for the entire charge at the time of their visit, they were as likely as a privately insured patient to secure an appointment.

Physicians refuse to take Medicaid patients in large part because the fees that Medicaid offers are meager—sometimes as little as $20 for an office visit. On average, a doctor treating a Medicaid patient in 2003 received just 69 percent of what CMS would pay him to provide the very same care to a senior on Medicare. Since Medicaid is administered by the states, reimbursements vary widely by state. And no surprise, a 2004 study reveals that in states like New York—where Medicaid offered just 45 percent of what Medicare would pay for the same procedure—doctors were far less likely to accept Medicaid patients than they were in, say, Arizona—where Medicaid actually paid a little more than Medicare. The pattern held nationwide, with

52 percent of physicians in low-fee states taking on new Medicaid patients, compared with 68 percent in high-fee states.[47]

Although basic medical services for the poor are available at community clinics across the country, specialty care is scarce for patients without health insurance. At one time, academic medical centers took care of a large share of the uninsured, but as reimbursements tighten, specialists at these institutions are treating more patients with private insurance—and fewer of the uninsured. A 2003 study by researchers at Boston Massachusetts Hospital confirmed the trend: Of 2,000 physicians surveyed nationwide, one in four said they had problems admitting patients to teaching hospitals or were forced to limit those patients' care.[48]

Even in New York, a city endowed with an embarrassment of specialists, it can be extraordinarily difficult to find one who will take a referral for an uninsured or Medicaid patient, says Dr. Neil Calman, a clinical professor of family medicine at Albert Einstein College of Medicine and founder of New York City's Institute for Urban Family Health, a not-for-profit that operates 13 health centers: "A lot of doctors just don't want to have anything to do with these patients."[49]

"If I want an echocardiogram for an uninsured patient, I don't know a single cardiologist in private practice in New York who will take him," Calman adds. "I can send the patient to a hospital clinic, but even they make it difficult. First, I have to send him to the hospital's GP clinic—despite the fact that I'm a general practitioner and have already seen him. Then the GP clinic will refer him to the hospital's cardiology clinic. And, finally, that clinic will refer him to the place where they do the echocardiograms. In other words, after the patient has seen me, he needs to make three separate appointments."

Mr. North

Calman recalls his experience with "Mr. North," a patient suffering from congestive heart failure.

In 1997 Neil Calman had been practicing family medicine in the Bronx for more than twenty years. He was no longer easily shocked. But, he admits, nothing prepared him for the day when James North sat quietly in an exam room, waiting to meet him. Calman remembers stopping dead in his tracks when he opened the exam room door and his new patient rose to greet him:

"His deep ebony, six-foot-three inch frame dwarfed my pale, five-foot-three presence. The tremendous hands of his 260-pound body grabbed my own outstretched right hand and shook it, accompanied by a baritone 'Good morning, Doc,' that reverberated through the room . . . I glanced at his face, trying to see through my initial discomfort, only to be greeted by my own face staring back at me from the silver, reflective sunglasses he wore beneath a baseball cap that covered his head and any hair that might have been growing on it." [50]

Mr. North then proceeded to explain that he had just been discharged from a hospital after suffering a severe heart attack. He was still barely able to walk a block without resting. He went on to "recite a list of the medications he was taking, with the precision of a medical student seeking to impress his new attending physician," Calman recalls. "He also knew the names of all the doctors who had taken care of him, including those of the physicians who were called in to consult during his hospital stay. My initial admiration for his facility in reciting this information was quickly replaced by my increasing intimidation by this man, whose size was clearly not his only outstanding feature.

"It was during Mr. North's second visit that I became aware of the suffering he had endured in his 50 years of life," Calman continues. "Not until I had completed the exam on his right eye did he save me the embarrassment of trying to see into his artistically matched left glass eye. His chest and abdomen were scarred from what I had come to recognize as multiple knife wounds. Now, left crippled by his recent heart attack, he was short of breath, even at rest."

North would become one of Calman's favorite patients, in part because of his "almost unnatural compliance with the interventions I recommended," in part because "he still intimidated me, and my continuing ability to care for him allowed me to feel special," Calman acknowledges. "I also loved watching him interact with my staff, because his commanding physical presence and intellect forced them to deliver a level of service I wish we could provide to all of our patients."

Yet Calman realized he could not "provide Mr. North with all that New York's great health care institutions have to offer.

"He knew that. He often tried to teach me that, and just as often was amazed that I was unable to accept it. It came up time and time again when I sent him for specialty consults, diagnostic tests, or even prescription refills. The same considerations my family or I would receive were rarely given to him."

Calman recalls the time that "the echocardiography lab where North had a scheduled appointment sent him home because he was 10 minutes late, having to stop every block to rest in the walk from his home to the hospital on a particularly windy day." And Calman knew that, although his 50-year-old patient might be a candidate for a heart transplant, and "reimbursement would be possible," the reimbursements rates would be "so far beneath those of private payers, and organ availability such a problem," that the likelihood of North ever receiving the transplant was "minute."

Mr. North would not live to see his 60th birthday.

How the System Decides Whom to Treat

Stories of patients like Buddy Rich and James North illustrate how in the United States, the marketplace decides who receives care. Or, as *The Wall Street Journal* put it in a 2003 headline: "The Big Secret in Health Care: Rationing Is Here."[51]

"Health-care rationing occurs every day in the U.S., in thousands of big and small decisions, made mostly out of sight of patients, according to rules that often aren't consistently applied," Wall Street's paper of record reported. "The people who make these decisions are harried doctors, Medicaid functionaries, hospital administrators, insurance workers and nurses. These are the gatekeepers of the American health-care system, the ones forced to say 'no' to certain demands for treatment."

Ad hoc rationing puts enormous pressure on doctors, nurses, and caseworkers who struggle with decisions about who should receive costly drugs and surgical procedures, who should be moved out of an expensive bed in an ICU and sent back to a nursing home, who should receive a third round of chemotherapy when the first two rounds have failed.[52]

"All you should be asking [doctors and nurses] to do is take care of sick people as quickly as possible," observes Robert Perry, chief executive officer of Philadelphia's Northeastern Hospital. Instead, hospital workers are forced to ration care on a case-by-case basis. "Health care is all backwards in this country. The biggest decisions are all made in the worst conditions," Perry adds.[53]

In most other developed countries, health care is rationed explicitly. Legislators debate and a policy is set. Typically, governments focus on the supply side, containing costs by capping prices, creating global budgets or limiting the supply of expensive equipment in order to discourage overuse.

Under Japan's universal health system, for instance, all citizens are covered equally and can go to any physician or hospital with no difference in cost; physicians are free to prescribe as they see fit. But the government keeps a lid on total spending by setting prices for all procedures, drugs, and devices, renegotiating the payment schedule with providers, usually on a biennial basis. Sometimes these prices reflect cultural values. For example, only about one-third as many surgeries are done in Japan as in the United States—in part due to a cultural antipathy to invasive procedures, in part because the fees paid for surgery are very low.

"Relatively inexpensive services such as ordinary consultations and prescribing drugs are profitable, but expensive procedures such as surgery and other high-tech treatments are often priced below actual cost," explains Naoki Ikegami, a professor at the Keio University School of Medicine in Tokyo. Thus, the government encourages more conservative practice patterns.

If surgery and certain high-tech treatments are unprofitable, why do Japanese hospitals and doctors provide them at all? "One answer is that physicians find that these services are professionally rewarding and feel a responsibility to provide the best care," Ikegami replies. "Another is that a reputation for good surgery and high-tech medicine is an advantage in competing for patients."[54] In other words, surgery becomes a loss leader.

The Japanese system also controls costs by lowering payments for procedures when volume soars. For example, Ikegami explains, in 2002 "the fee for magnetic resonance imaging (MRI) of the head was reduced by 30 percent from 16,600 Yen ($151) to 11,400 Yen ($104). In addition, under tight billing rules already in effect, if imaging was performed by MRI and by computed tomography (CT) scanning in the same calendar month, the CT scan could not be billed." Thus, the government blunted the cost of high-tech procedures, while discouraging overuse.[55]

This is not to suggest that Japan has found a final solution to health care inflation—or that a system founded on Japan's cultural preferences and biases would ever fly in the United States. The point is simply that in Japan, as in virtually every other industrialized nation, the rules for rationing are made publicly and apply to everyone—just as in the United States decisions about what Medicare will and will not cover apply to everyone over the age of 65. And, because Medicare's rules are spelled out in broad daylight, they are open to public debate.

By contrast, when U.S. hospitals and physicians decide how to allocate resources for patients under the age of 65, the decisions are usually made on an implicit, ad hoc basis, and often, as Northeastern's CEO points out, "under the worst possible conditions"—at the bedside and without enough evidence-based research to guide a decision as to whether further treatment would help the patient.

Instead, gatekeepers ask, "Would his insurance cover it?"

Some make the argument that case-by-case bedside rationing is preferable to letting evidence-based guidelines set one policy for all: "The strengths of implicit rationing are its discretion and flexibility," in responding to individual cases and circumstances, David Mechanic, director of the Institute for Health, Health Care Policy and Aging Research at Rutgers University wrote in 1997. "Explicit rationing," by contrast, "brings into a public forum conflicting needs and preferences, resulting in acrimony and political mobilization. . . ." The issues involved in allocating health resources are "incredibly difficult," he adds. Rather than trying to decide such complex issues in a public forum, "the fitting response is to muddle through, changing course as knowledge and experience guide us. If we are particularly thoughtful and lucky, perhaps we will be able to say that we have 'muddled through elegantly.' "[56]

But few Americans are comfortable with the idea that we ration care at all. Many believe that the uninsured should be covered by some form of national health insurance—and a surprising number say that they would be willing to pay higher taxes to assure universal coverage. In 2003 a Wall Street Journal Online/Harris Interactive Health-Care Poll showed that 58 percent of those polled claimed they "would be willing to forgo President's Bush's proposed tax cuts if the revenue would be used to provide health coverage to a large number of uninsured people."[57]

But in lieu of a national policy, the *Journal* is right: rationing is here, and without clear guidelines, the market decides who receives care—which means that ability to pay usually determines how much care a patient receives. *In other words, rather than limiting which services people receive, we limit which people receive the services.*

Of course no one told Buddy Rich that he couldn't have further treatment. He simply was told that treatment would cost a certain sum and that it was up to him to scrape up that amount.

The arbitrary nature of what happened to Buddy Rich becomes clear when you consider the "if only's":

If only Rich had happened to live in a state that offered Medicaid to childless adults, he might have qualified for help.[58]

If only Rich had happened to work for an employer who offered health insurance, he might have been covered.

If only his cancer had struck 10 or 15 years earlier, when the gap between incomes and the cost of health insurance was narrower, he might have been able to afford to buy his own insurance. But by 2002 the cheapest standard policy available to a man his age in North Carolina cost well over $3,000—clearly out of reach for a minimum-wage worker who at the time might have earned a little more than $10,000 a year before taxes, if he was lucky enough to find full-time work.[59]

If only his cancer had waited another five years before it developed, Rich would have been covered by Medicare.

If only Liz Dreesen had been the person making the decision at the outpatient clinic, she might have waived the down payment—or she might have admitted him as an inpatient.

But as luck would have it, none of these things happened. Thus a rationing system based on chance and circumstance determined that Rich would not get the care he needed. The decision had nothing to do with how sick he was, what is considered best practice, or how most Americans think health care dollars should be allocated.

Many assume that if a person can't afford care, Medicaid will cover him. But as former Oregon governor John Kitzhaber notes, Medicaid also rations care capriciously, mandating coverage "only for 'the deserving poor'—women who are pregnant, families with dependent children, and those who are blind or disabled. The 'undeserving poor'—indigent men and women who do not have children—are not eligible, no matter how impoverished they are."[60]

The Cost of Not Caring for the Uninsured

Even if a patient qualifies for Medicaid, states are at liberty to reconfigure who or what they cover in ways that make little sense. Kitzhaber offers a casebook example of irrational rationing: "In February of 2003, in order to save money, the Oregon legislature discontinued prescription drug coverage for a certain category of patients on its Medicaid program.

"As a consequence of this decision, Douglas Schmidt, a man in his mid-30s suffering from a seizure disorder, was no longer able to afford to purchase the medication which controlled his seizures. He subsequently went into a sustained grand mal seizure and ended up with severe brain damage and on a ventilator in a Portland hospital. He remained in the hospital for several months and then was transferred to a long-term care facility where he finally died in November 2003 when life support was withdrawn.

"Now the cost of his anti-seizure medication was $14 a day," Kitzhaber points out. "The cost of his care in the intensive care unit was over $7,500 a day and that cost was billed back to the state Medicaid program. So the legislature did not save *any* money by its decision. On the contrary, it increased its fiscal liability and, in order to absorb it, was forced to drop more people from coverage—perpetuating this kind of human tragedy and fiscal disaster.

"My point is simply this: we are going to pay these costs one way or another: either explicitly or implicitly. And by failing do so explicitly, the cost will ultimately be much higher in both economic and human terms."[61]

Studies of preventable hospitalizations confirm Kitzhaber's point: while any single uninsured patient is likely to receive less care than an insured patient, a larger percentage of uninsured patients become seriously ill because they did not receive the care that they needed in a timely fashion.[62]

Who pays for their delayed care? As always, the answer is "everyone." As noted earlier, hospitals pass the cost of uncompensated care onto insurers, who in turn shift the cost to their customers in the form of higher premiums. The bottom line, according to a study by Families USA, is that in 2005 the cost of paying for uncompensated care boosted health insurance premiums for a family by $922.[63]

But the insured do not foot the entire bill. State and local governments (i.e., taxpayers) picked up as much as $31 billion of the tab in 2003 according to the Kaiser Commission report on Medicaid and the uninsured. Indeed the study's authors conclude that since so much money is already being spent by government to care for the uninsured, "it should be possible to transfer a large share of these funds to a program that subsidizes insurance for the uninsured." But instead of helping the uninsured buy insurance, we pay hospitals for deferred care, "paying for treatment for the uninsured in the least efficient way possible," observes *Health Affairs* founding editor John Iglehart.[64]

Cutting Medicaid: the Irrational Way

At the beginning of 2005 President Bush proposed slashing the nation's Medicaid budget by $10 billion over a period of five years—leaving it largely up to the states to decide how and where to cut care.

Everything that we know about how dollars are squandered on overtreatment as well as the high cost of undertreatment would suggest that if Medicaid is going to ration care rationally, it needs to limit unnecessary procedures and unproven treatments, while emphasizing preventive care and chronic disease management. But this is not what many states seem to have in mind. Instead, early in 2005 politicians began to talk about paring care for Medicaid patients in bizarre and arbitrary ways.

In Utah, for example, an experimental plan devised under Secretary of Health and Human Services Michael Leavitt (while he was still governor of the state) covers doctor's visits and visits to the ER for a larger number of patients—while simultaneously eliminating reimbursements for extended hospitalization or specialty medical treatments, from dermatology to oncology. For catastrophic care, Medicaid patients with cancer are expected to rely on the generosity of doctors and hospitals willing to provide treatment free of charge.[65]

In Missouri, Governor Matt Blunt proposed that parents of children on Medicaid should be cut from the program if the family's annual income exceeds $4,800—that's right, $4,800, not $48,000.

Under Michigan's proposed program, impoverished adults who are not disabled or pregnant would lose hearing, vision, and therapy services. In addition, hospital coverage would be limited to 20 days a year—no matter how sick or poor the Medicaid patient might be.[66]

None of these proposals have anything to do with promoting effective care or reducing wasteful care. Instead, they simply take an ax to Medicaid budgets, blindly excluding categories of people—or whole areas of treatment—without rhyme or reason. If this is an example of "muddling through" the challenge of allocating scarce resources, it hardly can be called an "elegant" solution.

7

Doing Less and Doing It Right: Is Pay for Performance the Answer?

The scent of economic incentive is everywhere in medicine, occasionally rising to the level of stench; that's what's bound us into the fix we're in. But in small doses, could such incentives also fix the bind we're in?

—DR. JERRY AVORN[1]

Thoughtful reformers recognize that just as more care does not guarantee better care, taking an ax to health care budgets is not the answer. Thus many have adopted a new mantra: "Doing less and doing it right." The focus, they say, should be on the quality of health care, not the quantity. With that goal in mind, the Centers for Medicare and Medicaid Services (CMS) has embarked on an ambitious experiment that borrows two solutions from private industry: information technology (IT) and pay for performance (P4P).

Health care IT is not an idea whose time has come—it is long overdue, says Scott Wallace, president and chief executive officer of The National Alliance for Health Information Technology. While most U.S. industries make good use of computers to collect, manage, and distribute information, health care still relies heavily on pen, paper, phone, and those little yellow Post-it notes that all too often come fluttering out of a patient's file. Indeed, when it comes to medicine, the United States lags far behind other countries. In 2000, 90 percent of physicians in Sweden, 88 percent in the Netherlands, 62 percent in Denmark, 58 percent in the United Kingdom, 56 percent in Finland, and 48 percent in Germany were using electronic medical records.[2] Five years later roughly 80 percent of U.S. physicians were still shuffling through manila folders.

"My dog has better medical records than I do," complains Wallace. "My vet has a fully computerized system that records everything that has been done to Samantha, tracks all of her inoculations and immunizations, and sends us an e-mail reminder when we need to come in. If vets can put together the finances and train themselves to use these things, it would seem that human physicians could, too."[3]

Advocates of health care IT envision a paperless health care system in which all of a patient's vital information (medical history, X-rays, lab results, and prescriptions) would be gathered into a single database that could be transferred, with the stroke of a key, from doctor's office to hospital to pharmacy. Doctors and hospitals would then use those records to coordinate care, reduce errors, and chart a patient's progress. And over time, a database of electronic records showing how thousands of patients responded to various treatments could serve as a rich fund of information for researchers creating guidelines for evidence-based medicine.

Pay for performance, Washington's policy makers say, goes hand in hand with health information technology. Rather than paying hospitals and doctors for how *much* they do, CMS wants to use P4P to reward them for how *well* they do it. But how can Washington know which health care providers are lifting the quality of care? Reformers point out that if caregivers begin using electronic medical records, they can easily track and document improvements in their performance. Meanwhile, bonuses for quality will provide the extra dollars that doctors and hospitals desperately need to invest in IT. "Pay-for-performance initiatives . . . will help remove economic barriers to the adoption of electronic health records," declares David Brailer, the Bush administration's national coordinator for health information technology. "P4P will drive IT."[4]

But not everyone is impressed—particularly when it comes to P4P. " 'Pay for performance' is the kind of seductive, focus-group-tested catchphrase that has come to dominate much of health policy discourse, but is largely devoid of meaning," says former Medicare chief Bruce Vladeck, who during his years in Washington developed an ear for the hollow phrase. "The expectation that complex, decentralized social change should happen instantaneously by giving hospitals a bonus is mere political posturing. Human behavior is too complex and influenced by too many variables," Vladeck adds, "and the amount of money involved is too small compared to the total revenues providers receive."[5]

Vladeck is not P4P's only critic. Like virtually any suggestion for reforming health care, both P4P and IT have generated more than a little controversy, and as usual the debate centers on money: who will pay? Who will profit? And can filthy lucre really inspire excellence?

The Skeptics

Some fear that "dangling" financial incentives in front of medical professionals could undermine both medical professionalism and the patient-doctor relationship. "The very concept that we have to be rewarded or 'incentivized' to work better is demeaning," says Dr. David Rogers. "Caring, thoughtful and proud physicians and the medical societies that represent them should simply say 'no thanks' to P4P. The only thing we have left in medicine is our pride. Strip that away, and medical care in our country will suffer immensely."[6]

A 2004 editorial in *The New England Journal of Medicine* acknowledges that the very existence of performance bonuses could raise questions in a patient's mind: "Previously, patients took it for granted that their doctors would provide high-quality care as a matter of course."[7] What does it mean if we begin to pay doctors extra to do what everyone agrees they should be doing in the first place?

"Does this imply that we should tip the surgical nurse if we want to be sure that she counts the sponges?" asks one physician, ice in his voice.[8] Skeptics also worry that P4P could tempt doctors to shun the most complicated or least compliant patients. Others argue that P4P schemes put too much emphasis on what can be counted—and in medicine, what can be counted most easily is not always what counts most.

When it comes to IT, few question whether electronic medical records could improve quality. Here, the debate focuses on practical concerns about cost and execution: just how much hype is mixed with the hope? "The investment community has poured nearly a half-trillion dollars into failed health IT ventures that once claimed to be solutions," J. D. Kleinke, executive director of the Omnimedix Institute, a nonprofit health care research organization, observed late in 2005. Although the technology has improved, "many health care organizations are [still] spending vast sums on proprietary products that do not coalesce into a system-wide solution."[9]

Indeed, U.S. hospitals have been taking a bottom-up approach to IT, with every institution inventing its own solution. But for information technology to work, hospitals and doctors need to be able to talk to one another. Unless they agree upon data transmission standards, they will succeed only in creating islands of digital information. Yet when you talk to hospitals about integrating their systems, says John Quinn, a senior executive at Accenture, a technology consulting firm, "they roll their eyes and say, 'we'd just be happy to get two nursing stations to do the same thing, let alone two hospitals in our network.' "[10]

And even when hospitals and doctors agree on digital standards, a larger question looms: who will come up with the billions needed to create a paperless health care system?

Consider this: in 2005 the United Kingdom budgeted $10 billion to create a system of universal electronic medical records in a much smaller country where there is only one major payer—the government. In the United States we would need to commit "tens of billions" to accomplish what Medicare envisions, says Dr. Barry Hieb, a research director for Gartner, Inc., a consulting firm that specializes in information technology. And there has been no real sign, he adds, that political leaders are willing to provide anything even remotely close to that sum. "I applaud the federal government for wanting to put a focus on health care IT," says Hieb. "It's long overdue ... [but] are they going to really do something, or just tinker and fiddle around?"[11]

Hieb has reason to be concerned. While President George W. Bush has set a goal of establishing electronic health records for most Americans by 2015, as of the summer of 2005 his budget for the 2006 fiscal year allocated a paltry $125 million—not billion, but million—to health IT. In Congress, the Wired for Health Care Quality Act, a bill cosponsored by Senators Bill Frist and Hillary Clinton, merely matched Bush's meager bid, proposing that the nation spend $125 million in 2006, $155 million in 2007, and "such sums as are necessary from 2008 through 2010."

Meanwhile, in July of 2005, a panel that included Brailer, the administration's IT czar, estimated that developing a National Health Information Network would require $156 billion in capital costs over a five-year period—plus $48 billion in annual operating costs.[12] Who will foot the bill? Hospitals? Doctors? Insurers?

Putting the Cart Before the Horse?

Medicare's many critics wonder if CMS isn't putting the cart before the horse by launching pay-for-performance initiatives when hospitals and doctors have barely begun to gather the data needed for evidence-based medicine.[13] In order to pay for performance, one needs to be able to measure it, and without electronic records of outcomes, that is very difficult to do. Collecting data by hand from a heap of paper records, collating it, and interpreting it is both expensive and labor intensive.

"My sense is that the number one priority of this country should be to get the nation wired, and create a database that would let us have a marketplace based on quality and value," says George Halvorson, chairman and CEO of Kaiser Permanente, a nonprofit group practice health care plan that is becoming a leader in the use of information technology. "We will never be able to achieve real accountability for costs or quality without accurate, accessible, meaningful, and timely data."[14]

It is hard to argue with Halvorson. As discussed in chapter 5, we still don't know which treatments work best for a long list of the most common chronic conditions. Though the process of accumulating the data has begun, it's still early innings. For example, as we have seen, although there is wide agreement that we perform far too many angioplasties and bypass surgeries, there is still little hard evidence to support guidelines as to precisely when, and under what circumstances, the risks outweigh the benefits.[15]

Consider, too, testing for prostate cancer. While some pay-for-performance schemes reward doctors for screening patients for cancer, the impact in reducing mortality "still isn't proven for a number of cancers," cautions Dr. Elaine Jaffe of the National Cancer Institute.[16] PSA blood testing for prostate cancer stands out as a particularly ambiguous case. While screening has led to a dramatic rise in the number of new cases of prostate cancer that are detected, as of the fall of 2005 *there was still no evidence that the screening has led to fewer deaths.* (emphasis mine)[17] True, thanks to the test, the disease is detected earlier, but this simply means that more men walk around knowing that they have prostate cancer.

Moreover, because prostate cancer is most common in older men, and because it can be a slow-growing disease, many men will die of something else long before they begin to display symptoms. Nevertheless, once screening detects the signs of cancer, "most patients undergo some sort of treatment—radical surgery or radiation," notes Dr. H. Gilbert Welch, a professor of medicine at Dartmouth Medical School and codirector of the VA Outcomes Group in the Department of Veterans Affairs in White River Junction, Vermont.

And this is a case where the cure can be worse than the disease. "While only 1 percent die from the surgery, 17 percent need additional treatment because they have difficulty urinating following the surgery; 28 percent must wear pads because they have the opposite problem—they cannot hold their urine, and more than half are bothered by a loss of sexual function," Welch observes in his book, *Should I Be Tested for Cancer?: Maybe Not and Here's Why.* "Among men undergoing radiation, 19 percent still suffer from radiation damage to the rectum two months afterward, and over a third report diarrhea or bowel urgency as much as two years later."[18]

Does this mean that physicians should throw up their hands and forget the idea of evidence-based medicine until someday in the misty future when the uncertainties of medical science have been resolved? No. But it might mean that the idea of *paying* for quality is, at best, premature—at least until doctors have a better idea of what quality means. What is needed is data that only extensive electronic medical records could provide, showing how millions of patients fared when they did or did not receive treatment X, Y, or Z.

Medicare's Plan: Rewarding Physicians for P4P and IT

But whatever objections the critics raise, the Centers for Medicare and Medicaid Services has put its imprimatur on both P4P and IT. And since CMS pays 60 percent of all hospital bills and 20 percent of all doctors' bills, the initiatives it backs deserve a full hearing. More than any other payer,

CMS possesses the clout to rewrite the rules for how we value medical service.

CMS is not alone in its enthusiasms. Medicare is, in fact, following the private sector's lead. Across the country, private insurers and employers have been trying out reimbursement schemes meant to encourage hospitals and physicians to meet specific quality targets, and to use electronic records to track their progress. But those programs, doctors and researchers say, are too small to make much of a difference nationally, and the jury is still out on how well they work.[19]

"Until the government moves into this, what one individual insurer does isn't enough to move the market," says Karen Davis, president of The Commonwealth Fund.[20]

But now the government is moving: CMS has begun to put a little money on the table—albeit a very little. In 2003 Medicare announced its first pay-for-performance initiative, a pilot project that promised to distribute some $21 million in financial incentives over three years to roughly 280 hospitals that meet 34 performance targets—a list that includes giving beta-blockers to heart attack victims, lowering mortality rates following coronary artery bypass graft surgery, and reducing the number of post-op orthopedic patients who receive intravenous antibiotics for more than the recommended 24 hours.

Turning the program into a contest, Medicare explained that it will compare how well hospitals meet the performance goals, and pay institutions scoring in the top 10 percent an extra 2 percent. Those in the next 10 percent will collect a 1 percent bonus. At the other end of the scale, hospitals that do not meet minimum requirements by the third year may find their fees reduced by as much as 2 percent.[21]

Critics point out that very few of the performance targets address the problems of overtreatment. While CMS is rewarding health care providers to do "more" in the form of tests and procedures that they might overlook, there are few obvious incentives to do less. "Counting how many patients survived bypass surgery is one thing," says one New York City hospital executive. "But how many survived a surgery that they didn't need? That's the important number that you'll never see."[22]

Dr. Stephen Jencks, Medicare's director of quality coordination, concedes that the critics have a point: "I would say we are moving much more slowly on trying to prevent overuse than in trying to fix underuse," he ac-

knowledged at the end of 2004. "If I tell a physician he shouldn't do a surgery he wants to do, I personally would anticipate a lot more resistance than
if I told him he should give a medicine he wasn't thinking of giving."[23] Yet if
Medicare and other payers don't find ways to locate and discourage unnecessary treatment, pay for performance will only add another layer to health
care inflation.

Granted, in April of 2005, when Washington extended the program to
doctors, it tried to incorporate incentives for doing less. Pledging to pay
bonuses to 10 large physician group practices that care for some 200,000
Medicare beneficiaries, CMS announced that a physician group will win a
bonus if total Medicare spending for its patients—including the tab for hospitals—does not rise as fast as spending on other Medicare patients in town.
At the same time, CMS told doctors that they could take home an even bigger reward if they improved their performance in meeting 32 targets, such as
cancer screening and regular blood testing of diabetic patients to be sure
their blood sugar is under control.[24] But assuming that most doctors do not
already meet all 32 targets, the larger bonus encourages them to provide *more*
services—and yet somehow charge less, if they want to win the first bonus
as well.

This is not to say that a conscientious physician couldn't achieve both
goals through wise use of preventive medicine. But clearly, policy makers are
still sidestepping the embarrassing fact that well-insured patients routinely
receive billions of dollars' worth of unnecessary and ineffective treatments,
tests, and procedures. No one really wants to suggest that health care
providers should do less.

Is 2 Percent Enough?

Meanwhile, critics like Bruce Vladeck suggest that the financial incentives
CMS is offering may not be large enough to change behavior. A 2 percent
bonus might seem a handsome reward for a hospital operating on a 2 percent margin—but that assumes that health care providers will be able to raise
quality without spending a penny. In fact, hospitals must collect the data that
demonstrate their progress. And just persuading doctors to cooperate can be
a time-consuming and labor-intensive business, as the Hackensack University Medical Center discovered in 2004.

Dr. Peter Gross, chief of the department of internal medicine at Hackensack, acknowledges that it has not been all that easy to mold physician behavior. When Hackensack enrolled in Medicare's pilot project, the hospital tried asking doctors to use a standardized order form that listed the 34 measures that Medicare was monitoring. "But the doctors didn't want to use the sheet," says Gross. "They insisted they would just remember those items."[25] Of course, in many cases they didn't.

Then the hospital tried assigning specially trained nurses to follow the doctors around, check what care was provided, and remind them when they forgot a recommended treatment. "But even when the nurses put the forms down in front of them, some of the doctors wouldn't use them," Gross confides. "So we had to have our hospitalists [physicians who, unlike private practice doctors with privileges at Hackensack, actually work for the hospital] check up on what the other doctors had done."

Couldn't Hackensack simply have told private-practice physicians that if they wanted to treat their patients at the hospital, they had to comply with Medicare's standards? "Not unless every other hospital in Bergen County would say the same thing," says Gross. Otherwise, irate doctors might well take their business—and their patients—elsewhere.

Recycling Funds from the Bottom of the Pyramid to the Top

Nevertheless, in the first year of the program, Hackensack did succeed in meeting most of its performance targets, reducing the number of post-op orthopedic surgery patients who were receiving intravenous antibiotics for more than the recommended 24 hours, for example, from 25 percent to just 6 percent. On this issue, Dr. John Andronaco, chairman of the hospital's department of orthopedic surgery, took a stand: "When some surgeons protested that longer treatment is better, I'd tell them, 'You're entitled to your opinion, but there's no validity to it.' " Clinical research shows that after 24 hours the antibiotics provide no further protection against infection and may increase the risk of antibiotic resistance.[26]

But while a market leader like Hackensack boasts both the resources and the leadership to train extra nurses and do whatever else is needed to implement the program, what happens to hospitals in the middle of the pyramid?[27] A survey of 37 pay-for-performance schemes published in *Health Affairs* in 2004 points out that almost none of these so-called quality improvement initiatives actually give points for improvement. Instead, they reward health care providers only if they meet fixed goals.

Moreover, roughly half of all P4P initiatives follow Medicare's competitive model, designing the project as a medical Bake-Off and rewarding only those health care providers who come out on top. As a result, the researchers suggest, such programs may have little effect on the many providers who realize that they have little chance of winning—even if they improve. After all, retraining staff and collecting the data Medicare wants is an expensive process, and while "some lower quality providers may be sufficiently motivated to make the investments necessary to reach for bonuses, many may find that the costs exceed the modest financial benefits from doing so."[28]

In other words, P4P programs may simply redistribute funds from the bottom of the medical pyramid to the top, without either improving those in the lowest tier—or weeding them out.

"Financial Incentives Can Work Too Well"

But this, detractors say, is not the major flaw inherent in P4P schemes. The larger danger is that pay for performance may encourage hospitals and doctors to focus on a fairly arbitrary set of performance measures that are, as Bruce Vladeck observes, "limited indicators—not a sign of quality per se."

Without question, all available evidence suggests that beta-blockers protect heart attack victims, and, without question, diabetics' blood sugar levels should be monitored. But broader and more meaningful markers of quality are needed to define overall "quality of care." By concentrating on such narrow targets, the *Health Affairs* survey of P4P plans observes, there is a real risk that "gains in one area will come at the cost of losing ground in other quality areas . . . Inevitably the dimensions of care that will receive the most attention will be those that are most easily measured, *and not necessarily those that are most valued.*" (emphasis mine)

If everyone is eyeballing their checklist of 34 targets, will anyone have time to listen to Lew Silverman—or coordinate care for patients like Ann Berwick?

"The problem is that [financial] incentives can work too well," says Harvard Business School professor Michael Beer. "They motivate employees to focus excessively on doing what they need to do to gain rewards, sometimes at the expense of doing other things." In a 2004 paper titled "Promise and Peril in Implementing Pay-for-Performance," Beer and his coauthor describe the hazards of pay for performance by focusing on Hewlett-Packard's experiments with financial incentives.[29]

In the early 1990s, HP launched 13 P4P plans in 13 separate units of the company—at different types of sites, in different states. Within three years, all 13 plans were discontinued. Why was the program such a resounding failure? When Beer and coauthor Mark Cannon interviewed the managers who had tried to implement the initiatives, "the most striking finding," they reported, "was the size of the gap between the managers' expectations of benefits and the reality they experienced." It was not just that the dollar cost of P4P outweighed the benefits; it seems that financial incentives "threatened" both "trust" and "commitment."[30]

HP is not the only company that has been hoist by its own P4P petard. Most do not talk publicly about their frustration—and very few are candid enough to let anyone publish a case study of how they wasted money. But a June, 2004 survey of 350 companies by human resources consulting firm Hewitt Associates and World at Work, a trade association that focuses on compensation issues, reveals that only 83 percent of companies using pay for performance describe their programs as even "somewhat successful" in accomplishing their goals.[31]

This is not to say that financial incentives can't change behavior. "Do rewards motivate people? Absolutely. They motivate people to get the rewards," says Alfie Kohn, an outspoken critic of pop behaviorism that he describes as "Skinner-boxed" (a reference to the father of behavioral psychology, B. F. Skinner, a man who, Kohn observes, "conducted most of his experiments on rodents and pigeons and wrote most of his books about people.")[32]

But while bonuses may keep workers as focused on the cheese as any rat on any wheel, managers have found that aligning the cheese with the company's overarching goals is tricky. And if HP had trouble getting the rewards right for workers manufacturing printers, how much more difficult must it be for hospitals to set targets that will promote effective, compassionate care?

Cherry-Picking Patients

Granted, research on how P4P might work in a medical setting has barely begun. For this reason, observers like Dr. Kenneth Kizer, president of the National Quality Forum, a not-for-profit organization devoted to developing meaningful consensus-based national standards for measuring and reporting the quality of health care, isn't ready to dismiss P4P out of hand. But he is cautious: "Pay for performance warrants a careful look and judicious application," says Kizer. "Yet there is just so much that we don't know about it. If you're not measuring the right things, you can create perverse incentives—for instance, hospitals and doctors may cherry-pick who they care for, avoiding difficult cases."[33]

Kizer underlines the real danger that a system that rewards better outcomes will penalize doctors who treat the riskiest patients—and perhaps tempt some doctors to avoid such patients altogether. This seems to be exactly what happened in New York State when physicians were publicly "graded" on their angioplasty results, according to a 2005 study published in the *Journal of the American College of Cardiology*.

When researchers compared more than 80,000 patients who received angioplasties in New York to over 11,000 patients who underwent the procedure in Michigan—a state which does not require public reporting of outcomes—they found that high-risk New Yorkers were far less likely to receive angioplasties. By contrast, in Michigan a significant percentage of patients who underwent the procedure suffered from other conditions that raised their risk of dying, such as kidney problems, diabetes, lung disease, or vascular problems. Not surprisingly, the rate of mortality following treatment was roughly twice as high in Michigan. But when the data were recalculated, taking into account the fact that the Michigan patients were much sicker on average, researchers found no difference in mortality rates.

In other words, it seems that mortality rates were lower in New York not because physicians were more skilled, but simply because they were shying away from dicey patients. "Public reporting of angioplasty outcomes has been seen as a way to improve accountability, and to drive efforts to improve quality. But these data suggest that physicians may be selecting patients who are least likely to 'bring down their grade,' so to speak," observed Dr. Mauro Moscucci, director of interventional cardiology and the cardiac catheterization laboratory at the University of Michigan in Ann Arbor, and the lead author of the study.[34] And if the "grade" were attached to a P4P check, the temptation to cherry-pick might be even greater.

Of course, Moscucci acknowledged, it could be that New York doctors simply are better at selecting appropriate patients for the procedure.[35] The fact that doctors in New York were more cautious may mean that terminally ill patients were spared futile surgeries. Or it may mean that patients who could have been saved were shunned. Without more studies, we just don't know.

What is certain, however, is that in a P4P setting, not only high-risk patients but so-called noncompliant patients (those who don't follow doctors' orders) would drag down a physician's score. The question is this: do we really want to penalize doctors and hospitals willing to treat diabetics who can't always afford to refill their prescriptions?[36]

In theory, outcomes could be risk-adjusted to take into account differences in patient populations, but the pool of patients would have to be very large. "Even using the best risk-adjustment methods available, a physician would need to have over 100 diabetic patients for quality measurement scores on this disease to be reliable," observes Dr. Lawrence Casalino, "and that physician could dramatically improve his or her score simply by pruning the two diabetics with the highest blood sugars from the practice.[37]

This is one reason why P4P might work best in large organizations where hundreds of physicians treat thousands of patients: the pool would then be large enough for risk adjustment to work.

Measuring What Counts

When it comes down to it, P4P just isn't as easy as it sounds. It's one thing to grade "outcomes" for Toyotas as they roll off an assembly line, but in a medical setting, quantifying quality becomes a treacherous project.

By paying for quality, not quantity, P4P tries to redress the perverse incentives of fee-for-service medicine. But "there is a crucial distinction between removing financial incentives that inhibit well-motivated people from doing what is appropriate, and using financial incentives as the key motivator to induce appropriate behavior," observes health care economist Jeremiah Hurley. Financial incentives work best, he suggests, when there is a single, observable, measurable goal and a clear way to match the reward to the objective: "The more we move away from such idealized worlds, the more problematic financial incentives can be." [38]

Often, what matters most simply can't be counted. How, after all, do you score the outcome for a terminally ill patient who received palliative care against the outcome for a terminally ill patient who didn't? Both died—adding to the hospital's mortality rates. Interviewing the families about whether the patient received enough pain medication, and whether he was "treated with dignity" (which is what researchers did in the study that found end-of-life care in most hospitals "woefully inadequate") would no doubt yield invaluable information—but how could Medicare translate that narrative into dollars on a P4P scale?

Again, this is not to suggest that hospitals and doctors must wait for perfect answers. Monitoring whether heart attack victims are receiving aspirin, and trying to lift the numbers, makes sense. What is in question, however, is whether a doctor's or a hospital's compensation should turn on a set of 34 or 24 or 51 specific targets—markers that have been chosen not because they measure what is most important, but because these are the things that, in this early stage of outcomes research, most clinicians can agree on.

In some cases these markers are too crude to serve as a meaningful gauge of quality (did the patient live or die?). In other cases they are too narrow (did he receive antibiotics for 28 hours instead of 24?). To judge quality, we need measures that run both broader and deeper.

The Institute for Healthcare Improvement's Don Berwick puts it this way: "Our measurements will mislead us if we forget the stories." [39] The fact that Lew Silverman died does not begin to tell the story of his hospital care. If he had survived to be transferred to the nursing home, he might have raised the hospital's score on a report card that measured quality in terms of mortality rates following kidney failure. But that would not have made his care any better.

"Playing with Fire"

Although Berwick believes in accountability, he expresses deep misgivings about pay for performance as the market's answer to pain and suffering: "Just as measurement can pluck the heart from a story, accountability can pluck the soul from our intentions," he warns. "The leader who thinks it is enough to create report cards and contingent rewards, misses the biggest and hardest opportunity of leadership itself—to help people discover and celebrate the meaning in their work."[40]

Here Berwick circles back to his main theme: that the quality of health care will improve "not because someone buys right, or pays right, or judges right," but only if doctors, nurses, pharmacists, technicians, and hospital executives band together to reform the system from within. And he does not believe that bribing them is the way to do it.

In a 2005 interview with Dr. Robert Galvin, director of global health at General Electric—an interview that turned into a debate on pay for performance—Berwick crystallized his concerns. "We've got to support the culture and the underlying system that make healing, not scoring, the objective."

In particular, Berwick objects to offering financial incentives to individual doctors and nurses: "I would draw a very dark line between the incentives that apply to organizations, boards, executives and the bottom line of a company, where I do want incentives in place. I want it to be good for an organization to be safe, and I want it to be good for an organization to manage chronic illness carefully. . . ." But "at the individual level," Berwick insists, "I don't trust incentives at all. . . . I think that it feels good to be a good doctor and better to be a better doctor. When we begin to attach dollar amounts to throughputs and to individual pay, we are playing with fire. *The first and most important effect may be to begin to disassociate people from their work.*" (emphasis mine)[41]

A 1998 Harvard Business School study supports Berwick's suspicion that external financial incentives could undermine a health care provider's internal commitment to the larger project, suggesting that P4P can cast a pall over self-esteem, teamwork, and creativity, "crushing employees' intrinsic motivation—the strong internal desire to do something based on interests and passions."[42]

Yet to GE's Galvin, the logic of P4P seems obvious: "In private industry we would simply call it understanding what makes people tick."

But is money what makes health care professionals "tick"? Berwick doesn't believe it: "I don't think the way to get better doctoring and better nursing is to put money on the table in front of individual doctors and nurses." Instead, he continues to insist that what he calls "the will to excellence . . . the latent will in the workforce to do better" is the key. Time and again, Berwick has seen IHI's Breakthrough initiatives work without any financial incentives, precisely because so many hospital workers are so frustrated to find themselves laboring in a broken, wasteful system, which can make much of their work seem redundant or even pointless.

Imagine, for instance, being the nurse who brought Colace to Ann Berwick, night after night, knowing that she would just throw it away. Until someone wrote an order telling the nurse not to bring it, she had to continue the farce. And the systems of communication that should have brought that order were broken. Given a chance, Berwick suggests, that nurse would like nothing more than an opportunity to turn her hospital into a meaningful workplace. And it's not too much of a stretch to guess that such an opportunity might be worth more to her than a 2 percent raise.

Tapping into that desire, says Berwick, is "like drilling for oil. There is so much pent-up need in the health care work force that, without financial incentives, health care workers are eager to make a change."

But when Berwick made that argument, GE's Galvin countered that when his company talked to physician leaders about financial incentives in GE's P4P program, "Their message was that to motivate their practicing physicians, financial rewards were part of the equation. More than three thousand doctors are participating in this program," Galvin added, "and their message has been, 'Look, I could use some of this money for improvement. I could use some of this money to put investments into my practice.' "

Berwick remained unconvinced. "Of course when you're talking money to the doctors, they're going to talk money to you," he replied. "You say that we're playing baseball and they'll play baseball. But you've got to make sure it's baseball you want to play. That's what we've got to keep our eye on.

"The problem with pay-for-performance is not that it doesn't mold behavior," Berwick continued. "The problem is that it does mold behavior. You get exactly what you're paying for, which might not in the end, when you're finally on your deathbed, be exactly what you wish you'd gotten."

Or, as Alfie Kohn warns: "Excellence pulls in one direction, rewards in another. Tell people that their income will depend on their productivity or performance rating, and they will focus on the number."[43]

In the end, Bruce Vladeck suggests, "quality improvement strategies need to focus on reinforcing the norms and values of professional responsibility rather than on undermining them through the exercise of economic

muscle. Unless we can continue to assume that most providers and administrators want to do the right thing for most patients most of the time,"
Vladeck adds, "we are all sunk—and no amount of economic incentives can
salvage the situation." [44]

The Case for Paperless Medicine

Even while rejecting P4P as a Washington sound bite, Vladeck does support
IT, and suggests that rather than doling out rewards to individual hospitals
and physicians—and hoping that they plow the money into software—
Medicare might better make a direct contribution to the IT revolution by
giving doctors and hospitals funds specifically earmarked for computerized
medicine.

Here Vladeck stands squarely with the majority. While some quarrel over
the need for P4P, when it comes to IT, nearly everyone, from President
George W. Bush to Senator Hillary Clinton (a broad spectrum of opinion, to
be sure), agrees: electronic medical records are key to making sure that patients like Ann Berwick are spared the agonies and expense of redundant
tests, lost records, and medication errors. Information technology may not
be a final solution, but it is, at the very least, the clearest path to "doing less
and doing it right."

Electronic medical records provide a snapshot of a patient's progress,
making it easy to chart cholesterol levels or weight loss over a period of time.
And if five specialists are treating a patient, they can call up the same chart
on their laptops and see what drugs and tests other doctors have ordered—
making it much easier to coordinate care. Computerized health care also allows doctors to order drugs and lab tests online—greatly reducing the
number of errors caused by physicians' scrawl. Finally, as laptops replace
clipboards, nurses no longer have to spend hours trying to track down missing orders, lost lab results—or missing doctors.

Duke University's Dr. Robert Califf still remembers the doctor who was
missing in action following his mother's knee surgery. "After Vioxx was
taken off the market, the pain in my mother's knee was bad enough that she
decided to have a knee replacement," Califf recalls. "The surgery went
smoothly, but when she was transferred from orthopedics to rehab, her
chart was lost. And the hospitalist who last had it was so busy that they

couldn't find him for 12 hours. In the meantime, the nurses couldn't give my mother her pain medication because they didn't have the chart."[45] In a paperless hospital, that wouldn't happen. Anyone with a laptop could have retrieved her records.

Bringing Evidence-Based Medicine to the Bedside

Health IT also could address one of the most frightening—and least talked-about—threats to patients' welfare: idiosyncratic care. "Ask 135 doctors how they would treat a particular condition for a particular patient, and research shows them coming up with 82 separate treatments," reports George Halvorson, chairman and CEO of Kaiser Permanente, the California-based group practice health care program that has become a leader in the use of information technology.[46]

"Why?" Halvorson continues. "Because some physicians graduated from medical school last month. Others graduated a year ago, or 20 years ago, or 40 years ago. Some attended seminars on the topic. Others read articles on the topic. Some articles were recent. Some weren't. Some physicians were influenced by drug company sales representatives.

"So inconsistency happens," he concludes. "That's understandable, particularly when so many American doctors still function as solo practitioners or with a single partner. These doctors are trying to run a business, see a full load of patients, hire and fire staff . . . and then do all the necessary medical reading and learning."

This, Halvorson suggests, helps explain why doctors and hospitals often don't use the best scientific evidence available when treating even the most common medical conditions. He points to a 2003 study "that looked at 18,000 patient charts in communities across the country, comparing the care patients received to the best practice protocols agreed to by some of the best medical minds in the country. What they found is that only 55 percent of patients received care in keeping with the current best practices."

Given the uncertainties of medical science, perhaps this should not come as a surprise. After all, what the "best medical minds" agreed upon in 2003 might well be out of fashion by 2007. Still, there are some areas where the consensus is firm and endures for years. Yet even in cases "where the medical science was particularly clear and strongly supported by 'level one' research [which means that there are multiple, reaffirming, clinically valid studies that reach a common conclusion], the number of physicians following best practice protocols rose to only 57 percent," Halvorson points out.[47] Most often, doctors don't translate knowledge into practice, not because they disagree with the evidence, but because they are unaware of the latest studies. Indeed, in 2001 the Institute of Medicine roiled the medical world by disclosing that it can take 15 to 20 years for new scientific knowledge to percolate down into everyday medical practice.[48]

In a world where doctors are buried in paper, the lag is unavoidable, says Halvorson: "As medical science progresses exponentially, it is unfair to both physicians and patients to expect the physician's memory to be sufficient to keep all care practices and patient follow-up steps current and up to speed. Every doctor wants to do the right thing," he adds, "but there are now approximately 23,000 medical journals published each year. No single physician can be entirely current."

To stay abreast of evolving scientific knowledge, physicians need help "right at the point when patients are receiving care," says Halvorson. This is where "decision-support technology" comes into play, bringing the latest research to the bedside, and matching that research to the information on a patient's electronic medical record. "In the past, physicians have had to hunt down their own scientific updates through a relatively haphazard process that includes seminars, journal articles, and salespeople from drug companies and medical equipment manufacturers," he explains. "But we are now moving beyond that point to having search engines for physicians that can do a much more thorough, complete, and timely review of the available source and literature custom-tailored to individual patients."

At New York–Presbyterian Hospital, for instance, software suggests treatment plans for cardiac intensive-care patients by matching patient characteristics such as age, disease type, and medication history to the records of some 7,500 cardiac patients stored in a data repository. "This idea of a decision-support system is one of the outcomes we'd like to see from the introduction of electronic medical records," says Eric Brown, an analyst at Forrester Research, Inc. "It is taking your particular situation and plugging it into the database—not searching for all people who have had a heart attack, but all patients who have had a heart attack who look like you."[49]

Some physicians bridle at the idea of being handcuffed to evidence-based protocols, objecting to that what they call "cookbook medicine."

Many argue that medicine is an art which draws heavily on the individual physician's intuitions. "I don't need someone second-guessing me or telling me how to practice medicine," says a Manhattan specialist who has been flying solo for more than 25 years. But like most advocates of evidence-based medicine, Halvorson advocates guidelines, not hard-and-fast rules. "Rules-based medicine is wrong," he says. "But guidelines-based medicine is clearly superior to the kind of fiercely nonsystematic, idiosyncratic approach that creates 82 diferent treatments for just one patient."

The best large group practices, like Kaiser or the Mayo Clinic, routinely create guidelines for consistent standards of care, and the doctors in these groups rely on those standards. Knowing that other physicians are looking over your shoulder also makes a difference. "When you're all working with the same chart, and you know the other docs are going to see your notes on that chart—well, you'd be embarrassed if you weren't up to speed," confides one doctor.[50]

Working elbow to elbow, physicians in these large groups share their knowledge, and large groups also are more likely to have access to electronic databases.[51] By contrast, "it's easy for solo practitioners to fall behind without even knowing it," says Dr. Andrew Wiesenthal, Kaiser's IT expert.[52]

Wiesenthal speaks from experience. His 86-year-old father lives in Manhattan, where he is routinely seen by four or five separate specialists, each working alone. "It's frustrating as hell," says Wiesenthal. "Because of the atomized nature of care in New York, there is too little communication—and very little scrutiny. One doctor has no idea what another doctor is planning. I'm forced into the position of being the integrator; I have to call up all these doctors to try to square things away. I'm lucky—at least I'm a physician, so they take my calls.

"I know it doesn't have to be this way," he adds. "I've been in a system [Kaiser Permanente] for 25 years where we have a single medical record for each patient, and I can always tell what my colleagues are thinking. But when everyone is practicing solo, care can be of poor quality and no one knows. These doctors in Manhattan are quick to adopt new technologies that they can bill for," he adds, "but when it comes to things like keeping up to date on lipid management or statins . . ."

Wiesenthal recalls how his father, who takes statins (drugs that have been shown to lower both total cholesterol and low-density lipoprotein [LDL], or bad cholesterol), went from one specialist to the another, complaining about muscle pain. "And yet no one recommended taking him off the statins," says Wiesenthal, "even though muscle pain is a known side effect for a small percentage of patients"—particularly those over 80.[53] "If he were younger, you would want to keep him on them, but at his age, and given his cholesterol levels, the risk-benefit equation is different.[54] The doctors that I talk to in New York all seem smart," Wiesenthal adds, "but they fail to communicate, and some of them fail to keep up."

The Bell Curve

It is not only doctors who resist the idea that computerized standards should help guide a physician's decision making, George Halvorson admits: "Surveys show that the vast majority of patients say their strong personal preference would be for their doctors to be totally independent of any external influence relative to their pattern of care. That preference is understandable but unfortunate," he adds. "Most Americans just don't realize how inconsistent or even dangerous care can be. Even if they've heard it's inconsistent, the vast majority believe that their own personal physician is in the top 55 percent who are following current best practices.

"The situation is compounded," Halvorson adds, "by the fact that it is 'politically incorrect' and 'impolite' inside American health care to point out the disparities in both care outcomes and care practices. Health plans are afraid of making doctors angry if the topic is raised. Physicians tend not to point out the performance problems of other physicians."

Yet, privately, any physician can tell stories of incompetent and even reckless colleagues. "When my husband was training as a surgeon, one of the attending physicians liked to tell the residents, 'Anyone can operate drunk; only a real man can operate hungover,' Dr. Liz Dreesen recalls. "Everyone knew that he took calls from a bar behind the hospital."[55] Why didn't anyone say anything? In large part because "no one wanted to be sued," says Dreesen. As discussed in chapter 2, whistle-blowing doctors can be subject to harsh retribution.

In theory, peer review would weed out incompetence, but "it's very difficult to have peer review at a small hospital in a small town," says Dreesen, remembering her experience in a mill town in North Carolina. "I was used to academic medicine, where you have mortality and morbidity [M&M] conferences to openly discuss what went wrong when a patient runs into complications and dies. Everyone takes their licks because everyone makes mistakes."

But today at more than a few hospitals, peer review has devolved into what Dreesen describes as "screaming and shouting. At our hospital in North Carolina, the peer review for surgery was held in a hotel," she recalls. The person in charge didn't want any of the nurses or administrators overhearing us—because of the gossip factor.

"Some of the doctors provided very good care, but maybe 20 percent just weren't competent. This is true, not only in a small town in North Carolina, but even at the finest academic medical centers," Dreesen adds. "At Harvard—where I trained—there were certain surgeons who we would refer to as 'HODAD' [rhymes with gonad]."

HODAD?

"Hands of death and destruction," Dreesen explains. "With a surgeon, it's not so much about dexterity as confidence and quickness—the ability to make a decision in the middle of an operation. Inevitably, there are times when you operate expecting to find X, and when you open the patient up, you find Y—most commonly in emergency cases, but even in elective cases where the patient was pretty well worked up."

Liz Dreesen's experience is far from unique. The painful truth, observes Boston surgeon Atul Gawande, is that physicians, like electricians, Ivy League professors, and everyone else, live on a bell curve. "It used to be assumed that differences among hospitals or doctors in a particular specialty were generally insignificant," says Gawande. "If you plotted a graph showing the results" of all doctors or hospitals treating a particular disease, "people expected that the curve would look something like a shark fin, with most [hospitals or doctors] clustered around the best outcomes. But the evidence has begun to indicate otherwise. What you tend to find is a bell curve: a handful of teams with disturbingly poor outcomes for their patients" at one end, "a handful with remarkably good results," at the other end, "and a great undistinguished middle. . . .

"It is distressing for doctors to have to acknowledge the bell curve," he adds. "It contradicts the belief nearly all of us have that we are doing our job as well as it can be done. But evidence of the bell curve is starting to trickle out, to doctors and patients alike, and we are only beginning to find out what happens when it does." [56]

What is likely to happen, Gawande suggests, is that once we acknowledge that the bell curve exists, patients will demand to know more about how well their doctors and hospitals perform. But first we'll need much subtler ways of gauging performance. Today, Gawande points out, "report cards" on doctors and hospitals are crude. As an example, he cites what a website called HealthGrades reveals about his own career: "For $7.95 you will learn, for instance, that I am in fact certified in my specialty, have no criminal convictions, have not been fired from any hospital, have not had my license suspended or revoked, and have not been disciplined. This is no doubt useful to know. But it sets the bar a tad low, doesn't it?"

Gawande emphasizes how difficult it is "to figure out what to measure. . . . Death rates are a poor metric for how doctors do. . . . What one really wants to know is how we perform in typical circumstances. After I've done an appendectomy, how long does it take for my patients to fully recover? After I've taken out a thyroid cancer, how often do my patients have serious avoidable complications? How do my results compare with those of other surgeons?" Today, getting such data is an all but impossible task, he notes, because "medicine still relies heavily on paper records."

Monitoring Performance

Nevertheless, some hospitals have begun to track physicians' performance—even without IT—and the results can be startling. In the mid-1990s, Dr. Kim Adcock, the head of radiology at Kaiser Permanente Colorado, a division of the nonprofit Kaiser Foundation Health Plan, decided to review how well radiologists in his department were doing in reading mammograms. "We didn't yet have electronic medical records, so we had to do most of the work by hand," Adcock recalls.[57] But it was worth it. What they discovered was a head-turning difference in physicians' ability to pick out lumps at a very early stage. "One of our radiologists was finding cancers at about one-tenth the rate of the rest of the group—he had read 3,100 mammograms in the 18 months he was with us, and when we went back and reread all of his mammograms, we found 10 additional cancers," says Adcock.

When the monitoring was completed, "about half of the 21 physicians who had been reading mammograms immediately and voluntarily surrendered their mammography privileges," Adcock recalls. "Some were missing small lumps; others just weren't reading enough mammograms, so we didn't have enough data to tell if they were reading them well." Some doctors were reassigned to read other kinds of X-rays. "We tried remedial training of the radiologist who had done so poorly," he adds, "but he didn't cooperate, so we asked him to leave." Before long, the number of undetected cancers dropped from 14 percent to 6 percent.

"This happened even though the doctors reading the mammograms were all trained radiologists," Kaiser CEO Halvorson observes. "In the non-Kaiser Permanente world, those X-rays are often read by internists and family practitioners with much lower levels of training. Some do a superb job. Others do not."[58]

By 1998 Kaiser's Colorado outpost had electronic medical records, "and now our monitoring is much more comprehensive and much more detailed," Adcock reports. How do doctors respond to having their performance measured? "It makes them nervous," he acknowledges. "But I can't think too much about that. What makes a physician good is his selflessness—his concern for the welfare of the patient over his own welfare. Against that paradigm I really don't care too much about physicians' druthers. At the end of the day you can't rationally defend the idea that you don't want to be monitored because it's uncomfortable."

Halvorson agrees, though he acknowledges that such monitoring could be tricky in a different setting: "In large group practices like the Mayo Clinic, The Cleveland Clinic, or Geisinger, where an exclusive network of salaried physicians work for the plan, this kind of monitoring is much easier than it would be in a fee-for-service setting, where physicians have privileges at a hospital but aren't employed by the hospital."[59] Doctors in private practice might well bristle at the idea of being "graded" by other doctors.

Nevertheless, advocates of evidence-based medicine hope that with expanded use of IT to measure performance, it will become easier to lift the quality of care. "The bell curve will always be with us," says one hospital administrator, "but the goal is to diagnose problems on the far left of the curve and then move the entire curve to the right," so that performance in "the great undistinguished middle" is not just pretty good, but very good.[60]

Hurdles

By the summer of 2005, the case for marrying information technology to medicine seemed clear, and the media was heralding what some called "the e-health" revolution. "Backed by the Bush Administration, prodded by employers and under pressure to contain costs and improve service, the medical community is finally—and rapidly—plugging into the new world of electronic health records," *Time* magazine reported. "The U.S. government is leading this charge into the medical information age . . . Dr. Mark McClellan, director of the Centers for Medicare and Medicaid Services, is making paperless medicine mandatory for physicians who hope to participate in the agency's potentially remunerative pay-for-performance scheme." On the sidelines, the magazine noted, corporations like Siemens Medical Solutions, IBM, and General Electric were salivating, "betting billions on the market for health-information technology."[61]

But the IT revolution in health care was far from a done deal. The players still had not agreed on data-sharing standards that would allow IT systems to talk to one another. And the very fact that so many powerful companies were jousting for health care's IT dollars did not bode well for unanimity.

Indeed, J. D. Kleinke blames the lack of standards on a competitive market where "fractious health IT vendors" and other self-interested players "work at economic cross-purposes" in a fee-for-service system. There is "a collective business case for a national health IT system, but it is one well beyond the reach of the health care marketplace," says the author of *Oxymorons: The Myth of a U.S. Health Care System*. The "failure of the health IT market is rooted in economic problems . . . typical of fragmented industries," Kleinke declares, a "failure exacerbated by U.S. reliance on the zigzag of market forces to generate technology standards.[62]

"The problem is hardly unique to health care," adds Kleinke, who serves both as executive director of Omnimedix, a research institute that focuses on health IT, and as chairman of HealthGrades, a publicly traded health information company. "Numerous other U.S. IT-related industries limp along behind their counterparts in more highly regulated economies," Kleinke points out. "While U.S. wireless telephone carriers fought for more than a decade over which of two protocols to adopt, leaving all of us to 'roam' (where we could) across carriers, countries throughout the rest of the world had the luxury of saying: 'Use this one, and get on with it.' The same goes for broadband access, which is why the United States ranks sixteenth in the world for the percentage of citizens with broadband access, and why that access moves data at only 60 percent of the rate of the broadband installed in the rest of the industrialized world.

"This is hardly an argument for the virtues of command-and-control economies or industrial planning," Kleinke insists. "Rather it is an elucidation of the hidden costs . . . of relying on markets for IT standardization . . . Most Americans . . . probably are not aware of what they do not have, but U.S. technology markets are years behind those in Asia and several European countries, thanks to our reliance on messy markets to grind their way toward standardized technology platform design rather than [relying on] rational orderly design."[63]

"Rational orderly design" is, according to Kleinke, "precisely what David Brailer [the Bush administration's point man on IT] and [CMS administrator] Mark McClellan are attempting to inspire in the fractious IT vendor community, with more words than dollars, from their bully pulpits in Washington." Though here Kleinke expresses his skepticism that their words will suffice to nudge private-sector players toward a consensus. Rather than "waiting for the invisible hand of a market that [might] never appear," Washington should "get the job done," Kleinke declares.

But in the fall of 2005, Brailer made it clear that he had no intention of imposing mandatory IT standards on the health care industry. Instead, he announced that he hoped to coax the various players to "come together and agree on a national solution." Brailer acknowledged the size of the challenge: "Many organizations are developing standards, but they reflect the health care industry itself: they're highly fragmented. . . . If there are two ways to represent lab data or three ways to represent a prescription or five ways to represent a patient's physical findings . . . we have [all of these] permutations," he admitted. "It's the same problem as having railroads of a different gauge or VHS versus Betamax [videotape], although I think there's more at stake with health care than with videotapes.[64]

"Divergent stakeholder interests" are creating a "significant barrier to agreement," Brailer conceded. Nevertheless, he insisted, "we're not going to mandate standards. . . . I think the miracle of what we're doing—and it's experimental, it's risky—is that we have not dictated the outcome as a typical government regulation would. . . . What we're doing is a market-based process. We're going to bring the purchasers, public and private . . . and the providers to the table . . . It's difficult, it's complicated, it's messy, but it's so much preferable to the alternative."

At the same time, Brailer confessed, he was worried. "I'm worried about interoperability. In fact, I would tell you that I think the likely outcome—unless we're smart, aggressive and lucky—is for IT adoption to occur with lip service to interoperability." His worst fear: a wired maze in which hospitals, labs, and doctors' offices are not able to talk to one another. "Every medical office will be just an automated island."

And in 2005 he recognized that he faced a narrow window of opportunity: "We have a very low IT adoption rate now, and that gives us a onetime opportunity to put the foundation for interoperability in place before that adoption rate goes up. . . . I am concerned that if we don't take the opportunity today, it'll be lost for thirty years." If that happens, Brailer acknowledged, the patient would be the loser: "The consumer benefit is completely locked up in interoperability."

Physicians Rebel: Showdown at Cedars-Sinai

Assuming that Brailer's worst fears are not realized, and the market manages to coalesce around IT standards, hospitals and doctors still face a signal challenge: learning how to tap into a new system. Up to 30 percent of all experiments with electronic medical records fail, because they are not well designed and/or because physicians resist adapting to a new way of doing business.[65] The IT fiasco at Los Angeles' Cedars-Sinai Medical Center stands out as a rather spectacular example of what happens when a hospital ignores what business consultants call "human change management."

After several years of laying groundwork, Cedars-Sinai installed its $34 million computerized physician order entry system in the fall of 2002. Almost immediately, physicians began to protest that the system was slowing them down. Instead of scribbling orders at the patient's bedside, they had to find a computer, log in, check a list of the boxes to describe the patient's condition, and type in instructions for treatment and medication. The system wouldn't accept the smallest misspellings, and if a doctor asked for anything out of the ordinary, warnings flashed.

"They designed the system poorly, sold it poorly, jammed it down our throats, and then had the audacity to say everybody loves it and that it's a great system," fumes Dr. Dudley Danoff.[66] Only 40 of the 2,000 doctors with privileges at the hospital were involved in the planning. Administrators also made a mistake by opting for a " 'big bang' implementation rather than switching on one ward at a time," says Paul Hackmeyer, an obstetrician-gynecologist who practices at the hospital."[67]

"Meanwhile we have 2,000 physicians with varying degrees of computer competence practicing at the hospital—some who didn't know what a mouse is, others who were writing their own software," explains Dr. John Harold, Cedars-Sinai's chief of staff.[68] For physicians who were not part of the computer generation, the learning curve was steep.

Imagine trying to master a new computer program while working in an ICU. "Many information systems simply don't reflect the health care professional's hectic work environment, with its all too frequent interruptions from phone calls, pages, colleagues and patients," Joan Ash, an associate professor at Oregon Health & Science University, notes in a 2003 study of computerized physician order entry systems. "Instead they are designed for people who work in calm and solitary environments."[69]

At Cedars-Sinai time became the most contentious issue. Tasks that normally took a few minutes could consume half an hour. "Who's got five extra hours in a day?" asks pulmonary specialist Andrew S. Wachtel.[70] Most physicians with privileges at Cedars-Sinai are in private practice—many with offices in Beverly Hills—and for them, losing 30 minutes meant losing 30 billable minutes. "They were a lot more upset than doctors who work for the hospital," observes one insider.[71]

Quarrels over whether the computers were slowing work flow became so intense that one doctor clocked colleagues with a stopwatch to prove the delays were exaggerated. "The perception of time and actual time sometimes are not congruent," Michael Langberg, Cedars-Sinai's vice president and chief medical officer told *The Washington Post*. But, he admitted, "It almost doesn't matter what the actual time was."

Perceptions would fuel a rebellion that culminated in a heated showdown between physicians and hospital management in January of 2003. With several hundred doctors demanding an end to the experiment, management had no choice but to back down, scrapping the multimillion-dollar system just three months after it was installed. And Cedars-Sinai is not unique. Dr. David Classen of First Consulting Group, a health care and telecommunications firm, says he knows of at least six other hospitals that have pulled paperless systems in the face of physician resistance.[72]

Two and a half years later, Cedars-Sinai still wasn't sure when it would try again, though the hospital's chief of staff was certain that eventually the hospital would be fully wired. "The biggest problem was for physicians close to 50," Harold pointed out in 2005. "But between two years ago and now we've had a 30 percent turnover of our staff. Every five years this becomes less and less of an issue."[73]

Can Doctors Afford It?

Yet even if an MTV generation of physicians embraces IT, the steepest hurdle remains—cost. Bruce Vladect warns, "It's everyone's interest to underestimate how expensive information technology is."[74]

For physicians in a small group practice, the price of installing and implementing an electronic record-keeping system runs "from $6,000 to $12,000 per physician per year for five years," points out Dr. Thomas Lee, network president of Partners HealthCare, an integrated group of hospitals and physicians. A tidy sum, he notes, "especially if you consider that most doctors in private practice are small business owners, many of them trying to juggle higher practice costs without losing personal income at the same time that they're being asked to invest in technology."[75]

Information technology has swept through industries where huge corporations enjoy economies of scale which help them realize a return on an IT investment over a relatively short period of time. But health care is still, by and large, a cottage industry of independent hospitals and doctors vying for their share of a local market, with most care delivered by practices made up of fewer than 10 doctors.

To be sure, there are doctors and there are doctors. In 2003 the median income for primary care physicians, pediatricians, and doctors in family practice was roughly $157,000—which is to say that half of the doctors in the group earned less. And many of those at the bottom end of the scale were younger physicians still paying off medical school loans that averaged $100,000 to $135,000.[76]

General surgeons fared better, taking home an average of $264,000, while at the top of the ladder, orthopedic surgeons, cardiologists, pain specialists, oncologists, neurologists, hand surgeons, and radiologists often pulled in half a million dollars a year—sometimes much more.[77] "Overall, physicians in the U.S. today remain better compensated than physicians anywhere else in the world," Boston surgeon Atul Gawande observes. "Our earnings are more than seven times the average American employee, and the gap has grown over time. In most industrialized nations," he added, "the ratio is under three."[78]

As in the rest of the economy, the gap between those at the top of the physicians' pyramid and those at the bottom is enormous—and not easily explained. Yes, surgery requires more training than pediatrics, but not by a factor of five. In recent years some cardiologists, orthopedic surgeons, and ophthalmologists have been able to boost their incomes by moving more services out of the hospital and into their offices, where they offer lucrative imaging services and other diagnostic tests. Others offset declining reimbursements by consulting with drugmakers and device makers. But this is only part of the explanation as to why some doctors make so much more than others. Traditionally, doctors who invade the surface of the body—whether with a tube, a knife, or a tiny wire—have been paid more than those who listen, think, and diagnose. Is this because when we feel most vulnerable, we are ready to pay more? Whatever the reason, as we saw in chapter 5, even when Medicare recalibrated physicians' wages in the early nineties, doctors who practice "cognitive medicine" remained at the bottom of the pay scale.

"When you come down to it, incomes at the high end have less to do with years of training or the skill and labor involved—which is very hard to measure—and more to do with what the market will bear," says one Boston physician, pointing out that the best-paid doctors often don't take insurance and simply charge whatever they think their patients will pay.[79] In New York, an eye surgeon agrees. When asked how he chose his specialty, he replies: "What are your eyes worth?"[80] By the same logic, it's not too surprising that pain specialists and oncologists wind up near the top of the ladder.

Return on Investment

While a pediatrician earning $120,000 a year might well have to think long and hard about plowing $60,000 into information technology over five years, a cardiologist netting half a million should be able to afford state-of-the-art IT. But that does not mean that the investment makes sense as a business proposition. Indeed, from the point of view of an individual doctor or hospital, the "business case" for IT is shaky.

Without question, over the long term, if information technology is used to reduce hazardous, wasteful treatments, it should save money for the health care system as a whole. Indeed, Blackford Middleton, chairman of the Center for Information Technology Leadership, a nonprofit research organization affiliated with the Harvard Medical School, estimates that the country would reap savings of $44 billion a year from computerized systems that allowed physicians to order drugs online, by eliminating the 2 million "adverse drug events" that occur each year.[81]

But Middleton is assessing the savings for the larger society. For a hospital or a small group of physicians, IT is an investment that may never pay off. For by "doing less and doing it right," health care providers reduce their own revenues. "Let's say you do a really good job of keeping someone out of the hospital," one doctor says. "Or let's say you save someone a physician's visit. You save the system money, but nobody benefits from the savings."[82]

By "nobody" he means "nobody I know." Insurers and taxpayers—not to mention the patient himself—benefit when electronic medical records help health care providers do a better job of managing chronically ill patients. "But in the traditional fee-for-service system, it makes no financial sense at all for physicians or hospitals to invest in programs that would reduce patients' need for medical services," says Dr. Lawrence Casalino.[83] As an example, he points to a physician group or hospital that spends money on programs aimed at reducing the number of physician and emergency room visits asthma patients need. The physician group or hospital "invests the money and makes the effort, but the HMO [i.e., the insurer that pays the bills] reaps the reward."

"Programs that improve quality and are likely to save money—but only in the distant future—are even more problematic," says Casalino. "For example, a medical group [that] invests in a program to identify its diabetic patients, track whether each is receiving annual retinal exams, and contact them if they are not, may create savings by ultimately preventing severe diabetic retinopathy, which causes blindness. But these savings will not occur until 5 to 20 years in the future, by which time the patient is likely to be with another physician group."

Ideally, physicians and hospitals would be able and willing to make the up-front investment in IT in order to improve the quality of care. But few hospital administrators enjoy the luxury of being able to step back and think about how their decisions might affect the health care system as a whole. J. D. Kleinke sums up the problem: "The practical reality is that return on investment (ROI) is modest, at best, ephemeral for most and attainable only well past its investment horizon—a dressed up way of saying that it exceeds the political capital [and likely tenure] of its current CEO and CIO."[84]

Since insurers and other payers will reap the rewards of doing less in the form of lower medical bills, some experts suggest that they should help health care providers pay for IT. "The goal is to find ways so that the parties that realize the benefit will subsidize gaps in return on investment," explains Mike Kappel, senior vice president for strategic planning at McKesson Corporation, a firm that sells software to hospitals and insurers. And in some cases, insurers have done just that. "The three major insurers that dominate the Massachusetts market—Blue Cross [and] Blue Shield of Massachusetts, Tufts, and Harvard Pilgrim—have been structuring payments to encourage more adoption of electronic health records," says Dr. Thomas Lee of Partners HealthCare. And they all use the same basic approach: reserving 10 percent to 15 percent of a doctor's fee-for-service payments as a reward for achieving specific quality goals—including the adoption of new systems.

But Lee is quick to admit that these three Massachusetts plans enjoy an advantage over many other regions: they are all not-for-profits that emphasize quality initiatives, and some of the academic centers in Boston were already far ahead of the curve in terms of buying up the latest technology. "Outside of that elite, though, providers haven't been so quick to get on the tech bandwagon," *Managed Care* magazine reports in an article titled "Electronic Medical Records: High Hopes Meet Harsh Reality." Lee agrees: "It's terrific that the insurance companies are beginning to value electronic records, but it won't be sufficient to get the broad adoption we need. We need Medicare to provide other incentives."[85]

Not everyone is sure that will happen. "When it comes to spending, the current administration's priorities are elsewhere," says Gartner's Hieb.[86]

Nevertheless, despite the hurdles, one large hospital system has made a full transition into a paperless universe, and its success illustrates how well IT can work to improve quality—and under what conditions.

A System That Works

When Scott Wallace's 62-year-old father suffered a stroke in 1998, "he was massively overweight," Wallace recalls, "suffering from high blood pressure, elevated cholesterol, and borderline diabetes. He hadn't seen a doctor in probably a decade. Then he was admitted the hospital, and that's when the cascade began. Suddenly, he went from no physicians to, at one point, 21 physicians—with no obvious way of communicating with each other.[87]

"Once he was in the hospital, it became clear that he was suffering from a series of respiratory and kidney problems," Wallace continues—and this is when the specialists began to contradict one another. "Before long, we learned that the medications that the renal specialists thought were most important were impacting the medications that the pulmonologists recommended. They hadn't talked to each other. They were relying on my mother—who is almost completely deaf—to coordinate my father's care. They assumed that she would tell them anything important, and that anything she said was gospel."

After Wallace's father went home, the problems proliferated. "At one point, a cardiologist prescribed a medication that conflicted with what the neurologist had already given him, causing his heart to stop," Wallace recalls. "The squad picked him up and raced him to the hospital. There, a third set of doctors had to figure out what the first two had done.

"Over a period of four and a half years, this continued to happen, with my father winding up in the ER or the ICU each time," says Wallace. "Finally, when it happened a sixth time, a friend who is a doctor in Houston suggested that I come down and look at the hospital where he worked. So I flew from Chicago to Houston, and when I got there, I realized: 'It doesn't have to be this way.'

"At the time I knew nothing about electronic health records," says Wallace, who is now president and chief executive officer of the National Alliance for Health Information Technology. But he knew he liked what he saw in Houston: a fully computerized hospital, where doctors wheel their laptops to their patients' bedside and with a keystroke, pull up their medical records. When they prescribe a medication, they enter the order on their computer, and the system immediately checks it against the patient's records to see what other drugs he is taking.

"If the new drug could produce an adverse reaction, I'll get a message back, saying 'Did you realize that what you just ordered could cause seizure in combination with this other medication the patient is on?' " explains one doctor. "Of course, I didn't."[88]

When the order is accepted and the hospital pharmacist fills the prescription, the system generates a bar code that goes on the bottle identifying the medication, who it is for, when it should be administered, in what dose, and by whom. Each patient also has an ID bracelet with his own bar code, as does each nurse. Before giving the patient any medication, the nurse must first scan the patient's ID bracelet, then her own, then the bar code on the bottle. If she's trying to give the wrong drug to the wrong patient, the computer will tell her. It also creates a report showing exactly when she administered the medication.[89]

Wallace knew that this was the care he wanted for his father. And he also knew that he wouldn't have to fly him to Houston to get it. The hospital where his friend works is part of the largest health care network in the United States: the Department of Veterans Affairs (VA) system, which operates some 157 hospitals, 134 nursing homes, and 887 outpatient clinics nationwide—all of them fully wired.

"I transferred my father to the VA hospital near his home in Cincinnati, and once I got him in there, the nonsense ended," says Wallace. "For the past three and a half years he has had a single medical record, and each of his doctors has access to what all of the others are doing, with one rehab doctor coordinating his care.

"I don't think these were bad physicians at the other hospital," Wallace adds. "They were conscientious and concerned. But they were working in a system that is just insane—paying everyone to work independently, paying everyone for volume . . . The VA has a system that works."

The Turnaround

This was not always the case. In 1994 the VA's critics used words like "squalor" when describing the system. A quarter of the VA's hospital beds were empty, and in many regions of the country, veterans who could find care elsewhere did. In the debate over the Clinton health care plan, conservative activist Jarret B. Wollstein held the VA up as a symbol of government-run medicine: "To see the future of health care in America for you and your children under Clinton's plan," Wollstein warned, "just visit any Veterans Administration hospital. You'll find filthy conditions, shortages of everything, and treatment bordering on barbarism."[90]

That was the year that Kenneth Kizer, a physician with 48 years' experience, trained in emergency medicine and public health, became the Veterans Health Administration's undersecretary for health. The former director of California's Department of Health Services set out to reinvent the VA system: closing hospitals, opening community clinics, firing specialists, hiring primary care physicians, and ushering in a new era of computerized medicine. "While the rest of the country moved toward unfettered access to specialists, the VA focused on ensuring access to high-quality primary care," observes Dartmouth's Elliott Fisher. "Between 1994 and 1998 the number of veterans enrolled to receive care rose from 2.6 million to 3.1 million, and the number of beds in use fell by 55 percent."[91] Meanwhile, the VA created 300 community-based clinics, "without Congress having to appropriate a cent," Kizer recalls. "We did it all by redirecting resources, closing unused beds that we didn't really need, reducing the number of specialists in the system, and negotiating better prices for drugs."[92]

Kizer's success turned on his decision to combine an old-fashioned emphasis on primary care with 21st-century information technology. While putting fewer heads on beds, the VA began investing in IT, using computerized case management to practice evidence-based medicine in its new outpatient clinics. A 2005 Rand Corporation study broadcast the results: comparing medical records of 600 VA patients with those of about 1,000 non-VA patients with similar health problems, researchers found that chronically ill patients who came to the VA received 72 percent of recommended care, while patients in the control group received only 59 percent of recommended treatment.[93]

The VA also uses its database of patients' medical records for research. After a review of those records at the end of 2001, it sharply curtailed its use of COX-2 inhibitors like Vioxx—more than two years before Merck took Vioxx off the market. The Mayo Clinic and Kaiser Permanente also cut back on their use of these painkillers. After undertaking separate reviews of test data, all three institutions reached the same conclusion: for most patients Vioxx, Celebrex, and a related drug, Bextra, did not work any better than older pain relievers—or provide any extra safety benefits. "So even as the prescribing of COX-2 drugs by doctors in general was increasing," *The New York Times* later reported, "the use of these drugs by doctors working for organizations doing evidence-based studies was falling."[94]

When it comes to end-of-life care, the VA system again stands out. "Nowhere is the growth in hospice and palliative care as rapid as at the Veterans Health Administration, where officials are bracing for a surge in the number of veterans reaching the last phase of their lives," *Today's Hospitalist* reported at the end of 2004. "Every VA medical center has a palliative care consult team which may include social workers and chaplains as well as nurses and doctors. At many facilities, these teams not only work in the hospital, but visit nursing homes and even patient's homes."[95]

Well aware that physicians inhabit a bell curve, Kizer also used the system's electronic records to monitor the quality of care the VA's physicians provide, bringing in staff whose sole job was to record and compare surgeons' outcomes. As a result, the VA reduced postoperative deaths by 27 percent and postsurgical complications by 45 percent.[96]

The VA's transformation has won kudos from a host of admirers, including Don Berwick ("The Veterans Administration is setting the pace in the nation for demonstrating a real, systemic focus on quality," says Berwick. "It's especially impressive because this is a massive system that works in a fishbowl, is under tremendous scrutiny and has constrained resources."[97]) and President George W. Bush ("The VA has got an advantage because . . . all the administrators work for the same outfit—the same organization," Bush pointed out in a 2004 speech praising the VA's use of health care IT.[98])

Yet in the mainstream media, the VA's turnaround has received relatively little attention—in part because an all-volunteer army draws most of its recruits from a relatively small slice of the population.[99] Forty years ago nearly everyone knew someone who had fought in World War II. Today most journalists writing for national magazines or newspapers have no close contacts with veterans, and few have ever visited a friend or family member in a VA hospital. So perhaps it's not surprising that the revolution within the VA system has, until recently, gone largely unnoted.

Some say, though, that ideology has also played a role in deep-sixing the story: "A political consensus that firmly opposes turning health care over to the government—because the government is presumed incapable of doing anything well—doesn't want to hear that government hospitals are outperforming rival hospitals," *Slate*'s Timothy Noah suggested in the spring of 2005.[100]

But if the VA's success doesn't sell newspapers, its triumphs have been grabbing headlines in the less widely read pages of major medical journals: "Creating a Culture of Quality: The Remarkable Transformation of the Department of Veterans Affairs Health Care" (*Annals of Internal Medicine,* 2004); "Effect of the Transformation of the Veterans Affairs Health Care System on the Quality of Care" (*The New England Journal of Medicine,* 2003); "VA Hospitals Found Best in Overall Quality, but Not Every One Measures Up, Reviews Show" (*Health Care Strategic Management,* 2005); "Diabetes Care Quality in the Veterans Affairs Health Care System and Commercial Managed Care" (*Annals of Internal Medicine,* 2004).[101]

Admittedly, the studies concentrate on specific markers for quality; they cannot yet sound the depths of health care to measure overall quality of care. But what is astounding is that, despite a patient base comprised mainly of older veterans of Korea and Vietnam, and younger veterans of the volunteer army (who are considered high risk because of their age, socioeconomic status, and generally poor health), the VA system either matches or outperforms both fee-for-service Medicare and most private health plans in so many different studies.[102]

To be sure, the VA has not achieved a medical utopia. While studies in medical journals describe systemwide change, stories in the mainstream media tend to focus on human interest stories at local hospitals, and inevitably not every hospital offers top-drawer care. At the end of 2004, for example, the VA hospital in Denver received a report from the inspector general warning of unsanitary conditions that included several large holes in the walls of the recovery room, gauze strips that were not changed between patients, contaminated linens, medical carts left unlocked, and restrooms with feces and blood on the floor.[103]

These are the stories that set a television network's cameras whirring—especially when it is the nation's veterans who are subjected to substandard conditions. But the fact that these more dramatic stories overshadow the larger tale of continuous systemwide improvements is another reason why most people don't know that the VA is providing some of the most effective care to be found anywhere—and doing it on a very tight budget. Indeed, by 2005 many would say that the VA's budget is too tight. As noted in chapter 6, the VA must now turn many veterans away, and even vets who qualify for care sometimes complain of long waiting lines for appointments.

Nevertheless, the program deserves praise for its efficiency. By 2005 the number of patients the Veterans Administration was treating had doubled over 10 years to roughly 7 million. Meanwhile, the VA had cut costs by about half.[104] Testifying before the Senate and House Committee on Veterans' Affairs in the spring of 2005, James E. Sursely, national commander of the Disabled American Veterans, laid out some of the savings:

"When researchers compared VA health care expenditures for all health care provided for a one-year period to hypothetical payments under Medicare rates for the same services, they found hypothetical payments to Medicare providers would have been more than 20 percent greater than the cost of care at VA," Sursely reported. "They concluded . . . that the VA is able to provide a richer benefit package at a lower cost than veterans would be able to obtain through the private sector under the Medicare fee-for-service program."[105]

One reason the VA spends less is because it is allowed to negotiate with drug companies for deep discounts. Meanwhile, for reasons best understood by the pharmaceutical industry's lobbyists, the Medicare care legislation signed by President Bush at the end of 2003 explicitly prohibits Medicare from using its enormous purchasing power to bargain with drugmakers.

The VA has clout because it purchases about 5 percent of all of the drugs sold in the United States. "We were able to get sizable discounts, and had hoped that we could partner with other large groups and drive prices down further," Kizer recalls. "We also hoped to help improve safety—we thought that if we could get 10 percent of the market together, we could force the pharmaceutical companies to do something about drugs that look alike and sound alike. But unfortunately, we couldn't get enough players to go along. Health care just doesn't have a culture of collaboration."[106]

Why It Works

In a rare, long look at the VA system published in *Washington Monthly* in January of 2005, Phillip Longman chronicles the VA's successes and concludes by saying: *"The story of how and why the VA became the benchmark for quality medi-*

cine in the United States suggests that much of what we think we know about health care and medical economics is just wrong. It's natural to believe that more competition and consumer choice in health care would lead to greater quality and lower costs because in almost every other realm, it does . . . But when it comes to health care, it's a government bureaucracy that's setting the standard for maintaining best practices while reducing costs, and it's the private sector that's lagging in quality. . . . the unexpected reality needs examining if we're to have any hope of understanding what's wrong with America's health care system and how to fix it." (emphasis mine)[107]

As Longman points out, "more competition and consumer choice" are the hallmarks of most market-driven efforts at health care reform. Yet the VA has succeeded where others have failed in large part because it is *not* competing, and because its patients *aren't* shopping around, moving from one health care plan to another.

The VA is more likely to invest in information technology—and less likely to buy yet another PET scanner—because it is not vying with other hospitals or doctors for patients. Thus it can ignore the medical "arms-and-amenities" race. No need for valet parking or full body scanning. "We acquire what's needed by our population, but it's not a market-driven decision," says Dr. William Weeks, a psychiatrist and health services researcher at the VA Medical Center in White River Junction, Vermont. "We don't say, 'Gee, the hospital across town got this—I'd better be able to advertise that I have it too.' "[108]

And once vets establish a relationship with the VA, they are likely to stay in the system for many years—which means that, unlike most hospitals, health plans, or physicians' practices, the VA reaps the full benefit from its investment in quality improvement.[109] The money it spends on computerized systems that help it manage diabetic patients will pay off 15 or 20 years from now when those patients do not need to be hospitalized. Simply put, the VA has a financial incentive to take a long-term view of its investments in IT.

By contrast, Longman notes, the Administration hopes to simultaneously lift the quality of health care and contain costs "by moving American health care to an 'ownership' model, where individuals use much more of their own money to purchase their own health care, forcing health care providers to compete for their business." Yet, Longman observes, "shifting more costs to patients, and encouraging them to bargain and haggle for the 'best deal' will result in even more jumping from provider to provider. This, in turn, will give private sector providers even fewer incentives to invest in quality measures that pay off only over time."

In theory, competition would spur hospitals and doctors to invest in IT in order to attract savvy, well-insured patients. But in a market where too many hospitals barely stay afloat and small physician groups are squeezed by rising costs, investment decisions tend to be driven by the need for short-term profits. Spring for a PET scanner and it will immediately become a profit center. Sink millions into installing information technology and training staff how to use it, and the computers will become a cost center that will eat away at profits for years.

Kaiser Permanente

In truth, the VA system is not the only place where the business case for IT works. As J. D. Kleinke observes, Kaiser Permanente Health Plans stands out as another "glaring exception to the rule." Both Kaiser and the VA "have electronic medical records that are the envy of the rest of the health care system, and for reasons that are not coincidental," Kleinke observes. "Although one organization is a commercial health plan and the other is a government health plan," they enjoy many of the same advantages.

Like the VA, Kaiser is both the payer (the Kaiser Foundation Health Plan, a prepaid health plan) and a health care provider (the Permanente Medical Group), which means that Kaiser Permanente reaps the financial benefits of "doing less and doing it right." The nation's largest not-for-profit integrated delivery system, Kaiser insures more than 8 million members in nine states and the District of Columbia. And just as the VA owns hospitals and outpatient clinics staffed by VA doctors, Kaiser operates its own closed network of hospitals and physicians.

Like the VA, Kaiser enjoys a long-term relationship with its patients, giving it a vested interest in their long-term health. When compared to other health plans, patient satisfaction is high; in regions of the country where Kaiser is well established, the annual voluntary turnover rate (the rate at which members leave the program when given the opportunity each year) is less than 3 percent.[110] Even when they change jobs, patients in California are likely to find that their new employer offers Kaiser. "People are incredibly loyal to Kaiser," says Jack Mahoney, director of health care benefits at Pitney Bowes. "We couldn't operate in northern California without offering it— people wouldn't come to work for us. We rate HMOs for quality, and Kaiser is always the benchmark," he adds.[111] Many patients stick with the plan for years—sometimes for generations.

Because their doctors work on salary, both Kaiser and the VA have a relatively easy time converting them to a new system. Physicians are not worried about losing billable hours while they learn how to navigate new computers. And they know it's worth the effort because they work for the organizations full-time. "If I were in private practice, I might have admitting privileges at three or four hospitals, and I'd have to worry about integrating my system with each of theirs," says the VA's Weeks. "Furthermore, if I were in the private sector, I would be wary of investing in a system for my office because I wouldn't know what these hospitals were going to do."[112] But at the VA and Kaiser there is no financial risk for physicians: the organizations make the investment for them.

Health IT czar David Brailer points to Kaiser's computerized system as a "model that should be replicated nationwide."[113] Kaiser began wiring its hospitals in the midnineties, and by 1999 it had launched its own chronic care management program using a computerized disease registry, electronic caregiver support tools, and automatic prompts to improve early intervention. The system has already begun to pay off: due largely to the use of the IT-supported approaches, by 2004 heart disease was no longer the number one cause of death among Kaiser Permanente's members in northern California—although it remained so for the California population at large.[114]

But unless more physicians join very large group practices, it will be hard to duplicate Kaiser's success. When it comes to return on investment, both the VA and Kaiser enjoy enormous economies of scale. In 2005 Jonathan B. Perlin, the acting undersecretary for health, estimated that it costs the VA only about $78 per patient per year to operate its electronic health record— "roughly the equivalent of not repeating one blood test."[115] At Kaiser, Dr. Andrew Wiesenthal reported that Kaiser expected to complete installation of a new $3.2 billion IT system by the spring of 2007. The price tag includes training and upgrading software over a period of 10 years. "At $320 million a year, that's under $40 a member a year," Weisenthal notes. "We'll break even and begin making money on it after the first eight years."[116]

Who Will Pay?

If they had the funds, other health care providers might well be tempted to follow such successful models, and in the summer of 2005 Medicare announced that it would try to make IT more affordable by offering the VA's software, VistA, free of charge to any doctors who wanted to computerize their practice. The catch is that installing the software and learning to use it is a huge undertaking. Giving out a version of VistA is "a great idea," says Dr. David Kibbe, director of the Center for Health Information Technology at the American Academy of Family Physicians, a group that has been working on the project. "But at the beginning, there was a lot of wishful thinking. They said, 'We'll just release it.' I said, 'Where's the fairy dust?' "

Those who have tried to install VistA agree. Dr. Nancy Anthracite, a family physician in Washington, D.C., needed endless hours of help from a group of VistA enthusiasts who volunteered their time. Getting started with VistA was so daunting, says Anthracite, that even when the VA demonstrated its program at medical meetings, almost none of those in attendance wanted to use it on their own. "You go to meetings and they show you things doctors can do with VistA and everyone's going, 'Wow, wow, wow,' " she says. "But no one installs it." [117]

Medicare and its contractors have worked to make the program easier to use and to adapt it to an office practice. Even so, Gartner's Dr. Barry Hieb doubts that many doctors will take Medicare up on its offer. "The VA has done very good work, and there is a lot to learn from the VA system, but the software represents maybe 10 percent of the total cost," Hieb points out. "The consulting fees that physicians will have to pay to get it to work for their office will exceed any savings." [118]

This brings us back to Hieb's original question: Who will pay for health IT? Is Washington "going to really do something, or just tinker and fiddle around?" [119]

To J. D. Kleinke, chairman of HealthGrades and author of *Oxymorons: The Myth of a U.S. Health Care System,* the answer seems self-evident: "The federal government can and should write the huge check and be done with it. Even with the inevitable graft and corruption that would ensue, this massive public investment would pay for itself many times over." Meanwhile, he argues, "the clinical payoff in improved patient safety and quality of care could dwarf the financial benefits projected from our model."

IT would cost taxpayers billions, but "we are already burning that money today, a few dollars at a time, with every unnecessary medical test, procedure and drug that an interoperable system would preclude," Kleinke argues. "Those costs are bundled into all of our provider payments and then again into all of our health insurance premiums. This is why government, as the largest health care payer and insurer of last resort, should fund the solution itself, the same way it funded the many great public works projects that came to define the United States in its finest moments."[120]

Then Kleinke catches himself, and returns to Political Reality, circa 2005.

"Back in the real world," he admits, "the suggestion that the federal government fix this intractable problem by writing a check for a quarter of a trillion dollars is pure political fantasy. It makes economic and technical sense, and it is not without political precedent; however, no one in today's Washington with the political power to say so would keep that power after saying so. The very idea of a public works project (at least within our own borders) sounds like an artifact from an era eclipsed by nearly three decades of hostility toward government-based solutions to domestic problems, combined with a seemingly religious belief in marketplace solutions for all of them."

But if "the federal government cannot build and finance a health IT system for political reasons, it can do far more than trying to jawbone the private sector into building its own," Kleinke suggests. "It should continue to prod the private sector to come up with standards, and once those standards are set . . . it should require all government payers—Medicare, Medicaid, the Department of Defense, and the Federal Employees Health Benefits Program—to use an IT system built from those same standards. On the other side of the reimbursement table, the federal government should require that all providers adopt the same IT system to receive payment for all claims submitted for governmental reimbursement.

"When confronted with this proposal, the payer and provider lobbies would scream, on cue, 'Unfunded mandate,' " Kleinke acknowledges. And, he concedes, "the short answer to this objection is 'yes.' The long answer, and one that would require considerable political courage, is this: A mandate is a mandate for all, and payers and providers will pass the initial cost of the new system along in the form of higher charges and utilization rates for all of us, the same way they pass along the unfunded mandate of caring for the uninsured in the ER."[121]

Or, as Barry Hieb puts it, when he finally answers his own question, "Who will pay?": "Of course, in the end, the consumer will pay for it. It's always the consumer who pays."[122]

This is, as they say, "how we do things in the U.S." Though, in a sense, it makes very little difference whether "the government" or "the consumer" pays. For the consumer is also the taxpayer; the billions needed for health IT will come out of the same collective pocket. True, our tax system is more progressive than a health care system that passes the highest costs on to those who, through no fault of their own, suffer from painful, debilitating diseases like cancer, Alzheimer's, or multiple sclerosis. With that in mind, one might well argue that it would be fairer to let taxpayers foot the bill, according to their ability to pay, rather than leaving it to patients to fund IT— according to how unlucky they are.

Still, in the end, we are all in the same boat, whether or not we all want to admit it. As seen in chapter 6, we all wind up bearing the cost of medical care for those least able to pay, and as former governor John Kitzhaber puts it, until we are ready to "let people die on the ambulance ramp for lack of insurance coverage,"[123] it is not so much a question of who will pay, but rather, where we will find the roughly $160 billion in capital costs—plus $50 billion in annual operating costs—needed to create a fully wired 21st-century health care system.[124]

By doing less and doing it right, hospitals and doctors can recapture a fair portion of the more than 600 billion health care dollars that are frittered away each year on unproven, ineffective, and sometimes unwanted treatments. Across the country, thousands of caregivers already are trying to use evidence-based medicine to reduce hazardous waste. But that is only part of the answer.

In round figures, the cost of prescription drugs and devices sold to individuals, hospitals, nursing homes, and health plans accounts for roughly 15 percent of the nation's health care bill. The chapter that follows will take a look at how those drugs and devices are priced; why earnings shortfalls, rather than the cost of research and development, dictate price hikes for drugs; how the relationship between device makers and the surgeons who decide which devices to use is cloaked in secrecy; why some of the world's largest institutional investors believe that the pharmaceutical industry needs to find a new business model before it self-destructs; how the nation's largest device maker used the FDA to tell a prestigious medical journal what it could and couldn't publish; and why a surgeon who wanted to learn more about a device before he tried to implant it in a patient's spine was told, both by the FDA and by the manufacturer, that details about complications that other physicians encountered during clinical trials were "trade secrets."

The answers to all of these questions will help to explain why Americans pay so much more for everything from statins to stents than anyone else in the world—and why, even while laying out top dollar, we cannot be at all sure of the safety and quality of the drugs and devices we buy.

8

Device Makers, Drugmakers, and the FDA

My children, some in high school and college by then, often sided with the critics [of the pharmaceutical industry]. They listened to my logic, but I could tell they weren't convinced, and to tell you the truth, I wasn't either.
—DR. HANK McKINNELL, CEO, PFIZER[1]

In the past, Dr. Charles Rosen had looked forward to attending the North American Spine Society's annual meeting. A spine surgeon for 17 years and the founding director of the spine center at the University of California at Irvine, Rosen had attended NASS's first meeting. But in September of 2005, the 50-year-old couldn't help but feel apprehensive as he boarded the red-eye to Philadelphia. Over the past year Rosen had found himself at the center of what was becoming an increasingly bitter controversy over an artificial spinal disc manufactured by Johnson & Johnson. He had an uneasy feeling that some of his colleagues might be lying in wait for him.[2]

A device about the diameter of a quarter and made of two high-density plastic pieces sandwiched between two metal plates, the spinal disc, called "Charité," had been approved by the FDA 11 months earlier and now was being hailed by its promoters as a revolutionary alternative to fusion surgery for severe back pain. Fusion stops the painful motion of a severely degenerated disc and associated arthritic joints by "fusing" the adjoining vertebrae so that they grow together—sometimes with the help of metal rods and screws. By contrast, the artificial disc is designed to replace the old disc. After removing it, a surgeon slips the plastic disc in between the vertebrae as if sliding a coin into a slot.

The advantage of Charité, according to J&J, is that rather than immobilizing the spine, the artificial disc lets the body move naturally. Because fusion limits the spine's range of motion, it can transfer extra stress to discs above and below the fusion site, causing them to degenerate. Charité, by contrast, allows continued motion, offering hope—though as yet no proof—that adjacent discs might be less likely to deteriorate.

But Rosen was not at all sure that the artificial disc would prove safe over the long term. Charité had been used in Europe for nearly 17 years, and after reviewing mixed data from the Continent, he was concerned that thousands of patients could wind up prisoners of their own bodies—in chronic pain, with no solution.[3] "I don't know how anyone, in good conscience, could put these things in knowing the past history and the potential for so many failures," said Rosen. "It's just money over everything else, and it's just cruel."[4]

Still, Rosen realized, he could be wrong. That was one reason why he was attending the NASS conference: he hoped to learn more.

As Rosen checked into Philadelphia's Crowne Plaza hotel and gave his name to the clerk, his premonition that Charité was going to haunt him for the next few days was realized. "Are you the Dr. Rosen who asked the FDA to recall all of those *terrible* disc replacements," asked the man standing beside him at the desk, his voice heavy with sarcasm.

"That's me," Rosen acknowledged.

The man handed him a card, identifying himself as "Mark Mintzer, Patient Advocate."

Rosen had heard of Mintzer from one of his own patients, a man who came to him after a failed disc operation left him in excruciating pain—just one of several disc implant patients who had gone to Rosen for help. Mintzer, who also had a spinal disc implant, had been far luckier. His operation had been an enormous success, and now the 48-year-old former computer consultant had become a familiar name in chat rooms for back pain sufferers, where he referred potential patients to spinal surgeons.[5]

Later in the day, as Rosen wandered through the convention center,

MONEY-DRIVEN MEDICINE

things only got stranger. Outside all the meeting halls, signs announced that anyone attempting to record or film the presentations would be escorted out by security guards. Rosen couldn't remember ever having seen such a sign at past conferences. The next day, at a presentation about the artificial spinal discs, the moderator reminded the audience of the warning, and indicated that at least one person already had been removed from the conference.

It was not necessary for anyone to record anything, he explained, because a CD of all the presentations would be mailed out later. "What's the difference between recording the presentations now or getting a CD from NASS later?" Rosen asked himself. He couldn't help but wonder if the conference's organizers planned to edit the proceedings, eliminating any embarrassing questions that might be asked by the audience.

The next day, he went to hear a presentation on complications following Charité disc replacements. Afterward, Rosen asked the presenter what years the disc replacements were done, and he replied, "2000 to 2002." Rosen had barely finished thanking him, when suddenly, the moderator interrupted him: "Why do you want to know? What are you getting at?" he demanded.

Rosen wanted to think that he was just being paranoid—until the last day of the conference, when he went to hear another paper about disc replacements. As he entered the large room, he noticed huge projection screens on either side of the stage. But it didn't occur to him that he was about to see his own name blown up on one of them.

At first, it seemed like a normal panel discussion. Toward the end of the session one of the last speakers began to talk about evidence-based medicine, comparing disc replacements to fusions, and acknowledging that there was disagreement among spinal surgeons as to how well the implants worked. "He was bringing up pertinent questions—I was surprised," Rosen recalls. "This is why I had come to the conference." But then, suddenly, the tone of the presentation changed.

"The speaker warned us that we had better get used to evidence-based medicine, because it's here to stay," Rosen remembers. "And he suggested that if physicians didn't deal with it, other people would bring it up. Then, suddenly, he put a slide up on the two projector screens."

Rosen expected a diagram of the spinal disc. Instead, he was stunned to see page A1 of *The Wall Street Journal*, June 7, 2005. One story was circled:

J&J's New Device

For Spine Surgery

Raises Questions

Artificial Disk Aims to Help

Body's Natural Movement;

Some See Risk if It Slips

'Big Money Riding on This'

Rosen recognized the headline. And he could visualize the paragraph later in the piece where he was quoted saying that the FDA's approval of the disc "puts the American people potentially at great risk for receiving operations that could fail at a high rate and result in untreatable pain and disability."[6]

Rosen remembers what happened next: "The speaker pointed to the screen and said: *'Our dirty laundry should not be aired in public.'* It was clear that he was very angry," says Rosen. "Then he told us, *'If you do that'*—and he pointed to the *Journal* story—*'this will happen'*—and a second slide popped up on the screens."

The new slide displayed a page from a class action lawyer's website. Rosen didn't recognize the attorney's name, but he did recognize his own name. There it was, in the very first paragraph. Again he was quoted saying that he couldn't imagine using the spinal disc that Johnson & Johnson was promoting. At the bottom of the attorney's webpage was the pitch to clients: "If you or a loved one suffered complications after artificial disc surgery for back pain or Degenerative Disc Disease, you have legal rights. Fill out our contact form for a free case evaluation."

Rosen groaned. Given the size of the screen, it was hard to miss his name. Although he didn't know the lawyer, he recognized the source of the quote: a story that appeared on TheStreet.com. Melissa Davis, a well-respected reporter who covered the health care industry for the online financial news site, had interviewed him about Charité, and he'd told her what he thought. "Now someone is trying to associate my name with this ambulance chaser," Rosen later told a friend, "implying that I am a shill for a plaintiff's firm, and that my criticism of the disc can be written off as unethical and financially motivated."

"Where There Is Big Money,
There Are No Disinterested People"

The Wall Street Journal story made it clear that the debate over the disc had become acrimonious, and that some of Charité's most vocal fans—not to mention some of its critics—had a financial stake in the outcome.

Charité's detractors pointed to patients like 52-year-old Susan Whittaker, who woke up one morning a month after a disc replacement with a badly swollen leg. Tests showed that her Charité had slipped out of its niche between the bones of her spine and become intertwined with blood vessels. During a nine-hour surgery to remove the disc, she lost pints of blood. "I'm lucky to be alive—I almost died twice on the table," said Whittaker.[7]

Ten months later, Dr. Joseph Riina, the Indianapolis surgeon who performed Whittaker's disc replacement and emergency surgery, still didn't know why her disc had slipped out of place. "We've sent films to surgeons all over the country," said Riina, who has taught other doctors how to use the device. "No one has been able to give a reason for what happened. . . . It's like hip replacement; the first ones didn't always work."[8]

Critics worry not just about slippage but about wear and tear. They point out that that no one knows how soon an artificial disc might wear out, and everyone agrees that replacing a worn disc can be extremely tricky. In June of 2005, eight months after the FDA approved the device, Dr. John Peloza, a spine surgeon in Dallas, told *The Wall Street Journal* that J&J's device would be "a nightmare to fix."

Earlier in the year, at a packed meeting of spinal surgeons in Canada, the same Dr. Peloza had attacked Dr. Fred Geisler, a Chicago surgeon who served as a consultant to Johnson & Johnson, accusing Geisler of hyping J&J's device.

Now Geisler saw his chance to reply: "Peloza is aligned with Medtronic [a competing device maker] so he thinks the Medtronic disc is better," Geisler told the *Journal*. "There is big money riding on this. Where there is big money, there are no disinterested people."[9]

But in fact, there were some disinterested parties in the spinal disc controversy—and Rosen was one of them. He had never had any financial ties to any device maker or drug company. He didn't hire himself out as a consultant; he didn't invest in their stocks.

"I'm whistle-clean—the people who want to discredit me hate that," he said a week after the NASS conference. "In the past, company reps have begun to suggest that I might consult for their company, but I always nip the conversation in the bud. Why? Because it leaves me free and clear to decide what's best for my patients. I don't want to be beholden to any company. As a surgeon, I make a fair living. I don't need to compromise my objectivity in dealing with patients. If you consult, all of a sudden you get wrapped up in that whole guilt game.

Guilt game? "You try some device, and it seems to work," he explains. "That's great. But if you begin using it—and you have a reputable name— the rep comes to you and suggests that you become a 'consultant.' Of course, you're compensated somehow . . . I just can't imagine not feeling obligated if they were paying me some huge amount of money. They're not paying you because they like you, you know—they expect you to use their product and keep using it.

"The majority of doctors aren't willing to be bought," he adds. "I counted one day—there are only about two dozen surgeons who have been really pushing the disc replacements. Many of them *do* have a financial interest— and the company has been pushing hard to offer incentives. One surgeon at the conference told me, in confidence, that a J&J rep in her town offered her $1,000 for every disc that she implanted. He told her that they would list it as some type of fee for consulting. She refused—she's not going to use the disc. But she was scared. Like me, she was also very discouraged. We both found the whole meeting to be about industry and profit, not doctors and data."

Johnson & Johnson denied the allegation that one of its reps offered a surgeon a bounty.[10] But stories of kickbacks to spine surgeons are not limited to J&J. In 2001 a lawsuit brought by Scott A. Wiese, a former sales representative for J&J rival Medtronic, accused the company of trying to persuade surgeons to use its products with offers of first-class plane tickets to Hawaii and nights at the finest hotels. Some of those lucrative consulting contracts, the suit claimed, involved little or no work. Medtronic denied the accusations in the lawsuit, which it settled in 2002 for an undisclosed amount.

In interviews with *The New York Times,* two other former Medtronic employees confirmed the outlines of Wiese's story, revealing that Medtronic's sales representatives routinely offered enticements to surgeons to use the company's hardware, including visits to a strip club in Memphis. The former employees said they had spent as much as $1,000 per doctor for a night on the town, and a document provided by one of them listed about 80 surgeons who had consulting agreements with Medtronic that paid as much as $400,000 a year.

"It's a business deal," confided one of the employees, who declined to be named because he still works in the medical device industry. "It takes money to make money." [11]

NASS—A Secret Society?

By the time Rosen got back to the University of California at Irvine (UCI), he wasn't just discouraged—he was angry. The controversy was turning ugly, and personal. He had heard that his name was coming up in NASS subcommittee meetings: "Who is this guy?" one doctor asked. "What's his game?" Someone on the subcommittee was assigned to call one of Rosen's colleagues at UCI to check him out.

On the Web, someone spread a rumor that Rosen was "in cahoots" with Jim Cramer, the former hedge-fund manager turned TV host, suggesting that Cramer was shorting J&J and paying Rosen to talk down the device. Rosen had never spoken to Cramer and doesn't even watch the show.

At UCI, Rosen received full support from his colleagues. No one was troubled by the fact that he spoke his mind. Many agreed with him. Everyone believed that he had a right to his opinion: without open debate, medical science could not advance.

With that in mind, Rosen sat down to write a letter to the speaker at the NASS conference who had displayed the slides of the *Wall Street Journal* story and the plaintiff's attorney's website: "You mentioned at NASS that our 'dirty laundry shouldn't be aired in public,'" Rosen wrote. "I was unaware that NASS is a secret society . . . Certainly you cannot suggest that I not provide my honest and fact-driven opinion when someone asks me in an interview. [You are welcome to] debate my opinions with hard facts and data," Rosen added. "However, I find it inappropriate that you endeavored to publicly humiliate me based upon the use of public information."

Behind the Scenes: The FDA Panel Meets

Looking back on his experience at the conference, Rosen still isn't certain how he became the villain in this story. "The irony is that I got embroiled in this only because I wanted to *use* the disc," he explains. "I'm not a social crusader. It's just that I had been following the development of the artificial disc for 10 or 15 years, and I thought it might be suitable for some of my patients."

But before experimenting on patients, Rosen wanted to do what he calls "due diligence": "In my position, I want to make sure I know everything about a new device before I try it." So, in January of 2005, he sat down to read the 300-page transcript of the 2004 meeting where the FDA's Orthopaedic and Rehabilitation Devices Panel considered the application for Charité's premarket approval.

Rosen read the minutes of the meeting twice—and was disturbed by what he found. First, the clinical trial of 275 patients lasted only two years. Second, in the trial Charité had been compared to an outdated fusion procedure that was still in use when the trial was designed but not by the time Charité was approved. But what was most startling was that the results for the first 71 patients in the trial were not counted when deciding whether or not to approve the device. Although this first group represented roughly 25 percent of the patients in the trial, their outcomes were reported separately on the grounds that these early subjects were "training patients." [12]

The physicians were "just getting their feet wet," with those first 71 patients, Michael Courtney, project manager of the FDA's orthopedic branch, would later tell Rosen, explaining that surgeons implanting the device faced a steep learning curve.

"Just getting their feet wet?" asks Rosen. "How do you tell the child of a man who is now disabled that the doctor operating on his father was 'just getting his feet wet'? The arrogance of that . . ." [13]

Meanwhile, at the FDA panel meeting, J&J's representatives acknowledged that the rate of "adverse events" was higher among the training patients. For example, one patient had lost 1,800 cc of blood during the operation—"and that's a lot of blood." Rosen notes. "Put it this way: 1,000 cc is a liter—we're talking almost two liters of blood. What I would like to know is, which vein was cut and how? What was the problem with the approach? That's what I need to know so that I don't have the same problem if I decide to implant one of these discs."

The benefits of the disc also seemed ambiguous. Even among the later patients, 13 percent experienced "no change or an increase in pain" while 12 percent reported only "some pain relief" after the operation—which is to say that when it came to reducing pain, the implant proved, at best, marginally more successful than the fusion procedure it was supposed to replace. And since the long-term success of the operation remained unknown, it was, by definition, riskier.

Nevertheless, the FDA approved Charité—in large part because the agency had set a very low bar for approval. J&J was not required to show that Charité was superior to the outdated fusion procedure, only that it was "not inferior"—a standard that insures that the marketplace will be crowded with me-too devices which may not be better, but are almost always more expensive than the products they replace.[14]

Reading through the transcript, Rosen also discovered that approval was not, as advertised in most press reports, "unanimous." Two of the eight voting members on the panel had initially moved to postpone approval: they believed that a two-year trial did not provide adequate information on the sensitive device.

At the hearing, Charité's defenders countered that a two-year trial was sufficient because the disc had been used in Europe for nearly two decades. But when Rosen investigated further, he found that the disc's track record abroad was sketchy, at best. A 2003 article in the *European Spine Journal* summed up the state of the research: "Despite the fact that these devices have been implanted for almost 15 years . . . there are currently insufficient data to assess the performance of total disc replacement adequately. . . . Total disc replacement seems to be associated with a high rate of reoperations, and the potential problems that may occur with longer follow-up have not been addressed. Therefore, total disc replacements should be considered experimental procedures and should only be used in strict clinical trials."[15]

The high rate of reoperations posed the greatest problem. Charité was designed for younger patients: the ideal candidate, everyone agreed, would be in his midforties—which meant that at some point, the device might well wear out and have to be replaced. But no one knew how long it might last—10 years? 15 years? 20 years?

During the hearing, Dr. Paul McAfee, a consultant with J&J with a financial interest in the product, was candid: "I hope they will last 40 years. I tell my patients to look at the LeMaire data [from France], which goes back 11 years—which is pretty good" he added. But "honestly, to talk to the patients, 10 years is a pretty good outcome."

Rosen was shocked. Ten years would be pretty good? As other speakers acknowledged, if a surgeon was forced to go back in to try to replace the disc, he faced what one of the panel's experts described as a "potentially life-threatening operation."

"The problem is scar tissue," Rosen explains. "When you first implant a spinal disc you have to enter through the abdomen and navigate around the iliac veins and arteries, the major vessels that move blood throughout the body, in order to get access to the spinal column. The approach is done from the front of the body because the disc is in front of the spine. But after the initial operation, it's much harder to go back in. Scar tissue sets in, and it's very difficult to move the major veins and arteries to gain access to the spine. They can rip open—you can't imagine how quickly the whole wound fills up with a liter or two of blood.

"In a virgin operation, you can find the tear and fix it," he adds. "A second time, it's hidden by the scarring. By the time you find it, the person could be dead. We're talking about a couple of minutes here."

After hours of discussion, debate, and questions, one member of the committee finally took a stand: Dr. John Kirkpatrick, associate professor of orthopedic surgery at the University of Alabama, moved that the panel recommend against approving the device without more data. Before making his motion, Kirkpatrick pointedly reminded the panel of "a recent editorial in the NASS *Journal* discussing the fact that there are a number of spine surgeons who will do things on patients that they would never consider for themselves. This reminds me of what the FDA's purpose is," Fitzgerald added: "First, to protect the public."

Dr. Maureen Finnegan of the University of Texas Southwestern Medical Center, seconded the motion. Earlier in the all-day discussion, Finnegan had made it clear that she did not think there was enough data to approve a device that was going to have to last for years.[16] Responding to Finnegan's comment, five of the voting members of the panel concurred.[17]

But now Sally Maher, an attorney representing the device industry, jumped into the discussion. Noting that she was not a voting member of the panel, Maher declared that, nonetheless, "I have to take exception, Dr. Kirkpatrick, to what you're saying. I have some deep concerns that if you tell a company they can't launch something for five years after they have started developing it, you're going to put a stop to new product innovation in the medical device or the orthopedic world. And I'm wondering why you feel that that's more appropriate than having a postmarket study, where you can follow the device and look at what's happening after it comes to market."

Immediately, two voting members of the panel weighed in, agreeing with Maher. One cited the 17 years of clinical evidence from Europe—skipping past the fact that this data was less than encouraging. Another complimented J&J on having "gone out of its way to document every complication that has occurred," apparently unperturbed by the number of complications.

Now Dr. Finnegan was on the defensive: "I'm not sure that some of the panel members understand that just because we say [that we're not recommending approval] that doesn't mean this is going into the closet. 'Not approval' means that, at the present time, the panel is not comfortable with all of the data. . . . It just means that certain things have to be done before the FDA makes a decision . . ."

But clearly, other members of the panel were swayed by the argument that delay might dampen J&J's "spirit of innovation." Earlier, Dr. Choll Kim of the University of California, San Diego had agreed with Dr. Finnegan: "This is a complex device," said Kim. "It's the first of its kind and designed to last for a long time, and we can't get at that question [of how long it will last] until we wait."

Now, however, Kim seemed to have changed his mind: "I think by requiring much longer follow-up, [we] will deter companies from being able to produce these innovative materials—the burden will be too onerous," Kim declared.

And so, when it came down to a vote on Kirkpatrick's motion to delay approval, six panel members backed off. Once again citing extensive European experience with Charité, the panel voted 6 to 2 against postponing approval.

Ultimately, the group compromised, and voted unanimously to recommend approval—with the understanding that after bringing the device to market, J&J would have to meet a list of conditions which included five-year follow-ups on outcomes for patients in the clinical study, and mandatory training for surgeons who wanted to implant the device. Dr. Fernando Diaz, a professor of neurosurgery at Wayne State University, emphasized the need for intensive training: "Of all the things we do in spine surgery, this is going to be the one that will require the most supervision, monitoring and critical analysis."

J&J agreed, and when the device came to market, the company set out to train 3,000 physicians in the first year. "Before we make an initial sale to a physician, we tell him that he has go to our two-day training course," explains William Christianson, vice president for clinical and regulatory affairs of DePuy Spine, the division of J&J that produces Charité.[18] "The first half is a lecture, emphasizing selecting the right patients for the procedure, complications, and how to get reimbursed. The second half is hands-on training using animals. First the surgeons watch the procedure, then they do it themselves. They all do one operation, and they take home a CD-ROM."

But is one operation enough to become proficient? During the FDA trials, J&J considered the first five patients at each site "training patients." Meanwhile J&J consultant Dr. Paul McAfee cautioned surgeons that anyone planning to implant Charité faces a "steep learning curve."[19] Five training patients multiplied by the 3,000 surgeons who went home with J&J's CD-ROM means that up to 15,000 patients could find themselves lying face up on that learning curve.

Mark Mintzer, the patient who had a successful implant and now helps other patients find surgeons, is concerned: "I see a wave of patients going to inexperienced surgeons," Mintzer confided in the fall of 2005. "These surgeons are telling patients that the implant is little different from a fusion—and they've done hundreds of fusions. In fact the implant is very different. These doctors are misrepresenting their experience."[20]

Perhaps, rather than training 3,000 physicians in one year and sending them out to operate on thousands of patients while they "get their feet wet," it might have made more sense to limit the number of surgeons doing the operation to a small number who were involved in the original clinical trials. Their hospitals could be designated "centers of excellence" for disc replacement. And in those centers, experienced surgeons could begin training both their own students and physicians from other hospitals who had time for more than a one-day hands-on session.

But, as Rosen saw it, the problem was not just that thousands of inexperienced surgeons might do irreparable harm as they practiced on their patients. As he reread the transcript, he kept coming back to expert testimony offered by Dr. David Polly, chief of spine surgery at the University of Minnesota, reminding the panel that it was "inevitable" that over time some discs would have to be replaced, or, in the language of spine surgery, "revised":

"These revisions will be due to infection, dislodgement, malposition and eventually to wear or wear debris," said Polly. "It is imperative that implanting surgeons understand the difficulties associated with revision procedures and that these revisions are potentially life threatening," he added. "They must then ask themselves if they are prepared to undertake such revision cases. If they are not prepared to do so, then they must ask themselves if they ought to be implanting the device [in the first place].

"I know that my . . . regional referral center will be facing these difficult revision cases whether we ever implant a single device or not," he concluded, "and I expect this will be a daunting task."

Polly was not a voting member of the panel. He had been sent to the hearing by Medtronic, one of J&J's rivals, to add his expert opinion to the discussion. "Medtronic paid my expenses, and I think their concept was to have me say a series of negative things. But I wasn't willing to say that the disc shouldn't be approved," Polly explains. "I was willing to say that once the disc was implanted, replacements would be a serious challenge—and I said that.

"I think Charité is 'okay,' but I don't think it's perfect," he adds. "Will some things go wrong? Absolutely. Will some people will die? There have been two deaths since the disc came on the market. The next generation of 'follow-on' devices that companies are developing right now will be better," says Polly. "But somebody has to be first." [21]

"Trade Secrets"

After reading the transcript of the FDA panel's deliberations, Rosen was still undecided as to whether he should try the operation. He wanted to know more, and late in January of 2005, he contacted both the FDA and J&J.

Rosen was particularly interested in more detail on the "adverse events" that the first 71 patients in the two-year trial had suffered. Seven percent needed a second operation (vs. 5.4 percent of later patients); 33.8 percent suffered severe neurological pain (vs. 16.1 percent in the later group).

To Rosen's surprise, the FDA told him that if he wanted in-depth information, he would have to file under the Freedom of Information Act. Rosen did that and was informed that his request had been denied. According to the FDA's Michael Courtney, the results could not be released because they were "trade secrets."

Rosen appealed: "I am concerned that the initial results of the procedure as reflected in the 71 patients may be bad," he explained. "The public has a right to know whether this is the case or not. I, as a spine surgeon being asked to put these artificial discs in, have a right to know. I also have a right to know in order to handle the possible failures that may come to me."[22]

With that end in mind, Rosen began exchanging letters with William Christianson, vice president of clinical and regulatory affairs for DePuy Spine. Christianson forwarded summaries showing the percentage of patients who suffered problems such as "neurological pain"—but again, no detail. Were they still in pain after they healed from the surgery? Why had some patients needed a second surgery? Rosen was frustrated. He could try to avoid these outcomes—but only if he had some clue as to what went wrong. He wasn't going to operate in the dark.

"I chose not to respond to his request," Christianson explained in the fall of 2005. "I thought he was being unreasonable . . . And given his negative characterization of Charité [in the press] I thought that [if he had the information] he wouldn't give us a fair shake."[23]

When asked, in the same interview, whether patients who experienced "neurological pain" were still in pain months after they had healed, Christianson explained: "We checked the patients at 6 weeks, 3 months, 6 months, 12 months, and 2 years. At each point, some patients reported pain. We added them all up and the total was 33.8 percent in the trial group—and 16.1 percent in the later group."

The next question seemed obvious: "What share of the patients in either group were still experiencing neurological pain at the end of two years?"

Christianson refused to answer: "If I tell you that," he said, "you'll want to know how many experienced pain after one year."

This was true. But wouldn't any prospective patient want to know how many patients were in agony a year later?

"We gave that information to the FDA," said Christianson. "We do not have to release it." He was correct. Legally, the level of detail Rosen was asking for is considered proprietary information, and neither the FDA nor the company is required to make it public.

And to be fair, even if Rosen had that information, he still could not be certain whether Charité's benefits would outweigh its risks over the long term. But he would be in a much better position to outline the immediate risks when describing the operation to a prospective patient.

The Risk of Being "Left Behind"

By the fall of 2005, more than 3,000 of J&J's spinal discs had been implanted. Although only two of the nation's eight largest insurers had agreed to pay for the operation, some hospitals were willing to absorb the cost of the $11,500 device. Earlier in the year, Dr. John Boockvar, chief of neurosurgery at Wyckoff Heights Hospital in Brooklyn, told Dow Jones Newswires that his hospital gave him permission to implant the device even though insurance would not reimburse "because it was important to be on the leading edge." [24]

Patients who read favorable reports of Charité online or in the press were beginning to demand the operation. "Some doctors say they're worried they will lose business if they don't offer the Charité option to patients," *The Wall Street Journal* reported, quoting Dr. Bernard Guiot, director of the spine program at the University of South Florida. "There's a feeling that it isn't adequately proven, but there's anxiety about being left behind." [25]

As for Rosen, he had no plans to use Charité: "Based on the evidence we have, I don't think it works," he said. "I like to do the newest things in spine surgery, but I'm interested in practicing evidence-based medicine—and we don't have the evidence."

Not everyone agreed. In the fall of 2005, Cedars-Sinai hospital continued to plug the procedure both in radio ads and on its website. There, a 1,400-word advertorial for Charité managed to avoid using the word "risk" even once. Instead, the Beverly Hills hospital assured prospective patients that the "revolutionary" spinal implant was "routine and safe." [26]

By then Dr. John Regan had performed some 200 Charité operations at Cedars-Sinai with what he described as a "90% success rate." And he agreed that the procedure is "routine and safe—most of the time." Much depends on both patient selection and the skill of the surgeon, said Regan: "I wouldn't want to see every spine surgeon in the country doing this operation—but then I wouldn't want to see every spine surgeon in the country doing many spine operations."

Regan knew the procedure better than most. "I helped develop the technique and some of the surgical instruments used to implant the disc," he explained. As a result, he has received royalties from J&J. Although he declined to divulge just how much J&J paid him, Regan insisted that the royalties had not influenced his professional judgment about the procedure.[27]

* * * * * * * * * * * * * * *

Drugs and Devices: Prices and Profits

The story of the Charité disc captures the secrecy, the scientific uncertainty, the financial pressures, and the potential for conflict of interest that clouds the development, approval, and marketing of new drugs and medical devices in the United States.

The amount of money at stake is staggering. In 2006 drugmakers and device makers will take in well over $300 billion—or roughly 15 percent of the nation's health care dollars.

The prescription drug industry tends to downplay the cost of its products, pointing to government reports which suggest that drugs account for roughly 11 percent of health care spending. But in fact, that figure represents only those drugs sold directly to consumers at pharmacies and other outlets. (See pie chart on page xii: "What Are We Paying For?") Hospitals, doctors, nursing homes, and other health care facilities also buy drugs, and when those purchases are included, spending on prescription drugs alone could hit $270 billion to $280 billion in 2006.[28] Add on the $36 billion that hospitals and other health providers will lay out for devices such as spinal discs, stents, and artificial hips, and the total tab for prescription drugs and devices approaches $310 billion to $320 billion.[29]

And in recent years spending on drugs and devices has become the fastest-growing component of health care costs, with outlays for drugs alone doubling between 1995 and 2003, thanks to a combination of higher prices (driving 58 percent of the rise), plus greater demand.[30] Over that span, prescription drug prices jumped by an average of 7.4 percent a year—almost three times the inflation rate of 2.5 percent.[31] In 2004 spending on prescription drugs rose another 7.2 percent, with pharmaceuticals accounting for nearly one-quarter of the total increase in the nation's health care bill.[32] Meanwhile, Americans popped more pills: from 1993 to 2003 the number of prescriptions purchased climbed by 70 percent while the U.S. population grew by only about 13 percent.[33]

Over the same span, the device industry took off. From 1993 through 2003 the industry's average revenues rose by an eye-popping 23 percent a year.[34] Looking ahead, as bionic boomers begin to replace body parts, the market for everything from artificial knees and hips to cardiovascular devices like defibrillators and pacemakers is likely to snowball—assuming that boomers can afford all of that hardware.

Just as Americans shell out far more for prescription drugs than the citizens of other countries, we also pay a premium for devices. "Europeans spend an average of just $1,270 for an artificial hip—or about one-fourth of what Americans spend," points out Sanford Bernstein analyst Bruce Nudell.[35] Stents that sell for roughly $1,500 in Europe command $2,200 in the United States.[36] And spare body parts are fast becoming luxury items: by 2005 a single screw used in spinal surgery fetched as much as $1,600, while the latest in artificial knees cost close to $10,000.[37]

Why are prescription drugs and devices so expensive in the United States? Manufacturers argue that Americans must pay dearly because in other countries, where governments regulate prices, consumers pay too little. Without U.S. dollars, the industries' supporters argue, drugmakers and device makers would not be able to cover the cost of research and development. "Implicit in this claim is a kind of blackmail," former *New England Journal of Medicine* editor Dr. Marcia Angell observes. "If you want drug companies to keep turning out lifesaving drugs, you will gratefully pay whatever they charge. Otherwise, you may wake up one morning and find there are no more new drugs."[38]

The threat is absurd. The truth is that the pharmaceutical industry spends approximately one-and-a-half times as much on marketing and sales as it spends on research and development.[39] If manufacturers slashed their bloated ad budgets, they could accept lower prices for their drugs without touching R & D.

Drugmakers themselves know that they are spending far too much on promotion. As Sanford Bernstein stock analyst Richard Evans pointed out in chapter 2, they've reached a point of diminishing returns. "Up until 1998—and for many companies through 2000—you were being paid to hire that next sales rep; you were being paid to do that next consumer ad," Evans explained. "You were generating returns for your shareholders by doing that. It is a strategy that worked. After 2000, however, even industry insiders privately admitted that billions were being wasted."[40]

But no company wanted to be the first to cut back on advertising and risk losing market share. Drugmakers, after all, are public companies with shareholders who demand an immediate return on investment. And with the pipeline of truly innovative drugs drying up, marketing has become the heart of the business. Struggling to meet Wall Street's expectations, the industry has begun to focus on producing copycat versions of already popular drugs that are all but certain to win quick FDA approval. But it is not always easy to persuade consumers and doctors to pay more for a product that is—at best—only a little better than its rivals. This may help explain why Big Pharma's promotional spending jumped by nearly 20 percent in 2003, according to *Bloomberg News,* while outlays for R & D rose by just 7.1 percent.[41]

Wall Street also drives the industry's pricing decisions. On this point, Hank McKinnell, chairman and CEO of Pfizer, is refreshingly candid: "Defenders of the pharmaceutical industry typically trot out a standard reason why prescription medicines are as expensive as they are: because the drug companies need to recover the high costs of research and development." But "it's a fallacy to suggest that our industry, or any industry, prices a product to recapture the R & D budget," says McKinnell. "Business doesn't work like that. Those are 'sunk costs.' In other words, we spent the money, and it cannot be recovered no matter what we decide to do with pricing. . . .

"If we don't use sunk costs to determine the price of medicine, how do we decide what to charge?" he asks. "It's basically the same as pricing a car, a consumer product or an appliance. *What will it take to sustain investors' confidence in the risk and rewards of an industry?* . . . If we don't generate sufficient income in the eyes of our investors . . . they will shift their capital to companies that can put it to more productive use, our stock will go down, and we'll have less capital with which to work." (emphasis mine)[42]

One drug analyst, who prefers not to be named, elaborates. "Pharmaceutical companies use price increases to fill earnings gaps left when the patent on a successful drug expires." In the fall of 2005, he pointed to AstraZeneca as an example of a company "that has put prices up on a number of its key products in the last six to nine months—5 percent here, 6 percent there, sometimes more—to meet an earnings target set by the company to impress investors." It is a policy that draws criticism in certain quarters, he adds. "There are populations—and I'm not just talking about the Third World—but within the United States, who cannot afford these medicines."[43]

Nevertheless, as McKinnell points out, manufacturers must jack up prices to sustain profit margins. And investors who sock their savings into prescription drugs have become accustomed to very plump margins. From 1995 to 2002, pharmaceuticals took first prize as the nation's most profitable industry, reporting earnings that ranged from 13 percent to 18.6 percent of sales each and every year. Put those numbers in context: over the same span, the average Fortune 500 firm posted earnings that averaged just 3.1 percent to 5 percent of revenues. Granted, in 2004 drugmakers fell to third place (trailing "mining, crude oil production" and "commercial banks"), but even then, earnings equaled 16 percent of sales.[44]

Meanwhile, less fortunate Fortune 500 companies contributed to Big Pharma's fat margins as they bought drugs for their employees, creating what Dr. Jerry Avorn describes as "an unlikely and unsustainable economic arrangement that costs the other 98.5% of American businesses dearly. . . . For some large companies paying the drug bills of employees and retirees now consumes fully a quarter of their entire outlay for health care."[45] Put simply, by 2005 GM just couldn't afford to keep Pfizer's investors in the style to which they had become accustomed.

Even while drugmakers set records, in recent years large device makers have managed to do even better. In 2003 the industry posted net margins of almost 20 percent.[46] Like the pharmaceutical industry, the device industry is driven by Wall Street, says Dr. John Cherf, a knee surgeon at a specialty hospital in Chicago who also consults with other hospitals. Cherf, who has a business degree as well as an MD, understands how Wall Street works. Investors who bet on a medical device company know that they are taking a gamble—many devices will never come to market—and so they expect a commensurate reward.

Device makers have pulled out all the stops to meet investors' expectations, pricing and marketing their products as aggressively as any drugmaker. "They do what they're supposed to do—they're supposed to be wizards at sales and marketing, and they have done a marvelous job," says Cherf. "They've brought some incredible technology to the table, and they've made a lot of money. It's a wonderful story. But," he acknowledges, "it's probably not sustainable.

"Their margins are very, very high," Cherf explains, "and there is great price discrimination. We pay more than anyone around the world for the exact same thing. And at a time when the federal government is struggling to pay for Medicare, states are struggling to finance Medicaid—and other players in the health economy are not doing well. It just can't continue." In fact, these days, Cherf reports, hospitals are losing money on many implant procedures. "Studies that look at inpatient orthopedic departments show that only one in 10 is profitable, and the rising cost of devices is one of the big reasons."[47]

The Real Reason Prices Are So Much Higher in the United States

Large device makers would be hard-pressed to claim that they require 19 percent profit margins in order to cover the cost of R & D. Indeed, the largest sector of the medical device business, the $18 billion orthopedic implant industry, sinks just 6 percent of sales into developing new devices.[48]

In other words, device makers, like drugmakers, charge a pretty penny for the products they sell in the United States, not because they *must* (to recoup the enormous investment that they're making in scientific research), but simply "because they *can,*" says Kaiser Permanente CEO George Halvorson. *"And, ironically, because they can, they must."* (emphasis mine)

Halvorson explains: "Imagine what would happen if the CEO of a multinational pharmaceutical company suddenly announced, 'We are now charging unfairly high prices in the U.S. So starting Monday, I am going to bring our U.S. prices down 50 percent to align them with prices in Europe'?"[49] The executive's career might last slightly longer than a Cedars-Sinai radio spot promoting spinal discs.

Virtually every other developed nation regulates or negotiates prices for health care products, either by setting reimbursement rates for new drugs based on how they compare with existing products (Japan), capping profits (Britain), putting a ceiling on total spending (France), or insisting that once a product is on the market, prices cannot increase faster than the general inflation rate (Canada).[50] In the United States, by contrast, drugmakers and device makers are free to price their products at whatever the market will bear. And when it comes to a lifesaving pacemaker or a much-needed hip, what the market will bear can be unreasonably high—not to mention arbitrary.

Kaiser Permanente's CEO explains why: "Although the United States supposedly has a market-driven health care economy . . . basic and fundamental value-based market forces are blunted here." Halvorson illustrates his point by imagining how a drug company might set the price for a new arthritis drug in a country where it had to negotiate directly with the government. (One could envision the same scenario if Medicare were allowed were allowed to bargain with drugmakers to secure the best price possible for seniors.)

" 'We'd like two dollars a pill,' the manufacturer's salesperson might tell the minister of health.

" 'What good does the drug do?' the minister [or Medicare] asks.

" 'Well, it reduces arthritis inflammation.'

" 'Fine,' the minister [or a panel of physicians representing Medicare] responds. 'How much better is it than the old inflammation reduction drug we have now that costs us ten cents a pill?'

" 'Well,' the manufacturer replies, 'our tests show the new drug reduces pain 5 percent better than your current drug.' "

At that point, Halvorson, observes, classic market forces come into play. Value becomes relevant. Is a 5 percent improvement in pain relief worth a 2,000 percent increase in price?

" 'Sorry,' says the minister. 'Two dollars a pill isn't a good deal. We'll just keep using the old drug.'

" 'Let's not be hasty,' the manufacturer's representative might reply. 'Two dollars is just our American retail price. We can do better. How about 50 cents a pill? Would you buy them for your patients for 50 cents?' "

Halvorson envisions the health minister rejecting what would be a 500 percent markup for a 5 percent improvement in care. Ultimately, he imagines the manufacturer settling for 25 cents. Alternatively, the company might turn down 25 cents, and the drug would not be sold in that country.

"Market forces would keep it out," says Halvorson. "What market forces? A decision by the actual payer (in this case the government or Medicare) that the price of the drug exceeds its perceived value.

"By contrast," says Halvorson, "look at how that same drug manufacturer would set a price when that same drug is introduced in the United States. First the manufacturer would arbitrarily set a price, a highly profitable price." Then a division of attractive and highly trained salespeople armed with gifts ranging from doughnuts to bonus airline miles for frequent prescribers would descend on doctors' offices.[51] Meanwhile the company would run ads in various consumer and medical magazines touting the drug. Halvorson envisions the ad copy in *Time* magazine:

Pain Away—proven in clinical tests to measurably outperform every other available painkilling drug for arthritis. . . . Pain hurts. We can help. We're on your side. Pain Away. You need it.

"The actual and minor 5 percent pain level improvement statistic would not typically show up in the drug company ad," says Halvorson, "and certainly not as 5 percent. The typical reference would be that it is 'measurably better.'" Nor would the ad mention price.[52]

Of course some reformers argue that if Medicare and other insurers raised co-pays on overpriced drugs, individual consumers would no longer be seduced by such ads. Instead, price-wise consumers would exert market pressure by choosing the cheaper product. But how could consumers know that the new product was only incrementally better? In most cases, even the savviest patients would be hard-pressed to find the head-to-head evidence needed to compare similar drugs and devices.

For, as we saw in chapter 2, drugmakers prefer to test new products against placebos. And as in the case of the Charité disc, the FDA often demands no more than proof that the product in question is "no worse" than what is already available. The newest knee is not tested against the best already on the market. This leaves it to the individual consumer to cut through the ambiguity surrounding the risks and benefits of various potions and spare parts. One can imagine a patient asking himself: "Am I more depressed because I switched back to the cheaper pill—or am I just imagining the difference? Would I be better off with J&J's spinal disc, or the newer one, which is supposed to last longer—but has been on the market for only nine months?"[53]

Should the government intervene? Many Americans would be loath to see Washington's bureaucrats negotiating drug prices. While the loss of an arthritis pill that is only 5 percent more effective might not cause anyone great hardship, past experience with Beltway bean counters suggests that the government might shut the door on some truly valuable products, especially if those products would be of benefit to only a small percentage of voters.

But many taxpayers might feel comfortable if a panel of disinterested doctors represented Medicare in meetings with manufacturers, insisted on head-to-head outcomes research whenever possible, and then negotiated how much Medicare would be willing to pay for a drug or a device based on value—much the way FDA panels of physicians approve products. Except in this case, it would be essential that the doctors doing the bargaining have no financial interest in the company or its rivals.

Yet, as discussed in chapter 7, the Medicare prescription benefit bill negotiated behind closed doors at the end of 2003 specifically prohibits Medicare from bargaining for the kind of bulk discounts that the Veterans Administration wins. As a result, Medicare must fork over at least 50 percent more than the VA pays for half of the top 20 brand-name prescription drugs sold to seniors.[54] And because the complicated new law "forces the federal government to underwrite the costs of all marketed drugs, regardless of their clinical or economic value," the Medicare prescription benefit bill "seems destined to channel more and more dollars into the costliest (and hence most aggressively marketed) products," observes Dr. Jerry Avorn.[55]

Admittedly, the 2003 law does allow private insurers and pharmacy benefits managers (PBMs) that contract with Medicare to negotiate prices with drugmakers. But the bill does not require that any savings from these negotiations be passed on to Medicare's enrollees. And on this score, the pharmacy benefit managers' record might best be described as unsavory.

Traditionally, PBMs like Caremark Rx and Medco Health Solutions have acted as intermediaries for large employers and insurers by hammering out discounts from manufacturers. But the PBMs have consistently refused to reveal both the size of these rebates and any other payments that they may be receiving from the manufacturers—leading to well-founded suspicions that they were not always passing along discounts. PBMs also have been fined for taking kickbacks from drugmakers in return for steering consumers to pricier products.[56] Their track record illustrates the folly of thinking that the best way to avoid gouging in the health care marketplace is to hire one for-profit company to keep an eye on another. Too often, they find common interest, as one hand washes the other.

But that is only the first reason why Medicare would be better off eliminating the middlemen and negotiating directly with manufacturers. The second is this: with 29 million expected beneficiaries, Medicare has the clout to go up against Pfizer or Johnson & Johnson. By contrast, the HMOs and PBMs allowed to bargain with manufacturers under the new Medicare law represent much smaller buying blocks, giving them far less leverage at the negotiating table. "The discounted prices that even the largest HMOs win are seldom, if ever, anywhere near as low as Canadian retail prices," says Kaiser Permanente's George Halvorson.[57]

Device Makers, Surgeons, and Secrets

Much has been written about the pharmaceutical industry's shortcomings. Hard-hitting books like Dr. Jerry Avorn's *Powerful Medicines: The Benefits, Risks, and Costs of Prescription Drugs;* Dr. Marcia Angell's *The Truth About the Drug Companies: How They Deceive Us and What to Do About It;* and Katharine Greider's *The Big Fix: How the Pharmaceutical Industry Rips Off American Consumers* offer vivid portraits of an industry that, critics say, has become a vast marketing machine, far more interested in protecting the bloated sales of overpriced products than in protecting the patients who use those products. There is no need to reprise those stories of greed and recklessness here.

Though, in fairness to the industry, it is worth repeating Dr. Jerry Avorn's reminder that "Even though the proportion of revenues [that pharmaceutical companies] spend on research is not as large as their self-congratulatory television commercials imply, it is still true that billions of dollars are committed by the best companies to important biomedical investigation; they hire excellent scientists, from basic organic chemists to clinical specialists, to try to discover important new products and bring them to market. Even if too much of the industry's prodigious cash flow is diverted away from research and spent on marketing or on the development and protection of trivial 'me too' products, we still need to preserve that core of scientifically useful work . . . *In a way, we need to protect the companies from themselves—or more precisely, from domination by their marketing departments.*" (emphasis mine)[58]

That said, it seems time to devote more attention to device makers. Less has been written about the medical device industry, in part because it is a smaller (though increasingly powerful) sector of the health care economy, and in part because consumers are rarely aware of the spiraling cost of devices. When a stent maker doubles or triples the price of its product, the markup is hidden in the hieroglyphics of a hospital bill.

But by 2005 hospitals were beginning to question just how sky-high prices for a stent or a knee are set—and who is setting them.

Although hospitals pick up the tab for devices (and then pass it on to insurers and patients), when it comes to picking a brand, surgeons usually call the shots. And they have little incentive to be cost conscious. Quite the opposite: insofar as the surgeon often has a close personal and/or financial relationship with the device maker and its sales rep, he may well be reluctant to haggle for the best possible price.

Begin with the personal relationship: "The sales rep is my friend," declares Dr. John Cherf, the Chicago knee surgeon with an MBA. "The device companies hire people who are gregarious, high energy, and fun. And in the operating room, they help my staff." Cherf tries to keep an eye on how much his surgical center is paying for devices, but "you don't want to bite the hand that feeds you," he says. "You don't want to be too brutal." [59]

George Cipolletti, cofounder of Apex Surgical, a company that focuses on joint replacement products, agrees that the manufacturers' reps are technicians, trained not just to sell products, but to assist the surgeon's staff in the OR: "The rep can help get a surgeon out of a jam," explains Cipolletti, who once oversaw knee implant research for Johnson & Johnson. "Operating room staffs are not always reliable. There are times when, in the middle of surgery, the shift changes and you get a new scrub nurse." At that point, a rep who knows the sequence of the instruments the surgeon needs can be an invaluable aid. "In general, the rep is very well versed in how to use the device," says Cipolletti. "He can give the surgeon options: 'If this isn't working, try this . . .'" [60]

And the sales rep has every reason to steer surgeons toward his company's newest, costliest products. Reps work on commissions that run as high as 10 percent to 20 percent, and the salesman can make as much, if not more, from an operation as the surgeon. But to do that, the company salesman needs to tend to his friendship with the physician. In an interview with *The New York Times,* one former sales rep confided that he often paid the doctors' assistants $200 a case: " 'It was a bonus the surgeon didn't have to pay with his own money,' said the rep, who insisted on not being identified because he still worked in the industry and feared retribution." [61]

Clinching the connection, the surgeon may well have financial ties to the company itself. Morgan Stanley stock analyst Glenn Reicin caused a stir at Harvard's 5th Annual Alumni Healthcare Conference in November of 2004 by outing some of the most common arrangements. Reicin offered several examples of ties that bind, beginning with the case of an implant maker paying physicians $1,000 to complete a questionnaire that requires only 15 minutes of their time. Alternatively, a company may offer a surgeon as much as $1 million dollars a year to train his peers in how to use particular devices—with the understanding that he use only the company's products. In a third example, Reicin described an orthopedics medical practice that wants to expand its research capacity by hiring a fellow. So it establishes a not-for-profit foundation to fund a fellowship. One of the medical device companies sponsors the fellowship, which carries the company's title.

"Are these [arrangements] appropriate or not?" Reicin asked.

One member of the audience cut to the chase: "We need to define the doctor as an intermediary, not a customer. The patient expects the doctor to be his or her fiduciary representative." [62]

Not long after the conference, *HBS Working Knowledge,* a weekly online publication produced by the Harvard Business School, summed up Reicin's talk: "The medical device arena—so green in venture capital money, yet so gray in areas of conduct—may prove tempting to [New York State attorney general] Eliot Spitzer if companies don't reexamine their own selling models, and soon."

In his talk, Reicin underlined just how green the sector has become. " 'We see a shifting of funds from the pharma sector to devices,' he explained. 'A couple years ago, there was a trillion dollars in market capitalization in the domestic pharma sector and only $300 million or so in the medical device sector.' " But "more recently," Reicin explained, "investors have been concluding that the drug business is riskier than the franchise model of medical devices, because drug patents eventually expire. It is true that medical devices have a very quick product cycle," *HBS Working Knowledge* noted, "but, Reicin said, device companies also develop lasting relationships with their customers and create sustainable franchises. . . . 'The relationships between the doctor and the rep are very cozy,' Reicin added." [63]

The *HBS Working Knowledge* piece, titled "Trouble Ahead: Ethics and Medical Devices," would prove prescient. Four months later, federal prosecutors subpoenaed three orthopedic implant makers—Biomet, Stryker, and the DePuy unit of Johnson & Johnson—seeking "any and all consulting contracts, professional service agreements or remuneration agreements" with orthopedic surgeons dating back to January of 2002. [64]

The probe came after years of spiraling prices. From 1991 to 2004, these implant makers boosted the price tags on their products by 132 percent, according to *Orthopedic Network News.* Over the same period, Medicare increased payments for joint replacement by just 16 percent. [65]

Orthopedic implant makers are not the only device makers who have sparked interest at the Justice Department: in October of 2005, the nation's three big makers of implantable heart devices—Medtronic, the Guidant Corporation, and St. Jude Medical—acknowledged that they, too, had received subpoenas. According to Medtronic, the subpoenas sought information related to possible violations of federal antifraud and antikickback statutes, which prohibit payments or "provision of benefit, if any, to anyone in a position to recommend purchases of" pacemakers and other cardiac devices.[66]

Defending financial ties between manufacturers and surgeons, Dr. Stuart L. Weinstein, president of the American Academy of Orthopaedic Surgeons, argues that since doctors are intimately involved in developing new devices and techniques, "there have to be these close relationships between surgeons and industry." And when surgeons consult, they must be paid for their time.[67]

But when relationships between physicians and manufacturers are shrouded in secrecy, one can't help but understand why hospitals are uneasy. Hospital officials at Louisiana State University Health Sciences Center in Shreveport, for instance, say that they were startled to discover that Sulzer Medical had agreed to pay Dr. William Overdyke, an assistant professor at the center who oversaw knee replacements, $75,000 a year to consult on product design while also "promoting and educating other surgeons" on the virtues of Sulzer products. Though officials might have wondered why, from 2000 to the middle of 2001, whenever a patient needed a spare part, Overdyke and the residents he supervised used one made by Sulzer—especially since, before signing with Sulzer, Overdyke and his residents usually used products made by Wright Medical Technology. (At that time, Overdyke had a contract with Wright.)

Another clue that the hospital missed: around the time that Overdyke became involved with Sulzer, one of the hospital's distributors, MD Medical, also changed its representation to Sulzer. A founder of MD Medical would later become Dr. Overdyke's wife.

Overdyke insisted that Sulzer's knee was the best available, and he was never accused of directly profiting from using Sulzer's implants. But state investigators would determine that he had violated Louisiana's ethics laws, which forbid state employees from doing business with companies when they have financial ties with the companies in question. Ultimately, Dr. Overdyke was hit with $100,000 in fines, though if he had not worked for a state hospital, he probably never would have been punished. As R. Gray Sexton, the counsel for the state's ethics board, observes: the case "involved conditions routinely tolerated in private hospitals across the nation."

Not only are hospitals often unaware of financial ties between device makers and surgeons, many hospitals are hazy on just how much they are paying for devices—and whether they are paying more than the going market price. Traditionally, device makers have viewed pricing as a trade secret, and as a result, prices are "all over the lot," industry insiders say. Indeed, the cost of a given device might vary by thousands of dollars from one hospital to the next. In the New York area, for example, one hospital paid $8,000 more for a DePuy hip than a competitor, according to a recent survey by the Greater New York Hospital Association. "[There has] almost been a black box around what people pay," Timothy Glennon, an executive with the association, told *The New York Times*.[68]

Recently, the hospital industry has begun to fight back. Realizing that secrecy helps drive prices skyward, hospitals have begun to call for a free exchange of information. Some have turned to consultants like Amerinet and MedAssets, which provide information about what other hospitals are paying.

But these efforts at transparency "are drawing fierce resistance," the *Times* reported in September of 2005. At that point Guidant, the nation's second largest manufacturer of cardiac implants, had sued two consultants, accusing them of sharing confidential price information. One of the consultants countersued, alleging Guidant has tried to buy doctors' loyalty with consulting agreements and other kickbacks. Each denied the other's charges.[69]

Presumably, Guidant would be among the first to denounce the idea of government regulating device prices. Waving the flag of free market competition, device makers uniformly insist on their right to charge what they wish, and "let the market" decide if the price is right. Yet by refusing to disclose what it is charging other hospitals, Guidant makes it impossible for a buyer to make an informed decision.

Exploiting the Erosion of the Alliance
Between Hospital and Doctor

Nevertheless, hospitals have been reluctant to question the devices surgeons choose, in part because it's important that a surgeon use the device that he knows best, and in part because hospitals know that surgeons operating at their institutions could easily take their patients elsewhere. As a result, hospitals have been paying an average of $5,200 for a knee and $6,000 for a hip, says John Cherf, while Medicare reimburses the hospital just $10,000 for the entire operation. "They shouldn't be paying more than 35 percent of that $10,000 for the device itself," he adds.[70]

Not surprisingly, Blair Childs, an executive vice president with the device makers trade group AdvaMed, objects to the notion that hospitals are being gouged: "Physicians are a very discriminating customer," Childs told *The New York Times*. "It's not like you're selling to a bunch of stooges."[71]

A surgeon himself, Cherf is not suggesting that doctors are easily duped, just that they're not terribly concerned about the economic problems of the hospitals where they operate: "The device industry has done a brilliant job of exploiting the erosion of the traditional alliance between hospital and doctor," he says.[72]

As we saw in chapter 2, that alliance has been tested by the pressures of a competitive marketplace where health care dollars are scarce, and both hospitals and doctors struggle to protect their own interests. Surgeons, in particular, complain about difficulties scheduling operating rooms and delays between surgeries that cost them billable time.[73] For their part, hospitals have tried to make it illegal for surgeons to build their own surgical centers, saying that specialty hospitals skim much-needed business from community hospitals.

Cherf sides with the physicians: "Hospitals need to understand who their customer is—the doctor who admits patients. Hospitals should make surgeons' lives better," says Cherf, adding that surgeons have legitimate complaints about error rates and inefficiencies at general hospitals. "I operate in a specialty surgical center where just two languages are spoken: neurosurgery and orthopedic surgery," says Cherf. "General hospitals should be building more of these 'focused factories' themselves. If they're too expensive for one hospital to finance, maybe three or four should get together to build the facilities surgeons need. But today, general hospitals are still too entrenched in the single 'big box' theory."[74]

Cherf may be right that for too long hospitals have ignored surgeons' needs. Certainly, letting scrub nurses' shifts change in the middle of an operation seems less than supportive.

Today, however, hospitals are trying to make amends as they reach out to enlist doctors in their fight against exorbitant and erratic pricing. In 2005 Aurora Health Care, for example, recruited Dr. Steven Kaplan, a prominent Milwaukee surgeon, when it realized that the cost of artificial hips and knees was eating up 80 percent of what Medicare paid the hospital system for an entire joint replacement surgery.

First, the hospital system needed to hire a consulting firm to figure out how much it *should* be paying for implants. Then it persuaded Kaplan to become its "physician champion." After looking at Aurora's books, Kaplan tumbled to what was going on. "In most of the cases, the implant rep in the operating room was making more than the surgeon," says Kaplan. "When I was able to point that out to other doctors, they were ready to listen. . . . I had the right selling tools."[75]

In exchange for the surgeons' cooperation, the hospital system began to offer doctors extra support in the form of designated orthopedic teams in the operating rooms and educational programs for implant patients. The collaborative effort worked: with the physicians' help, Aurora was able to bring the average price of a hip down from $8,000 to $4,300.

In the process, Aurora negotiated the cuts with every one of its vendors, so orthopedic surgeons still had access to their favorite devices. "We supported an 'all-play' program with the understanding that, if the vendors decided not to play [and offer the discounts], we would exclude them," explains Ken Peterson, vice president of systems logistics management for Aurora's 12-hospital system. "All of them ended up playing."[76]

"It's going to be a win-win situation for everybody—except the implant companies," says Kaplan. But "they've been winning for a long time."[77]

Hoping to enlist more doctors in their campaign to contain runaway device prices, some hospitals have begun to discuss sharing savings with their surgeons. In 2005 HCA, the nation's largest for-profit chain, sought federal approval for a "gain-sharing" plan that would encourage its orthopedic surgeons to select less expensive devices by giving them 10 percent to 20 percent of the dollars saved.

Predictably, the idea of gain sharing has sent both the device industry and its investors into a swivet. "This will probably start a whole new round of investor fear regarding the medical device industry and its ability to maintain healthy pricing," said Morgan Stanley stock analyst Glenn Reicin, referring to the Hospital Fair Competition Act of 2005, sponsored by Senators Charles Grassley and Max Baucus.[78]

Apex Surgical's George Cipolletti objects for other reasons: "Gain sharing is no different from a surgeon getting a check from the manufacturer," says Cipolletti. "Money is still driving the surgeon's decision when he picks a device. Doctors think about too many different things," Cipolletti adds. "I want them to get back to making medical decisions based on what's good medicine."[79]

The "Best Knee"

Cipolletti has a point. Just as a sales rep may sell a surgeon on the most expensive device, whether or not it is best for the patient, gain sharing may tilt him in the direction of the least expensive, without the doctor even being conscious of his bias.

The uncertainty surrounding most new devices makes it very difficult to sort out motives. As Cipolletti acknowledges, the difference between an older product and a new, improved version can prove elusive. "If you talk to a statistician, he'll tell you that if you already have a knee that is giving good results 90 percent of the time, and you're trying to improve on it with a knee that will give equally good results 95 percent of the time, you'll need an enormous amount of patience to prove the difference."[80]

In truth, "there is no such thing as a 'best knee,'" Chicago knee surgeon John Cherf declares. "Three things make for a successful operation: (a) selecting the right patient for the right operation—that's 10 percent of it; (b) selecting the right device—that might count for 5 percent; and (c) surgical technique—that's 80 percent to 85 percent of it. The human input is critical," says Cherf. "Think of it this way: if you gave Tiger Woods 20-year-old golf clubs, and gave me the newest clubs, he'd still kick my butt."[81]

Even Cipolletti, the device maker who oversaw knee research at J&J, agrees: "90 percent of success is determined not by the device itself, but by how good the surgeon is at implanting that particular device—how much experience he has with it. If you were having knee surgery, that's what I would tell you to ask the surgeon."[82]

"I'd hate to say that medical devices are commodity products," adds Cherf, "but there is not a lot of long-term data differentiating their products. If manufacturers are raising prices on the newest devices claiming that they're better, there should be a warranty."[83]

Yet, as Kaiser Permanente CEO George Halvorson points out, few medical researchers would be willing to risk betting their own money on their newest products or procedures. In some cases, he reports, when health care plans have been asked to cover a new, as yet unproven treatment, they have said: " 'Try it. If it works, we'll pick up the bill. If it fails, then it's your cost, not ours.' "

Researchers virtually never take the bet because they "know that most research fails," says Halvorson. "So having their personal incomes tied to the actual success of their unproven care isn't at all attractive. There is some irony in the fact that the same researchers who enthusiastically extend hope to individual patients are, almost without exception, far too practical about the actual value of their experimental care to risk their own income."[84]

Nevertheless, manufacturers must "constantly roll out new products—and promise superior results—in order to justify the premium prices that have made them so profitable in the past," observes TheStreet.com's Melissa Davis.[85] "A lot of technological innovation serves shareholders more than patients," says Stan Mendenhall, the editor and publisher of *Orthopedic Network News*.[86] FDA data support his assertion, showing that most orthopedic devices approved in recent years gained clearance through the agency's 510(k) process for being "substantially equivalent" to items already available. Since 2000 the big orthopedic implant companies have gained regulatory approval for just five hips and one knee that qualify as "breakthrough devices."[87]

Despite the lack of hard evidence that a high-end knee is better, surgeons often want to try the newest, most sophisticated products. After all, as spine surgeon Dr. Bernard Guiot points out, "nobody wants to be left behind." Meanwhile, patients themselves frequently are convinced that what is newest must be superior.

Yet the industry's detractors argue that device makers are merely creating the illusion of success by keeping outcomes data under wraps and avoiding head-to-head comparisons.[88] "Industry is proposing new designs and new technologies almost every day—with increasing costs—and no real progress has been made," Italian physician Paolo Gallinaro wrote in the journal *Orthopedics* in January of 2005. "We all agree that scientific advances" often involve "taking a small step forward," Gallinaro acknowledges. "This means that we also must take the risk of occasionally taking a small step backwards. But haven't we taken too many steps back and only a few forward?" He points out that each of the materials used in hip joint replacement surgery has its drawbacks: "Highly cross-linked polyethylene shows 'wear and surface cracking' when examined by an independent bioengineering laboratory. Metal-on-metal raises concerns due to hypersensitivity reactions, and ceramic can break.[89]

"If this is state of the art, why is our attention to the aforementioned problems diverted to new acrobatic toys like 'building a ship in the bottle,' i.e., minimally invasive surgery [MIS]?" he asks. Instead of constantly inventing new procedures, Gallinaro suggests, we should concentrate on improving the devices already on the market.

Yet from a marketer's point of view, new ideas are essential. And certainly, the idea of "minimally invasive" (or mini-incision) hip replacement sounds attractive. One would think that smaller incisions would mean fewer infections and fewer complications—and this is exactly what industry-sponsored research suggests.[90]

But an independent study conducted by orthopedic surgeons at Stanford University Medical Center who received no grants or support from industry found no significant benefits to MIS. Instead, the study—published in *The Journal of Bone and Joint Surgery* in 2004—revealed that the patients who received MIS faced "a significantly higher risk of wound complications" and were more likely to experience poor implant positioning and fit.

The researchers were concerned: "If other studies of the mini-incision technique also show more component malposition and more serious postoperative complications than the standard-incision technique, then the long-term results of the mini-incision arthroplasty may be jeopardized," they wrote. "Until the safety and efficacy of mini-incision total hip replacement are confirmed in the peer-reviewed literature by other investigators, we are concerned about the widespread use of the technique." In 2005 other studies of minimally invasive hip replacement published in the same journal continued to emphasize "catastrophic complications," while indicating that, at least over the short term, MIS seemed to offer no benefit in terms of post-op outcomes.[91]

Wall Street analysts took note. "During the past several years, Zimmer [Holdings, the world's largest manufacturer of knee and hip implants] has cast itself as the minimally invasive surgery company," Morgan Stanley's Glenn Reicin noted in January of 2005. But "we believe concerns may arise regarding high complication rates and poor outcomes for those patients undergoing MIS single-incision hip replacement."[92]

Critics like Dr. Gallinaro suggest that rather than crowding the market-place with new products and procedures, device makers need to consolidate what they already know, pulling the information together into databases that would let doctors and patients compare long-term outcomes. Such databases, called "registries," are commonplace in most developed countries. By tracking actual failure rates, they throw a spotlight on problematic devices so that they can be identified and avoided. Sweden established the first registry in 1979, and this, researchers say, may be one reason why the failure rate of joint replacement in Sweden is half what it is in the United States.[93]

Some industry insiders argue that Americans would never submit to being listed in a registry because it would mean giving up their right to privacy. But in Sweden no one is forced to sign up. Patients have a choice—though the vast majority agree to enroll because they realize that down the line, if there is a problem with the device, the registry gives doctors an easy way to track them down. In the United States, by contrast, orthopedic surgeons complain that they have limited access to long-term scientific data. Despite repeated recommendations to start a joint registry here, the United States doesn't have one—largely because device makers don't want one.

"Since new products are not necessarily better than brand X, you have to hype them right," Cipolletti observes mildly. "If you actually have outcomes research, it's much harder to do that."[94]

The lack of a registry demonstrates how the culture of secrecy that permeates the medical device industry, shrouding both pricing and financial relationships between manufacturers and surgeons, extends into an area that threatens patient safety. Manufacturers are reluctant to hold their products up to the spotlight because they are afraid of exposing their flaws—even though they know that, in some cases, those defects may prove deadly.

Patient Safety and Wall Street's Imperatives

On a balmy March day in 2005, two college students were riding mountain bikes through the red rock canyons outside Moab, Utah, when Jessica Lemieux, who was riding ahead of her boyfriend, Joshua Oukrop, "heard him call out, 'Hold on, I need to . . . ' When she turned, he was already falling backward, his bike tumbling on top of him," *The New York Times* later reported. Before she could begin to take in what was happening, he had stopped breathing.[95]

When Oukrop's physicians at the Minneapolis Heart Institute Foundation learned of his death, they were stunned. Four years earlier Oukrop, who suffered from a genetic heart disease, had had a defibrillator, a device that uses jolts of electricity to shock an erratically beating heart back to a normal rhythm, surgically implanted in his chest. Joshua's physicians checked it every three months. In fact, they had examined it in January—just two months before the fatal bike trip—and found no problems.

It turned out that the device had short-circuited while trying to deliver high-voltage therapy to Joshua's heart. The FDA later reported that "the problem [was] caused by deterioration of electrical insulation in the device that can only be detected after the device has already malfunctioned. The device does not give any sign of impending failure and there is no test that predicts whether the device will fail."[96]

Joshua's defibrillator had been made by Guidant, the nation's second-largest maker of defibrillators and pacemakers. When a company official told Dr. Barry Maron, one of Joshua's doctors at the Minneapolis Heart Institute, what had happened, Maron called Dr. Robert Hauser, a senior consulting cardiologist at the institute. Hauser searched the Manufacturer and User Facility Device Experience (MAUDE) database maintained by the FDA, which contains reports of adverse events involving medical devices. There, buried in the data, Hauser found other reports from Guidant of instances in which the same defibrillator had short-circuited in exactly the same way. Neither the FDA nor the company had alerted doctors to the problem.

Maron and Hauser faced a crisis of conscience. Forty-seven other patients using the same device were followed at the institute—including Joshua's father, who suffered from the same genetic disease. "We became very concerned," Maron recalls. "We were keeping a secret not just from our patients and their physicians, but also from all the patients with the device and their physicians."

On May 12, four Guidant officials came to Maron's office. " 'What are we going to do about this?' " Maron asked. " 'We are in an untenable situation ethically and morally with our patients. How are we going to get the word out?' "

"The Guidant officials replied: 'Well, we are not. We don't think we need to. And we don't think it's advisable.' " Guidant's emissaries expressed doubt that the patients would be able to understand the medical issues involved in determining whether or not to replace the devices.

"I said, 'I think this is the biggest mistake you will ever make,' " Maron remembers. "They said they didn't agree."[97]

They were wrong. Before the year was out Guidant would be the target of a criminal investigation.

It would turn out that Guidant had identified the design flaw in the defibrillator that Joshua used in February of 2002, a full three years before the 21-year-old died. When the company discovered the problem, it quietly made manufacturing changes in April and November of that year—*and then continued to sell devices that had been manufactured before the changes were made, while issuing no public statements about the problem or the corrections.*

The company didn't let the public in on its secret until May 23, 2005—hours before *The New York Times* published an article about Oukrop's death, headlined: "Maker of Heart Device Kept Flaw from Doctors."[98]

The day after the *Times* broke the story, Wall Street weighed in with a shrug: "It's a gray area—you can't be issuing alerts or recalls every time you have a glitch," said Thomas Gunderson, a securities analyst with Piper Jaffray. Investors also appeared to dismiss the news: the company's stock slipped just 48 cents to $73.75 a share.[99]

Meanwhile, Dr. Joseph M. Smith, the chief medical officer of Guidant's cardiac rhythm management division, explained that the company had not seen any compelling reason to issue an alert because the failure rate was very low. The company was aware of "only" 25 other cases (out of 26,000) in which the defibrillator that Joshua used had been affected by the same flaw. Smith rejected any suggestion that financial or liability concerns had influenced the company's decision, saying that Guidant believed that publicizing the issue could cause more harm than good: after all, surgery to replace the defibrillator also could pose risks.[100] What patients didn't know wouldn't worry them.

Dr. Barry Maron rejected the company's explanation: "Replacing the device poses an extraordinarily low risk—approaching zero," he said, pointing out that the devices need to be replaced every five years anyway, because their batteries wear out. Both of Joshua's doctors said that if they had known of the problem earlier, they would have changed the defibrillator.[101] At the Mayo Clinic, Dr. Robert Rea, the director of the implantable cardiac service, agreed: "I think it very likely that we will change a lot of these devices."[102]

Joshua's father Lee Oukrop had his own Guidant defibrillator replaced less than two months after his son died. "Whoever made this decision at Guidant, I pray he doesn't have a son who this happens to," said Oukrop, who was haunted by the reassurances he gave his 17-year-old son before the implant: "I sat down with my son and I gave him my personal guarantee that this device would save his life, that he would be around for many, many years," Oukrop said. "I told him, 'You've got to have it, this will save your life.'"[103]

In the end, it was not up to the company to weigh the risk-benefit equation and decide what patients should and shouldn't know, says Gordon Rudd, a partner with Zimmerman Reed in Minneapolis, a law firm that handles medical device product liability cases: "If they see a pattern of a problem, they should alert patients and let patients and doctors make an informed decision."[104]

But Guidant had a compelling financial reason to keep news of the defect under wraps. In December of 2004—three months before Joshua Oukrop's death—Johnson & Johnson had announced that it planned to acquire the device maker for $25.4 billion. Wall Street matchmakers had been trying to pair Guidant with Johnson & Johnson for years. Finally, the marriage was about to become a reality. The two already had comarketed J&J's drug-coated stents, and now Guidant's pacemakers and implantable defibrillators would fill a hole in J&J's growing device portfolio.[105] Little wonder that Guidant didn't want its suitor to learn of the possible blemish on the dowry: in 2004 implantable defibrillators accounted for nearly half of Guidant's $3.8 billion in total sales.

As for J&J, the company realized that cutting-edge devices could jumpstart its earnings. The cardiac implant market was growing at about 20 percent a year, and Guidant's earnings were forecast to rise 16 percent in 2006 and 31 percent in 2007.[106] J&J was willing to pay handsomely for the opportunity. When the rumors started circulating that J&J might be ready to tie the knot with the Indianapolis device maker, Guidant was trading at $65 a share; by the time the deal was sealed, J&J had agreed to pay $76, a nice premium for Guidant's shareholders.

One can only imagine the gnashing of teeth in Indianapolis five months later when Guidant executives heard that a dogged *New York Times* reporter was digging into the defibrillator death. Over the next six months, Barry

Meier would publish some 33 stories about the failure of Guidant's defibrillator—and the fact that, for more than three years, the company had kept quiet about the problem while continuing to sell the defective defibrillators that it had in stock.

Insisting that it had done nothing wrong, Guidant tried, at first, to characterize the student's death as a tragic but rare accident. Within weeks, however, the company was forced to admit that the same type of electrical defect that destroyed Joshua's defibrillator also caused other Guidant heart devices to malfunction. Ultimately Guidant admitted that it was aware of two recent deaths involving those other devices. And since autopsies have become rare, and defibrillators are not routinely evaluated after a patient dies, Guidant would have to acknowledge that the actual rate of failure could be higher, and that the number of associated deaths might be underreported.[107]

Covering up a scandal is like ignoring a tumor—inevitably, it spreads. On June 18, 2005, Guidant announced that it was recalling some 29,000 implanted heart devices. The recalls focused new attention on other skeletons in Guidant's closet. In June of 2003 Endovascular Technologies, a subsidiary of Guidant, had pleaded guilty to 10 felony counts and agreed to pay $92.4 million in civil and criminal penalties related to its Ancure Endograft system, a stent graft device used to treat abdominal aortic aneurysms. The company admitted that it had lied to the government and hidden thousands of serious health problems, including 12 deaths.[108]

On Wall Street, in the spring of 2005, Guidant's defenders would continue to rally around the device maker, arguing that the defibrillator's failure rate was very low. There is no such thing as a "perfect device," they pointed out—and they were right. But it was the pattern of secrecy and deceit that would be Guidant's undoing.

In June investors began filing lawsuits, alleging that Guidant and its executives had purposefully covered up the problem. (Nimble investors managed to sue while simultaneously rallying 'round.) The revelation that Guidant executives unloaded millions of dollars of company stock shortly before the scandal broke didn't help their case. For example, on May 17, 2005, Beverly Lorell, Guidant's chief medical and technology officer, sold 23,300 shares for $1.71 million. On May 23, 2005, the day before Guidant made the front page of the *Times,* she sold another 22,667 shares for $1.68 million.[109]

As for Johnson & Johnson, when the *Times* story appeared in May of 2005, J&J seemed unperturbed. After all, Guidant's shares hadn't tanked—

and it's the company's share price, not the integrity of its products, that usu-ally makes or breaks a Wall Street merger. But at the end of September, a *New York Times* story headlined, "Guidant Case May Involve Criminal In-quiry" may have given J&J pause. Two weeks later headlines indicated that J&J was "Rethinking the Cost of a Deal," and in October, five months after the story broke, Guidant shares plummeted, losing more than 20 percent of their value.[110] Evidence of short-circuiting heart implants and dead patients was not enough to drive Guidant's investors away. They didn't defect until they began to suspect that J&J might not pay a premium for their shares.

At that point, Guidant had recalled or issued safety notices on some 100,000 pacemakers and defibrillators, and had agreed to pay for replace-ments at $25,000 a pop.[111] Both federal and state authorities had launched in-vestigations into the cover-up. New York State attorney general Eliot Spitzer stalked the company.

Guidant's reputation was in tatters, its financial health threatened by lawsuits, but Johnson & Johnson couldn't take its eyes off the lucrative cardiac implant market. And so in November it agreed to take Guidant to the altar after all—but at a discount. Under the new terms, J&J would pur-chase Guidant for $21.5 billion, or $63.08 a share, down $4 billion from the original price.

Then came a final plot twist. In December a second suitor stepped for-ward, and Johnson & Johnson rival Boston Scientific offered $24.7 billion for Guidant's hand. A bidding war ensued. When it was all over, a month later, Boston Scientific had agreed to pay $27 billion, $1.6 billion more than J&J's original offer, even while prosecutors widened their probe.

Where Was the FDA?

At the tail end of the sorry story of Guidant and its defibrillator, just one loose end remains: Where was the FDA? Companies that manufacture de-fibrillators and pacemakers are required to file annual reports with the FDA that say how often, and why, their devices fail. And in February of 2005, Guidant had submitted just such a report, disclosing data which showed that the defibrillator that Joshua Oukrop used was short-circuiting at the rate of about one a month.

The FDA didn't issue an alert about the defibrillator until June—after *The*

New York Times forced Guidant to share its story with the public. At first the FDA warning was relatively mild, but ultimately the agency turned up the volume, acknowledging that while the short circuits were rare, they posed a significant risk because they could render a defibrillator useless, just when it is most needed—i.e., when the patient's heart was signaling that it was in desperate need of a stabilizing jolt.

The FDA did not make its data about the defibrillator's shortcomings public in February for the same reason that it refused to give Dr. Charles Rosen detailed information about the Charité disc: the agency labels the information it receives from companies "confidential." Noting that the FDA receives thousands of reports from manufacturers, Dr. Daniel G. Schultz, the director of the FDA's Center for Devices and Radiological Health, told *The New York Times* that it would tie up too many of the agency's resources to review the massive amounts of data sent in each year in order to sort out which should be deemed trade secrets and which could be routinely released.[112]

For its part, Guidant point outs that it made all required disclosures to the FDA, including notifying the agency in its 2003 annual report about the manufacturing change that it made in 2002. But the February 2005 report was the first of the annual filings to say that a number of devices had failed because of electrical short circuits.

Guidant also regularly sent performance reports to doctors, but in those notices the company provided only a "survival rate" for each model over time, without giving the cause of the failure. Like Rosen, many physicians believe that the warnings that they need to see are buried in the details of exactly what went wrong. It's important to know whether a device failed because its battery ran out, or because it short-circuited when it tried to save a patient's life. "Device failures that are abrupt and catastrophic are more critical than ones that happen slowly or don't interfere with life-saving functions," says Los Angeles cardiologist Dr. Charles Swerdlow.[113]

Digging for the truth, the *Times* did what Dr. Charles Rosen had done when he wanted to know more about the Charité disc: the newspaper requested copies under the Freedom of Information Act of the detailed filings that Guidant had sent to the FDA. The agency refused, telling the *Times* just what it had told Rosen: the annual reports contained proprietary information. But it would turn out that the newspaper had more clout than a physician. When the *Times* appealed that decision, the FDA, without citing a specific reason, reversed its position in September of 2005, releasing much of the data.

"Those filings show the wide gap between the data provided to the FDA and that given to doctors," the *Times* reported. For each defibrillator model it sold, Guidant gave the agency three to four pages of information citing specific reasons for device failure, including memory problems and prematurely low batteries, and how many units failed for what reason. In its 2004 filing, for example, the company reported that over a 12-month period the defibrillator Joshua Oukrop used had suffered an "electrical short" almost once a month.

This might seem an eye-stopping fact, but it was buried in a chart on page 60 of a 96-page section of numbing numbers on Guidant's defibrillators. Some might fault the company for not spotlighting the statistic, both in reports to the FDA and in letters to doctors. Others would say the FDA should shoulder the responsibility for not sounding the alarm. "They probably didn't even read the report," said Joshua's doctor Dr. Robert Hauser.[114]

Whatever Happened to the FDA?

In 2002 Alistair Wood, a respected clinical pharmacologist at Vanderbilt University, was close to being nominated by President George W. Bush to fill the long-vacant job of FDA commissioner. But some industry executives, along with free-market enthusiasts that included members of the editorial board at *The Wall Street Journal,* objected. When Senator Bill Frist was asked why Wood was dropped from consideration for the top post at the FDA, he summed up the opposition: "There was a great deal of concern that he put too much emphasis on safety."[115] (Dr. Mark McClellan, brother of White House press secretary Scott McClellan and son of the Republican comptroller of Texas and former mayor of Austin, got the job.)[116]

One cannot help but remember that at the daylong FDA panel meeting on J&J's spinal disc, Charité, only Dr. John Kirkpatrick stressed that the FDA's "first purpose" is "protecting the public." Other members of the panel seemed more concerned with accommodating the company's desire to get the product to market as quickly as possible.

Certainly, getting new drugs and devices to the public in a timely fashion is important—particularly those products that, unlike Charité, offer a clear and proven advantage over older rivals. But while it is the manufacturer's job to push for early approval, it is the FDA's responsibility to hold back as it presses questions about safety. Ideally, that push and pull creates a dialogue that will balance risks and benefits. But if the manufacturer and the FDA's experts all sit on the same side of the table, no one represents the public's primary need for safety.

Over the past decade, the FDA's critics claim that the agency has abdicated its role as the public's protector. The agency's priorities started to shift, they suggest, in 1992—when the supposedly independent watchdog agency began to depend on the very companies that it regulates for a major chunk of its funding.

That was the year that the pharmaceutical industry finally succeeded in persuading Congress to pass the Prescription Drug User Fee Act (PDUFA)—a law that aimed to speed up the drug approval process by letting manufacturers fund drug approvals. In the late 1980s everyone from AIDS activists to *The Wall Street Journal*'s editorial board pummeled the FDA for dragging its heels when approving potentially lifesaving drugs. Money was a large part of the problem: the agency just didn't have the funds to hire enough reviewers. Under PDUFA, that would change.

The 1992 law opened the door to industry funding in exchange for faster reviews. Under the original agreement, drugmakers promised to give the agency $200 million in 1993—but only if the FDA spent a specified level of money on new drug approvals. For the industry this was "chump change," Dr. Marcia Angell points out, "more than offset by the added income of getting to the market sooner." But for the agency, the industry's dollars provided funding that an understaffed and underfinanced FDA sorely needed. Ten years later Congress would offer the same deal to device makers, passing the Medical Device User Fee and Modernization Act (MDUFMA) of 2002.

But rather than serving as "additional" funding, the manufacturers' contributions would become essential—and begin to dictate how the FDA spends its money. The problem was twofold: First, in the years that followed passage of PDUFA Congress cut back on its support, and the agency became more and more dependent on the dollars it received from industry. By 2004 user fees paid for more than half of the Center for Drug Evaluation and Research's annual budget of almost $500 million.[117] Second, the 1992 law stipulated that the FDA's financing of new drug reviews, adjusted for inflation, would never fall below 1992 levels (later revised to 1997 levels).[118]

Because congressional financing lagged far behind the agency's needs, over the next decade the FDA was forced to shift dollars from other programs into the review program in order to fund it at the levels that PDUFA promised. As the years passed, the agency spent more and more of its budget on getting drugs to market, and less and less on monitoring drug safety. The numbers tell the story: in 1992, the agency's drug center spent 53 percent of its budget on new drug reviews. The rest went to survey programs, laboratories, and other efforts that helped ensure that drugs already on the market were safe. In 2003, 79 percent of the agency's drug center budget went to new drug reviews.[119]

In the process the FDA has met or exceeded nearly all of the PDUFA goals. By 2003 drug approval time had been cut in half.[120] But insiders say that the FDA's independence has been compromised.

Dr. Jerry Avorn reprises a conversation between a senior FDA official and an agency scientist whose concerns about the safety of a particular drug had "attracted the ire of its manufacturer":

" 'You need,' " the scientist's boss told him, " 'to understand that the pharmaceutical industry is our client.'

" 'That's odd,' the scientist responded. 'I always thought our clients were the people of the United States.' " [121]

Even observers like Dr. Eve Slater, former senior vice president of Merck Research Laboratories, and a former assistant secretary for health at the Department of Health and Human Services in the Bush administration until her resignation in 2003, warns that "the FDA must evolve beyond satisfying the appetite of industry for faster approval." In a 2005 article published in *The New England Journal of Medicine,* Slater wrote: "We must envision the FDA as more than a counterpart to the pharmaceutical industry. It is time for the agency to realize its full potential as protector and promoter of the public health." [122]

Some say that if the FDA is going to recover its independence, it will need more money from Congress. Not everyone agrees. Avorn argues that what the agency needs more than money is a backbone. When doubts emerge about a medicine's safety, the agency needs to insist that drugmakers pay for independent tests, says Avorn. If companies balk, the agency "needs to call a press conference and issue a public notice saying, 'There are unresolved issues and we are trying to get the company to do a clinical trial and doctors should take that into account,' " says Avorn. "The FDA has moral authority and extraordinary public relations power if they chose to use it."[123]

Inside the FDA, old hands agree. Morale is low.[124] The biggest problem, longtime employees say, is the lack of follow-up on products like the Guidant defibrillator after they have been approved. Particularly when products are sped to market, their flaws may not become apparent until tens of thousands of patients have begun using them.

Alistair Wood, the clinical pharmacologist who was once a candidate for FDA commissioner, proposed a solution to the problem in 1998 in a paper published in *The New England Journal of Medicine*. Under the present system, Wood and his coauthors pointed out, once a drug is approved for marketing, the doctors and patients assume that it is safe, unless case reports of adverse effects call that assumption into question. The problem is that there is no systematic approach to detecting problems after the product goes to market. The FDA normally relies on voluntary goodwill reporting by manufacturers and physicians.

But it is often all but impossible for individual physicians to recognize that a patient's symptoms are linked to the new drug or device—a doctor would have to see a large number of patients using the same product to recognize a pattern. And the story of Guidant's defibrillator underscores how reluctant manufacturers are to advertise adverse events.[125]

This is why Wood and his colleagues called for an independent, systematic review of products after they had been approved by the FDA. They proposed that manufacturers be required to collect data in ongoing observational studies and send that information to a drug safety board that would have enough funds to mount its own studies and hold open hearings. Indeed, the paper's authors went so far as to recommend that the board should have access to comparative data on competitors' products.[126]

Others have floated similar proposals, and by 2005 the FDA had begun to require postmarketing studies of drugs that had been "fast-tracked." But it is not at all clear that either manufacturers—or the agency—took the requirement seriously. When Massachusetts Representative Edward Markey's staff reviewed 91 studies that the FDA ordered on 42 products approved between 1993 and October 2004, the staff discovered that as of 2005 half the studies still were not done. Twenty-one of the unfinished studies had not even been begun. The oldest outstanding study had been ordered in 1996.

"It is outrageous that drug companies and the FDA have been dragging their feet when it comes to conducting required postmarketing studies," Markey observed. "They are laughing at the FDA, and sometimes it seems as if the FDA is treating it as a joke as well."[127]

A Device Maker Lobbies the FDA

Dr. Lazar Greenfield understands why the FDA doesn't get long-term follow-up information, despite the requirements: "Once the product is on the market, that's it. The companies feel that they are in business," says Greenfield, a professor of vascular surgery at the University of Michigan.[128] He understands how the device industry works better than most, both because he's renowned as the inventor of the Greenfield filter—a device that captures blood clots before they can be transported to the lung—and because from 2003 to 2004 he became an eyewitness to the inner workings of the FDA.

On sabbatical from Michigan, Greenfield, an internationally recognized expert in vascular surgery, spent six months as a visiting scholar at the FDA.[129] "One of the reasons that I went to the FDA was to get the agency more involved in tracking long-term experience with devices," says Greenfield. "Only 1 percent of the information the FDA gets is from physicians—the rest comes from the companies themselves. And while the FDA does get adverse-event reports, sorting through them is a real challenge. They get 100,000 a year, and those are reviewed by nurses, many of whom have very little operational experience."

While at the FDA, Greenfield met Dr. Dale Tavris, head of epidemiology in the FDA device center's office of postmarket surveillance. Tavris had been working hard trying to get follow-up data from Medtronic, the nation's largest medical-device manufacturer, about its AneuRx stent graft—a device used to take pressure off an abdominal aortic aneurysm (a bulge in the wall of the main artery leading from the heart) so that the aneurysm won't rupture.

For years, the only way to treat an abdominal aortic aneurysm was by opening up a patient's abdomen. This meant making an incision from the breastbone to the navel, removing the bowels and placing them outside the body to gain access to the aneurysm, then sewing a synthetic-fabric tube inside the aorta in the area of the bulge. Blood would then flow through the fabric tube, making it less likely that the artery would burst.

In the late 1990s device makers developed a far less invasive alternative, using devices like Medtronic's AneuRx stent graft, a 5-inch metal-and-fabric cylinder that can substitute for the synthetic tube used in the abdominal surgery. Like the tube, the device forms a new channel for blood and takes pressure off the bulge. In this case, however, the surgeon does not have to slice the abdomen open. He can slide the Medtronic device into the body through a small incision in the thigh—a much easier procedure for a frail patient.

But while the initial operation involves fewer risks than more invasive surgery, the question remained as to whether, over time, the device might either leak or "migrate," drifting away from the spot where it was implanted. This is why Dale Tavris needed follow-up data from the manufacturer.

"Medtronic was very reluctant to provide the data," Greenfield recalls. "And much of what the FDA did get turned out to be completely unusable. Dale Tavris finally had to go back to the company and ask for raw data—before they processed it internally.

"The way Medtronic was reporting the data was really biased," Greenfield explains. "They were claiming that patients who they hadn't heard from were still living and well—that all deaths that they didn't follow up on were due to causes unrelated to the implant. They consistently sanitized the information, but Dale sorted it out, and was able to see a pattern of problems, over time."

The FDA then set out to prepare a letter to doctors comparing the risks and benefits of the new treatment to the older surgery. Studies and interviews with vascular surgeons indicated that at top hospitals, the short-term mortality rate for the more invasive abdominal surgery was low, with just 1 percent to 2 percent of patients dying in the hospital during or after the operation. At two highly regarded programs, the University of Michigan and The Cleveland Clinic, the death rate was only about 1 percent.[130] At community hospitals, by contrast, the rate appeared to be in the 4 percent to 6 percent range. But the FDA decided to use the lower 1 percent to 2 percent mortality rate to compare abdominal surgery to the Medtronic implant on the grounds that the patients in Medtronic's AneuRx sample also were treated at high-volume hospitals with good surgery results.

Setting the numbers side by side, the AneuRx stent graft looked dicey. In the initial period after the Medtronic device was implanted about 1.5 percent of patients died as a result of aneurysms. This was no better than the mortality rate for invasive abdominal surgery at high-volume hospitals. And in subsequent years, the data suggested a 0.4 percent annual death rate for patients with the implant. There with no evidence of that rate slowing over time.

Based on the available evidence, the FDA concluded that the Medtronic device should be used on frail and/or elderly patients whose chance of dying during or shortly after the invasive surgery was greater than 2 percent. Other patients, who were at less risk of dying on the operating table, and more likely to live longer (running the long-term risk that the device would leak or migrate), would be better off undergoing the more invasive abdominal surgery.

Predictably, Medtronic cried foul. And in August of 2002, the FDA met with a group of prominent surgeons who agreed with the company. But the agency was not convinced by their arguments.

Undeterred, Medtronic continued its campaign, and 14 months later, in October of 2003, the company brought another group of leading vascular surgeons to an FDA meeting—including the then-president of the Society for Vascular Surgery. "Medtronic had helped fund the Society's aneurysm-screening program," *The Wall Street Journal* later reported. "Of the other two surgeons present, one was on Medtronic's scientific advisory board, but the other wasn't a Medtronic consultant." These experts all agreed that the FDA draft presented an unfairly negative picture of AneuRx by exaggerating the safety of the more invasive abdominal surgery.[131]

Dale Tavris, who had helped draft the FDA notice, was present at the meeting and began asking the experts pointed questions. Medtronic's champions were aggressive, and at times the meeting became "confrontational," says one FDA insider.[132] But while Tavris stuck by his guns, higher-ranking FDA officials reportedly "appeared more conciliatory and agreed to re-examine the surgical statistics."[133]

Greenfield thinks he knows what happened. "Whenever a company feels squeezed, they simply call the congressional people they support—and before long, the congressmen are on the phone to the FDA, saying, 'Back off.' "

For whatever reason, the FDA did back down. And at the tail end of 2003, more than a year after it began negotiating the language of the letter with Medtronic, the agency issued a watered-down public-health notice. The agency's most straightforward recommendation—that the devices should not be used on relatively healthy patients whose risk of dying from the abdominal surgery is less than 2 percent—had disappeared. Instead, the FDA vaguely recommended using AneuRx in patients who meet "the appropriate risk-benefit profile," and went on to list factors for doctors to consider in making the decision.

Greenfield questions the objectivity of some of the surgeons who offered glowing reports of the AneuRx stent graft. "Some of these surgeons, riding the crest of the wave, were heavily involved with the company. I think it's unhealthy to have a financial involvement with a manufacturer," he adds. "I never got any royalties from my invention," says Greenfield, referring to the Greenfield filter, the device that he introduced in 1972.

In 2005 the Greenfield filter remained the industry standard and "the fact that I didn't get royalties turned out to be a decided advantage," Greenfield confides. "I could criticize things the company was doing with a device that had my name on it. Over the years, they had various engineers come along who wanted to modify it [and presumably market the 'new improved' product at a higher price]. I simply wouldn't let them do any of it until the modifications had been tested in the laboratory."

A Device Maker Censors
What a Medical Journal Can Publish

It seemed that Medtronic had won the AneuRx publicity wars—at least until the spring of 2004, when the company discovered that Greenfield, Tavris, and two of Tavris's colleagues at the FDA had written a paper titled "Aneurysm-Related Mortality Rates in the U.S. AneuRx Clinical Trial" that was about to appear in the prestigious *Journal of Vascular Surgery*. In the peer-reviewed paper, which was previewed on the journal's website, the authors used the same Medtronic data that the FDA used in its public health notice—but they returned to the conclusions of the original draft, recommending that the patients most likely to benefit from the AneuRx stent would be older, weaker patients with "higher surgical risk" and "lower life expectancy."[134]

Medtronic, believing that it had a deal with the FDA, felt blindsided.

In a letter to the FDA dated May 20, 2004, the company pointed out that it had reached an agreement with the agency about the public-health notice issued in December of 2003, and that the article about to be published in the journal went "well beyond" the notice, "in some cases reverting to the position[s] in the initial draft . . . which we . . . believed were wrong and which were ultimately eliminated in the final version" of the notice.[135]

In fact, in the paper, Greenfield and the FDA researchers went out of their way to be fair, noting that their conclusions were based on data from "the early years of experience [with the Medtronic device] in the U.S. when users of AneuRx were going through their 'learning curve' . . . Much has been learned since then that may improve outcome of patients treated with AneuRx," they wrote in 2004. But, they observed, Medtronic stopped submitting data in October of 2002—just three years after the device was approved.[136]

"You would expect that when the company heard about our paper, they would have said, 'We have additional new data since 2002'—data that would either confirm our conclusion or rebut it. But they didn't do that," says Greenfield.

In fact, "the company has never questioned or contested the data that was to be included in the proposed *Journal of Vascular Surgery* article . . . regarding the AneuRx stent graft," Medtronic spokesman Rob Clarke explained in December of 2005.[137] Instead, "what we disputed was the data on the more invasive procedure that suggested a mortality rate of only 1 percent to 2 percent.[138]

Medtronic also claimed that the article contained "proprietary information" that the FDA had no right to disclose, though according to Greenfield "the article had been vetted for confidential information" before it was sent out. "It is not unusual for FDA scientists to submit papers for publication in medical journals," he adds. "They are encouraged to do so." In such cases "the paper goes through freedom of information, and is cleared—which is what happened with this paper. There was no proprietary information—the data in the paper was the data that had already been posted in the public letter on the FDA website. We just came to a different conclusion." [139]

Nevertheless, Medtronic's lawyers moved quickly to quash the article, firing off a letter to the *Jounal* demanding that its editors remove the preview of the article from their website and warning that "disclosure of . . . proprietary information and breach of confidentiality protections are subject to both criminal and civil sanctions which will be pursued vigorously if this situation if not remedied." [140]

In the meantime, the FDA commissioner's office became involved in the controversy, Greenfield recalls. "There was a guy there named Dan Troy, who had become very influential in deciding the commissioner's position on various matters."

Dan Troy had become the FDA's chief counsel in August of 2001. A conservative Bush appointee and protégé of Judge Robert Bork of the U.S. Court of Appeals, Troy was a longtime foe of FDA regulation. In the 1990s he had represented the Brown & Williamson Tobacco Corp. in its effort to fend off the FDA, and just months before joining the agency, he had defended Pfizer in another battle with regulators. A *U.S. News & World Report* headline summed up his career change: "Mr. Outside Moves Inside: Daniel Troy Fought the FDA for Years; Now He's Helping to Run It."[141]

During the first two years of the Bush administration, Troy operated in a power vacuum. The FDA had no permanent commissioner, and "while the White House and Congress publicly argued over who should lead the agency it was being quietly transformed by appointees such as Troy, who needed no congressional confirmation," *The Boston Globe* observed.[142] *U.S. News* corroborated the report, saying that Troy "operated as the de facto head of the FDA" between September of 2001 and November of 2002. During that time, the magazine added, Troy held "at least 50" closed-door meetings with representatives of drug companies and others regulated by the FDA. When *U.S. News* sought records of those meetings under the Freedom of Information Act, it was informed by Troy's office that there were "no minutes, no memos, no nothing." Troy resigned his FDA post without explanation on November 16, 2004.

But in the spring of 2003, Troy was still chief counsel, and when Medtronic complained about the article that had been accepted for publication in the *Journal of Vascular Surgery*, "Dan Schultz, the acting director of the FDA's Center for Devices and Radiological Health, was told to write a letter to the medical journal requesting that the paper be withdrawn," Greenfield recalls. "He was very unhappy about this."

Off the record, Schultz told a colleague that he felt "compromised,"[143] though publicly he would insist that the FDA did not intervene in order to please or placate Medtronic. Rather, "the way in which the information was presented in the article was somewhat different from the way in which the information was presented in a previously issued public health notification," he explained. "When I was asked to take a look at all of that together, I felt that the article needed to be pulled."[144]

"These are very good people—but they're midlevel. Their hands are tied," says Greenfield who, unlike FDA employees, is free to speak his mind.

To the shock of many in the medical community, the *Journal of Vascular Surgery* did not print the article. "Since when has the FDA begun telling medical journals what they can and can't publish?" one surgeon asked.[145]

But the *Journal of Vascular Surgery*'s editors did speak out in a special editorial in August of 2004, saying that cancelling the article "in response to objections by a manufacturer of a device regulated and approved by the FDA is very disturbing." The editors went on to say that they were "extremely disappointed by the actions of the FDA and Medtronic Inc., which have prevented the publication of an article containing data that we believe are important to readers of the journal."

"As editors, we are responsible for preserving the rights of authors to communicate appropriately reviewed scientific information and for preventing corporate influence of this process," said Jack Cronenwett, a professor at Dartmouth Medical School and one of the editors of the journal. "In this case we were unable to do so."[146]

End of an Era?

For years drugmakers and device makers have enjoyed fabulous success. Under siege, they have nonetheless warded off threats of tighter regulation, registries, caps on price increases, and imports from Canada. But despite that success—or perhaps because of it—by 2005 both industries were riding for a fall. Great success, after all, breeds excess.

"I think even the drug industry may be beginning to realize that you can't simply stomp around and do whatever you want—without consequences. People get cheesed off—demanding Canadian imports and all the rest of it," one Wall Street drug analyst observed late in 2005. "In a sense they've reaped their whirlwind."[147]

Despite the billions spent on TV ads, by November of 2005, it was getting harder and harder to sell the public on pricey products. "A lot of the demand that the industry has created over the years has been through promotion, and for that promotion to be effective, there has to be trust," said Richard Evans, a stock analyst at Sanford C. Bernstein.[148] "That trust has been lost," Evans added, referring to revelations that Merck had failed to follow up on signs that its best-selling drug, Vioxx, led to increased risk of heart attack or stroke, while other drugmakers concealed the results of clinical trials which showed that patients who took antidepressants might run an increased risk of suicidal thoughts.[149]

Big Pharma's popular support was waning. In the fall of 2005 Merck had lost one high-profile trial, won another, and still faced a firing squad of plaintiffs' attorneys intent on winning large awards for patients who took Vioxx. Meanwhile, a Harris Interactive survey disclosed that only 44 percent of the U.S. public viewed the industry as doing a good job for its consumers— down from 79 percent just seven years earlier.[150] Even America's most popular drug, Lipitor, was under attack, the subject of a lawsuit filed in U.S. District Court in Boston, claiming Pfizer deceptively marketed the drug to women and the elderly, without proof that the drug lowers the risk of heart disease for these groups.[151]

This not to say that the industry was on the skids. Pfizer alone expected to make about $8 billion in profit in 2005 on sales of roughly $51 billion. But investors were restless. In the fall of 2005, shares of market leader Pfizer were near their lowest levels since 1997, and a broad index of drug stocks has fallen 25 percent in five years.[152]

Drugmakers had done their best to keep profits high: from January of 2000 through December of 2004 they hiked prices on 96 frequently used drugs by nearly 25 percent.[153] But during this span, they were finding fewer and fewer promising new drugs to bring to market. In the third quarter of 2005, Pfizer acknowledged that spending on research and development was down 6 percent from the same period a year earlier, and said it expected its research budget to stay flat or decline in the years ahead.[154]

Revenues already had begun to slow. In 2004, after nine years of solid double-digit growth, industry sales grew by just 8.3 percent. Some saw sluggish sales ahead. In 2005 Datamonitor PLC, a business information company, predicted that drugmakers could expect revenues to grow by an average of only 2.2 percent annually for the rest of the decade. "The pharmaceutical industry is in the process of transformation," longtime Pfizer board member Stanley O. Ikenberry told *BusinessWeek*. "We have to reexamine all the assumptions that pharmaceutical companies have made for as long as I can remember."[155]

Now drugmakers were forced to talk about cutting costs. In the summer of 2005, Wyeth announced that it was trimming its sales force. "The marketplace has changed, and frequent visits are not well received anymore," said company spokesman Doug Petkus.[156] This was an understatement. Physicians were so fed up with seeing sales reps in their waiting room that drugmakers were committing "death-by-salesman," quipped Sanford Bernstein stock analyst Richard Evans.[157] Even Pfizer reluctantly admitted that it planned to shrink its massive sales force, mainly through attrition.[158]

Some on Wall Street suggested that drugmakers could and should make far deeper cuts. "Companies have just been slavishly following what everyone else is doing," observed one drug analyst. "If you have profit margins of 25 percent—who cares how much you spend? Nobody is rigorously calculating whether they are getting return on investment." [159]

By 2005 institutional investors with enormous sums at stake were beginning to mutter that the industry should "rethink its business model," the same analyst confided. "These investors tend to be pension funds, with long-term liabilities to be concerned about. They recognize that health care stocks represent 10 percent of their assets under management," and that if share prices fall, "you could easily see that 10 percent become 5 percent." Worried that after years of aggressive marketing and pricing Big Pharma is about to "reap its whirlwind," these investors are beginning to say, " 'You can't carry along this path, or you're going to meet quite a bit of resistance.' "

"Of course, no one wants to rethink the business model," he admits. "It has worked quite well—in the sense of generating profits. But if you did think about it, you would see a great deal of waste."

For example, some investors point out that drugmakers could save millions by making intelligent use of information technology to capture data in doctors' offices. Others ask why Big Pharma is not the low-cost producer of its own products. Why is it that the generics take away its sales after a patent expires? "In any other industry, if you are the manufacturer, you would strive to make the product as efficiently as it is humanly possible to make it," says the analyst. "But pharmaceutical companies don't seem concerned with driving down their own costs"—largely because they have been able to make enormous profits without worrying about efficiency.

Further belt-tightening is in order, he suggests. "It might mean doing clinical trials in Poland, Ukraine, or South Africa—where you can do them for 20 to 30 percent less than in the United States. It might require shifting manufacturing to Singapore or India. I'm not saying any of this is comfortable," he adds. "But the drug industry doesn't have a divine right to comfort—any more than any other industry."[160]

Institutional investors realize that these ideas are controversial, but what is important is that it is not the industry's scolds, but rather some of its biggest investors, who are talking about radical changes in how drugmakers do business.

Will CMS Begin to Use Its Clout?

Looking ahead to 2010, the biggest question for the pharmaceutical industry is this: how will the new Medicare prescription drug bill play out? Many see the complicated new law as a bonanza for the drug industry. Or, as a *Pittsburgh Post-Gazette* headline put it in November of 2005: "While Seniors Scratch Heads, Big Pharma Licks Chops."[161]

Others are not so sure. How many seniors will sign up? Will HMOs negotiate deeper discounts? And will Medicare finally exercise some muscle in deciding what drugs to cover?

Thanks to the new prescription drug benefit, the "federal government's share of the national drug bill will rise from 13 percent to over 40 percent," *Medical Marketing & Media,* a pharmaceutical trade publication, predicts. "The Centers for Medicare and Medicaid Services (CMS) will thus control the purse strings and have the clout to bring about major reform in the country's healthcare system. As administrator of the agency since March 2004, Dr. Mark McClellan . . . has made it quite clear that he intends to introduce rational, economic-based decision-making into healthcare."

"Let's face it," McClellan said in a Webcast on September 29, 2004, "the only way we can continue to justify the payments required for truly innovative new drugs is by generating evidence that demonstrates the benefits of these treatments and that gives patients and doctors timely and specific information about how to use these treatments with confidence that they will get better outcomes as a result."

"Enter the era of outcomes research which is already a factor in other countries, but has not yet caught a strong wind in the U.S.," suggests *Medical Marketing & Media.* "CMS will champion reforms such as head-to-head clinical trials and more robust health outcomes data. Products that prove themselves superior will earn generous reimbursement deals. Those products that do not stand out will be limited to receiving a small, fixed percentage of the cost as their profit margin. When competing products are deemed to be 'functional equivalents,' CMS will select the lowest cost alternative. CMS's stance on the relative worth of drugs will no doubt form a model for other payers."[162]

For CMS to begin inquiring into the cost-effectiveness of new products would require a striking shift of ideology on the part of the Bush administration. Nevertheless, as Washington struggles to pay for the trillion-dollar Medicare drug benefit, device makers, along with drugmakers must consider the unpleasant possibility that CMS will begin asking questions about value before agreeing to reimburse for new products.

Device makers also must worry about how Justice Department investigations will affect their relationships with surgeons, and whether the prospect of gain-sharing between hospitals and physicians will become a reality. "Implant prices cannot continue to spiral," Dr. John Cherf, the knee surgeon with an MBA, said in the fall of 2005. "I tell analysts at money management firms—I would sell these stocks. They're all down double digits. It is coming to an end—it is not sustainable."

Cherf is not alone. Ray Elliott, chief of Zimmer Holdings, the world's largest manufacturer of knee and hip implants, alarmed investors at a Bank of America conference in the fall of 2005: "There's a lot of bell-and-whistle stuff in this industry over the last five or six years where you got pretty good money for stuff that was pretty fluffy . . . ," Elliott declared. "If [you think] you're going to take [a device] and spray it red and add $1,000 to it and say, 'This is still the good old days,' it's not going to happen anymore."[163]

Perhaps 5 or 10 years from now, we'll look back and say that 2006 marked the end of an era for both device makers and drugmakers. In the meantime, some see the second half of the decade as the beginning of a brave new era for HMOs. In the years ahead, many of Wall Street's forecasters predict, the insurance industry's giants could wind up taking home the pot of gold at the end of the Medicare prescription drug rainbow. And at the same time, they say, managed care companies should be able to turn a nice profit by selling younger Americans on a new form of high-deductible, low-premium insurance. Optimists call it "consumer-driven health care."

WHERE WE ARE NOW: EVERYONE OUT OF THE POOL

With the Medicare Prescription Drug, Improvement, and Modernization Act (MMA) of 2003, Washington made what might best be described as a last-ditch effort to find a market solution to runaway health care inflation. Hoping to nudge seniors into the marketplace, the law offers them a prescription drug benefit—but only if they sign up with a private insurer. Meanwhile it encourages Americans under the age of 65 to take responsibility for funding their own health care by setting up tax-free Health Savings Accounts (HSAs). Using the money in those accounts, the law's architects suggest, consumers can pick and choose what health care products and services they want to use, just as seniors are free to select from a Chinese menu of prescription drug benefits and managed care plans.

All in all, it would be fair to say that MMA represents a true believer's vision of how market-driven medicine should work: corporations offer consumers a smorgasbord of choices, and the savvy shopper selects the best possible product at the lowest possible price. Or, if he can't afford the best possible product, at least he can choose the product that best fits his pocketbook. Ergo: prices should fall, while quality climbs—thanks to the wisdom of crowds roaming an efficient market.

Medicare Advantage = Medicare + Choice Redux?

Critics call it faith-based policy making. Begin with MMA's "new" vision for Medicare: a program that combines a prescription drug benefit with private sector managed care in an insurance plan called Medicare Advantage.[1] This is not the first time that Medicare has attempted to hand seniors off to private insurers. In 1997 Medicare began giving beneficiaries a choice between standard Medicare (with the government paying medical bills directly) and Medicare + Choice (a program that paid HMOs to provide Medicare benefits to seniors). The hope was that, in a competitive market, managed care plans would find innovative ways to cut Medicare's costs while enhancing benefits.

Unfortunately, in the first go-round, it didn't work out that way. Rather than saving the government money, Medicare + Choice (M+C) proved more expensive than traditional Medicare. Problems began when private insurers figured out how to shun the sickest seniors by charging high co-pays for items like hospital care, chemotherapy, radiation therapy, oxygen, and dialysis. Thus HMOs wound up with a relatively healthy pool of customers. Meanwhile Medicare paid the plans a lump sum per enrollee—without adjusting for the fact that insurers had winnowed out so many of the most expensive patients. As a result, in 2003 Medicare shelled out roughly 4 percent more for M+C enrollees than it would have spent if those seniors had remained in traditional fee-for-service Medicare—where they would have used relatively few services.[2]

Even so, many insurers groused that Medicare's payments weren't rich enough to keep up with the soaring cost of care, and HMOs began bailing out of the program. From 1998 to 2003, the number of private M+C plans was cut in half. Insurers that didn't abandon their Medicare patients drove them away by hiking both co-pays and deductibles. Over the five years ending in 2003, the list of beneficiaries enrolled in M+C plunged from 6.2 million to 4.6 million.[3]

To be sure, it was tough for HMOs to try to deliver on the benefits that they promised while simultaneously turning a profit. As former Medicare administrator Bruce Vladeck pointed out in chapter 2, private insurers' administrative costs are, of necessity, much higher than Medicare's.[4] (See pie charts on pages xi and xii, "Who Is Paying" and "What Are We Paying For?")

Just enrolling and disenrolling beneficiaries is expensive as consumers play musical chairs, moving in and out of plans. And while Medicare doesn't need to advertise, rival HMOs must trumpet their products. Indeed, in the fall of 2005 Dow Jones Newswires reported that managed care companies such as UnitedHealth Group Inc. and Humana Inc. were spending tens of millions of dollars on marketing, expanding call centers, and installing new technology as they prepared for a flood of Medicare enrollees shopping for the new prescription drug benefit.[5]

When M+C plans pulled out of the Medicare market, seniors were blind-sided. Many were bitter. Yet despite earlier disappointments, at the end of 2005 it appeared that a fair number were willing to give Medicare Advantage a try. And no wonder. Vying for new customers, companies like Aetna, Paci-fiCare Health Systems, UnitedHealth Group, and Humana were offering some very attractive deals including extras like vision benefits, gym member-ships, and low premiums—or even no premiums. Often plans include pre-scription drug benefits at no extra charge.[6]

But if insurers couldn't afford to provide the benefits promised under M+C, why do they think they can be so generous under Medicare Advan-tage? Because the new law boosts the government's payments to insurers by some $46 billion over 10 years.

Washington's largesse began in 2004 and varies by region. In places like New York's Nassau County, the windfall meant that Medicare hiked reim-bursements to HMOs by 24.5 percent. At the time, Leslie V. Norwalk, acting deputy administrator of the federal Centers for Medicare and Medicaid Ser-vices, said the goal was "to get plans back in the program" and to give bene-ficiaries more choices, including preferred provider managed care plans that let patients go out of a plan's network of hospitals and doctors.[7]

All in all, Medicare is paying a premium to move patients into the private sector. A 2004 study by Mathematica Policy Research, an independent re-search center, calculates that Washington will be shelling out an average of 7 percent more than it spends per senior under traditional Medicare. This in turn sheds some light on why the price tag for the prescription drug program is turning out to be so much higher than advertised. Originally, the adminis-tration calculated that the new plan would cost about $400 billion over the first 10 years. By the fall of 2005, that number had been revised to $724 billion—and some said that was a conservative estimate. According to the Congressional Budget Office the 10-year tab is likely to mount to $1 trillion.[8]

But wait a minute—wasn't the whole point of privatization to contain health care spending by taking advantage of an efficient marketplace?

The government has "pretty much given up on the argument that the HMO's save money," notes Lori Achman, a research analyst at Mathematica.[9]

Is that true? "Implicitly, yes," says Wall Street's Sheryl Skolnick. "They have given up the argument that HMOs can do it for less, though there is a hope HMOs may provide extra benefits."[10]

In the end, MMA offers an expensive case study in privatization for the sake of privatization, says Princeton economist and *New York Times* columnist Paul Krugman. He compares the Medicare Modernization Act to a 2005 bill introduced by Senator Rick Santorum that would have forced the National Weather Service to limit the weather information directly available to the public. "Although he didn't say so explicitly, he wanted the service to funnel that information through private forecasters instead," Krugman explains. "Santorum's bill didn't go anywhere," he adds. "But it was a classic attempt to force gratuitous privatization: involving private corporations in the delivery of public services even when those corporations have no useful role to play. The Medicare drug benefit," Krugman concludes, "is an example of gratuitous privatization on a grand scale."[11]

Nearly everyone agrees that many seniors need some sort of drug benefit, but why not just provide it through traditional Medicare? "It didn't have to be like this," an editorial in *The Atlanta Journal-Constitution* lamented in the fall of 2005. "Forty years after its creation, Medicare has proved itself to be a well-administered and cost-effective government program. . . . Extending that basic model to include prescription drug coverage would have been comparatively simple, cheap and efficient.

"Unfortunately, though, we can't bring ourselves to acknowledge Medicare's success," the editorial continues, "because doing so would mean challenging the accepted wisdom" that health care financed through the government "must always be a disaster. Apparently we would rather design a complex, largely unworkable and hugely expensive Rube Goldberg machine that diverts huge profits to private industry, because that's exactly what we've done."[12]

On the other side of the debate, those who believe in the market's magic counter that while HMOs may not save Medicare any money, over the long run competition will lead to better benefits and higher-quality care. With that hope in mind, Congress has agreed to pay even higher premiums to HMOs that court and care for the sickest seniors. Ideally, managed care plans tailored to the special needs of the chronically ill will do a better job of coordinating patients' care. "These people have the highest needs and make up most of the [Medicare] budget," says Lois Quam, head of Ovations, United-Health's division for its Medicare and other elderly-care services. "Therein lies the opportunity to improve their health and, as a byproduct, keep them out of the hospital and save money." [13]

Moreover, even if the move to private plans doesn't save the Medicare trust fund any money, Medicare director Mark McClellan suggests that the HMOs will reduce costs for seniors themselves. "When beneficiaries' out-of-pocket costs are counted," he argues, "spending in traditional Medicare is 'significantly higher' than in Medicare Advantage." So while higher reimbursements to the HMOs may cost taxpayers more, McClellan suggests that society as a whole will save money. [14]

Along the way, MMA is expected to create wealth for the private sector. In 2005 CIBC World Markets analyst Carl McDonald predicted that the new drug benefit would boost 2006 revenue at seven of the largest health insurers by at least $4.45 billion, and lift earnings by 2 percent to 4 percent. By September of 2005, managed-care stocks had shot up 20 percent to 50 percent in nine months, thanks in part to high hopes for Medicare Advantage.

That fall, Fulcrum Global Partners' Sheryl Skolnick agreed that the new program could lead to a big payoff for insurers. But never one to jump onto a bandwagon, Skolnick also saw risks ahead—both for HMOs and for patients. First, there is the real possibility that Congress will cut the promised subsidies. In 2005 some members of Congress already were complaining that Medicare was overpaying insurers.

"The question is this," says Skolnick: "Will the government continue to be a consistent business partner? The answer is: as long as the money lasts— sure. After that, no way." [15]

On the other hand, "Congress has learned that when you create a benefit, you can't just slash it to ribbons," says Skolnick. "There has to be some commitment to that benefit over time." Moreover, she notes, insurers are protected by the fact that they are locked into the plan for only a year at a time. If

Congress pulls back, they can either bail out—or jack up co-pays, deductibles, and premiums.

For seniors, this is the greatest risk. "Some of the plans appear too good to be true," Skolnick acknowledges. "Looking at them, one wonders, how will they make money on it?"

Cynics suggest that insurers could be playing a game of bait and switch. Down the road, they warn, seniors may well discover that their benefits have been trimmed, while out-of-pocket expenses climb. Whether or not the changes are draconian, it's inevitable that as insurers experiment with a new product, they will be taking a nip here and a tuck there. "In July of 2006," Skolnick predicts, "every single one of the plans will be rebid."

Skolnick's prophecy conjures up a Medicare beneficiary's worst nightmare: If plans continue to adjust their offerings, seniors could find themselves once again sorting through a bewildering array of options—year after year after year. At some point, many might well just give up and go back to traditional Medicare—if the Medicare trust fund hasn't been too badly eroded by the costs of the new program.

"Choice" was supposed to be the hallmark of private sector Medicare, but late in 2005, seniors attempting to comb through the details of as many as 67 prescription drug plans were overwhelmed. Some were baffled; others were just plain mad. At the end of a long meeting outlining the new options, one 80-year-old woman stood up, ramrod straight, said, "This is ridiculous," and walked out.[16]

Her indignation is understandable. While Medicare has set minimum requirements for the prescription benefit, there is no standard plan. Different insurers cover different drugs. Many divide drugs into tiers and charge different co-pays for each tier: drugs in tier one may require a $5 co-pay, while drugs in tier three call for a $55 co-pay. Co-pays can be raised on 60 days' notice. In addition, some insurers cover certain drugs only for a limited period of time: 60 days, say, or 90. Others require "step therapy": patients must try the least expensive drug in a particular category before a more expensive one is covered. Finally, some require preauthorization for particular drugs, which means that patients must go to the doctor each time they need a refill.[17]

"The number of choices has created tremendous confusion," says Skolnick. "The basic benefit designed by Medicare was not very good," she adds, and so in an effort to snag seniors, insurers have come up with endless variations on the theme. "Frankly," Skolnick observes, "as anti-free market as this sounds, fewer choices of better products would be a better idea.

"We're a long way off from people declaring this program a success or a failure," she concluded late in 2005. "It will take at least two or three years before we find out."

Deciding How Medicare Dollars Are Spent

From a politician's point of view, one of the great advantages of fobbing off Medicare onto the private sector is that it provides "a wonderful opportunity for public officials to delegate difficult decisions [about Medicare coverage] to presumably independent private actors," Bruce Vladeck observes. "Not having to make pricing or coverage decisions under the glare of congressional committees or the Administrative Procedures Act is an enormously attractive prospect."[18] If seniors complain, Congress has an easy explanation: "The market decided."

In fact, the insurance company will have decided. This, of course, is precisely what fueled the revolt against managed care in the nineties. Suddenly, bean counters at HMOs were determining who needed a biopsy—and who didn't. It quickly became apparent that, in the mind of the American public, HMOs lack the standing to set health care policy. Insurers are not physicians. They are not scientists. They are not even elected officials.

Managed care executives themselves have expressed discomfort about the role they play in setting health care priorities: "We find ourselves [becoming] private regulators and making public policy by HMO," Alan Hoops, then chief executive officer of PacifiCare, the HMO giant based in Santa Ana, California, told *The Los Angeles Times* in 1998. "We're in the business of constantly passing judgment on the societal value of a given protocol. We are making very difficult decisions on questions that, frankly, have no right answer," he added, acknowledging the essential ambiguity of modern medicine.[19]

As medical technologies advance at warp speed, the question of what is "medically necessary" takes both scientists and medical ethicists into ever more uncertain territory. Should insurers have covered bone marrow transplants for breast cancer victims? Should they cover Viagra and infertility treatments? How do we allocate scarce health care dollars?

How much reconstructive surgery is truly needed for children with severe facial disfigurement?" the *LA Times* asked. "Surgeons could simply restore normal functions or do more elaborate, and more costly, work that would dramatically improve patients' lives. "Do we reconstruct the entire face or simply improve it?" asks John Golenski, a medical ethicist and executive director of George Mark Children's House in San Leandro, California. "How to draw those lines is not clear in any insurance organization I've ever worked with."

"At the center of such questions is the fact that health care economics have become a zero-sum game," the *LA Times* observed. "The drive to rein in medical costs means that when a health plan or employer decides to pay for a treatment"—be it Viagra, fertility treatments, or plastic surgery for a child born with a hole where his nose should be—"everyone pays—in higher premiums or lost coverage. . . . As health care is increasingly dominated by large, publicly traded corporations intent on maximizing profits for shareholders, should insurers be taking the lead on issues of such importance to society? Can the competitive marketplace handle these issues in a way that society will find acceptable?"

Granted, when insurers review questions about medical need and cost effectiveness, they consult with their own physician administrators, as well as doctors, pharmacists, and other health professionals. Nevertheless, in a for-profit setting where shareholders' interests must be weighed, "benefit decisions don't happen in a vacuum in which good medicine and science always win out," the *LA Times* concluded.

Complicating matters, an HMO's decision-making process is far from transparent. Once again the specter of "trade secrets" rears its ugly head. HMOs often argue that information about how they decide what to cover and what to exclude is "competitive" and could be used by rivals. It's "not well understood how health plans make their decisions, and part of the problem is that they tend to cloak their benefit decisions in secrecy," says Golenski.[20]

At the end of the nineties, HMOs backed off. In the face of widespread consumer dissatisfaction coupled with ugly publicity, most insurers loosened their regulations. Indeed, as discussed in chapter 2, the most popular managed care plans opened up their networks and began rubber-stamping requests for treatments.

But today, as Medicare patients desperate for a drug benefit begin to stream into the private sector, managed care plans are once again positioned to have a huge impact on the allocation of health care dollars. To be sure, the insurance industry's expanded role has been presented under the guise of consumer choice. According to the new program's backers, insurers won't be deciding what benefits Medicare's dollars should cover: seniors will make that judgment themselves when they pick a plan.

The truth is that insurance companies will design those plans. And as Apex Surgical's George Cipolletti points out: "When you're doing product development, you have two options—try to design something that you think will give a better result—or what you know people want." [21]

Cipoletti is an inventor, and so when he designs an artificial knee, he tries to fashion something that will give a better result. Insurers, however, are not inventors: they are businesspeople and their decisions tend to be profit-driven. Inevitably, they will design Medicare Advantage plans that include the drugs that they think seniors will find most attractive, whether or not research suggests that those drugs promise the best results. Ideally, for-profit managed care plans would invest in outcomes research, committing capital to the expensive clinical trials needed to sort out the very best drugs, devices, and treatments for chronic diseases. But insurers have little incentive to sink millions into research that would attract the sickest patients. No one wants to become known as the best HMO for diabetics; it would be too expensive.

Consider, by contrast, how the Veterans Administration determines which drugs to cover. At the VA, medical staff review drugs for effectiveness and cost, using their own database of how thousands of patients have reacted to various medications. On that basis, as noted earlier, the VA's doctors decided that Vioxx was no more effective than far less expensive alternatives and sharply limited their use of the drug in 2001—more than two years before Merck took it off the market. Two other not-for-profit health care providers, the Mayo Clinic and Kaiser Permanente, came to the same conclusion. In each case, physicians were making a medical decision. [22]

For-profit insurers, on the other hand, must view medical decisions as marketing decisions. And in 2001 insurers knew that if they refused to cover a drug as popular as Vioxx, they could count on losing customers. Few dared exclude the drug from their formularies. Those who support market-driven medicine would say that the insurers made the correct decision: in the marketplace, the customer is always right.

But in the bizarre bazaar where health care products are sold, the information that customers receive is imperfect—at best—and at worst, deceptive. Consider the television ads featuring ice skater Dorothy Hamill promoting Vioxx—and later revelations by *The New England Journal of Medicine* that Merck's researchers excised data about three Vioxx patients who suffered heart attacks shortly before publishing a crucial study.[23] Even consumer advocates would be hard-pressed to justify spending public money (i.e., Medicare dollars) on a pricey product that became popular, not because prudent, informed reviews of the research showed it was better than its rivals, but because jazzed-up, direct-to-consumer ads propelled it to the top of the charts.[24]

HSAs and High-Deductible Insurance

While paving the way for private-sector Medicare, the Medicare Modernization Act of 2003 also created health savings accounts (HSAs) for younger Americans—tax-free accounts designed to let consumers take charge of their own health care dollars. Like 401(k)s and IRAs, HSAs give workers and their employers a chance to squirrel away pre-tax dollars. But the deal is even sweeter: when employees withdraw the money from an HSA to cover medical expenses, they don't have to pay taxes on either the principal or the compounded dividends and capital gains that have accumulated over the years. Moreover, "medical expenses" includes items often not covered by health insurance, including dental work, contact lenses, psychoanalysis, in-vitro fertilization, and certain home improvements.[25]

There is just one catch: to be eligible for an HSA, the consumer must enroll in a high-deductible health plan (HDHP)—an insurance plan that carries a deductible of at least $1,050 for individual coverage and $2,100 for family coverage. (Typically, deductibles are higher: in 2005, the average HDHP carried a $1,901 deductible for an individual and $4,070 for a family.)[26]

HDHPs are pitched as "affordable insurance." Because benefits kick in only after the customer has spent more than $1,000 out of his own pocket, premiums are lower. Moreover, HDHPs' architects say, the plans are designed to empower the consumer, giving him a chance to tell the market what he wants, while managing his own health care dollars in what President George W. Bush describes as a new "ownership society."

As a tax shelter, the combination of an HSA and an HDHP has no peer, at least for healthy, wealthy Americans. In 2006 a family with cash to spare could put away up to $5,450 a year, tax-free, sign up for a low-cost, high-deductible policy that will cover catastrophes—and then pay for checkups, flu shots, mammograms, eye exams, annual physicals, and the occasional childhood accident out of a separate savings account.

Why not use the $5,450 in the HSA to cover these medical expenses? Because if you don't touch the HSA, you can carry it over to the next year. Thus, a family that has enough free cash to cover a deductible of, say, $5,000 to $10,000 a year can look forward to rolling over $5,450 a year, year after year, letting it compound tax-free for decades.

As a gift from the government (actually, a remarkably generous present from other less fortunate but always hopeful taxpayers), the HSA cannot be beat. A family that tucks $5,450 into an HSA for 30 years, and earns 7 percent a year on their investments, will wind up with a nest egg worth well over half a million dollars—tax-free.[27] If that family had put the same money into a 401(k) or an IRA, they would have to pay taxes on every dollar that they withdrew. But by sinking their savings into an HSA, they ensure that 30 years of investment gains will never be touched by the IRS.

Of course, not everyone can afford to take full advantage of the tax haven. Many, if not most, middle-class and upper-middle-class families will need to tap their HSAs to cover ongoing medical expenses. In fact, if someone in the household is chronically ill, it's likely that the family's annual medical expenses will exceed $5,450, forcing them to make up the difference between that $5,450 and a deductible which may run as high as $10,000.

At that point, a family may discover that some expenses don't count toward their deductible. This is what happened to Eve Stacey, a stay-at-home mother in Woodinville, Washington, after she went to her gynecologist for a routine checkup. It turned out that the $345 bill couldn't be applied to the $1,500 annual deductible on Stacey's "affordable" plan. If the visit were for a specific medical problem, it would have counted, but under her plan, regular checkups with her internist or gynecologist are excluded.[28]

Some HDHPs discourage preventive care. Others don't cover medications for chronic conditions such as diabetes and asthma. Many offer only limited coverage for physical therapy, rehabilitation, prescription drugs, and mental health care. In other words, while a health savings account works wonderfully as a tax shelter for the affluent, as an insurance policy a high-deductible health plan can leave something to be desired.

Can HDHPs Expand Access While Curbing Inflation?

Nevertheless, the plans' promoters recommend HDHPs, not just for families who can afford to take advantage of a Health Savings Account, but for low-income families who in the past could not afford any form of health insurance. Not everyone agrees. Low-cost HDHPs can prove high risk, warns Karen Pollitz, project director at Georgetown University's Health Policy Institute. Even after the worker meets the deductible, she points out, some policies require co-pays that can run as high as 10 percent to 20 percent of the cost of hospitalization and drugs.

Granted, the law caps how much a family can be required to shell out in co-pays and deductibles—in 2006 the maximum is $10,500. But there are exceptions to that rule. The maximum does not include money a family must pay after exceeding a million-dollar life-time limit on benefits, for example, or limits on specific benefits such as maximum days covered or maximum dollar reimbursements.[29]

Pollitz cautions against low-premium policies that feature $1,000 deductibles and little or no drug coverage because, typically, these Swiss-cheese policies are riddled with out-of-pocket cost obligations: "Leaving the back door open is what will bankrupt you" if you get sick, she warns, suggesting that families who want an HDHP pick a policy with a relatively high deductible (of say, $5,000) that clearly covers 100 percent of all costs after the deductible is met. "Just make sure you can afford the $5,000," she advises.

And read the fine print. "The bookkeeping can be pretty complicated throughout the claims payment process," Pollitz says. While consumers enrolled in managed care plans usually don't see provider bills, and only pay co-payments and premiums, "You are on your own [with] high-deductible health plans," notes Pollitz.[30]

Despite the caveats, market enthusiasts contend that low-premium HDHPs will improve access to care, while simultaneously curbing health care inflation. Ignoring evidence that supply tends to drive demand for health care services, the plans' advocates focus on the demand side of the equation, arguing that insured Americans spend so much on health care because they are spending other people's money. High deductibles, they say, will force them to become more prudent consumers.

There are a few wrinkles to this theory. First, high-deductible plans are not a solution to the nation's soaring health care bill because health care expenses are concentrated among patients whose costs exceed even a $5,000 deductible. By most estimates, 30 percent of Americans account for 90 percent of total health care spending.[31] Typically, they are chronically ill, and their bills quickly outstrip their deductibles. After that, the deductible has no effect on how much they spend.

Second, when it comes to widening access to care, just because a family has an HDHP plan does not mean that they can afford to use it. In many cases families who don't have traditional insurance don't have $5,000 to cover a deductible. The HDHP leaves them with two choices: put off care, or go to the doctor and go into debt (assuming that the doctor or hospital will treat them without asking for the deductible up front).

Economists who trust the market tend to believe that consumers always act in their own self-interest and therefore will seek medical help when they really need it. (Economists are the only social scientists who assume that man is rational. Anthropologists, psychologists, and sociologists know better.) The truth is that, especially when they are under financial pressure, humans do not always act prudently. Indeed, when co-pays and deductibles are high, patients "are almost as likely to cut back on essential care as on elective or discretionary services," notes a study published in *Health Affairs* in 2005, making cost-sharing "at best a blunt tool," for containing costs.[32]

"Thrill-Seeker" Insurance

Despite the drawbacks of HDHPs for many middle-income families, these plans are likely to attract not only the very wealthy, but the very young and very lucky. Childless 20-something singles often go without insurance, gambling that they won't get sick. For them, a bare-bones high-deductible plan might well seem a reasonable alternative to no insurance at all—especially if they don't need maternity benefits and use few prescription drugs.

Taking their cue from retailers and consumer-products makers, insurers are targeting these younger customers as they divide the uninsured into specialized markets, "using many of the same market-research tools that go into developing new shampoos and snack foods," *The Wall Street Journal* reports, quoting Andy Slavitt, managing director for UnitedHealth's newly created Center for Affordable Consumer Health: " 'The people who develop potato chips know just how crunchy the chip has to be and how much air to put in the bag, but we've been at a much cruder level in health care,' Slavitt confides. Now, however, he reports proudly, 'We're thinking more like a retailer thinks.' "[33]

Following the same creative line of thought, in 2004 Blue Cross of California launched Tonik, a line of health insurance whose Thrill-Seeker, Part-time Daredevil and Calculated Risk-Taker plans trawl for the uninsured members of the generation that invented reality TV. The plans are cheap, not only because they require higher deductibles, but because they carry many restrictions and exclude some standard benefits, such as maternity coverage.[34]

Some physicians believe that these insurance policies are dangerous even for the young and healthy because their slick marketing camouflages gaping holes in coverage. "They are specifically catering to an ignorant population that has little understanding about what insurance is and what it should do," says Ruth Haskins, an obstetrician-gynecologist who is legislative committee chairman for the California branch of the American College of Obstetricians and Gynecologists. Insurance, after all, is supposed to protect against the unforeseen. The 26-year-old who isn't planning on getting pregnant still could. A 24-year-old who feels lucky is more likely to wind up in a traffic accident than his middle-aged father—and when he does, he may well need both the physical therapy and prescription drugs that his policy doesn't cover.

But the plans' detractors say that high-deductible plans pose an even greater threat to society as a whole: both HDHPs and health savings accounts present individual solutions to what is, in the end, a collective problem—the fact that health care is becoming unaffordable for so many Americans. By attracting both the youngest and most affluent customers, these plans are likely to skim many of the healthiest customers from the larger insurance pool. As a result, risk pools could become unbalanced—which means that costs would rise for everyone else. Indeed, some policy makers warn that if high-deductible plans succeed in siphoning off low-risk customers, premiums for the comprehensive coverage that the average family needs could spiral out of sight.

Traditionally, insurance protects families against financial disaster by gathering everyone into the same pool. By contrast, today's market-driven insurance segregates patients into market niches. The newlywed who wants a policy that covers pregnancy will find it more expensive because she is no longer part of the same pool as her friend who has no plans to have children. A 50-year-old woman with a history of breast cancer in need of a policy that puts no cap on drug benefits may not be able to afford it—though her 24-year-old son can qualify for a low-cost Thrill-Seeker plan.

High-deductible plans, like health savings accounts, are designed for an atomized society where the individual consumer is expected to take care of himself. Health care economist James Robinson acknowledges the trade-off: "The language of individual ownership weakens society's sense of collective responsibility for its most vulnerable members."[35] Not every insurer believes that this is the optimal solution to a health care crisis that involves everyone. As Dr. John Kitzhaber pointed out in chapter 6, in the end we all wind up paying for those who were left out of the pool.

Yet even insurers who have doubts about HDHPs feel forced to offer them: "We have begun to get into these less comprehensive low-cost, high-deductible plans—with some reluctance," confides Dr. Jay Crosson, executive director of Kaiser's Permanente Federation. "But if you don't play that game, you lose the younger, healthier customers. We need to have a balanced membership, so we have begun to market a plan with a $1,000 deductible.

"Is this sound public policy? No," says Crosson. "We're doing what we're doing at the moment because it is a business necessity. We have no idea that this is a long-term solution to anything. It just is what it is."[36]

Contradictions: Private Health Care, Public Funding

The irony is that while trying to find individual solutions to what is, inescapably, a collective crisis, we finance our health care system collectively—with our tax dollars. As the pie chart on page xi shows ("Who Is Paying?"), taxpayers pick up 51 percent of the nation's health care bill by funding Medicare, Medicaid and SCHIP, veterans' programs, and private insurance for government employees, while also providing subsidies for state and local hospitals.

And that's not all. Taxpayers also underwrite the insurance that private sector employers buy for their workers. In 2004, for example, when employers laid out roughly $443 billion for health benefits for their employees and retirees, employers deducted the $443 billion from their taxable income as part of the cost of doing business—just like wages. But while employees pay taxes on their wages, neither current employees nor retirees are required to declare their health benefits as part of their income. As a result, a study published in *Health Affairs* calculates that in 2004 the government lost $108.5 billion in tax revenues, and another $66.4 billion in payroll taxes for Social Security and Medicare, for a total of $174.9 billion. And the cost of employer-based insurance is growing fast: by 2010 forgone income taxes alone are expected to surpass $180 billion.[37]

In 2004 who made up for that $174.9 billion in lost revenues? Other taxpayers, who must cough up income and payroll taxes even if they aren't fortunate enough to work for an employer who offers health benefits. The subsidy is skewed in favor of families earning more than $100,000 a year, the study's authors point out, both because they are more likely to have employer coverage and because they are in a higher tax bracket, and so benefit more from tax-free perks.

Add that $174.9 billion to the $950 billion that taxpayers spent funding Medicare and other public programs in 2004, and their contributions equal roughly 60 percent of what Americans spent on health care that year.[38]

When all is said and done, the United States has a "private" health care system that is bankrolled by the public. It is private only in the sense that it is privately controlled—by insurance companies that decide what treatments to cover, drugmakers and device makers that determine which diseases to research and which devices to develop (while also censoring what information the FDA divulges about that research), and hospitals that ration care in an ad hoc fashion as they decide whom they can treat and whom they must turn away.[39]

Consumer-Driven Medicine

Thus, in the world of corporate medicine, power has shifted from the physician to the private sector. In the process, physicians have been stripped of their standing as professionals. Insurers address them as vendors ("Dear Health Care Provider"), drugmakers and device makers see them as customers (someone you might take to lunch or a strip club), while hospital executives view them variously as rivals, troublemakers, or rainmakers. And with the advent of "consumer-driven medicine," consumers (aka patients) are encouraged to see their doctors as overpaid retailers.

Regina Herzlinger's award winning *Market-Driven Health Care: Who Wins, Who Loses in the Transformation of America's Largest Service Industry* is seen by many as the popular bible for the "consumer-driven" movement. Herzlinger hails the American consumer as the force behind an efficient market. These savvy shoppers want "good prices, many choices, top quality, fast delivery, and excellent service—all the time," she explains, quoting a furniture retailer who sums up their mantra: " 'I want it the way I want it and when I want it—and I want it instantly.' "[40]

Her empowered consumer is an individual who values mastery and convenience. He does not want to wait an hour for a doctor because of someone else's emergency. Indeed, he is not burdened with a collective sensibility. (Herzlinger quotes G. Kirk Raab, "the then-CEO of the fabled biotechnology company Genentech," describing how he slammed his thumb in his car trunk and "spent ninety minutes waiting in agony to see a noted hand surgeon. 'I almost blew my cork,' " says Raab, with what Herzlinger describes as "admirable restraint." Perhaps Raab could have seen a less noted hand surgeon a little sooner, but he wanted what he wanted when he wanted it.)[41]

Herzlinger depicts the "health care activist" as the patient who takes control of his own destiny, pointing to Janine Jacinto Sharkey, who told *Town & Country* "how she custom-designed the types of incisions that removed her breast cancer tumor, faxed questions that arose from her research about breast cancer to her surgeons and even selected the classical music to be played in the operating room. 'I'm not the kind of person to sit there and allow someone else to dictate to me,' " Sharkey says.[42]

Consumer-driven medicine goes hand in hand with health savings accounts and high-deductible plans because it, too, envisions the patient in the driver's seat—shaping the market by choosing the services and products that best suit his needs. "When consumers pay directly, innovators respond to their needs—that's how a market works," says Herzlinger, somewhat optimistically. (Writing in 1997, she holds out the American automobile industry as a prime example of an innovative industry that has responded to consumers' needs.)[43]

Finally, by taking advantage of the age of information, the resourceful health care shopper becomes his own expert, choosing the procedures, doctors, and hospitals that fit his purse and priorities. Indeed, as *The Wall Street Journal* put it in 2002: "New rating systems around the country are starting to make it possible for people to shop for a hospital the way they shop for . . . mutual funds."[44]

Did we learn nothing from the nineties?

Just as most people are not cut out to be their own money managers, the majority are not well suited to becoming their own physicians. In the 21st century, we have instant access to a world of information—but information is not knowledge. All of the mutual fund rating systems in the world could not save the small investor from disaster if he bought a five-star high-tech fund at the market's high. And if it is difficult for the layman to avoid the hype while chasing hope on Wall Street, consider the dilemma of the seriously ill patient facing the mysteries of his own mortality.

The consumer-driven movement seems to overlook the "uncertainty" that Dr. Atul Gawande described in chapter 1 as the "core predicament" of medicine, "the thing that makes being a patient so wrenching, being a doctor so difficult, and being part of a society that pays the bills so vexing."[45]

Patients, naturally, would prefer to believe that all the ills that flesh is heir to have a solution that can be found on a website somewhere—if one is just persistent, asks enough questions, and finds the "right doctor." But even the very best doctors are practicing an infant science in what Dr. Eric Cassell rightly calls "a sea of doubt and uncertainty," so that "judgment must inevitably be made on the doctor's personal experience of past cases; the comparison of the present size, sound or feeling of something with what is remembered, and on what a clinician believes to be the problem, based sometimes on very scanty evidence."[46]

In other words, much of what a doctor knows is intuitive—something he feels or smells or vaguely remembers as a sensate experience—not something that he can easily articulate. And even when that experiential knowledge is added to what he has read and learned—he still doesn't know nearly enough. "One of the barriers to informed consent is lack of information," notes Carl Schneider, a professor of law and internal medicine in *The Practice of Autonomy: Patients, Doctors, and Medical Decisions*. "Both patient and physician are working with many unknowns and uncertainties. Yet how far do most patients understand the pervasiveness of that uncertainty? Even when it is explained to them, do they believe it?" Schneider asks.

Probably not. Few are willing "to appreciate, for example, that diagnostic uncertainty often means that treatments must be chosen before the disease is identified and that treatment itself can be a diagnostic tool," says Schneider.[47]

Empowering the Physician

There is much to be said for Herzlinger's portrait of the patient who takes an active interest in his own health by quitting smoking, exercising, embracing moderation—and asking questions.

But what the consumer movement seems to ignore is that *before patients can reclaim their rightful place as the center—and indeed as the raison d'être—of our health care system, we must once again empower doctors. Physicians must be free to practice patient-centered medicine—based not on corporate imperatives, doctors' druthers, or even patients' demands, but on what scientific evidence suggests would be in the best interests of the patient. In other words, society needs to recognize doctors as professionals.*

There is much to regret about the loss of the world described in chapter 1, when physicians held sway over what we now call the health care "industry." This is not to say that anyone would wish to return to the day when the individual doctor reigned sovereign. The Lone Ranger Who Is Always Right is an anachronism. Today forward-looking professionals realize that they must collaborate to create the evidence-based guidelines needed to shape best practices in the century ahead.

But consumer-driven medicine often seems to accept the corporate model of health care as a world where the patient is a customer and the physician is a retailer selling his services. He is not the patient's advocate. To the contrary, consumer activists tend to paint him almost as an adversary: the arrogant know-it-all who keeps the patient waiting and then brushes by his questions. In this world "caveat emptor" always applies. The consumer must *demand* the best care because he cannot count on the doctor to provide it.

And in fact, if the patient assumes that health care is an industry like any other, then the consumer advocates are right: the patient cannot expect the marketplace to put his interests first. Corporate retailers like Wal-Mart and McDonald's are expected to be honest, but they are not expected to be selfless: they are not expected to put their customers' interests *ahead* of their shareholders'. But physicians are not retailers, and health care is not a retail industry or even a service industry in the ordinary sense of the term.

Trust

Everything comes back to trust. As Kenneth Arrow, the father of health care economics, put it in chapter 1, "Uncertainty as to the quality of the product is perhaps more intense here than in any other [market]," and this is what makes the purchase of health care so different from any other purchase—it is, perforce, a transaction based on trust.[48] Whether the patient's belief in the doctor's superior knowledge and complete professionalism is wholly justified is not the question. It is simply that without it, the health care market could not function. No one would ever go under the knife or submit to chemotherapy or any other painful or invasive procedure. The physician's power lies with what Arrow calls his "moral authority"—authority grounded in the belief that, as a professional, he will put his patients' interest first.[49]

In a 2005 essay questioning the consumer-driven model, Robert Berenson quotes health economist Victor Fuchs, noting that Fuchs "understands that the patient/physician relationship is very different from the one we accept in commercial marketplaces because it requires patients and health professionals to work cooperatively rather than as adversarial buyers and sellers. Mutual trust and confidence contribute to the efficiency of production. Thus the model of atomistic competition . . . often is not the right goal for health care."[50]

But while patient and doctor may share decision making, Berenson suggests that the physician is usually in the better position to grapple with the complexity of medical decisions. And while "shared clinician/patient decision-making . . . is one thing; cost-sharing-induced consumers' decisions are something else altogether." If the patient's choice is money driven, research suggests that the odds are only 50-50 that he will make the best medical decision. "In many ways," Berenson points out, "the consumer-directed movement is in conflict with [making] progress toward . . . evidence based medicine."

Finally, Berenson argues that however much advocates of consumer-directed care talk about consumer sovereignty, they "do not speak the language of the public" because they ignore the reality of how most patients actually make medical decisions. In practice, most patients want to "place their trust in professionals to bear primary responsibility."

Certainly, 21st century patients want to be informed. They want to know how sick they are, how long the sickness will last, what the treatment is supposed to do, what side effects to expect, and the possible advantages of treatment X over treatment Y. But while they do not want to be in the dark, once they have been informed, many have no desire, no interest even, in making the final decision.

In *The Practice of Autonomy*, Carl Schneider turns to his own experience to illustrate the point: "A few years ago my dentist thought I was a candidate for the delights of a root canal. The endodontist did what endodontists do and presented me with the facts of my case. I said that was interesting, but did I need a root canal? He told me that was my decision. I replied that I understood that, but that I would be glad of a recommendation. He made it clear that he could not and should not decide this medical issue for me. I asked what he would do if it were his tooth. He told me that his values might not be my values, so that what he might do could not be relevant for me. I was baffled (even after hearing all his information, I had no idea how to think about the question), morally reproved (why was I so debased as to refuse responsibility for this important decision?), irritated (why was I being required to make a basically technical decision?) and even bored (this was not the kind of issue about which I could work up any interesting or even useful ideas). But the endodontist was adamant, sturdy in the righteousness of his cause."[51]

Schneider's example takes consumer-directed health care to its absurd extreme. But even in far more serious situations, many patients do not want the final power to set the course of treatment. They want a doctor—even if they are themselves doctors. Schneider tells the story of Franz Ingelfinger, an editor of *The New England Journal of Medicine*, cruelly stricken with the very illness he had specialized in as a physician.

Ingelfinger wrestled desperately with the uncertainties of his situation, gathering conflicting information from physician friends throughout the country—a barrage of well-intentioned but contradictory advice. " 'As a result, not only I but my wife, my son and daughter-in-law (both doctors), and other family members became increasingly confused and emotionally distraught,' he recalled. 'Finally, when the pangs of indecision had become nearly intolerable, one wise physician friend said, "What you need is a doctor.' "

" 'He was telling me to forget the information I already had and the information I was receiving from many quarters, and to seek instead a person who would dominate, who would tell me what to do, who would in a paternalistic manner assume responsibility for my care. When that excellent advice was followed, my family and I sensed immediate and immense relief. The incapacity of enervating worry was dispelled, and I could return to my usual anxieties.' " [52]

Reflecting on their own experiences as patients, many doctors report that what patients want most from their physicians is competence and compassion. While the marketplace emphasizes "consumer choice," Schneider suggests that evidence-based medicine should instead make "patient welfare" its priority in a system that is "patient-centered" but not necessarily "consumer-driven."

"It may now be time for bioethics to accelerate a shift that seems already to have begun—away from patient choice and toward changing the medical care system so that it delivers a better product," Schneider suggests. "To put the point provocatively, it may be time to think about giving patients what we think they want, but have not been able to secure for themselves. We might even consider giving patients what we think they would want if they thought about it." [53]

This is a modest proposal. It's not enough to prevent the abuses or cure the excesses of money-driven medicine, but at least it changes the terms of the discussion, making it clear that the doctor is not marketing a commodity, he is practicing his profession—and as a member of the healing profession, his responsibility is to give his patient not what he thinks the patient wants, but what he has reason to believe will yield the best result.

NOTES

PREFACE

1. "Troubled National Health Systems Search for Solutions: Best Practices Identified in Global Healthcare Report," PricewaterhouseCoopers Health Research Institute, 7 November 2005.

2. Interview with the author. Of course, as health care spending rises, so will GDP. Like all consumer spending, health care spending contributes to GDP. But the problem is that historically, health care spending has been growing roughly 2 percent faster than GDP—year after year.

   Nevertheless an argument can be made that, during periods of pervasive unemployment, rising health care spending is not a drag on the economy, but instead functions as a stimulus, just like spending on housing. Moreover, "even under conditions of full employment . . . a diversion of real resources from other economic activities to health care might improve economic welfare in society," note Uwe E. Reinhardt, Peter S. Hussey, and Gerard F. Anderson in "U.S. Health Care Spending in an International Context," *Health Affairs,* May/June 2004.

   But, the authors observe, *everything depends on "the value of the added health care gained relative to the opportunity costs represented by the value of other output given up."* (emphasis mine) And while medical spending may "on the whole" be worth the increased costs, the authors observe that "the 'whole' may hide individual medical interventions of dubious clinical and economic merit." (See chapter 5, "When More Care Is Not Better Care.")

3. See "Exhibit 1.1: Increases in Health Insurance Premiums Compared to Other Indicators, 1988–2005," *Employer Health Benefits 2005 Annual Survey,* (Menlo Park: The Henry J. Kaiser Family Foundation). See www.kff.org.

4. In "U.S. Health Care Spending in an International Context," Reinhardt, Hussey, and Anderson point out that if health care spending continues to rise just 2 percent faster than GDP, the U.S. economy might be able to sustain rising health care inflation until 2040. But

at that point, medical spending trends would "force the United States to make do with actual reductions in the non-health GDP per capita overall." And, of course, if current trends persist, there is no guarantee that health care spending won't rise 2½ percent or 3 percent faster than GDP.

Moreover, as the authors observe, even if health care inflation might be sustainable for another 30 years at *a macroeconomic level,* the crisis is far more immediate for individual employers and employees. Taking the problem to the level of an individual private business, Reinhardt et al. suggest that their reader "consider a private business firm whose line of business and workforce skill mix is such that it can tolerate only a maximum total compensation of $35,000 per worker per year. At higher compensation levels, the firm would lose money on employing such a worker. . . .

"If we assume that these workers' productivity . . . rises at an average rate of 1.5 percent and that the prices of the firm's output inflate at the general price inflation in the economy of about 2.5 percent, then one can plausibly assume that the total wage base per worker in this industry will increase at an average annual rate of 4 percent over the next decade, to about $50,000" in 10 years. Meanwhile, health care premiums have been rising by double digits over the past several years. Even if premiums grew by "only" 10 percent for the next decade, the typical family's coverage would cost about $21,000 per year, or 42 percent of the total wage base of $50,000 projected for that year.

"In the end," they point out, "such a firm would be likely to cease offering its employees health insurance, and the income of these workers would be too small to absorb health insurance premiums in excess of $20,000. They would be likely to join the ranks of the uninsured. This prospect puts U.S. policymakers at a crossroads."

Of course, health insurance premiums may not rise by 10 percent a year over the next decade. But in the first four years of the 21st century, double-digit increases have been the rule, not the exception. From 2001 to 2004 rates climbed 59 percent, with premiums rising 11.2 percent in 2004. (See survey by The Henry J. Kaiser Family Foundation and the Health Research and Educational Trust reported in *Bloomberg News,* September 2004.) Moreover, there is no guarantee that productivity will rise by an average of 1.5 percent annually.

In other words, at some point, the cost of insuring a low-income employee will represent an impossibly large share of his compensation. At that point, politicians face difficult and unpopular choices. "One approach," the authors suggest, "would be to persuade the upper half of families in the nation's income distribution to help purchase adequate health insurance for families in the lower third. . . . it would, of course, involve added taxes and transfers flowing through government budgets . . ." Alternatively, the United States could "embrace as official policy . . . a multitier health system in which a person's health care experience would be allowed to vary by his or her ability to pay for health care."

5. *Employer Health Benefits 2005 Annual Survey.*

6. John Holahan and Allison Cook, "Changes in Economic Conditions and Health Insurance Coverage, 2000–2004," Web Exclusive, *Health Affairs,* 1 November 2005. "About 55 percent of the uninsurance growth was among whites; and about 73 percent among native-born citizens," the authors note.

7. *Paying a Premium: The Added Cost of Care for the Uninsured,* report, Families USA, 8 June 2005.

Analysis of the percentage of the uninsured earning more than $50,000 was done by the Blue Cross Blue Shield Association and reported by William L. Jews, "Covering the Uninsured May Not Require Additional Funds After All," *Baltimore Business Journal,* 31 May 2004.

8. That year, average premiums for an individual hit $4,024. *(Employer Health Benefits 2005 Annual Survey.)* In 2004 median household income stood at $44,389.

9. Although tax breaks help the self-employed, those who must insure themselves usually don't get the discounts that come with group insurance and are likely to pay considerably more than the average premium.

10. *Employer Health Benefits 2005 Annual Survey.*

11. Liz Szabo, "Child's cancer can batter family's finances," *USA Today,* 30 August 2005. Szabo notes that about half of health plans set caps on coverage, citing a 2004 report by The Kaiser Family Foundation and the Health Research and Educational Trust. Moreover, some health plans that have no general cap do limit coverage for particular types of procedures, according to Larry Akey, spokesman for America's Health Insurance Plans.

12. Julie Appleby, "Even the Insured Can Buckle Under Health Care Costs," *USA Today,* 20 August 2005.

13. "Toyota's Profits Rise on Global Sales," Associated Press, 4 November 2005.

14. The GM chairman noted that in 2005, health care expenses were adding $1,500 to the cost of each GM vehicle. This puts GM at a "significant disadvantage versus foreign-based competitors," Wagoner said, echoing comments made by the Standard and Poor's and Fitch ratings services after both reduced the company's bond rating to junk status. (John Porretto, "GM Plans to Cut 25,000 U.S. Jobs by 2008," Associated Press, 7 June 2005.)

15. NFIB noted that 65 percent of 4,603 members surveyed called health costs a "critical" problem, up from 47 percent in 2000. (Jim Hopkins, "Rising Benefit Costs Hurt Small Businesses' Financial Health, *USA Today,* 6 June 2004.)

16. Justin Lahart, "On the Gurney," *The Wall Street Journal,* 6 July 2004. For data on profits per vehicle for GM, Ford, Chrysler, Nissan, and Toyota, see Bush Bernard, "Smyrna Nissan Plant Sets Efficiency Record," *Middle Tennessee News & Information,* 11 June 2004.

Automakers are not the only employers squeezed by rising premiums. According to the National Survey of Employer-Sponsored Health Plans, 2004 (compiled by Mercer Human Resource Consulting), the cost of insuring an employee has risen from $3,644 a year in 1994 to $6,215 in 2003. (The numbers below include all medical, dental, and other health benefits for all covered employees and dependents, as well as employer and employee contributions.)

HEALTH BENEFIT COSTS PER ACTIVE EMPLOYEE, 1994–2004

Year	Total Health Benefit Costs
1994	$3,644
1995	$3,653
1996	$3,703
1997	$3,594
1998	$3,817
1999	$4,097
2000	$4,430
2001	$4,924
2002	$5,646
2003	$6,215
2004	$6,679

17. In "Health Care Reform in Japan: The Virtues of Muddling Through" (*Health Affairs,* May/June 1999), Naoki Ikegami and John Creighton Campbell point out that rates of crime, high-speed motor vehicle accidents, HIV virus, and poverty are all appreciably lower than in the United States. But, they report, the most important factor explaining the difference in health care spending is that the Japanese government sets fees for all procedures and services in ways that reflect the country's cultural values while encouraging less expensive care. While patients can go to any doctor or hospital that they wish—and doctors can treat patients freely, as they see fit—certain types of care are favored by the fee schedules. For example, "Routine outpatient care (including drug dispensing) is covered by more generous fees than those for high-tech inpatient care." Also, only about one-third as much surgery is done in Japan as in the U.S.—reflecting both "a cultural antipathy for invasive procedures" and the fact that "fees paid for surgery are very low." The authors note that although the Japanese health care system is weak in some aspects of quality (particularly with regard to high-tech care), this does not seem to have had a major adverse effect on the overall health of patients: "by any measure, the Japanese population is quite healthy."

18. These comparative spending numbers are from 2002—the most recent numbers available in the summer of 2005. See Gerard F. Anderson, Peter S. Hussey, Bianca K. Frogner, and Hugh R. Waters, "Health Spending in the United States and the Rest of the Industrialized World," *Health Affairs,* July/August 2005.

19. Anderson et al., "Health Spending in the United States." The researchers also noted that "not every OECD country experiences waiting lists, although every country spends much less than the United States on health care. The OECD Waiting Times project identified twelve OECD countries that considered waiting times for elective surgery to be a high priority but also identified seven countries besides the United States that did not perceive that they had a problem with waiting times. Health spending in the twelve countries with waiting lists averaged $2,366 per capita, while in the seven countries without waiting lists, it averaged $2,696—both much less than U.S. spending of $5,267 per capita."

20. In 2001 payments in the United States, were 14 percent below payments in Canada and 36

percent less than payments in the United Kingdom. See Anderson et al., "Health Spending in the United States." According to the researchers, probably the best gauge of "the magnitude of malpractice awards" is total payments divided by total population. By that measure, spending in the United States ($16 per capita) is only somewhat higher than in the United Kingdom ($12 per capita) and Australia ($10).

The authors go on to acknowledge that it is very difficult to pin down the numbers: "The comparison of one single year of data across countries obscures changes that are occurring over time. For example, Canadian payments in 2001 included one for a large class-action suit. Excluding that suit, Canadian payments averaged $249,750 (PPP) in 2001. In the United States, malpractice insurance companies are legally required to report all award payments to the NPDB, which is maintained by the Health Resources and Services Administration (HRSA). Some settlements may not be reported if the settlement does not name a specific physician. HRSA also has very little infrastructure for enforcement of the regulation." See J. T. Hallinan, "Attempt to Track Malpractice Cases Is Often Thwarted," *The Wall Street Journal,* 27 August 2004. The average reported here does not include installments of multipart payments that are disbursed in years other than 2001. HRSA reports that "most cases" do not include multipart payments. Total payments for 2001 using the NPDB were $4.4 billion. The U.S. Government Accountability Office (GAO) has estimated payments at $5.2 billion. (*Medical Malpractice Insurance: Multiple Factors Have Contributed to Increased Premium Rates,* report no. GAO-03-702 [Washington, D.C.: GAO, 27 June 2003].) The private consulting firm Tillinghast–Towers Perrin has estimated $24.6 billion in payments and the costs associated with settling claims against physicians. Its estimate was based on analysis of a proprietary database. (Tillinghast–Towers Perrin, *U.S. Tort Costs: 2003 Update,* February 2003, www.towersperrin.com/tillinghast/publications/reports/2003_Tort_Costs_Update/Tort_Costs_Trends_2003_Update.pdf [8 April 2005]). The Physician Insurers Association of America (PIAA), an association of physician-owned insurance companies, estimates that the average payment for claims against its beneficiaries was $310,215.

But even taking the highest estimates, malpractice costs represent a small fraction of health care spending.

21. These figures do not include the legal costs of defending malpractice claims. Legal costs are estimated to average $27,000 per claim in the United States, which adds approximately $1.4 billion in costs to the $4.4 billion paid in settlements and judgments. The costs of underwriting insurance against malpractice claims are estimated at an additional 12 percent, or $700 million. In sum, the cost of defending U.S. malpractice claims, including awards, legal costs, and underwriting costs, are estimated at $6.5 billion in 2001—equaling just 0.46 percent of total health spending.

22. Anderson et al. point out that "One estimate of this cost has come from HHS, which estimates that $70–126 billion (5–9 percent) in health spending per year would be saved if malpractice tort reform, similar to policies in California, were passed at the national level. This estimate was constructed by extrapolating the findings from a study by Daniel Kessler and Mark McClellan. They found lower hospital spending for Medicare patients hospitalized for two diagnoses (acute myocardial infarction and ischemic heart disease) in states with certain types of tort reform. However, the Congressional Budget Office

(CBO) was unable to replicate these results using a broader set of diagnoses. The CBO also found mixed evidence for defensive medicine in the published literature; it thus concluded that 'savings from defensive medicine would be small' following tort reform. These two widely divergent conclusions by two government agencies underscore the uncertainty around the contribution of defensive medicine to health spending. If the upper estimate of 9 percent were accurate, and for some reason little defensive medicine were practiced in other countries, it could explain some of the differential in per capita health spending between the United States and other OECD countries. Given the number of malpractice claims observed, however, defensive medicine is likely to exist in other countries as well."

23. Anderson et al. acknowledge that in other countries, malpractice insurance is more affordable: "British and Canadian physicians are protected from malpractice litigation risks by a single national organization, with premiums subsidized by the government. Australia has a private insurance system more similar to the U.S. system, but the Australian government subsidizes physicians' malpractice premiums and reinsures high-cost claims." This might well mean that individual physicians in these countries are less upset about the malpractice issue, but it doesn't suggest that they would be less likely to order the extra test or procedure. For it is the threat of a large judgment, combined with the loss of reputation and time, that most doctors cite when explaining their major reasons for practicing defensive medicine—not the cost of the insurance premiums per se.

24. Karen Davis, invited testimony, Senate Appropriations Committee Subcommittee on Labor, Health and Human Services, Education and Related Agencies, Hearing on Health Care Access and Affordability: Cost Containment Strategies, 11 June 2003.

25. Interview with the author.

26. National Coalition on Health Care, *Building a Better Health Care System: Specifications for Reform*, 2004.

27. *Building a Better Health Care System*. It is worth noting that coalition members issuing the report included the American Academy of Family Physicians, the American Academy of Pediatrics, the American Cancer Society, AT&T, the AFL-CIO, Blue Shield of California, BellSouth, Kellogg Company, CalPERS, the New York State Teachers' Retirement System, the Presbyterian Church, the Episcopal Church, the United States Conference of Catholic Bishops, the Union of American Hebrew Congregations, Pfizer, Qwest Communications, and Verizon.

28. Yet *The Wall Street Journal* reported that public support for just such price controls was growing. By the fall of 2004, a Harris poll showed that well over half of all consumers polled favored government price controls on both hospital charges and prescription drugs—and fully 48 percent said the government should regulate doctors' fees as well.

In the Harris poll of a cross-section of adults conducted between August 10 and 15, 2004, respondents were asked first if they thought that "the prices of most of the following products and services are fair and reasonable, somewhat high or unreasonably high?" and second, "Would you favor or oppose federal government price controls of the following products and services?

Sixty-six percent of poll respondents said prescription-drug prices are unreasonably high, up from 57 percent who felt that way in a survey done a year earlier, and 60 percent said they favored federal government price controls on prescription drugs. Sixty-four percent felt hospital charges were unreasonably high, with 55 percent favoring price controls of hospitals. Finally, the share of Americans who thought doctor bills were unreasonably high rose to 55 percent—up from 43 percent a year earlier. On the question of the government regulating prices charged by doctors, the public was split with 48 percent in favor and 46 percent opposed. ("Americans Feel Controls Needed to Curb High Health-Care Costs," *The Wall Street Journal Online News Roundup,* 9 September 2004.)

29. Sarah Lueck, "Coalition Floats Ideas to Tame Rocketing Costs of Health Care," *The Wall Street Journal,* 21 July 2004.

CHAPTER 1

1. Paul Starr, *The Social Transformation of American Medicine* (New York: Basic Books, 1982), 3.

2. Thomas Rice, *The Economics of Health Reconsidered,* 2nd ed. (Chicago: Health Administration Press, 2002), 133.

3. Atul Gawande, *Complications: A Surgeon's Notes on an Imperfect Science* (New York: Picador, 2003), 7, 229.

4. Kenneth J. Arrow, "Uncertainty and the Welfare Economics of Medical Care," *The American Economic Review,* December 1963. In 1963 the Ford Foundation Program in Economic Development commissioned Arrow to write what turned out to be a seminal essay, breaking ground for the study of modern health care economics. Although there have been many changes in health care since then, Arrow's work continues to be citied in law, economics, and medical journals.

5. Gawande, 229. In "Are Market Forces Strong Enough to Deliver Efficient Health Care Systems? Confidence Is Waning" Len M. Nichols, Paul B. Ginsburg, Robert A. Berenson, Jon Christianson, and Robert E. Hurley observe that even today, when data on quality of care and outcomes are improving, "much of medical practice remains in gray areas . . . and is likely to remain so for quite some time" *(Health Affairs,* March/April 2004.) While stressing "the need for state-of-the-art evidence-based medicine and technology assessment information, as well as for data comparing quality among providers," they note, "no one should think that comparative quality and effectiveness information alone are the long-awaited silver bullets for our health care system." Because much of medical practice remains in those gray areas where evidence is ambiguous, "hard choices about competing resource uses and social values in the face of irreducible uncertainty lie ahead."

6. Rice, 83. Rice estimates that only 25 percent of health care dollars are spent on products and services that are purchased "relatively frequently" by the typical household. These might include eyeglasses, regular pediatric checkups, dental care, or prescription drugs for a chronic illness. Typically, in these cases the consumer is not seriously ill, and he can rely on his own experience to draw comparisons. (Rice cites a U.S. Federal Trade Commission conference for the 25 percent estimate.) The other 75 percent of health care dollars are spent on products and services that are "provided frequently by the physician, but used infrequently by a patient, including most surgical procedures" or "services that even a physician provides infrequently—unusual and experimental procedures."

7. If truth be told, Arrow acknowledges, at various points in the past "the actual differential knowledge possessed by physicians may not have been much." During the first third of

the 20th century, many serious diseases remained virtually as mysterious to the physician as to they were to the patient. *"But from the economic point of view,"* Arrow stresses, *"it is the subjective belief of both parties, as manifested in their market behavior, that is relevant."* (emphasis mine) (Arrow, "Uncertainty and the Welfare Economics of Medical Care," *The American Economic Review,* December 1963.)

Today belief in the medical profession's claims of superior knowledge and pure, unwavering commitment to the patient's best interests are met with increasing skepticism. Yet by and large, supply still drives demand in the health care market. In a 2003 article, Arrow argues that while much has changed in the 40 years since he wrote his original essay, what remains of the physician's "power" still rests on that perception of "moral authority."

"I am not denying that moral authority may be based on illusions, and that those illusions will be carefully fostered," Arrow adds. "But I want to emphasize that social norms [such as the expectations about a physician's lack of self-interest] are based on . . . perceived mutual gains, and that one must be wary of assuming that these perceptions are not based as much on reality as on other perceptions." (Arrow, "Reflections on the Reflections," in *Uncertain Times: Kenneth Arrow and the Changing Economics of Health Care,* Peter J. Hammer, Deborah Haas-Wilson, Mark A. Peterson, and William M. Sage, eds. [Durham: Duke University Press, 2003], 325.)

8. This probably explains why, despite rising skepticism about the medical profession in general, a wave of recent empirical studies confirm that interpersonal trust in a specific, known physician remains at remarkably high levels. Even in the face of medical errors, "most patients take a generally optimistic view of physicians' benevolent motivations," which makes them "capable of extraordinary, perhaps excessive, levels of forgiveness," writes one researcher. "Trust induces patients to view poor performance in the most positive light, as unintended or unavoidable isolated events that do not undermine their fundamental assumptions about their physicians' intentions and abilities." (Mark A. Hall, "Arrow on Trust," in *Uncertain Times,* 262.) Who would want to think otherwise? Hall, a professor of law and public health at Wake Forest University who has conducted his own two-year study of patients' trust in HMOs, cites numerous studies that suggest that demographics, health status, preferred role in medical decision making, and even patients' general level of cynicism about people or social institutions have little or no effect on the level of trust in one's own physician: "Contrary studies. . . . which suggest that trust is rapidly diminishing . . . refer to trust in the medical profession as a whole," Hall writes. "This captures only trust at a social, institutional or system level, not interpersonal trust, which has a distinctly differently psychological basis. . . ."

9. "Southern political barons" who "weren't about to vote for any system that extended health care to blacks" also played a role, notes Chris Farrell in *Deflation: What Happens When Prices Fall* (New York: HarperBusiness, 2004), 169.

10. Starr, 216.

11. Starr, 216.

12. Starr, 16.

13. Rice, 224.

14. Starr, 300.

15. George D. Lundberg with James Stacey, *Severed Trust: Why American Medicine Hasn't Been Fixed* (New York: Basic Books, 2000), 83–86.

16. Interview with the author.

17. In his groundbreaking study of health care economics, "Uncertainty and the Welfare Economics of Medical Care" Kenneth J. Arrow makes it clear that "virtually all the special aspects of this [the health care] industry, in fact, stem from the prevalence of trust." See also Mark A. Hall, "Arrow on Trust" for a discussion of how Arrow's emphasis on trust anticipates the 21st century's renewed interest in trust. Hall contrasts our recent recognition of the therapeutic aspects of trust to the late 20th-century vision of patients as "consumers engaged in market transactions"—a view that ignores the "brute reality of seeking care in a debilitating state of illness." For further discussion of the patient as consumer, and the importance of trust in the doctor-patient relationship, see chapter 3, "For-Profit Hospitals," and "Where We Are Now: Everyone Out of the Pool."

18. Interview with the author.

19. Starr, 295.

20. Consumers Union, amicus curiae brief, *Dan Morales, Attorney General of the State of Texas v. Blue Cross and Blue Shield of Texas* (October 1997).

21. Starr, 295.

22. See C. A. Kulp, *Casualty Insurance* (New York: Ronald Press, 1956).

23. James C. Robinson, *The Corporate Practice of Medicine: Competition and Innovation in Health Care* (Berkeley: University of California Press, 1999), 21. See also T. L. Delbanco, K. C. Meyers, and E. A. Segal, "Paying the Physician's Fee: Blue Shield and the Reasonable Charge," *The New England Journal of Medicine* 301 (1979): 1314–1320.

24. Starr, 385.

25. Robinson, interview with the author.

26. Starr, 311.

27. Odin W. Anderson and Jacob J. Feldman, *Family Medical Costs and Voluntary Health Insurance: A Nationwide Survey* (New York: McGraw-Hill, 1956), 11.

28. Rosemary A. Stevens, "Health Care in the Early 1960s," *Health Care Financing Review*, Winter 1996.

29. Robinson, *Corporate Practice of Medicine*, 22.

30. Peter A. Corning, *The Evolution of Medicare . . . From Idea to Law*, chapter 4, "The Fourth Round—1957 to 1965." (Washington, D.C.: Social Security Administration, 1969). Corning originally wrote *The Evolution of Medicare* under contract for the Social Security Administration in 1969. Since then, the SSA has republished his study online: see www.ssa.gov/history/corningchap4.html.

31. Corning, chapter 4.

32. Lundberg, interview with the author.

33. Corning, chapter 4.

34. See Corning, chapter 4, and Frank J. Primich, MD, "Book Review: *Code Blue: Health Care in Crisis* by Edward R. Annis, M.D." This review appeared in *The Freeman: Ideas on Liberty* published by The Foundation for Economic Education, September 1994.

35. Howard Wolinsky and Tom Brune, *The Serpent on the Staff: The Unhealthy Politics of the American Medical Association* (New York: Tarcher/Putnam, 1994), 47, 48. Wolinsky and Brune

note that physicians' salaries began to climb only after WWII. At that point, doctors' incomes began to rise at a rate of 5.9 percent a year, twice the consumer price index. By 1965 doctors' average annual earnings hit nearly $30,000—about five times the median average income.

36. Interview with Roger Mudd, *The Health Quarterly,* 5 May 1992 (transcript available from Journal Graphics, Inc., Denver, CO).

37. Carol S. Weissert and William G. Weissert, *Governing Health: The Politics of Health Policy,* 2nd ed. (Baltimore: The Johns Hopkins University Press, 2002), 291.

38. Wolinsky and Brune, 49, 47.

39. Starr, 369–70.

40. Lundberg, interview with the author.

41. Lundberg, interview with the author; see also Lundberg, *Severed Trust,* 31, 32, 87.

42. Kelly J. Devers, Linda R. Brewster, and Lawrence P. Casalino compare hospital competition prior to 1983 to hospital competition both in the 1990s and in the 21st century in "Changes in Hospital Competitive Strategy: A New Medical Arms Race?" *Health Services Research,* February 2003. The authors note that while some evidence of more complementary competitive behavior was reported (e.g., hospitals less likely to add a service as the number of neighboring hospitals increased), this occurred only in a few basic service areas such as emergency and maternity care. As evidence, they point to H. S. Luft, J. C. Robinson, D. W. Garnick, S. C. Maerki, and S. J. McPhee. "The Role of Specialized Services in Competition among Hospitals." *Inquiry* 23, no. 1 (1986); and M. A. Morrisey, "Competition in Hospital and Health Insurance Markets: A Review and Research Agenda." *Health Services Research* 36, no. 1 (2001): 191–222.

43. Robinson, *Corporate Practice of Medicine,* 3.

44. Starr, 384.

45. Wolinsky and Brune, 49.

46. Wolinsky and Brune, 49–50.

47. Alice M. Rivlin, "Agreed: Here Comes National Health Insurance," *The New York Times Magazine,* 21 July 1974.

48. Starr, 381.

49. "It's Time to Operate," *Fortune,* January 1970.

50. Starr, 382.

51. Benson R. Roe, "The UCR Boondoggle: A Death Knell for Private Practice?" *The New England Journal of Medicine,* 305 (July 1981).

52. "It's Time to Operate."

53. "$60-Billion Crisis in Health Care," *Business Week,* 17 January 1970; Ronald Anderson, Joanna Kravits, and Odin W. Anderson, "The Public's View of the Crisis in Medical Care: An Impetus for Changing Delivery Systems?" *Economic and Business Bulletin* 24 (1971): 44–52.

54. Harold M. Schmeck Jr., "President Warns of 'Massive Crisis' in Health Care," *The New York Times,* 11 July 1969.

55. Harold M. Schmeck Jr., "Nixon Sees Passage in '74 of a Health Insurance Plan," *The New York Times,* 6 February 1974.

56. Schmeck, "Nixon Sees Passage."

57. Deirdre Shesgreen, "Universal Health Care Is a Political Hot Potato," *St. Louis Post-Dispatch,* 16 October 2004.

58. Wolinsky and Brune, 224, 39, 43; Starr, 398. Wolinsky and Brune point out that by the late eighties, the American College of Physicians had broken with the AMA, and by the early nineties, the College of Physicians released its own version of health care reform—a version that was far different from the AMA's. The ACP plan invited government to take a greater role in health care and called for a national budget to limit health care costs. When the AMA rejected the idea, the ACP publicly criticized the AMA in a statement AMA delegates later characterized as "inaccurate, unprofessional and insulting." Finally, in 1994, the independent American College of Surgeons parted company with the AMA when the chairman of the ACS board of regents, representing 55,000 members, told the House Committee on Education and Labor that it would support a single-payer, Canadian-style health care system because it provided "the best assurances that patients would be able to seek care from any doctor of their choice." The AMA's president-elect expressed "astonishment" at the surgeons' position, Wolinsky and Brune report, yet "the stand by the surgeons and others—representing more than 350,000 physicians, far more than the AMA's membership—again demonstrated that if there is one Voice of Medicine, it was not the AMA."

59. Starr, 404; Martin Plissner, "Health-Care Bill Fantasy," *Slate,* 5 June 2001.

60. Starr, 405.

61. Robinson, *Corporate Practice of Medicine,* 3.

62. Starr, 417.

63. Interview with Roger Mudd, *The Health Quarterly,* 20 May 1992.

64. Debra L. Roth and Deborah Reidy Kelch, *Making Sense of Managed Care Regulation in California 2001,* prepared for the California HealthCare Foundation (9–10); Mark Schlesinger and Bradford Gray, "A Broader Vision for Managed Care, Part 1: Measuring the Benefit to Communities," *Health Affairs,* May/June 1998; Lynn R. Gruber, Maureen Shadle, and Cynthia L. Polich, "From Movement to Industry: The Growth of HMOs," *Health Affairs,* Summer 1988.

65. Marcia Angell, "The Truth About the Drug Companies," *The New York Review of Books,* 15 July 2004.

66. By 2004 *St.Elsewhere* had given way to *Scrubs,* a far more cynical comedy, which parodies both science and the ideals of medicine. Or, as The Center for Nursing Advocacy puts it, this is a medical program that "poses the question, what if a hospital was staffed by insult comics?" ("Scrubs," The Center For Nursing Advocacy, www.nursingadvocacy.org/media).

67. Starr, 448, 449.

68. See chapter 8, "Device Makers, Drugmakers, and the FDA" for a discussion of conflict of interest and the entrepreneurial physician.

69. Richard Evans, interview with the author.

70. See preface.

71. Casalino, interview with the author. Casalino originally made the remark in a review of *The Economic Evolution of American Health Care* in *The New England Journal of Medicine,* 10 May 2001.

72. Interview with the author. See chapter 3, "For-Profit Hospitals: A flaw in the Business Model?" on the relationship between supply and demand in health care.

73. Elliott S. Fisher, "Health Care in America: Is More Better?" See www.dartmouthatlas.org. In a study published in the 18 February 2003 issue of *Annals of Internal Medicine,* Fisher and his colleagues compared regional differences in per capita Medicare spending in numerous regions across the United States and then looked at how the patients in those different areas fared. Previous research has shown that Medicare spending varies widely in different regions of the country. In this study researchers compared outcomes. While the study showed that those who lived in the higher-spending areas did tend to go to the doctor more, have more tests, see specialists more often, and were hospitalized more often, there was no evidence of lower death rates or better health status. Indeed, the study suggested that in some cases more care led to higher mortality rates. (See chapter 5, "When More Care Is Not Better Care.")

74. Marcia Angell, "The Forgotten Domestic Crisis," *The New York Times,* 13 October 2002.

75. Daniel Callahan, *False Hopes: Why America's Quest for Perfect Health Is a Recipe for Failure* (New York: Simon & Schuster, 1998), 40.

76. Interview with the author.

77. Evans, interview with the author. In *The Profit Motive and Patient Care: The Changing Accountability of Doctors and Hospitals* (Cambridge: Harvard University Press, 1991), 21, Bradford H. Gray, director of the Division of Health and Science Policy at The New York Academy of Medicine, observes that the best Wall Street analysts enjoy a unique perspective on the health care industry: "Although compliance with reporting requirements provides investors with important information about a company's performance, it offers little insight into such matters as the cost or quality of services in company-owned facilities or service to patients who lack the means to pay. Information about these matters sometimes comes to light through the work of investment analysts, who often learn much that is otherwise not made public by companies."

CHAPTER 2

1. Arnold S. Relman, review of *The Institute of Medicine Report on the Quality of Health Care Crossing the Quality Chasm: A New Health System for the 21st Century* in *The New England Journal of Medicine,* 30 August 2001.

2. There is always a temptation to idealize the health care system of the past. While at its best, it encouraged collaboration, doctors and hospitals often had different agendas. Moreover, within the profession many solo practitioners valued their independence above all else. This meant that the majority did not readily learn from one another. That said, the *model* was one of collaboration rather than competition. Doctors did not see themselves as opportunistic entrepreneurs, and hospitals did not advertise for patients. The Mayo Clinic— one of the first health care "co-ops"—was viewed as the gold standard for what the practice of medicine should be. Most actors in the system genuinely believed that they always put the patients' interests ahead of their own interests—and probably most did.

3. James Buchan makes the point in *Frozen Desire: The Meaning of Money* (New York: Welcome Rain, 2001), 180: "That the economists can explain neither prices nor the rate of interest nor even agree what money is reminds us that we are dealing with belief not science."

4. Michael E. Porter and Elizabeth Olmsted Teisberg, "Redefining Competition in Health Care," *Harvard Business Review,* June 2004. Porter and Teisberg do, however, believe that markets *should* be able to deliver more efficient care.

5. "At times providers are paid even more when the quality of care is worse, such as when complications occur as the result of error," the Medicare Payment Advisory Commission complains. Medicare Payment Advisory Committee (MedPAC), *Report to the Congress: Variation and Innovation in Medicare,* June 2003, 108. On Duke's program, see Regina Herzlinger, professor of business administration, Harvard Business School, participant in Federal Trade Commission Department of Justice Hearings, 27 May 2003. See also Regina Herzlinger, "A Better Way to Pay," *Modern Healthcare,* 11 December 2000; and Joanne Lynn, director, The Washington Home Center for Palliative Care Studies, FTCDOJ Hearings, 30 May 2003. ("There are now six randomized control trials showing better ways of taking care of patients with advanced heart failure," Lynn observed. "Every single one of those programs has folded at the end of the grant funding because it is not sustainable under Medicare.")

In Utah, 10 hospitals had a similar experience after applying new guidelines for treating pneumonia: the cost savings in those 10 small rural hospitals totaled more than $500,000 per year, but an analysis of net operating income showed a loss to the facilities of over $200,000 annually. See Brent James, executive director, Institute for Health Care Delivery Research, Intermountain Health Care, participant in the FTCDOJ hearings, 28 May 2003. For detail on all of the above, see *Improving Health Care: A Dose of Competition,* a report by the Federal Trade Commission and the Department of Justice, July 2004, chapter 1, "An Overview."

6. Lawrence Casalino, interview with the author. For more on the processes that would allow a physician to monitor a chronically ill patient and keep him out of the hospital, see the discussion of health information technology in chapter 7, "Doing Less and Doing It Right: Is Pay for Performance the Answer?"

7. Joanne Andiorio, interview with the author.

8. Casalino, interview with the author. See also *Emerging Health Care Market Trends: Insights from Communities,* "Session Two: Providers' Response to the Retreat from Managed Care," Center for Studying Health System Change, 10 December 2001, www.hschange.org/CONTENT/394/.

9. Andiorio, interview with the author.

10. By 2003 research showed that some managed care plans had begun to move toward disease management programs that emphasized intensive management for high-risk patients, though the programs had not been in operation long enough to provide evidence of cost savings. (Glen P. Mays, Gary Paxton, and Justin White, "Managed Care Rebound?: Recent changes in Health Plans' Cost Containment Strategies," Web Exclusive, *Health Affairs,* 11 August 2004.)

11. The HMO model might have worked "in a less ruthlessly competitive market," suggests *Business Week* columnist and *American Prospect* coeditor Robert Kuttner. In the past, "non-profit prepaid group plans, with an ideology of service as well as consumer accountability, [have offered] genuine opportunities to spend the same health dollars more efficiently and compassionately," Kuttner argues, pointing to Group Health Cooperative of Puget

Sound, an HMO owned by its consumer-members, as an example of an HMO where patient satisfaction had been "consistently high."

But Puget Sound had no obligation to outside investors, and its consumer-owners had no incentive to pursue market share as an end in itself. By contrast, for-profit HMOs operating in a competitive marketplace have a fiduciary responsibility to their shareholders to push for ever larger market share and ever higher profits. Growth is their mandate. In that context, dollars saved are less likely to be "recycled within the HMO" to improve the health of its members, Kuttner points out, and "more likely to be diverted—to shareholders, or new acquisitions, or lower premiums" to make a particular HMO more attractive to employers. Meanwhile, in the fierce market of the nineties, where cost cutting and growth became paramount, "HMOs like Group Health of Puget Sound [were] under pressure to match the false economies of cheaper for-profit competition, lest they be dropped by large employers as too expensive," Kuttner suggests. *Everything For Sale: The Virtues and Limits of Markets* (New York: Knopf, 1997), 134.

12. On the advantages and disadvantages of broader networks, see Michael E. Chernew, Walter P. Wodchis, Dennis P. Scanlon, and Catherine G. McLaughlin, "Overlap in HMO Physician Networks," *Health Affairs,* March/April 2004.

13. Interview with the author. This is not to say that doctors no longer find themselves on the phone with an insurance company, arguing for permission to hospitalize a patient. But by 2005 many plans had moved back to a fee-for-service payment system, and a good number allowed patients to see specialists without a referral—though there were some signs that health plans were once again beginning to tighten their rules.

14. Controversy about bone marrow transplants for women with breast cancer raged for years—another example of how the uncertainties of medical science make it extremely difficult, even for professionals, to measure the quality of care. (For a full discussion of this procedure, see chapter 5, "When More Care Is Not Better Care.")

15. "Summary of Findings," *Employee Health Benefits 2005 Annual Survey* (Menlo Park: The Henry J. Kaiser Family Foundation). See www.kff.org.

16. James C. Robinson, *The Corporate Practice of Medicine: Competition and Innovation in Health Care* (Berkeley: University of California Press, 1999), 37, 229, 211.

17. Robinson, 228. Robinson does not pretend that unmanaged competition is a perfect example of free market competition—which, after all, exists only on paper. His point is simply that as more and more employers move away from the most restrictive HMOs and toward a varied offering of plans that provide the maximum number of choices, market competition is far less managed than it was in the nineties.

18. Robinson, interview with the author.

19. "Summary of Findings."

20. Interview with the author. As noted in the preface, by 2005 the average annual premium for family coverage stood at $10,800. As a very rough definition of average family income, I use median annual income, or $44,389. In 2004 half of all U.S. families earned more; half earned less. Since the cost of living varies so widely nationwide, a range of $25,000 to $75,000 is often used to define "middle class." But even using that definition, families earning $75,000—before taxes—may easily find annual premiums of $10,880 unaffordable, especially if they live in a region where the cost of housing is high. In some cases em-

ployers share the burden, but as noted in the preface, more and more employers are shifting costs to employees—or dropping coverage altogether.

21. Roger Yu, "The New Piece of Health Insurance: Plans with Lower Premiums Are Intended to Fit Small Firms but Coverage Limits Have Raised Concern in Medical Circles," *The Dallas Morning News,* 8 June 2004. Insurance plans that carry a high deductible are marketed as another alternative for families who cannot afford the $10,000 to $13,000 annual premium for a family plan. The problem here is that these are the very same families who can least afford to cover a deductible of $5,000. While high-deductible plans work well for more affluent families, they don't increase access to care for those who are now being priced out of the system. Moreover, numerous studies show that when deductibles and copayments rise, consumers put off needed care, particularly preventive care and the ongoing treatment for chronic diseases needed to avoid complications down the line. See "Where We Are Now: Everyone Out of the Pool."

22. Relman, review of *The Institute of Medicine Report.*

23. The Institute for Health and Socioeconomic Policy, *Stripping Away the Myth of a U.S. Health Care System,* 15 September 2003. IHSP is a nonprofit research and policy organization overseen by an advisory board drawn from Albert Einstein School of Medicine, Boston University, Harvard University, and the University of California.

24. The Harris Poll #38, "Supermarkets, Food Companies, Airlines, Computers and Banks Top the List of Industries Doing Good Job for Their Consumers," 28 May 2004.

25. Dinah Wisenberg Brin, "Hospitals' Charity-Care Levels Hard to Pinpoint" Dow Jones Newswires, 23 May 2005.

26. Robert J. Blendon, Cathy Schoen, Catherine M. DesRoches, Robin Osborn, Kinga Zapert, and Elizabeth Raleigh, "Confronting Competing Demands to Improve Quality: A Five-Country Hospital Survey," *Health Affairs,* May/June 2004.

27. See J. Robinson and H. Luft, "The Impact of Hospital Market Structure on Patient Volume, Average Length of Stay and the Cost of Care," *Journal of Health Economics* 4 (1985): 333–56; C. Adams, "Medical Arms Race: Excess Technology Adds to Soaring Cost," *New Orleans Times Picayune,* 16 October 1984; H. Luft et al., *Hospital Volume, Physician Volume, and Patient Outcomes: Assessing the Evidence, Health Administration Press Perspectives* (Ann Arbor: Health Administration Press, 1990); Julie Appleby, "Hospitals Fight for Turf in Medical Arms Race," *USA Today,* 19 February 2002; and Daniel P. Kessler and Mark B. McClellan, "Is Hospital Competition Socially Wasteful?" Stanford Graduate School of Business, August 2000. See www.gsb.stanford.edu/community/bmag/sbsm0008/faculty _research_health.html.

28. Kelly J. Devers, Linda R. Brewster, and Lawrence P. Casalino, "Changes in Hospital Competitive Strategy: A New Medical Arms Race?" *Health Services Research,* February 2003. As part of the Center for Studying Health System Change's ongoing field study, researchers visited 12 representative communities every two years, beginning in 1996, interviewing local health care leaders, including some 140 hospital executives, focusing on changes in hospital market conditions and competitive strategy. By 2001 HMO enrollments were slowing, and broader provider networks had become the norm, reducing the threat of exclusion from insurers' networks. As a result, the researchers found hospitals returning to the "retail strategies" designed to attract doctors and patients in the eighties. Once again

they were trying to outdo rivals by investing in the plants and equipment that would bring in the most desirable customers.

29. Kelly Devers, "The Return of the Medical Arms Race," *Emerging Health Care Market Trends: Insights from Communities,* Session Two.

    In 2004 Dr. Lawrence Casalino, one of the study's coauthors, reported that the arms race had not slowed. "Given the financial pressures, they really don't have any choice," he said (interview with the author). On Wall Street, Gary Taylor, hospital analyst at Banc of America Securities, confirmed that hospitals were once again making large capital investments. "In the survey we just did, I was a little surprised," he observed in June of 2004. "For the third year in a row, we had a huge majority of hospitals talking about planning to add capacity in the next few years. This year, maybe 85 percent of the urban hospitals planned to add capacity in the next two years. And 60 percent of the rural hospitals were planning on expansion. I would have guessed that the number would be 30." ("Wall Street Comes to Washington," Center for Studying Health System Change conference, 24 June 2004, hschange.org/CONTENT/688/?conf-17.)

30. For example, an AHRQ (Agency for Healthcare Research and Quality) research study of elderly patients who had any of 14 high-risk cardiovascular or cancer surgeries published in *The New England Journal of Medicine* in 2002 showed that they fared better in more experienced hospitals that did a higher volume of the particular procedure. When patients underwent surgery for cancer of the esophagus, for instance, only 8 percent of those in high-volume hospitals died, while 20 percent of those in low-volume hospitals did not survive. When patients underwent surgery for cancer of the pancreas, respective mortality rates were 4 percent and 16 percent. (J. Birkmeyer, A. Siewers, E. Finlayson, et al., "Hospital Volume and Surgical Mortality in the United States," *The New England Journal of Medicine,* April 2002.)

31. Atul Gawande, *Complications: A Surgeon's Notes on an Imperfect Science* (New York: Picador, 2003), 19. Nevertheless, there is "as yet no compelling evidence that specialty surgical centers offer either better or more economical care," observes Dr. Lawrence Casalino. The jury is still out, he explains, because such centers have become popular only in recent years (interview with the author). Nevertheless, proponents argue that in addition to the advantage of allowing surgical teams to focus on a few procedures, these smaller, freestanding hospitals offer physicians more control over their working environment. In a larger, more congested community hospital, emergencies often derail operating room schedules.

32. Larry Stepnick, "The New Competitive Landscape: Board and CEO Strategies for Dealing with Emerging Threats," white paper WP-2003-SM, The Governance Institute, summer 2003. See www.governanceinstitute.com.

33. Stepnick, "The New Competitive Landscape."

34. Reed Abelson, "Hospitals Battle For-Profit Groups for Patients," *The New York Times,* 30 October 2002.

35. "Doctor-Owned Specialty Hospitals Spur Investor Interest, Capitol Hill Worries," *BNA's Health Care Policy Report* 11, no. 16 (2003): 532–533.

36. Lawrence P. Casalino, Kelly J. Devers, and Linda R. Brewster, "Focused Factories? Physician-Owned Special Facilities," *Health Affairs,* November/December 2003. Reporting on

interviews conducted from 2001 to 2004 with leaders of the three to four of the largest medical groups, hospitals, and health plans in each of twelve randomly selected areas, the authors observe that while medical group leaders emphasized their desire to improve the quality of care, "we were unable to elicit much specific information about processes [established to boost quality], and hospital and health plan respondents stated that they were not aware of them. Some physician-leaders of specialty facilities argued that they would like to implement more processes to improve care, but that because they do not reward quality, Medicare and commercial health plans fail to give physicians an incentive to make the investment. Even without such processes, the authors noted, facilities might well improve quality simply because their physicians and other staff work together daily providing the same services again and again. However, if creating specialty facilities leads to excess capacity in a community and service volume decreases in these facilities or in general hospitals (or both), quality could decline along with volume."

37. "Even if the moratorium is extended," observes Banc of America Securities' Taylor, "this will not be the end of physician-owned specialty hospitals. I suspect that there are some very smart attorneys and lawyers out there who are being fairly active in terms of developing some structures that are going to be able to move forward despite the moratorium. You'll see some legal structures created that get around how the law is written right now." ("Wall Street Comes to Washington" conference, Center for Health System Change, 24 June 2004.) See webcast at www.rwjf.org/newsroom/activitydetail.jsp?id=10086 &type=3.)

38. Stepnick, "The New Competitive Landscape."

39. Fewer, larger regional centers of excellence might better serve the community's interests, suggests health care economist Tom Rice (Rice, *The Economics of Health Reconsidered,* 2nd ed. [Chicago: Health Administration Press, 2002], 148–9).

40. Stepnick, "The New Competitive Landscape."

41. "Wall Street Comes to Washington."

42. Devers, "The Return of the Medical Arms Race." Research done at Stanford's Graduate School of Business by economist Daniel Kessler and fellow Stanford economist and physician Mark McClellan reveals that in the eighties, when the medical arms race was going full force, competition among hospitals "led to higher costs and [only] somewhat better health outcomes for elderly Americans with heart disease." By contrast, in the nineties, when HMOs were forcing hospitals to compete on price, "competition led to substantially lower costs and significantly lower rates of mortality and cardiac complications." Noting that the benefits were most visible in states with high HMO enrollments, Kessler and McClellan suggest that "the spillover effects from increasingly efficient treatment of privately insured patients in HMOs may have favorably affected the treatment of Medicare patients by mediating the effects of hospital competition in a way that enhances medical productivity. In particular, managed care appears to increase efficiency by reducing the tendency of hospital competition to result in a 'medical arms race' of expenditure growth." See Kessler and McClellan, "Is Hospital Competition Socially Wasteful?"

43. Michelle Rogers, "The Great Heart Race," *HealthLeaders,* February 2004.

44. Rogers, "The Great Heart Race."

45. Kelly Devers, Linda R. Brewster, and Paul B. Ginsburg, "Specialty Hospitals: Focused

Factories or Cream Skimmers?" Center for Studying Health System Change, Issue Brief No. 52, April 2003.

46. Tom Malasto, interview with author; see also Rogers, "The Great Heart Race."

47. Daniel Callahan, *False Hopes: Why America's Quest for Perfect Health Is a Recipe for Failure* (New York: Simon & Schuster, 1998), 227.

48. Appleby, "Hospitals Fight for Turf in Medical Arms Race"; Rogers, "The Great Heart Race."

49. Appleby, "Hospitals Fight for Turf in Medical Arms Race."

50. Joe Manning, "Area Hospitals Spend $7.4 Million on Ads," *Milwaukee Journal Sentinel,* 2 April 2004.

51. Rice, *The Economics of Health Reconsidered,* 242–245. Rice cites the following studies: "OECD Health Data 2001: A Comparative Analysis of 30 Countries" (Paris: OECD); Technological Change in Health Care (TECH) Research Network, published in "Technological Change Around the World: Evidence from Heart Attack Care," *Health Affairs,* May/June 2001; R. B. Saltman and J. Figueras, "Analyzing the Evidence on European Health Care Reforms, *Health Affairs,* March/April 1998; Mark McClellan and Daniel Kessler for the TECH Investigators, "A Global Analysis of Technological Change in Health Care: The Case of Heart Attacks," *Health Affairs,* May/June 1999; D. K. Verrilli, R. Berenson, and S. J. Katz, "A Comparison of Cardiovascular Procedure Use Between the United States and Canada," *Health Services Research,* and J. V. Tu, L. Pashos, C. D. Naylor et al., "Use of Cardiac Procedures and Outcomes in Elderly Patients with Myocardial Infarction in the United States and Canada," *The New England Journal of Medicine* 336, no. 21 (1997): 1500–05. The last study, which focused on elderly patients in the United States and in Ontario, Canada, showed angioplasty five times as common in the U.S.—and coronary artery bypass surgery seven times as common, yet there was virtually no difference in one-year mortality (34.3 percent in the United States vs. 34.4 percent in Ontario) and only a slight difference after 30 days (21.4 percent in Ontario vs. 22.4 percent in the U.S.).

52. Thomas Riles, interview with the author.

53. Jack Mahoney, interview with the author.

54. Interview with the author.

55. James Orlikoff, interview with the author.

56. Interview with the author.

57. Steve Hymon, "Doctors Refusing Calls to the ER in Dispute Over Pay, State Report Finds," The State, *Los Angeles Times,* 29 May 2003.

58. Orlikoff, interview with the author. In "Financial Pressures Spur Physician Entrepreneurialism," (*Health Affairs,* March/April 2004) Hoangmai H. Pham et al. confirm that "most commonly physicians in [the 12 markets studied] refused to take calls in emergency departments or demanded extra pay from hospitals for doing so. In addition, the authors noted that after "confronting . . . physicians who shirked traditional obligations such as Emergency Department care," hospitals in some markets "accommodated them." Their report was based on data from 270 interviews conducted between September of 2002 and May of 2003 with three to four of the largest hospitals, health plans, and multi and single-specialty physicians groups in each of 12 representative markets nationwide.

59. Robert Rosen, interview with the author.

60. Rosen, interviews with the author. Unless otherwise indicated, all further quotations are drawn from these interviews. See also Joanne Kaufman, "Strong Medicine: The Uncut Version," *New York,* 13 October 2003.

61. Geeta Anand and Ron Winslow, "Transformation of Heart Care Is Putting Specialists At Odds," *The Wall Street Journal,* 10 September 2003. Since surgeons' fees represent only a small part of the total cost of the procedure, cardiovascular surgery remains a money-maker for most hospitals.

62. Interview with the author.

63. Thomas Riles, interviews with the author. Unless otherwise indicated, all quotations that follow are from those interviews.

64. See Riles's remarks above.

65. Kaufman, "Strong Medicine: The Uncut Version."

66. Anand and Winslow, "Transformation of Heart Care Is Putting Specialists At Odds."

67. Kaufman, "Strong Medicine: The Uncut Version."

68. See Jerry Avorn, *Powerful Medicines: The Benefits, Risks, and Costs of Prescription Drugs* (New York: Knopf, 2004), 288, and Marcia Angell, *The Truth About the Drug Companies: How They Deceive Us and What to Do About It* (New York: Random House, 2004), 123–124. Up until 1997 the FDA required drug advertisers to provide full information about side effects, making a 30-second spot difficult—if not downright frightening. But when it loosened the restrictions, the FDA ruled that drug companies would only have to mention the major risks, and refer to a toll-free phone number or other source for additional information.

69. Anna Wilde Mathews, "FDA to Review Drug Marketing to Consumers," *The Wall Street Journal,* 2 August 2005.

70. Richard Evans, interview with the author. Also see "The Other Drug War," *Frontline,* PBS, 19 June 2003.

71. David Pauly, "Drug Companies' Cost of Pushing Pills Rivals R&D," *Bloomberg News,* 26 August 2004.

72. In *The Truth About the Drug Companies: How They Deceive Us and What to Do About It,* Dr. Marcia Angell points out that $5.5 billion is probably a lowball figure since "it is unlikely to cost only $62,500—$5.5 billion divided by 88,000—for each sales representative's salary, benefits, travel costs, and gift-giving (116). Angell also cites the U.S. General Accounting Office's critical report on direct-to-consumer advertising, which contains the industry's claims about its promotional spending, *Prescription Drugs: FDA Oversight of Direct-to-Consumer Advertising Has Limitations,* 28 October 2002, GAO-03-177 (www.gao.gov).

73. Amy Barrett, "Pfizer's Funk," *BusinessWeek,* 28 February 2005.

74. Evans, interview with the author. See Avorn, *Powerful Medicines,* 429, note 206. Avorn points out that at the time, most estimates put the industry's direct promotion to prescribers at about $20 billion annually, with another $2 billion spent each year on company-sponsored educational events designed to promote product sales. An additional $3 billion was devoted to direct-to-consumer advertising. Adding in a modest expenditure for the administration of these programs, the total for promotion-related activities came to nearly $30 billion of the industry's $200 billion in revenues.

75. Scott Hensley, "Some Drug Makers Are Starting to Curtail TV Ad Spending" *The Wall*

Street Journal, 16 May 2005. For a full discussion of how even Pfizer had begun to talk about cutting marketing cost, see chapter 8, "Device Makers, Drugmakers, and the FDA."

76. Evans, interview with the author.

77. Avorn, *Powerful Medicines,* 290.

78. Mahoney, interview with the author.

79. According to The Kaiser Family Foundation, retail prices "increased an average of 7.4% a year—more than double the average inflation rate of 2.5%—a change which reflects both manufacturers hiking prices of existing drugs and persuading consumers to switch to newer, higher-priced drugs." (Kaiser Family Foundation, *Prescription Drug Trends,* October 2004.) Kaiser cites the National Association of Chain Drug Stores, "Industry Facts-at-a-Glance," at www.nacds.org.

80. Families USA used EDGAR (the SEC's Electronic Data Gathering Analysis and Retrieval System) to review the financial report submitted to the SEC by nine of the largest U.S.-based pharmaceutical companies. (*Profiting from Pain: Where Prescription Drug Dollars Go* [Washington, D.C.: Families USA, 2002].) For a full discussion of the industry's profits, see chapter 8, "Device Makers, Drugmakers, and the FDA."

81. Pauly, "Drug Companies' Cost of Pushing Pills Rivals R&D."

82. For example, a footnote in an industry report to the General Accounting Office notes that marketing costs "do not include educational meetings arranged by pharmaceutical companies for physicians which are not generally considered promotional activities." Indeed, the drug industry now pays for roughly 60 percent of the cost of the "continuing medical education" that most states require that doctors receive throughout their professional lives. When doctors attend "educational" conventions at luxurious resorts, the drug company's contribution is nearly always described as an "unrestricted educational grant"—a phrase meant to suggest that there are no strings attached to its gift. But in fact, drug company sponsors often have a hand in putting together the graphics and other educational materials for the conference. It's difficult to measure just how far the conflict of interest goes: suffice to say that research shows that doctors prescribe more of the sponsors' drugs after these meetings. "If it were otherwise," notes Dr. Marcia Angell in *The Truth About the Drug Companies* (138–141), "the industry would not spend the huge sums that it does on these programs."

83. The Kaiser Family Foundation, *Prescription Drug Trends,* May 2003.

84. "The Other Drug War 2003: Drug Companies Deploy an Army of 675 Lobbyists to Protect Profits," Public Citizen Congress Watch, 2003, www.citizen.org. In *The Truth About the Drug Companies,* Angell points out that these lobbyists are well pedigreed: in 2002 they included 26 former members of Congress, and another 342 who had been on congressional staffs or otherwise connected with government officials. Twenty had been congressional chiefs of staff. Two were former chairmen of the Republican National Committee.

85. "Pharmaceutical Industry Spent $800 Million on Lobbying Over Seven Years, Report Says," *Medical News Today,* 8 July 2005.

86. Clifton Leaf, "Why We're Losing the War on Cancer—and How to Win It," *Fortune,* 22 March 2004. In his article, Leaf makes it clear that the problem is pervasive, not only in industry but in academia—where research has become more and more closely tied to commerce. See chapter 8, "Device Makers, Drugmakers, and the FDA."

87. Andrew Pollack, "No Cure, but Drugs May Turn Cancer into Manageable Illness," *The New York Times*, 6 June 2004.

88. Genie Kleinerman, interview with the author.

89. Leaf, "Why We're Losing the War on Cancer—and How to Win It." Leaf points to a study published in the August of 2004 issue of the *British Medical Journal* that underlines the problem: after poring over the results of trials of 12 new anticancer drugs that had been approved for the European market from 1995 to 2000, and comparing them with standard treatments for their respective diseases, researchers could find "no substantial advantages—no improved survival, no better quality of life, no added safety—with any of the new agents. All of them, though, were several times more expensive than the old drugs. In one case, the price was 350 times higher."

90. Casalino, interview with the author.

91. Pollack, "No Cure, but Drugs May Turn Cancer into Manageable Illness."

92. Kleinerman, interview with the author.

93. Donald Rumsfeld, *The NewsHour with Jim Lehrer*, PBS, 17 August 2004. But the conversation did not end there: "They get homogenized," Rumsfeld insisted (referring back to his earlier comment that if researchers lunched together and discussed their ideas, they would wind up "all thinking alike").

"All right," Lehrer said, clearly anxious to move on to another point. (Practicing what he preached, Rumsfeld had made his point clear: there would be no give-and-take of ideas in this discussion.)

94. In the *Duke Law & Technology Review*, Melissa Ganz explains: "Since the MMA's new discount drug plan will be privately administered, the insurance industry will benefit directly from an estimated $46 billion that will be 'pumped' into managed care by the government over the next ten years. Moreover, greater government reimbursement—upwards of 25%—and increases in the number of enrollees in participating insurance plans will lead to greater overall revenues. In fact, investors seem to already be placing their bets that HMOs will experience a 2–5% increase in after-tax profits. Fewer than five million of the 40 million Medicare beneficiaries, about 12 percent, are in private plans. The administration predicts that the proportion will grow to 35 million by 2007, as beneficiaries enroll in HMOs and PPOs." See Milt Freudenheim, "Using Medicare Billions, H.M.O's Again Court Elderly," NewYorkTimes.com, 9 March 2004; Alan M. Schlein, "Medicare Reform Bill—Loved, Hated, Hailed and Decried. What's In It for You?" *Fifty Plus*, January 2004.

95. Commenting on the Medicare legislation, Dr. David Himmelstein, an associate professor of medicine at Harvard and coauthor of an *International Journal of Health Services* Health Research Group study on administrative costs in U.S. medicine, notes: "At present, Medicare's overhead is less than 4 percent. But all of the new Medicare money—$400 billion—will flow through private insurance plans whose overhead averages 12 percent. So insurance companies will gain $36 billion from this bill." In testimony before the Senate Appropriations Subcommittee on Labor, Health, and Human Services, Karen Davis, president of The Commonwealth Fund, draws a similar conclusion, estimating that administrative expenses for private insurance in the United States are two-and-one-half times as high as those for public programs. ("American Health Care: Why So Costly?" in-

vited testimony before the Senate Appropriations Subcommittee on Labor, Health, and Human Services, Hearing on Health Care Access and Affordability: Cost Containment Strategies, 11 June 2003.)

96. Marcia Angell, "The Forgotten Domestic Crisis," *The New York Times,* 13 October 2002.

97. Bruce Vladeck, interview with the author. Unless otherwise indicated, all quotations that follow are drawn from that interview.

98. This is not a criticism, simply a matter of law. Public relations aside, as a legal entity a corporation has a single mandate: to create profits for its shareholders, without legal or moral obligation to the welfare of workers, the environment, or the well-being of society as a whole. A corporation that ignores that duty leaves itself open to suit by its shareholders. See Joel Bakan, *The Corporation: The Pathological Pursuit of Profit and Power* (New York: Free Press, 2004).

99. Robert Maltbie, "Long Oxford Health, Short Affymetrix," Forbes.com, 5 June 2003.

100. "HMOs Earn $10.2 Billion in 2003, Nearly Doubling Profits, According to Weiss Ratings," Business Wire, 30 August 2004.

101. Sandra Ward, "WellPoint's Winning Ways," *Barron's,* 25 July 2005.

102. "Healthcare News: Insurance Companies' Profit Summaries" MediCo Unlimited, 27 July 2005. See www.medicounlimited.com/news.htm.

103. Vladeck summed up the 15–20 percent differential in prepared testimony before the House Committee on Energy and Commerce's Subcomittee on Health, 8 April 2003.

104. Vladeck, interview with the author.

105. Vince Galloro and Laura B. Benko, "Are They Worth It?" modernhealthcare.com, 21 October 2005.

106. Vladeck, interview with the author.

107. Dugan Barr, interview with the author; see also "Open Heart Profiteering?" *CBS Evening News,* 6 May 2003.

108. Sabin Russell, Kevin Fagan, and Carolyn Said, "Unneeded Open-heart Surgeries, and Complex, Expensive Diagnostic Probes," *San Francisco Chronicle,* 2 November 2002. See also "Open Heart Profiteering?"

109. See chapter 3, "For-Profit Hospitals: A Flaw in the Business Model?"

110. Steve Twedt, "The Cost of Courage: How the Tables Turn on Doctors," *Pittsburgh Post-Gazette,* 26 October 2003.

111. Orlikoff, interview with the author.

112. Bill Monnig, interview with author; see also Mark Taylor, "Storm Warning: 'Rainmaker' Doctors Bring in Big Bucks for Hospitals, but When Oversight Goes Awry, They Also Can Bring a Deluge of Legal Problems," *Modern Health Care,* 17 November 2003.

113. Dr. Edward Dench Jr.'s story is based on interviews with the author.

114. For further discussion of the tension between medicine as a business and medicine as a profession see chapter 6, " 'Too Little, Too Late': The Cost of Rationing Care," and chapter 8; "Device Makers, Drugmakers, and the FDA."

115. Powers's story is based on interviews with Steve Twedt, "The Cost of Courage: Centre County Hospital Critics Soon Unwanted," *Pittsburgh Post-Gazette,* 28 October 2003. In interviews with the author, Dench, who also appears in "The Cost of Courage," confirmed her story.

116. Robert Martin, interview with the author.

117. Twedt recounts the details of the Curleys' suit in "The Cost of Courage: Centre County Hospital Critics Soon Unwanted."

118. Twedt, "The Cost of Courage."

119. Dench, interview with the author.

120. Twedt, " 'Disruptive' physician tells her story to AMA," *Pittsburgh Post-Gazette,* 13 June 2004.

121. Twedt, interview with the author. See also "The Cost of Courage," *Pittsburgh Post-Gazette,* 26 October 2003.

122. Twedt, interview with the author.

123. Kieran Walshe and Stephen M. Shortell, "When Things Go Wrong: How Health Care Organizations Deal With Major Failures," *Health Affairs,* May/June 2004.

124. Mary Anderlik, "Introduction to Patient Safety," *Health Law News,* March 2000.

125. Walshe and Shortell, "When Things Go Wrong."

126. Blendon et al., "Confronting Competing Demands to Improve Quality: A Five-Country Hospital Survey." The 2003 survey of executives at larger general and pediatric hospitals was jointly developed by researchers at the Harvard School of Public Health, The Commonwealth Fund, and Harris Interactive.

On the question of competition, 64 percent of U.S. hospital executives reported that they were "very concerned" or "somewhat concerned" about losing market share to other hospitals, with 55 percent revealing that they were "very concerned" that specialty hospitals would skim patients. In the other four countries, less than 17 percent of executives worried about losing market to general hospitals, while less than 7 percent were concerned that specialty treatment centers would siphon off patients.

On the question of reporting medical errors, 40 percent of U.S. hospital executives and 31 percent of their Australian counterparts opposed disclosure—compared to just 15 percent in the U.K., 18 percent in Canada, and 25 percent in New Zealand. At the same time, 88 percent of U.S. hospitals reported that they had a written policy for informing patients and their families of preventable errors—though only 24 percent reported that they thought their hospitals' programs for finding and addressing preventable medical errors were "very effective."

127. Dench, interview with the author.

128. Len M. Nichols, Paul B. Ginsburg, Robert A. Berenson, Jon Christianson, and Robert E. Hurley, "Are Market Forces Strong Enough to Deliver Efficient Health Care Systems? Confidence is Waning," *Health Affairs,* (March/April 2004).

129. Dench, interview with the author.

130. Devers, "The Return of the Medical Arms Race."

131. David Dranove and Richard Lindrooth, "Hospital Consolidation and Costs: Another Look at the Evidence," *Journal of Health Economics* 22, no. 6 (2003).

132. Porter and Teisberg, "Redefining Competition in Health Care."

133. Cory Capps and David Dranove, "Hospital Consolidation and Negotiated PPO Prices," *Health Affairs,* March/April 2004.

134. Sid Abrams, interview with the author. Unless otherwise noted, the quotations that follow are drawn from that interview.

135. Vanessa Fuhrmans, "Attacking Rise in Health Costs, Big Company Meets Resistance," *The Wall Street Journal*, 13 July 2004.

136. Rhonda L. Rundle, "Prosecutor Accuses Hospital of Bribing Doctors," *The Wall Street Journal*, 11 June 2004. The *Journal* cites a Washington think tank, the Center for Studying Health System Change, as the source of information on the increase in hospital costs.

137. Fuhrmans, "Attacking Rise in Health Costs, Big Company Meets Resistance."

138. Chris Rauber, "Sutter Shows Healthy Profit," *San Francisco Business Times*, 30 April 2004.

139. "Sutter Health Announces 2003 Financial Performance," news release, Sutter Health, 30 April 2004.

140. Rauber, "Sutter Shows Healthy Profit."

141. *America's Least and Most Expensive Hospitals*, 18 August 2003. The full 48-page report, which was done by the Institute for Health and Socioeconomic Policy (IHSP), is no longer available online.

142. Fuhrmans, "Attacking Rise in Health Costs, Big Company Meets Resistance."

143. Mahoney, interview with the author.

144. Robinson, *The Corporate Practice of Medicine*, 51.

145. Report of the Council on Medical Service, "Impact of the Health Maintenance Organization Act of 1973," American Medical Association CMS Report 4 - A-04 (June 2004).

146. Sandra Ward, "WellPoint's Winning Ways," *Barron's*, 25 July 2005.

147. Report of the Council on Medical Service, AMA.

148. "Wall Street Comes to Washington."

149. Deborah Weymouth, interview with the author.

150. Abrams, interview with the author.

151. Robinson, *The Corporate Practice of Medicine*, 229.

152. Joseph Schumpeter, *Capitalism, Socialism, and Democracy* (New York: Harper & Row, 1975 [orig. pub. 1942]), 82–85.

153. "The Father of Creative Destruction: Why Joseph Schumpeter Is Suddenly All the Rage in Washington," *Wired*, March 2002. It's worth noting that by 2002, the phrase had become a cliché in Silicon Valley, but in Washington, where not everyone realized that the nineties had ended, it was still alive.

154. Schumpeter himself understood the dangers of such turbulence. As Robert Kuttner points out, while "casual readers (or non-readers) may remember Schumpeter as the prophet of creative destruction . . . the usual cartoon of Schumpeter gets his meaning backwards. Schumpeter's concern was how a market system could endure *despite* its many propensities toward ruinous competition. He was no advocate of creative destruction." (*Everything For Sale*, 26.)

155. See Robinson's description of "unmanaged competition" earlier in this chapter.

156. See chapter 5, "When More Care Is Not Better Care," for further discussion of what medical ethicist Daniel Callahan describes as "therapeutic relentlessness."

In *False Hopes* (56), Callahan takes a skeptical view of 20th century "progress for its own sake." Yet he notes that while medical progress may have had its failures—and its limits—"The idea of medical progress has had an easier time of it than other forms of progress. It has not had to live down nuclear weapons, as physics has had to do; and if the eugenics movements of the late nineteenth and early twentieth centuries scarred the reputation of the biological sciences, more recent genetic medicine has worked hard, and with great success, to overcome that bad memory by putting something scientifically and morally better in its place. Medical progress, moreover, has produced such palpably important gains in human health during the twentieth century that it has only now and then been subject to the fundamental criticism and disillusionment that progress in general had to put up with in the early decades of this century."

157. Here the coalition quotes Dr. David Lawrence, former chairman and CEO of Kaiser Permanente. (See "Building a Better Health Care System, Specifications for Reform," A Report from the National Coalition on Health Care, 2004.) For a fuller discussion of the need to focus on "treating what we do know how to treat" while avoiding "overzealous care," see chapter 5, "When More Care Is Not Better Care."

158. Avorn, *Powerful Medicines,* 364.

159. "The idea, rarely articulated, is that there is no need for anyone to have oversight over what we know or what we prescribe, since with all those competing companies hawking their wares and touting the advantages of each, the practicing physician can just evaluate all the claims and counterclaims in order to decide what are the best drugs to use," Avorn writes. "The marketplace model has a logical corollary: no one has to worry about the impact of our prescribing on the public's health or the public till. Individual physicians, patients and payers, each pursuing their own interests, will take care of all that as well"—a proposition he describes as "naive." (*Powerful Medicines,* 304.)

160. Looking back in October of 2004, *The Wall Street Journal* reported: "The long path to withdrawal of Vioxx began in 2000 when *The New England Journal of Medicine* published the results of a Merck trial called Vigor. It showed that patients taking the drug were four times as likely—0.4% to 0.1%—to have a heart attack or stroke as patients taking naproxen.

"In early 2001, at a meeting of an FDA advisory panel, Merck argued that the difference might reflect the protective effects of naproxen and not danger from its drug. The committee ended up recommending that the issue be noted on Vioxx's label, and members called for follow-up research to clear up the questions."

Steven E. Nissen, a cardiologist at The Cleveland Clinic, attended the meeting and was troubled by the data. Back at the clinic, he discussed his concerns with Eric Topol, chairman of cardiovascular medicine. They decided to take a closer look by examining data from several trials of patients who had taken Vioxx and other painkillers.

They published their findings in the *Journal of the American Medical Association* in August of 2001, saying the "available data raise a cautionary flag about the risk of cardiovascular events" with COX-2 inhibitors. Vioxx, they said, appeared especially risky. The authors called for more studies to look specifically at heart-safety issues, but Merck and other companies didn't start any—at least not publicly.

In 2004 Merck would say that in 2001 it was already conducting the study that would ultimately lead to Vioxx's withdrawal. Nevertheless, the *Journal* reported, "As concerns rose, Merck vigorously defended Vioxx. It attacked the Cleveland Clinic's data as inadequate. One study in which Merck researchers participated suggested that Vioxx was associated with a higher risk of heart attacks." This study appeared in the spring of 2004 in *Circulation,* a journal published by the American Heart Association—"but without the name of a Merck scientist who participated. The company withdrew the employee's name from the list of authors because it disagreed with the study's conclusion." (Barbara Martinez, Anna Wilde Mathews, Joann S. Lublin, and Ron Winslow, "Merck Pulls Vioxx from Market After Link to Heart Problems: Drug's Demise Raises Concerns About Company's Future; Loss of $2.5 Billion in Sales; Patients Are Left in Quandary," *The Wall Street Journal,* 1 October 2004.)

161. Avorn, *Powerful Medicines,* 292–3.

162. Brooke A. Masters and Marc Kaufman, "Painful Withdrawal for Makers of Vioxx," *The Washington Post,* 18 October 2004. Here Dr. Topol also estimates that Vioxx caused 30,000 to 100,000 heart attacks and strokes.

163. Drugmakers generally eschew such head-to-head comparisons, preferring to test their newest products against placebos. And the FDA requires only that they demonstrate that their product is effective and safe—not whether it is safer than or more effective than a less expensive rival. For a fuller discussion see chapter 8, "Device Makers, Drugmakers, and the FDA".

164. See chapter 8, "Device Makers, Drugmakers, and the FDA" for a discussion of physicians' financial ties to the products that they test.

165. Rashi Fein, "Social and Economic Attitudes Shaping American Health Policy," *Milbank Quarterly* 349, (1980); 376–82.

166. Marietta Cauchi, "Health Care Seen as Growth Area for Buyout Firms," Dow Jones Newswires, 30 June 2004.

167. In *Everything For Sale: The Virtues and Limits of Markets,* 129, Robert Kuttner observes that "The epidemic of reorganization [in health care] is driven substantially by entrepreneurs who see profit opportunities in assets temporarily undervalued by markets . . . there are countless instances of hospitals being sold and then resold, acquisitions followed by spin-offs, and huge windfall profits. All of this is 'efficient' only if one believes that everything markets do is efficient by definition. It doesn't necessarily produce the optimal configuration of health facilities, which is a social good beyond the comprehension of markets."

CHAPTER 3

1. Gerard F. Anderson, Peter S. Hussey, Bianca K. Frogner, and Hugh R. Waters, "Health Spending in the United States and the Rest of the Industrialized World," *Health Affairs,* July/August 2005. Percentages reflect health care spending in 2002, the latest Organisation for Economic Co-operation and Development (OECD) figures available in 2005.

2. David M. Cutler, *Your Money or Your Life: Strong Medicine for America's Health Care System* (New York: Oxford University Press, 2004). In 2005 the Centers for Medicare and Medicaid Services estimated that the United States was spending over $6,400 per person.

3. Cynthia Smith, Cathy Cowan, Stephen Heffler, Aaron Catlin the National Health Accounts Team, "National Health Spending in 2004," *Health Affairs,* January/February 2006.

4. Alison Evans Cuellar and Paul J. Gertler, "How the Expansion of Hospitals Has Affected Consumers," *Health Affairs,* January/February 2005. See chapter 4, "Not-for-Profit Hospitals," for a further discussion of hospital errors, economic pressures, and nursing shortages undermine care.

5. Interview with the author.

6. In 2003 the price of hospital services rose by 8 percent; in 2004 hospitals hiked prices by

another 7 percent (Bradley Strunk, et al., "Tracking Health Care Costs" *Health Affairs,* 21 June 2005). It's worth noting that from 2002 to 2004 hospital spending rose not so much because baby boomers were using more services—in 2004, for example, utilization rose by only 2.9 percent—but because prices of those services were climbing as hospitals tried to make up for cuts in Medicare reimbursements and the high cost of caring for the uninsured.

HOSPITAL SPENDING TREND, 1994–2004

	Annual percent change per capita		
Year	Spending on hospital services	Hospital prices	Quantity of services used
1994	3.7	4.0	−0.3
1995	2.8	3.7	−0.8
1996	2.7	1.8	1.0
1997	4.1	1.7	2.3
1998	5.3	1.9	3.3
1999	9.0	2.5	6.3
2000	8.2	3.3	4.7
2001	13.0	3.6	9.0
2002	11.8	5.2	6.2
2003	9.9	8.0	1.7
2004	10.1	7.0	2.9

Note: Estimates differ from past reports because of data revisions by Milliman and the BLS.
Sources: Data on hospital spending are from the Milliman Health Cost Index ($0 deductible) and include both hospital inpatient and outpatient services. Hospital prices are from the Bureau of Labor Statistics (BLS) "all other payers" Producer Price Index (PPI) series for general and surgical hospitals (data accessed 15 April 2005). See Strunk, "Tracking Health Care Costs."

7. Uwe Reinhardt, "Does the Aging of the Population Really Drive the Demand for Health Care?" *Health Affairs,* November/December 2003. See also "The Authors Respond," Letters, *Health Affairs,* January/February 2004, as well as David Shactman, Stuart H. Altman, Efrat Eilat, Kenneth E. Thorpe, and Michael Doonan, "The Outlook for Hospital Spending," *Health Affairs,* November/December 2003. Shactman et al. note the importance of "half-way technologies" in boosting hospital spending: "Most medical breakthroughs in the past fifty years have been 'half-way technologies.' They treat the symptoms of disease at considerable cost, particularly in the hospital. Examples include some of the current technologies used to treat cancer, including chemotherapy." In contrast, "full technologies" either cure or prevent disease.

8. While Reinhardt acknowledges that "the projected increase in the fraction of elderly in the total population from the current 12.7 percent to about 20 percent by 2030 is hardly a trivial matter," when it comes to explaining the rise in health care costs, it is not the central factor. The baby boomers' "propensity to consume," even while still in their 30s and 40s,

counts as a bigger piece of the equation. Indeed, studies reveal that in the nineties, health care outlays by middle-aged boomers (ages 31–50) were growing nearly 2.5 times as fast as spending by seniors (over the age of 65).

The lure of new technology helps explain why boomers consume more, Reinhardt notes, and "blaming Medicare's future economic pressures mainly on demographic factors beyond policymakers' control is an evasion of more important challenges." (For a discussion of "half-way technologies," see chapter 2, "Market-Driven Medicine: The Cost of Competition," and Schactman et al., note 7 above.)

For a fuller discussion of rising hospital costs and how, in the hospital industry, supply drives demand, see chapter 1, "The Road to Corporate Medicine," and chapter 5, "When More Care Is Not Better Care." For a discussion of how technology drives costs, see chapter 8, "Device Makers, Drugmakers, and the FDA."

As the table below shows, payroll increases have slowed but still remain well above wage increases in other industries—as they must if hospitals hope to attract skilled workers. (See Strunk et al., "Tracking Health Care Costs" for a discussion of the table.)

HOSPITAL PAYROLL COSTS, HOURS WORKED, AND UNDERLYING WAGE RATES, 1994–2004

| | Annual percent change per capita | | |
| | Hospitals | | |
Year	Payroll[a]	Total hours worked[b]	Average hourly wage	All industries, average hourly wage
1994	0.9	−1.8	2.8	2.6
1995	2.5	−0.9	3.4	2.8
1996	2.3	−0.5	2.8	3.3
1997	4.0	1.7	2.3	3.9
1998	4.0	1.2	2.8	4.0
1999	2.2	−0.9	3.2	3.6
2000	3.5	0.2	3.3	4.0
2001	8.1	1.9	6.1	3.8
2002	6.6	1.3	5.2	2.9
2003	6.3	2.0	4.2	2.7
2004	6.0	1.2	4.8	2.1

Note: Estimates may differ from past reports because of data revisions by the BLS.

[a]Product of total hours worked and average hourly wage.

[b]Product of total production workers (excludes executives and managers) and average hours per week of production workers.

Source: U.S. Department of Labor, Bureau of Labor Statistics (BLS), National Employment, Hours, and Earnings series for general medical and surgical hospitals (data accessed 15 April 2005).

9. See chapter 5, "When More Care Is Not Better Care," for evidence that while people who live in regions with more hospitals and more specialists receive more health care, more health care does not mean better health—even after adjusting for demographic and environmental factors.

10. "Data Trends, Supply Costs for U.S. Hospitals Show Substantial Three-Year Rise," Solucient: Insight to Better Healthcare, August 2005. See www.solucient.com. The most prosperous hospitals "may make 8% or 10%," observes former Medicare administrator Bruce Vladeck, "not by cunning management, but by being located in a place where the vast majority of their patients are well-insured and hospitals can charge top dollar for their services." (Interview with the author.)

Meanwhile, the majority barely get by on margins of 3 percent to 6 percent. A hospital's income is as fickle as the politicians who vote on Medicare and Medicaid reimbursements, and because it is so difficult to plan ahead, hospitals need a buffer: to be considered "financially healthy, a hospital needs a net margin of 4% to 6%," says Martin Arrick, managing director at Standard & Poor's. (Melanie Evans, "Good News, Bad News; Hospitals' Net Profit Margin Up, Operating Margin Down," *Modern Healthcare,* 1 November 2004.) Meanwhile, even the most successful hospitals typically achieve margins of only 6 percent to 8 percent. (See, for example, Commission to Study Maine's Hospitals, *Report to the Legislature,* February 2005.)

Finally, the way for-profit hospitals report margins can confuse the issue of hospital profits. Typically, for-profits claim margins that are significantly higher than not-for-profits, in part because for-profits generally prefer to report earnings before subtracting interest, taxes, depreciation, and amortization from their bottom line (what accountants call EBITDA.) These earnings will look higher than earnings under generally accepted accounting principles (GAAP), particularly if the hospital is paying interest on a heap of debt or is making significant capital expenditures.

See also: Stewart H. Altman, et al., "Could U.S. Hospitals Go the Way of U.S. Airlines?" *Health Affair,* January/February 2006; "The Second Annual IHSP Hospital 200: Hospitals, Big Pharma, HMOs and the Health Care War Economy," Institute for Health and Socioeconomic Policy, 8 September 2004; "Slowdown in Health-Care Spending Rise May Be Over," Dow Jones Newswires, 2 December 2004.

11. A 2002 report by the Joint Commission on Accreditation of Healthcare Organizations found that a lack of sufficient nursing staff is a factor in about one-quarter of patients' injuries or deaths in hospitals. Another 2002 study of 168 hospitals by the University of Pennsylvania found the risk of dying following surgery rose 7 percent for each patient over four assigned to a nurse. (Kim Norris, "Nurse-to-Patient Ratio Equals Conflict," *Detroit Free Press,* 21 August 2004.)

See also Jack Needleman, PhD, Peter Buerhaus, PhD, RN, Soeren Mattke, MD, MPH, Maureen Stewart, BA, and Katya Zelevinsky, "Nurse-Staffing Levels and the Quality of Care in Hospitals," *The New England Journal of Medicine,* 30 May 2002. In this study, researchers found "an association between the proportion of total hours of nursing care provided by registered nurses or the number of registered-nurse–hours per day and six outcomes among medical patients. These were the length of stay and the rates of urinary tract infections, upper gastrointestinal bleeding, hospital-acquired pneumonia, shock or cardiac arrest, and failure to rescue (the death of a patient with one of five life-threatening complications—pneumonia, shock or cardiac arrest, upper gastrointestinal bleeding, sepsis, or deep venous thrombosis). The evidence was weaker for failure to rescue than for the other five measures. As in other studies, higher levels of staffing by registered nurses were associated with lower rates of failure to rescue among surgical patients, among whom we also found an association between a higher proportion of registered-nurse–hours and lower rates of urinary tract infections."

12. William J. Baumol, "Macroeconomics of Unbalanced Growth," *American Economic Review* 62 (1967): 415–426. As *New Yorker* columnist James Surowiecki points out, Baumol's disease may help explain why government often seems so much less efficient than the private sector: "Some of the most important services that the government provides—education, law enforcement, health care—are the hardest to make more productive. To keep providing the same quality of services [as wages rise, along with the cost of living], government has to get more expensive. People pay more in taxes and don't get more in return, which makes it look as though the public sector, at least compared with the private sector, is inept and bloated. But it could be that the government is merely stuck in inherently low-productivity-growth businesses. It's not inefficient. It's just got a bad case of Baumol's disease." ("What Ails Us," The Talk of the Town, *The New Yorker,* 7 July 2003.)

13. Kenneth R. Wing with Michael S. Jacobs and Patricia C. Kuszler, *The Law and American Health Care* (1998), 6. (Available online only from Seattle University School of Law. For a link to chapter 1, see http://www.law.seattleu.edu/fachome/wing, click on "class assignments," then click on "chapter 1 The Law and American Health Care."

14. Wing, *The Law and American Health Care,* 8. See also Sherwin Nuland's *Doctors: The Biography of Medicine* (reissue, New York: Vintage, 1995). Sherwin Nuland quotes Halsted's 1913 description of how he came to use rubber gloves: "In the winter of 1889 and 1890—I cannot recall the month—the nurse in charge of my operating room complained that the solutions of mercuric chloride produced a dermatitis of her arms and hands. As she was an unusually efficient woman, I gave the matter my consideration and one day in New York requested the Goodyear Rubber Company to make as an experiment two pair of thin rubber gloves with gauntlets. On trial these proved to be so satisfactory that additional gloves were ordered. In the autumn, on my return to town, an assistant who passed the instruments and threaded the needles was also provided with rubber gloves to wear at the operations. At first the operator wore them only when exploratory incisions into joints were made. After a time the assistants became so accustomed to working in gloves that they also wore them as operators and would remark that they seemed to be less expert with bare hands than with the gloved hands."

According to Nuland, "this is very likely the most famous paragraph ever printed in the literature of surgery, not only for its description of the introduction of rubber operating gloves, but also because it is the only instance of the beginning of a researcher's love affair being recorded in a medical journal." On June 4, 1890, Halsted married the "unusually efficient woman," one Caroline Hampton.

15. Much of that money flowed from the now defunct Hill-Burton program, which grew out of legislation passed in 1946. Under the bill, Congress directed the Surgeon General to

evaluate the national need for new hospitals and to approve funding for hospitals applying for construction. By 1976 many in Washington felt that the hospital industry had reached a point of excess capacity, and Hill-Burton was phased out.

16. Paul Starr, *The Social Transformation of American Medicine* (New York: Basic Books, 1982), 334.

17. For a description of how President Johnson made the decision, see chapter 1, "The Road to Corporate Medicine."

18. Although HCA was the first *hospital* chain, seven years earlier, two young attorneys, David A. Jones and Wendell Cherry, formed a nursing home company to make some extra money. They opened their first nursing home in 1962 and later named the company Extendicare. By 1972 it had become the nation's largest chain of nursing homes, and in 1974 it changed its name to Humana. Humana would go on to be the first for-profit hospital company to take over a teaching hospital.

19. Starr, 428, 430.

20. Starr, 430, 431.

21. Maggie Mahar, "Tomorrow's Hospital—For Profit or Not, It Will Be Radically Different," *Barron's,* 10 January 1994.

22. Sheryl Skolnick, interview with the author.

23. Jeff Villwock, interview with the author.

24. Starr, 442.

25. In 2004 for-profits owned 16 percent of the market.

26. "Anger over Salaries of Health Care Execs," *Los Angeles Times,* 14 June 1992.

27. Donna K. H. Walters, "Hospital Maverick Riding High: Profit Quadrupled at National Medical Enterprises during the 1980s," *Los Angeles Times,* 13 May 1991.

28. See chapter 1, "The Road to Corporate Medicine."

29. For a discussion of this decision, see chapter 1, "The Road to Corporate Medicine." For a discussion of the problems with Medicare's pricing and needed reforms, see chapter 4, "Not-For Profit Hospitals: 'No Margin, No Mission'?"

30. Bradford H. Gray, *The Profit Motive and Patient Care: The Changing Accountability of Doctors and Hospitals* (Cambridge: Harvard University Press, 1991), 43. Gray notes that over this span the total number of for-profit hospitals remained more or less constant, indicating that industrywide, hospital owners were moving out of the general care business and into the specialty business.

31. Sonia L. Nazario, "Abiding Suspicion: Allegations of Fraud, Malpractice Still Haunt Operator of Hospitals—National Medical Profit Push Is Alleged to Have Led to Unneeded Treatment—CEO Calls Charges Unfair," *The Wall Street Journal,* 8 January 1993.

32. Nazario, "Abiding Suspicion." Bowen left NME in 1988 and later filed a lawsuit charging that the company hadn't paid what he claimed were millions of dollars in fees due him. The suit was settled out of court.

33. Nazario, "Abiding Suspicion."

34. John David Deaton, testimony before a hearing of the House Subcommittee on Crime and Criminal Justice, Federal Document Clearing House, 19 July 1994; Holcomb B. Noble, "10 Texas Psychiatrists Sue Ex-Patients over Fraud Accusations," *The New York Times,* 24 February 1995; Mark Smith, "Few Doctors Lost Licenses over Scandal/Psychi-

atric Hospitals Accused of Filling Beds 'at Any Cost,' " *Houston Chronicle,* 24 March 1997; Eugene H. Methvin, "Cuckoo's Nest," *National Review,* 15 July 1996.

35. Jim Moriarty, interview with the author.

36. Leon Bing, *A Wrongful Death: One Child's Fatal Encounter with Public Health and Private Greed* (New York: Villard, 1997), 68, 79, 189–90, 191–2.

37. Bing, *A Wrongful Death,* 232.

38. David R. Olmos, "NME Admits Responsibility in Girl's Suicide: The Company's Extraordinary Acknowledgment Is Made in an Out-of-Court Settlement," *Los Angeles Times,* 26 July 1994.

39. Smith, "Few Doctors Lost Licenses over Scandal."

40. Nazario, "Abiding Suspicion."

41. Peter Kerr, "U.S. Raids Hospital Operator," *The New York Times,* 27 Aug 1993.

42. Benjamin Mark Cole, "Corporate 'Doctor' for Health Care Firm; Jeffrey Barbakow Tapped to Remedy What Ails National Medical Enterprises," *Los Angeles Business Journal,* 25 April 1994.

43. Donna K. H. Walters, "Triage Comes First for New CEO of Hospitals: Colleagues Say Jeffrey Barbakow Can Handle What Ails National Medical Enterprises, but Some Wonder if a Sell-off Is One Prescription," *Los Angeles Times,* 13 May 1993.

44. Andrea Adelson describes Barbakow's admiration for Eamer's entrepreneurial achievements in "The Job, Thankless; the Challenge, Huge. Let's Go," *The New York Times,* 31 July 1994.

45. Walters, "Triage Comes First for New CEO of Hospitals."

46. Adelson, "The Job, Thankless."

47. Kerri S. Smith, "FBI Raids Psychiatric Hospital in Over-billing Investigation. Multistate Inquiry into Alleged Scam Focuses on Owner of Louisvilles Centennial Peaks Facility," *Rocky Mountain News,* 27 August 1993.

48. In *The Profit Motive and Patient Care* Bradford H. Gray links this view of a company to the changing view of the corporation following the takeover binge of the eighties. He quotes sociologist Paul Hirsch: "During the past decade, professional managers have been sharply reminded that they are hired agents for the owners of the corporation. Top management and boards of directors of large business firms have experienced a loss of power and autonomy to set the firm's future course. As the corporation itself is increasingly defined as a salable bundle of liquid assets, rather than as a producer of goods and services, top executives' incentives are channeled to accord priority to . . . financial and share price goals, over and above a commitment to the firm's product or products." ("From Ambushes to Golden Parachutes: Corporate Takeovers as an Instance of Cultural Framing and Institutional Integration," *American Journal of Sociology,* January 1986.)

49. In "The Job, Thankless," Andrea Adelson describes how Barbakow responded to the FBI raid.

50. Sonia L. Nazario, "National Medical Case Shows How Lax Some Insurers Are in Fighting Fraud," *The Wall Street Journal,* 8 January 1993.

51. M. Smith, "Few Doctors Lost Licenses over Scandal."

52. "NME Loans to Eamer Revealed Management: Outgoing Exec Received Millions from

National Medical Enterprises at Time of His Departure," *Los Angeles Times,* 29 September 1993.

53. Sandy Lutz, "Hope Springs Eternal," *Modern Healthcare,* 29 April 1996.

54. Ron Shinkman and Bruce Japsen with John Morrissey, "Purchase of OrNda Adds Bulk to No. 2 Chain Tenet: But Some Analysts Question Whether $3.1 Billion Deal Is Good Fit," *Modern Healthcare,* 21 October 1996.

55. David R. Olmos, "Tenet to Buy Rival OrNda for $3.2 Billion: Merged Company Would Be Southland's Biggest Hospital Operator. Analysts' Reaction Is Mixed," *Los Angeles Times,* 18 October 1996; Lisa Eckelbecker, "Tenet-OrNda Combination Could Pack Greater Punch," Worcester (MA) *Sunday Telegram,* 3 November 1996. For a discussion of the fear that free-market competition in the health care industry has turned into a free-for-all, see chapter 2, "Market-Driven Medicine: The Cost of Competition."

56. Sandy Lutz, "Playing the Name Game," *Modern Healthcare,* 6 March 1995.

57. Constance Clarke, "An Unbalanced Portrait of NME's New Chief," Letters, *The New York Times,* 28 August 1994.

58. See James Surowiecki, "The Financial Page: Perk Hogs," *The New Yorker,* 14 June 2004.

59. It is worth noting that a 2001 survey of the nation's 40 most prestigious teaching hospitals done by Clark Consulting revealed that the average CEO earned an average of just $800,000. Another survey of compensation at 57 U.S. academic medical centers, done by New York–based consultancy William M. Mercer, Inc., put the median CEO salary, including bonus, at just $397,500. (See Sarah A. Klein, "CEOs in the Pink Despite Red Ink; Hospital Bosses Pocket Fat Salaries," *Crain's Chicago Business,* 1 September 2003.)

Barbakow, of course, was running a hospital chain rather than a stand-alone hospital. But even compared to other chain operators, his salary was high: two years later, the median cash compensation for a CEO running a hospital system was just $625,000. (Julie Appleby, "Non-profit Hospitals' Top Salaries May Be Due for a Check-up," *USA Today,* 24 September 2004.)

In recent years, CEO salaries at not-for-profit hospitals have begun to raise eyebrows. But even the most generous rarely pay a CEO more than $1.3–$1.5 million. Meanwhile, in 2003, salary and exercised options brought HCA CEO Jack Bovender's total compensation to $3.7 million, Tenet Healthcare's Trevor Fetter took in $6.1 million, Health Management Associates Joseph Vumbacco earned $6.9 million, and Universal Health Services' Alan Miller brought home $16.2 million. (Appleby, "Non-profit Hospitals' Top salaries.")

60. "Tenet CEO Receives Lucrative Boost to Pension Benefits," The Associated Press, 27 August 2002.

61. Clifford Hewitt, interview with the author. See also Don Lee, "Tenet's Aggressive Corporate Culture Fed Crisis, Insiders Say . . ." *Los Angeles Times,* 12 December 2002.

62. "The Top 25 Managers of the Year," *BusinessWeek,* 14 January 2002.

63. Rhonda L. Rundle and Anna Wilde Mathews, "Tenet Reaped Outsize Gains From Flaw in Medicare System," *The Wall Street Journal,* 11 November 2002.

64. Estimates of just how much outlier payments contributed to Tenet's bottom line vary. In 2003 *Barron's* put the number at "25% or more in 2001 and in 2002." (Thomas Donlan, "A Time to Heal," 22 December 2003).

65. Though, as Princeton economist Uwe Reinhardt observes, corporate hospitals have played a role in making the rules so complex. "If the private-sector executives who chafe under the complexity of government regulation wished to discover the culprits behind that complexity, and if they wanted to be brutally honest with themselves, they would look into the mirror first," Reinhardt argues, "look at Congress next, and only then look at the government bureaucrats who administer the laws hatched out by the former two." Corporate lobbyists have insisted that "federal laws respect the idiosyncratic needs of so many diverse constituents." In other words, the rules are virtually incomprehensible in part because so many exceptions have been written into them, in response to "entreaties by individuals and single institutions. . . .

"While, in theory, there is something lovely about this enormous respect for individuals and single institutions," Reinhardt writes, "it does infuse our laws with an administrative complexity that borders on the criminal in this sense: It has the capacity of criminalizing the behavior of perfectly decent citizens who would never break laws that they can actually understand." ("Columbia/HCA: Villain or Victim?" *Health Affairs,* March/April 1998).

66. Jeff Villwock, interview with the author. Because the uninsured do not belong to a formal group, no one negotiates a group discount for them. Meanwhile, everyone else—insurers, Medicare and Medicaid—win steep discounts for their patients. As a result, a hospital's sticker prices become largely irrelevant, says Villwock. "When I'm valuing a hospital, I never look at the undiscounted or 'gross' charges—the amount that a hospital would receive if everyone paid full price. No one cares. You look at the net revenues—the amount that the hospital actually takes in.

"Yet Tenet doubled or tripled its gross charges. Why?" Villwock asks. "There could be only one reason: because they knew this would hike their outlier payments." For more on the high prices paid by the uninsured see chapter 6, " 'Too Little, Too Late': The Cost of Rationing Care."

67. The survey was done by the Institute for Health and Socioeconomic Policy for the California Nurses Association. For the 48-page report, see their website, http://www .calnurses.org/research.

68. Lee, "Tenet's Aggressive Corporate Culture Fed Crisis, Insiders Say."

69. Don Lee, "Tenet Shares Tumble 14% After Downgrade: An Analyst's Report Raises Questions about the Hospital Company's Medicare Reimbursements and Whether It Can Sustain Its Stellar Growth," *Los Angeles Times,* 29 October 2002.

70. Villwock, interview with the author.

71. Tony Ginocchio, interview with the author.

72. Bob Wooten, interview with the author.

73. Steven Hunt, interview with the author.

74. Alex Breitler, "FBI Reviews Doctors' Files: Affidavit Suggests Unnecessary Heart Procedures Performed," *Redding Record Searchlight (CA),* 1 November 2002. Some reformers suggest that if consumers are in the driver's seat, and doing their homework, they can find the best value for their health care dollar. In truth, evaluating the quality of health care is an extraordinarily complicated process, and at this point in time the online report cards that consumers rely on do not begin to reflect that complexity. Some would say that imperfect

information is better than no information. But a little knowledge can be a dangerous thing. For a fuller discussion of the hazards of relying on report cards for hospitals and doctors, see chapter 5, "When More Care Is Not Better Care."

75. Mark A. Hall, "Arrow on Trust," in *Uncertain Times: Kenneth Arrow and the Changing Economics of Health Care,* Peter J. Hammer, Deborah Haas-Wilson, Mark A. Peterson, and William M. Sage, eds., (Durham: Duke University Press, 2003), 262, 263. To buttress the argument, Hall cites Howard Brody, "The Doctor as Therapeutic Agent: A Placebo Effect Research Agenda" in *The Placebo Effect: An Interdisciplinary Exploration,* Anne Harrington, ed., (Cambridge: Harvard University Press, 1997); J. V. Basmajian, "Debonafide Effects vs. Placebo Effects," Proceedings of the Royal College of Physicians, Edinburgh 1999; and Edmund D. Pellegrino and David C. Thomasma, *The Virtues in Medical Practice* (New York: Oxford University Press, 1993).

76. Others would argue that taking control is more therapeutic because it reduces stress and enhances the immune response. In *The Practice of Autonomy: Patients, Doctors, and Medical Decisions* (New York: Oxford University Press, 1998), 20, Carl E. Schneider quotes Anne Hawkins talking about "the recent discovery, popularized by media channels, . . . that passive, compliant patients fare less well in surviving serious illness than their aggressive and non-compliant counterparts" (Anne Hunsaker Hawkins, *Reconstructing Illness: Studies in Pathography* [West Lafayette, IN: Purdue University Press, 1993], 65). "Pathography" is Hawkins's term for patient memoirs.

For fuller discussion of the issue of trust and patient autonomy see chapter 1, "The Road to Corporate Medicine."

77. For further discussion of research showing a high rate of unnecessary cardiac procedures in the United States, see chapter 2, "Market-Driven Medicine: The Cost of Competition," and chapter 5, "When More Care Is Not Better Care."

78. Moriarty, interview with the author.

79. See also Dr. Thomas Riles, chief of surgery at NYU Medical Center, commenting on unnecessary cardiac procedures in chapter 2, "Market-Driven Medicine: The Cost of Competition." In "No More Knife Guys," *AARP, The Magazine* (November and December 2004), Kelly Griffin quotes both Graboys and Cleveland Clinic cardiologist Steven Nissen, who describes the "fireman mentality" among too many of his colleagues. And, as Griffin points out, "the numbers support his concern." The U.S. is home to only 5 percent of the world's population but performs almost half of the invasive coronary procedures (angioplasties and bypass surgeries) worldwide. "Angioplasty is generally a last resort for high-risk patients in Canada and Europe, but in the U.S. it's frequently step one," says Dr. William Boden, professor of medicine at the University of Connecticut School of Medicine. "Neither bypass (in which a healthy blood vessel is grafted around the blockage) nor angioplasty has been shown to prevent heart attacks," Griffin explains. "Bypass surgery makes it less likely that a heart attack will prove fatal—but only in patients with the most severe disease (for example, those with a blockage in the left main coronary artery, which supplies a large portion of the heart with blood). For patients with less-severe disease, bypass has never been found to enhance survival compared with non-surgical treatments." As for angioplasty, William Boden says, "There are no studies—none, zero—to date that have demonstrated that it improves survival compared to medication."

Proponents of the less-is-more philosophy don't dispute that some high-risk patients benefit from more aggressive treatment. The problem, they say, is that this approach is also used on low-risk patients who would do very well with nonsurgical therapies.

80. Thomas Riles, Interview with the author. See Riles's comments on unnecessary procedures in chapter 2, "The Cost of Competition: An Overview."

81. Hunt, interview with the author.

82. Sabin Russell, Kevin Fagan, and Carolyn Said, "Unneeded Open-Heart Surgeries and Complex Expensive Diagnostic Probes," *San Francisco Chronicle,* 2 November 2002.

83. Skolnick, interview with the author. Unless otherwise indicated, the stories that follow are based on that interview.

84. Melissa Lee and John Metaxas, "When Companies Behave Badly to Analysts," CNBC, 29 April 2004. An HMA spokesman claimed that the company had been waiting to hear from Skolnick. For three years? In an interview with the author, Skolnick was definite: "Their head of investor relations lied."

85. In January of 2003 Fleet Boston, which had been Robertson Stephens's corporate parent, paid $33 million to settle charges that its Robertson Stephens unit had issued biased research and allocated "hot" IPOs (initial public offerings) to certain clients in exchange for commissions that ran 4,000 percent higher than commissions customarily paid by the firm's clients. ("SEC Sues Robertson Stephens Inc. for Profit Sharing in Connection with 'Hot' IPOs Firm, Former Research Analyst Separately Charged in Connection with Misleading Research Reports; Firm to Pay Total of $33 Million To Settle All Charges," press release, Securities and Exchange Commission, 9 January 2003.)

86. Melissa Davis, "Insider Sales Cloud the Tenet Tale," The Street.com, 24 November 2002. Alan Abelson, "Winner Took All," *Barron's,* 11 November 2002. "In Mackey's defense," Davis points out, "Weakley has said his questions took on a specific nature only after he sold his shares and that he never discussed the matter with Mackey personally. Instead, Weakley said he broached the subject roughly a week after Mackey's sale with then-CFO Dennis—one of only two insiders who actually bought Tenet stock (in non-option transactions) that year."

87. See "Et Tu, Barbakow?" Recent Commentaries, Tenet Shareholder Committee, 30 June, 2004.

88. In "Top Lawyer Bailed Before Tenet Tanked," TheStreet.Com, 14 August 2003, Melissa Davis points out that in 2000, Tenet's executives sold only about $3 of stock for every $1 they spent buying the company's shares. The next year, they unloaded $100 of stock for every $1 they purchased. In 2002, when Barbakow executed his big sale, they cashed in $275 worth of shares for every dollar that they invested.

TENET HEALTHCARE: INSIDER SALES IN 2002

Date	Insider	Shares Sold	Profit
Jan. 9	Director Sanford Cloud	2,500	$109,000
Jan. 11	Exec V.P. Raymond Mathiasen	100,000	4.82 million

Date	Insider	Shares Sold	Profit
Jan. 14	Director		
	Michael Focht	125,000	5.38 million
Jan. 15	COO		
	Thomas Mackey	151,666	6.75 million
Jan. 16	Chairman		
	Jeffrey Barbakow	2,000,000	111 million
April 4	Director		
	Bernice Bratter	5,000	200,100
April 19	Director		
	Van Honeycutt	5,000	178,100
Aug. 16	Honeycutt	7,500	168,150
Aug. 19	Cloud	10,000	360,000
Oct. 4	Director		
	Robert Kerrey	30,000	638,400
Oct. 4	Mackey	277,500	9.92 million
Oct. 8	Kerrey	18,000	213,100
Oct. 16	Director		
	Maurice DeWald	7,500	275,000

Source: Melissa Davis, "Insider Sales Cloud the Tenet Tale."

89. Donlan, "A Time to Heal." The remark was made by Trevor Fetter, the former Tenet CFO who would replace Barbakow.

90. Tenet Shareholder Committee, "Tenet Healthcare: A Roller Coaster Careening Down a Broken Track," 15 July 2003.

91. In "Tenet Healthcare: A Roller Coaster Careening Down a Broken Track," the shareholders attribute the numbers on Redding's profits to a *Los Angeles Times* article (1 November 2002), "Tenet's Stock Hammered on News of Probe," where Don Lee and Ronald W. White report that the Redding Medical Center "generated a net profit margin of 38%—and pretax net income of $94 million—in the year ended June 30 [2002], according to unaudited reports filed with the state."

92. Davis, "Insider Sales Cloud the Tenet Tale."

93. In July of 2003, both the Tenet Shareholder Committee and Senator Charles Grassley, chairman of the Senate Finance Committee, called on Tenet to make the report public. But a month later, when the $54 million settlement was finalized, the Mercer report still had not surfaced. See letter written by Senator Charles Grassley, addressed to Edward Kangas, Chairman, Tenet Healthcare, 31 October 2003, and reprinted in a Senate Finance Committee press release dated 3 November 2003, "Grassley Urges Tenet to Provide More Documents to the Committee."

94. And indeed, investor sentiment began to improve. At the end of 2003, in a story titled "A Time to Heal," *Barron's* predicted that Tenet appeared to be on the road to recovery. "The stock has a firm floor, too," the story observed, noting that once a health care company

had paid its fines, it could look forward to rising from the ashes of its past crimes. After all, "Tenet stock quintupled after the company recovered from its previous debacle (in the early 90s, when Barbakow rode to the rescue, changing NME's name to Tenet), and [investors] would love to see it happen again." What the story didn't mention is that NME was reincarnated as Tenet and little had changed in the corporate culture.

95. Moriarty, interview with the author.

96. Sam Stanton and Danny Walsh, "Redding's Doctors Won't Be Changed," *The Sacramento Bee,* 10 November 2005.

97. Lisa Rapaport, "Tenet to Pay $395 Million to Settle Heart Surgery Suits," *The Sacramento Bee,* 21 December 2004.

98. Gary Taylor, an analyst at Banc of America Securities, was one of a number of observers who had urged Tenet to look outside the company for a new CEO. "People want to see new management, and I think they will be cynical of the board's desire to make wholesale changes if they're not going to bring in a completely new management team." (Victoria Colliver, "SEC Demands Tenet Records as Investigation Heats Up," *San Francisco Chronicle,* 10 July 2003.)

99. Vince Galloro, "Strong Tenets: For the Acting CEO at No. 2 Hospital Chain, Three R's Could Be Relationships, Risk-taking and Responsibility," *Modern Healthcare,* 2 June 2003.

100. In 2003 Tenet's board agreed to pay Fetter a salary of $848,539, a bonus of $262,500, and additional compensation totaling $1.28 million—mostly a relocation reimbursement. In addition, he received $3.73 million in restricted stock and options to buy 350,000 shares at $14.98 a share by September 15, 2013.

101. Barbakow filed the lawsuit on June 4, 2004. "Et Tu, Barbakow?"

102. Chris Knap, "CEO of San Diego Hospital Indicted for Allegedly Paying Kickbacks," *The Orange County Register,* 7 June 2003; Rhonda L. Rundle, "Prosecutor Accuses Hospital of Bribing Doctors," *The Wall Street Journal,* 11 June 2004.

103. "Tenet Healthcare Corporation," Hoover's Company In-depth Records, 28 September 2005; Vince Galloro, "Feds Subpoena Iasis; A Whistle-blower Lawsuit May Be Behind Investigation," *Modern Healthcare,* 26 September 2005.

104. Gilbert M. Gaul, "Bad Practices Net Hospitals More Money; High Quality Often Loses Out in the 40-Year-Old Program," *The Washington Post,* 24 July 2005.

105. Melissa Davis, "Florida Heart Surgery Law Bugs Tenet Healthcare," TheStreet.com, 6 July 2004. Davis reported that "By March of 2001—years after the problem erupted—special consultants were clearly suggesting one of the most expensive remedies possible. 'The problem is persisting because the old, wet materials in the roof were never removed when the roof was repaired,' wrote C. D. Mampe, a DM Associates consultant with more than three decades of experience. 'Since there is little or no air movement in the roof structure, this area will never dry out, and the fungus gnat problem will persist. . . . The ultimate solution is to open up the roof, remove all wet organic materials and replace the roof.'

"Just one month later, the long-time exterminators who hired the consultant found themselves terminated from the job. But a replacement firm sounded similarly troubled when it took over.

" 'There are several areas of high priority such as the intensive care and operating rooms,' Michael Brimanson of Bug Stoppers wrote in October of 2001. 'We feel these areas should be treated as a zero-tolerance area for insects. . . . The facility will require a considerable amount of attention and dedication.'

"Bug Stoppers promised to 'meet or exceed' the hospital's requirements for $5,900 per month.

"But Sandra Perdew, the CFO of yet another firm, was still listing serious deficiencies the following year. She mentioned fly-infested mops and slime in the surgical trash room. She said the entire sterile processing room was 'in poor condition and certainly in need of cleaning and maintenance.' She noted that the the general surgery unit had holes in the wall and cups of Pepsi on the trash can. She also mentioned concerns about the decontamination room and the nurses' lounge.

" 'The maintenance and structural issues (in the area) that we went over . . . remain the same,' she wrote in February of 2002. 'It is imperative that we work together to get this problem under control.' "

106. Melissa Davis, "Some Accuse Tenet of Skimping on Care," TheStreet.com, 28 April 2003.
107. Gaul, "Bad Practices Net Hospitals More Money."
108. Melissa Davis, "Critics See Long Road Ahead," TheStreet.com, 14 October 2005.
109. Letter from Senator Charles Grassley to Trevor Fetter, acting chief executive officer and president, Tenet Healthcare Corporation, September 5, 2003. See www.tenetshareholder committee.org.
110. Moriarty, interview with the author.
111. In a seminal 2001 study of corporate accounting during the bull market, The Jerome Levy Forecasting Center, a highly respected, nonpartisan, independently funded consulting firm revealed that corporations systematically defrauded investors by overstating their earnings throughout the bull market of the 1980s and 1990s. The report points out that both the press and the public were reluctant to face the fact that the problem was systemic, preferring to believe that just a few bad apples were corrupting the system:

"Over the past ten years the financial media have spotlighted case after case of earnings misrepresentations. . . . *[but] the focus of public concern remained on finding the bad apples; little attention was paid to the quality of the entire bushel,*" the study's authors wrote. "*Just how widespread and serious was the overstatement of aggregate corporate profits?*" they asked. "*The answer is startling. The evidence indicates that corporate operating earnings for the S&P 500 have been significantly exaggerated for nearly two decades—by about 10 percent or more early in this period and by over 20 percent in recent years. These figures are conservative—the magnitude of the overstatement may be considerably larger.*" (Walter M. Cadette, David A. Levy, and Srinivas Thiruvadanthai, "Two Decades of Overstated Corporate Earnings: The Surprisingly Large Exaggeration of Aggregate Profits," The Jerome Levy Forecasting Center, 2001.)

It was easier to believe that a few corrupt CEOs were puffing up earnings statements. To admit that the entire system had been gamed—and not just in the late nineties, but throughout much of the bull market—meant questioning the ideology of the times. That ideology was grounded in "the efficient market hypothesis"—the firm, deluded belief that markets are always right. But if the market was operating on tainted information, just how efficient could it be?

Nevertheless, throughout the final two decades of the 20th century, the efficient market hypothesis has led to a naive faith in "the corporate model," a model which included the notion that corporations should "manage" their earnings—a euphemism for cooking their books in a way that would allow them to meet Wall Street's soaring expectations, quarter after quarter, year after year. Indeed, companies like GE boasted of smoothing their earnings—even though this meant obscuring the underlying reality of the business. In fact, the corporate model was a frictionless construct created by economists living at some remove from the messy reality of running a business. (The efficient market hypothesis also sprang from the groves of academe.)

Meanwhile, belief in the corporate model became embedded in corporate law: rather than putting limits on what a corporation could do, the law provided the loopholes needed to "manage earnings." This is why, contrary to the conventional wisdom, most of the financial legerdemain of the nineties, including Enron's errant bookkeeping, was, in fact, perfectly legal. For a full discussion of both corporate fraud and the Levy report, see Maggie Mahar, *Bull! A History of the Boom and Bust, 1982–2004,* (New York: HarperCollins, 2004), chapter 16.

112. Tenet was the nation's second-largest chain while HealthSouth was the largest owner of rehab hospitals and outpatient surgical centers. When these facilities are included in the pool with acute-care hospitals, HealthSouth was number 3 in the industry.

113. See Paul Davies, "Leadership (A Special Report)—Patient Growth: A Hospital Chain Discovers the Benefits of a Go-Slow Approach," *The Wall Street Journal,* 25 October 2004. Unlike many hospital companies, Universal Health Services is not financed by hot money. More than half of its shares are owned by four institutional investors. As a result, the company has not had to worry about currying favor on Wall Street by achieving short-term goals. But while the company has avoided fraud, it has not succeeded in finding a way to harness the profit motive to deliver both hospital services and profits for investors. At the beginning of 2005, rising labor costs, bad debt, and competition from physician-owned specialty hospitals were squeezing its profit margins even while the company hiked prices (Stock Report: Universal Health Services, Standard & Poor's, 15 January 2005). Citing pressure on already lower-than average profit margins, S&P recommended selling the stock. "They don't seem able to stabilize the deterioration in their business or predict it," Skolnick observed early in 2005 (interview with the author.)

114. In an interview with the author, a California physician repeated the CEO's comment. For further discussion of how the line between for-profits and not-for-profits has blurred, and questions about the latter's tax-exempt status, see chapter 4, "Not-for Profit Hospitals: 'No Margin, No Mission'?"

115 Carl Ginsburg, "The Patient as Profit Center: Hospital Inc. Comes to Town," *The Nation,* 18 November 1996.

116. David S. Hilzenrath, "Hospital Chain Adopts a Bigger-Is-Better Strategy," *The Washington Post,* 7 March 1994.

117. Mahar, "Tomorrow's Hospital."

118. Martin Gottlieb and Kurt Eichenwald, "A Hospital Chain's Brass Knuckles and the Backlash," *The New York Times,* 17 May 1997.

119. In "A Hospital Chain's Brass Knuckles . . ." Gottlieb and Eichenwald report that company records showed "that at least 90 percent of 1995 bonuses were based on financial perfor-

mance. . . . Ten percent of the bonus was discretionary. But the company suggested that this be based on revenue-producing yardsticks like 'growth in admissions and surgery cases.' " Of course, not-for-profit hospitals also hand out bonuses, but they tend to be much smaller, the *Times* reported, citing the Hay Group, a management consulting firm that specializes in human resources, and far more likely to reward other nonfinancial achievements "like low death rates and programs to benefit local communities."

120. Kris Hundley, "As Columbia/HCA Grows . . ." *St. Petersburg Times;* Hilzenrath, "Hospital Chain Adopts a Bigger-Is-Better Strategy"; Ginsburg, "The Patient as Profit Center."

121. Darren Puscas, report on HCA, Polaris Institute. The report cites *Corporate Crime Reporter,* 13 October 1997.

122. Gottlieb and Eichenwald, "A Hospital Chain's Brass Knuckles and the Backlash."

123. Hilzenrath, "Hospital Chain Adopts a Bigger-Is-Better Strategy."

124. See chapter 5, "When More Care Is Not Better Care," on how excess capacity can lead to unnecessary care. That said, when a hospital company in Nashville decides to shutter a hospital in Florida, the corporate priorities that drive the decision may or may not happen to coincide with the needs of the community in Florida. Often, money-losing hospitals provide a vital community service, serving a population that otherwise might not receive adequate care.

125. Ginsburg, "The Patient as Profit Center."

126. Hewitt, interview with the author.

127. "Doctoring the Books," *The NewsHour with Jim Lehrer,* PBS, 31 July 1997.

128. "Part of the company's strategy was to offer doctors special opportunities to invest in Columbia subsidiaries in their markets, sometimes helping arrange low-interest loans to cover the investments. In theory, the arrangement would give doctors an incentive to help cut costs. But analysts and rivals say that if doctors have a stake in the profitability of Columbia hospitals, they are more likely to send patients Columbia's way—and less likely to base their referrals on issues of price and quality." (Hilzenrath, "Hospital Chain Adopts a Bigger-Is-Better Strategy.") Meanwhile, federal law prohibits health care providers from steering Medicare and Medicaid patients to certain hospitals in return for a financial inducement. Columbia claimed that it was violating no laws—though its practices had not been tested in court. And in filings with the SEC, the company itself warned that its partnerships "may not be in strict compliance with all such conditions . . ." (Hilzenrath).

It was not only the for-profit industry's critics, but some of its founders who criticized the whole idea of giving doctors financial incentives to drum up business, arguing that this distorted the doctor-patient relationship. "I recall vividly a speech delivered in the mid-1980s by then HCA chairman Don McNaughton in which he announced as company policy that no physician affiliated with HCA should hold an equity position in the company, so that the physician would be in appearance as well as in fact the faithful agent strictly of the patient," writes Uwe Reinhardt. "Presumably, the late Thomas Frist Sr. and Thomas Frist Jr., both founders of HCA, stood firmly behind this policy at the time. In fact, it is not at all surprising that among Thomas Frist Jr.'s first announcements upon retaking the reins of Columbia/HCA last year was the severance of any financial ties between the firm and its affiliated physicians." ("Columbia/HCA: Victim or Villain?")

129. Thomas Frist Jr.'s "style" has been described as "that of a country-gentleman." See for example, Christina Sponselli, "Scott Is Out; Frist Is In: Where Does Columbia/HCA Go from Here?" Nurseweek.com, 10 September 1997.

130. "Until early this year, he attended Mr. Scott's pivotal management-committee meetings at 7 a.m. Mondays, and sat in on 8:30 a.m. weekly 'development' meetings that focused on acquisitions and partnerships," the *Journal* pointed out. (Lucette Lagnado, Eva M. Rodriguez, and Greg Jaffe, "What He Knew: How 'Out of the Loop' Was Dr. Frist During Columbia's Expansion?—Hospital Giant's New CEO Had a Top Title but Says He Deferred to Mr. Scott—Making the 7 A.M. Meetings," 4 September 1997.

131. "Can Dr. Frist Cure This Patient?" *Business Week,* 17 November 1997.

132. In the past, HCA had agreed to pay a $475,000 settlement with the state of Texas involving allegations that its psychiatric hospitals engaged in questionable billing, admitting, and marketing practices, and improperly paid physicians and others for patient referrals, according to the state attorney general's office. HCA admitted to no wrongdoing.

133. Lagnado, Rodriguez, and Jaffe, "What He Knew: How 'Out of the Loop' Was Dr. Frist During Columbia's Expansion?"

134. See Alderson's attorneys' website: www.phillipsandcohen.com/CM/Custom/TOC Whistleblowerrewardsstories.asp.

135. Skolnick, interview with the author.

136. Lagnado, Rodriguez, and Jaffe, "What He Knew: How 'Out of the Loop' Was Dr. Frist During Columbia's Expansion?"

137. To be fair, although he was a heart transplant surgeon before joining Congress, Senator Frist has never played a role in running HCA—though in a regrettable moment, he once compared conversations with his father about the family company to "benign versions of the Godfather and Michael Corleone," as the two discussed how medical power had shifted from housecall doctors to corporate administrators. (Michael Kranish, "First Responder Meet President Bush's Medicine Man," *The Boston Globe,* 29 October 2002.) And because he held so much HCA stock, some would accuse Senator Frist of conflict of interest—particularly when he led a fight for caps on malpractice awards. In April of 2004, The Foundation for Taxpayer & Consumer Rights reported that "Majority Leader Frist's Senate financial disclosures reveal that he, and his wife and children, hold millions of dollars in HCA stock. Documents filed with the Senate Office of Public Records at the end of the year 2000 indicate that HCA stock worth at least $10,150,000, and up to $30,350,000 or more, was transferred into Frist family blind trusts in December, 2000. The trust agreements note that the assets initially contributed by [Frist] to this Trust are concentrated in the stock of HCA, the Healthcare Company . . . Recent reports show that [Senator Frist's brother] Thomas F. Frist Jr. holds over 5.5 million shares of HCA stock, worth approximately $240 million. He is HCA's largest non-institutional shareholder. . . . Because Senator Frist has refused to recognize his conflict, it is up to the Senate Select Committee on Ethics to require he step aside for pending votes on liability caps, and specifically prohibit advocacy by the Senator for any further legislation which would directly benefit his family's hospital chain and insurance company and increase his personal fortune." ("Senate Ethics Committee Should Ban Frist from Hospital Liability Debate, Says Ethics Complaint Filed Today: Conflict of Interest Requires Majority Leader's Im-

mediate Recusal," press release, The Foundation for Taxpayer & Consumer Rights, 6 April 2004.)

138. Bill Lewis, "HCA Execs Faced Attorney's Query," Tennessean.com, 19 December 2002.

139. In an effort to distance itself from its past, Columbia/HCA first changed its name, in May of 2000, to The HealthCare Company, and later, to HCA. (Two midlevel HCA executives, Robert Whiteside of Brentwood, HCA's former director of reimbursement, and Jay Jarrell, former chief executive officer of HCA's Southwest Florida division, were sentenced to prison terms in 1999. But in 2002 the 11th U.S. District Court of Appeals overturned the conviction, saying that the government had failed to make its case. (Graham Brink, "Court Clears Ex-HCA Executives," *St. Petersburg Times,* 26 March 2002.)

140. David D. Kirkpatrick, "Senate Leader Explains His Sale of a Stock That Then Plummeted," *The New York Times,* 22 September 2005.

141. Greg Farrell, "SEC Subpoenas Frist's documents in Investigation of Health Stock Sale," *USA Today,* 14 October 2005.

142. The hospital administrators' annual meeting took place at the Disney theme park. (Andrew Parker, "HealthSouth to Pay $325m," *Financial Times* (FT.Com), 3 January 2005.)

143. John Helyar, "The Insatiable King Richard," *Fortune,* 7 July 2003.

144. Helyar, "The Insatiable King Richard."

145. Dan Morse, Chad Terhune, and Ann Carms, "Clean Sweep: HealthSouth's Scrushy Is Acquitted," *The Wall Street Journal,* 29 June 2005.

146. For example, in *Uncertain Times: Kenneth Arrow and the Changing Economics of Health Care,* Jack Needleman cites a string of studies which show that "for-profits charges are higher and they are more likely to 'upcode' [i.e., pad] Medicare claims, [though] nonprofits in heavily for-profit markets are nearly as likely to do so"—suggesting that in markets where the two compete, for-profits have established norms that not-for-profits emulate in order to compete. (In his essay, "The Role of Nonprofits," Needleman points to research by F. A. Sloan, G. A. Picone, D. H. Taylor, and S. Y. Chou, "Hospital Ownership and Cost and Quality of Care: Is There a Dime's Worth of Difference?" *Journal of Health Economics,* January 2001; Bradford Gray, *The Profit Motive and Patient Care: The Changing Accountability of Doctors and Hospitals;* S. Hall and T. G. McGuire, "Ownership and Performance: The Case of Outpatient Mental Health Clinics," *Medical Care,* December 1987; E. Silverman and J. Skinner, "Are For-Profits Hospitals Really Different? Medical Upcoding and Market Structure," Cambridge, Massachusetts, National Bureau of Economic Research, February 2001.)

147. The survey of the nation's 100 most expensive hospitals, commissioned by the California Nurses Association, showed that from 2000 to 2001, 64 of the top 100 were located in these three states. The study, which was done by the Institute for Health and Socioeconomic Policy, also revealed that nationwide, the average hospital marked up its sticker prices (before discounts to insurers) by 206 percent. ("America's Least and Most Expensive Hospitals: A New Study Links High Hospital Prices to Higher Profits," press release, California Nurses Association, 11 June 2003.) For the full study see http://www.calnurses .org.

148. Cuellar and Gertler, "How the Expansion of Hospital Systems Has Affected Consumers." Significantly, when not-for-profits banded together they followed the same

pattern—though in 2000, only 51 percent of not-for-profits belonged to a system, compared to 77 percent of investor-owned hospitals. See also J. White, R. E. Hurley, and B. C. Strunk, "Getting Along or Going Along? Health Plan-Provider Contract Showdowns Subside," Issue Brief no. 74, Center for Health System Change, January 2004.

In "Strategic Hospital Alliances: Impact on Financial Performance," Jan P. Clement, Michael J. McCue, et al. also found that when acute care hospitals formed alliances, "their revenues increase but their costs do not decrease. . . . they are not more effective at cost control." *(Health Affairs,* November/December 1997.)

For further discussion of the effect of consolidation on both hospital and insurance prices, see chapter 2, "Market-Driven Medicine: The Cost of Competition."

149. Cuellar and Gertler, "How the Expansion of Hospital Systems Has Affected Consumers." At present, most other research leads to the same conclusion: it is very difficult to say whether, as a group, for-profit hospitals offer better or worse care. (See Jack Needleman, "The Role of Nonprofits in Health Care," in *Kenneth Arrow and the Changing Economics of Health Care,* 249–250, for references to other research attempting to compare the quality of nonprofits and for-profits.)

Pointing to disasters like Redding, detractors nevertheless suggest that when the quest for profits becomes paramount, investor-owned hospitals put patients second. But the ambiguities of medical care continue to make definitions of "quality" elusive. Until researchers are able to accumulate more hard evidence on what practices lead to the best outcomes—and what exactly counts as a "good outcome"—the jury remains out as to whether not-for-profits, as a group, offer better care. What is far easier to document is that investor-owned hospitals are more expensive. See Needleman, 250.

For a fuller discussion of why the ambiguity of medicine makes it so difficult to measure quality, and the progress that nonetheless is being made in refining "outcomes research," see chapter 5, "When More Care Is Not Better Care," and chapter 7, "Doing Less and Doing It Right: Is Pay for Performance the Answer?"

150. At the time, Columbia/HCA was supposedly one of the most efficient chains in the country. Why, then, were its prices so high? Because, despite Rick Scott's best efforts, in 1995 Columbia was spending only 1.5 percent less than its rivals when providing hospital services. William O. Cleverly, head of the Ohio State research center that analyzed the data, sums up the findings: "Columbia has much higher prices and slightly lower costs. The reason they make more money, the majority of it, is related to prices, not cost." (Gottlieb and Eichenwald, "A Hospital Chain's Brass Knuckles and the Backlash.") The analysis showed that before discounts, HCA was charging 35 percent more than its competitors.

In "Columbia/HCA: Villain or Victim?" *(Health Affairs,* March/April 1998), Uwe Reinhardt also points to HCA's remarkably low occupancy rates as evidence that the company returned profits to its investors not by tightening and strengthening operations, but by boosting prices: "In 1995 the company's median occupancy rate was only 42 percent," Reinhardt observes, which means that half of the company's hospitals had an occupancy rate even lower than that. That occupancy rate is far below the ratio of close to 60 percent for the hospital sector as a whole.

"If Columbia/HCA did contribute to the consolidation of the hospital sector, it would have done so mainly by frightening other hospitals into preemptive mergers, rather than through consolidation in its own ranks," Reinhardt continues.

"That in 1995 Columbia/HCA achieved a median profit margin of 9.6 percent on its hospitals, in spite of their low occupancy rates may seem a miracle, were it not for two factors that boosted these margins. First, there is a difference between a company's operating costs and the prices it charges its customers. That distinction is frequently overlooked by commentators who have imputed to Columbia/HCA a genius for lowering its operating costs. Low operating costs translate themselves into low prices only when customers bestir themselves to harvest these economies. But even in markets with many price-sensitive payers—notably in California—hospitals still can act like airlines, namely, as profit-maximizing price discriminators who charge different customers different prices for the same service and whose profit margins per service vary strictly with payers' ability to offer the hospital countervailing market power. Although Columbia/HCA undoubtedly gave some vigilant purchasers steeply discounted prices, I am not aware of any study that showed Columbia/HCA hospitals to be uniformly the low-price provider of health care overall (that is, for all customers) in the local markets in which it operated."

151. Skolnick, interview with the author.
152. James Robinson, interview with the author.
153. Gray, *The Profit Motive and Patient Care,* 49–52, 22–23.
154. Skolnick, interview with the author.
155. Gray, interview with the author.
156. "Eventually the government realized what was happening," says Gray. "They saw it first with nursing homes: owners would keep them for a certain number of years, until the depreciation and interest costs had declined, then sell them off." In other words, reimbursements for interest and depreciation were rich enough to become the raison d'être for owning a facility. (Gray, interview with the author.) See also *The Profit Motive and Patient Care,* 33.
157. Gray, *The Profit Motive and Patient Care,* 33.
158. *1985 Directory of the Federation of American Hospitals* (Little Rock: Federation of America Hospitals, 1984) and *American Hospital Association, Hospital Statistics* (Chicago: American Hospital Association, 1985).
159. Rosemary Stevens, *In Sickness and Wealth: American Hospitals in the Twentieth Century* (New York: Basic Books, 1989), 337.
160. Scrushy made his mark building up a respiratory therapy unit at a hospital where Lifemark had contracted to run the unit. After Lifemark was acquired in 1983, Scrushy led four colleagues out the door to start a chain of outpatient clinics based in Birmingham. (Helyar, "The Insatiable King Richard.")
161. Gray, *The Profit Motive and Patient Care,* 33.
162. Gray, *The Profit Motive and Patient Care,* 36. Even in the 1980s, the average hospital's profit margin stood at only 2 percent.
163. Gray, *The Profit Motive and Patient Care,* 40.
164. Gray, *The Profit Motive and Patient Care,* 39.
165. Gray, *The Profit Motive and Patient Care,* 37.

166. Gail Garfinkel Weiss, "How to 'Fire' a Patient: When You Dismiss a Patient, Choose Your Words Carefully. Here's What to Say," Clip and Copy, *Medical Economics,* 5 December 2003.

167. The study on the number of uninsured, released in December of 2004, was led by researchers at the University of Minnesota's School of Public Health who analyzed data from the federal Centers for Disease Control and Prevention. See "Hospital Uncompensated Care Up Again in '03," AHANews.com, 29 November 2004; "Study: 20M U.S. Workers Uninsured," CBSNews.com, 23 December 2004.

168. Robinson, interview with the author.

169. James C. Robinson, "Bond Market Skepticism and Stock Market Exuberance in the Hospital Industry," *Health Affairs,* January/February 2002.

170. Robinson, interview with the author.

171. Gerard Anderson, interview with the author.

172. See chapter 7, "Doing Less, but Doing It Right: Is Pay for Performance the Answer?" for a full discussion of health information technology.

173. Skolnick, interview with the author.

174. For Rice's argument that, in the health care industry, supply is in the driver's seat, see chapter 1, "The Road to Corporate Medicine."

175. Here, Rice follows Kenneth Arrow, the founder of health care economics, who originally pointed out that in the health care industry, the supplier has so much power because the consumer is in a uniquely vulnerable position. He cannot test out the product, he cannot return it, and there are no warranties. As a result, for the transaction to go forward, the buyer must trust the seller. "Whether the patient's confidence in the supplier's superior knowledge and complete professionalism is justified is not the question," Arrow emphasizes—it is simply that, without it, the transaction could not go forward.

   A customer might purchase a car from a salesman whom he views as less than completely trustworthy—relying on his own knowledge to pick the best vehicle and strike the best deal. But even the most well-educated consumer will not willingly lie down on a operating table and open his shirt unless he has decided, rightly or wrongly, that he can trust the surgeon standing over him. (For Arrow's full argument, see chapter 1, "The Road to Corporate Medicine.")

CHAPTER 4

1. Associated Press, "Advertising Lures Hospital Patients," *The New York Times,* 26 October 1981.

2. John Dorschner, "Stand-Alone Hospitals Struggle to Survive, Make Bids for Patients," *The Miami Herald,* 24 May 2004.

3. Mark McDougle, interview with the author.

4. Jerry Avorn, *Powerful Medicines: The Benefits, Risks, and Costs of Prescription Drugs* (New York: Knopf, 2004), 411.

5. Robin J. Larson, Steven Woloshin, and H. Gilbert Welch, "Advertising by Academic Medical Centers," *Annals of Internal Medicine,* 28 March 2005.

6. Lisa Schwartz, interview with the author.

7. Kenneth Wing with Michael S. Jacobs and Patricia C. Kuszler, *The Law and American Health Care* (1998), 12. (Available online only. For a link to chapter 1, see http://www.law

.seattleu.edu/fachome/wing, click on "class assignments," then click on "chapter 1 The Law and American Health Care."

8. Bradford H. Gray, *The Profit Motive and Patient Care: The Changing Accountability of Doctors and Hospitals* (Cambridge: Harvard University Press, 1991), 69. See also Robert D. Reischauer, "CBO Testimony Before the Subcommittee on Housing and Community Development Committee on Banking, Finance and Urban Affairs U.S. House of Representatives," 17 May 1979.

9. Gray, *The Profit Motive and Patient Care,* 69.

10. Gray, *The Profit Motive and Patient Care,* 70.

11. Gray, *The Profit Motive and Patient Care,* 7.

12. In 2001 tax-exempt bonds provided 54 percent of hospital capital, while bank loans contributed 7 percent. Another 16 percent came from leasing, while the remainder came from other sources "where volume is more difficult to ensure," stated the Healthcare Financial Management Association in its 2003 report, *Financing the Future, Report 1: How Are Hospitals Financing the Future? Access to Capital in Health Care Today.*

"For example," the report noted, "sales of medical office buildings were up 22 percent in 2002, in part fueled by an increasing number of hospitals selling assets to deleverage their balance sheets."

13. Joel S. Weissman, "The Trouble with Uncompensated Hospital Care," *The New England Journal of Medicine,* 24 March 2005; Marsha Regenstein and Jennifer Huang, The National Public Health and Hospital Institute, "Stresses to the Safety Net: The Public Hospital Perspective," The Kaiser Commission on Medicaid and the Uninsured, 6 June 2005. In 2002 teaching hospitals provided nearly two-thirds of all uncompensated care, according to the National Association of Urban Hospitals. (Ellen J. Kugler, executive director, National Association of Urban Hospitals, letter to Mark B. McClellan, administrator, Centers for Medicare and Medicaid Services, 9 July 2004.)

14. Jill R. Horwitz, "Making Profits and Providing Care: Comparing Nonprofit, For-Profit and Government Hospitals" *Health Affairs,* May/June 2005.

15. Gray, *The Profit Motive and Patient Care,* 71.

16. J. M. Teno et al.: "Family Perspectives on End-of-Life Care at the Last Place of Care," *Journal of the American Medical Association,* 7 January 2004.

17. Gautam Naik, "Unlikely Way to Cut Hospital Costs: Comfort the Dying," *The Wall Street Journal,* 10 March 2005.

18. Roger Hughes, interview with the author. See also Jodie Snyder, "Valley Hospital Boom Under Way," *The Arizona Republic,* 1 May 2005, and Patricia Kirk, "Rising with the Rooftops," *Retail Traffic,* 1 November 2003.

19. Snyder, "Valley Hospital Boom Under Way."

20. Susanna Moon, "Construction—and Costs—Going Up; Even as Expenses Mount, Pressured by Rising Commodity Prices, Health Care Building Continues to Boom," *Modern Healthcare,* 7 March 2005.

21. Lisa Greene, "Hospital Boom Is Sheer Survival," *The St. Petersburg Times,* 16 May 2004.

22. Joanne Kaufman, "Strong Medicine: The Out-of-Towners," *New York* magazine, 24 March 2003. In 2005 *The New York Times* reported that a state audit showed that "mismanagement, sloppy accounting practices and wasteful spending at Westchester Medical Cen-

ter . . . contributed to staggering financial losses between 2001 and 2004 . . . The audit also showed that former executives at the hospital were spending lavishly on things like restaurants, hotels and florists—with scant controls or documentation—as the medical center's finances were deteriorating." (Lisa W. Foderaro, "Audit Finds Fiscal Mess at Hospital in Westchester," 2 September 2005.)

23. McDougle, interview with the author.

24. Interview with the author.

25. W. Douglas Weaver, "Is Onsite Surgery Backup Necessary for Percutaneous Coronary Interventions?" *Journal of the American Medical Association,* 27 October 2004.

26. Paul Davies, "Hospitals Build Deluxe Wings for New Moms," *The Wall Street Journal,* 8 February 2005.

27. Rachel Brand, "Baby Grand: Hospitals Race to Replace Sterile Wards with Lavish Suites," *Rocky Mountain News,* 5 March 2005.

28. Brand, "Baby Grand: Hospitals Race to Replace Sterile Wards with Lavish Suites."

29. David C. Goodman, Elliott S. Fisher, George A. Little, Thérèse A. Stukel, Chiang-hua Chang, and Kenneth S. Schoendorf, "The Relation Between the Availability of Neonatal Intensive Care and Neonatal Mortality," *The New England Journal of Medicine,* 16 May 2002.

30. Kevin Grumbach, "Specialists, Technology and Newborns—Too Much of a Good Thing," *The New England Journal of Medicine,* 16 May 2002.

31. Bradley C. Strunk, Paul B. Ginsburg, and John P. Cookson, "Tracking Health Care Costs: Declining Growth Trend Pauses in 2004," Web Exclusive, *Health Affairs,* 21 June 2005. In the midnineties managed care put a lid on increases in hospital spending, but by 1999 insurers were backing off, hospitals gained leverage in contract negotiations, and both total spending on hospital services and the prices hospitals charged began to levitate. See chapter 3, "For-Profit Hospitals: A Flaw in the Business Model?"

32. Hughes, interview with the author.

33. Sheryl Skolnick, interview with the author.

34. Skolnick, interview with the author. See also Melissa Davis, "Some See Stunted Growth for Hospitals," TheStreet.com, 20 May 2004.

35. Nancy Opiela, "Health Care Costs a Nightmare for Retirement Dreams," *Journal of Financial Planning,* February 2005.

36. *Employer Health Benefits, 2005 Annual Survey,* (Menlo Park: The Kaiser Family Foundation and Health Research Educational Trust). See www.kff.org.

37. "The Impact of the Erosion of Retiree Health Benefits on Workers and Retirees," EBRI Issue Brief, March 2005.

38. For further discussion of the holes and ambiguities in many "affordable" insurance plans, see "Where We Are Now: Everyone Out of the Pool."

39. David L. Koch, "Article Hits Home," Web Exclusive eLetter, *Health Affairs,* 14 June 2005.

40. "Encouraging Workers to Save: The 2005 Retirement Confidence Survey," EBRI Issue Brief, April 2005.

41. Hilary Smith, "Where the Big Borrowers Live," MSN Money, 20 June 2005. The report on debt was based on data compiled from approximately 3 million consumers by credit-reporting agency Experian.

42. Carmen DeNavas-Wait, Bernadette D. Proctor, and Cheryl Hill Lee, "Income, Poverty and Health Insurance Coverage in the United States: 2004," Current Population Reports, U.S. Census Bureau, August 2005. $44,389 represents joint income for all "households," including single-person households, families with children, and married couples. The median joint income for families with children was $55,327 (meaning that half of all families earned less than that amount), with average income of $23,848 per family member.

43. "Encouraging Workers to Save: The 2005 Retirement Confidence Survey."

44. Moon, "Construction—and Costs—Going Up."

45. Donald Berwick, "Kevin Speaks," keynote address at the fourth annual National Forum on Quality Improvement in Health Care, 7 December 1992, reprinted in *Escape Fire: Designs for the Future of Health Care* (San Francisco: Jossey Bass, 2004), 7; Donald Berwick, "Quality Comes Home," keynote address at the sixth annual National Forum on Quality Improvement in Health Care, 4 December 1994, reprinted in *Escape Fire,* 58. In the speech, Berwick noted that he borrowed the phrase "The competition that matters is against disease" from Dr. Paul Batalden of the Dartmouth Medical School.

CHAPTER 5

1. Elliott. S. Fisher, David E. Wennberg, Thérèse A. Stukel, Daniel J. Gottlieb, F. L. Lucas, and Étoile L. Pinder, "The Implications of Regional Variations in Medicare Spending, Part 1: The Content, Quality, and Accessibility of Care," *Annals of Internal Medicine,* 18 February 2003.

2. Maureen Silverman's story is based on interviews with the author. Silverman also has published a longer, first-person memoir of her father's death, and the author drew on this memoir as well. To protect the privacy of Silverman's family, all names have been changed.

3. At the source's request, the name of the hospital also has been changed.

4. Jack Wennberg, interview with the author.

5. "These variations cannot reasonably be attributed to differences in illness," researchers noted. "During the last six months of life most people are ill, regardless of where they live." Nor do sunny climes explain the fluctuations. While only 14 percent of patients in Sun City, Arizona, wound up in intensive care, 45 percent of patients in Sun City, California, and 49 percent in Sun City, Florida, were admitted to an ICU. (John E. Wennberg, Elliott S. Fisher, and Jonathan S. Skinner, "Geography and the Debate Over Medicare Reform," Web Exclusive, *Health Affairs,* 13 February 2002.)

   For data, see "The Quality of Medical Care in the United States: A Report on the Medicare Program," *The Dartmouth Atlas of Health Care 1999* (Chicago: American Health Association Press, 1999), where J. E. Wennberg and M. M. Cooper report that after adjusting for age, sex, and race, Medicare spent $8,414 per patient in the Miami hospital referral region in 1996—nearly two and a half times the $3,341 spent that year in the Minneapolis region.

6. Elliott Fisher, interview with the author. Elliott S. Fisher, et al., "The Implications of Regional Variations in Medicare Spending, Part 1: The Content, Quality, and Accessibility of Care."

7. J. E. Wennberg and D. E. Wennberg, eds., *The Dartmouth Atlas of Health Care in Michigan*

(Hanover, New Hampshire: Center for the Evaluative Clinical Sciences, Dartmouth Medical School, 2000).

8. J. Wennberg and Cooper, eds., "The Quality of Medical Care in the United States: A Report on the Medicare Program," 196–7.

9. Wennberg, Fisher, and Skinner, "Geography and the Debate Over Medicare Reform," where the authors explain that their lifetime calculation assumes that the relative differences in Medicare spending persist, life expectancy conditional on reaching age 65 is 15 years, the discount rate is 3 percent, and the annual rate of growth in real per capita Medicare spending is 2 percent. See also D. Wennberg and J. Skinner, "Medicare Transfers Across States: Winners and Losers," *National Tax Journal,* September 2000.

10. J. Wennberg et al., "Geography and the Debate Over Medicare Reform."

11. In "Geography and the Debate Over Medicare Reform," J. Wennberg and colleagues explain how they adjusted for the underlying health of the population in a particular region: "We created an 'illness index' that uses regional rates of heart attack, stroke, hip fracture, cancer, gastrointestinal hemorrhage, and death of Medicare beneficiaries to quantify the underlying disease burden in a region. These measures were chosen because the hospitalization records for the illnesses are accurate reflections of their true incidence in the population; nearly every elderly person with a hip fracture ends up in the hospital. (Not surprisingly, the Social Security Administration is assiduous about measuring mortality accurately.)

"Using regression analysis, we found that the health of enrollees in Grand Junction, Colorado, one of the healthiest regions in the United States, implies that their per capita Medicare spending should be about 20 percent below the national average. By contrast, the regression suggests that those living in Birmingham, Alabama, one of the least healthy regions, should receive about 24 percent above the national average. . . ."

Yet "those regional differences in underlying health explain just 27 percent of the (weighted) variation in Medicare spending across regions. Consequently, illness-adjusted Medicare spending differs greatly across regions. Other studies with homogeneous patient populations (such as those with hip fracture or heart attack) confirm that substantial differences in Medicare use and spending across U.S. regions are largely independent of beneficiaries' need for services."

12. Fisher, et al., "The Implications of Regional Variations in Medicare Spending, Part 1. On the question of how much fear of a lawsuit boosts hospital spending, Fisher et al. cite D. P. Kessler and M. B. McClellan, "Do Doctors Practice Defensive Medicine?" *The Quarterly Journal of Economics,* May 1996.

13. Fisher, interview with the author. Even in a single city, differences in how much time patients spend in the hospital correlate with supply. Research shows that in a given city each hospital has a certain number of patients who are "loyal" to that hospital, and when the ratio of available hospital beds to the number of loyal patients is high, those patients are likely to receive more hospital care. Also see John E. Wennberg, Elliott S. Fisher, Laurence Baker, Sandra M. Sharp, and Kristen K. Bonner, "Evaluating the Efficiency of California Providers in Caring for Patients with Chronic Illnesses," *Health Affairs,* 16 November 2005.

14. The study surveyed care and outcomes in 306 cities and counties nationwide. (Fisher et al.,

"The Implications of Regional Variations in Medicare Spending, Part 1," and "Part 2: Health Outcomes and Satisfaction with Care," *Annals of Internal Medicine,* 18 February 2003.)

Numerous studies have shown that extra care does not seem to lower mortality rates in high-treatment regions. Still, researchers acknowledge, mortality rates are a very crude measure of medical outcomes: just because a patient did not die does not mean that he was well-served by a more conservative regimen. Perhaps patients who spend more time in the hospital and consult with more specialists wind up not simply alive, but healthier and more satisfied.

Part 2 of this study tested this hypothesis, following patients for up to five years after their initial hospitalization. In "Health Outcomes and Satisfaction with Care," the authors describe how they measured functioning, using the Health Activities and Limitations Index (HALex) developed by the National Center for Health Statistics and found no difference between high-treatment and low-treatment regions. Interviews with patients did show some differences in how happy patients were with their care, with patient satisfaction significantly higher in the Northeast than in the South. But, the authors reported, "the study did not reveal a consistent pattern of greater satisfaction in areas where more was spent on hospital care."

In the end, then, the study confirmed earlier findings: patients in high-treatment areas were, by and large, no healthier and no more satisfied than their peers.

15. Fisher, interview with the author. See Fisher et al., "The Implications of Regional Variations in Medicare Spending, Part 1: The Content, Quality and Accessibility of Care," and "Part 2: Health Outcomes and Satisfaction with Care." The study also showed that hospitals that treated one disease aggressively tended to treat the other two conditions with equal intensity. See Elliott S. Fisher, David E. Wennberg, Thérèsè A. Stuckel, and Daniel J. Gottlieb, "Variations in the Longitudinal Efficiency of Academic Medical Centers," Web Exclusive, *Health Affairs,* 7 October 2004.

16. Donald M. Berwick, "My Right Knee," plenary address, 15th annual National Forum on Quality Improvement in Health Care, 4 December 2003).

17. Elliott S. Fisher, and H. Gilbert Welch, "Avoiding the Unintended Consequences of Growth in Medical Care: How Might More Be Worse?" *Journal of the American Medical Association,* 3 February 1999.

18. Elliott S. Fisher, "Medical Care—Is More Always Better?" *The New England Journal of Medicine,* 23 October 2003.

19. In cases where they disagree, physicians tend to follow what was considered best practice at the medical schools where they trained—the fact that doctors tend to settle in the same region where they trained explains some of the geographic variation. But, as J. Wennberg points out, it does not explain different practice patterns in cases where clinical evidence quite clearly shows that extra treatment brings no benefit.

20. J. E. Wennberg, "Dealing with Medical Practice Variations: A Proposal for Action," *Health Affairs,* summer 1984.

21. John Wennberg, "Variation in Use of Medicare Services Among Regions and Selected Academic Medical Centers," Duncan W. Clarke Lecture, New York Academy of Medicine, New York City, 24 January 2005.

22. Of the seven hospitals surveyed (UCLA Medical Centers, Johns Hopkins, Mount Sinai, Duke University Medical Center, Massachusetts General Hospital, Mayo Clinic Hospitals, and St. Louis University Hospital), patients received the most intensive care at UCLA and Mount Sinai. (John E. Wennberg, Elliott S. Fisher, Thérèse A. Stukel, and Sandra M. Sharp, "Use of Medicare Claims Data to Monitor Provider-Specific Performance Among Patients with Severe Chronic Illness," Web Exclusive, *Health Affairs,* 7 October 2004.) For a study of academic medical centers which suggests that patients who receive more aggressive care fare no better, see Fisher et al., "Variations in the Longitudinal Efficiency of Academic Medical Centers."

    The study of the seven top-rated geriatric centers also showed that patients treated at Mount Sinai and UCLA were more likely to die in the hospital while those at Johns Hopkins or the Mayo Clinic were more likely to be admitted to a hospice—a fact which, as the authors point out, "calls into question the validity of *U.S. News & World Report*'s use of inpatient mortality rates as a basis for evaluating hospital quality in managing chronic illness." See chapter 7, "Doing Less and Doing It Right: Is Pay for Performance the Answer?" on the difficulties involved in measuring quality—and the limited usefulness (from a consumer's point of view) of various hospital "report cards" and rankings.

    For a separate discussion of wide variations in treatment patterns at 77 hospitals that appeared in the 2001 *U.S. News & World Report* "best hospital list" for heart and pulmonary disease, cancer and geriatric services, see John E. Wennberg, Elliott S. Fisher, Thérèsè A Stukel, Jonathan S. Skinner, Sandra M. Sharp, Kristen K. Bonner, "Use of Hospitals, Physician Visits and Hospice During the Last Six Months of Life Among Cohorts Loyal to Highly Respected Hospitals in the United States," BMJ.com, 13 March 2004.

23. Victor R. Fuchs, "More Variation in Use of Care, More Flat-of-the-Curve Medicine," Web Exclusive, *Health Affairs,* 7 October 2004.

24. Fuchs, "More Variation in Use of Care, More Flat-of-the-Curve Medicine."

25. Katherine Baicker and Amitabh Chandra, "Medicare Spending, the Physician Workforce, and Beneficiaries' Quality of Care," Web Exclusive, *Health Affairs,* 7 April 2004. To compare quality of care, the Dartmouth economists used the 24 quality measures developed by the Medicare Quality Improvement Organization (QIO) and computed at the state level by Steve Jencks. These measures use samples of patient discharge records for the treatment of six common medical conditions (acute myocardial infarction, breast cancer, diabetes mellitus, heart failure, pneumonia, and stroke) and capture interventions and evaluation "for which there is strong scientific evidence and professional consensus that the process of care either directly improves outcomes or is a necessary step in a chain of care that does so," such as the prescription of warfarin for atrial fibrillation or biennial eye examinations for diabetics. Jencks and his colleagues then ranked states for each measure and averaged the ranks (weighting each measure equally) to compute each state's overall rank. See S. F. Jencks et al., "Quality of Medical Care Delivered to Medicare Beneficiaries: A Profile at State and National Levels," *Journal of the American Medical Association,* 4 October 2000; S. F. Jencks, E. D. Huff, and T. Cuerdon, "Change in the Quality of Care Delivered to Medicare Beneficiaries, 1998–1999 to 2000–2001, *Journal of the American Medical Association,* 15 January 2003; E. A. McGlynn et al., "The Quality of Health Care Delivered to Adults in the United States," *The New England Journal of Medicine,* 26 June 2003.

26. Gina Kolata, "Program Coaxes Hospitals to See Treatments Under Their Noses," *The New York Times,* 25 December 2004.

27. Fisher, interview with the author.

28. Interview with the author.

29. Gina Kolata, "Patients in Florida Lining Up for All That Medicare Covers," *The New York Times,* 13 September 2003.

30. This is a special problem for retirees in low-spending states who belong to a Medicare HMO. Because Medicare reimbursements to HMOs are tied to the local history of fee-for-service spending per Medicare beneficiary, HMOs in a state like Minnesota receive less from Medicare than HMOS in a high-spending state. This in turn means that HMOs in Minnesota are less likely to offer extras like drugs benefits or prescription glasses. Attempts have been made to redress the inequities, but inevitably this only has led to further complications and controversy.

31. Jonathan Skinner and John E. Wennberg, "Perspective: Exceptionalism or Extravagance? What's Different About Health Care in South Florida?" Web Exclusive, *Health Affairs,* 13 August 2003.

32. The 1999 *Dartmouth Atlas,* a compilation of data on supply and use of health care, showed an abundant supply of hospital beds per 1,000 residents in cities like New Orleans and Hattiesburg, Mississippi, (4.6 in each city—roughly twice as many as in the average low-spending region), and that in these cities roughly a fifth of Medicare beneficiaries saw 10 or more specialists during the last six months of life, while between 27 percent and 33 percent were admitted to an ICU.

33. Bruce Vladeck, interview with the author; "Everything New Is Old Again," Web Exclusive, *Health Affairs,* 7 October 2004.

34. Thomas Rice, interview with the author. Rice stresses that while he believes that excess capacity is important, it is not the whole explanation as to how supply drives care. But he is convinced that if problems of waste in health care spending are to be addressed, the answer is to look at supply, focusing, for example, on "the comparative effectiveness of new technology."

35. See www.ftc.gov/ogc/healthcarehearings/docs/030527fisher.pdf. For further discussion, see J. Wennberg, "Variation in Use of Medicare Services Among Regions and Selected Academic Medical Centers: Is More Better?"

36. J. Wennberg, "Variation in Use of Medicare Services Among Regions and Selected Academic Medical Centers: Is More Better?"

37. For statistics on these cities see J. Wennberg and Cooper, eds., "The Quality of Medical Care in the United States: A Report on the Medicare Program."

    Within a single city with several hospitals, researchers have found a mirror image of the national pattern. Typically, a certain number of city's residents are loyal to a particular hospital, and if the supply of beds relative to the number of patients who use that hospital is high, they will use it more often than patients who are loyal to a hospital with fewer beds per patients in their base.

38. J. Wennberg, interview with the author.

39. See Skinner and J. Wennberg, "Perspective: Exceptionalism or Extravagance? What's Different About Health Care in South Florida?" As evidence that consumer preference is not

driving the high spending pattern, Skinner and Wennberg point out that although patients in Miami are likely to receive far more intensive care during the final six months of life than patients in other areas, they are not more likely to undergo hip replacements, back surgery, or angioplasty—"If anything rates of these procedures seem to be lower in Miami than in the other Florida regions, and even the United States as a whole."

The difference is that while patients' and physicians' preferences are more likely to play a role in deciding whether or not they want hip replacement surgery, when it comes to treatment in the final six months of life, supply seems to be the driving force.

40. Ken Terry, "Wennberg on Supply: Why Treatment Varies So Greatly," *Medical Economics,* 10 February 1997.

41. Fisher, interview with the author. See also Fisher et al., "Variations in the Longitudinal Efficiency of Academic Medical Centers."

42. Larry Beresford et al., *Promoting Excellence in End of Life Care,* The Robert Wood Johnson Foundation, October 2002.

43. J. Wennberg, interview with the author. See also Terry, "Wennberg on Supply." For a discussion of how insured patients who can't get appointments with their doctors are driving rising ER visits, see chapter 6, " 'Too Little, Too Late': The Cost of Rationing Care."

44. To the contrary, J. Wennberg notes, as researchers gather more hard data on outcomes they find that frequent one-on-one visits may not be the best way to manage chronically ill patients: "In one study [where] doctors made periodic telephone calls to patients instead of scheduling regular follow-up visits, patients in the study group experienced fewer hospitalizations and lower mortality than controls," Wennberg reports. "In three other studies planned group visits to doctors were offered instead of one-to-one follow-up visits for patients with chronic illness: those offered group visits achieved better control of diabetes, lower rates of use of emergency rooms and specialists visits, and improvement in other outcomes . . ." As evidence, Wennberg cites:

J. Wasson, C. Gaudette, F. Whaley, A. Sauvigne, P. Baribeau, and H. G. Welch, "Telephone Care as a Substitute for Routine Clinic Follow-up" *Journal of the American Medical Association,* 1 April 1992;

E. H. Wagner, L. C. Grothaus, N. Sandhu, et al., "Chronic Care Clinics for Diabetes in Primary Care: A System-wide Randomized Trial," *Diabetes Care,* April 2001;

M. Trento, P. Passera, M. Tomalino, M. Bajardi, F. Pomero, A. Allione, et al. "Group Visits Improve Metabolic Control in Type 2 Diabetes: A 2-year Follow-up." *Diabetes Care,* June 2001;

E. A. Coleman, T. B. Eilertsen, A. M. Kramer, D. J. Magid, A. Beck, and D. Conner, "Reducing Emergency Visits in Older Adults with Chronic Illness. A Randomized, Controlled Trial of Group Visits" [see comments], *Effective Clinical Practice,* March/April 2001;

A. Beck, J. Scott, P. Williams, B. Robertson, D. Jackson, G. Gade et al., "A Randomized Trial of Group Outpatient Visits for Chronically Ill Older HMO Members: The Cooperative Health Care Clinic" *Journal of the American Geriatrics Society* 45 (1997): 543–549.

45. Skinner, interview with the author.

46. J. Wennberg, "Variation in Use of Medicare Services Among Regions and Selected Academic Medical Centers."

47. Diane Meier, interview with the author. See also Diane Meier, "Variability in End of Life Care," Editorial, *BMJ USA,* 15 May 2004.

48. Fitzhugh Mullan, "Wrestling with Variation: An Interview with Jack Wennberg," Web Exclusive, *Health Affairs,* 7 October 2004.

49. Mullan, "Wrestling with Variation: An Interview with Jack Wennberg."

50. Managed care companies often reimburse hospitals on a per diem basis. And while Medicare now pays a lump sum per diagnosis (or DRG) rather than paying fee-for-service, a hospital's revenues soar when it does more. In "Lumpers and Splitters: Different Approaches to Understanding Variations Research," Robert A. Berenson points to "congestive heart failure—the leading cause of hospitalization for the Medicare population" as an example of how hospitals "lack a business case to invest in approaches that would effectively decrease admissions for this 'bread and butter' diagnosis." Although not as lucrative as "certain surgical diagnoses, for hospitals not at full capacity, the marginal revenues for CHF patients certainly exceed the marginal costs," Berenson points out. "Avoidable CHF admissions are important to hospitals' bottom lines. So even though communities hospitals would seem to be the right locus for housing the various disease management–type activities that would support community physicians in caring for patients with chronic conditions [without hospitalizing them], for the most part, hospitals understandably have not stepped up to the challenge. Similarly, Medicare's physician fee schedule based on classical FFS reimbursement pays for face to face visits with patients with CHF—but not for most of the activities that constitute good chronic care management. The fee schedule reimburses for care transactions, but not for care coordination." (Web Exclusive, *Health Affairs,* 7 October 2004.)

51. The most common definition is the one used by the Office of Technology Assessment of the U.S. Congress and the Institute of Medicine of the National Academy of Sciences, which defines medical technology as any "techniques, drugs, equipment and procedures used by health care professionals in delivering medical care to individuals, and the systems within which such care is delivered." (See Richard D. Lamm, and Duane H. Bluemke, "High-tech Health Care and Society's Ability to Pay," *Healthcare Financial Management,* September 1990.) In his classic essay "The Sorcerer's Broom: Medicine's Rampant Technology," Eric J. Cassell makes the point: "In addition to the instruments and devices usually considered as technology, we should include, for the sake of understanding, high-power medications—cardiac, antimicrobial, psychotropic, or whatever—that greatly extend our therapeutic power" (*The Hastings Center Report,* 1 November 1993).

52. Robert Califf, interview with the author, and see Robert M. Califf, "Defining the Balance of Risk and Benefit in the Era of Genomics and Proteomics," *Health Affairs,* January/February 2004. See also Kolata, "Program Coaxes Hospitals to See Treatments Under Their Noses."

53. The agency was originally named the Agency for Health Care Policy and Research (AHCPR). (John E. Wennberg, "Practice Variations and Health Care Reform: Connecting the Dots," Web Exclusive, *Health Affairs,* 7 October 2004, and Mullan, "Wrestling with Variation: An Interview with Jack Wennberg.")

54. George Lundberg, with James Stacey, *Severed Trust: Why American Medicine Hasn't Been Fixed* (New York: Basic Books, 2000), 282, 311.

55. J. Wennberg, interview with the author.

56. Fisher, interview with the author.

57. Mullan, "Wrestling with Variation: An Interview with Jack Wennberg."

58. Lundberg with Stacey, *Severed Trust,* 90–91.

59. Shannon Brownlee, "Bad Science and Breast Cancer," *Discover,* 1 August 2002.

60. "Position Statement on High-Dose Chemotherapy with Bone Marrow Transplant or Stem Cell Support," October 2003, www.natbcc.org.

61. Uwe Reinhardt, "Does the Aging of the Population Really Drive the Demand for Health Care?" *Health Affairs,* November/December 2003.

62. J. Wennberg, "Variation in Use of Medicare Services Among Regions and Selected Academic Medical Centers."

63. A. Mark Fendrick, Letters to the Editor, *Health Affairs,* September/October 2002.

64. Len M. Nichols, Paul B. Ginsburg, Robert A. Berenson, Jon Christianson, and Robert E. Hurley, "Are Market Forces Strong Enough to Deliver Efficient Health Care Systems? Confidence Is Waning," *Health Affairs,* March/April 2004.

65. J. Wennberg, interview with the author.

66. Ceci Connolly, "Studies Raise Questions on Value of Intensive Care," *The Washington Post,* 8 October 2004.

67. Karen Davis, "Achieving a High Performance Health System," President's Message, 2003 Annual Report, The Commonwealth Fund. Davis points to two other studies which suggest that more care may not be better care, including an analysis of the cost and quality of care at American hospitals done by the Institute for Healthcare Improvement, which documented a three- to fivefold difference in cost and quality for different diagnoses but no systematic relationship between quality and cost. ("Move Your Dot: Measuring Evaluating and Reducing Hospital Mortality Rates," Institute for Healthcare Improvement, 2003.) "The findings are provocative," says Davis, "yet more refined analysis will be needed to develop effective solutions."

68. Robert Galvin, " 'A Deficiency of Will and Ambition': A Conversation with Donald Berwick," Web Exclusive, *Health Affairs,* 12 January 2005.

69. Berwick, "Dirty Words and Magic Spells," address given to the 12th annual National Forum on Quality Improvement in Health Care, 5 December 2000, collected in *Escape Fire,* 233.

70. Atul Gawande, "The Bell Curve," *The New Yorker,* 6 December 2004. For the list of the 100 most powerful, see modernhealthcare.com, 13 June 2005.

71. Berwick, "Why the Vasa Sank," address given to the ninth annual National Forum on Quality Improvement in Health Care, 9 December 1997.

72. Berwick, "Plenty," address given to the 14th annual National Forum on Quality Improvement in Health Care, 10 December 2002.

73. Berwick originally told the tale of his wife's illness in an address given to the 11th annual National Forum on Quality Improvement in Health Care, 7 December 1999, collected in *Escape Fire,* 183ff. Unless otherwise indicated, the details of the story that follows taken from that speech.

74. Berwick recounted the story of his encounter with the nurse to Neil Swidey, "Even the

Revolutionary Donald Berwick Says Our World-Class Hospitals and Doctors Are Delivering Health Care That Is Unsafe and Unreliable," *The Boston Globe,* 4 January 2004.

75. Interview with the author.

76. Berwick, "Dirty Words and Magic Spells," 220.

77. Swidey, "Even the Revolutionary Donald Berwick Says Our World-Class Hospitals and Doctors Are Delivering Health Care That Is Unsafe and Unreliable."

78. Frank Davidoff, introduction to *Escape Fire,* xx.

79. Berwick, "Plenty."

80. Berwick, "A Discussion with Donald Berwick," AHCJ Sixth National Conference, 2 April 2005.

81. As noted in chapter 4, "Not-for-Profit Hospitals: 'No Margin, No Mission' " only 20 percent of U.S. community hospitals invest in palliative care aimed at reducing both the pain and the terror of dying. In other developed countries—particularly the United Kingdom—palliative care programs are much more common.

82. Berwick, "Dirty Words and Magic Spells," 231.

83. Berwick, "Dirty Words and Magic Spells," 221.

84. Interview with the author.

85. Berwick, "Plenty."

86. Luke Schockman, "Medical Centers in Area Feel Pull of MRI Devices," Toledoblade.com, 2 May 2005.

87. The estimate, made by consulting firm Booz Allen Hamilton, was reported in *The Wall Street Journal* by David Armstrong, "MRI and CT Scanners Offer Doctors Way to Profit on Scans," 5 May 2005.

88. In fact, Dr. H. Gilbert Welch points out, "cancer screening tends to miss the fastest-growing and most aggressive forms of cancer." (H. Gilbert Welch, *Should I Be Tested for Cancer?: Maybe Not and Here's Why* [Berkeley; University of California Press, 2004]), 19–21. On false negatives, see David Dobbs, "Buried Answers," *The New York Times Magazine,* 24 April 2005.

89. Gawande cites the 1998 and 1999 studies and quotes Lundberg in *Complications: A Surgeon's Notes on an Imperfect Science* (New York: Picador, 2002), 199. See also Lundberg, *Severed Trust,* 253–4.

90. Gawande, *Complications,* 199.

91. Gawande, *Complications,* 199.

92. David Dobbs, "Buried Answers," *The New York Times Magazine,* 24 April 2005.

93. The data comes from Last Acts, a coalition to improve care and caring near the end of life.

94. Ellen Fox, "Rethinking Doctor Think: Reforming Medical Education by Nurturing Neglected Goals," in *The Goals of Medicine: The Forgotten Issues in Health Care Reform,* Mark J. Hanson and Daniel Callahan, eds., (Washington, D.C.: Georgetown University Press, 1999), 187–8.

95. Meier, interview with the author. See also Edward Doyle, "Profiles in Palliative Care: How the Rapid Growth of Inpatient Palliative Care Services May Affect Hospitalists," *Today's Hospitalist,* December 2004.

96. Meier, interview with the author.

97. Daniel Callahan, *False Hopes: Why America's Quest for Perfect Health Is a Recipe for Failure* (New York: Simon & Schuster, 1998), 21, 78.

98. Fox, "Rethinking Doctor Think: Reforming Medical Education by Nurturing Neglected Goals."

99. Jerry Avorn, *Powerful Medicines: The Benefits, Risks, and Costs of Prescription Drugs* (New York: Knopf, 2004), 322.

100. Robert H. LeBow, *Health Care Meltdown: Confronting the Myths and Fixing Our Failing System* (Boise, ID: JRI Press, 2002), 69.

101. Gawande explains how the system was devised in "Piecework," *The New Yorker,* 4 April 2005. Although private insurers follow the fee schedule, Gawande explains, the multipliers they used to convert the relative values into dollars vary "depending on the deals they struck with local physicians."

102. Daniel Q. Haney, "Critical Condition: U.S. Health Care in Crisis, Doctors Unhappy with Medicare's Effort to Redistribute Medical Wealth," Associated Press, 25 August 1993.

103. Fisher, interview with the author. For a fuller discussion of paying doctors for performance, see chapter 7, "Doing Less and Doing It Right: Is Pay For Performance the Answer?"

104. Meier, interview with the author.

105. Liz Dreesen, interview with the author.

106. Kenneth Boyd, "Old Age: Something to Look Forward To?" in *The Goals of Medicine: The Forgotten Issues in Health Care Reform,* 158–9. Boyd cites M. Sonnenblick, Y. Friedlander, and A. Steinberg, "Dissociation Between the Wishes of Terminally Ill Parents and Decisions by Their Offspring," *Journal of the American Geriatrics Society* 41 (1993): 599–604.

107. Haim Hazan, *Old Age: Constructions and Deconstructions* (Cambridge: Cambridge University Press, 1994), 72.

108. Dreesen, interview with the author.

109. Meier, interview with the author.

110. Mark J. Hanson, "The Idea of Progress and the Goals of Medicine" in *The Goals of Medicine: The Forgotten Issues in Health Care Reform,* 146; Eric J. Cassell, "The Sorcerer's Broom: Medicine's Rampant Technology."

111. Elliott S. Fisher, and H. Gilbert Welch, "Avoiding the Unintended Consequences of Growth in Medical Care: How Might More Be Worse?"

CHAPTER 6

1. Institute of Medicine Committee on the Consequence of Uninsurance, *Care Without Coverage: Too Little, Too Late* (Washington, D.C.: National Academy Press, 21 May 2002). See www.iom.edu.

2. Paul H. Wise, "The Transformation of Child Health in the United States," *Health Affairs,* September/October 2004.

3. According to the "Employee Benefit Research Institute Estimates from the March Current Population Survey, 2004 Supplement," in 2003 two-thirds of uninsured children lived in families earning less than 200 percent of the poverty level ($38,968 for a family of four in 2004); in two-thirds of the households where the children lacked coverage, the head of the family had worked full-time all year. One-third of all uninsured children lived below

the poverty level—$19,484 for a four-person household in 2004. See also Vanessa Fuhrmans, "Health Insurers' New Target," *The Wall Street Journal*, 31 May 2005.

4. John K. Iglehart, "To What Are Children Entitled?: Coming Challenges," *Health Affairs*, September/October 2004.

5. Donna Cohen Ross and Laura Cox, *Beneath the Surface: Barriers Threaten to Slow Progress on Expanding Health Coverage of Children and Families*, (Menlo Park: The Henry J. Kaiser Family Foundation, October 2004.)

6. Bob Herbert, "Hide and Seek in Florida, *The New York Times*, 5 March 2004.

7. Lisa Sprague, "Veterans' Health Care: Balancing Resources and Responsibilities," *National Health Policy Forum*, 1 April 2004.

8. Phillip Longman, "The Best Care Anywhere," *Washington Monthly*, January/February 2005.

9. The exact terms of eligibility also depend on geographic location. (Sprague, "Veterans' Health Care: Balancing Resources and Responsibilities.")

10. Maggie Fox, "Nearly 1.7 Million Veterans Lack Health Care—Study," Reuters, 19 October 2004.

11. In 2005, 47 million Americans were uninsured for the entire year (Families USA, "Paying a Premium: The Added Cost of Care for the Uninsured," 8 June 2005.) See also Joel S. Weissman, "The Trouble with Uncompensated Care," *The New England Journal of Medicine*, 24 March 2005; Todd Gilmer and Richard Kronick, "It's the Premiums, Stupid: Projections of the Uninsured Through 2013," Web Exclusive, *Health Affairs*, 5 April 2005.

    While predicting that 56 million Americans will be uninsured by 2013, Gilmer and Kronick acknowledge that it is very hard to predict health care inflation: If managed care comes back into vogue, and gatekeepers tighten the rules, inflation could slow, despite the spiraling cost of medical technology. Nevertheless, they point out that their projections are conservative insofar as they are based on the optimistic assumption that in the 10 years years ending in 2013, health care spending will rise by only 7.4 percent a year—while personal income grows by 4.6 percent. In other words, they are hoping that in the years ahead health care inflation will slow by about a third (from 1999 to 2002 spending on health care grew 9.8 percent annually) while wages rise twice as fast as in recent years (from 1999 to 2002, income climbed by just 2.2 percent a year.)

12. Kenneth Thorpe, interview with the author; Kenneth E. Thorpe and David Howard, "Health Insurance and Spending Among Cancer Patients," Web Exclusive, *Health Affairs*, 9 April 2003.

13. Thorpe, interview with the author.

14. Evan M. Melhado, interview with the author. See also review of *The Economics of Health Reconsidered* in *Journal of Health Politics, Policy and Law*, 1 February 2000.

15. Jack Hadley, and John Holahan, *The Cost of Not Covering the Uninsured—Project Highlights*, The Kaiser Commission on Medicaid and the Uninsured, June 2003.

16. Institute of Medicine, *Care Without Coverage: Too Little, Too Late*.

17. This story is based on the author's interview with Dr. Donald Lefkowits (who would ultimately treat Martinez) and Marsha Austin's description of Martinez's condition in "Denver Hospitals Turn Away Sick, Injured People as Result of Screening Process," *The Denver Post*, 29 June 2003.

    Martinez had been visiting his mother in a small town outside of Santa Fe when he was attacked. Martinez didn't live in New Mexico, however; he lived in the Denver area with his girlfriend. That's why, after getting his jaw X-rayed in Santa Fe, he got on a bus and rode six hours. He wanted to get home to Denver—home where he thought he could get help.

18. Lefkowits, interview with the author. See also Austin, "Denver Hospitals Turn Away Sick, Injured People as Result of Screening Process."

19. Andi Atwater quotes Young in "Emergency Rooms Debate Care Options," *Southwest Florida News-Press*, 6 March 2005.

20. Ironically, Lefkowits works for a for-profit hospital: Rose Medical is half-owned by HCA, the nation's largest hospital chain, and half-owned by the physicians who staff the facilities. "The physicians set medical policy," says Lefkowits, "and I've never felt any pressure to turn away uninsured patients who need care. Our physicians' group doesn't have any outside shareholders—so there's no outside pressure," he adds. "The profits that the group makes are distributed among the physicians." (Interview with the author.)

21. Lefkowits, interview with the author.

22. Ceci Connolly, "Emergency Care Under Strain: Hospital Filtering Out Non-urgent Patients," *The Washington Post*, 27 April 2004.

23. Austin, "Denver Hospitals Turn Away Sick."

24. In Florida, for example, nonprofit Munroe Regional Medical Center and HCA-owned West Marion Community Hospital sent a proposal to the Florida Agency for Health Care Administration in 2005, outlining their plans to begin referring nonemergency cases to other facilities. Patients who want to stay in the ER will have to pay cash.

    In his reply, Health Care Administration Secretary Alan Levine was clear: if a screening determines a patient does not have a medical emergency, "the hospital's services ends." (Atwater, "Emergency Rooms Debate Care Options.")

25. Atwater, "Emergency Rooms Debate Care Options."

26. Maggie Fox, "Poor Uninsured Don't Fill Emergency Rooms," Reuters, 19 October 2004; Ellen J. Weber, et al., "Does Lack of a Usual Source of Care or Health Insurance Increase the Likelihood of an Emergency Department Visit?" *Annals of Emergency Medicine*, January 2005.

27. In "Insured Americans Drive Surge in Emergency Department Visits," Peter J. Cunningham and Jessica H. May report that insured Americans accounted for most of the 16 percent increase in ED visits between 1996–97 and 2000–01. (Center for Studying Health System Change, Issue Brief No. 70, October 2003.) See www.hschange.com/CONTENTS.

28. A 2004 survey of physician appointment wait times in 15 metropolitan areas conducted by Merritt, Hawkins & Associates, a national physician search firm, found that patients seeking an appointment with a cardiologist, a dermatologist, a gynecologist, or an orthopedic surgeon typically had to wait two weeks—or longer. *Summary Report: 2004 Survey of Physician Appointment Wait Times*, Merritt, Hawkins & Associates.

29. Arthur Kellerman, interview with the author. Also see Ceci Connolly, "Emergency Care Under Strain."

30. Connolly, "Emergency Care Under Strain."

31. Connolly, "Emergency Care Under Strain."

32. Weissman, "The Trouble with Uncompensated Hospital Care."

33. *Paying a Premium: The Added Cost of Care for the Uninsured,* (Washington, D.C.: Families USA, June 2005). Government support includes Medicaid and Medicare Disproportionate Share Hospital payments from the federal government and various state and local government programs.

34. John Dorschner, "Emergency Rooms Have to Accept You for Treatment, but a Lack of Specialists May Mean You Won't Get the Care You Need," *The Miami Herald,* 26 December 2004.

35. Marsha Regenstein, and Jennifer Huang, *Stresses to the Safety Net: The Public Hospital Perspective,* The Henry J. Kaiser Family Foundation, Commission on Medicaid and the Uninsured, June 2005.

36. Austin, "Denver Hospitals Turn Away Sick."

37. Connolly, "Emergency Care Under Strain."

38. In 2004, a group of plaintiffs attorneys filed civil lawsuits against more than a dozen not-for-profit hospitals, charging that they had violated their obligation as charities by overcharging the uninsured. See Reed Abelson and Jonathan D. Glater, "Suits Challenge Hospital Bills of Uninsured," *The New York Times,* 17 June 2004.

39. Lucette Lagnado, "Hospitals Try Extreme Measures to Collect Their Overdue Debts," *The Wall Street Journal,* 30 October 2003.

40. Weissman, "The Trouble with Uncompensated Care."

41. Elisabeth Benjamin, Kat Gabriesheski, and Anna Pomykala, *State Secret: How Government Fails to Ensure that Uninsured and Underinsured Patients Have Access to State Charity Funds,* Health Law Unit, The Legal Aid Society, 2004.

42. John Kitzhaber, "Community Hospitals in the 21st Century: Reexamining Our Operating System," opening session, The Estes Park Institute, Naples, Florida, October 2004.

43. Liz Dreesen, interview with the author. The patient's name has been changed to protect his privacy.

44. Laura B. Benko, "Survival Guide for Healthcare Executives: Show Them the Money; Requiring Payment Upfront Protects Hospitals from Getting Stuck with the Bill," *Modern Healthcare,* 8 November 2004.

45. Guy Boulton, "Hospitals No Longer Willing to Hold Bill," *Tampa Tribune,* 27 June 2004.

46. More specifically, the students were told to say that they had been diagnosed with community-acquired pneumonia (pneumonia severity index class II) and asymptomatic accelerated hypertension. (Brent R. Asplin, Karin V. Rhodes, Helen Levy, Nicole Lurie, A. Lauren Crain, Bradley P. Carlin, and Arthur L. Kellermann, "Insurance Status and Access to Urgent Ambulatory Care Follow-Up Appointments," *The Journal of the American Medical Association,* 14 September 2005.)

47. Stephen Zuckerman, Joshua McFeeters, Peter Cunningham, and Len Nichols, "Changes in Medicaid Physician Fees, 1998–2003: Implications for Physician Participation," Web Exclusive, *Health Affairs,* 23 June 2004.

48. Judith Graham, "Needy Patients Find Door Shut When Searching for Specialist," *Chicago Tribune,* 23 May 2005.

49. Neil Calman, interview with the author.

50. Neil Calman originally told this story in "Out of the Shadow," *Health Affairs,* January/February 2000. The author interviewed him after James North had died.

51. Geeta Anand, "The Big Secret in Health Care: Rationing Is Here," *The Wall Street Journal,* 12 September 2003.

52. See Bernard Wysocki Jr., "At One Hospital, a Stark Solution for Allocating Care: Galveston Facility Cuts Drugs, Treatments for the Uninsured," *The Wall Street Journal,* 23 September 2003; Antonio Regalado, "To Sell Pricey Drug, Eli Lilly Fuels a Debate over Rationing," *The Wall Street Journal,* 18 September 2003; Lucette Lagnado, "What Is a Bet on Life Worth?" *The Wall Street Journal,* 18 June 2003.

53. Anand, "The Big Secret in Health Care."

54. Naoki Ikegami and John Creighton Campbell, "Health Care Reform in Japan: The Virtues of Muddling Through, *Health Affairs,* May/June 1999.

55. Naoki Ikegami and John Creighton Campbell, "Japan's Health Care System: Containing Costs and Attempting Reform," *Health Affairs,* May/June 2004.

56. David Mechanic, "Muddling Through Elegantly: Finding the Proper Balance in Rationing," *Health Affairs,* September/October 1997.

57. "Many Would Pass the Buck to Help Cover Uninsured," *The Wall Street Journal,* 26 May 2003.

58. *Who's Uninsured in North Carolina and Why?* (Washington, D.C., Families USA, November 2003). See www.familiesusa.org.

59. See *Who's Uninsured in North Carolina and Why?* for estimates of the cost of insurance in North Carolina in 2002. In 2005 www.ehealthinsurance.com showed that the best standard plan available to a 60-year-old man who lived in Rich's county would cost $3,300 a year—though it would not cover lab tests, hospitalization, or outpatient surgery until Rich had paid a $5,000 deductible. Nor is it clear that Rich was in sufficiently good health to qualify, and even if he did, the policy probably would not cover most preexisting conditions. Even then, the policy would cover only 80 percent of his bills if he stayed in-network, 50 percent if he went out-of-network.

    For further discussion of the many holes in high-deductible insurance plans, see chapter 4, "Not-for-Profit Hospitals: No Margin, No Mission?" and "Where We Are Now: Everyone Out of the Pool."

61. Kitzhaber, "Community Hospitals in the 21st Century: Reexamining Our Operating System."

62. One of the largest studies, conducted in 2001, looked at hospital discharge data in nine states, and discovered that uninsured adults were 33–82 percent more likely to be hospitalized for an avoidable condition than insured adults, depending on the state. See Jack Hadley, "Sicker and Poorer: The Consequences of Being Uninsured," The Kaiser Commission on Medicaid and the Uninsured, May 2002, for this study and references to other studies which show the uninsured are far more likely to be hospitalized for conditions that could have been treated in an ambulatory setting—if they had been treated earlier.

63. *Paying a Premium.* The report looked at health insurance premiums for families who have insurance through their private employers and concluded that premiums were $922 higher due to the cost of health care for the uninsured that is not paid for by the uninsured themselves or by other sources of reimbursement.

64. Iglehart was quoted in the Colorado Community Health Network newsletter, February 2003. The Kaiser report can be found at www.kff.org/content/2003/20030212.

65. Kirk Johnson and Reed Abelson, "Model in Utah May Be Future for Medicaid," *The New York Times,* 24 February 2005.

66. Robert Pear, "Governors Prepare to Fight Medicaid Cuts," *The New York Times,* 27 February 2005.

CHAPTER 7

1. Jerry Avorn, *Powerful Medicines: The Benefits, Risks, and Costs of Prescription Drugs* (New York: Knopf, 2004), 401.

2. Humphrey Taylor and Robert Leitman, "European Physicians Especially in Sweden, Netherlands and Denmark, Lead U.S. in Use of Electronic Medical Records," *Healthcare News,* 8 August 2002.

3. Scott Wallace, interview with the author. Of course, as Wallace is quick to admit, his veterinarian's system is dramatically simpler—and cheaper—than the system a physician would need. Samantha doesn't see 20 specialists; she doesn't have health insurance; she has never been hospitalized, and she receives her medication directly from her vet. Thus, the vet doesn't need a system that talks to other vets, insurers, pharmacies, or hospitals. See also Amanda Gardner, "U.S. Sets Sights on Electronic Health Records: Aims to Catch Up with Industry, Make Health History Portable," *HealthDay,* 26 July 2004.

4. "Physicians, Business, Government & Industry Embrace Common Strategy to Improve Health Care: Pay-for-Performance," press release, Bridges to Excellence, 28 March 2005; "President Bush's IT Doctor," *BusinessWeek Online,* 29 March 2005.

5. Bruce Vladeck, interview with the author. See also Bruce C. Vladeck, "Ineffective Approach," Letters, *Health Affairs,* March/April 2004. Vladeck is not alone in questioning whether relatively small financial incentives will change behavior. A survey of pay-for-performance programs published in *Health Affairs* shows that "most programs put 5 percent or less of compensation at risk for performance on quality and many simultaneously target ten or more separate clinical areas," leaving the researchers to "wonder if the incremental reward for quality for any one provider will be sufficient to motivate the kind of change that is needed." (Meredith B. Rosenthal, Rushika Fernandopulle, HyunSook Ryu Song, and Bruce Landon, "Paying for Quality: Providers' Incentives for Quality Improvement," *Health Affairs,* March/April 2004.)

6. David Wessel, "Pay-for-Performance Strikes a Nerve or Two," *The Wall Street Journal,* 8 February 2005.

7. Arnold M. Epstein, Thomas H. Lee, and Mary Beth Hamel, "Paying Physicians for High-Quality Care," *The New England Journal of Medicine,* 22 January 2004.

8. Interview with the author.

9. J. D. Kleinke, "Dot-Gov: Market Failure and the Creation of a National Health Information Technology System," *Health Affairs,* September/October 2005.

10. John Carroll, "Electronic Medical Records: High Hopes Meet Harsh Reality," *Managed Care,* November 2004. When Quinn made the comment, he was chief technology officer of Capgemini Health.

11. Barry Hieb, interview with the author. See also Carroll, "Electronic Medical Records: High Hopes Meet Harsh Reality."

12. Rainu Kaushal, David Blumenthal, Eric G. Poon, et al., and the Cost of National Health

Information Network Working Group, "The Costs of a National Health Information Network," *Annals of Internal Medicine,* 2 August 2005.

13. In 2005, it appeared that only about 19 percent of U.S. hospitals and roughly 20 percent of the nation's licensed doctors have even begun to use electronic medical records. See GAO report number GAO-05-309R, "Health and Human Services' Estimate of Health Care Cost Savings Resulting from the Use of Information Technology," 17 February 2005. Here, the GAO estimates that 19 percent of hospitals use electronic medical records, citing the 15th annual leadership survey of the Healthcare Information and Management Systems Society.

In "U.S. Will Offer Doctors Free Electronic Records System" *(The New York Times,* 21 July 2005), Gina Kolata reported that "20 to 25 percent of the 650,000 civilian doctors working outside the military and the VA hospital system use EMR." Meanwhile, *Medical Economics* estimated that only 15 percent of primary care physicians have electronic records. (Ken Terry, "EHRs: Where Are We Now?: Uncle Sam Doesn't Want to Pay for It, but He Wants You to Buy an EHR Anyway. Our Consultants' Recommendations? Wait a While" [20 May 2005].)

14. George Halvorson, interview with the author. See also George C. Halvorson, "Wiring Health Care," *Health Affairs,* September/October 2005.

15. For a discussion of angioplasties and bypass surgery see chapter 2, "Market-Driven Medicines: The Cost of Competition," and chapter 3, "For-Profit Hospitals: A Flaw in the Business Model?"

16. Sharon Begley, "Early Cancer Detection Doesn't Always Give Patient an Advantage," *The Wall Street Journal,* 26 August 2005.

17. H. Gilbert Welch, *Should I Be Tested for Cancer? Maybe Not and Here's Why,* (Berkeley: University of California Press, 2004), 61–62.

18. Welch, *Should I Be Tested for Cancer?* 63.

19. In "Paying for Quality: Providers' Incentives for Quality Improvement," Rosenthal et al. estimate that individual payers in the private sector have put aside "more than $200 million for these programs in 2004," yet the authors note that most of these programs put 5 percent or less of compensation at risk for performance on quality, and many simultaneously target ten or more separate clinical areas.

"Moreover, because few sponsors command a large share of the average provider's business, the quality incentive is further diluted by competing incentives. Improving quality of care in the U.S. health care system has some elements of a public good problem," they observe. "Investments by one payer accrue benefits to other payers because of nonexclusive contracting (overlapping networks), and by corollary no individual payer will invest enough in trying to bridge the quality chasm. Purchasing coalitions and other multilateral entities such as . . . Leapfrog [a consortium of employers] have emerged to overcome this problem in part, but our data suggest that most paying-for-quality initiatives are relatively small in scale."

See also Gina Kolata and Reed Abelson, "A Bonus for Health, Payable to the Doctor," *The New York Times,* 15 April 2005.

20. David Wessel, "Paying for Better Care, Not More: Medicare Joins the P4P Movement," *The Wall Street Journal,* 3 February 2005.

21. Government Innovators Network (produced by the Ash Institute for Democratic Governance and Innovation at Harvard's John F. Kennedy School of Government), explains how the penalties work. At the end of the first year, baselines will be set for the bottom 20 percent and the bottom 10 percent. These levels remain static, and CMS and Premier expect that all hospitals will be above the baselines by the final year of the demonstration. If any hospitals are below the 10 percent baseline in the third year of the demonstration, they will get a 2 percent reduction in Medicare payments for the clinical area involved, and those between 20 and 10 percent will get a 1 percent reduction. ("Medicare pay-for-performance demonstration shows significant quality of care improvements," *US Fed News,* 9 May 2005.)

22. Interview with the author.

23. Gina Kolata, "Program Coaxes Hospitals to See Treatments Under Their Noses," *The New York Times,* 25 December 2004.

24. Wessel, "Paying for Better Care, Not More: Medicare Joins the P4P Movement."

25. Peter Gross, interview with the author. See also Kolata, "Program Coaxes Hospitals to See Treatments Under Their Noses."

26. Gross, interview with the author. See also Kolata, "Program Coaxes Doctors to See Treatments Under Their Noses," and Kolata and Abelson, "A Bonus for Health, Payable to the Doctor."

27. In December, while rating Hackensack's bond issue A2, Moody's described the medical center as "the dominant provider . . . in an affluent service area." (Moody's Investor Service, "Moody's Affirms A2 Rating to Hackensack University Medical Center," press release, 22 December 2003.)

28. Rosenthal et al., "Paying for Quality: Providers' Incentives for Quality Improvement."

29. Michael Beer and Mark D. Cannon, "Promise and Peril in Implementing Pay-for-Performance," *Human Resource Management,* spring 2004.

30. Beer and Cannon suggest that since HP's culture is one that "historically placed more emphasis on management [that relied on "commitment" and "trust" rather than "on monetary incentives"] HP may have been quicker to abandon programs that threatened trust and commitment. They also note that the problems HP encountered "are supported by findings that executives in high team-oriented cultures, when compared with exectives who perceived their cultures as less team-oriented, observed more rather than fewer unintended negatives outcomes (damage to teamwork, gaming, etc.) as a result of executive incentive systems."

    The authors are not saying that P4P can't work. To the contrary, they emphasize that it can motivate, but they conclude "little attention has been given to whether the benefits outweigh the costs or the 'fit' of these programs with high-commitment cultures like Hewlett-Packard was at the time. . . . While pay-for-performance systems theoretically promise many motivation and performance benefits, researchers and managers have underappreciated the costs incurred when these systems are implemented, particularly in high-commitment systems."

31. "Measurable Goals, Clear Communication Key to Performance-Based Incentive Programs," *RSM McGladrey Advantage,* February 2005.

32. Alfie Kohn, "Why Incentive Plans Cannot Work," *Harvard Business Review,* 1 September 1993.

33. Kenneth Kizer, interview with the author.

34. "Doctor 'Report Cards' May Keep Some Heart Patients from Getting Angioplasties, U-M Study Suggests," press release, Blue Cross Blue Shield of Michigan, 6 June 2005.

35. Serena Gordon, "Study: Public Disclosure Makes Docs More Cautious," *HealthDay,* 8 June 2005.

36. A study by University of Michigan and Veterans Affairs researchers found that about one in five older diabetes patients cannot afford necessary medications. The study's results were "disturbing," said John D. Piette, lead author of a report titled, "Problems Paying Out-of-Pocket Medication Costs Among Older Adults with Diabetes," which was published in the February 2004 issue of *Diabetes Care.* "This is a major healthcare threat to millions of people," he said. (Quoted in Martin Sipkoff, "Pharmacists Can Help Patients Who Can't Afford Diabetes Meds," *Drug Topics* online, 1 October 2004.)

37. Lawrence P. Casalino, "Markets and Medicine: Barriers to Creating a 'Business Case for Quality'," *Perspectives in Biology and Medicine,* winter 2003. On the number of patients needed to assess quality of care, Casalino cites T. P. Hofer et al., "The Unreliability of Individual Physician 'Report Cards' for Assessing the Costs and Quality of Care of a Chronic Disease, *Journal of the American Medical Association,* 9 June 1999.

38. Jeremiah Hurley, review of David M. Cutler's *Your Money or Your Life: Strong Medicine for America's Health Care System* in *Journal of Health Politics, Policy and Law,* August 2005.

39. Donald M. Berwick, "Dirty Words and Magic Spells," address to the 12th annual National Forum on Quality Improvement in Health Care, 5 December 2000, collected in *Escape Fire: Designs for the Future of Health Care* (San Francisco: Jossey-Bass, 2003), 237.

40. Berwick, "Dirty Words and Magic Spells," 231.

41. Robert Galvin, "Interview: 'A Deficiency of Will and Ambition': A Conversation with Donald Berwick," Web Exclusive, *Health Affairs,* 12 January 2005.

42. Stephen Taub, " 'Pay for Performance' Underperforming," CFO.com, 17 June 2004; Teresa M. Amabile, "How to Kill Creativity," *Harvard Business Review,* September-October 1998.

43. Kohn, "Why Incentive Plans Cannot Work."

44. Vladeck, interview with the author, and see "Ineffective Approach."

45. Robert Califf, interview with the author.

46. Halvorson cites A. O. Berg, "Variations Among Family Physicians' Management Strategies for Lower Urinary Tract Infection in Women: A Report from the Washington Family Physicians Collective Research Network," *The Journal of the American Board of Family Practices,* September-October 1991.

47. George C. Halvorson and George J. Isham, *Epidemic of Care: A Call for Safer, Better, and More Accountable Health Care* (San Francisco: Jossey-Bass, 2003), 19–34.

48. The Institute of Medicine, *Crossing the Quality Chasm: A New Health System for the 21st Century* (Washington, D.C.: National Academies Press, 2001).

49. Heather Havenstein, "Health Care System Turns to IT for Patient Care Plans; Suggested Treatment Is Based on Data About Similar Patients," *Computerworld,* 8 August 2005.

50. Interview with the author.

51. Research shows that solo practitioners are less likely to use recommended care protocols to manage chronically ill patients, and are less likely to use information technology. See

L. Casalino et al., "External Incentives, Information Technology, and Organized Processes to Improve Health Care Quality for Patients with Chronic Diseases," *The Journal of the American Medical Association,* 22 January 2003; Alain C. Enthoven and Laura A. Tollen, "Competition in Health Care: It Takes Systems to Pursue Quality and Efficiency," Web Exclusive, *Health Affairs,* 7 September 2005.

52. Andrew Wiesenthal, interview with the author.

53. "Statins: The Bandwagon Effect," UC Berkeley Wellness Letter, www.wellnessletter.com, October 2004.

54. In 2005 the most recent evidence suggested unresolved questions about the risks and benefits of statins for older patients. In one large clinical trial, published in the British medical journal *Lancet* in 2002, researchers found statins lowered the incidence of cardiac "events," including heart attacks, among 70- to 82-year-olds with heart disease or known risk factors. *But the study found no effect on longevity.* "Although statins are recommended for men and women, young and old, they've been shown to extend life in only one group: middle-age men at high risk for heart disease," Beatrice Golomb, a cardiologist at UC, San Diego, pointed out in 2005. "For all other groups, the existing evidence says that your life will not be extended." And while only a tiny percentage of patients on statins develop drug-related muscle pain, such pain can be a signal for rhabdomyolysis, a serious condition that can lead to kidney failure and death. (See "Using Crestor—and All Statins—Safely," *Harvard Heart Letter,* 1 September 2005; Alex Barnum, "Doubts Raised on Wider Sales of Statins; Over-the-Counter Marketing Push for Cholesterol Drug," *San Francisco Chronicle,* 24 January 2005.)

55. Liz Dreesen, interview with the author.

56. Atul Gawande, "The Bell Curve," *The New Yorker,* 6 December 2004.

57. Kim Adcock, interview with the author.

58. Halvorson and Isham, *Epidemic of Care,* 176.

59. Halvorson, interview with the author.

60. Interview with the author.

61. Bill Saporito, "The e-Health Revolution: How a Bipartisan Bill from Hillary Clinton and Bill Frist Could Help Jump-start a New Kind of Health-Care Reform," *Time,* 27 June 2005.

62. Kleinke, "Dot-Gov: Market Failure and the Creation of a National Health Information Technology System."

63. As evidence, Kleinke cites the International Telecommunications Union, "ITU's New Broadband Statistics for 1 January 2005," 13 April 2005.

64. Robert Cunningham, "Action Through Collaboration: A Conversation with David Brailer," *Health Affairs,* September/October 2005.

65. Carroll, "Electronic Medical Records: High Hopes Meet Harsh Reality," where Brailer puts the failure rate at "30% to 50%."

66. Dudley Danoff, quoted in "Doctors Pull Plug on Paperless System at Cedars-Sinai Medical Center in Los Angeles," *AMNews,* 17 February 2003.

67. Paul Hackmeyer, quoted in Ceci Connolly, "Cedars-Sinai Doctors Cling to Pen and Paper," *The Washington Post,* 21 March 2005.

68. John Harold, interview with the author.

69. Joan Ash, quoted in "Most Hospitals Don't Use Latest Ordering Technology," available online at http://www.eurekalert.org/pub_releases/2003-11/ohs-mhd112403.php.

70. Connolly, "Cedars-Sinai Doctors Cling to Pen and Paper."

71. Interview with the author.

72. "Doctors Pull Plug on Paperless System at Cedars-Sinai Medical Center in Los Angeles."

73. Harold, interview with the author.

74. Vladeck, interview with the author.

75. Carroll, "Electronic Medical Records: High Hopes Meet Harsh Reality."

76. Christine Wiebe, "Doctor Pay Surveys Reveal Growing Gaps," *Medscape Business of Medicine,* March 2005; Paul Jolly, "Medical School Tuition and Young Physicians' Indebtedness," *Health Affairs,* March/April 2005.

77. Atul Gawande, "Piecework: Medicine's Money Problem," *The New Yorker,* 4 April 2005.

78. Gawande, "Piecework."

79. In "Piecework" Gawande gives the example of a general surgeon who does not take insurance and charges $8,500 to remove a gall bladder. Most insurers will pay $700. For an operation to stop severe reflux of stomach acid, insurers pay $1,100, Gawande reports. His acquaintance charges $12,000 and "has no shortage of patients." Because they are paying so much, his patients assume that he must be very good.

80. Interview with the author.

81. Carroll, "Electronic Medical Records: High Hopes Meet Harsh Reality."

82. Gina Kolata, "Health Plan That Cuts Costs Raises Doctors' Ire," *The New York Times,* 11 August 2004.

83. Casalino, "Markets and Medicine: Barriers to Creating a 'Business Case for Quality.' "

84. Kleinke, "Dot-Gov: Market Failure and the Creation of a National Health Information Technology System."

85. Carroll, "Electronic Medical Records: High Hopes Meet Harsh Reality."

86. Hieb, interview with the author.

87. Wallace, interview with the author; see also Gardner, "U.S. Sets Sights on Electronic Health Records."

88. Bill Weeks, interview with the author.

89. See Phillip Longman's description of how the computerized order entry system works in "The Best Care Anywhere," *Washington Monthly,* January/February 2005.

90. Longman quotes Wollstein in "The Best Care Anywhere."

91. Elliott S. Fisher, "Medical Care—Is More Always Better?" Editorial, *The New England Journal of Medicine,* 23 October 2003.

92. Kizer, interview with the author.

93. "VA Hospitals Found Best in Overall Care Quality, but Not Every One Measures Up, Reviews Show," *Health Care Strategic Management,* 1 January 2005.

94. Barry Meier, "Doctors, Too, Ask: Is This Drug Right?" *The New York Times,* 30 December 2004.

95. Edward Doyle, "Profiles in Palliative Care," *Today's Hospitalist,* December 2004.

96. Gawande, "The Bell Curve"; Christopher J. Gearon, "Military Might," *U.S. News & World Report,* 18 July 2005.

97. Gilbert M. Gaul, "Revamped Veterans' Health Care Now a Model," *The Washington Post,* 22 August 2005.

98. Office of the Press Secretary, "President Bush Touts Benefits of Health Care Information Technology," Department of Veterans Affairs Medical Center, 27 April 2004.

99. A notable exception is a lengthy article by Phillip Longman that appeared in *Washington Monthly,* "The Best Care Anywhere." In March, Timothy Noah wrote about Longman's story in *Slate* (see note 100), and later that year, both *U.S. News & World Report* and *The Washington Post* picked up on the story (see notes above).

100. Timothy Noah, "The Triumph of Socialized Medicine," *Slate,* 8 March 2005.

101. Sheldon Greenfield, and Sherrie H. Kaplan, "Creating a Culture of Quality: The Remarkable Transformation of the Department of Veterans Affairs Health Care System," editorial, *Annals of Internal Medicine,* 17 August 2004; A. K. Jha, J. B. Perlin, K. W. Kizer, and R. A. Dudley, "Effect of the Transformation of the Veterans Affairs Health Care System on the Quality of Care, *The New England Journal of Medicine* 29 May 2003; "VA Hospitals Found Best in Overall Care Quality, but Not Every One Measures Up, Reviews Show;" Sheldon Greenfield, Sherrie H. Kaplan, Eve A. Kerr, et al., "Diabetes Care Quality in the Veterans Affairs Health Care System and Commercial Managed Care: The TRIAD Study," *Annals of Internal Medicine,* 17 August 2004.

102. See the medical journal studies cited above as well as Gaul, "Revamped Veterans' Health Care Now a Model."

103. "VA Hospitals Found Best in Overall Care Quality, but Not Every One Measures Up, Reviews Show."

104. Gaul, "Revamped Veterans' Health Care Now a Model."

105. Statement of James E. Sursely, National Commander, Disabled American Veterans, before the Senate and House Committee on Veterans' Affairs, 8 March 2005. Sursely was quoting from a study published in *Medical Care Research and Review* at the end of 2004: "Value for Taxpayers' Dollars: What VA Care Would Cost at Medicare Prices."

106. Kizer, interview with the author.

107. Longman, "The Best Care Anywhere."

108. Weeks, interview with the author.

109. At one time, many veterans avoided VA hospitals, but in recent years the numbers show that vets are pouring into the VA system, and sticking with it, with much of the increased demand predating both Afghanistan and Iraq—which suggests that the vets' preference for VA clinics and hospitals coincides with the department's new reputation for quality.

110. In 2005, when the state of California rated the state's 10 largest commercial HMOs in four general categories (preventive care, treatment and recovery, care of chronic illnesses, and patient satisfaction), as well as about 30 subcategories, Kaiser Permanente's Southern California unit scored the highest among the HMOs, receiving 10 out of 12 possible stars. Kaiser's northern California unit, which came in first a year earlier, ranked second, with nine stars. (Laura Benko, "California Rates HMOs," *Modern Healthcare,* 19 September 2005.) On turnover at Kaiser, see David Lawrence, "Gatekeeping Reconsidered," *The New England Journal of Medicine,* 2 November 2001.

111. Jack Mahoney, interview with the author.

112. Weeks, interview with the author.

113. Rebecca Vesely, "Kaiser Earns Praise for Its Info System," *The Oakland Tribune,* 3 August 2005.

114. George C. Halvorson, "Epilogue," in *Toward a 21st-Century Health System: The Contributions and Promise of Prepaid Group Practice,* Alain C. Enthoven and Laura A. Tollen, eds. (San Francisco: Jossey-Bass, 2004), 258.

115. Gaul, "Revamped Veterans' Health Care Now a Model."

116. Wiesenthal, interview with the author.

117. Kolata, "U.S. Will Offer Doctors Free Electronic Records System."

118. Hieb, interview with the author.

119. Hieb, interview with the author. See also Carroll, "Electronic Medical Records: High Hopes Meet Harsh Reality."

120. Kleinke, "Dot-Gov: Market Failure and the Creation of a National Health Information Technology System."

121. Kleinke, "Dot-Gov."

122. Hieb, interview with the author.

123. See chapter 6.

124. Kaushal et al., "The Costs of a National Health Information Network."

CHAPTER 8

1. Hank McKinnell with John Kador, *A Call to Action: Taking Back Healthcare for Future Generations* (New York: McGraw-Hill, 2005), 11–13. "Dinner at the McKinell house had some interesting moments in the 1990s," McKinnell writes. "The pharmaceutical industry was the target of scorching criticism from HIV/AIDS activists who saw us blocking the way for impoverished people who needed medicines . . . Perhaps at that moment the seeds for this book started to take shape . . ." By 2001 "Dinners at the McKinnell home became more heated," he reports. "We are sitting on a failed health system. It is a failure economically and politically, and for the sake of our children I want to find a better way."

2. Charles Rosen—unless otherwise indicated, the story that follows is based on interviews with the author.

3. For an excellent summary of data available from Europe as well as the FDA trial in the United States, see Jeffrey A. Tice, assistant adjunct professor of medicine, division of general internal medicine, University of California, San Francisco, "Artificial Disc Replacement for Degenerative Disc Disease of the Lumbar Spine," assessment, California Technology Assessment Forum, 16 February 2005.

4. Melissa Davis, "J&J Discs Face Backlash," TheStreet.com, 13 May 2005.

5. Mintzer reports that he has no affiliation with any device maker. His clients are patients who pay him to present their case to surgeons and, in some cases, accompany them to their surgery (interview with the author).

6. Rhonda L. Rundle and Scott Hensley, "J&J's New Device for Spine Surgery Raises Questions," *The Wall Street Journal,* 7 June 2005.

7. Rundle and Hensley, "J&J's New Device for Spine Surgery Raises Questions."

8. In an interview with the author in October of 2005, Dr. Riina still didn't know what had

gone wrong, and drew the analogy to hip replacement. For the original story, see Rundle and Hensley, "J&J's New Device for Spine Surgery Raises Questions."

9. "Peloza confirmed that he was a Medtronic consultant, but says that didn't affect his view of the Charité," *The Wall Street Journal* reported. (Rundle and Hensley, "J&J's New Device for Spine Surgery Raises Questions.")

10. In an interview with the author, Johnson & Johnson's William P. Christianson, vice president of clinical and regulatory affairs, DePuy Spine, Inc. (the division of J&J that is marketing the disc), denied the allegation that a rep offered anyone a kickback. "We do not conduct ourselves that way," Christianson declared—although he acknowledged that the company couldn't be sure what an individual rogue rep might do to boost his own performance.

11. Reed Abelson and Melody Petersen, "An Operation to Ease Back Pain Bolsters the Bottom Line, Too," *The New York Times,* 31 December 2003.

12. Transcript, Orthopaedic and Rehabilitation Devices Panel of the Medical Devices Advisory Committee, Food and Drug Administration, 2 June 2004, can be found at www .fda.gov. All further quotations from the panel meeting are taken from this transcript.

13. When the author checked with the FDA about Courtney's comment that the surgeons were "just getting their feet wet" with the first 71 patients, she received an e-mail reply from an FDA spokesperson: "The Charité study was designed to have non-randomized roll-in patients (71 patients) that were primarily used for training. The informed consent for these patients clearly stated their role in the study, and we analyzed these patients for safety."

14. Because the cost of medical devices varies so widely from one hospital to the next (see discussing of pricing later in this chapter), there is some controversy over whether Charité is more expensive than fusion. The total cost of implanting the disc is "roughly the same price as the alternative—spinal fusion," according to J&J's Christianson, and at least one surgeon confirms that opinion.

15. M. de Kleuver, F. Oner, and W. Jacobs, "Total Disc Replacement for Chronic Low Back Pain: Background and a Systematic Review of the Literature," *European Spine Journal,* April 2003. During the FDA panel hearing, Dr. Andre van Ooij, a spinal surgeon from Maastricht, the Netherlands, offered additional information, reporting on his experience using Charité while treating 49 patients over a period of eight years. According to Dr. Van Ooij, the patients suffered a high rate of complications. But since Medtronic, J&J's rival, had sent Dr. Van Ooij to the panel meeting, paying all of his travel expenses, it was difficult to know to what degree his testimony was biased.

16. "I would have to say that if this device was going to [fulfill] its main purpose over a short-term—that is a two to three year period . . . then the data does suggest that this is probably safe," said Finnegan. "Unfortunately, this device is designed for a much longer period of time and I do not think that there is data present at the present time to say . . . it is safe for the lifetime that it is predicted to be necessary for."

17. Choll Kim, of the University of California, San Diego, seemed to agree with Finnegan. "This is a complex device," said Kim. "It's the first of its kind and designed to last for a long time, and we can't get at that question until we wait." Following Kim's remark, four of the eight voting members of the panel said that they concurred: Sanjiv S.

Naidu, Pennsylvania State College of Medicine; Marcus P. Besser, Thomas Jefferson University; Brent A. Blumenstein, TriArc Consulting; and Kirkpatrick.

18. Christianson, interview with the author.

19. Stephen Hochschuler, and Paul McAfee, "Issues to Consider Before Having Artificial Disc Surgery," spine-health.com, 17 November 2004.

20. Mintzer, interview with the author.

21. David Polly, interview with the author.

22. Letter from Charles Rosen to Office of Management Programs, Division of Freedom of Information, 4 February 2005.

23. Christianson, interview with the author. Instead of sending the information, Christianson offered to meet with Rosen so that they could "review the data in an appropriate context." Rosen replied: "As an Associate Clinical Professor of Surgery, having performed spine surgery for 16 years on all aspects of the spine, I do not need you to interpret surgical data in 'the appropriate context.' This suggests you wish me to review the data with a certain bias, and only with you or your agent present, instead of just sending it to me."

24. Daniel Rosenberg, "J&J Artificial Spinal Disc Runs into Insurance Issues," Dow Jones Newswires, 24 February 2005.

25. Rundle and Hensley, "J&J's New Device for Spine Surgery Raises Questions."

26. "A Program of Excellence in Artificial Disc Replacement (ADR)" can be found on Cedars-Sinai's website in October of 2005 (www.csmc.edu/7072.html).

27. John Regan, interview with the author. In that interview, he reported the 90 percent success rate; confirmed that in his experience, the surgery was "routine and safe" but indicated that it was not for all patients (nor all surgeons), and declined to say how much he had received from J&J. In an earlier interview with *The Wall Street Journal,* Regan said that the royalty payments did not influence his professional judgment. He confirmed this in the interview with the author.

28. As the table below shows, in 2004 IMS Health, a company that tracks the pharmaceutical industry, reported total U.S. drugs sales at $235.367 billion.

In 2005 IMS projected that compound annual growth rate for the prescription drug market in the United States would be between 7 percent and 10 percent from 2005 to 2009. On that basis, drug sales would hit $270 billion to $280 billion in 2006. (For projections, see Ana-Maria Zaugg and Diana Conmy, "The IMS Health Report: Pressure Zone," *Medical Marketing & Media,* 1 May 2005. Note: Others project slower growth—much depends on how the Medicare prescription drug bill affects the industry.

2004 YEAR-END U.S. PRESCRIPTION AND SALES INFORMATION AND COMMENTARY (WWW.IMSHEALTH.COM/IMS/PORTAL/FRONT/ARTICLEC/ 0,2777,6599_3665_69890098,00.HTML)

	Total U.S. Sales (U.S. $Millions)*	% Growth +/-	% Market Share
Chain Stores	$84,132	6.4%	35.7%
Mail Service	$33,877	17.9%	14.4%
Independent Pharmacies	$33,410	5.2%	14.2%

	Total U.S. Sales (U.S. $Millions)*	% Growth +/–	% Market Share
Non-Federal Hospitals	$24,768	7.7%	10.5%
Clinics	$21,887	11.6%	9.3%
Food Stores	$20,755	6.8%	8.8%
Long-Term Care	$8,160	5.0%	3.5%
Federal Hospitals	$3,608	4.7%	1.5%
Home Health	$2,445	12.0%	1.0%
HMOs	$1,508	–1.7%	0.6%
Others	$817	2.8%	0.3%
Total U.S. Market	$235,367	8.3%	100%

* Represents total dispensed prescriptions, including insulin dispensed through chain, food store, independent long-term care, and mail service pharmacies.

Source: IMS Health, National Sales Perspectives™, February 2005

29. Bear Stearns device industry analyst Milton Hsu provides a breakdown: "In the U.S., the market for orthopedic devices is roughly $18 billion; ophthalmologic devices account for another $10 billion; stents, $5 billion; and cardiac devices, $3.1 billion." (interview with the author.)

30. Jerry Avorn, *Powerful Medicines: The Benefits, Risks, and Costs of Prescription Drugs* (New York: Knopf, 2004), 217.

31. *Out of Bounds: Rising Prescription Drug Prices for Seniors,* (Washington, D.C.: Families USA, July 2003.)

32. Bradley C. Strunk, Paul B. Ginsburg, and John P. Cookson, "Tracking Health Care Costs: Declining Growth Trend Pauses in 2004," Web Exclusives, *Health Affairs,* 21 June 2005.

33. The Kaiser Family Foundation, "Prescription Drug Trends," October 2003. Three factors drove the rise in spending on prescription drugs from 1993 to 2003: Increased consumption (accounting for 42 percent of the increase), manufacturers' price hikes (25 percent), and successful marketing persuading consumers to switch to higher-priced drugs (34 percent). (Source: KFF analysis of price and utilization data from IMS Health and expenditure data from Centers for Medicare and Medicaid Services at www.cms.hhs.gov/statistics/nhe/default.asp [National Health Accounts].)

34. Health Care Industry Market Update: "Wall Street's View of Medical Device and Supply Manufacturers," CMS (Centers for Medicare and Medicaid), 5 December 2003.

35. Melissa Davis, "Zimmer, Peers Brace for Pricing Storm," TheStreet.com, 12 July 2005.

36. Thomas M. Burton, "Medtronic Wins Europe's Backing for Coated Stent," *The Wall Street Journal,* 1 August 2005.

37. Reed Abelson, "Possible Conflicts for Doctors Are Seen on Medical Devices," *The New York Times,* 22 September 2005.

38. Marcia Angell, *The Truth About the Drug Companies: How They Deceive Us and What to Do About It* (New York: Random House, 2004), 37.

39. Since sales and marketing are bundled together with administrative costs, it is difficult to

tease out just how much pharmaceutical companies spend on promotion, but one Wall Street analyst put the cost at roughly 20 percent to 25 percent of sales (interview with the author). Meanwhile, the industry itself reported spending just 17.7 percent of revenues on R & D in 2003. (See Pharmaceutical Research and Manufacturers of America, Pharmaceutical Industry Profile, various years, at www.phrma.org/publications.)

40. Richard Evans, interview with the author.

41. David Pauly, "Drug Companies' Cost of Pushing Pills Rivals R&D," *Bloomberg News,* 26 August 2004. Over the preceding five years, drug makers boosted promotional spending by 103 percent while R & D climbed by only about 58 percent. See chapter 2, "The Cost of Competition: An Overview."

42. McKinnell, *A Call to Action,* 46–47.

43. Interview with the author. See also Sally Hardcastle, "Pfizer Sees Future in New Drugs, *BBC News,* U.K. Edition, 1 February 2005, http://news.bbc.co.uk/1/hi/business/4226477.stm.

44. "Prescription Drug Trends Fact Sheet"—November 2005 Update, www.kff.org.

45. Avorn, *Powerful Medicines,* 407, 219.

46. Health Care Industry Market Update: "Wall Street's View of Medical Device and Supply Manufacturers."

47. John Cherf, interview with the author.

48. Melissa Davis, "Orthopedics Probe's Deep Roots," TheStreet.com, 5 April 2005. Davis cites Morgan Stanley analyst Glenn Reicin, who, at the time, estimated that the orthopedic implant industry was an $11 billion industry. Later estimates put it at $18 billion.

49. George C. Halvorson and George J. Isham, *Epidemic of Care: A Call for Safer, Better, and More Accountable Health Care* (San Francisco: Jossey-Bass, 2003), 88.

50. Angell, *The Truth About the Drug Companies,* 219–220.

51. In *Powerful Medicines,* 320, Avorn describes how drugmaker Wyeth initiated a "bonus miles program" in which each prescription written for one of its drugs generated points a doctor could trade in for trips to vacation destinations. (When this scam came to light, Wyeth was forced to pay large settlements to Medicaid programs around the country for bribing physicians.)

52. Halvorson and Isham, *Epidemic of Care,* 90–91.

53. Arguably, a panel of doctors and device experts who had the power to insist on clinical evidence of how a product had affected a large pool of patients would be in a much better position to decide whether the new drug or device was worth a premium—and to convey that information to consumers.

54. "Rising Cost of Prescription Drugs," National Priorities Project, 31 July 2004.

55. Avorn, *Powerful Medicines,* 219.

56. In 2004, for example, Medco Health Solutions, the nation's largest PBM, agreed to pay states $29.3 million for failing to pass on savings either to health plans or to consumers. (Linda Loyd, "Medco Settles with U.S., 20 States," *The Philadelphia Inquirer,* 27 April 2004.) See also Milt Freudenheim, "Critics Attack Secret Deals By Middlemen to Buy Drugs," *The New York Times,* 20 December 2003; Freudenheim, "Pharmacy Benefit Companies Won't Disclose Fees," *The New York Times,* 10 January 2003.

Meanwhile, in 2005 PBMs continued to resist revealing discounts. (Vanessa

Fuhrmans, "Employers Join to Push Drug Managers for Full Disclosure," *The Wall Street Journal,* 10 August 2005; Barbara Martinez, "Caremark Closes In on a Settlement," *The Wall Street Journal,* 27 May 2005.)

57. Halvorson and Isham, *Epidemic of Care,* 91.

58. Avorn, *Powerful Medicines,* 233.

59. Cherf, interview with the author.

60. George Cipolletti, interview with the author.

61. Abelson, "Possible Conflicts for Doctors Are Seen on Medical Devices."

62. Martha Lagace described Reicin's presentation in Harvard Business School's *HBS Working Knowledge* ("Trouble Ahead: Ethics and Medical Devices," 22 November 2004). In response to the author's query, Reicin confirmed that *Working Knowledge* had given an accurate account. See also Davis, "Orthopedics Probe's Deep Roots."

63. Lagace, "Trouble Ahead: Ethics and Medical Devices."

64. Melissa Davis, "Justice Probe Hammers Stryker, Biomet," TheStreet.com, 31 March 2005.

65. See Davis, "Orthopedics Probe's Deep Roots."

66. Thomas R. Burton, "U.S. Seeks Data from Medtronic, St. Jude, Guidant," *The Wall Street Journal,* 26 October 2005.

67. Abelson, "Possible Conflicts for Doctors Are Seen on Medical Devices."

68. Abelson, "Possible Conflicts for Doctors Are Seen on Medical Devices."

69. Abelson, "Possible Conflicts for Doctors Are Seen on Medical Devices."

70. Cherf, interview with the author.

71. Abelson, "Possible Conflicts for Doctors Are Seen on Medical Devices."

72. Abelson, "Possible Conflicts for Doctors Are Seen on Medical Devices."

73. For example, see Mary Flood, "Dissatisfied Doctors Open a Full-Service Hospital," *The Wall Street Journal,* 11 August 1999.

74. Cherf, interview with the author.

75. Melissa Davis, "Hospitals Turn Tables on Implants," TheStreet.com, 20 June 2005.

76. Davis, "Hospitals Turn Tables on Implants."

77. Davis, "Hospitals Turn Tables on Implants." Davis points out that Aurora isn't the first hospital system to extract discounts from device makers. The Milwaukee hospital system based its strategy on a successful campaign carried out earlier by BayCare Health System in Florida.

78. "Senate Bill Raises Fears Among Medtech Investors," Reuters, 12 May 2005.

79. Cipolletti, interview with the author.

80. Cipolletti, interview with the author.

81. Cherf, interview with the author.

82. Cipolletti, interview with the author.

83. Cherf, interview with the author.

84. Halvorson and Isham, *Epidemic of Care,* 57.

85. Melissa Davis, "Competition Limps Toward Knee Implant Market," TheStreet.com, 27 September 2005.

86. Abelson and Petersen, "An Operation to Ease Back Pain Bolsters the Bottom Line, Too."

87. Davis, "Zimmer, Peers Brace for Pricing Storm."

88. Melissa Davis, "Biomet Gains Hinge on Old Standby," TheStreet.com, 12 May 2005.

89. Paolo Gallinaro, "Where Have All the Flowers Gone?" *Orthopedics,* January 2005.

90. See Davis, "Biomet Gains Hinge on Old Standby."

91. Steven T. Woolson, et al:, "Comparison of Primary Total Hip Replacements Performed with a Standard Incision or a Mini-Incision, *The Journal of Bone and Joint Surgery,* 1 July 2004; see also Thomas K. Fehring and J. Bohannon Mason, "Catastrophic Complications of Minimally Invasive Hip Surgery: A Series of Three Cases," *The Journal of Bone and Joint Surgery,* 1 April 2005; Luke Ogonda et al., "A Minimal-Incision Technique in Total Hip Arthroplasty Does Not Improve Early Postoperative Outcomes: A Prospective, Randomized, Controlled Trial," *The Journal of Bone and Joint Surgery,* 1 April 2005.

92. Davis, "Orthopedics Probe's Deep Roots."

93. Davis, "Orthopedics Probe's Deep Roots." However, Cipolletti points out, the rate of "device failure" is just one way to measure whether a new device marks an improvement over an older product. "There are other factors like gait, back pain, or a limp that U.S. patients complain about," says Cipolletti. "European patients are less likely to complain." (Interview with the author.)

94. Cipolletti, interview with the author.

95. This description of Oukrop's death is based on Barry Meier's account in *The New York Times:* "Repeated Defect in Heart Devices Exposes a History of Problems," 20 October 2005.

96. Robert Steinbrook, "The Controversy over Guidant's Implantable Defibrillators," *The New England Journal of Medicine,* 21 July 2005.

97. Steinbrook, "The Controversy over Guidant's Implantable Defibrillators."

98. Steinbrook, "The Controversy over Guidant's Implantable Defibrillators." Here Steinbrook refers to Barry Meier's "Maker of Heart Device Kept Flaw from Doctors," *The New York Times,* 24 May 2005.

99. Jim McCartney, "Guidant Assesses the Fallout; Medical, Financial Communities Differ on Device Maker's Delayed Disclosure of Potential Flaw," *St. Paul Pioneer Press,* 25 May 2005.

100. Meier, "Maker of Heart Device Kept Flaw from Doctors."

101. Meier, "Maker of Heart Device Kept Flaw from Doctors."

102. Barry Meier, "F.D.A. Meets with Maker of Flawed Heart Device," *The New York Times,* 25 May 2005.

103. Meier, "Maker of Heart Device Kept Flaw from Doctors."; Jennifer Bjorhus, " 'This Will Save Your Life'; That's What Lee Oukrup Told His Son of the Defibrillator That Failed," *St. Paul Pioneer Press,* 25 May 2005.

104. McCartney, "Guidant Assesses the Fallout."

105. "Lex: Johnson & Johnson," FT.com, 8 December 2004.

106. Marilyn Alva, "J&J Eyes $24 Bil Buy of Guidant to Give Pep to Its Tired Growth," *Investor's Business Daily,* 8 December 2004.

107. Steinbrook, "The Controversy over Guidant's Implantable Defibrillators."

108. The Guidant subsidiary stopped selling the system in March of 2001, made changes, and reintroduced it to the market in August of 2001 (Steinbrook, "The Controversy over Guidant's Implantable Defibrillators.")

109. Steinbrook, "The Controversy over Guidant's Implantable Defibrillators."

110. Barry Meier, "Guidant Case May Involve Crime Inquiry," *The New York Times,* 29 Septem-

ber 2005; Andrew Ross Sorkin and Barry Meier, "Rethinking the Cost of a Deal," *The New York Times,* 19 October 2005.

111. Scott Hensley, "J&J to Pay $4 Billion Less for Guidant in Revised Deal," *The Wall Street Journal,* 15 November 2005.

112. Barry Meier, "F.D.A. Had Report of Short Circuit in Heart Devices," *The New York Times,* 12 September 2005.

113. Meier, "F.D.A. Had Report of Short Circuit in Heart Devices." Meier notes that Swerdlow is a consultant to Medtronic, one of Guidant's prime rivals.

114. Meier, "FDA Had Report of Short Circuit in Heart Devices."

115. Avorn, *Powerful Medicines,* 381.

116. See Angell, *The Truth About the Drug Companies,* 212.

117. Marc Kaufman and Brooke A. Masters, "FDA Is Flexing Less Muscle: Some Question Its Relationship with Drugmakers," *The Washington Post,* 18 November 2004. In a nod to the critics, PDUFA's 2002 funding package would set aside $75 million over five years (or $15 million a year) from user fees to add more than 100 positions to the drug safety office—but the lion's share of industry's contributions continued to be earmarked for faster drug approvals.

118. Gardiner Harris, "At F.D.A., Strong Drug Ties and Less Monitoring," *The New York Times,* 6 December 2004.

119. Harris, "At F.D.A., Strong Drug Ties and Less Monitoring."

120. "Fiscal Year 2003 Performance Report to the President and the Congress for the Prescription Drug User Fee Act of 1992" (available at http://www.fda.gov/oc/pdufa/report2003/default.htm).

121. Avorn, *Powerful Medicines,* 93.

122. Eve E. Slater, "Today's FDA," Sounding Board, *The New England Journal of Medicine,* 352, no. 3 (20 January 2005).

123. Harris, "At F.D.A., Strong Drug Ties and Less Monitoring."

124. Interviews with the author.

125. David J. Malenka, Aaron V. Kaplan, Sandra M. Sharp, and John E. Wennberg make this point about the weakness of the current postmarketing surveillance system in "Postmarketing Surveillance of Medicare Devices Using Medicare Claims," *Health Affairs,* July/August 2005.

126. Alastair J. J. Wood, C. Michael Stein, Raymond Woosley, "Making Medicines Safer—The Need for an Independent Drug Safety Board," Sounding Board, *The New England Journal of Medicine,* (17 December 1998).

127. Jennifer Corbett Dooren, "Drug Makers Seen as Slow to Finish Postmarket Studies," Dow Jones Newswires, 1 June 2005.

128. Lazar John Greenfield, interview with the author. Unless otherwise indicated, the quotations that follow are based on that interview.

129. Greenfield has authored more than 360 scientific articles in peer-reviewed journals, 128 book chapters, and 2 textbooks. He has served on the editorial boards of 15 scientific journals and on an NIH Study Section. He is a fellow of the American College of Surgeons and has served on its board of governors, its advisory council for vascular surgery, and as first vice president. He has been elected president of the American Surgical Asso-

ciation, the American Venous Forum, the American Association of Vascular Surgery, and the Halsted Society. In 1995 Dr. Greenfield was elected to the Institute of Medicine of the National Academies. In 1996 he was designated a Johns Hopkins Society Scholar, and in 1999 he received the Rice University Distinguished Alumnus Award.

130. Anna Wilde Mathews and Thomas M. Burton, "After Medtronic Lobbying Push, the FDA Had Change of Heart: Agency Squelches an Article Raising Doubts on Safety of Device to Repair Artery, Threat of 'Criminal Sanction,' " *The Wall Street Journal,* 9 July 2004.

131. Mathews and Burton, "After Medtronic Lobbying Push, the FDA Had Change of Heart."

132. Interview with the author.

133. Mathews and Burton, "After Medtronic Lobbying Push, the FDA Had Change of Heart."

134. Dale R. Tavris, Chih-hsin Liu, Thomas P. Gross, Lazar John Greenfield, "Aneurysm-Related Morality Rates in the U.S. AneuRx Clinical Trial," paper accepted by *Journal of Vascular Surgery* in March of 2004.

135. Mathews and Burton, "After Medtronic Lobbying Push, the FDA Had Change of Heart."

136. Tavris et al., "Aneurysm-Related Morality Rates in the U.S. AneuRx Clinical Trial."

137. Rob Clarke, interview with the author and e-mail to the author. Clarke also stated that Medtronic had continued to send the FDA updates as recently as January of 2005.

138. Clarke, interview with the author. As noted earlier, in an effort to draw an apples-to-apples comparison, the FDA researchers decided to use the mortality rates from high-volume hospitals, and made that point clear in the article accepted by *The Journal of Vascular Surgery.*

139. Greenfield, interview with the author.

140. Mathews and Burton, "After Medtronic Lobbying Push, the FDA Had Change of Heart."

141. Stacey Schultz, "Mr. Outside Moves Inside: Daniel Troy Fought the FDA for Years; Now He's Helping to Run It," *U.S. News & World Report,* 24 March 2003.

142. Michael Kranish, "FDA Counsel's Rise Embodies U.S. Shift," *The Boston Globe,* 22 December 2002.

143. Interview with the author.

144. James G. Dickinson, "CDRH's Schultz Seeks More Postmarket Reports," *Medical Device & Diagnostic Industry,* October 2004.

145. Interview with the author.

146. Anna Wilde Mathews, "FDA's Withdrawal of AneuRx Paper Draws Criticism," *The Wall Street Journal,* 6 August 2004.

147. Interview with the author.

148. Alex Berenson, "Big Drug Makers See Sales Decline with Their Image," *The New York Times,* 14 November 2005.

149. In October of 2004, *The Wall Street Journal* summed up the story of how Merck avoided following up on what it knew about Vioxx: "The long path to withdrawal of Vioxx began in 2000 when the *New England Journal of Medicine* published the results of a Merck trial called Vigor. It showed that patients taking the drug were four times as likely—0.4% to 0.1%—to have a heart attack or stroke as patients taking naproxen.

    "In early 2001, at a meeting of an FDA advisory panel, Merck argued that the difference might reflect the protective effects of naproxen and not danger from its drug. The committee ended up recommending that the issue be noted on Vioxx's label, and members called for follow-up research to clear up the questions.

"Steven E. Nissen, a cardiologist at the Cleveland Clinic, attended the meeting and was troubled by the data. Back at the clinic, he discussed his concerns with Eric Topol, chairman of cardiovascular medicine . . . They decided to take a closer look by examining data from several trials of patients who had taken Vioxx and other painkillers."

When they published their findings in *The Journal of the American Medical Association* in August of 2001, they warned that the "available data raise a cautionary flag about the risk of cardiovascular events" with COX-2 inhibitors, saying that Vioxx appeared especially risky.

In 2004 Merck would say that in 2001 it was already conducting the study that would ultimately lead to Vioxx's withdrawal. Nevertheless, the *Wall Street Journal* reported, "As concerns rose, Merck vigorously defended Vioxx. It attacked the Cleveland Clinic's data as inadequate. One study in which Merck researchers participated suggested that Vioxx was associated with a higher risk of heart attacks." This study appeared in the spring of 2004 in *Circulation,* a journal published by the American Heart Association, "but without the name of a Merck scientist who participated. The company withdrew the employee's name from the list of authors because it disagreed with the study's conclusion." (Barbara Martinez, Anna Wilde Mathews, Joann S. Lublin, and Ron Winslow, "Expiration Date: Merck Pulls Vioxx from Market After Link to Heart Problems: Drug's Demise Raises Concerns About Company's Future; Loss of $2.5 Billion in Sales; Patients Are Left in Quandary," *The Wall Street Journal,* 1 October 2004.)

150. Zaugg and Conmy, "The IMS Health Report: Pressure Zone."
151. Paula L. Stepankowsky, "Drug Makers Are Expected to Post Profit Gains, but Worries Persist," Dow Jones Newswires, 5 October 2005.
152. Berenson, "Big Drug Makers See Sales Decline, with Their Image."
153. "Brand Price Increases Continue to Outpace Those for Generics, GAO Says," *Generic Line,* 21 September 2005. From January of 2000 through December of 2004, patients without prescription drug coverage paid an average of 24.5 percent more for 96 frequently used drugs, according to the GAO.
154. Berenson, "Big Drug Makers See Sales Decline with Their Image."
155. Amy Barrett, "Pfizer's Funk," cover story, *Businessweek,* 28 February 2005.
156. Ransdell Pierson, "Wyeth Cuts Sales Force, Visits to Docs," Reuters, 20 June 2005.
157. Barrett, "Pfizer's Funk."
158. Pierson, "Wyeth Cuts Sales Force, Visits to Docs."
159. Interview with the author.
160. Interview with the author.
161. Thomas Ginsberg, "While Seniors Scratch Heads, Big Pharma Licks Chops," *Pittsburgh Post-Gazzette,* 6 November 2005.
162. Zaugg and Conmy, "The IMS Health Report: Pressure Zone."
163. Melissa Davis, "Biomet, Zimmer Clash on Pricing Picture," TheStreet.com, 13 October 2005.

WHERE WE ARE NOW: EVERYONE OUT OF THE POOL

1. If they choose, Medicare beneficiaries can select a stand-alone prescription benefit without joining a managed care plan, but they still must buy it from a private insurer.

2. Brian Biles, Geraldine Dallek, and Lauren Hersch Nicholas, "Medicare Advantage: Déjà Vu All Over Again?" Web Exclusive, *Health Affairs,* 15 December 2004. The authors note that in recent years, Medicare has developed an improved risk-adjustment system that is now being phased in through 2007, but even this improved system will account for only half of the difference of the costs of plan enrollees in 2005.

3. Biles et al., "Medicare Advantage: Déjà Vu All Over Again?"

4. Karen Davis, president of The Commonwealth Fund, in invited testimony before the Senate Appropriations Committee's Subcommittee on Labor, Health and Human Services, Education, and Related Agencies, estimated that private insurers' administrative costs are 2 1/2 times higher (hearing on Health Care Access and Affordability: Cost Containment Strategies, 11 June 2003.) See also the pie charts on pages xi and xii ("Who Is Paying?" and "What Are We Paying For?"). As the charts show, while private insurers pick up only about 30 percent of the national health care bill, they retain roughly 15 percent of what they receive (equal to roughly 4.5 percent of the total pie) to cover administrative costs and profits. By contrast, the government (i.e., taxpayers) pays for roughly 51 percent of all health care costs, but keeps only about 5 percent of what it receives (or 2.2 percent of the total) to cover administrative costs.

5. Peter Loftus, "Insurers Bet Big on New Drug Benefit," Dow Jones Newswires, 7 September 2005.

6. Vanessa Fuhrmans and Sarah Lueck, "Insurers Sweeten Health Plans for Seniors," *The Wall Street Journal,* 8 November 2005.

7. Milt Freudenheim, "H.M.O.'s Return for a Piece of Medicare Pie," *The New York Times,* 9 March 2004.

8. "Our Opinion: Medicare Suffers a Drug Overdose," editorial, *The Atlanta Journal-Constitution,* 20 November 2005.

9. Freudenheim, "H.M.O.'s Return for a Piece of Medicare Pie."

10. Sheryl Skolnick, interview with the author.

11. Paul Krugman, "A Private Obsession," *The New York Times,* 18 November 2005.

12. "Our Opinion: Medicare Suffers a Drug Overdose."

13. Vanessa Furhmans, "Fierce Bidding for Drug Benefit," *The Wall Street Journal,* 23 September 2005.

14. Fuhrmans and Lueck, "Insurers Sweeten Health Plans for Seniors."

15. Skolnick, interview with the author.

16. Author's interview with a middle-aged woman who had taken her own mother to the meeting.

17. Cindy V. Culp, "Seniors Face Bewildering Array of Choices in Drug Plan," Cox News Service, 20 November 2005.

18. Bruce C. Vladeck, "The Struggle for the Soul of Medicare," *Journal of Law, Medicine & Ethics,* fall 2004.

19. David R. Olmos, "Viagra Shows the Potency of Insurers: This Drug and Other Medical Breakthroughs Raise Questions About How Companies Decide What to Cover and How That Affects People's Lives," *Los Angeles Times,* 7 June 1998.

20. Olmos, "Viagra Shows the Potency of Insurers."

21. George Cipoletti, interview with the author.

22. Barry Meier, "Doctors, Too, Ask: Is This Drug Right?" *The New York Times,* 30 December 2004.

23. "They did not disclose all they knew," said Gregory Curfman, the journal's executive editor, referring to a study published in *The New England Journal of Medicine* in November of 2000. "There were serious negative consequences for the public health as a result of that." Merck denied that it had done anything improper. (Alex Berenson, "Medical Journal Criticizes Merck Over Vioxx Data," *The New York Times,* 9 December 2005.)

24. In "Which Way for Competition? None of the Above," Robert A. Berenson points to Vioxx's successful promotional campaign as "a prime example" of how "in many ways, the consumer-directed movement is in conflict with developing progress toward reliance on evidence-based medicine." *Health Affairs,* November/December 2005.

25. "Medical and Dental Expenses for Use in Preparing 2005 Returns," Department of the Treasury, Internal Revenue Service, Publication 502.

26. *Employer Health Benefits 2005 Annual Survey,* (Menlo Park, CA: The Henry J. Kaiser Family Foundation, www.kff.org).

27. Since the amount that a family is allowed to contribute to an HSA will rise each year with inflation, the total value of a nest egg in 30 years would be far more than $500,000.

28. Sarah Rubenstein, "As Health Deductibles Increase, So Does Consumers' Confusion," *The Wall Street Journal,* 28 January 2005.

29. Christopher J. Gearon, "High Deductible, High Risk 'Consumer-Directed' Plans a Health Gamble," *The Washington Post,* 18 October 2005. For details on what is not included in the cap on deductibles and copays, see "All About HSAs," Department of the Treasury, 25 November 2005 (www.treas.gov).

30. Gearon, "High Deductible, High Risk 'Consumer-Directed' Plans a Health Gamble."

31. Alain C. Enthoven and Laura A. Tollen, "Competition in Health Care: It Takes Systems to Pursue Quality and Efficiency," Web Exclusive, *Health Affairs,* 7 September 2005.

32. Cathy Schoen, Michelle M. Doty, Sara R. Collins, and Alyssa L. Holmgren, "Insured but Not Protected: How Many Adults Are Underinsured?" Web Exclusive, *Health Affairs,* 14 June 2005.

33. Vanessa Fuhrmans, "Health Insurers' New Target—Companies Go After the Uninsured with Cheaper Plans, Clever Marketing, but Benefits Are Sparser," *The Wall Street Journal,* 31 May 2005.

34. Fuhrmans, "Health Insurers' New Target—Companies Go After the Uninsured with Cheaper Plans, Clever Marketing, but Benefits Are Sparser."

35. Robinson, who supports the concept (with some reservations), goes on to observe that while leaving the vulnerable exposed, creation of health savings accounts "emphasizes the importance of individual effort in generating the economic resources that underlie any system of care. The HSA moves the nation another step toward a personalized and privatized health care system." ("Health Savings Accounts—The Ownership Society in Health Care," *The New England Journal of Medicine,* 22 September 2005.)

36. Jay Crosson, interview with the author.

37. Eduardo Porter, "Health Care for All, Just a (Big) Step Away," *The New York Times,* 18 December 2005.

38. John Sheils and Randall Haught, "The Cost of Tax-Exempt Health Benefits in 2004,"

Web Exclusive, *Health Affairs,* 25 February 2004. Of course, other taxpayers didn't necessarily pay more taxes to make up for the subsidy. They may simply have received fewer services and faced greater uncertainty regarding the fate of Medicare and Social Security.

39. In the world of money-driven medicine, important medical research can be ignored. In December of 2005, *The Wall Street Journal* reported on how, for years, U.S. researchers paid little or no attention to celiac disease, a gastrointestinal ailment that can debilitate patients with diarrhea, fatigue, nausea, and weight loss as their intestines lose the ability to absorb nutrients, leaving it to European researchers to investigate and treat the disease:

"Lack of [financial] incentives . . . played a role," the *Journal* reported. "Treating celiac disease usually requires little more than a strict dietary regimen . . . As a result, it attracted little attention from drug companies. . . .

"Celiac disease isn't the only medical condition to fall into an American blind spot," the *Journal* added. "It took a decade or more for U.S. doctors to accept a 1982 Australian discovery that most stomach ulcers are caused by the bacterium Helicobacter pylori. The discovery made it possible to replace expensive drug and surgical treatments with a cheap course of antibiotics. It won the Nobel Prize for two scientists this year." (David P. Hamilton, "Belatedly, an Illness of the Intestines Gets Notice in U.S.: Long Well-Known in Europe, Celiac Disease May Affect Up to 3 Million Americans," *The Wall Street Journal,* 9 December 2005.)

40. Regina Herzlinger, *Market-Driven Health Care: Who Wins, Who Loses in the Transformation of America's Largest Service Industry,* (Cambridge, Massachusetts: Perseus Books, 1997), 7.

41. Herzlinger, *Market-Driven Health Care,* 18.

42. Herzlinger, *Market-Driven Health Care,* 50.

43. Herzlinger, *Market-Driven Health Care,* 84. In 1997 Herzlinger argued that the consumer revolutionaries' desire for mastery, and the information boom it created, has completely reshaped many industries. "The mighty American automobile industry, for example, nearly collapsed from the repeated negative evaluations that, conversely, caused the Japanese and German car industries to boom. For years, its cars were almost universally rated as clunkier and less reliable than their foreign counterparts. Finally, the industry restructured itself to produce vehicles whose quality and cost stand up to foreign competition" (12–13). By 2005 many consumers were less than happy with the exorbitantly expensive gas-guzzling automobiles that Detroit had invented, and the U.S was once again losing market share to foreign cars. The SUV may be a prime example of a designer creating a product that, to paraphrase George Cipolletti, "gives people what they think they want rather than what will give the best result."

44. Bernard Wysocki Jr., "Keeping Score: New Ratings Allow Patients to Shop for Best Hospitals," *The Wall Street Journal,* 1 May 2002.

45. Atul Gawande, *Complications: A Surgeon's Notes on an Imperfect Science* (New York: Picador, 2003), 229. (For a discussion of medicine's uncertainty, see chapter 1 of this book.)

46. Eric J. Cassell, "The Changing Concept of the Ideal Physician," *Daedalus,* spring 1996.

47. Carl E. Schneider, *The Practice of Autonomy: Patients, Doctors, and Medical Decisions* (New York: Oxford University Press, 1998), 53.

48. Kenneth J. Arrow, "Uncertainty and the Welfare Economics of Medical Care," *The American Economic Review,* December 1963.

49. In a 2003 article, Arrow argues that while much has changed in the 40 years since he wrote his original essay, what remains of the physician's "power" still rests on that perception of "moral authority."

   "I am not denying that moral authority may be based on illusions, and that those illusions will be carefully fostered," Arrow adds. "But I want to emphasize that social norms [such as the expectations about a physician's lack of self-interest] are based on . . . perceived mutual gains, and that one must be wary of assuming that these perceptions are not based as much on reality as on other perceptions." (Kenneth Arrow, "Reflections on the Reflections," in *Uncertain Times: Kenneth Arrow and the Changing Economics of Health Care,* Peter J. Hammer, Deborah Haas-Wilson, Mark A. Peterson, and William M. Sage, eds. (Durham: Duke University Press, 2003).

50. Robert A. Berenson, "Which Way for Competition? None of the Above," *Health Affairs,* November/December 2005.

51. Schneider, *The Practice of Autonomy,* 16–17.

52. Franz J. Ingelfinger, "Arrogance," *The New England Journal of Medicine,* 25 December 1980.

53. Schneider, *The Practice of Autonomy,* 211.

INDEX